Lecture Notes in Computer Science   5215

Commenced Publication in 1973
Founding and Former Series Editors:
Gerhard Goos, Juris Hartmanis, and Jan van Leeuwen

Editorial Board

Franck Cassez   Claude Jard (Eds.)

Formal Modeling
and Analysis
of Timed Systems

6th International Conference, FORMATS 2008
Saint Malo, France, September 15-17, 2008
Proceedings

 Springer

Volume Editors

Franck Cassez
CNRS/IRCCyN
1 rue de la Noë, BP 92101
44321 Nantes Cedex 3, France
E-mail: franck.cassez@cnrs.irccyn.fr

Claude Jard
ENS de Cachan, Campus de Ker-Lann
35170, Bruz Cedex, France
and
IRISA, Campus de Beaulieu
35042 Rennes Cedex, France
E-mail: Claude.Jard@bretagne.ens-cachan.fr

Library of Congress Control Number: Applied for

CR Subject Classification (1998): D.2, C.3, F.3, D.3, F.2

LNCS Sublibrary: SL 1 – Theoretical Computer Science and General Issues

ISSN   0302-9743
ISBN-10   3-540-85777-X Springer Berlin Heidelberg New York
ISBN-13   978-3-540-85777-8 Springer Berlin Heidelberg New York

Springer is a part of Springer Science+Business Media

springer.com

© Springer-Verlag Berlin Heidelberg 2008
Printed in Germany

Typesetting: Camera-ready by author, data conversion by Scientific Publishing Services, Chennai, India
Printed on acid-free paper   SPIN: 12519675   06/3180   5 4 3 2 1 0

Preface

This volume consists of the proceedings of the Sixth International Conference on Formal Modelling and Analysis of Timed Systems (FORMATS 2008). The main goal of this series of conferences is to bring together diverse communities of researchers that deal with the timing aspects of computing systems. Both fundamental and practical aspects of timed systems are addressed. Further, three invited talks that survey various aspects of this broad research domain were presented at the conference: "Composing Web Services in an Open World: QoS Issues" (Albert Benveniste); "Recent Results in Metric Temporal Logic" (Joël Ouaknine); "Comparing the Expressiveness of Timed Automata and Timed Extensions of Petri Nets" (Jiri Srba).

FORMATS 2008 was co-located with QEST 2008 (Fifth International Conference on the Quantitative Evaluation of SysTems) and took place in Saint-Malo, France, during September 14–17, 2008. Detailed information about FORMATS 2008 can be found at http://formats08.inria.fr/, while, the generic link for the QEST conference series is http://www.qest.org. This was a great opportunity for researchers of both communities to share their scientific interests in timed systems.

This year we received 37 submissions and the Programme Committee selected 17 submissions for presentation at the conference. FORMATS 2008 used the EasyChair conference system to manage the reviewing process. The topics dealt with by the accepted papers cover: the theory of timed and hybrid systems, analysis and verification techniques and case studies. We wish to thank the Programme Committee members and the other reviewers for their competent and timely review of the submissions. We also wish to sincerely thank the three invited speakers, Albert Benveniste, Joël Ouaknine, and Jiri Srba, for accepting our invitation and providing extended abstracts of their talks to be included in the proceedings. As always, the Springer LNCS team provided excellent support in the preparation of this volume.

July 2008

Franck Cassez
Claude Jard

Organization

Programme Chairs

Franck Cassez   CNRS, IRCCyN, France
Claude Jard   ENS de Cachan, IRISA, France

Programme Committee

Eugene Asarin   LIAFA, University of Paris 7 and CNRS, France
Patricia Bouyer   CNRS, LSV, France
Ed Brinksma   ESI, University of Twente and Eindhoven
     University of Technology, The Netherlands
Franck Cassez   CNRS, IRCCyN, France
Flavio Corradini   University of Camerino, Italy
Deepak D'Souza   CSA, IISc, Bangalore, India
Martin Fränzle   University of Oldenbourg, Germany
Goran Frehse   University of Grenoble 1, Verimag, France
Claude Jard   ENS de Cachan, IRISA, France
Joost-Pieter Katoen   RWTH Aachen University, Germany
Bruce Krogh   Carnegie Mellon University, USA
Salvatore La Torre   University of Salerno, Italy
Insup Lee   University of Pennsylvania, USA
Rupak Majumdar   UCLA, USA
Brian Nielsen   CISS and Aalborg University, Denmark
Joël Ouaknine   Oxford University, UK
Paritosh Pandya   TIFR, India
Paul Pettersson   Mälardalen University, Sweden
Jean-François Raskin   ULB, Belgium
P.S. Thiagarajan   National University of Singapore
Stavros Tripakis   Cadence Research Labs and Verimag/CNRS,
     Berkeley, USA
Frits Vaandrager   Radboud University Nijmegen, The Netherlands
Farn Wang   National Taiwan University, Taiwan
Wang Yi   Uppsala University, Sweden
Tomohiro Yoneda   NII, Tokyo, Japan

Local Organization

Léna Baudoin, INRIA, France
Laurence Dinh, INRIA, France
Claude Jard, ENS de Cachan, IRISA, France
Elisabeth Lebret, INRIA, France

Sponsors

The organization of FORMATS 2008 was supported by: CNRS, ENS-Cachan, INRIA. FORMATS 2008 was financially supported by: CNRS, ENS-Cachan, INRIA, GDR ASR et MACS du CNRS: groupe AFSEC, Université de Rennes 1, Rennes Métropole, Région Bretagne.

External Reviewers

Erika Abraham

David Arney

Henrik Bohnenkamp

Diletta Romana Cacciagrano

Thomas Chatain

Taloue Chen

Vivien Chinnapongse

Martin De Wulf

Maria Rita Di Berardini

Amir Hossein Ghamarian

Nan Guan

Christoph Haase

Tingting Han

Loïc Hélouët

Maneesh Khattri

Daniel Klink

Pavel Krcal

Didier Lime

Birgitta Lindström

Kamal Lodaya

Morgan Magnin

Junkil Park

Pavithra Prabhakar

Jan-David Quesel

Rajarshi Ray

Pierre-Alain Reynier

Oliviero Riganelli

Olivier Henri Roux

Pritam Roy

Prahladavaradan Sampath

Cristina Seceleanu

Jeremy Sproston

Ingo Stierand

Jagadish Suryadevara

Tino Teige

Luca Tesei

Louis-Marie Traounez

Table of Contents

Session 3. Case Studies

Session 4. Model-Checking of Probabilistic Systems

Session 5. Verification and Test

Session 6. Time Petri Nets

Some Recent Results in Metric Temporal Logic

Joël Ouaknine and James Worrell

Oxford University Computing Laboratory, UK
{joel,jbw}@comlab.ox.ac.uk

Abstract. Metric Temporal Logic (MTL) is a widely-studied real-time extension of Linear Temporal Logic. In this paper we survey results about the complexity of the satisfiability and model checking problems for fragments of MTL with respect to different semantic models. We show that these fragments have widely differing complexities: from polynomial space to non-primitive recursive and even undecidable. However we show that the most commonly occurring real-time properties, such as invariance and bounded response, can be expressed in fragments of MTL for which model checking, if not satisfiability, can be decided in polynomial or exponential space.

1 Introduction

Linear temporal logic (LTL) is a popular formalism for the specification and verification of concurrent and reactive systems [28]. Most approaches that use LTL adopt a discrete model of time, where a run of a system produces a sequence of observations. Such a model is inadequate for real-time systems, where a run of a system is modelled either as a sequence of events that are time-stamped with reals or as a trajectory with domain the set $\mathbb{R}_+$ of non-negative reals.

In fact, interpretations of LTL on the reals were considered long before temporal logic became popular in verification. For example, the celebrated result of Kamp [20] that LTL with the "until" and "since" modalities is expressively complete for the first-order monadic logic over $(\mathbb{N}, <)$ also holds for the structure $(\mathbb{R}_+, <)$. A more recent development has been the extension of LTL to allow specifying quantitative or metric properties over the reals [21,23]. For example, when specifying the behaviour of a real-time system one may want to stipulate deadlines between environment events and corresponding system responses: every *alarm* is followed by a *shutdown* event in 10 time units unless *all clear* is sounded first.

The most widely known such extension is *Metric Temporal Logic (MTL)* in which the modalities of LTL are augmented with timing constraints [21]. For example, the informally stated property above might be rendered

$$\Box(alarm \rightarrow (\Diamond_{(0,10)}\, allclear \vee \Diamond_{\{10\}}\, shutdown))$$

in MTL. Here $\Diamond_{(0,10)}$ means *sometime in the next 10 time units*, while $\Diamond_{\{10\}}$ means *in exactly 10 time units*.

F. Cassez and C. Jard (Eds.): FORMATS 2008, LNCS 5215, pp. 1–13, 2008.
© Springer-Verlag Berlin Heidelberg 2008

An alternative approach to extending LTL is embodied in *Timed Propositional Temporal Logic (TPTL)* [6]. TPTL is a version of first-order temporal logic in which first-order variables range over the time domain and there is a restricted form of quantification, called *freeze quantification*, in which every variable is bound to the time of a particular state. In TPTL the above property could be written

$$\Box x.(\text{alarm} \rightarrow (\Diamond y.(\text{allclear} \land y - x < 10) \lor \Diamond z.(\text{shutdown} \land z - x = 10))).$$

Here x is bound to the time of the *alarm* event, y is bound to the time of the *allclear* event, and z is bound to the time of the *shutdown* event.

The relative expressiveness of MTL and TPTL is investigated in [8]. In particular it was shown there that MTL corresponds to a proper subset of the two-variable fragment of TPTL. In general it seems that the extra expressiveness of TPTL compared to MTL makes it harder to identify interesting decidable fragments of the former.

Yet another approach to reasoning about metric properties of computations is to work within the framework of monadic predicate logic [5,17,18,31]. For example, Hirshfeld and Rabinovich [17] introduce the *Quantitative Monadic Logic of Order (QMLO)*, a fragment of first-order monadic logic over $(\mathbb{R}_+, <, +1)$. QMLO carefully restricts the use of the $+1$ function to a type of *bounded quantification*. For example, given a QMLO formula φ with one free variable,

$$(\exists t)_{>t_0}^{<t_0+1}\varphi \equiv \exists t(t_0 < t < t_0 + 1 \land \varphi(t))$$

denotes a formula with free variable t_0. It turns out that QMLO has the same expressiveness as a well-known decidable subset of MTL [17].

In this paper we concentrate on Metric Temporal Logic, although naturally many of the ideas we develop apply more widely. We survey a wide variety of complexity and decidability results for fragments MTL and show that these fragments have widely differing complexities: from PSPACE to non-primitive recursive and even undecidable. Reinforcing the message of [15], our objective is to illustrate that great care must be exercised in extending LTL to handle metric properties if one is to avoid a blow-up in the complexity of verification.

2   Metric Temporal Logic

Given a set P of atomic propositions, the formulas of MTL are built from P using Boolean connectives, and time-constrained versions of the *until* operator U as follows:

$$\varphi ::= p \mid \neg\varphi \mid \varphi \land \varphi \mid \varphi\, U_I\, \varphi,$$

where $I \subseteq (0, \infty)$ is an interval of reals with endpoints in $\mathbb{N} \cup \{\infty\}$. We sometimes abbreviate $U_{(0,\infty)}$ to U, calling this the *unconstrained* until operator.

Further connectives can be defined following standard conventions. In addition to propositions $\top$ (true) and $\bot$ (false), and to disjunction $\lor$, we have the *constrained eventually* operator $\Diamond_I \varphi \equiv \top\, U_I\, \varphi$, the *constrained always* operator $\Box_I \varphi \equiv \neg \Diamond_I \neg \varphi$, and the *constrained dual until* operator $\varphi_1\, \tilde{U}_I\, \varphi_2 \equiv \neg((\neg\varphi_1)\, U_I\, (\neg\varphi_2))$. Admitting only $\tilde{U}_I$ as an extra connective one can transform any MTL formula into an equivalent *negation normal form*, in which negation is only applied to propositional variables.

Sometimes MTL is presented with past connectives (e.g., constrained versions of the "since" connective from LTL) as well future connectives [5]. However we do not consider past connectives in this paper.

Next we describe two commonly adopted semantics for MTL.

Continuous Semantics. Denote by $\mathbb{R}_+$ the set of nonnegative real numbers. Given a set of propositions P, a *signal* is a function $f \colon \mathbb{R}_+ \to 2^P$ mapping $t \in \mathbb{R}_+$ to the set $f(t)$ of propositions holding at time t. We say that f has *finite variability* if its set of discontinuities has no accumulation points. Given an MTL formula φ over the set of propositional variables P, the satisfaction relation $f \models \varphi$ is defined inductively, with the classical rules for atomic propositions and Boolean operators, and with the following rule for the "until" modality, where f^t denotes the signal $f^t(s) = f(t+s)$:

$$f \models \varphi_1\, U_I\, \varphi_2 \text{ iff for some } t \in I,\ f^t \models \varphi_2 \text{ and } f^u \models \varphi_1 \text{ for all } u \in (0,t).$$

Pointwise Semantics. In the *pointwise semantics* MTL formulas are interpreted over *timed words*. Given an alphabet of events Σ, a timed word ρ is a finite or infinite sequence $(\sigma_0, \tau_0)(\sigma_1, \tau_1)\ldots$ where $\sigma_i \in \Sigma$ and $\tau_i \in \mathbb{R}_+$, such that the sequence (τ_i) is strictly increasing and *non-Zeno* (i.e., it is either finite or it diverges to infinity). The requirement of non-Zenoness is closely related to the condition of finite variability in the continuous semantics. It reflects the intuition that a system has only finitely many state changes in bounded time interval.

Given a (finite or infinite) timed word $\rho = (\sigma, \tau)$ over alphabet 2^P and an MTL formula φ, the satisfaction relation $\rho, i \models \varphi$ (read ρ satisfies φ at position i) is defined inductively, with the classical rules for Boolean operators, and with the following rule for the "until" modality:

$$\rho, i \models \varphi_1\, U_I\, \varphi_2 \text{ iff there exists } j \text{ such that } i < j < |\rho|,\ \rho, j \models \varphi_2,\ \tau_j - \tau_i \in I,$$
$$\text{and } \rho, k \models \varphi_1 \text{ for all } k \text{ with } i < k < j.$$

The pointwise semantics is less natural if one thinks of temporal logics as encoding fragments of monadic logic over the reals. On the other hand it seems more suitable when considering MTL formulas as specifications on timed automata. In this vein, when adopting the pointwise semantics it is natural to think of atomic propositions in MTL as referring to events (corresponding to state changes) rather than to states themselves.

For example, consider the specification of a traffic light. In the continuous semantics one might introduce propositions such as *green* and *red* to denote the *state* of the light. Then one could write a formula $\Box(green \to (green\, U_{(0,5)}\, red))$ to say that whenever the light is green it stays green until turning red in at most five time units. By contrast, in the pointwise semantics one would introduce propositions referring to *events*. For example, suppose the propositions *green* and *red* hold of events that respectively turn the traffic light green and red. Then the specification $\Box(green \rightarrow (\neg red\ U_{\{5\}}\ red))$ says that after the traffic light turns green it next becomes red after exactly 5 time units.

Decision Problems. This paper focuses on the following two fundamental decision problems:

- The *satisfiability problem*, asking whether a given MTL formula φ is satisfiable by some signal (or timed word).
- The *model-checking problem*, asking whether a given timed automaton A satisfies a given MTL formula φ, *i.e.*, whether all signals (or timed words) accepted by A satisfy φ (see [3] for details).

We consider satisfiability and model checking for various fragments of MTL, relative to the continuous semantics and both the finite-word and infinite-word variants of the pointwise semantics.

3   Alternating Timed Automata

In this section we review the notion of *alternating timed automata*. This class of automata is closely related to MTL and plays a key role in decision procedures for the latter over the pointwise semantics. (By contrast, over the continuous semantics it generally seems possible to avoid the use of automata in decision procedures [17].)

Following [22,27] we define an alternating timed automaton to be an alternating automaton augmented with a single clock variable[1], which is denoted x. Given a finite set S of *locations* we define a set of formulas $\Phi(S, x)$ by the grammar:

$$\varphi ::= \varphi_1 \wedge \varphi_2 \mid \varphi_1 \vee \varphi_2 \mid s \mid x \sim c \mid x.\varphi,$$

where $c \in \mathbb{N}$, $\sim \in \{<, \leq, \geq, >\}$, and $s \in S$. A term of the form $x \sim c$ should be thought of as a *clock constraint*, whereas the expression $x.\varphi$ is a binding construct corresponding to the operation of resetting the clock x to 0.

In an alternating timed automaton the transition function maps each location $s \in S$ and event $a \in \Sigma$ to an expression in $\Phi(S, x)$. Thus alternating automata allow two modes of branching: existential branching, represented by disjunction, and universal branching, represented by conjunction.

Formally an *alternating timed automaton* is a tuple $A = (\Sigma, S, s_0, F, \delta)$, where

- Σ is a finite alphabet
- S is a finite set of locations
- $s_0 \in S$ is the initial location
- $F \subseteq S$ is a set of accepting locations
- $\delta : S \times \Sigma \rightarrow \Phi(S, x)$ is the transition function.

---

[1] Virtually all decision problems, and in particular language emptiness, are undecidable for alternating automata with more than one clock.

Before stating the formal definition of a run of an alternating timed automaton, we give an example of how an MTL formula can be translated into an equivalent automaton.

Example 1. The MTL formula $\square(a \rightarrow \Diamond_{\{1\}}b)$ ('for every a-event there is a b-event exactly one time unit later') can be expressed by the following automaton A. Let A have two locations $\{s,t\}$ with s the initial and only accepting location, and transition function δ given by the following table:

	a	b
s	$s \wedge x.t$	s
t	t	$(x=1) \vee t$

Location s represents an invariant. When an a-event occurs, the conjunction in the definition of $\delta(s,a)$ results in the creation of a new thread of computation, starting in location t. Since this location is not accepting, the automaton must eventually leave it. This is only possible if a b-event happens exactly one time unit after the new thread was spawned.

We now proceed to formally define a run of an alternating timed automaton A. A *state* of A is a pair (s,v), where $s \in S$ is a location and $v \in \mathbb{R}_+$ is a *clock value*. Write $Q = S \times \mathbb{R}_+$ for the set of all states of A and define a *configuration* to be a finite subset of Q. A configuration $M \subseteq Q$ and a clock value $v \in \mathbb{R}_+$ defines a Boolean valuation on $\Phi(S,x)$ as follows:

- $M \models_v \varphi_1 \wedge \varphi_2$ if $M \models_v \varphi_1$ and $M \models_v \varphi_2$
- $M \models_v \varphi_1 \vee \varphi_2$ if $M \models_v \varphi_1$ or $M \models_v \varphi_2$
- $M \models_v s$ if $(s,v) \in M$
- $M \models_v x \sim c$ if $v \sim c$
- $M \models_v x.\varphi$ if $M \models_0 \varphi$.

A *tree* is a non-empty prefix closed set of *nodes* $T \subseteq \mathbb{N}^*$. A run of an alternating timed automaton A on a timed word $\rho = (\sigma, \tau)$ consists of a tree T and a *labelling* $l : T \rightarrow Q$ of the nodes of T by states of A such that: *(i)* $l(\varepsilon) = (s_0, 0)$ (the root is labelled by the initial state); and *(ii)* for each node $t \in T$ with $l(t) = (s,v)$, we have that $M \models_{v'} \delta(s, \sigma_n)$, where $n = |t|$ is the depth of t, $v' = v + (\tau_n - \tau_{n-1})$ and $M = \{l(t \cdot n) : t \cdot n \in T, n \in \mathbb{N}\}$ is the set of labels of the children of t. Finally, an infinite run is accepting if every infinite branch contains infinitely many accepting locations, while a run on a finite word ρ is accepting if every node at depth $|\rho|$ is accepting.

Example 1 can be generalised to show that for each MTL formula φ there is an alternating timed automaton A_φ such that $\{\rho : \rho \models \varphi\}$ is the set of timed words accepted by A. We refer the reader to [27] for details.

Well-quasi-order on Configurations. Recall that a *quasi-order* $(W, \preccurlyeq)$ consists of a set W together with a reflexive, transitive relation $\preccurlyeq$. An infinite sequence $w_1, w_2, w_3, \ldots$ in $(W, \preccurlyeq)$ is said to be *saturating* if there exist indices $i < j$ such that $w_i \preccurlyeq w_j$. $(W, \preccurlyeq)$ is said to be a *well-quasi-order (wqo)* if every infinite sequence is saturating.

Recall that the set of states of a classical (non-deterministic) timed automaton admits a finite quotient: the so called *clock regions construction* [1,2]. In the case of alternating timed automata this generalises to a well-quasi-order on the set of configurations as we shortly explain. This well-quasi-order is important in establishing the termination of several decision procedures for MTL, e.g., in [26,27].

Given an alternating timed automaton A, let c_{max} be the maximum clock constant in the description of A. Given configurations C and D, define $C \preccurlyeq D$ if there is an injection $f : C \to D$ such that: *(i)* $f(s, u) = (t, v)$ implies $s = t$ and either $\lfloor u \rfloor = \lfloor v \rfloor$ or $\lfloor u \rfloor, \lfloor v \rfloor > c_{max}$; *(ii)* if $f(s, u) = (s, u')$ and $f(s, v) = (t, v')$, then $frac(u) \leq frac(v)$ iff $frac(u') \leq frac(v')$. This quasi-order can be shown to be a well-quasi-order using Higman's Lemma [19,27].

4   Decidable Sublogics: Continuous Semantics

It is well known that both model checking and satisfiability for MTL in the continuous semantics are highly undecidable (Σ_1^1-complete) [3]. In this section we explain how this undecidability arises, we discuss some of the syntactic restrictions that have been imposed to recover decidability, and we state the complexity of model checking and satisfiability for the resulting fragments of MTL.

4.1   Punctuality

From one point of view, the source of undecidability in MTL is the excessive precision of the timing constraints. In particular, MTL allows so-called *punctual* formulas, such as $\Diamond_{\{1\}}p$, in which the constraint is a singleton interval. Using such punctual formulas, given an arbitrary Turing machine M with input X, one can construct an MTL formula $\varphi_{M,X}$ such that the signals satisfying $\varphi_{M,X}$ encode accepting computations of M on X. Thus one reduces the halting problem to the MTL satisfiability problem.

Assume that the set of atomic propositions P includes a proposition for each tape symbol and control state of M. A configuration of M is then encoded by a sequence of propositions holding in a unit-length time interval in a given signal. The formula $\varphi_{M,X}$ includes a component φ_{INIT} to ensure that the first configuration agrees with X and a component φ_{TRAN} that ensures that successive configurations respect the transition function of M. For example, the punctual formula $p \leftrightarrow \Diamond_{\{1\}}p$ is used in φ_{TRAN} to indicate that a given tape cell is unchanged from one configuration to the next. Since there is no *a priori* bound on the length of M's computations φ_{TRAN} appears in $\varphi_{M,X}$ under the scope of the "always" operator $\Box$.

Researchers were thus led to propose syntactic subsets of MTL in which punctual formulas are not expressible. For example, the sub-logic $MTL_{0,\infty}$ [3,15] arises by requiring that the constraining interval I in any temporal modality either has left endpoint 0 or right endpoint ∞. This logic allows one to speak about the earliest or latest times that a formula becomes true; for example $\Box(p \to \Diamond_{(0,5)}q)$

is an $\mathsf{MTL}_{0,\infty}$ formula saying that every p-state is followed by a q-state within 5 time units. Satisfiability and model checking for $\mathsf{MTL}_{0,\infty}$ are both PSPACE-complete. Thus the addition of upper- and lower-bound timing constraints to LTL incurs no complexity blow-up.

A more general fragment of MTL that prohibits punctual specifications is *Metric Interval Temporal Logic (MITL)*. This is the subset of MTL in which the constraining interval I in any temporal modality is required to be non-singular. Alur, Feder and Henzinger [3] describe an exponential translation of MITL formulas into equivalent non-deterministic timed automata, leading to an EXPSPACE decision procedure for both model checking and satisfiability. It was shown in [18] that over the continuous semantics $\mathsf{MTL}_{0,\infty}$ and MITL are equally expressive, although the latter is exponentially more succinct. Over the pointwise semantics, however, MITL is strictly more expressive than $\mathsf{MTL}_{0,\infty}$ [15].

A version of MITL called *Quantitative Temporal Logic (QTL)* has been introduced by Hirshfeld and Rabinovich [17]. This logic simply augments LTL with the modality $\Diamond_{(0,1)}$ (and the correspond past modality). They show that QTL has the same expressiveness as the version of MITL with both "until" and "since" and give a PSPACE decision procedure for the satisfiability problem. In contrast to the approach of [3] this procedure does not involve automata, but rather goes via a satisfiability preserving translation of QTL into LTL. For each QTL formula φ using set of atomic propositions P one can define an LTL formula $\widetilde{\varphi}$, over an augmented set of propositions $P \cup Q$, such that a signal $f : \mathbb{R}_+ \to 2^{P \cup Q}$ satisfies $\widetilde{\varphi}$ iff there exists a piecewise-linear monotone bijection $g : \mathbb{R}_+ \to \mathbb{R}_+$ such that $f \circ g$ satisfies φ. Intuitively, sets of signals that are definable in QTL (or MITL) are also definable in LTL up to some stretching.

4.2   Boundedness

A complementary route to obtaining decidable subsets of MTL has recently been propounded in [9,10]. The idea is that rather than ban constraining intervals that are *too small*, one bans constraining intervals that are *too big*. (Note in this regard that the undecidability proof for MTL described above involved both the punctual "eventually" connective $\Diamond_{\{1\}}$ and the unbounded "always" connective $\Box$.) Thus [10] defines BMTL to be the subset of MTL in which all constraining intervals have finite length. For example, $\varphi \equiv \Box_{(0,10)}(p \leftrightarrow \Diamond_{\{1\}}q)$ is a BMTL formula.

As with MITL, the satisfiability and model checking problems for BMTL are EXPSPACE-complete. However, unlike MITL, it is not the case that BMTL formulas can be translated into equivalent timed automata. Indeed a variation on a well-known result tells us that the set of signals satisfying the example formula φ above cannot be the language of a timed automaton [2,7].

Note that the above-defined encoding of Turing machines in MTL does not, when restricted to BMTL, yield EXPSPACE-hardness. Since we encode Turing-machine configurations in unit-length intervals, a BMTL version of the formula $\varphi_{M,X}$, described above, that has size polynomial in $|X|$ can only encode computations for which the number of steps is exponential in $|X|$. To achieve EXPSPACE-hardness requires a slightly different idea, although still crucially using punctuality.

Given a 2^n-space-bounded Turing machine M with input X, we construct in logarithmic space a BMTL formula $\varphi_{M,X}$ that is satisfiable if and only if M accepts X. The definition of $\varphi_{M,X}$ involves a set of atomic propositions $P \cup \dot{P}$, where P is as in the undecidability proof for MTL and $\dot{P} = \{\dot{p} : p \in P\}$. The dot is used as a pointer to aid in simulating M. The idea is to encode the entire computation of M in a single time unit, rather than encoding one configuration per time unit. In any signal satisfying $\varphi_{M,X}$ the sequence of propositions holding in the time interval $[0, 1)$ is meant to encode the computation history of M on input X. In this time interval we assume that the dot superscript decorates the first tape cell of each configuration of the computation.

The definition of $\varphi_{M,X}$ involves a formula

$$\varphi_{COPY} = \bigwedge_{p \in P} \Box_{[0,2^{|X|}]}(p \to \Diamond_{\{1\}}(p \vee \dot{p}))$$

$$\wedge \bigwedge_{p,q \in P} \Box_{[0,2^{|X|}]}((\dot{p}\, U_{(0,1)}\, q) \leftrightarrow \Diamond_{\{1\}}(p\, U_{(0,1)}\, \dot{q})),$$

that copies the sequence of propositions holding in each unit-duration time interval into the subsequent time interval, at the same time moving the dot superscript 'one place to the right'. Thus the sequence of propositions holding in each subsequent time interval $[k, k+1)$, $k = 1, \ldots, 2^{|X|} - 1$, should also represent the computation history of M on X. The only difference is that in the interval $[k, k+1)$ the dot decorates exactly those propositions encoding the contents of the k-th tape cell in each configuration in the computation history.

In addition to φ_{COPY}, $\varphi_{M,X}$ has another component φ_{CHECK}. For a given unit-length time interval $[k, k+1)$, φ_{CHECK} uses the dots as pointers to check the correctness of the k-th tape cell in each configuration. Thus, in $2^{|X|}$ time units the whole computation is checked.

4.3   Flatness

MITL and BMTL represent two different approaches to obtaining decidable metric temporal logics, and they have incomparable expressive power. In particular, BMTL is not capable of expressing invariance—one of the most basic safety specifications. To repair this deficiency [10] consider the syntactic property of *flatness* as a generalisation of boundedness. The term flatness here is motivated by by similarities with logics introduced in [12,13]. Intuitively an MTL formula is flat if no punctual subformula appears within the scope of a connective that involves unbounded universal quantification over the time domain. In fact the most natural way to state the results of [10] is in terms of the dual notion to flatness, called *coflatness*.

The condition of coflatness applies to formulas in negation normal form. Recall that such formulas feature the constrained dual until operator $\widetilde{U}_I$ in addition to the constrained until operator. Formally we say an MTL formula in negation normal form is *coflat* if *(i)* in any subformula of the form $\varphi_1 \, U_I \, \varphi_2$, either I is bounded or φ_2 is in MITL, and *(ii)* in any subformula of the form $\varphi_1 \, \tilde{U}_I \, \varphi_2$, either I is bounded or φ_1 is in MITL. If we write CFMTL for the sublogic of coflat formulas then CFMTL includes both BMTL and MITL, is closed under $\Box_I$ for arbitrary I (invariance), and is closed under U_I for bounded I (bounded liveness). Thus, for specifications, coflatness is a very natural and mild restriction.

The formula $\Box(req \rightarrow \Diamond_{(0,1)}(acq \wedge \Diamond_{\{1\}} rel))$ says that every time a lock is requested, it is acquired within one time unit, and released after exactly one further time unit. This formula is in CFMTL, but is not in BMTL (due to the unconstrained $\Box$) nor is it in MITL (due to the punctual $\Diamond_{\{1\}}$).

The main result of [10] is that the model-checking problem for CFMTL is EXPSPACE-complete; moreover this result holds irrespective of whether the constants in the timing constraints are encoded in unary or binary. In the case that constants are encoded in unary, the proof of EXPSPACE-hardness follows the same idea as the EXPSPACE-hardness proof for BMTL satisfiability. The matching upper bound is via a translation to LTL that incurs an exponential blow-up. Thus for the most commonly occurring specification patterns, such as invariance and bounded response, punctuality can be accommodated while model checking remains in EXPSPACE.

We emphasise that the above refers to model checking and not satisfiability. In fact the satisfiability problem for CFMTL is undecidable for the simple reason that all the formulas used in the proof of undecidability of satisfiability for MTL are coflat. (Note that CFMTL is not closed under negation.)

5 Decidable Sublogics: Pointwise Semantics

From another point of view, the source of undecidability in MTL is the richness of the semantic model. A natural restriction on the semantics is to interpret the logic on timed words in which all timestamps are integers. Indeed it is often argued that integer time suffices for most applications [16]. With respect to integer-valued timed words, satisfiability and model checking for MTL are easily seen to be EXPSPACE-complete, matching the complexity of MITL over the continuous semantics. The exponential blow-up over LTL arises from the possibility to write timing constraints succinctly in binary. We note that such succinct timing constraints are also the cause of the exponential blow-up in the complexity of MITL over MTL: if timing constraints are written in unary then model checking and satisfiability for MITL in the continuous semantics are both PSPACE-complete.

Keeping with timed words, but now allowing timestamps to be arbitrary real numbers, the situation becomes more delicate. Over finite timed words both model checking and satisfiability for MTL are decidable but not primitive recursive [27]. Over infinite timed words both problems are undecidable. Thus in the pointwise semantics the situation between decidability and undecidability is finely balanced.

The decidability of satisfiability and model checking for MTL over finite timed words was proved in [27] by giving a procedure for deciding language emptiness for alternating timed automata over finite words. That procedure used forward reachability analysis to search for an accepting computation tree on a given automaton. The well-quasi-order on configurations identified in Section 3 was used to prove the termination of such a search.

At this point it is instructive to see why the undecidability proof for MTL over the continuous semantics fails over the pointwise semantics. Consider the formula $\Box(a \leftrightarrow \Diamond_{\{1\}}a)$. For a timed word to satisfy this formula every a-event should be followed by another a-event after exactly one time unit. However the formula does not force every a-event to be preceded by an a-event one time unit earlier (for the reason that the former might not be preceded by any event exactly one time unit earlier). Thus if we try to encode computations of a Turing machine as timed words in MTL, we find that we can only encode the computations of a machine with $insertion$ $errors$.

In fact, when considering such erroneous computation devices it is more convenient to talk about a class of computing devices called $insertion$ $channel$ $machines$ $with$ $emptiness$-$testing$, or $ICMET$ [25]. Such devices consist of a finite control together with a fixed number of unbounded channels (or queues). Transitions between control states can write messages to the tail of a channel, read messages from the head of a channel, or perform an emptiness test on a channel.[2] There is a formal duality between such ICMETs and $lossy$ $channel$ $machines$ [30].

The $control$-$state$ $reachability$ $problem$ for ICMETs asks whether a given ICMET has a finite computation starting from the initial state and ending in an accepting control state. The $recurrent$-$state$ $problem$ for ICMETs asks whether a given ICMET has an infinite computation that visits an accepting state infinitely often. The control-state reachability problem is decidable, but not primitive recursive, while the recurrent-state problem is undecidable [25,27,30].

As suggested above, one can encode finite computations of ICMETs using MTL formulas over finite timed words; thus one shows that satisfiability and model-checking for MTL over finite timed words are not primitive recursive. Similarly one can reduce the recurrent-state problem for ICMETs to the satisfiability and model checking problems for MTL over infinite words, showing that the latter two problems are undecidable. In particular the formula $\Box\Diamond p$ is used to encode the fact that a computation visits an accepting state infinitely often.

5.1 Safety

The last remark above suggests that one might recover decidability over infinite timed words by restricting to safety properties. This approach was taken

---

[2] In contrast to models of asynchronous communication, we assume that the same finite control automaton writes to and reads from the channels.

in [26,27] which defined a syntactic fragment of MTL called *Safety MTL (SMTL)*. An MTL formula in negation normal form is said to be in SMTL if in any subformula of the form $\varphi_1 \; U_I \; \varphi_2$ the interval I is bounded. No restrictions are placed on the dual until connective $\widetilde{U}$. For example, if $\varphi \in$ SMTL then $\Box\varphi$ and $\Diamond_{(0,5)}\varphi$ are both in SMTL. Informally the requirement for a formula to be in SMTL is that all eventualities be bounded.

Following the classical semantic definition of safety property in the untimed setting, a set Π of infinite timed words is said to be a safety property if any timed word $\rho \notin \Pi$ has a finite prefix ρ', such that no extension of ρ' lies in Π. Due to the assumption that timed words are non-Zeno, Henzinger [14] calls such properties 'safety relative to the divergence of time'. (In a dense-time model a bounded-response property, such as $\Diamond_{(0,5)}p$, can only be considered a safety property thanks to the assumption of non-Zenoness.) All SMTL formulas define semantic safety properties.

Continuing the thread of ideas from above, the undecidability proof for MTL over infinite timed words does not apply to SMTL, since the latter cannot encode a *recurrent* computation of an ICMET. One can reduce the *termination problem* for ICMETs [11] to the satisfiability problem for SMTL, but the former is decidable though non-elementary. In fact one can again use alternating timed automata and the well-quasi-order from Section 3 to show that both satisfiability and model checking for SMTL are decidable [26,27].

Similarly to CFMTL, SMTL is suitable for defining invariance and time-bounded response properties. Comparing the two logics, we note that SMTL is more permissive in its use of $\widetilde{U}$, but less permissive in its use of U (cf. Section 4). Notwithstanding this superficial similarity, there is a chasm between the respective complexities of the model checking problem. Model checking for SMTL is non-primitive recursive [27] while it is EXPSPACE-complete for CFMTL.

6 Summary

We summarise the relationships between the various logics introduced in Sections 4 and 5 in the following diagram (where $\hookrightarrow$ indicates a syntactic inclusion):

$$
\begin{array}{ccc}
\text{BMTL} \hookrightarrow & \longrightarrow \text{SMTL} \hookleftarrow & \\
\text{LTL} \hookrightarrow \text{MTL}_{0,\infty} \hookrightarrow \text{MITL} \hookrightarrow & \text{CFMTL} \hookrightarrow & \text{MTL}
\end{array}
$$

We also summarise complexity results for model-checking and satisfiability for different fragments of MTL in Table 1. In this table results that refer to the pointwise semantics are shaded in grey; all other results refer to the continuous semantics. The legend 'MTL (fin.)' in the last row stands for MTL over finite timed words.

Table 1. Complexity of fragments of MTL

	Model Checking	**Satisfiability**
LTL	PSPACE-c.	PSPACE-c.
$MTL_{0,\infty}$	PSPACE-c.	PSPACE-c.
MITL	EXPSPACE-c.	EXPSPACE-c.
BMTL	EXPSPACE-c.	EXPSPACE-c.
SMTL	Non-Prim.-Rec.	Non-Elem.
CFMTL	EXPSPACE-c.	Undec.
MTL	Undec.	Undec.
MTL (fin.)	Non-Prim.-Rec	Non-Prim.-Rec

References

1. Alur, R., Courcoubetis, C., Dill, D.L.: Model-checking for real-time systems. In: Proceeding of LICS 1990. IEEE Comp. Society Press, Los Alamitos (1990)
2. Alur, R., Dill, D.: A theory of timed automata. Theoretical Computer Science 126, 183–235 (1994)
3. Alur, R., Feder, T., Henzinger, T.A.: The benefits of relaxing punctuality. Journal of the ACM 43, 116–146 (1996)
4. Alur, R., Henzinger, T.A.: Logics and models of real time: A survey. In: Proceedings of Real Time: Theory in Practice. LNCS, vol. 600. Springer, Heidelberg (1992)
5. Alur, R., Henzinger, T.A.: Real-time logics: complexity and expressiveness. Information and Computation 104, 35–77 (1993)
6. Alur, R., Henzinger, T.A.: A really temporal logic. Journal of the ACM 41, 181–204 (1994)
7. Alur, R., Madhusudan, P.: Decision Problems for Timed Automata: A Survey. In: Bernardo, M., Corradini, F. (eds.) SFM-RT 2004. LNCS, vol. 3185. Springer, Heidelberg (2004)
8. Bouyer, P., Chevalier, F., Markey, N.: On the Expressiveness of TPTL and MTL. In: Ramanujam, R., Sen, S. (eds.) FSTTCS 2005. LNCS, vol. 3821. Springer, Heidelberg (2005)
9. Bouyer, P., Markey, N., Ouaknine, J., Worrell, J.: The Cost of Punctuality. In: Proceedings of LICS 2007. IEEE Computer Society Press, Los Alamitos (2007)
10. Bouyer, P., Markey, N., Ouaknine, J., Worrell, J.: On Expressiveness and Complexity in Real-time Model Checking. In: Proceedings of ICALP 2008. LNCS. Springer, Heidelberg (to appear, 2008)
11. Bouyer, P., Markey, N., Ouaknine, J., Schnoebelen, P., Worrell, J.: On Termination for Faulty Channel Machines. In: Proceedings of STACS 2008 (2008)
12. Comon, H., Cortier, V.: Flatness is not a Weakness. In: Clote, P.G., Schwichtenberg, H. (eds.) CSL 2000. LNCS, vol. 1862. Springer, Heidelberg (2000)
13. Demri, S., Lazić, R., Nowak, D.: On the Freeze Quantifier in Constraint LTL: Decidability and Complexity. Information and Computation 205(1), 2–24 (2007)
14. Henzinger, T.A.: Sooner is safer than later. Processing Letters 43, 135–141 (1992)
15. Henzinger, T.A.: It's about time: Real-time logics reviewed. In: Sangiorgi, D., de Simone, R. (eds.) CONCUR 1998. LNCS, vol. 1466. Springer, Heidelberg (1998)
16. Henzinger, T.A., Manna, Z., Pnueli, A.: What good are digital clocks? In: Kuich, W. (ed.) ICALP 1992. LNCS, vol. 623. Springer, Heidelberg (1992)

17. Hirshfeld, Y., Rabinovich, A.M.: Logics for Real Time: Decidability and Complexity. Fundam. Inform. 62(1), 1–28 (2004)
18. Henzinger, T.A., Raskin, J.-F., Shobbens, P.-Y.: The regular real-time languages. In: Larsen, K.G., Skyum, S., Winskel, G. (eds.) ICALP 1998. LNCS, vol. 1443. Springer, Heidelberg (1998)
19. Higman, G.: Ordering by divisibility in abstract algebras. Proc. of the London Mathematical Society 2, 236–366 (1952)
20. Kamp, J.A.W.: Tense logic and the theory of linear order. Ph.D. Thesis, UCLA (1968)
21. Koymans, R.: Specifying real-time properties with metric temporal logic. Real-time Systems 2(4), 255–299 (1990)
22. Lasota, S., Walukiewicz, I.: Alternating timed automata. In: Sassone, V. (ed.) FOSSACS 2005. LNCS, vol. 3441. Springer, Heidelberg (2005)
23. Ostroff, J.: Temporal logic of real-time systems. Research Studies Press, Taunton
24. Ouaknine, J., Worrell, J.: On the language inclusion problem for timed automata: Closing a decidability gap. In: Proceedings of LICS 2004. IEEE Computer Society Press, Los Alamitos (2004)
25. Ouaknine, J., Worrell, J.: Metric temporal logic and faulty Turing machines. In: Aceto, L., Ingólfsdóttir, A. (eds.) FOSSACS 2006. LNCS, vol. 3921. Springer, Heidelberg (2006)
26. Ouaknine, J., Worrell, J.: Safety metric temporal logic is fully decidable. In: Hermanns, H., Palsberg, J. (eds.) TACAS 2006. LNCS, vol. 3920. Springer, Heidelberg (2006)
27. Ouaknine, J., Worrell, J.: On the Decidability and Complexity of Metric Temporal Logic over Finite Words. Logicical Methods in Computer Science 3(1) (2007)
28. Pnueli, A.: The temporal logic of programs. In: Proceedings of FOCS 1977. IEEE Computer Society Press, Los Alamitos (1977)
29. Raskin, J.-F., Schobbens, P.-Y.: State-clock logic: a decidable real-time logic. In: Maler, O. (ed.) HART 1997. LNCS, vol. 1201. Springer, Heidelberg (1997)
30. Schnoebelen, P.: Verifying lossy channel systems has nonprimitive recursive complexity. Information Processing Letters 83(5), 251–261 (2002)
31. Wilke, T.: Specifying timed state sequences in powerful decidable logics and timed automata. In: Langmaack, H., de Roever, W.-P., Vytopil, J. (eds.) FTRTFT 1994 and ProCoS 1994. LNCS, vol. 863. Springer, Heidelberg (1994)

Composing Web Services in an Open World: Issues of Quality of Service*

Albert Benveniste

Inria-Rennes; Irisa, Campus de Beaulieu, 35042 Rennes cedex, France
http://www.irisa.fr/distribcom/benveniste/

Abstract. Orchestrating Web services has become the method of choice for building new services on top of existing ones. One area of interest for this technology is business processes. Languages and methods have been developed and are now getting widely used, BPEL being the typical instance. When exposing the profile of a Web service, Quality of Service (QoS) must be specified. Besides security aspects, QoS involves a variety of parameters related to performance, query throughput, as well as quality of the returned data. How should QoS be handled in this context of Web Services Orchestrations? A number of novel and not so well identified issues occur that make this topic deviating from QoS for networks in a substantial way.

Firstly, since Web services aim at hiding details for the external world, no information regarding the infrastructure or resources supporting a Web service is generally exposed. This prevents from using classical resource based performance models. Contracts are preferred instead. Contracts expose what a service offers, in terms of both function and QoS; in turn, contracts may or may not assume certain constraints on how the service should be invoked.

A second important feature is that, unlike in networks, the control in orchestrations may depend on the carried data. Consequently performance and data interfere, which can cause orchestrations to become non-monotonic with respect to QoS—improving the QoS of some called service may degrade the overall QoS of the orchestration. Unfortunately, relying on QoS contracts implicitly assumes monotonicity.

In a contract-based framework, a central question is to relate the contract that the orchestration can offer to its customers, to the contracts it has established with its subcontractors regarding the called services. This is not so simple when dealing with Web Services Orchestrations because actual QoS parameters vary a lot for different calls and are better described by means of a probability distribution. I shall discuss probabilistic soft contracts and how to compose them. Such contracts must be monitored by the orchestration for possible violations. I shall advocate using testing techniques from statistics for this purpose.

Orchestration reconfiguration (e.g., to cope with breaching) is another important issue that is beyond the scope of my presentation, however.

---

* This work was partially funded by the ANR national research program DocFlow (ANR-06-MDCA-005) and the project CREATE ActivDoc. This talk is based on joint work with Anne Bouillard, Stefan Haar, Claude Jard, and Sidney Rosario.

F. Cassez and C. Jard (Eds.): FORMATS 2008, LNCS 5215, p. 14, 2008.

Comparing the Expressiveness of Timed Automata and Timed Extensions of Petri Nets

Jiří Srba*

Department of Computer Science, Aalborg University,
Selma Lagerlöfs Vej 300, 9220 Aalborg East, Denmark
srba@cs.aau.dk

Abstract. Time dependant models have been intensively studied for many reasons, among others because of their applications in software verification and due to the development of embedded platforms where reliability and safety depend to a large extent on the time features. Many of the time dependant models were suggested as real-time extensions of several well-known untimed models. The most studied formalisms include Networks of Timed Automata which extend the model of communicating finite-state machines with a finite number of real-valued clocks, and timed extensions of Petri nets where the added time constructs include e.g. time intervals that are assigned to the transitions (Time Petri Nets) or to the arcs (Timed-Arc Petri Nets). In this paper, we shall semi-formally introduce these models, discuss their strengths and weaknesses, and provide an overview of the known results about the relationships among the models.

1 Introduction

In formal modelling and verification of software and hardware systems there is an obvious need for considering time features and hence the study of so-called *time dependant models* has become increasingly important. The overall research in this area is motivated, among others, by the development of embedded platforms which use time features and should be reliable and correct [53].

As mentioned in [83], majority of these formalisms rely on the assumption of *orthogonality* between discrete and continuous (time delay) changes which significantly simplifies the underlying semantics of time dependant models. A run of the system can be then seen as a sequence of steps where continuous time progress and discrete events alternate. We are going to adopt such an approach also in this paper.

In what follows, we shall take a closer look at three prominent examples of time dependant systems, namely Networks of Timed Automata (NTA), Time Petri Nets (TPN) and Timed-Arc Petri Nets (TAPN). These models have existed for a relatively long period of time but they have been developed to a large extent

---

* The author is supported in part by a grant of the Ministry of Education of the Czech Republic, project No. 1M0545.

F. Cassez and C. Jard (Eds.): FORMATS 2008, LNCS 5215, pp. 15–32, 2008.

independently of each other, even though they share many common features. Citing [21]: "In spite of many technical resemblances and their overlapping application domains, few material was available until recently comparing expressiveness of these ... models." Fortunately, there has recently been a growing interest in mutual comparisons of different models that include real-time constructs. One reason for this development could be the recent availability of efficient verification tools for timed automata, which stimulates the translation approaches from TPN and TAPN to TA, rather than the development TPN/TAPN verification techniques that resemble those already available for timed automata.

In this paper we will, by means of examples, introduce the models of timed automata, time Petri nets and timed-arc Petri nets. Then we provide an overview of decidable and undecidable problems related to these models and present a summary of their strengths and weaknesses. Finally, we give an up-to-date overview of work that aims at comparing the relative expressive power of these models. In the last section we finish with a few concluding remarks and the possible future development in this area.

2   Time Dependant Models

Time dependant models are often obtained by extending the untimed ones with time constructs that enable to manipulate in different ways the passing of time. Two well-studied approaches include the extension of finite automata resp. networks of communicating finite automata with a number of real-valued clocks and different timed extensions of Petri nets.

2.1   Timed Automata and Networks of Timed Automata

Timed Automata. Timed automata were introduced by Alur and Dill [6, 7] and have by now been recognized as one of the classical formalisms for modelling real-time systems with dense time.

A *timed automaton* (TA) is a finite-state machine extended with a finite number of synchronous clocks. Transitions in the automaton are conditioned on the clock values and taking a transition can affect (reset) the values of selected clocks. A typical transition in a timed automaton looks like

$$\ell \xrightarrow{g,a,r} \ell'$$

where ℓ and ℓ' are *locations* (or *states*) of the automaton, g is a clock *guard*, a is a *label* (or *action*) of the transition, and r is a subset of clocks that are reset when the transition is taken. Guards are defined by the abstract syntax

$$g ::= x \bowtie k \mid x - y \bowtie k \mid g \wedge g$$

where x, y are elements from a given finite set of *clocks*, k is an integer, and $\bowtie \in \{\leq, <, \geq, >, =\}$. A timed automaton which does not contain any guard of the form $x - y \bowtie k$ is called *diagonal-free*.

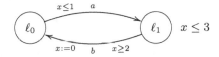

Fig. 1. Example of TA

Guards can be also associated with locations and then they are called *invariants*. Invariants restrict the amount of time that can be spent in a given location and we usually consider only invariants given by the abstract syntax: $g ::= x \leq k \mid x < k \mid g \wedge g$.

A *configuration* of a timed automaton is a pair of a location and a *clock valuation*, which is a function assigning to each clock a nonnegative real number (the time that has elapsed since the last clock reset). Consider an example of a timed automaton in Figure 1 where ℓ_0 is a given initial location.

Starting from the configuration $(\ell_0, [x = 0])$ where the value of the clock x is zero, we can delay for any nonnegative real number d and reach the valuation $(\ell_0, [x = d])$. This is called a *time elapsing step*. As long as we are in the configuration where $d \leq 1$, we can also perform a *discrete step* by taking the transition labelled by a. This is because the guard $x \leq 1$ is satisfied. We then reach the configuration $(\ell_1, [x = d])$. In the location ℓ_1 we can now delay for at most $3 - d$ time units because of the invariant $x \leq 3$ associated with the location ℓ_1. As soon as the value of the clock x is at least 2 we can also take the discrete transition labelled with b and return to the initial configuration $(\ell_0, [x = 0])$ because the value of the clock x is reset to 0 by taking this transition.

Networks of Timed Automata. Single timed automata can be also run in parallel. A *network of timed automata* (NTA) is a parallel composition of a finite number of timed automata where the actions are partitioned into the set of output (suffixed with !) and input (suffixed with ?) actions. A component in the parallel composition can make a discrete step under an action $a!$ only if there is another component ready to make a discrete step under the complementary action $a?$. In this case the two parallel components perform a handshake synchronization and move simultaneously to their new locations. Other types of synchronization, e.g. in the style of Arnold-Nivat [10] via synchronization functions, are also possible and studied. The parallel components may also perform a time elapsing step and in this case all the clocks age in a synchronous manner. Networks of timed automata are not more expressive than a single timed automaton (which can be shown by a standard product construction) but they are exponentially more concise.

2.2 Petri Nets

Untimed Petri Nets. Petri nets (PN) were first suggested in early sixties by Carl Adam Petri in his PhD thesis [73] and have since then become a popular and wide-spread model of distributed systems with many applications and a large number of academic as well as industrial tools (see [51] for an updated list). One

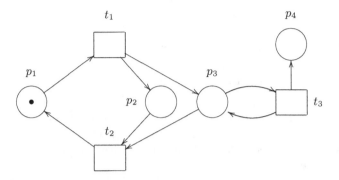

Fig. 2. Example of PN

of the main advantages of this model is its intuitive graphical representation. Consider an example of a Petri net in Figure 2.

The circles are called *places*, boxes are called *transitions* and arrows (also called *arcs*) can connect only a place to a transition, or a transition to a place. The dot in the place p_1 is called a *token* and it is connected with the behaviour of the net. One place can hold several tokens. A token assignment to the places is called a *marking*. A transition t, in a given marking, that has a token in every of its input places (those connected to t by an arc) is called *enabled* and can *fire* by consuming one token from every of its input places and producing a new token to every of its output places (having an incoming arc from the transition t).

In our example the transition t_1 is enabled and when it fires it consumes the token in the place p_1 and produces two new tokens, one into the place p_2 and the other into the place p_3. Now either the transition t_2 can fire and return the net to its initial marking, or the transition t_3 can fire, consume the token from p_3, and produce a new token into the places p_3 and p_4. Now the transition t_3 can fire again, leaving the token in p_3 and producing a second token into the place p_4. It is easy to see that by repeatedly firing the transition t_3, an arbitrary large number of tokens will be placed into p_4. This net is hence an example of so-called *unbounded net*.

Formally, a net is called *bounded* or *safe* if the number of tokens in all reachable markings is bounded by some a priori given constant. A special case when every place in any reachable marking contains at most one token is called *1-safe*.

Remark 1. Despite the infinite state-spaces of unbounded Petri nets, several properties like marking reachability, coverability, boundedness and others are still decidable (for an overview see e.g. [47, 46]), while strong bisimilarity and some other related problems are undecidable [54]. In order to compare the expressive power of Petri nets (and their extensions with time) with finite automata-based models, we usually consider only bounded nets. They are still useful for modelling and analyzing many real-life problems (for an overview of different case studies see e.g. [52]).

Extending Petri Nets with Time. Unlike timed automata, Petri nets offer several options where the time constructs can be associated to. For example *timed transitions Petri nets* were proposed in [76] where transitions are annotated with their durations. A model in which time parameters are associated with places is called *timed places Petri nets* and it was introduced in [82]. For an overview of the different extensions see e.g. [32, 72, 88].

In this paper we shall focus on two other, perhaps the most studied, extensions called Time Petri Nets of Merlin and Faber [66, 67] introduced in 1976 and the model of Timed-Arc Petri Nets first studied around 1990 by Bolognesi, Lucidi, Trigila and Hanisch [26, 50].

2.3   Time Petri Nets

In Time Petri Nets (TPN) [66, 67] each transition has an associated time interval which gives the earliest and latest firing time of the transition since it became enabled. One can think of this as every transition having an associated real-valued clock, which gets initialized at the moment the transition becomes enabled. The transition can fire as soon as the clock value reaches the earliest firing time and it *must* fire no later than the latest firing time, unless the transition got disabled by the firing of some other transition. This means that TPN can express *urgent* behaviour (also called the *strong* semantics). The precise semantics of the behaviour is, however, not completely obvious and several different variants can be considered [17]. It seems that the *intermediate semantics* is the most often used one. Here all transitions disabled after consuming the tokens of the transition being fired, as well as the firing transition itself, are reinitialized.

Consider the following example of TPN presented in Figure 3. It uses the underlying untimed net from Figure 2 enriched with time intervals on transitions. Assume that the clocks x_1, x_2 and x_3 are associated to the transitions t_1, t_2 and t_3, respectively. In the initial marking the clock x_1 gets initialized to the value 0 and as the firing interval of t_1 is $[2, 4]$, the only possible behaviour of the net is to delay any time between 2 and 4 time units and then fire the transition t_1. This produces two new tokens into p_2 and p_3 and the clocks x_2 and x_3 get initialized at the same time. Now the net has to wait for another 3 time units and latest by

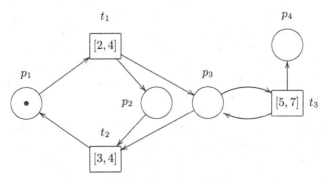

Fig. 3. Example of TPN

4 time units the transition t_2 must fire and we reach the initial marking. This implies that t_3 is never firable and unlike the underlying untimed net, the TPN in our example is bounded and even 1-safe. Assume now that the time interval $[5, 7]$ associated with t_3 is replaced by $[2, 8]$. Now after firing t_1 and starting the clocks x_2 and x_3, the transition t_3 is ready to fire already after two time units, and after another 1 time unit both t_2 and t_3 are enabled. Note that after firing t_3 both x_2 and x_3 get reinitialized to 0 because we adopted the intermediate semantics. In other semantics the clock x_2 might not get restarted.

2.4   Timed-Arc Petri Nets

The last extension of Petri nets that we consider in this paper is called *Timed-Arc Petri Nets* (TAPN) [26, 50]. Here the time entity (also called *age*) is associated with tokens. We can think of this as if every token in the net had its own private clock. The arcs from places to transitions are labelled by time intervals which restrict the age of tokens that can be used to fire a given transition. When new tokens are produced, their age is set by default to 0. The usually considered semantics is *non-urgent* (or *weak*), which means that tokens can grow older even if this disables the firing of certain transitions (sometimes for ever). Consider the following TAPN in Figure 4 with the same underlying untimed net as in Figure 2.

In the initial marking there is one token of age 0 in the place p_1. As the age of the token does not belong to the interval $[2, 4]$, the transition t_1 is not enabled yet, but only after two time units. Then anytime within another 2 units the transition can fire and produce two new tokens of age 0 into the places p_2 and p_3. Note, however, that due to the non-urgent semantics it is possible that the age of the token in p_1 grows beyond 4 and hence the transition t_1 gets disabled for ever. Should this happen, the token in the place p_1 is called *dead*. Assume now that we are in a marking with two tokens of age 0 in the places p_2 and p_3. After waiting for two time units, the transition t_3 becomes enabled and if it fires it resets the age of the token in the place p_3 to 0 and produces a new fresh token into the place p_4. By waiting for another two time units the age of the token in the place p_2 reaches the value 4 and the tokens in the places p_3 and p_4 will be of age 2. Now, for example, the transition t_2 can fire, consuming the tokens in places p_2 and p_3 and producing a fresh one into the place p_1. Another possible behaviour (due to the non-urgent semantics) is that the transition t_3 keeps firing for ever after arbitrary delays between 2 and 8 time units. This shows that our TAPN is unbounded and moreover every token in the place p_4 will have its own unique age. This demonstrates that unlike for TA and TPN, we cannot rely only on a finite number of clocks associated with a given automaton/net.

Our example also shows that every time the transition t_3 fires, the age of the token in p_3 is reset to 0. In some applications this might be undesirable and hence in [84] the model was extended with so-called *read-arcs*, which allow to test for a presence of a token in a certain place but do not change its age. It was later shown in [30] that this extension is not only convenient from the modelling point of view but it also extends the expressiveness of the model.

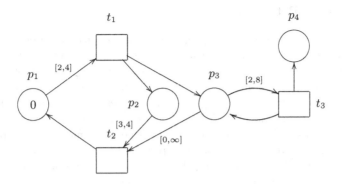

Fig. 4. Example of TAPN

3 Overview of Known Decidability Results

In this section we shall mention a selection of positive and negative decidability results for our three time dependant models.

3.1 Networks of Timed Automata

The *region graph* construction provides a universal tool for arguing about the decidability of several problems on timed automata [6, 7]. Using this technique it was shown, e.g., that reachability is decidable in PSPACE for TA [7] as well as for NTA [5], untimed language equivalence for TA is decidable in PSPACE [7], and untimed bisimilarity for TA is decidable in EXPTIME [59]. Practically more efficient algorithms are usually achieved by considering *zones* instead of regions (see e.g. [16]). Somewhat surprisingly even timed bisimilarity for timed automata is decidable. Using region graphs on a product construction, timed bisimilarity was shown to be decidable in EXPTIME [41].

Unfortunately, timed language equivalence for timed automata is undecidable [7]. In fact, even the universality problem (whether a given timed automaton generates *all* timed traces) is undecidable.

3.2 Time Petri Nets

It is known that even very simple classes of timed nets extended with the notion of urgency have the full Turing power [55] (can simulate e.g. Minsky two-counter machines) and hence most of the verification problems for TPN like reachability and boundedness are undecidable. For additional remarks see also [23, 74].

On the other hand, for bounded nets the *state class method* [24] can be often used to derive decidability results. Regarding the complexity, it is known that reachability (and also TCTL model-checking) of bounded TPN is PSPACE-complete [27].

3.3   Timed-Arc Petri Nets

In spite of the fact that reachability is decidable for ordinary Petri nets [65], it is undecidable for timed-arc Petri nets [78], even in the case when tokens in different places are not required to age synchronously [69]. On the other hand, coverability, boundedness and other problems remain decidable for TAPN [77, 3, 1], which are also known to offer 'weak' expressiveness, in the sense that TAPN cannot simulate Turing machines [25]. Coverability is decidable even for TAPN extended with read-arcs [30]. These results hold due to the monotonicity property (adding more tokens to the net does not restrict the possible executions) and the application of well-quasi-ordering (for a general introduction see [48]) resp. better-quasi-ordering [2] techniques.

When we consider the subclass of 1-safe TAPN, it is known that the reachability problem is no more difficult than in untimed 1-safe Petri nets and hence it is decidable in PSPACE [84]. This is the case also for 1-safe TAPN with read-arcs.

4   Strengths and Weaknesses of the Models

This section aims at providing a comparison of the three models w.r.t. to their modelling capabilities and their applicability for verification purposes.

4.1   Networks of Timed Automata

Pros. Timed automata are nowadays a widely used modelling formalism with rich theoretical foundations and a number of developed verification tools like UPPAAL [58], KRONOS [37], IF [38] and CMC [57]. A number of case studies (see e.g. [9, 14] for an overview) demonstrate that timed automata are a suitable formalism for modelling of systems of industrial sizes and the tools have already reached a reasonable degree of maturity and efficiency. A combination of an easily understandable syntax and semantics together with the support for C-like constructs and data structures (e.g. in the tool UPPAAL) makes this a widely applicable and successful approach to modelling and verification of time dependant systems.

Cons. On the other hand, timed automata are less convenient for modelling of certain types of applications like work-flow management systems, production lines with shared resources and other systems which require e.g. a dynamic creation of new processes. Here models based on Petri nets are most commonly used. It is also known that e.g. TPN are exponentially more concise than NTA [31, 29], so even though timed automata are as expressive as bounded Petri net based models, the size of TA models for certain time dependant systems might be unnecessarily large. As claimed in [45] timed automata also lack a support for high level composable graphical patterns to support systematic design of complex systems. The explicit use of invariants in timed automata also causes problems: during the design of a specification it is easy to introduce time deadlocks (time cannot progress and no transition is firable). This is usually interpreted as an inconsistency of the specification and should be avoided. However, such specification errors cannot occur neither in TPN (urgency is applicable only as long as some discrete transitions are still enabled) nor in TAPN (time is always allowed to progress). For further discussion on this issue see [83].

4.2 Time Petri Nets

Pros. The model of TPN has been around for several decades and it has proven to be useful for modelling of a wide range of real-time systems including work-flow processes, scheduling problems and others [11, 15, 68, 75]. It has an implicit notion of urgency suitable for modelling many real-life problems and implicitly avoids the construction of ill-defined timed systems. There are available a few public verification tools like TINA [22] and ROMEO [81].

Cons. Unbounded TPN are too expressive (have full Turing power) and are hence unsuitable for automatic verification. This means that most of the verification approaches are limited to bounded nets. Also the modelling power is restricted as TPN cannot model some useful features like e.g. a dynamic creation of new processes which carry their own time information. In fact the number of time clocks (associated to the transitions) is limited in advance by the structure of the net and lacks more flexibility. Last, the exact semantics is not only more difficult to understand than for the other two models but it also offers several variants [17]. Different papers use different variants of the semantics, though the intermediate semantics described also in this paper seems most common. This is in contrast with the conclusion drawn in [17] where the authors give arguments why other policies like e.g. the *persistent atomic semantics* should be preferred over the intermediate semantics. The current TPN tools are relatively new, have a limited number of constructs like data structures which include e.g. arrays, and they lack hierarchical modelling features.

4.3 Timed-Arc Petri Nets

Pros. TAPN are particularly suitable for modelling of manufacturing systems, work-flow management and similar applications. It is the author's opinion that TAPN offer a more intuitive semantics than TPN; at least there are no competing variants of the semantics. TAPN provide an easy to understand interplay between the token game and the associated time features. For modelling of certain applications, especially systems where a number of identical time processes share the same pattern of behaviour [3, 4] but also others [70, 79, 80, 71], TAPN provide a convenient modelling formalism. By simply adding more and more tokens to the net, more and more processes (each carrying its own clock) can be modelled without any change to the net itself. Neither TPN nor NTA provide this feature. As several problems like e.g. coverability are decidable even for unbounded TAPN, a parametric reasoning is possible [3].

Cons. One of the major weaknesses of TAPN is the lack of the possibility to model urgent behaviour. This might be one of the reasons, together with the fact that the model was introduced much later than TPN, why TAPN deserved less attention among the scientists. Currently there are no publicly available tools, though some prototype implementations already exist.

5   Relationships among the Models

In this section we will provide an overview of the expressiveness results for the studied models. As already mentioned, unbounded TPN and TAPN generate infinite state-spaces and e.g. the reachability problem is undecidable for both of them. Hence to draw a fair comparison between the nets and timed automata, most of the work focuses on the relationship between *bounded* or *1-safe* nets and timed automata. There are some exceptions like e.g. the work in [40] which translates unbounded TPN into UPPAAL-like NTA extended with unbounded integer arrays.

From TA/NTA to TPN. A translation from diagonal-free TA without invariants and strict constraints to 1-safe TPN preserving weak timed bisimulation was suggested by Haar et al. in [49]. In the paper they, however, consider only weak (non-urgent) semantics for TPN. Bérard et al. give in [18] a linear translation from diagonal-free TA with invariants to 1-safe TPN up to timed language equivalence. They also show that TA are strictly more expressive than TPN w.r.t. weak timed bisimilarity and in [19] (see also a forthcoming journal article [20]) they identify a strict subclass of TA which is equivalent with bounded TPN w.r.t. weak timed bisimilarity. In [21] Berthomieu et al. suggest to extend the TPN model with priorities and show that this is enough to establish an equivalence with NTA w.r.t. weak timed bisimilarity. Another reduction from TA to TPN, which includes also diagonal constraints and updates to integral values, was presented by Bouyer et al. in [31]. The reduction preserves timed language equivalence and works in linear resp. quadratic time, depending on what features of TA are included. This work, however, does not include invariants in TA. In [31] the authors also provide a translation from NTA to TPN, which preserves timed language equivalence, but introduces new deadlocks into the system behaviour.

From TPN to TA/NTA. Haar et al. provided in [49] a translation from 1-safe TPN to TA preserving weak timed bisimilarity. It improved the complexity of the previously known work based on enumerative methods [23, 24] and their translation is polynomial but only in the size of the TPN reachability graph. On the other hand, they allow only non-strict intervals and consider the weak (non-urgent) semantics for TPN, while the other papers focus on the standard strong (urgent) semantics. Another approach by Lime and Roux [62] extends these results to bounded TPN but also requires first a construction of the state class graph of the given bounded TPN. An extended version of their paper [63] provides an efficient reduction technique to decrease the number of clocks in the resulting timed automaton. A structural translation from TPN to NTA preserving weak timed bisimilarity, which does not require the construction of the state class graph, was proposed by Cassez and Roux in [40]. Their reduction uses NTA extended with arrays of (unbounded) integers and enables to translate even unbounded TPN into the extended NTA. If the input net is bounded, the values in the integer arrays are bounded too and automatic verification is hence possible. An implementation of the translation is available as a part of the TPN tool Romeo [81] and the results seem promising as documented on several case studies [40]. A possible problem with this approach is a potentially high number of clocks in the produced NTA. Recently D'Aprile et al. suggested in [44] an alternative technique for the translation from TPN to TA. Their method bypasses the construction of the state class graph (as used e.g. in [49, 62]) by considering only the underlying untimed reachability graph. It preserves timed bisimulation and TCTL properties. According to the experiments carried out by the authors, it is competitive with the other approaches on a number of case studies. On the other hand, it requires the underlying untimed net to be bounded, while the other approaches require only TPN boundedness. Empirical methods to deal with this limitation are outlined in the paper. Yet another approach is presented in [43] by Cortés et al. where the authors translate a more general model of TPN called PRES+ into UPPAAL-like timed automata, suggest several optimizations of the reduction, and provide two case studies. Their reduction works only for 1-safe nets and unfortunately there is no argument about the correctness of the translation.

From TA/NTA to TAPN and Backwards. The first result (we are aware of) which compares the expressive power of TA and TAPN is by Sifakis and Yovine [83] from 1996. They provide a translation of 1-safe timed-arc Petri nets (with urgent behaviour) into timed automata (with invariants) which preserves strong timed bisimilarity but their translation causes an exponential blow up in the size. Srba established in [84] a strong relationship (up to isomorphism of timed transition systems) between NTA without invariants and a superclass of 1-safe TAPN extended with read-arcs. When we are interested only in the reachability questions, the reductions work in polynomial time. Recently Bouyer et al. in [30] presented a reduction from bounded TAPN (with read-arcs) to 1-safe TAPN (with read-arcs) which preserves timed language equivalence (over finite words, infinite words and non-Zeno infinite words). This demonstrates that NTA without invariants and bounded TAPN with read-arcs are timed language equivalent. The authors in [30] also provide a number of expressiveness results for several subclasses of TAPN with read-arcs.

From TPN to TAPN and Backwards. We are aware of only few detailed studies comparing TPN and TAPN. In [42] Cerone and Maggiolio-Schettini study several timed extensions of bounded Petri nets w.r.t. language equivalence. Regarding the two classes of our main focus they show that TPN and TAPN are language equivalent w.r.t. weak (non-urgent) semantics and that TPN form a subclass of TAPN when considering the strong (urgent) semantics. In [35] Boyer and Vernadat show that the inclusion of TPN in TAPN is strict (in the strong semantics).

A further comparison of the different classes w.r.t. weak timed bisimilarity is provided in [34]. We should note that all the work mentioned so far in this paragraph uses the so-called single server semantics [36] for TAPN where the timing information to be remembered in every marking is constant. However, TAPN are mostly studied with the multi-server semantics where each token carries its own timing information. In this case, as concluded in [33], TPN express timed behaviour and TAPN express time behaviour *and* time constraints.

6   Conclusion

We have introduced three popular models of time dependant systems, compared their relative strengths and weaknesses and presented an overview of the known relationships across these models. Even though these formalisms share many common features and there exist mutual translations between the models, it is hard to say what should be *the* model for time dependant systems. Different applications might be modelled in different modelling formalisms with a very varying effort for a human modeller to create such models. We should also note that due to their complexity, the modelling tricks used in the translations between the different models are often unsuitable for a direct use by a human modeller. Nevertheless, the possibility of automatically translating all the time dependant models studied in this paper to e.g. a network of timed automata offers the option of creating hybrid tools that will enable to enter real-time models (or even their subparts) in all kinds of different formalisms, depending on the preference of the human modeller, and still have a clearly defined semantics and a support for automatic verification.

The tools for timed automata verification seem to be most developed at the moment. So while adding additional modelling features to Petri net based models, researchers should check whether these features can be translated to their TA counter-parts and the verification techniques/tools can be reused for them, rather than rediscovered. For example in the theory of TA there has been recently lots of research on extending timed automata with price/cost [60, 8, 28] and studying timed games [64, 39, 13, 12] as well as on-line testing [56, 61]. There is also a tool support implementing many of these theoretical results. Let us mention e.g. the tool UPPAAL-CORA [85] for cost-optimal reachability, UPPAAL-TIGA [86] for timed games and UPPAAL-TRON [87] for on-line testing. It is likely that the existing translations from TPN and TAPN to NTA can be extended with such features and a future research might focus on studying efficient translation approaches that include several of these new aspects.

Acknowledgements. I would like to thank to Patricia Bouyer, Franck Cassez, Alexandre David and Olivier H. Roux for their comments on a draft of this paper.

References

[1] Abdulla, P.A., Mahata, P., Mayr, R.: Dense-timed Petri nets: Checking zenoness, token liveness and boundedness. Logical Methods in Computer Science 3(1), 1–61 (2007)

[2] Abdulla, P.A., Nylén, A.: Better is better than well: On efficient verification of infinite-state systems. In: Proceedings of 15th Annual IEEE Symposium on Logic in Computer Science (LICS 2000), pp. 132–140 (2000)

[3] Abdulla, P.A., Nylén, A.: Timed Petri nets and BQOs. In: Colom, J.-M., Koutny, M. (eds.) ICATPN 2001. LNCS, vol. 2075, pp. 53–70. Springer, Heidelberg (2001)

[4] Abdulla, P.A., Deneux, J., Mahata, P., Nylén, A.: Forward reachability analysis of timed Petri nets. In: Lakhnech, Y., Yovine, S. (eds.) FORMATS 2004 and FTRTFT 2004. LNCS, vol. 3253, pp. 343–362. Springer, Heidelberg (2004)

[5] Aceto, L., Laroussinie, F.: Is your model checker on time? On the complexity of model checking for timed modal logics. Journal of Logic and Algebraic Programming, 52–53, 7–51 (2002)

[6] Alur, R., Dill, D.: Automata for modelling real-time systems. In: Paterson, M. (ed.) ICALP 1990. LNCS, vol. 443, pp. 322–335. Springer, Heidelberg (1990)

[7] Alur, R., Dill, D.: A theory of timed automata. Theoretical Computer Science 126(2), 183–235 (1994)

[8] Alur, R., La Torre, S., Pappas, G.J.: Optimal paths in weighted timed automata. Theoretical Computer Science 318(3), 297–322 (2004)

[9] Amnell, T., Behrmann, G., Bengtsson, J., D'Argenio, P.R., David, A., Fehnker, A., Hune, T., Jeannet, B., Larsen, K.G., Möller, M.O., Pettersson, P., Weise, C., Yi, W.: UPPAAL: Now, next, and future. In: Cassez, F., Jard, C., Rozoy, B., Dermot, M. (eds.) MOVEP 2001. LNCS, vol. 2067, pp. 99–124. Springer, Heidelberg (2001)

[10] Arnold, A.: Finite Transition Systems. Prentice-Hall, Englewood Cliffs (1994)

[11] Barreto, R., Cavalcante, S., Maciel, P.: A time Petri net approach for finding pre-runtime schedules in embedded hard real-time systems. In: Proceedings of the 24th International Conference on Distributed Computing Systems Workshops - W7: EC (ICDCSW 2004), pp. 846–851. IEEE Computer Society, Los Alamitos (2004)

[12] Behrmann, G., Cougnard, A., David, A., Fleury, E., Larsen, K.G., Lime, D.: UPPAAL-Tiga: Timed games for everyone. In: Aceto, L., Ingolfdottir, A. (eds.) Proceedings of the 18th Nordic Workshop on Programming Theory (NWPT 2006). Reykjavik University, Reykjavik (2006)

[13] Behrmann, G., Cougnard, A., David, A., Fleury, E., Larsen, K.G., Lime, D.: Uppaal-tiga: Time for playing games. In: Damm, W., Hermanns, H. (eds.) CAV 2007. LNCS, vol. 4590, pp. 121–125. Springer, Heidelberg (2007)

[14] Behrmann, G., David, A., Larsen, K.G.: A tutorial on uppaal. In: Bernardo, M., Corradini, F. (eds.) SFM-RT 2004. LNCS, vol. 3185, pp. 200–236. Springer, Heidelberg (2004)

[15] Bender, D.F., Combemale, B., Crégut, X., Farines, J.-M., Berthomieu, B., Vernadat, F.: Ladder metamodeling and PLC program validation through time Petri nets. In: Schieferdecker, I., Hartman, A. (eds.) ECMDA-FA 2008. LNCS, vol. 5095, pp. 121–136. Springer, Heidelberg (2008)

[16] Bengtsson, J., Yi, W.: Timed automata: Semantics, algorithms and tools. In: Desel, J., Reisig, W., Rozenberg, G. (eds.) Lectures on Concurrency and Petri Nets. LNCS, vol. 3098, pp. 87–124. Springer, Heidelberg (2004)

[17] Bérard, B., Cassez, F., Haddad, S., Lime, D., Roux, O.H.: Comparison of different semantics for time Petri nets. In: Peled, D.A., Tsay, Y.-K. (eds.) ATVA 2005. LNCS, vol. 3707, pp. 293–307. Springer, Heidelberg (2005)

[18] Bérard, B., Cassez, F., Haddad, S., Lime, D., Roux, O.H.: Comparison of the expressiveness of timed automata and time Petri nets. In: Pettersson, P., Yi, W. (eds.) FORMATS 2005. LNCS, vol. 3829, pp. 211–225. Springer, Heidelberg (2005)

[19] Bérard, B., Cassez, F., Haddad, S., Lime, D., Roux, O.H.: When are timed automata weakly timed bisimilar to time Petri nets? In: Ramanujam, R., Sen, S. (eds.) FSTTCS 2005. LNCS, vol. 3821, pp. 273–284. Springer, Heidelberg (2005)

[20] Bérard, B., Cassez, F., Haddad, S., Lime, D., Roux, O.H.: When are timed automata weakly timed bisimilar to time Petri nets? Theoretical Computer Science (forthcoming, 2008)

[21] Berthomieu, B., Peres, F., Vernadat, F.: Bridging the gap between timed automata and bounded time Petri nets. In: Asarin, E., Bouyer, P. (eds.) FORMATS 2006. LNCS, vol. 4202, pp. 82–97. Springer, Heidelberg (2006)

[22] Berthomieu, B., Ribet, P.-O., Vernadat, F.: The tool TINA — construction of abstract state spaces for Petri nets and time Petri nets. International Journal of Production Research 42(14), 2741–2756 (2004)

[23] Berthomieu, B., Diaz, M.: Modeling and verification of time dependent systems using time Petri nets. IEEE Trans. Software Eng. 17(3), 259–273 (1991)

[24] Berthomieu, B., Menasche, M.: An enumerative approach for analyzing time Petri nets. In: Proceedings of IFIP Congress 1983 on Information Processing, vol. 9, pp. 41–46. Elsevier Science Publishers, Amsterdam (1983)

[25] Bolognesi, T., Cremonese, P.: The weakness of some timed models for concurrent systems. Technical Report CNUCE C89-29, CNUCE–C.N.R (1989)

[26] Bolognesi, T., Lucidi, F., Trigila, S.: From timed Petri nets to timed LOTOS. In: Proceedings of the IFIP WG 6.1 Tenth International Symposium on Protocol Specification, Testing and Verification (Ottawa 1990), pp. 1–14. North-Holland, Amsterdam (1990)

[27] Boucheneb, H., Gardey, G., Roux, O.H.: TCTL model checking of time Petri nets. Technical Report IRCCyN number RI2006-14, Nantes Cedex, 2006, updated in (2008)

[28] Bouyer, P., Brinksma, E., Larsen, K.G.: Staying alive as cheaply as possible. In: Alur, R., Pappas, G.J. (eds.) HSCC 2004. LNCS, vol. 2993, pp. 203–218. Springer, Heidelberg (2004)

[29] Bouyer, P., Chevalier, F.: On conciseness of extensions of timed automata. Journal of Automata, Languages and Combinatorics 10(4), 393–405 (2005)

[30] Bouyer, P., Haddad, S., Reynier, P.-A.: Timed Petri nets and timed automata: On the discriminating power of zeno sequences. Information and Computation 206(1), 73–107 (2008)

[31] Bouyer, P., Reynier, P.-A., Haddad, S.: Extended timed automata and time Petri nets. In: Proceedings of the 6th International Conference on Application of Concurrency to System Design (ACSD 2006), pp. 91–100. IEEE Computer Society, Los Alamitos (2006)

[32] Bowden, F.D.J.: Modelling time in Petri nets. In: Proceedings of the Second Australia-Japan Workshop on Stochastic Models (1996)

[33] Boyer, M., Diaz, M.: Non equivalence between time Petri nets and time stream Petri nets. In: Proceedings of the 8th International Workshop on Petri Nets and Performance Models (PNPM 1999), pp. 198–207. IEEE Computer Society, Los Alamitos (1999)

[34] Boyer, M., Roux, O.H.: Comparison of the expressiveness of arc, place and transition time Petri nets. In: Kleijn, J., Yakovlev, A. (eds.) ICATPN 2007. LNCS, vol. 4546, pp. 63–82. Springer, Heidelberg (2007)

[35] Boyer, M., Vernadat, F.: Language and bisimulation relations between subclasses of timed Petri nets with strong timing semantic. Technical Report No. 146, LAAS (2000)

[36] Boyer, M., Diaz, M.: Multiple enabledness of transitions in Petri nets with time. In: Proceedings of the 9th international Workshop on Petri Nets and Performance Models (PNPM 2001), pp. 219–228. IEEE Computer Society, Los Alamitos (2001)

[37] Bozga, M., Daws, C., Maler, O., Olivero, A., Tripakis, S., Yovine, S.: Kronos: A model-checking tool for real-time systems. In: Y. Vardi, M. (ed.) CAV 1998. LNCS, vol. 1427, pp. 546–550. Springer, Heidelberg (1998)

[38] Bozga, M., Graf, S., Ober, I., Ober, I., Sifakis, J.: The IF toolset. In: Bernardo, M., Corradini, F. (eds.) SFM-RT 2004. LNCS, vol. 3185, pp. 237–267. Springer, Heidelberg (2004)

[39] Cassez, F., David, A., Fleury, E., Larsen, K.G., Lime, D.: Efficient on-the-fly algorithms for the analysis of timed games. In: Abadi, M., de Alfaro, L. (eds.) CONCUR 2005. LNCS, vol. 3653, pp. 66–80. Springer, Heidelberg (2005)

[40] Cassez, F., Roux, O.H.: Structural translation from time Petri nets to timed automata. Journal of Systems and Software 79(10), 1456–1468 (2006)

[41] Čerāns, K.: Decidability of bisimulation equivalences for parallel timer processes. In: Probst, D.K., von Bochmann, G. (eds.) CAV 1992. LNCS, vol. 663, pp. 302–315. Springer, Heidelberg (1993)

[42] Cerone, A., Maggiolio-Schettini, A.: Time-based expressivity of timed Petri nets for system specification. Theoretical Computer Science 216(1-2), 1–53 (1999)

[43] Cortés, L.A., Eles, P., Peng, Z.: Verification of real-time embedded systems using Petri net models and timed automata. In: Proceedings of the 8th International Conference on Real-Time Computing Systems and Applications (RTCSA 2002), pp. 191–199 (2002)

[44] D'Aprile, D., Donatelli, S., Sangnier, A., Sproston, J.: From time Petri nets to timed automata: An untimed approach. In: Grumberg, O., Huth, M. (eds.) TACAS 2007. LNCS, vol. 4424, pp. 216–230. Springer, Heidelberg (2007)

[45] Dong, J.S., Hao, P., Qin, S.C., Sun, J., Yi., W.: Timed patterns: TCOZ to timed automata. In: Davies, J., Schulte, W., Barnett, M. (eds.) ICFEM 2004. LNCS, vol. 3308, pp. 483–498. Springer, Heidelberg (2004)

[46] Esparza, J.: Decidability and complexity of Petri net problems — an introduction. In: Reisig, W., Rozenberg, G. (eds.) APN 1998. LNCS, vol. 1491, pp. 374–428. Springer, Heidelberg (1998)

[47] Esparza, J., Nielsen, M.: Decidability issues for Petri nets — a survey. Bulletin of the European Association for Theoretical Computer Science 52, 245–262 (1994)

[48] Finkel, A., Schnoebelen, P.: Well-structured transition systems everywhere! Theoretical Computer Science 256(1–2), 63–92 (2001)

[49] Haar, S., Kaiser, L., Simonot-Lion, F., Toussaint, J.: Equivalence of timed state machines and safe TPN. In: Proceedings of the 6th International Workshop on Discrete Event Systems (WODES 2002), pp. 119–126. IEEE Computer Society, Los Alamitos (2002)

[50] Hanisch, H.M.: Analysis of place/transition nets with timed-arcs and its application to batch process control. In: Ajmone Marsan, M. (ed.) ICATPN 1993. LNCS, vol. 691, pp. 282–299. Springer, Heidelberg (1993)

[51] Heitmann, F., Moldt, D., Mortensen, K.H., Rölke, H.: Petri nets tools database quick overview (Accessed: 11.6.2008),
http://www.informatik.uni-hamburg.de/TGI/PetriNets/tools/quick.html

[52] Heitmann, F., Moldt, D., Mortensen, K.H., Rölke, H.: Applications of Petri nets (Accessed: 15.6.2008),
http://www.informatik.uni-hamburg.de/TGI/PetriNets/applications

[53] Henzinger, T.A., Sifakis, J.: The discipline of embedded systems design. Computer 40(10), 32–40 (2007)

[54] Jančar, P.: Undecidability of bisimilarity for Petri nets and some related problems. Theoretical Computer Science 148(2), 281–301 (1995)

[55] Jones, N.D., Landweber, L.H., Lien, Y.E.: Complexity of some problems in Petri nets. Theoretical Computer Science 4(3), 277–299 (1977)

[56] Krichen, M., Tripakis, S.: Black-box conformance testing for real-time systems. In: Graf, S., Mounier, L. (eds.) SPIN 2004. LNCS, vol. 2989, pp. 109–126. Springer, Heidelberg (2004)

[57] Laroussinie, F., Larsen, K.G.: CMC: A tool for compositional model-checking of real-time systems. In: Proceedings of the FIP TC6 WG6.1 Joint International Conference on Formal Description Techniques for Distributed Systems and Communication Protocols (FORTE XI) and Protocol Specification, Testing and Verification (PSTV XVIII), pp. 439–456. Kluwer, B.V (1998)

[58] Larsen, K.G., Pettersson, P., Yi, W.: Uppaal in a Nutshell. International Journal on Software Tools for Technology Transfer 1(1–2), 134–152 (1997)

[59] Larsen, K.G., Yi, W.: Time-abstracted bisimulation: Implicit specifications and decidability. Information and Computation 134(2), 75–101 (1997)

[60] Larsen, K.G., Behrmann, G., Brinksma, E., Fehnker, A., Hune, T., Pettersson, P., Romijn, J.: As cheap as possible: Efficient cost-optimal reachability for priced timed automata. In: Berry, G., Comon, H., Finkel, A. (eds.) CAV 2001. LNCS, vol. 2102, pp. 493–505. Springer, Heidelberg (2001)

[61] Larsen, K.G., Mikucionis, M., Nielsen, B.: Online testing of real-time systems using Uppaal. In: Grabowski, J., Nielsen, B. (eds.) FATES 2004. LNCS, vol. 3395, pp. 79–94. Springer, Heidelberg (2005)

[62] Lime, D., Roux, O.H.: State class timed automaton of a time Petri net. In: Proceedings of the 10th International Workshop on Petri Net and Performance Models (PNPM 2003), pp. 124–133 (2003)

[63] Lime, D., Roux, O.H.: Model checking of time Petri nets using the state class timed automaton. Journal of Discrete Events Dynamic Systems — Theory and Applications (DEDS) 16(2), 179–205 (2006)

[64] Maler, O., Pnueli, A., Sifakis, J.: On the synthesis of discrete controllers for timed systems (an extended abstract). In: STACS 1995. LNCS, vol. 900, pp. 229–242. Springer, Heidelberg (1995)

[65] Mayr, E.W.: An algorithm for the general Petri net reachability problem (preliminary version). In: Proceedings of the 13th Ann. ACM Symposium on Theory of Computing, pp. 238–246. Assoc. for Computing Machinery (1981)

[66] Merlin, P.M.: A Study of the Recoverability of Computing Systems. PhD thesis, University of California, Irvine, CA, USA (1974)

[67] Merlin, P.M., Faber, D.J.: Recoverability of communication protocols: Implications of a theoretical study. IEEE Transactions on Communications 24(9), 1036–1043 (1976)

[68] Montano, L., Peñalvo, F.J.G., Villarroel, J.L.: Using the time Petri net formalism for specification, validation, and code generation in robot-control applications. International Journal of Robotic Research 19(1), 59–76 (2000)

[69] Nielsen, M., Sassone, V., Srba, J.: Properties of distributed timed-arc Petri nets. In: Hariharan, R., Mukund, M., Vinay, V. (eds.) FSTTCS 2001. LNCS, vol. 2245, pp. 280–291. Springer, Heidelberg (2001)

[70] Pelayo, F.L., Cuartero, F., Valero, V., Macia, H., Pelayo, M.L.: Applying timed-arc Petri nets to improve the performance of the MPEG-2 encoding algorithm. In: Proceedings of the 10th International Multimedia Modelling Conference (MMM 2004), pp. 49–56. IEEE Computer Society, Los Alamitos (2004)

[71] Pelayo, F.L., Cuartero, F., Valero, V., Pelayo, M.L., Merayo, M.G.: How does the memory work? by timed-arc Petri nets. In: Proceedings of the 4th IEEE International Conference on Cognitive Informatics (ICCI 2005), pp. 128–135 (2005)

[72] Penczek, W., Pólrola, A.: Advances in Verification of Time Petri Nets and Timed Automata: A Temporal Logic Approach. Springer, Heidelberg (2006)

[73] Petri, C.A.: Kommunikation mit Automaten. PhD thesis, Darmstadt (1962)

[74] Popova-Zeugmann, L.: On time Petri nets. Elektronische Informationsverarbeitung und Kybernetik 27(4), 227–244 (1991)

[75] Popova-Zeugmann, L., Heiner, M., Koch, I.: Time Petri nets for modelling and analysis of biochemical networks. Fundamenta Informatica 67(1-3), 149–162 (2005)

[76] Ramchandani, C.: Performance Evaluation of Asynchronous Concurrent Systems by Timed Petri Nets. PhD thesis, Massachusetts Institute of Technology, Cambridge (1973)

[77] Valero Ruiz, V., de Frutos Escrig, D., Marroquin Alonso, O.: Decidability of properties of timed-arc Petri nets. In: Nielsen, M., Simpson, D. (eds.) ICATPN 2000. LNCS, vol. 1825, pp. 187–206. Springer, Heidelberg (2000)

[78] Valero Ruiz, V., Cuartero Gomez, F., de Frutos Escrig, D.: On non-decidability of reachability for timed-arc Petri nets. In: Proceedings of the 8th International Workshop on Petri Net and Performance Models (PNPM 1999), pp. 188–196 (1999)

[79] Ruiz, V.V., Pardo, J.J., Cuartero, F.: Translating TPAL specifications into timed-arc Petri nets. In: Esparza, J., Lakos, C.A. (eds.) ICATPN 2002. LNCS, vol. 2360, pp. 414–433. Springer, Heidelberg (2002)

[80] Ruiz, V.V., Pelayo, F.L., Cuartero, F., Cazorla, D.: Specification and analysis of the MPEG-2 video encoder with timed-arc Petri nets. Electronic Notes Theoretial Computer Science 66(2) (2002)

[81] Seidner, Ch., Gardey, G., Lime, D., Magnin, M., Roux, O.: Romeo: A tool for time Petri net analysis (Accessed: 11.6.2008), http://romeo.rts-software.org/

[82] Sifakis, J.: Use of Petri nets for performance evaluation. In: Proceedings of the Third International Symposium IFIP W.G. 7.3., Measuring, Modelling and Evaluating Computer Systems, Bonn-Bad Godesberg, pp. 75–93. Elsevier Science Publishers, Amsterdam (1977)

[83] Sifakis, J., Yovine, S.: Compositional specification of timed systems. In: Puech, C., Reischuk, R. (eds.) STACS 1996. LNCS, vol. 1046, pp. 347–359. Springer, Heidelberg (1996)

[84] Srba, J.: Timed-arc Petri nets vs. networks of timed automata. In: Ciardo, G., Darondeau, P. (eds.) ICATPN 2005. LNCS, vol. 3536, pp. 385–402. Springer, Heidelberg (2005)

[85] UPPAAL-Cora (Accessed: 18.6.2008), http://www.cs.aau.dk/~behrmann/cora/
[86] UPPAAL-Tiga (Accessed: 18.6.2008), http://www.cs.aau.dk/~adavid/tiga/
[87] UPPAAL-Tron (Accessed: 23.6.2008), http://www.cs.aau.dk/~marius/tron/
[88] Wang, J.: Timed Petri Nets, Theory and Application. Kluwer Academic Publishers, Dordrecht (1998)

Infinite Runs in Weighted Timed Automata with Energy Constraints

Patricia Bouyer[1,*], Uli Fahrenberg[2], Kim G. Larsen[2],
Nicolas Markey[1,*], and Jiří Srba[2,**]

[1] Lab. Spécification et Vérification, CNRS & ENS Cachan, France
{bouyer,markey}@lsv.ens-cachan.fr
[2] Dept. of Computer Science, Aalborg University, Denmark
{uli,kgl,srba}@cs.aau.dk

Abstract. We study the problems of existence and construction of infinite schedules for finite weighted automata and one-clock weighted timed automata, subject to boundary constraints on the accumulated weight. More specifically, we consider automata equipped with positive and negative weights on transitions and locations, corresponding to the production and consumption of some resource (*e.g.* energy). We ask the question whether there exists an infinite path for which the accumulated weight for any finite prefix satisfies certain constraints (*e.g.* remains between 0 and some given upper-bound). We also consider a game version of the above, where certain transitions may be uncontrollable.

1 Introduction

The overall motivation of the research underlying this paper is the quest of developing weighted (or priced) timed automata and games [3,2] into a universal formalism useful for formulating and solving a broad range of resource scheduling problems of importance in application areas such as, *e.g.*, embedded systems. In this paper we introduce and study a new resource scheduling problem, namely that of constructing infinite schedules or strategies subject to boundary constraints on the accumulation of resources. More specifically, we propose finite and timed automata and games equipped with positive as well as negative weights, respectively weight-rates. With this extension, we may model systems where resources are not only consumed but also occasionally produced or regained, *e.g.* useful in modelling autonomous robots equipped with solar-cells for energy-harvesting or with the ability to search for docking-stations when energy-level gets critically low. Main challenges are now to synthesize schedules or strategies that will ensure indefinite safe operation with the additional guarantee that energy will always be available, yet never exceeds a possible maximum storage capacity.

As a basic example, consider the weighted timed automaton in Fig. 1a) with infinite behaviours repeatedly delaying in ℓ_0, ℓ_1 and ℓ_2 for a total of precisely

---

* This author is partially supported by project DOTS (ANR-06-SETI-003).
** This author is partially supported by grant no. MSM-0021622419.

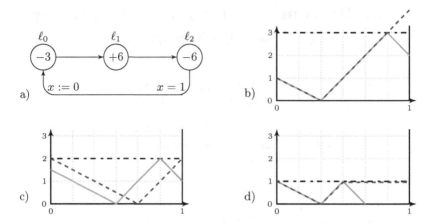

Fig. 1. a) Weighted Timed Automaton (global invariant $x \leq 1$). b) $U = +\infty$ and $U = 3$. c) $U = 2$. d) $U = 1$ and $W = 1$.

one time-unit. The negative weights (-3 and -6) in ℓ_0 and ℓ_2 indicate the rates by which energy will be consumed, and the positive rate ($+6$) in ℓ_1 indicates the rate by which energy will be gained. Thus, for a given iteration the effect on the amount of energy remaining will depend highly on the distribution of the one time-unit over the three locations. Let us observe the effect of lower and upper constraints on the energy-level on so-called bang-bang strategies, where the behaviour remains in a given location as long as permitted by the given bounds. Fig. 1b) shows the bang-bang strategy given an initial energy-level of 1 with no upper bound (dashed line) or 3 as upper bound (solid line). In both cases, it may be seen that the bang-bang strategy yields an infinite behaviour.

In Fig. 1c) and d), we consider the upper bounds 2 and 1, respectively. For an upper bound of 2, we see that the bang-bang strategy reduces an initial energy-level of $1\frac{1}{2}$ to 1 (solid line), and yet another iteration will reduce the remaining energy-level to 0. In fact, the bang-bang strategy—and it may be argued, any other strategy—fails to maintain an infinite behaviour for any initial energy-level *except for* 2 (dashed line). With upper-bound 1, the bang-bang strategy—and any other strategy—fails to complete even one iteration (solid line).

We also propose an alternative *weak* notion of upper bounds, which does not prevent energy-increasing behaviour from proceeding once the upper bound is reached but merely maintains the energy-level at the upper bound. In this case, as also illustrated in Fig. 1d) (dashed line), the bang-bang strategy is quite adequate for yielding an infinite behaviour.

In this paper, we ask the question whether some, or all, of the infinite paths obey the property that the weight accumulated in any finite prefix satisfies certain constraints. The *lower-bound problem* requires the accumulated weight never drop below zero, the *interval-bound problem* requires the accumulated weight to stay within a given interval, and in the *lower-weak-upper-bound problem* the accumulated weights may not drop below zero, with the additional feature that the weights never accumulate to more than a given upper bound; any increases above this bound are simply truncated. We also consider a game version of the above setting, where certain transitions may be uncontrollable.

For finite weighted automata, we show that the lower- and lower-weak-upper-bound problems are decidable in polynomial time. In the game setting we prove these problems to be P-hard but decidable in NP ∩ coNP. The interval-bound problem is on the other hand NP-hard but decidable in PSPACE and in the game setting it is EXPTIME-complete. For one-clock weighted timed automata, the lower- and lower-weak-upper-bound problems remain in P, but the interval-bound problem in the game setting is already undecidable.

Related Work. Recently, extensions of timed automata with costs (or prices) to measure quantities like energy, bandwidth, etc. have been introduced and subject to significant research. In these models—so-called *priced* or *weighted timed automata*—the cost can be used to measure the performance of a system allowing various optimization problems to be considered. Examples include cost-optimal reachability problem in a single-cost setting [2,3], as well as in a multi-cost setting [20], or the computation of (mean-cost or discounted) cost-optimal infinite schedules [6,16]. Also games where players try to optimize the cost have been considered [1,7,13,5,10], and several model-checking problems have been studied [12,5,9,11]. It is worth noticing that in these last frameworks (model-checking and games), most of the problems are undecidable, and they can be solved algorithmically only for the (restricted) class of one-clock automata.

However, in the priced extensions considered so far, only non-negative costs are allowed restricting the types of quantities one can measure. The only exception concerns the optimal-cost reachability problem, which has been solved even when negative costs are allowed [4], but the proof is basically not much more involved than with only non-negative costs. In the current work, we pursue this line of research, and focus on non-trivial problems that can be posed on timed automata with arbitrary costs, which allow to model interesting problems on timed systems with (bounded) resources.

Due to space limitations, most proofs had to be omitted in this paper. A long version is available as [8].

2 Models and Problems

2.1 Weighted Automata and Games

A *weighted automaton* is a tuple $A = (S, s_0, T)$ consisting of a set of locations (or states) S, an initial location (state) $s_0 \in S$, and a set of transitions $T \subseteq S \times \mathbb{R} \times S$. A transition (s, p, s') is customarily denoted $s \xrightarrow{p} s'$, where $p \in \mathbb{R}$ is the *weight* of that transition. We implicitly consider only *non-blocking* automata where every location has at least one outgoing transition. If S and T are finite sets and $T \subseteq S \times \mathbb{Z} \times S$ then A is called a *finite* weighted automaton.

A run in A starting from $s \in S$ is a finite or infinite sequence $s = s_1 \xrightarrow{p_1} s_2 \xrightarrow{p_2} s_3 \xrightarrow{p_3} \cdots$. We write $\mathsf{Runs}(A, s)$ for the set of all runs in A starting from s. Given a finite run $\gamma = s_1 \xrightarrow{p_1} \cdots \xrightarrow{p_{n-1}} s_n$, we write $\mathsf{last}(\gamma)$ to denote its final location s_n.

Definition 1. *Let $A = (S, s_0, T)$ be a weighted automaton, $c \in \mathbb{R}$, $b \in \mathbb{R} \cup \{\infty\}$, and let $\gamma = s_1 \xrightarrow{p_1} \cdots \xrightarrow{p_{n-1}} s_n \in \mathsf{Runs}(A, s_1)$. The accumulated weight with initial credit c under weak upper bound b is $p_{c \downarrow b}(\gamma) = r_n$, where $r_1, \ldots, r_n \in \mathbb{R}$ are defined inductively by $r_1 = \min(c, b)$, $r_{i+1} = \min(r_i + p_i, b)$.*

So for computing $p_{c \downarrow b}(\gamma)$, costs are accumulated along the transitions of γ, but only up to a maximum accumulated cost b; possible increases above b are simply discarded. The case $b = \infty$ is special; we will denote $p_c(\gamma) = p_{c \downarrow \infty}(\gamma) = c + \sum_{i=1}^{n-1} p_i$. Also, we will write $p(\gamma) = p_0(\gamma)$.

A *weighted game* is a tuple $G = (S_1, S_2, s_0, T)$ where S_1 and S_2 are two disjoint sets of locations, and $A_G = (S_1 \cup S_2, s_0, T)$ is a weighted automaton. Note that we only introduce *turn-based* weighted games here.

A run of G is a run of A_G, and we write $\mathsf{Runs}(G)$ for $\mathsf{Runs}(A_G)$. A strategy σ for Player i, where $i = 1$ or $i = 2$, maps each finite run γ ending in S_i to a transition departing from $\mathsf{last}(\gamma)$. Given a location s in G and a strategy σ for Player i, an outcome of σ from s is any run $s_1 \xrightarrow{p_1} s_2 \xrightarrow{p_2} \cdots \xrightarrow{p_{n-1}} s_n$ starting in s such that for any k, if $s_k \in S_i$ then $s_k \xrightarrow{p_k} s_{k+1} = \sigma(s_1 \xrightarrow{p_1} s_2 \xrightarrow{p_2} \cdots \xrightarrow{p_{k-1}} s_k)$.

We are now able to formulate the problems which we shall be concerned with.

The lower-bound problem: Given a weighted game G and an initial credit c, does there exist a strategy for Player 1 such that any infinite outcome γ from the initial state of G has $p_c(\gamma') \geq 0$ for all finite prefixes γ' of γ?

The lower-weak-upper-bound problem: Given a weighted game G, a weak upper bound b and an initial credit $c \leq b$, does there exist a strategy for Player 1 such that any infinite outcome γ from the initial state of G has $p_{c \downarrow b}(\gamma') \geq 0$ for all finite prefixes γ' of γ?

The interval-bound problem: Given a weighted game G, an upper bound b, and an initial credit $c \leq b$, does there exist a strategy for Player 1 such that any infinite outcome γ from the initial state of G has $0 \leq p_c(\gamma') \leq b$ for all finite prefixes γ' of γ?

Note that by Martin's determinacy theorem [21], our games are *determined*: Player 1 has a strategy for winning one of the above games if, and only if, Player 2 does not have a strategy for making Player 1 lose.

Special variants of the above problems are obtained when one of the sets S_1 and S_2 is empty. In case $S_2 = \emptyset$, they amount to asking for the *existence* of an infinite path adhering to the given bounds; in case $S_1 = \emptyset$, one asks whether *all* infinite paths stay within the bounds. The former problems will be referred to as *existential* problems, the latter as *universal* ones.

2.2   The Timed Setting

A *weighted timed automaton* is a tuple $A = (Q, q_0, C, I, E, rate)$, with Q a finite set of locations, $q_0 \in Q$ the initial location, C a finite set of clocks, $I \colon Q \to \Phi(C)$ location invariants, $E \subseteq Q \times \Phi(C) \times 2^C \times Q$ a finite set of transitions, and $rate \colon Q \to \mathbb{Z}$ location weight-rates. Here the set $\Phi(C)$ of clock constraints φ is defined by the grammar $\varphi ::= x \bowtie k \mid \varphi_1 \wedge \varphi_2$ with $x \in C$, $k \in \mathbb{Z}$ and

$\bowtie \; \in \; \{\leq, <, \geq, >, =\}$. The semantics of a weighted timed automaton A is given by a weighted automaton $\llbracket A \rrbracket$ with states (q, v), where $q \in Q$ and $v \colon C \to \mathbb{R}_{\geq 0}$, and transitions of two types:

- *Delay transitions* $(q, v) \xrightarrow{p}_t (q, v + t)$ for some $t \in \mathbb{R}_{\geq 0}$. Such a transition exists whenever $v + t' \models I(q)$ for all $t' \in [0, t]$, and its weight is $p = t \cdot rate(q)$.
- *Switch transitions* $(q, v) \xrightarrow{0}_e (q', v')$, where $e = (q, g, r, q')$ is a transition of A. Such a switch transition exists whenever $v \models g \wedge I(q)$, $v' = v[r \leftarrow 0]$, and $v' \models I(q')$. Switch transition have always the weight 0.

A *run* of A is a sequence $(q_1, v_1) \xrightarrow{p_1}_{t_1} (q_1, v_1') \xrightarrow{0}_{e_1} (q_2, v_2) \xrightarrow{p_2}_{t_2} (q_2, v_2') \cdots$ of alternating delay and switch transitions in $\llbracket A \rrbracket$. We write $\mathsf{Runs}(A)$ for the set of all runs of A. The accumulated weight (with initial credit c and weak upper bound b) for runs of a weighted timed automaton are given by Definition 1.

A *weighted timed game* is a tuple $G = (Q, q_0, C, I, E_1, E_2, rate)$ such that $A_G = (Q, q_0, C, I, E_1 \cup E_2, rate)$ is a weighted timed automaton. States and runs of a weighted timed game are those of the underlying weighted timed automaton, and we again write $\mathsf{Runs}(G)$ for $\mathsf{Runs}(A_G)$.

Given a weighted timed game G, a strategy for Player i ($i \in \{1, 2\}$) is a partial function σ mapping each finite run of $\mathsf{Runs}(A_G)$ to $E_i \cup \{\lambda\}$, where $\lambda \notin E_1 \cup E_2$ is the "wait" action. For a finite run γ ending in (q, v), it is required that if $\sigma(\gamma) = \lambda$ then $(q, v) \xrightarrow{p}_t (q, v + t)$ for some $t > 0$, and if $\sigma(\gamma) = e$ then $(q, v) \xrightarrow{0}_e (q', v')$.

Given a state $s = (q, v)$ of a weighted timed game G and a strategy σ for Player i, the set $\mathsf{Out}(\sigma, s)$ of outcomes of σ from s is the smallest subset of $\mathsf{Runs}(G, s)$ such that

- (q, v) is in $\mathsf{Out}(\sigma, s)$;
- if $\gamma \in \mathsf{Out}(\sigma, s)$ is a finite run ending in (q_n, v_n), then a run of the form $\gamma \to (q_{n+1}, v_{n+1})$ is in $\mathsf{Out}(\sigma, s)$ if either
  - $(q_n, v_n) \to_e (q_{n+1}, v_{n+1})$ with $e \in E_{3-i}$,
  - $(q_n, v_n) \to_e (q_{n+1}, v_{n+1})$ with $e = \sigma(\gamma) \in E_i$, or
  - $(q_n, v_n) \to_t (q_{n+1}, v_{n+1})$ with $t \in \mathbb{R}_{\geq 0}$, and $\sigma(\gamma \to_{t'} (q_n, v_n + t')) = \lambda$ for all $t' \in [0, t)$;
- an infinite run is in $\mathsf{Out}(\sigma, s)$ if all its finite prefixes belong to $\mathsf{Out}(\sigma, s)$.

A weighted timed game $G = (Q, q_0, C, I, E_1, E_2, r)$ is said to be *turn-based* if the set of edges leaving any $q \in Q$ is a subset of either E_1 or E_2. In that case, the semantics of G is a (turn-based, infinite) weighted game as introduced in the previous section. However, weighted timed games introduced above are more general than turn-based ones, and we shall later use the more general notion.

For weighted timed games, we will be interested in the same three problems as in the previous section; the existence of a strategy whose outcomes are infinite runs remaining within given bounds. As in the previous section, we have the special cases of *existential* and *universal* problems.

3   Fixed-Point Characterization

Let us introduce some terminology. For the lower-bound problem, we say that an infinite path γ is *c-feasible* for some initial credit $c < +\infty$, if $p_c(\gamma') \geq 0$ for all finite prefixes γ' of γ, and that γ is *feasible* if it is c-feasible for some c.

Given a weighted game (S_1, S_2, s_0, T) and $b \in \mathbb{R}_{\geq 0}$, we define three predicates $L, W_b, U_b : S \times \mathbb{R}_{\geq 0} \to \{tt, ff\}$ to be the respective maximal fixed points to the following equations:

$$L(s,c) = 0 \leq c \wedge \begin{cases} s \in S_1 \implies \exists s \xrightarrow{p} s' \in T : L(s', c+p) \\ s \in S_2 \implies \forall s \xrightarrow{p} s' \in T : L(s', c+p) \end{cases}$$

$$W_b(s,c) = 0 \leq c \leq b \wedge \begin{cases} s \in S_1 \implies \exists s \xrightarrow{p} s' \in T : W_b(s', \max(b, c+p)) \\ s \in S_2 \implies \forall s \xrightarrow{p} s' \in T : W_b(s', \max(b, c+p)) \end{cases}$$

$$U_b(s,c) = 0 \leq c \leq b \wedge \begin{cases} s \in S_1 \implies \exists s \xrightarrow{p} s' \in T : U_b(s', c+p) \\ s \in S_2 \implies \forall s \xrightarrow{p} s' \in T : U_b(s', c+p) \ . \end{cases}$$

The right-hand side of each of these equations defines a monotone functional on the power set lattice of $S \times \mathbb{R}_{\geq 0}$, hence indeed the maximal fixed points exist. Also, if the weighted game under investigation is *image finite*, i.e. if the sets $\{(p, s') \mid s \xrightarrow{p} s' \in T\}$ are finite for all states s, then it can be shown that these respective functionals are continuous, implying that the maximal fixed points can be obtained as the limits of the iterated application of the respective functionals to the maximal element $S \times \mathbb{R}_{\geq 0}$ of the power set lattice. The proof of the lemma below is immediate from the definition of the predicates.

Lemma 2. *Let (S_1, S_2, s_0, T) be a weighted game and $s \in S_1 \cup S_2$, $b, c \in \mathbb{R}_{\geq 0}$. Then $(s, c) \in L$ (or $(s, c) \in W_b$, or $(s, c) \in U_b$) if and only if there exists a strategy for Player 1 such that any infinite path γ from s consistent with the strategy is c-feasible for the lower-bound problem (or lower-weak-upper-bound problem, or interval-bound problem, respectively).*

For the lower-bound problems, the above fixed-point characterization can be stated in a different way by defining recursively the *infimum credits* sufficient for feasibility—note that such a notion does not make sense for the interval-bound problem, as here the set of sufficient credits is not necessarily upward-closed. For a given weighted game (S_1, S_2, s_0, T) and $b \in \mathbb{R}_{\geq 0}$, let $L, W_b : S \to \mathbb{R} \cup \{\infty\}$ be the functions defined as respective minimal fixed points to the following equations:

$$L(s) = \begin{cases} \min\{L(s') - p \mid s \xrightarrow{p} s'\} & \text{if } s \in S_1 \\ \max\{L(s') - p \mid s \xrightarrow{p} s'\} & \text{if } s \in S_2 \end{cases}$$

$$W_b(s) = \begin{cases} \min\left(b, \min\{W(s') - p \mid s \xrightarrow{p} s'\}\right) & \text{if } s \in S_1 \\ \min\left(b, \max\{W(s') - p \mid s \xrightarrow{p} s'\}\right) & \text{if } s \in S_2 \ . \end{cases}$$

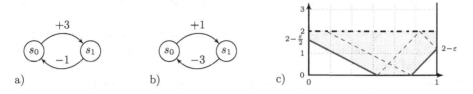

Fig. 2. a), b) Weighted automata with and without feasible paths. c) One fixed-point iteration on the weighted timed automaton of Fig. 1.

Proposition 3. We have $L(s,c)$ if and only if $c \geq L(s)$, and $W_b(s,c)$ if and only if $W_b(s) \leq c \leq b$.

The following lemma shows that for finite weighted games, there is a predescribed upper limit for the values of L and W_b. This implies that the fixed-point computations can be terminated after a finite number of iterations. For *timed* games, the second part of the next example below shows that this is *not* necessarily the case.

Lemma 4. Let (S_1, S_2, s_0, T) be a finite weighted game and $b \in \mathbb{R}_{\geq 0}$. Let $M = \sum\{-p \mid s \xrightarrow{p} s' \in T, p < 0\}$. Then for any state s, $L(s) < \infty$ if and only if $L(s) \leq M$, and $W_b(s) < \infty$ if and only if $W_b(s) \leq M$.

Example 5. Consider the weighted automata in Fig. 2a) and 2b). Let us attempt to compute L using iterative application of the recursive definition. For a) we find the following fixed points after two iterations: $L(s_0) = 0$ and $L(s_1) = 1$. For b) we get the following sequence of decreasing approximations: $L^{2n}(s_0) = L^{2n+1}(s_0) = 2n$ and $L^{2n}(s_1) = L^{2n-1}(s_1) = 2n+1$. Hence clearly $L(s_0) = L(s_1) = \infty$, though this fixed point is not reached within a finite number of iteration.

In Fig. 2c) we reconsider the weighted timed automaton from Fig. 1 under the interval-bound problem with upper bound 2. If we assume that after n iterations of the fixed-point computation, $U_2^n((\ell_2, 1), c) = tt$ if and only if $c \in [2 - \varepsilon, 2]$ for some ε, then $U_2^{n+1}((\ell_0, 0), c) = tt$ if and only if $c \in [2 - \frac{1}{2}\varepsilon, 2]$. The largest fixed point—$U_2((\ell_2, 1), c) = tt$ if and only if $c = 2$—is only reached as the limit of this infinite sequence of approximations. $\square$

4   Lower-Bound Problems

In this section we treat the lower-bound and lower-weak-upper-bound problems for finite automata, one-clock timed automata, and for finite games. For one-clock timed games, these problems are open.

4.1   Finite Weighted Automata

For a given finite weighted automaton $A = (S, s_0, T)$, we denote by $\mathsf{MinCr}(\gamma)$, for a path γ in A, the minimum $c \geq 0$ for which γ is c-feasible, and by $\mathsf{MinCr}(s)$, for a state $s \in S$, the minimum of $\mathsf{MinCr}(\gamma)$ over all feasible paths γ emerging from s.

A *cycle* $\gamma = s_0 \to s_1 \to \cdots \to s_0$ in A is *non-losing* if $p(\gamma) \geq 0$ (or equivalently, $p_c(\gamma) \geq c$ for any initial credit c). A *lasso* λ from a given state s_0 is an infinite path of the form $\gamma_1(\gamma_2)^\omega$, where $\gamma_1 = s_0 \to s_1 \to \cdots \to s_{i-1}$, $\gamma_2 = s_i \to \cdots \to s_k \to s_i$, and $s_{i-1} \to s_i$ are paths in A, and with $s_i \neq s_j$ whenever $i \neq j \leq k$. It is clear that if a lasso $\gamma_1(\gamma_2)^\omega$ constitutes a feasible path then the cycle γ_2 must be non-losing.

Lemma 6. *Let $A = (S, s_0, T)$ be a finite weighted automaton and $s \in S$. For any feasible path γ from s, there exists a feasible lasso λ also from s such that $\mathsf{MinCr}(\lambda) \leq \mathsf{MinCr}(\gamma)$.*

Proof. Let $c = \mathsf{MinCr}(\gamma)$, and assume first that there is a cycle π in γ such that $p(\pi) \geq 0$. Write $\gamma = \gamma_1 \pi \gamma_2$, then $\lambda = \gamma_1 \pi^\omega$ is a feasible lasso from s, and $\mathsf{MinCr}(\lambda) \leq \mathsf{MinCr}(\gamma)$.

Assume now that there is no cycle π in γ with $p(\pi) \geq 0$. We can write $\gamma = \gamma_1 \gamma_2$, where γ_2 only takes transitions that appear infinitely often along γ. As there is no cycle with non-negative weight in γ, the weights of prefixes of γ_2 decrease to $-\infty$. Hence there is a prefix γ_2' of γ_2 such that $p(\gamma_2') < -p(\gamma_1)$. But then the accumulated weight of $\gamma_1 \gamma_2'$, which is a prefix of γ, is negative, which contradicts the feasibility of γ. $\square$

Thus, determining $L(s, c)$ corresponds to determining whether there is a feasible lasso λ out of s with $\mathsf{MinCr}(\lambda) \leq c$. This may be done in polynomial time in the size of the weighted automaton using a slightly modified Bellman-Ford algorithm. Hence, this allows us to solve the existential lower-bound and lower-weak-upper-bound problems in polynomial time. The corresponding universal problems can be solved using very similar techniques that we do not detail here (see the full version). Hence we get the following result.

Theorem 7. *For finite weighted automata, the existential and universal lower-bound and lower-weak-upper-bound problems are decidable in P. Also, $\mathsf{MinCr}(s_0)$ is computable in polynomial time.*

4.2   One-Clock Weighted Timed Automata

Let A be a one-clock weighted timed automaton. Without loss of generality we shall assume that for any location, the value of the (single) clock x is bounded by some constant M (see [3]). Let $0 \leq a_1 < a_2 < \ldots < a_n < a_{n+1} = M$ where $\{a_1, \ldots, a_n\}$ are the constants occurring in A. Then the one-dimensional *regions* of A are all elementary open intervals (a_i, a_{i+1}) and singletons $\{a_i\}$ (see [19]). In particular, two states (q, v) and (q, v') of A are time-abstract bisimilar whenever v and v' belong to the same region.

A *corner-point region* is a pair $\langle \rho, e \rangle$, where ρ is a region and e an end-point of ρ. We say that $\langle \rho', e' \rangle$ is the *successor* of $\langle \rho, e \rangle$ if either ρ' is the successor region of ρ and $e = e'$ or $\rho = \rho' = (a, b)$, $e = a$, and $e' = b$. Now the *corner-point abstraction* [3,6], $\mathsf{cpa}(A)$, of A is the finite weighted automaton with states

$(q, \langle \rho, e \rangle)$ and with transitions $(q, \langle \rho, e \rangle) \rightarrow (q', \langle \rho', e' \rangle)$ if $\rho \models I(q)$, $q' \models I(q')$ and one of the following applies:

- $q = q'$ and $\langle \rho', e' \rangle$ is the successor of $\langle \rho, e \rangle$, or
- $(q, \varphi, \emptyset, q') \in E$ with $\rho \models \varphi$ and $\langle \rho', e' \rangle = \langle \rho, e \rangle$, or
- $(q, \varphi, \{x\}, q') \in E$ with $\rho \models \varphi$, $\rho' = \{0\}$ and $e' = 0$.

The weight of the first (delay) transition is $rate(q) \cdot (e' - e)$, the weights of the two last (discrete) transitions are 0. The above corner-point abstraction is sound and complete with respect to the lower-bound problem in the following sense (proof in the full version):

Proposition 8. *Let A be a one-clock weighted timed automaton.*

Completeness: *Let γ be an infinite run in A from $(q_0, 0)$ which is c-feasible for some $c < +\infty$. Then there exists a c-feasible infinite run γ' from $(q_0, \langle \{0\}, 0 \rangle)$ in $\mathsf{cpa}(A)$.*

Soundness: *Let γ' be an infinite run in $\mathsf{cpa}(A)$ from $(q_0, \langle \{0\}, 0 \rangle)$ which is c-feasible for some $c < +\infty$. Then, for any $\varepsilon > 0$, there exists a $(c+\varepsilon)$-feasible infinite run γ from $(q_0, 0)$ in A.*

Let us introduce the *lower-bound* (and lower-weak-upper-bound) *infimum problem* to be the problem as to whether for a given initial credit c, $L(s_0, c + \varepsilon)$ $(W_b(s_0, c + \varepsilon))$ holds for any $\varepsilon > 0$. Based on the above propositions we have:

Theorem 9. *For one-clock weighted timed automata, the existential and universal lower-bound and lower-weak-upper-bound infimum problems are decidable in P. Also, $\mathsf{MinCr}(s_0)$ may be computed in polynomial time.*

Proof (sketch). For the existential problem, note that for a given one-clock weighted timed automaton A, the size of $\mathsf{cpa}(A)$ is polynomial in the size of A, as the regions are constructed from the constants appearing in A. Then apply Theorem 7. For the universal problem, note that Proposition 8 can be modified to show that for any run in A there exist a run in $\mathsf{cpa}(A)$ which has always less remaining credit (within any region we simply choose to do the delay at the location with the smallest rate rather than the largest one). □

4.3 Finite Weighted Games

Recall that a strategy σ is said to be *memoryless* if $\sigma(\gamma)$ only depends on $\mathsf{last}(\gamma)$ for any finite path γ. The proof of the following lemma can be found in the full version.

Lemma 10. *Let (S_1, S_2, s_0, T) be a finite weighted game. Let $b \in \mathbb{N} \cup \{\infty\}$ and $c \in \mathbb{N}$. If there exists a strategy σ for Player 1 which ensures that $p_{c \downarrow b}(\gamma') \geq 0$ for any finite prefix γ' of any infinite outcome γ of σ, then there is also a memoryless strategy with the same property. Symmetrically, if Player 2 has a strategy to ensure that for any outcome γ of σ, there is a finite prefix γ' of γ such that $p_{c \downarrow b}(\gamma') < 0$, then she has a memoryless strategy with the same property.*

Proposition 11. *For finite weighted games, the lower-bound and lower-weak-upper-bound problems are decidable in* NP ∩ coNP.

Proof. The NP algorithm consists in nondeterministically guessing a memoryless strategy, pruning the transitions that are not selected by that strategy in G, and checking whether for any finite prefix γ of any infinite execution, we have $p_{c \downarrow b}(\gamma) \geq 0$, which is polynomial (Theorem 7). If Player 1 has a winning strategy, then this algorithm will answer positively.

The coNP algorithm follows from the determinacy of the game: if Player 1 has no winning strategy, then Player 2 has one, which can be chosen memoryless. It can then be guessed and checked in nondeterministic polynomial time. □

For the lower-bound problem, we can do better, and prove its equivalence with the mean-payoff problem.

Proposition 12. *The mean-payoff game problem is log-space equivalent to the lower-bound problem, and is log-space reducible to the lower-weak-upper-bound problem.*

Proof (sketch). Mean-payoff games are defined as follows [17]: given a weighted game $G = (S_1, S_2, s_0, T)$ and an integer m, is there a strategy for Player 1 s.t. for any infinite outcome $s_0 \xrightarrow{p_0} s_1 \xrightarrow{p_1} \cdots$, we have $\liminf_{n \to \infty} \sum_{j \leq n} p_j / n \geq m$. By shifting all weights by $-m$, we can simplify the problem by assuming $m = 0$. An important feature of mean-payoff games is that they admit memoryless winning strategies in case they admit winning strategies [15].

Transforming a mean-payoff problem into a lower-bound (or lower-weak-upper-bound) problem is easy: the mean weight of an infinite path is negative iff its accumulated weight is $-\infty$. Hence a winning strategy for Player 1 for the mean-payoff problem is also winning in the lower-bound (or lower-weak-upper-bound) problem, provided that the initial credit is sufficient (at least the opposite of the sum of all negative weights).

Conversely, given an instance $G = (S_1, S_2, s_0, T)$ of the lower-bound problem (assuming the initial credit is zero, by possibly adding an extra initial transition setting the initial credit), we construct an equivalent instance of the mean-payoff problem as follows: each transition $t = s \xrightarrow{p} s'$ is replaced by a new uncontrollable state s_t and three transitions $s \xrightarrow{p} s_t$, $s_t \xrightarrow{0} s'$ and $s_t \xrightarrow{0} s_0$. In other words, at each transition of the original game, Player 2 is given the opportunity to go back to the initial state. If the accumulated weight goes below zero at some point, Player 2 will decide to go back to the initial state. Since strategies can be assumed to be memoryless, there will be a periodic outcome with negative mean weight. □

The exact complexity of the mean-payoff problem is not known, but it is P-hard and in UP ∩ coUP [17]. Hence we get the following theorem.

Theorem 13. *For finite weighted games, the lower-bound problem is P-hard and in* UP ∩ coUP *(thus in* NP ∩ coNP*). The lower-weak-upper-bound problem is P-hard and in* NP ∩ coNP.

5   Interval-Bound Problems

We shall now study the interval-bound problems for the finite and timed cases.

5.1   Finite Weighted Automata

The following theorem summarizes all our results on the various interval-bound problems for finite weighted automata and games.

Theorem 14. *Under the interval-bound constraint,*

1. *the universal problem for finite weighted automata is decidable in* P *,*
2. *the existential problem for finite weighted automata is decidable in* PSPACE *and* NP *-hard, and*
3. *the problem for finite weighted games is* EXPTIME *-complete.*

The complete proofs of all the results mentioned in this theorem can be found in the full version. We only mention some ideas, and then give the complete NP -hardness proof, as we think this can be rather instructive.

1. Using Bellman-Ford-like algorithms, we detect whether there is a negative (resp. positive) cycle or a shortest (resp. longest) path whose cost becomes negative (resp. goes above the maximal bound of the interval). This can be done in polynomial time.
2. From a finite weighted automaton, we can construct a finite graph whose set of states is a pair (s, c) with s a state of the automaton, and c a cost value (in the interval $[0, b]$), and in which $(s, c) \rightarrow (s', c')$ is a transition whenever $s \xrightarrow{c'-c} s'$ is a transition of the weighted automaton. Guessing an infinite path in that graph gives a solution to the existential problem. This can be done in polynomial space (due to the encoding of b in binary). The NP -hardness proof will be detailed below.
3. Similarly as for the PSPACE upper bound, we construct the graph described above, and we add alternation: a state belonging to Player 1 (resp. 2) becomes existential (resp. universal). The interval-bound problem for finite weighted games reduces to an alternating graph accessibility problem (see [14]) which can be solved in P , hence the EXPTIME upper bound (the exponential blow-up is still due to the encoding of b in binary). EXPTIME -hardness is by reduction from the problem of countdown games which was very recently shown to be EXPTIME -complete [18].

Proof (of the NP *-hardness).* We reduce the NP-complete problem SUBSET-SUM (see *e.g.* [22]) into our existential interval-bound problem. An instance of SUBSET-SUM is a pair (A, t) where $A \subseteq \mathbb{N}$ is a finite set and $t \in \mathbb{N}$. The question is whether there is a subset of A which adds exactly to t. Assume a given instance of SUBSET-SUM (A, t) where $A = \{t_1, t_2, \ldots, t_n\}$. We construct a weighted automaton (S, s_0, T) where $S = \{s_0, s_1, \ldots, s_n\}$ and where $T =$

$\{s_i \xrightarrow{t_{i+1}} s_{i+1} \mid 0 \le i < n\} \cup \{s_i \xrightarrow{0} s_{i+1} \mid 0 \le i < n\} \cup \{s_n \xrightarrow{-t} s_0\}$. The construction is depicted below.

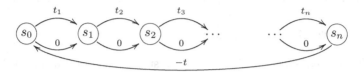

Now consider the existential interval-bound problem with upper bound t, and let the initial credit be 0. It is clear that there is an infinite path with the accumulated weight staying between 0 and t if and only if the SUBSET-SUM problem has a solution.   □

5.2   Timed Games

We prove in this section that the interval-bound problem for timed games is undecidable, even for games involving only one clock.

Theorem 15. *The interval-bound problem is undecidable for one-clock weighted timed games.*

Proof (sketch). This is achieved by simulating a two-counter machine. If c_1 and c_2 are the values of the counters, the accumulated weight along runs of the simulating weighted timed game will be $E(c_1, c_2) = 5 - 1/(2^{c_1} 3^{c_2})$, and we will work with the upper bound of 5. We start with accumulated weight 4 (encoding that the two counters are initialized to 0).

We will describe modules that increment respectively decrement a counter, and then informally describe how we can test that the value of a counter is zero. We assume that there is a global invariant $x \le 1$ in all the modules. Moreover, for the purpose of this reduction, a *configuration* is a triple (ℓ, x, W) where ℓ is a discrete location, x is the value of the clock, and W is the accumulated weight.

We first assume we have a module ok that is winning for Player 1 as soon as this module is entered with an accumulated weight in $[0, 5]$ (it is nothing more than a location, with weight-rate 0, and a controllable self-loop that checks whether $x = 1$ and resets clock x).

We now consider the module Mod_n that is described in Fig. 3 (n is an integer that will be fixed later in the set $\{2, 3, 12, 18\}$). A strategy in Mod_n for Player 1 which has the property that any outcome either reaches a module ok or exits the module while always satisfying the lower- and upper-bound conditions will be said to be *locally safe* in that module.

Let $e \in [0, 1]$ with $0 \le ne \le 30$. Consider the following strategy σ_n, depicted on Fig. 4:

– from location $(m, 0, 5 - e)$, it delays during $(5 - e)/6$ time units in m, then leaves to m_1 (thus to configuration $(m_1, (5 - e)/6, 0)$);
– from m_1, it directly goes to m_2;

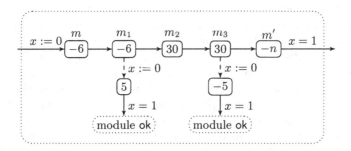

Fig. 3. Generic module Mod_n

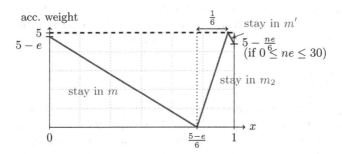

Fig. 4. The effect of (strategy σ_n in) module Mod_n

- from $(m_2, (5-e)/6, 0)$, it waits for $1/6$ time units and then leaves to m_3 (hence to configuration $(m_3, 1 - e/6, 5)$);
- from $(m_3, 1 - e/6, 5)$, it directly goes to m';
- in m', it delays until $x = 1$, and fires the last transition to the next module.

In Mod_n, from locations m_1 (resp. m_3), Player 2 can decide to bring the game to the first (resp. second) vertical branch, and the only way to stay safe is to arrive in m_1 (resp. m_3) with accumulated cost 0 (resp. 5) and to leave in 0-delay. This is precisely what does strategy σ_n, which is then the unique locally safe strategy in module Mod_n.

Proposition 16. *Starting from configuration $(m, 0, 5 - e)$ in Mod_n, with $0 \leq ne \leq 30$, Player 1 has a unique locally safe strategy. Under that strategy, the only outcome that visits m' exits the module with accumulated weight $5 - ne/6$.*

In the sequel, we use the following modules: $\text{Inc}(c_1) = \text{Mod}_3$, $\text{Inc}(c_2) = \text{Mod}_2$, $\text{Dec}(c_1) = \text{Mod}_{12}$, and $\text{Dec}(c_2) = \text{Mod}_{18}$. When starting with accumulated weight $5 - e$ in module $\text{Inc}(c_1)$, the accumulated weight when leaving this module is $5 - e/2$, hence $\text{Inc}(c_1)$ increments the counter c_1. Similarly, $\text{Inc}(c_2)$ increments c_2, and $\text{Dec}(c_1)$ and $\text{Dec}(c_2)$ decrement the respective counters. In the last two modules, no check is performed whether the counter to be decremented actually has a positive value.

We briefly describe how such a test can be done. First we construct a module that has two output branches, one where the two counters are equal to 0, and one where one of the counters is positive. This is to Player 1 to decide in which branch we go, but Player 2 can easily check that this is correct (checking that the two counters are equal to zero reduces to checking that the accumulated weight is 4, whereas checking that one of the counters is positive reduces to checking that the accumulated cost be in the open interval $(4, 5)$). Then, using that module, we can for instance implement a test that counter c_2 is equal to zero as follows: either both counters are equal to zero, or under the assumption that one of the counters is positive, and by decrementing the first counter, we will eventually reach a point where both counters are equal to zero. For lack of space, we do not detail the construction of those modules, which use ideas quite similar to Mod_n.

Hence, fixing $\mathcal{M}$ to be a two-counter machine, we can construct a one-clock weighted timed game $G_{\mathcal{M}}$ which is a positive instance of the interval-bound problem if and only if $\mathcal{M}$ has an infinite computation.   □

6   Conclusion

A summary of the results proved in this paper is provided in the following table. The fields in gray remain open. Matching the complexity lower and upper bounds for some of the problems is left open: the lower-bound problems for finite games are strongly related to the well known open problem of complexity of mean-payoff games; closing the gap between NP -hardness and containment in PSPACE for the existential interval-bound problem seems intricate and it is a part of our future work.

	games		existential problem		universal problem	
	finite	1-clock	finite	1-clock	finite	1-clock
L	∈ UP ∩ coUP P-h (Th. 13)		∈ P (Th. 7)	∈ P (Th. 9)	∈ P (Th. 7)	∈ P (Th. 9)
L+W	∈ NP ∩ coNP P-h (Th. 13)		∈ P (Th. 7)	∈ P (Th. 9)	∈ P (Th. 7)	∈ P (Th. 9)
L+U	EXPTIME-c (Th. 14)	Undec. (Th. 15)	∈ PSPACE NP-h (Th. 14)		∈ P (Th. 14)	

Note that the results related to Theorem 9 hold for the initial credits arbitrarily close (for any given $\varepsilon > 0$) to the given ones.

References

1. Alur, R., Bernadsky, M., Madhusudan, P.: Optimal reachability in weighted timed games. In: Díaz, J., Karhumäki, J., Lepistö, A., Sannella, D. (eds.) ICALP 2004. LNCS, vol. 3142, pp. 122–133. Springer, Heidelberg (2004)
2. Alur, R., La Torre, S., Pappas, G.J.: Optimal paths in weighted timed automata. In: Di Benedetto, M.D., Sangiovanni-Vincentelli, A.L. (eds.) HSCC 2001. LNCS, vol. 2034, pp. 49–62. Springer, Heidelberg (2001)

3. Behrmann, G., Fehnker, A., Hune, T., Larsen, K.G., Pettersson, P., Romijn, J., Vaandrager, F.: Minimum-cost reachability for priced timed automata. In: Di Benedetto, M.D., Sangiovanni-Vincentelli, A.L. (eds.) HSCC 2001. LNCS, vol. 2034, pp. 147–161. Springer, Heidelberg (2001)
4. Bouyer, P., Brihaye, Th., Bruyère, V., Raskin, J.-F.: On the optimal reachability problem. Formal Methods in System Design 31(2), 135–175 (2007)
5. Bouyer, P., Brihaye, Th., Markey, N.: Improved undecidability results on weighted timed automata. Inf. Proc. Letters 98(5), 188–194 (2006)
6. Bouyer, P., Brinksma, E., Larsen, K.G.: Staying alive as cheaply as possible. In: Alur, R., Pappas, G.J. (eds.) HSCC 2004. LNCS, vol. 2993, pp. 203–218. Springer, Heidelberg (2004)
7. Bouyer, P., Cassez, F., Fleury, E., Larsen, K.G.: Optimal strategies in priced timed game automata. In: Lodaya, K., Mahajan, M. (eds.) FSTTCS 2004. LNCS, vol. 3328, pp. 148–160. Springer, Heidelberg (2004)
8. Bouyer, P., Fahrenberg, U., Larsen, K.G., Markey, N., Srba, J.: Infinite runs in weighted timed automata with energy constraints. Research Report LSV-08-23, Laboratoire Spécification et Vérification, ENS Cachan, France (2008), http://www.lsv.ens-cachan.fr/Publis/RAPPORTS_LSV/PDF/rr-lsv-2008-23.pdf
9. Bouyer, P., Larsen, K.G., Markey, N.: Model-checking one-clock priced timed automata. In: Seidl, H. (ed.) FOSSACS 2007. LNCS, vol. 4423, pp. 108–122. Springer, Heidelberg (2007)
10. Bouyer, P., Larsen, K.G., Markey, N., Rasmussen, J.I.: Almost optimal strategies in one-clock priced timed automata. In: Arun-Kumar, S., Garg, N. (eds.) FSTTCS 2006. LNCS, vol. 4337, pp. 345–356. Springer, Heidelberg (2006)
11. Bouyer, P., Markey, N.: Costs are expensive! In: Raskin, J.-F., Thiagarajan, P.S. (eds.) FORMATS 2007. LNCS, vol. 4763, pp. 53–68. Springer, Heidelberg (2007)
12. Brihaye, Th., Bruyère, V., Raskin, J.-F.: Model-checking for weighted timed automata. In: Lakhnech, Y., Yovine, S. (eds.) FORMATS 2004 and FTRTFT 2004. LNCS, vol. 3253, pp. 277–292. Springer, Heidelberg (2004)
13. Brihaye, Th., Bruyère, V., Raskin, J.-F.: On optimal timed strategies. In: Ramanujam, R., Sen, S. (eds.) FSTTCS 2005. LNCS, vol. 3821, pp. 49–64. Springer, Heidelberg (2005)
14. Chandra, A.K., Kozen, D.C., Stockmeyer, L.J.: Alternation. J. ACM 28(1), 114–133 (1981)
15. Ehrenfeucht, A., Mycielski, J.: Positional strategies for mean payoff games. Int. J. Game Theory 8(2), 109–113 (1979)
16. Fahrenberg, U., Larsen, K.G.: Discount-optimal infinite runs in priced timed automata (submitted, 2008)
17. Jurdziński, M.: Deciding the winner in parity games is in UP∩co-UP. Inf. Proc. Letters 68(3), 119–124 (1998)
18. Jurdziński, M., Laroussinie, F., Sproston, J.: Model checking probabilistic timed automata with one or two clocks. In: Grumberg, O., Huth, M. (eds.) TACAS 2007. LNCS, vol. 4424, pp. 170–184. Springer, Heidelberg (2007)
19. Laroussinie, F., Markey, N., Schnoebelen, Ph.: Model checking timed automata with one or two clocks. In: Gardner, P., Yoshida, N. (eds.) CONCUR 2004. LNCS, vol. 3170, pp. 387–401. Springer, Heidelberg (2004)
20. Larsen, K.G., Rasmussen, J.I.: Optimal conditional scheduling for multi-priced timed automata. In: Sassone, V. (ed.) FOSSACS 2005. LNCS, vol. 3441, pp. 234–249. Springer, Heidelberg (2005)
21. Martin, D.: Borel determinacy. Annals Math. 102(2), 363–371 (1975)
22. Papadimitriou, C.H.: Computational Complexity. Addison-Wesley, Reading (1994)

Concavely-Priced Timed Automata

(Extended Abstract)

Marcin Jurdziński and Ashutosh Trivedi

Department of Computer Science, University of Warwick, UK

Abstract. Concavely-priced timed automata, a generalization of linearly-priced timed automata, are introduced. Computing the minimum value of a number of cost functions—including reachability price, discounted price, average time, average price, price-per-time average, and price-per-reward average—is considered in a uniform fashion for concavely-priced timed automata. All the corresponding decision problems are shown to be PSPACE-complete. This paper generalises the recent work of Bouyer et al. on deciding the minimum reachability price and the minimum ratio-price for linearly-priced timed automata.

A new type of a region graph—the boundary region graph—is defined, which generalizes the corner-point abstraction of Bouyer et al. A broad class of cost functions—concave-regular cost functions—is introduced, and the boundary region graph is shown to be a correct abstraction for deciding the minimum value of concave-regular cost functions for concavely-priced timed automata.

1 Introduction

A system is *real-time*, if the correctness of some of its operations critically depend on the time at which they are performed. Numerous safety-critical systems are real-time, including medical systems such as heart pacemakers, and industrial process controllers such as nuclear reactor protective systems. Ensuring the correctness of real-time systems is of paramount importance. Timed automata [4] are a popular and well-established formalism for modelling real-time systems.

A timed automaton is a finite automaton accompanied by a finite set of real-valued variables called *clocks*. The states of a timed automaton are traditionally called *locations*, and the configurations of a timed automaton, consisting of a location and a valuation of clock variables, are called states. A state is called a *corner state*, if the values of all clock variables are integers. Clock variables may appear in guards of transitions of a timed automaton, where they can be compared against integers. The syntax of timed automata also allows clock values to be reset to zero after executing a transition.

Given a timed automaton and an initial state, the reachability problem is to decide whether there exists a run starting from the initial state and leading to a final state of the timed automaton. The safety-violation property of a real-time system can be modeled as a reachability problem on a timed automaton. The reachability problem for timed automata is in PSPACE (in fact, it is PSPACE-complete) by a reduction to the non-emptiness problem for a finite state automaton, called the *region graph*, whose size is exponential in the size of a timed automaton [4,2]. A natural optimization problem over timed automata is to minimize time to reach a final state. Minimum- and maximum-time

F. Cassez and C. Jard (Eds.): FORMATS 2008, LNCS 5215, pp. 48–62, 2008.
© Springer-Verlag Berlin Heidelberg 2008

reachability was shown to be decidable in [14]. It was shown to be PSPACE-complete in [3,16]. A more general problem of two-player reachability-time games was shown to be decidable in [6] and proved EXPTIME-complete in [15,13]. An efficient algorithm to solve minimum-time reachability problem on timed automata appeared in [19], where the initial state was restricted to be a corner state.

The *linearly-priced* timed automata [7] (LPTA), also known as weighted timed automata, are an extension of timed automata, and are quite useful in modeling scheduling problems [11,1] for real-time systems. A linearly-priced timed automaton augments a timed automaton with price information, such that the price of waiting in a location is proportional to the waiting time, hence the name linearly-priced timed automata. The problem of finding a minimum price (time) schedule can be modeled as a minimum reachability-price problem over a linearly-priced timed automaton. This problem is known to be a PSPACE-complete [10] if the start state is a corner state. Alur et al. [5] give an EXPTIME algorithm to solve the problem with an arbitrary initial state by giving a non-trivial extension of the region graph. Larsen et al. [17,7] give a symbolic algorithm to solve the problem, although with some restrictions on the initial state (a corner state with all clocks set to zero). Note that PSPACE-hardness results hold for timed automata with at least three clocks. For timed automata with one clock, reachability-time and reachability-price problems are known to be NL-complete, while the complexity of these problems for two-clock timed automata remains open.

On the other hand, the problem of finding a minimum-price (or minimum-time) infinite schedule can be modelled by the minimum average-price problem on a priced timed automaton. Since the total price of an infinite run can be unbounded, a natural measure of optimality is average price per transition or average price per time unit. Bouyer et al. [11] show that a more general problem of average reward per transition over multi-priced timed automata is PSPACE-complete if the start state is a corner state.

In this paper we introduce the *concavely-priced* timed automata, a generalization of the linearly-priced timed automata, which arguably can be used to model a larger class of scheduling problems. The definition of a concavely-priced timed automaton is such that it allows price functions which are concave in a certain sense. In this paper, we show that deciding the minimum value of the reachability price, discounted price, average time, average price, price-per-time average, and price-per-reward average is PSPACE-complete for arbitrary start states (i.e., including non-corner states).

2   Optimization Problems on Finite Priced Graphs

Consider a finite graph $G = (S, E, F)$, where S is a set of states, $E \subseteq S \times S$ is a set of directed edges, such that every state has at least one outgoing edge, and $F \subseteq S$ is a set of final states. An *run* (path) in G is a sequence $\langle s_0, s_1, s_2, \ldots \rangle \in S^\omega$, such that for all $i \geq 1$, we have $(s_{i-1}, s_i) \in E$. We write Runs and Runs$_{\text{fin}}$ for the sets of infinite and finite runs, respectively, and we write Runs(s) and Runs$_{\text{fin}}(s)$ for the sets of infinite and finite runs starting from state $s \in S$, respectively. For a run $r = \langle s_0, s_1, s_2, \ldots \rangle$, we define $\text{Stop}(r) = \inf_{i \geq 0} \{i : s_i \in F\}$.

Let Cost : Runs $\to \mathbb{R}$ be a cost function that for every run $r \in$ Runs determines its cost Cost(r). We then define the *minimum cost* function Cost$_* : S \to \mathbb{R}$, by Cost$_*(s) =$

$\inf_{r \in \text{Runs}(s)} \text{Cost}(r)$. The *minimization problem* for that cost function Cost is: given a state $s \in S$ and a number $D \in \mathbb{Q}$, determine whether $\text{Cost}_*(s) \leq D$.

A *priced graph* (G, π) consists of a graph G and a price function $\pi : E \to \mathbb{R}$; and a *price-reward graph* (G, π, ϱ) consists of a graph G and price and reward functions $\pi, \varrho : E \to \mathbb{R}$, respectively. Let $r = \langle s_0, s_1, s_2, \ldots \rangle \in \text{Runs}$, and for every $n \geq 1$, let $\pi_n(r) = \sum_{i=1}^{n} \pi(s_{i-1}, s_i)$ and $\varrho_n(r) = \sum_{i=1}^{n} \varrho(s_{i-1}, s_i)$. We further assume that the graph is reward-diverging i.e. $|\varrho_n(r)| \to \infty$ as $n \to \infty$.

The following list of cost functions gives rise to a number of corresponding minimization problems.

1. *Reachability:* $\text{Reach}(r) = \pi_N(r)$ if $N = \text{Stop}(r) < \infty$, and $\text{Reach}(r) = \infty$ otherwise.
2. *Discounted:* $\text{Discounted}(\lambda)(r) = (1 - \lambda) \sum_{i=1}^{\infty} \lambda^{i-1} \pi(s_{i-1}, s_i)$, where $\lambda \in (0, 1)$ is the *discount factor*.
3. *Average price:* $\text{AvgPrice}(R) = \limsup_{n \to \infty} \pi_n(r)/n$.
4. *Price-per-reward average:* $\text{PriceRewardAvg}(r) = \limsup_{n \to \infty} \pi_n(r)/\varrho_n(r)$.

A *positional strategy* is a function $\sigma : S \to S$, such that for every $s \in S$, we have $(s, \sigma(s)) \in E$. We write Σ for the set of positional strategies. A run from state $s \in S$ according to strategy σ is the unique run $\text{Run}(s, \sigma) = \langle s_0, s_1, s_2, \ldots \rangle$, such that $s_0 = s$, and for every $i \geq 1$, we have $\sigma(s_{i-1}) = s_i$. A positional strategy is *optimal* for a cost function $\text{Cost} : \text{Runs} \to \mathbb{R}$ if for every state $s \in S$, we have $\text{Cost}_*(s) = \text{Cost}(\text{Run}(s, \sigma))$. Observe that existence of an optimal positional strategy for a cost function means that, from every starting state, there is a run that minimizes the cost, and that is a simple path leading to a simple cycle.

Theorem 1. *For every finite priced graph, and for each of the reachability, discounted, and average price cost functions, there is an optimal positional strategy.*

For every finite price-reward graph, there is an optimal positional strategy for the price-per-reward average cost function.

3 Concavely-Priced Timed Automata

We assume that, wherever appropriate, sets $\mathbb{N}$ of non-negative integers and $\mathbb{R}$ of reals contain a maximum element ∞, and we write $\mathbb{N}_+$ for the set of positive integers and $\mathbb{R}_\oplus$ for the set of non-negative reals. For $n \in \mathbb{N}$ we write $[\![n]\!]_\mathbb{N}$ for the set $\{0, 1, \ldots, n\}$, and $[\![n]\!]_\mathbb{R}$ for the set $\{r \in \mathbb{R} : 0 \leq r \leq n\}$ of non-negative reals bounded by n. For a real number $r \in \mathbb{R}$, we write $|r|$ for its absolute value, we write $\lfloor r \rfloor$ for its integer part, i.e., the largest integer $n \in \mathbb{N}$, such that $n \leq r$, and we write $\lceil r \lfloor$ for its fractional part, i.e., we have $\lceil r \lfloor = r - \lfloor r \rfloor$. For sets X and Y, we write $[X \to Y]$ for the set of functions $F : X \to Y$, and $[X \rightharpoonup Y]$ for the set of partial functions $F : X \rightharpoonup Y$. For a function $f : X \to Y$ we write $\text{dom}(f)$ for the domain of function f.

For a point $x = (x_1, x_2, \ldots, x_n) \in \mathbb{R}^n$, we define its norm by $\|x\| = \max_{i=1}^{n} |x_i|$. For a point $x \in \mathbb{R}^n$, the open ball $B(x, r)$, with the center x and the radius $r > 0$, is defined by $B(x, r) = \{y : y \in \mathbb{R}^n \text{ and } \|x - y\| < r\}$. An $x \in \mathcal{D} \subseteq \mathbb{R}^n$ is an *interior point* of $\mathcal{D}$ if there is an $r > 0$, such that $B(x, r) \subseteq \mathcal{D}$. The set of all interior points of $\mathcal{D}$ is called the *interior* of $\mathcal{D}$, and it is denoted by $int(\mathcal{D})$. A set $\mathcal{D} \subseteq \mathbb{R}^n$ is *open* if $int(\mathcal{D}) = \mathcal{D}$. A set $\mathcal{D} \subseteq \mathbb{R}^n$ is *closed* if its complement $\mathbb{R}^n \setminus \mathcal{D}$ is open. The *closure* of a set $\mathcal{D} \subseteq \mathbb{R}^n$ is defined as $clos(\mathcal{D}) = \mathbb{R}^n \setminus int(\mathbb{R}^n \setminus \mathcal{D})$. We sometimes denote closure of a set $\mathcal{D}$ by $\overline{\mathcal{D}}$.

3.1 Concave and Quasi-Concave Functions

A set $\mathcal{D} \subseteq \mathbb{R}^n$ is *convex* if for all $x, y \in \mathcal{D}$ and $\theta \in [0, 1]$, we have $\theta x + (1 - \theta)y \in \mathcal{D}$. A function $f : \mathbb{R}^n \rightarrow \mathbb{R}$ is *concave* (on its domain $dom(f) \subseteq \mathbb{R}^n$), if $dom(f) \subseteq \mathbb{R}^n$ is a convex set, and for all $x, y \in \mathbb{R}^n$ and $\theta \in [0, 1]$, we have $f(\theta x + (1 - \theta)y) \geq \theta f(x) + (1 - \theta)f(y)$. A function f is *convex* if the function $-f$ is concave. A function is *affine* if it is both convex and concave. The α-*superlevel set* of a function $f : \mathbb{R}^n \rightarrow \mathbb{R}$ is defined as $S^{\alpha}(f) = \{x \in dom(f) : f(x) \geq \alpha\}$, and the α-*sublevel set* of f is defined as $S_{\alpha}(f) = \{x \in dom(f) : f(x) \leq \alpha\}$.

Proposition 2 ([12]). *If a function is concave then its superlevel sets are convex; and if it is convex then its sublevel sets are convex.*

The following properties of concave functions are of interest in this paper.

Lemma 3. 1. *(Non-negative weighted sum) If $f_1, f_2, \ldots, f_k : \mathbb{R}^n \rightarrow \mathbb{R}$ are concave and $w_1, w_2, \ldots, w_k \geq 0$, then their w-weighted sum $\mathbb{R}^n \ni x \mapsto \sum_{i=1}^{k} w_i \cdot f_i$ is concave (on its domain $\bigcap_{i=1}^{k} dom(f_i)$).*
   2. *(Composition with an affine map) If $f : \mathbb{R}^n \rightarrow \mathbb{R}$ is concave, $A \in \mathbb{R}^{n \times n}$, and $b \in \mathbb{R}^n$, then the function $\mathbb{R}^n \ni x \mapsto f(Ax + b)$ is concave (on its domain $\{x : Ax + b \in dom(f)\}$).*
   3. *(Pointwise minimum and infimum) If functions $f_1, f_2, \ldots f_k : \mathbb{R}^n \rightarrow \mathbb{R}$ are concave, then their pointwise minimum $\mathbb{R}^n \ni x \mapsto \min_{i=1}^{k} f_i(x)$ is concave (on its domain $\bigcap_{i=1}^{k} dom(f_i)$).*
   Let $f : \mathbb{R}^n \times Z \rightarrow \mathbb{R}$, where Z is an arbitrary (infinite) set. If for all $z \in Z$, the function $\mathbb{R}^n \ni x \mapsto f(x, z)$ is concave, then the function $\mathbb{R}^n \ni x \mapsto \inf_{z \in Z} f(x, z)$ is concave (on its domain $\bigcap_{z \in Z} dom(f(\cdot, z))$).

A function $f : \mathbb{R}^n \rightarrow \mathbb{R}$ is *quasi-concave* (on its domain $dom(f) \subseteq \mathbb{R}^n$), if $dom(f)$ is a convex set, and for all $x, y \in dom(f)$ and $\theta \in [0, 1]$, we have $f(\theta x + (1 - \theta)y) \geq \min\{f(x), f(y)\}$. A function f is *quasi-convex* if the function $-f$ is quasi-concave.

Proposition 4 ([12]). *A function is quasi-concave if and only if its superlevel sets are convex; and it is quasi-convex if and only if its sublevel sets are convex.*

The following properties of quasi-concave functions are of interest in this paper.

Lemma 5 ([18]). *For $h_1, h_2 : \mathbb{R}^n \rightarrow \mathbb{R}$, the function $\mathbb{R}^n \ni x \mapsto h_1(x)/h_2(x)$ is quasi-concave (on its domain $dom(h_1) \cap dom(h_2)$) if at least one of the following holds:*

   1. h_1 *is nonnegative and convex, and h_2 is positive and convex;*
   2. h_1 *is nonpositive and convex, and h_2 is negative and convex;*
   3. h_1 *is nonnegative and concave, and h_2 is positive and concave;*
   4. h_1 *is nonpositive and concave, and h_2 is negative and concave;*
   5. h_1 *is affine and h_2 is non-zero and affine;*
   6. h_1 *is concave, and h_2 is positive and affine;*
   7. h_1 *is convex, and h_2 is negative and affine.*

3.2   Lipschitz-Continuous Functions

A function $f : \mathbb{R}^n \to \mathbb{R}^m$ is Lipschitz-continuous on its domain $\text{dom}(f)$, if there exists a constant $K \geq 0$, called a Lipschitz constant of f, such that $\|f(x) - f(y)\| \leq K\|x - y\|$ for all $x, y \in \text{dom}(f)$; we then also say that f is K-continuous. The following properties of Lipschitz-continuous functions are of interest in this paper.

Lemma 6.   *1. If for every $i = 1, 2, \ldots, k$, the function $f_i : \mathbb{R}^n \to \mathbb{R}^m$ is K_i-continuous and $w_i \in \mathbb{R}$, then the function $\mathbb{R}^n \ni x \mapsto \sum_{i=1}^n w_i f_i(x)$ is K-continuous for $K = \sum_{i=1}^k |w_i| K_i$.*

2. If $f_1 : \mathbb{R}^n \to \mathbb{R}^m$ and $f_2 : \mathbb{R}^m \to \mathbb{R}^k$ are K_1-continuous and K_2-continuous, respectively, then their composition, $\mathbb{R}^n \ni x \mapsto f_2(f_1(x))$, is K-continuous for $K = K_1 K_2$.

3. Let $f_1, f_2 : \mathbb{R}^n \to \mathbb{R}$ be K_1-continuous and K_2-continuous, respectively; let f_1 and f_2 be bounded, i.e., there is a constant $M \geq 0$, such that for all $x \in \text{dom}(f_1) \cap \text{dom}(f_2)$, we have $|f_1(x)|, |f_2(x)| \leq M$; and let f_2 be bounded from below, i.e., there is a constant $N > 0$, such that for all $x \in \text{dom}(f_2)$, we have $f_2(x) \geq N$. Then the function $\mathbb{R}^n \ni x \mapsto f_1(x)/f_2(x)$ is K-continuous for $K = (NK_1 + MK_2)/N^2$.

3.3   Timed Automata

Clock Valuations, Regions, and Zones.   Fix a constant $k \in \mathbb{N}$ for the rest of this paper. Let C be a finite set of *clocks*. A (k-bounded) *clock valuation* is a function $\nu : C \to [\![k]\!]_\mathbb{R}$; we write V for the set $[C \to [\![k]\!]_\mathbb{R}]$ of clock valuations. If $\nu \in V$ and $t \in \mathbb{R}_\oplus$ then we write $\nu + t$ for the clock valuation defined by $(\nu + t)(c) = \nu(c) + t$, for all $c \in C$. For a set $C' \subseteq C$ of clocks and a clock valuation $\nu : C \to \mathbb{R}_\oplus$, we define $\text{Reset}(\nu, C')(c) = 0$ if $c \in C'$, and $\text{Reset}(\nu, C')(c) = \nu(c)$ if $c \notin C'$.

Note 7. Clocks in timed automata are usually allowed to take arbitrary non-negative real values, while we restrict them to be bounded by some constant k, i.e., we consider only *bounded* timed automata models. We can make this restriction for technical convenience and without significant loss of generality.

The set of *clock constraints* over the set of clocks C is the set of conjunctions of *simple clock constraints*, which are constraints of the form $c \bowtie i$ or $c - c' \bowtie i$, where $c, c' \in C$, $i \in [\![k]\!]_\mathbb{N}$, and $\bowtie \in \{<, >, =, \leq, \geq\}$. There are finitely many simple clock constraints. For every clock valuation $\nu \in V$, let $\text{SCC}(\nu)$ be the set of simple clock constraints which hold in $\nu \in V$. A *clock region* is a maximal set $P \subseteq V$, such that for all $\nu, \nu' \in P$, $\text{SCC}(\nu) = \text{SCC}(\nu')$. In other words, every clock region is an equivalence class of the indistinguishability-by-clock-constraints relation, and vice versa. Note that ν and ν' are in the same clock region iff all clocks have the same integer parts in ν and ν', and if the partial orders of the clocks, determined by their fractional parts in ν and ν', are the same. For all $\nu \in V$, we write $[\nu]$ for the clock region of ν.

A *clock zone* is a convex set of clock valuations, which is a union of a set of clock regions. Note that a set of clock valuations is a zone iff it is definable by a clock constraint. For $W \subseteq V$, we write $\overline{W}$ for the smallest closed set in V which contains W. Observe that for every clock zone W, the set $\overline{W}$ is also a clock zone.

Let L be a finite set of *locations*. A *configuration* is a pair (ℓ, ν), where $\ell \in L$ is a location and $\nu \in V$ is a clock valuation; we write Q for the set of configurations. If $s = (\ell, \nu) \in Q$ and $c \in C$, then we write $s(c)$ for $\nu(c)$. A *region* is a pair (ℓ, P), where ℓ is a location and P is a clock region. If $s = (\ell, \nu)$ is a configuration then we write $[s]$ for the region $(\ell, [\nu])$. We write $\mathcal{R}$ for the set of regions. A set $Z \subseteq Q$ is a *zone* if for every $\ell \in L$, there is a clock zone W_ℓ (possibly empty), such that $Z = \{(\ell, \nu) : \ell \in L$ and $\nu \in W_\ell\}$. For a region $R = (\ell, P) \in \mathcal{R}$, we write $\overline{R}$ for the zone $\{(\ell, \nu) : \nu \in \overline{P}\}$.

Timed Automata. A *timed automaton* $T = (L, C, S, A, E, \delta, \xi, F)$ consists of a finite set of locations L, a finite set of clocks C, a set of *states* $S \subseteq Q$, a finite set of *actions* A, an *action enabledness function* $E : A \to 2^S$, a *transition function* $\delta : L \times A \to L$, a *clock reset function* $\xi : A \to 2^C$, and a set of *final states* $F \subseteq S$. We require that S, F, and $E(a)$ for all $a \in A$, are zones.

Clock zones, from which zones S, F, and $E(a)$, for all $a \in A$, are built, are typically specified by clock constraints. Therefore, when we consider a timed automaton as an input of an algorithm, its size should be understood as the sum of sizes of encodings of L, C, A, δ, and ξ, and the sizes of encodings of clock constraints defining zones S, F, and $E(a)$, for all $a \in A$. Our definition of a timed automaton may appear to differ from the usual ones [4,9]. The differences are, however, superficial and mostly syntactic.

For a configuration $s = (\ell, \nu) \in Q$ and $t \in \mathbb{R}_\oplus$, we define $s + t$ to be the configuration $s' = (\ell, \nu + t)$ if $\nu + t \in V$, and we then write $s \to_t s'$. For an action $a \in A$, we define $\text{Succ}(s, a)$ to be the configuration $s' = (\ell', \nu')$, where $\ell' = \delta(\ell, a)$ and $\nu' = \text{Reset}(\nu, \xi(a))$, and we then write $s \xrightarrow{a} s'$. We write $s \xrightarrow{a} s'$ if $s \xrightarrow{a} s'$; $s, s' \in S$; and $s \in E(a)$. For technical convenience, and without loss of generality, we will assume throughout that for every $s \in S$, there exists $a \in A$, such that $s \xrightarrow{a} s'$.

For $s, s' \in S$, we say that s' is in the future of s, or equivalently, that s is in the past of s', if there is $t \in \mathbb{R}_\oplus$, such that $s \to_t s'$; we then write $s \to_* s'$. For $R, R' \in \mathcal{R}$, we say that R' is in the future of R, or that R is in the past of R', if for all $s \in R$, there is $s' \in R'$, such that s' is in the future of s; we then write $R \to_* R'$. We say that R' is the *time successor* of R if $R \to_* R'$, $R \neq R'$, and for every $R'' \in \mathcal{R}$, we have that $R \to_* R'' \to_* R'$ implies $R'' = R$ or $R'' = R'$; we then write $R \to_{+1} R'$ or $R' \leftarrow_{+1} R$. Similarly, for $R, R' \in \mathcal{R}$, we write $R \xrightarrow{a} R'$ if there is $s \in R$, and there is $s' \in R'$, such that $s \xrightarrow{a} s'$.

We say that a region $R \in \mathcal{R}$ is *thin* if for every $s \in R$ and every $\varepsilon > 0$, we have that $[s] \neq [s + \varepsilon]$; other regions are called *thick*. We write $\mathcal{R}_{\text{Thin}}$ and $\mathcal{R}_{\text{Thick}}$ for the sets of thin and thick regions, respectively. Note that if $R \in \mathcal{R}_{\text{Thick}}$ then for every $s \in R$, there is an $\varepsilon > 0$, such that $[s] = [s + \varepsilon]$. Observe also, that the time successor of a thin region is thick, and vice versa.

A *timed action* is a pair $\tau = (t, a) \in \mathbb{R}_\oplus \times A$. For $s \in Q$, we define $\text{Succ}(s, \tau) = \text{Succ}(s, (t, a))$ to be the configuration $s' = \text{Succ}(s + t, a)$, i.e., such that $s \to_t s'' \xrightarrow{a} s'$, and we then write $s \xrightarrow{a}_t s'$. We write $s \xrightarrow{a}_t s'$ if $s \to_t s'' \xrightarrow{a} s'$, and we then say that $(s, (t, a), s')$ is a *transition* of the timed automaton. If $\tau = (t, a)$ then we write $s \xrightarrow{\tau} s'$ instead of $s \xrightarrow{a}_t s'$, and $s \xrightarrow{\tau} s'$ instead of $s \xrightarrow{a}_t s'$.

The Reachability Problem. A finite run is a sequence $\langle s_0, \tau_1, s_1, \tau_2, \ldots, \tau_n, s_n \rangle \in S \times ((\mathbb{R}_\oplus \times A) \times S)^*$, such that for all i, $1 \leq i \leq n$, we have that (s_{i-1}, τ_i, s_i) is a transition, i.e., that $s_{i-1} \xrightarrow{\tau_i} s_i$. For a finite run $r = \langle s_0, \tau_1, s_1, \tau_2, \ldots, \tau_n, s_n \rangle$, we define Length$(r) = n$, and we define Last$(r) = s_n$ to be the state in which the run ends. We write Runs$_{\mathrm{fin}}$ for the set of finite runs, and Runs$_{\mathrm{fin}}(s)$ for the set of finite runs starting from state $s \in S$. An infinite run of a timed automaton is a sequence $r = \langle s_0, \tau_1, s_1, \tau_2, \ldots \rangle$, such that for all $i \geq 1$, we have $s_{i-1} \xrightarrow{\tau_i} s_i$. For an infinite run r, we define Length$(r) = \infty$. For a run $r = \langle s_0, \tau_1, s_1, \tau_2, \ldots \rangle$, we define Stop$(r) = \inf\{i : s_i \in F\}$. We write Runs for the set of infinite runs, and Runs(s) for the set of infinite runs starting from state $s \in S$.

The *reachability problem* for timed automata is the following: given a timed automaton $\mathcal{T}$ and an initial state $s \in S$, decide whether there is a run $r \in$ Runs(s), such that Stop$(r) < \infty$. The following is a well known result.

Theorem 8 ([4]). *The reachability problem for timed automata is PSPACE-complete.*

Strategies. A *strategy* is a function $\sigma : $ Runs$_{\mathrm{fin}} \to \mathbb{R}_{\oplus} \times A$, such that if Last$(r) = s \in S$ and $\sigma(r) = \tau$ then $s \xrightarrow{\tau} s'$. We write Σ for the set of strategies. A run according to a strategy σ from a state $s \in S$ is the unique run Run$(s, \sigma) = \langle s_0, \tau_1, s_1, \tau_2, \ldots \rangle$, such that $s_0 = s$, and for every $i \geq 1$, we have $\sigma(\mathrm{Run}_i(s, \sigma)) = \tau_{i+1}$, where $\mathrm{Run}_i(s, \sigma) = \langle s_0, \tau_1, s_1, \ldots, s_{i-1}, \tau_i, s_i \rangle$.

Since for every run $r \in$ Runs(s), there is a strategy $\sigma \in \Sigma$, such that Run$(s, \sigma) = r$, the reachability problem can be equivalently stated in terms of strategies: given a timed automaton $\mathcal{T}$ and an initial state $s \in S$, decide whether there is a strategy $\sigma \in \Sigma$, such that Stop$(\mathrm{Run}(s, \sigma)) < \infty$.

We say that a strategy σ is *positional* if for all finite runs $r, r' \in$ Runs$_{\mathrm{fin}}$, we have that Last$(r) = $ Last(r') implies $\sigma(r) = \sigma(r')$. A positional strategy can be then represented as a function $\sigma : S \to \mathbb{R}_{\oplus} \times A$, which uniquely determines the strategy $\sigma^{\infty} \in \Sigma$ as follows: $\sigma^{\infty}(r) = \sigma(\mathrm{Last}(r))$, for all finite runs $r \in$ Runs$_{\mathrm{fin}}$. We write Π for the sets of positional strategies.

3.4 Priced Timed Automata

A *priced timed automaton* $(\mathcal{T}, \pi)$ consists of a timed automaton $\mathcal{T}$ and a price function $\pi : S \times \mathbb{R}_{\oplus} \times A \to \mathbb{R}$ that, for every state $s \in S$ and a timed move $(t, a) \in \mathbb{R}_{\oplus} \times A$, determines the price $\pi(s, t, a)$ of taking the timed move (t, a) from state s, i.e., of the transition $(s, (t, a), \mathrm{Succ}(s, (t, a)))$. In a *linearly-priced* timed automaton [7], the price function is represented as a function $p : L \cup A \to \mathbb{R}$, that gives a *price rate* $p(\ell)$ to every location $\ell \in L$, and a price $p(a)$ to every action a; the price of taking the timed move (a, t) from state $s = (\ell, \nu)$ is then defined by $\pi(s, (t, a)) = p(\ell) \cdot t + p(a)$.

In this paper we consider *concavely-priced* timed automata, a generalization of linearly-priced timed automata. Unlike for linearly-priced timed automata, we do not specify explicitly how the price function $\pi : S \times \mathbb{R}_{\oplus} \times A$ is represented; for conceptual simplicity it is convenient to think of it as a black box. We do, however, require that there is a constant $K > 0$, given as a part of the input, such that for all actions $a \in A$ and for all regions $R, R' \in \mathcal{R}$, the function $\pi^a_{R, R'} : (s, t) \mapsto \pi(s, t, a)$ is concave and K-continuous on $D_{R, R'} = \{(s, t) \in S \times \mathbb{R}_{\oplus} : s \in R \text{ and } (s + t) \in R'\}$.

Notice that every linearly-priced timed automaton is a concavely-priced timed automaton. In the rest of the paper we reserve the term priced timed automata to refer to concavely-priced timed automata.

We also consider *concave price-reward timed automata* (T, π, ϱ), where the *price* and *reward* functions $\pi, \varrho : S \times \mathbb{R}_\oplus \times A \to \mathbb{R}$ satisfy the following properties: there is a constant $K > 0$, given as a part of the input, such that for all actions $a \in A$ and for all regions $R, R' \in \mathcal{R}$, the functions $(s, t) \mapsto \pi(s, t, a)$ and $(s, t) \mapsto \varrho(s, t, a)$ are K-continuous, and concave and convex, respectively, on $\{(s, t) \in S \times \mathbb{R}_\oplus : s \in R \text{ and } (s + t) \in R'\}$. Moreover, for technical convenience we require that the timed automaton is *structurally non-Zeno* with respect to ϱ, i.e., for every run $r = \langle s_0, \tau_1, s_1, \tau_2, \ldots, \tau_n, s_n \rangle \in \mathrm{Runs}_{\mathrm{fin}}$, such that $s_0 = (\ell_0, \nu_0)$, $s_n = (\ell_n, \nu_n)$, and $\ell_0 = \ell_n$ (i.e., such that the run r forms a cycle in the finite graph of the locations and transitions of the timed automaton), we have that $\sum_{i=1}^n \varrho(s_{i-1}, \tau_i) \geq 1$.

4   Optimization Problems on Priced Timed Automata

The fundamental reachability problem for timed automata can be, in a natural way, generalized to a number of optimization problems on priced timed automata. Let Cost : Runs $\to \mathbb{R}$ be a cost function that for every run $r \in$ Runs determines its cost $\mathrm{Cost}(r)$. We then define the *minimum cost* function $\mathrm{Cost}_* : S \to \mathbb{R}$, by

$$\mathrm{Cost}_*(s) = \inf_{r \in \mathrm{Runs}(s)} \mathrm{Cost}(r) = \inf_{\sigma \in \Sigma} \mathrm{Cost}(\mathrm{Run}(s, \sigma)).$$

The *minimization problem* for that cost function Cost is: given a state $s \in S$ and a number $D \in \mathbb{Q}$, determine whether $\mathrm{Cost}_*(s) \leq D$.

The following list of cost functions gives rise to a number of corresponding minimization problems. Let $r = \langle s_0, \tau_1, s_1, \tau_2, \ldots \rangle \in$ Runs, where $\tau_i = (t_i, a_i)$ for all $i \geq 1$. Moreover, for π and ϱ, the price and reward functions, respectively, of a priced (or price-reward) timed automaton, and for every $n \geq 1$, let: $T_n(r) = \sum_{i=1}^n t_i$, $\pi_n(r) = \sum_{i=1}^n \pi(s_{i-1}, \tau_i)$, and $\varrho_n(r) = \sum_{i=1}^n \varrho(s_{i-1}, \tau_i)$.

1. *Reachability*: $\mathrm{Reach}(r) = \pi_N(r)$ if $N = \mathrm{Stop}(r) < \infty$, and we define $\mathrm{Reach}(r) = \infty$ otherwise.
2. *Discounted*: $\mathrm{Discounted}(\lambda)(r) = (1 - \lambda) \sum_{i=1}^\infty \lambda^{i-1} \pi(s_{i-1}, \tau_i)$, where $\lambda \in (0, 1)$ is the *discount factor*.
3. *Average time*: $\mathrm{AvgTime}(r) = \limsup_{n \to \infty} T_n/n$.
4. *Average price*: $\mathrm{AvgPrice}(r) = \limsup_{n \to \infty} \pi_n(r)/n$.
5. *Price-per-time average*: $\mathrm{TimeAvgPrice}(r) = \limsup_{n \to \infty} \pi_n(r)/T_n(r)$.
6. *Price-per-reward average*: $\mathrm{PriceRewardAvg}(r) = \limsup_{n \to \infty} \pi_n(r)/\varrho_n(r)$.

The following is the main result of the paper.

Theorem 9. *The minimization problems for reachability, discounted, average time, average price, price-per-time average, and price-per-reward average cost functions, for concavely-priced and concave price-reward timed automata, as appropriate, are PSPACE-complete.*

The reachability problem for timed automata can be easily reduced, in logarithmic space, to the minimization problems discussed above so, by Theorem 8, they are all PSPACE-hard. In Sections 5 and 6 we prove that they are all in PSPACE, and hence we establish the main Theorem 9.

5   Region Graphs

We say that a run $r = \langle s_0, (t_1, a_1), s_1, (t_2, a_2), \ldots \rangle$ of a timed automaton $\mathcal{T}$ is of type $\Lambda(r) = \langle R_0, (R'_1, a_1), R_1, (R'_2, a_2), \ldots \rangle$, if for all $i \in \mathbb{N}$, we have $[s_i] = R_i$ and $[s_i + t_{i+1}] = R'_{i+1}$. We write Types for the set of run types, and we write Types(R) for the set of run types starting from region $R \in \mathcal{R}$.

For $\Lambda = \langle R_0, (R'_1, a_1), R_1, (R'_2, a_2), \ldots \rangle \in$ Types, $s \in R_0$, and $\bar{t} = \langle t_1, t_2, \ldots \rangle \in \mathbb{R}^\omega_\oplus$, we define PreRun$^\Lambda_s(\bar{t}) = \langle (s_0, R_0), (R'_1, t_1, a_1), (s_1, R_1), (R'_2, t_2, a_2), \ldots \rangle$, where $s_0 = s$, and for $i \in \mathbb{N}$, we have $(s_i + t_{i+1}) \xrightarrow{a_{i+1}} s_{i+1}$. For $s, s' \in S$, $R, R'', R' \in \mathcal{R}$, $t \in \mathbb{R}_\oplus$, and $a \in A$, we also say that $\big((s, R), (R'', t, a), (s', R')\big)$ is a pre-transition if $(s + t) \xrightarrow{a} s'$.

5.1   Region Graph $\widetilde{\mathcal{T}}$

Let $\mathcal{T}$ be a timed automaton. We define the *region graph* $\widetilde{\mathcal{T}}$ to be the finite edge-labelled graph $(\mathcal{R}, \widetilde{\mathcal{M}})$, where the set $\mathcal{R}$ of $\mathcal{T}$ is the set of vertices, and the labelled edge relation $\widetilde{\mathcal{M}} \subseteq \mathcal{R} \times \mathcal{R} \times A \times \mathcal{R}$ is defined by $\widetilde{\mathcal{M}} = \{(R, R'', a, R') : R \to_* R'' \xrightarrow{a} R'\}$.

Let $\widetilde{S} = \{(s, R) \in S \times \mathcal{R} : s \in R\}$ be the set of states of $\widetilde{\mathcal{T}}$. For $(s, R), (s', R') \in \widetilde{S}$ and $(R'', t, a) \in \mathcal{R} \times \mathbb{R}_\oplus \times A$, we say that $\big((s, R), (R'', t, a), (s', R')\big)$ is a transition in $\widetilde{\mathcal{T}}$ if: it is a pre-transition, $(s + t) \in R''$, and $(R, R'', a, R') \in \widetilde{\mathcal{M}}$. We then also say that there is an (R'', t, a)-transition from state (s, R) in $\widetilde{\mathcal{T}}$.

A run of $\widetilde{\mathcal{T}}$ is a sequence $\langle (s_0, R_0), (R'_1, t_1, a_1), (s_1, R_1), (R'_2, t_2, a_2), \ldots \rangle$, such that for all $i \in \mathbb{N}$, we have that $\big((s_i, R_i), (R''_{i+1}, t_{i+1}, a_{i+1}), (s'_{i+1}, R'_{i+1})\big)$ is a transition in $\widetilde{\mathcal{T}}$. We write Runs$^{\widetilde{\mathcal{T}}}$ for the set of runs of $\widetilde{\mathcal{T}}$, and for $(s, R) \in \widetilde{S}$, we write Runs$^{\widetilde{\mathcal{T}}}(s, R)$ for the set of runs of $\widetilde{\mathcal{T}}$ whose initial state is (s, R).

The timed automaton $\mathcal{T}$ and the region graph $\widetilde{\mathcal{T}}$ are equivalent in the following sense.

Proposition 10. *For every $s \in S$ and $(t, a) \in \mathbb{R}_\oplus \times A$, there is a (t, a)-transition from s in $\mathcal{T}$ if and only if there is a $([s + t], t, a)$-transition from $(s, [s])$ in $\widetilde{\mathcal{T}}$.*

Let $(\mathcal{T}, \pi)$ be a concavely-priced timed automaton. We define the price function $\widetilde{\pi} : \widetilde{S} \times (\mathcal{R} \times \mathbb{R}_\oplus \times A) \to \mathbb{R}$ in the following way. For $(s, R) \in \widetilde{S}$ and $(R'', t, a) \in \mathcal{R} \times \mathbb{R}_\oplus \times A$, such that there is a (R'', t, a)-transition from (s, R) in $\widetilde{\mathcal{T}}$, we define $\widetilde{\pi}\big((s, R), (R'', t, a)\big) = \pi(s, t, a)$. For a concave price-reward automaton $(\mathcal{T}, \pi, \varrho)$, we define functions $\widetilde{\pi}$ and $\widetilde{\varrho}$ in an analogous way.

5.2   Boundary Region Graph $\widehat{\mathcal{T}}$

Define the finite set of *boundary timed actions* $\mathcal{A} = [\![k]\!]_\mathbb{N} \times C \times A$. For $s \in Q$ and $\alpha = (b, c, a) \in \mathcal{A}$, we define $t(s, \alpha) = b - s(c)$; and we define Succ(s, α) to be the state

$s' = \mathrm{Succ}(s, \tau(\alpha))$, where $\tau(\alpha) = (t(s, \alpha), a)$; we then write $s \xrightarrow{\alpha} s'$. We also write $s \xrightarrow{\alpha} s'$ if $s \xrightarrow{\tau(\alpha)} s'$. Note that if $\alpha \in \mathcal{A}$ and $s \xrightarrow{\alpha} s'$ then $[s'] \in \mathcal{R}_{\mathrm{Thin}}$. Observe that for every thin region $R' \in \mathcal{R}_{\mathrm{Thin}}$, there is a number $b \in [\![k]\!]_{\mathbb{N}}$ and a clock $c \in C$, such that for every $R \in \mathcal{R}$ in the past of R', we have that $s \in R$ implies $(s + (b - s(c)) \in R'$; we then write $R \to_{b,c} R'$. For $\alpha = (b, c, a) \in \mathcal{A}$ and $R, R' \in \mathcal{R}$, we write $R \xrightarrow{\alpha} R'$ or $R \xrightarrow{a}_{b,c} R'$, if $R \to_{b,c} R'' \xrightarrow{a} R'$, for some $R'' \in \mathcal{R}_{\mathrm{Thin}}$.

Let $\mathcal{T}$ be a timed automaton. We define the *boundary region graph* $\widehat{\mathcal{T}}$ to be the finite edge-labelled graph $(\mathcal{R}, \widehat{\mathcal{M}})$, where the set $\mathcal{R}$ of $\mathcal{T}$ is the set of vertices, and the labelled edge relation $\widehat{\mathcal{M}} \subseteq \mathcal{R} \times \mathcal{R} \times \mathcal{A} \times \mathcal{R}$ is defined in the following way. For $\alpha = (b, c, a) \in \mathcal{A}$ and $R, R'', R' \in \mathcal{R}$, we have $(R, R'', \alpha, R') \in \widehat{\mathcal{M}}$ if one of the following conditions holds:

- $R \to_{b,c} R'' \xrightarrow{a} R'$; or
- there is an $R''' \in \mathcal{R}$, such that $R \to_{b,c} R''' \to_{+1} R'' \xrightarrow{a} R'$; or
- there is an $R''' \in \mathcal{R}$, such that $R \to_{b,c} R''' \leftarrow_{+1} R'' \xrightarrow{a} R'$.

Let $\widehat{S} = \{(s, R) \in S \times \mathcal{R} : s \in \overline{R}\}$ be the set of states of $\widehat{\mathcal{T}}$. For $(s, R), (s', R') \in \widehat{S}$ and $(R'', t, a) \in \mathcal{R} \times \mathbb{R}_{\oplus} \times A$, we say that $\big((s, R), (R'', t, a), (s', R')\big)$ is a transition in $\widehat{\mathcal{T}}$ if: it is a pre-transition, and there is an $\alpha = (b, c, a)$, such that $t = b - s(c)$, $(s + t) \in \overline{R''}$, and $(R, R'', \alpha, R') \in \widehat{\mathcal{M}}$.

A run of $\widehat{\mathcal{T}}$ is a sequence $\langle (s_0, R_0), (R'_1, t_1, a_1), (s_1, R_1), (R'_2, t_2, a_2), \ldots \rangle$, such that for all $i \in \mathbb{N}$, we have that $\big((s_i, R_i), (R''_{i+1}, t_{i+1}, a_{i+1}), (s'_{i+1}, R'_{i+1})\big)$ is a transition in $\widehat{\mathcal{T}}$. We write $\mathrm{Runs}^{\widehat{\mathcal{T}}}$ for the set of runs of $\widehat{\mathcal{T}}$, and for $(s, R) \in \widehat{S}$, we write $\mathrm{Runs}^{\widehat{\mathcal{T}}}(s, R)$ for the set of runs of $\widehat{\mathcal{T}}$ whose initial state is (s, R).

Let $(\mathcal{T}, \pi)$ be a concavely-priced timed automaton. We define the price function $\widehat{\pi} : \widehat{S} \times (\mathcal{R} \times \mathbb{R}_{\oplus} \times A)$ in the following way. Recall that for $a \in A$ and $R, R'' \in \mathcal{R}$, the function $\pi^a_{R,R''} : (s, t) \mapsto \pi(s, a, t)$ defined on the set $D_{R,R''} = \{(s, t) : s \in R \text{ and } (s+t) \in R''\}$ is continuous. We write $\overline{\pi^a_{R,R''}}$ for the unique continuous extension of $\pi^a_{R,R''}$ to the closure $\overline{D_{R,R''}}$ of the set $D_{R,R''}$. For $(s, R) \in \widehat{S}$ and $(R'', t, a) \in \mathcal{R} \times \mathbb{R}_{\oplus} \times A$, such that there is an (R'', t, a)-transition from (s, R) in $\widehat{\mathcal{T}}$, we define $\widehat{\pi}\big((s, R), (R'', t, a)\big) = \overline{\pi^a_{R,R''}}(s, t)$. For a concave price-reward automaton $(\mathcal{T}, \pi, \varrho)$, we define functions $\widehat{\pi}$ and $\widehat{\varrho}$ in an analogous way.

Proposition 11. *If $r \in \mathrm{Runs}^{\widetilde{\mathcal{T}}} \cap \mathrm{Runs}^{\widehat{\mathcal{T}}}$ then $\widetilde{\pi}(r) = \widehat{\pi}(r)$.*

Thanks to the above proposition we can, and sometimes will, abuse notation by writing $\pi(r)$ instead of $\widetilde{\pi}(r)$ or $\widehat{\pi}(r)$ for $r \in \mathrm{Runs}^{\widetilde{\mathcal{T}}}$ or $r \in \mathrm{Runs}^{\widehat{\mathcal{T}}}$, respectively.

5.3 Optimization Problems on the Region Graphs $\widetilde{\mathcal{T}}$ and $\widehat{\mathcal{T}}$

For a cost function $\mathrm{Cost} : \mathrm{PreRuns} \to \mathbb{R}$, we define the *minimum cost* functions $\mathrm{Cost}^{\widetilde{\mathcal{T}}}_* : \widetilde{S} \to \mathbb{R}$ and $\mathrm{Cost}^{\widehat{\mathcal{T}}}_* : \widehat{S} \to \mathbb{R}$, by:

$$\mathrm{Cost}^{\widetilde{\mathcal{T}}}_*(s, R) = \inf_{r \in \mathrm{Runs}^{\widetilde{\mathcal{T}}}(s, R)} \mathrm{Cost}(r), \quad \text{and} \quad \mathrm{Cost}^{\widehat{\mathcal{T}}}_*(s, R) = \inf_{r \in \mathrm{Runs}^{\widehat{\mathcal{T}}}(s, R)} \mathrm{Cost}(r).$$

The corresponding *minimization problems* are: given a state $s \in S$ and a number $D \in \mathbb{Q}$, determine whether $\mathrm{Cost}^{\tilde{T}}_*(s, [s]) \leq D$ and $\mathrm{Cost}^{\hat{T}}_*(s, [s]) \leq D$, respectively.

The following list of cost functions gives rise to a number of minimization problems. Let $r = \langle(s_0, R_0), (R'_1, t_1, a_1), (s_1, R_1), (R'_2, t_2, a_2), \ldots\rangle$ be a run of $\tilde{T}$ or $\hat{T}$. For all $n \in \mathbb{N}$, define $T_n(r) = \sum_{i=1}^n t_i$; $\pi_n(r) = \sum_{i=1}^n \pi((s_{i-1}, R_{i-1}), (R'_i, t_i, a_i))$; and $\varrho_n(r) = \sum_{i=1}^n \varrho((s_{i-1}, R_{i-1}), (R'_i, t_i, a_i))$. With those notations, we define the reachability, discounted, average time, average price, price-per-time average, and price-per-reward average cost functions, on the sets of runs of $\tilde{T}$ and $\hat{T}$, in exactly the same way as for runs of the timed automaton T; see Section 4.

The following is an easy corollary of Proposition 10.

Proposition 12. *If Cost is any of the reachability, discounted, average time, average price, price-per-time average, or price-per-reward average cost functions, then for all $s \in S$, we have $\mathrm{Cost}^{T}_*(s) = \mathrm{Cost}^{\tilde{T}}_*(s, [s])$.*

The following theorem is one of the main technical results of the paper.

Theorem 13. *If Cost is any of the reachability, discounted, average time, average price, price-per-time average, or price-per-reward average cost functions, then for all $s \in S$, we have $\mathrm{Cost}^{\tilde{T}}_*(s, [s]) = \mathrm{Cost}^{\hat{T}}_*(s, [s])$.*

Observe that for every state $s \in S$, the number of states reachable from s in the boundary region graph $\hat{T}$ is at most proportional to the size of $\hat{T}$, and hence finite. By Theorem 1, it follows that optimal positional strategies exist in $\hat{T}$ for all above-mentioned cost functions. Therefore, and since a run from a state according to a positional strategy in $\hat{T}$ can be guessed, and its cost computed, in PSPACE (with respect to the size of the input, i.e., a timed automaton T), it suffices to prove Theorem 13 in order to obtain the main Theorem 9. We dedicate Section 6 to the proof of Theorem 13.

6   Correctness of the Bounded Region Graph Abstraction

6.1   Approximations of Cost Functions

For $n \in \mathbb{N}$, we write $\mathrm{Runs}^{\tilde{T}}(n)$ and $\mathrm{Runs}^{\hat{T}}(n)$ for the sets of runs of $\tilde{T}$ and $\hat{T}$, respectively, of length n. Also, for a run $r \in \mathrm{Runs}^{\tilde{T}}$ or $r \in \mathrm{Runs}^{\hat{T}}$, and $n \in \mathbb{N}$, we write $\mathrm{Prefix}(r, n)$ for the finite run consisting of the first n transitions of r. For $r \in \mathrm{Runs}^{\tilde{T}}$, we sometimes abuse notation—for the sake of brevity—by writing $\mathrm{Cost}_n(r)$ instead of $\mathrm{Cost}_n(\mathrm{Prefix}(r, n))$; the same applies to runs in $\mathrm{Runs}^{\hat{T}}$.

We say that a sequence of functions $\langle \mathrm{Cost}_n : \mathrm{PreRuns}(n) \to \mathbb{R} \rangle_{n \in \mathbb{N}}$ approximates a cost function $\mathrm{Cost} : \mathrm{Runs}^{\tilde{T}} \to \mathbb{R}$ or $\mathrm{Cost} : \mathrm{Runs}^{\hat{T}} \to \mathbb{R}$, respectively, if for all $r \in \mathrm{Runs}^{\tilde{T}}$, or for all $r \in \mathrm{Runs}^{\hat{T}}$, respectively, we have that $\mathrm{Cost}(r) = \limsup_{n \to \infty} \mathrm{Cost}_n(r)$.

6.2 Cost Functions and Finite Run Types

Let $\Lambda = \langle R_0, (R'_1, a_1), R_1, (R'_2, a_2), R_2, \ldots \rangle$ be a run type. For a state $s \in R_0$ and $(t_1, t_2, \ldots, t_n) \in \mathbb{R}_\oplus^n$, we define $\mathrm{PreRun}^\Lambda_{n,s}(t_1, t_2, \ldots, t_n) = \mathrm{Prefix}(\mathrm{PreRun}^\Lambda_s(\bar{t}), n)$, where the first n elements of $\bar{t} \in \mathbb{R}_\oplus^\omega$ are $t_1, t_2, \ldots, t_n$. We define $\Delta^\Lambda_{n,s} \subseteq \mathbb{R}_\oplus^n$ to consist of the tuples $(t_1, t_2, \ldots, t_n) \in \mathbb{R}_\oplus^n$, such that $\mathrm{PreRun}^\Lambda_{n,s}(t_1, t_2, \ldots, t_n) \in \mathrm{Runs}^{\widetilde{T}}(n)$.

Proposition 14. *For every state $s \in S$, a run type $\Lambda \in \mathrm{Types}([s])$, and $n \in \mathbb{N}$, the set $\Delta^\Lambda_{n,s}$ is a polytope.*

Proposition 15. *Let $R \in \mathcal{R}$, $\Lambda \in \mathrm{Types}(R)$, $s \in R$, and $n \in \mathbb{N}$. There is a 1-to-1 correspondence between runs—starting from s, of type Λ, and of length n—in $\widehat{T}$, and vertices of $\overline{\Delta^\Lambda_{n,s}}$.*

More precisely, $r = \langle (s_0, R_0), (R'_1, t_1, a_1), (s_1, R_1), \ldots, (R'_n, t_n, a_n), (s_n, R_n) \rangle$ is a run (of type Λ) in $\widehat{T}$ if and only if there is a vertex $(t_1, t_2, \ldots, t_n)$ of $\overline{\Delta^\Lambda_{n,s}}$, such that $r = \mathrm{PreRun}^\Lambda_{n,s}(t_1, t_2, \ldots, t_n)$.

The following is a well-known result [8].

Proposition 16. *Let $f : \Delta \to \mathbb{R}$ be a continuous quasi-concave function, where $\Delta \subseteq \mathbb{R}^n$ is a polytope. Let $\overline{f}$ be the unique continuous extension of f to the closure $\overline{\Delta}$ of Δ.*

- *There exists a vertex v of $\overline{\Delta}$, such that $\overline{f}(v) = \inf_{x \in \Delta} f(x)$.*
- *For every $\varepsilon > 0$, there exists $x \in \Delta$, such that $f(x) \leq \overline{f}(v) + \varepsilon$.*

Let a sequence $\langle \mathrm{Cost}_n \rangle_{n \in \mathbb{N}}$ approximate a cost function Cost. We define the function $\mathrm{Cost}^\Lambda_{n,s} : \Delta^\Lambda_{n,s} \to \mathbb{R}$ by $\mathrm{Cost}^\Lambda_{n,s}(t_1, t_2, \ldots, t_n) = \mathrm{Cost}_n(\mathrm{PreRun}^\Lambda_{n,s}(t_1, t_2, \ldots, t_n))$.

The following can be derived from Propositions 15 and 16.

Corollary 17. *Let $\mathrm{Cost}^\Lambda_{n,s}$ be quasi-concave on $\Delta^\Lambda_{n,s}$.*

1. *For every run $\widetilde{r} \in \mathrm{Runs}^{\widetilde{T}}(s)$ of type Λ, and for every $n \in \mathbb{N}$, there is a run $\widehat{r} \in \mathrm{Runs}^{\widetilde{T}}(s)$ of type Λ, such that $\mathrm{Cost}_n(\widehat{r}) \leq \mathrm{Cost}_n(\widetilde{r})$.*
2. *For every run $\widehat{r} \in \mathrm{Runs}^{\widetilde{T}}(s)$, and for every $\varepsilon > 0$, there is a run $\widetilde{r} \in \mathrm{Runs}^{\widetilde{T}}(s)$ of type Λ, such that $\mathrm{Cost}_n(\widetilde{r}) \leq \mathrm{Cost}_n(\widehat{r}) + \varepsilon$.*

Consider pre-runs $r = \langle (s_0, R_0), (R'_1, t_1, a_1), (s_1, R_1), (R'_2, t_2, a_2), \ldots \rangle$ and $r' = \langle (s'_0, R_0), (R'_1, t'_1, a_1), (s'_1, R_1), (R'_2, t'_2, a_2), \ldots \rangle$ of the same type. We define $r - r' = (s_0 - s'_0, t_1 - t'_1, s_1 - s'_1, t_2 - t'_2, \ldots)$, where for all $i \in \mathbb{N}$, the expression $(s_i - s'_i)$ stands for the finite sequence $\langle s_i(c) - s'_i(c) \rangle_{c \in C}$. For a sequence $\overline{x} = \langle x_i \rangle_{i \in \mathbb{N}} \in \mathbb{R}^\omega$ of reals, we define $\|\overline{x}\| = \sup_{i \in \mathbb{N}} |x_i|$.

Proposition 18. *For every run $\widehat{r} \in \mathrm{Runs}^{\widetilde{T}}(s)$, and for every $\varepsilon > 0$, and there is a run $\widetilde{r} \in \mathrm{Runs}^{\widetilde{T}}(s)$, such that $\|\widehat{r} - \widetilde{r}\| \leq \varepsilon$.*

Proof. Let $\widehat{r} = \langle (s_0, R_0), (R'_1, t_1, a_1), (s_1, R_1), (R'_2, t_2, a_2), \ldots \rangle \in \mathrm{Runs}^{\widehat{T}}$. Note that since $\widehat{r} \in \mathrm{Runs}^{\widehat{T}}$, for every $i \in \mathbb{N}$, there are $b_i \in [\![k]\!]_\mathbb{N}$ and $c_i \in C$, such that $t_i = b_i - s_{i-1}(c_i)$. Let $\widetilde{r} = \langle (s'_0 = s_0, R_0), (R'_1, t'_1, a_1), (s'_1, R_1), (R'_2, t'_2, a_2), \ldots \rangle \in \mathrm{Runs}^{\widetilde{T}}$ (of the same type as $\widehat{r}$) be such that for all $i \in \mathbb{N}$, we choose $t'_i \in \mathbb{R}_\oplus$ so that $|t'_i - (b_i - s'_{i-1}(c_i))| < \varepsilon - \|s_{i-1} - s'_{i-1}\|$. It then follows that for all $i \in \mathbb{N}$, we have $\|s_i - s'_i\| < \varepsilon$, and hence $\|\widehat{r} - \widetilde{r}\| \leq \varepsilon$. $\qquad\square$

6.3 Concave-Regular Cost Functions

A cost function Cost : PreRuns $\to$ $\mathbb{R}$ is *concave-regular* if it satisfies the following properties.

1. *(Quasi-concavity).* For every region $R \in \mathcal{R}$ and for every run type $\Lambda \in \mathrm{Types}(R)$, there is $N \in \mathbb{N}$, such that for every state $s \in R$ and for every $n \geq N$, the function $\mathrm{Cost}_{n,s}^{\Lambda}$ is quasi-concave on $\Delta_{n,s}^{\Lambda}$.
2. *(Regular Lipschitz-continuity).* There is a constant $K \geq 0$, such that for every region $R \in \mathcal{R}$ and for every positional run type $\Lambda \in \mathrm{Types}(R)$, there is $N \in \mathbb{N}$, such that for every state $s \in R$ and for every $n \geq N$, the function $\mathrm{Cost}_{n,s}^{\Lambda}$ is K-continuous on $\Delta_{n,s}^{\Lambda}$.
3. *(Uniform convergence).* There is $\chi : \mathbb{N} \to \mathbb{R}$, such that $\lim_{n \to \infty} \chi(n) = 0$, and for every state $s \in S$, run $\widehat{r} \in \mathrm{Runs}^{\widehat{T}}(s, [s])$, and $n \in \mathbb{N}$, we have $\mathrm{Cost}_{*}^{\widehat{T}}(s, [s]) \leq \mathrm{Cost}_{n}(\widehat{r}) + \chi(n)$.

Theorem 19. *If Cost : PreRuns $\to$ $\mathbb{R}$ is concave-regular then for all states $s \in S$, we have $\mathrm{Cost}_{*}^{\widetilde{T}}(s, [s]) = \mathrm{Cost}_{*}^{\widehat{T}}(s, [s])$.*

Proof. First we prove that for all $s \in S$, we have $\mathrm{Cost}_{*}^{\widehat{T}}(s, [s]) \leq \mathrm{Cost}_{*}^{\widetilde{T}}(s, [s])$. It suffices to show that for every run $\widetilde{r} \in \mathrm{Runs}^{\widetilde{T}}(s, [s])$, we have $\mathrm{Cost}_{*}^{\widehat{T}}(s, [s]) \leq \mathrm{Cost}(\widetilde{r})$.

Let $\widetilde{r} \in \mathrm{Runs}^{\widetilde{T}}(s, [s])$ be a run in $\widetilde{T}$ of type Λ. By the quasi-concavity property of Cost, there is $N \in \mathbb{N}$, such that for all $n \geq N$, the function $\mathrm{Cost}_{n,s}^{\Lambda}$ is quasi-concave on $\Delta_{n,s}^{\Lambda}$. Hence—by the first part of Corollary 17—for every $n \geq N$, there is a run $\widehat{r_n} \in \mathrm{Runs}^{\widehat{T}}(s, [s])$ of type Λ, such that $\mathrm{Cost}_{n}(\widehat{r_n}) \leq \mathrm{Cost}_{n}(\widetilde{r})$.

By the uniform convergence property of Cost, there is a function $\chi : \mathbb{N} \to \mathbb{R}$, such that $\lim_{n \to \infty} \chi(n) = 0$ and for all $n \in \mathbb{N}$, we have $\mathrm{Cost}_{*}^{\widehat{T}}(s, [s]) \leq \mathrm{Cost}_{n}(\widehat{r_n}) + \chi(n)$. Hence—combining the last two inequalities—we get $\mathrm{Cost}_{*}^{\widehat{T}}(s, [s]) \leq \mathrm{Cost}_{n}(\widetilde{r}) + \chi(n)$, for $n \geq N$. Taking the limit supremum of both sides of the last inequality yields:

$$\mathrm{Cost}_{*}^{\widehat{T}}(s, [s]) \leq \limsup_{n \to \infty} \left(\mathrm{Cost}_{n}(\widetilde{r}) + \chi(n) \right) = \mathrm{Cost}(\widetilde{r}).$$

Next we prove that for all $s \in S$, we have $\mathrm{Cost}_{*}^{\widetilde{T}}(s, [s]) \leq \mathrm{Cost}_{*}^{\widehat{T}}(s, [s])$. It suffices to argue that for every $s \in S$ and $\varepsilon > 0$, there is a run $\widetilde{r} \in \mathrm{Runs}^{\widetilde{T}}(s, [s])$, such that $|\mathrm{Cost}(\widetilde{r}) - \mathrm{Cost}_{*}^{\widehat{T}}(s, [s])| \leq \varepsilon$.

Let $\varepsilon > 0$ and let $\widehat{r} \in \mathrm{Runs}^{\widehat{T}}(s, [s])$, so that $\mathrm{Cost}(\widehat{r}) \leq \mathrm{Cost}_{*}^{\widehat{T}}(s, [s]) + \varepsilon/2$, and hence $|\mathrm{Cost}(\widehat{r}) - \mathrm{Cost}_{*}^{\widehat{T}}(s, [s])| \leq \varepsilon/2$. Let $\widetilde{r} \in \mathrm{Runs}^{\widetilde{T}}$ be such that $\|\widetilde{r} - \widehat{r}\| \leq \varepsilon'$, for some $\varepsilon' > 0$ to be chosen later; existence of such $\widetilde{r} \in \mathrm{Runs}^{\widetilde{T}}(s, [s])$ follows from Proposition 18.

By the regular Lipschitz-continuity of Cost, there is $K \geq 0$ and $N \in \mathbb{N}$, such that for all $n \geq N$, we have: $|\mathrm{Cost}_{n}(\widetilde{r}) - \mathrm{Cost}_{n}(\widehat{r})| \leq K\|\widetilde{r} - \widehat{r}\| \leq K\varepsilon'$. Hence—by choosing $\varepsilon' > 0$ so that $\varepsilon' \leq \varepsilon/(2K)$—we obtain that:

$$|\mathrm{Cost}_{n}(\widetilde{r}) - \mathrm{Cost}_{n}(\widehat{r})| \leq \varepsilon/2,$$

for $n \geq N$. Recall, however, that we have chosen $\widehat{r} \in \mathrm{Runs}^{\widehat{T}}(s, [s])$ so that:

$$|\mathrm{Cost}(\widehat{r}) - \mathrm{Cost}_*^{\widehat{T}}(s, [s])| \leq \varepsilon/2.$$

From the last two inequalities it follows that $|\mathrm{Cost}(\widetilde{r}) - \mathrm{Cost}_*^{\widehat{T}}(s, [s])| \leq \varepsilon$.   □

Theorem 20. *Reachability, discounted, average time, average price, price-per-time average, and price-per-reward average cost functions are concave-regular for concavely-priced (or concave price-reward, as appropriate) timed automata.*

Note that the key Theorem 13 follows immediately from Theorems 19 and 20.

References

1. Abdeddaïm, Y., Maler, O.: Job-shop scheduling using timed automata. In: Berry, G., Comon, H., Finkel, A. (eds.) CAV 2001. LNCS, vol. 2102, pp. 478–492. Springer, Heidelberg (2001)
2. Alur, R., Courcoubetis, C., Dill, D.: Model-checking in dense real-time. Information and Computation 104(1), 2–34 (1993)
3. Alur, R., Courcoubetis, C., Henzinger, T.A.: Computing accumulated delays in real-time systems. Formal Methods in System Design 11(2), 137–155 (1997)
4. Alur, R., Dill, D.: A theory of timed automata. In: Theoretical Computer Science, vol. 126, pp. 183–235 (1994)
5. Alur, R., La Torre, S., Pappas, G.J.: Optimal paths in weighted timed automata. Theoretical Computer Science 318(3), 297–322 (2004)
6. Asarin, E., Maler, O.: As soon as possible: Time optimal control for timed automata. In: Vaandrager, F.W., van Schuppen, J.H. (eds.) HSCC 1999. LNCS, vol. 1569, pp. 19–30. Springer, Heidelberg (1999)
7. Behrmann, G., Fehnker, A., Hune, T., Larsen, K.G., Pettersson, P., Romijn, J., Vaandrager, F.W.: Minimum-cost reachability for priced timed automata. In: Di Benedetto, M.D., Sangiovanni-Vincentelli, A.L. (eds.) HSCC 2001. LNCS, vol. 2034, pp. 147–161. Springer, Heidelberg (2001)
8. Bertsekas, D.P., Nedić, A., Ozdaglar, A.E.: Convex Analysis and Optimization. Athena Scientific (2003)
9. Bouyer, P.: Weighted timed automata: Model-checking and games. Electr. Notes Theor. Comput. Sci. 158, 3–17 (2006)
10. Bouyer, P., Brihaye, T., Bruyère, V., Raskin, J.: On the optimal reachability problem on weighted timed automata. Formal Methods in System Design 31(2), 135–175 (2007)
11. Bouyer, P., Brinksma, E., Larsen, K.G.: Optimal infinite scheduling for multi-priced timed automata. Formal Methods in System Design 32(1), 3–23 (2008)
12. Boyd, S., Vandenberghe, L.: Convex Optimization. Cambridge University Press, Cambridge (2004)
13. Brihaye, T., Henzinger, T.A., Prabhu, V.S., Raskin, J.: Minimum-time reachability in timed games. In: Arge, L., Cachin, C., Jurdziński, T., Tarlecki, A. (eds.) ICALP 2007. LNCS, vol. 4596, pp. 825–837. Springer, Heidelberg (2007)
14. Courcoubetis, C., Yannakakis, M.: Minimum and maximum delay problems in real-time systems. In: FMSD 1992, vol. 1, pp. 385–415. Kluwer, Dordrecht (1992)
15. Jurdziński, M., Trivedi, A.: Reachability-time games on timed automata. In: Arge, L., Cachin, C., Jurdziński, T., Tarlecki, A. (eds.) ICALP 2007. LNCS, vol. 4596, pp. 838–849. Springer, Heidelberg (2007)

16. Kesten, Y., Pnueli, A., Sifakis, J., Yovine, S.: Decidable integration graphs. Information and Computation 150(2), 209–243 (1999)
17. Larsen, K.G., Behrmann, G., Brinksma, E., Fehnker, A., Hune, T., Pettersson, P., Romijn, J.: As cheap as possible: Efficient cost-optimal reachability for priced timed automata. In: Berry, G., Comon, H., Finkel, A. (eds.) CAV 2001. LNCS, vol. 2102, pp. 493–505. Springer, Heidelberg (2001)
18. Mangasarian, O.L.: Nonlinear Programming. McGraw-Hill Series in Systems Science. McGraw-Hill, New York (1969)
19. Niebert, P., Tripakis, S., Yovine, S.: Minimum-time reachability for timed automata. In: MED 2000. IEEE Comp. Soc. Press, Los Alamitos (2000)

Average-Price and Reachability-Price Games on Hybrid Automata with Strong Resets*

Patricia Bouyer[1], Thomas Brihaye[2], Marcin Jurdziński[3], Ranko Lazić[3],
and Michał Rutkowski[3]

[1] LSV, CNRS & ENS de Cachan, France
[2] Institut de Mathématiques, University of Mons-Hainaut, Belgium
[3] Department of Computer Science, University of Warwick, UK

Abstract. We introduce and study hybrid automata with strong resets. They generalize o-minimal hybrid automata, a class of hybrid automata which allows modeling of complex continuous dynamics. A number of analysis problems, such as reachability testing and controller synthesis, are decidable for classes of o-minimal hybrid automata. We generalize existing decidability results for controller synthesis on hybrid automata and we establish new ones by proving that average-price and reachability-price games on hybrid systems with strong resets are decidable, provided that the structure on which the hybrid automaton is defined has a decidable first-order theory. Our proof techniques include a novel characterization of values in games on hybrid systems by optimality equations, and a definition of a new finitary equivalence relation on the states of a hybrid system which enables a reduction of games on hybrid systems to games on finite graphs.

1 Introduction

Hybrid systems and automata. Systems that exhibit both discrete and continuous behavior are referred to as *hybrid systems* [1]. Continuous changes to the system's state are interleaved with discrete ones, which may alter the constraints for future continuous behaviors. *Hybrid automata* are a formalism for modeling hybrid systems [2]. Hybrid automata are finite automata augmented with continuous real-valued variables. The discrete states can be seen as modes of execution, and the continuous changes of the variables as the evolution of the system's state over time. The mode specifies the continuous dynamics of the system, and mode changes are triggered by the changes in variable's values.

Verification and controller synthesis. Formal verification of hybrid systems is an active field of research in computer science (e.g. [3,4,5,6,7]). When augmented with price information, they can serve as models for resource consumption. The price does not constrain the behavior of the system, but gives quantitative information about it. This research directions ha recently received substantial attention. Timed automata[3] have

---

* This research was supported in part by EPSRC project EP/E022030/1.

F. Cassez and C. Jard (Eds.): FORMATS 2008, LNCS 5215, pp. 63–77, 2008.

been extended with price information [8,9]. Similarly, the model of o-minimal[1] hybrid systems has been extended with price functions [10].

The designer of the system often lacks full control over its operation. The behavior of the system is a result of an interaction between a controller and the environment. This gives rise to the *controller synthesis* problem, where the goal is to design a program such that, regardless of the the environment's behavior, the system behaves correctly and optimally. A game-based approach to the controller synthesis problem was first proposed by Church [11], and was applied to hybrid automata [12,10] and timed automata [13]. There are two players, *controller* and *environment*, and they are playing a zero-sum game. The game is played on the hybrid automaton and consists of rounds. In this paper, we use player Min to denote the controller and player Max to denote the environment. These are standard player names in zero-sum games. In each round, Min proposes a transition. Based on that, and in accordance with the game protocol, Max performs this or another transition.

Hybrid games with strong resets. We are considering a subclass of hybrid automata: hybrid automata with strong resets (HASR). In order to represent the automaton finitely, we require that all the components of the system are first-order definable over the ordered field of reals. The term "strong resets" comes from the property of the system that all the continuous variables are non-deterministically reset after each discrete transition. As opposed to timed automata, where flow rates are constant, and reseting of the variables upon a discrete transition is not compulsory [3], HASR allow for rich continuous dynamics [5,10,12]. In the game setting, we allow only for alternating sequences of timed and discrete transitions [12,10]. Allowing an arbitrary number of continuous transitions prior to a discrete one, without the requirement of o-minimality, renders it impossible to construct a bisimulation of finite index [14,15].

Contributions. We are considering hybrid games with strong resets which generalize the previously studied *o-minimal hybrid games* [12,10]. The o-minimality assumption, together with the decidability of the first-order theory, was crucial in establishing previous decidability results [10].

For controller synthesis, only *reachability-price* games were studied so far [10]. However, the decidability result was limited to o-minimal hybrid games, where the price function is positive and non-decreasing. In this work, we extend the previous results to arbitrary price functions. Moreover, we show decidability of solving average-price games which, until now, were studied only in a discrete time setting [16].

In order to characterize the concept of *game value*, we use a technique of *optimality equations* [17]. For each game we introduce a set of equations. We prove that, if a pair of functions from the states to real numbers satisfies those equations, then the values of those functions are actually game values. We also show how to find solutions to such equations. This technique is new in the area of infinite state systems and we believe that its introduction contributes to the value of our results.

---

[1] O-minimality refers to the underlying algebraic structure. A structure is said to be *o-minimal* if every first-order definable subset of its domain is a finite union of points and intervals.

We introduce a new equivalence relation over the state space of the game. This equivalence is coarser then the previously considered in this context [12,10] and also induces a finite bisimulation.

To compute solutions to the optimality equations, we construct a finite priced graph, using the introduced equivalence relation. We prove that we can derive solutions to the original problem from solutions to the finite problem. Both average-price and reachability-price games on finite graphs are known to be decidable.

It is worth noting that our results can be easily extended to *relaxed hybrid automata* [7], where the strong reset requirement is replaced by a requirement that every cycle in the control graph has a transition that resets all the variables. This extension can be achieved by a refinement of the equivalence relation and a minor modification of the finite graph obtained from it. We decided against considering this more general model, as it would have a negative impact on the clarity of presentation and exposition of our results.

Organization of the paper. The paper is organized as follows. Sec. 2 introduces notions of computability, definability, and zero-sum games. We recall the known results for finite average-price and reachability-price games. Sec. 3 introduces zero-sum hybrid games with strong resets. We characterize game values using optimality equations, and prove that if these equations have solutions then the games are determined and almost-optimal strategies exist. In the rest of the paper we are showing that the solutions to the optimality equations indeed exist. A finite abstraction over the state space of the hybrid game is introduced in Sec. 4. It is used to construct a finite priced game graph. In Sec. 5, we show that solutions to optimality equations for finite average-price and reachability-price games on this graph coincide with solutions to the optimality equations for their hybrid analogues.

2 Preliminaries

We introduce key notions and results that will be used further in the paper, such as computability, definability, decidability, and two-player zero-sum games on priced graphs. We also briefly summarize known results for average-price and reachability-price games on finite graphs.

Throughout the paper $\mathbb{R}_\infty$ denotes the set of real numbers augmented with positive and negative infinities, and $\mathbb{R}_+$ and $\mathbb{R}_\oplus$ denote the sets of positive and non-negative reals, respectively. If $G = (V, E)$ is a graph then for for a vertex v we write vE to denote the set $\{v' : (v, v') \in E\}$.

2.1 Computability and Definability

Computability. Let $f : X \to \mathbb{R}$ be a partial function, which is defined on a set $D \subseteq X \subseteq \mathbb{R}^n$. We say that f is *computable* if $f(x)$ is rational for every rational $x \in D$, and there exists an algorithm that computes it given x. It is *approximately computable* if for every rational $x \in D$, and every $\varepsilon > 0$, we can compute a $y \in \mathbb{R}$ such that $|y - f(x)| < \varepsilon$. It is *decidable* if the following problem is decidable: given a rational $x \in D$ and $c \in \mathbb{Q}$, decide whether $f(x) \leqslant c$. A set $X \subseteq \mathbb{R}^n$ is *decidable* if there is an algorithm that, given a rational x, can decide whether $x \in X$.

Proposition 1. *If a function is decidable then it is approximately computable. If a decidable set contains a rational element, then there is an algorithm that outputs one.*

Earlier definitions apply to the broadly accepted *Turing machine* model of computation. When dealing with real computation, the *Blume-Shub-Smale (BSS)* model [18,19] can also be considered. In the BSS model all real numbers are among the valid inputs and outputs.

Definability. Let $\mathcal{M} = \langle \mathbb{R}, 0, 1, +, \cdot, \leqslant \rangle$ be the field of reals We will say that a set $X \subseteq \mathbb{R}^n$ is *definable* in $\mathcal{M}$ if it is *first-order definable* in $\mathcal{M}$. The *first-order theory of* $\mathcal{M}$ is the set of all first-order sentences that are true in $\mathcal{M}$. A well known result by Tarski [20] is that the first-order theory of the ordered field of reals is decidable.

It is possible to enrich the structure $\mathcal{M}$ with more operations (e.g., trigonometric functions, exponential function, etc.), but decidability of the respective first-order theory might be broken. Decidability of $\mathcal{M}$ is necessary to establish Cor. 19 and 21, and Thm 22. Unlike results in [6,10,12], definability over $\mathcal{M}$ is not necessary to establish determinacy and existence of almost-optimal strategies (Thms 7, 11, 17, and 20). These results are a direct consequence of the "strong reset" property mentioned in the introduction.

Note that, if a real partial function is definable it is decidable, and if a set is definable it is decidable.

2.2 Zero-Sum Games

Priced game graphs. Let S be a set of *states*, $E \subseteq S \times S$ be an *edge relation*, and $\pi : E \to \mathbb{R}$ a *price function*. A *priced game graph* is $\Gamma = ((S, E), S^{\mathsf{Min}}, S^{\mathsf{Max}}, \pi)$, where $S = S^{\mathsf{Min}} \uplus S^{\mathsf{Max}}$. Note that S and E do not have to be finite or even countable.

A run of Γ is a sequence $\rho = \langle s_0, s_1, \ldots \rangle$ of elements of S, where $\rho(0) = s_0$ is called the initial state, and $(s_i, s_{i+1}) \in E$ for all $i \in \mathbb{N}$. A finite run is a finite sequence $\rho = \langle s_0, \ldots, s_k \rangle$ of elements of S, satisfying the same conditions. We write Runs (Runs$_{\mathsf{fin}}$) to denote the set of all runs (finite runs) of Γ.

Strategies. A *strategy* for player Min is a function $\mu : \mathsf{Runs}_{\mathsf{fin}} \to S$, such that for every $\rho = \langle s_0, s_1, \ldots, s_n \rangle \in \mathsf{Runs}_{\mathsf{fin}}$, if $s_n \in S^{\mathsf{Min}}$ then $(s_n, \mu(\rho)) \in E$. A *positional strategy* for player Min is a function $\mu : S^{\mathsf{Min}} \to S$ that satisfies the same conditions. A positional strategy μ naturally induces the strategy $\mathsf{Runs}_{\mathsf{fin}} \ni \langle s_0, s_1, \ldots, s_n \rangle \mapsto \mu(s_n) \in S$, which, for simplicity, we also refer to as μ. (Positional) strategies for player Max are defined analogously. We write Σ_{Min} and Σ_{Max} for the sets of strategies for player Min and Max, respectively, and we write Π_{Min} and Π_{Max} for the sets of their positional strategies. For $s \in S$ and strategies $\mu \in \Sigma_{\mathsf{Min}}$ and $\chi \in \Sigma_{\mathsf{Max}}$, we define the run starting at s and following μ and χ by $\mathsf{Run}(s, \mu, \chi) = \langle s_0, s_1, s_2, \ldots \rangle$, where $s_0 = s$ and for all $i \geq 0$, $\mu(s_0, \ldots, s_i) = s_{i+1}$ if $s_i \in S^{\mathsf{Min}}$, and $\chi(s_0, \ldots, s_i) = s_{i+1}$ if $s_i \in S^{\mathsf{Max}}$.

Let $\mathsf{P}_* : \mathsf{Runs} \to \mathbb{R}_\infty$ and $\mathsf{P}^* : \mathsf{Runs} \to \mathbb{R}_\infty$ be *lower* and *upper payoff functions*, respectively. In a two-player zero-sum game, player Min wants to minimize the value of P^* of a play and player Max wants to maximize the value of P_* of the play. We require that $\mathsf{P}^* \geqslant \mathsf{P}_*$, and if $\mathsf{P} = \mathsf{P}_* = \mathsf{P}^*$ then we call P the *payoff function*. Payoff functions define a *zero-sum game* on a priced game graph Γ.

Example 2. Let us consider a very simple priced game graph, consisting of one vertex and two edges. One of these edges bears a price of 0, and the other one the price of 1. For the sake of the definition completeness, we say that the set of vertices of player Min is empty.

If we use the average-price payoff functions (see Sec. 2.3 for the definition) and consider an infinite run ρ of the form $\underbrace{10}_{2 \cdot 2^0} \underbrace{1100}_{2 \cdot 2^1} \underbrace{11110000}_{2 \cdot 2^2} \ldots$ one can see, after a brief calculation, that $\mathsf{P}_*(\rho) = 1/2$ which is not equal to $\mathsf{P}^*(\rho) = 2/3$.

Determinacy. We define lower value $\mathsf{Val}_*(s) = \sup_{\chi \in \varSigma_{\mathrm{Max}}} \inf_{\mu \in \varSigma_{\mathrm{Min}}} \mathsf{P}_*(\mathsf{Run}(s, \mu, \chi))$, and upper value $\mathsf{Val}^*(s) = \inf_{\mu \in \varSigma_{\mathrm{Min}}} \sup_{\chi \in \varSigma_{\mathrm{Max}}} \mathsf{P}^*(\mathsf{Run}(s, \mu, \chi))$, for all $s \in \mathsf{S}$. Note that $\mathsf{Val}_* \leqslant \mathsf{Val}^*$, and if these values are equal, then we will refer to them as the value of the game from this state, denoted by $\mathsf{Val}(s)$. We will also say that the game from this state is *determined*. We say that it is *positionally determined*, if $\mathsf{Val}(s) = \sup_{\chi \in \varPi_{\mathrm{Max}}} \inf_{\mu \in \varSigma_{\mathrm{Min}}} \mathsf{P}_*(\mathsf{Run}(s, \mu, \chi)) = \inf_{\mu \in \varPi_{\mathrm{Min}}} \sup_{\chi \in \varSigma_{\mathrm{Max}}} \mathsf{P}^*(\mathsf{Run}(s, \mu, \chi))$.

For all $\mu \in \varSigma_{\mathrm{Min}}$ and $s \in \mathsf{S}$, we define $\mathsf{Val}^\mu(s) = \sup_{\chi' \in \varSigma_{\mathrm{Max}}} \mathsf{P}^*(\mathsf{Run}(s, \mu, \chi'))$. Analogously, for $\chi \in \varSigma_{\mathrm{Max}}$ we define $\mathsf{Val}_\chi(s) = \inf_{\mu' \in \varSigma_{\mathrm{Min}}} \mathsf{P}_*(\mathsf{Run}(s, \mu', \chi))$. For $\varepsilon > 0$, we say that $\mu \in \varSigma_{\mathrm{Min}}$ is ε-*optimal* if for every $s \in \mathsf{S}$, we have that $\mathsf{Val}^\mu(s) \leqslant \mathsf{Val}^*(s) + \varepsilon$. We define ε-optimality of strategies for Max analogously.

Decidability and computability. We will say that a zero-sum game on a game graph $\varGamma$ is *decidable* if the partial function $\mathsf{Val} : \mathsf{S} \to \mathbb{R}$ is decidable. A game has *computable ε-optimal strategies* if there exist ε-optimal strategies for both players, which are computable.

2.3 Average-Price and Reachability-Price Games on Finite Graphs

We recall the known results that will be used later, when discussing hybrid games. We characterize the game values using optimality, equations and recall strategy improvement algorithms, used for finding solutions to these equations. The games are determined (Thms 3 and 4), decidable and have computable optimal strategies (Cor. 5).

Average-price games. The goal of player Min in the *average-price game* on $\varGamma$ is to minimize an average price per step in a run, and the goal of player Max is to maximize it. For every run $\rho = \langle s_0, s_1, s_2, \ldots \rangle$, we define $\mathsf{P}_*(\rho) = \liminf_{n \to \infty} (1/n) \sum_{i=0}^{n-1} \pi(s_i, s_{i+1})$, and $\mathsf{P}^*(\rho) = \limsup_{n \to \infty} (1/n) \sum_{i=0}^{n-1} \pi(s_i, s_{i+1})$.

Optimality equations for average-price games. Let $\varGamma$ be a priced game graph, and let $G, B : \mathsf{S} \to \mathbb{R}$. We say that the pair of functions (G, B) is a solution of *optimality equations* for the average-price game $\varGamma$, denoted by $(G, B) \models \mathsf{Opt}_{\mathrm{Avg}}(\varGamma)$, if the following conditions hold for all states $s \in \mathsf{S}^{\mathrm{Min}}$:

$$G(s) = \min_{(s,s') \in \mathsf{E}} \{G(s')\}, \quad B(s) = \min_{(s,s') \in \mathsf{E}} \{\pi(s, s') - G(s) + B(s') : G(s') = G(s)\},$$

and the analogous two equations hold, with max instead of min in both, for all $s \in \mathsf{S}^{\mathrm{Max}}$. The two functions G and B are called *gain* and *bias*, cf. [17]. Solutions of the gain-bias optimality equations for a finite game graph always exist and they are used to establish positional determinacy of average-price games. For every state $s \in S$, the gain of s is uniquely determined by optimality equations and it is equal to the value of the average-price game starting from s.

Theorem 3. *For every* finite *priced game graph* Γ, *there is a pair of functions* $G, B :$ $S \rightarrow \mathbb{R}$, *such that* $(G, B) \models Opt_{Avg}(\Gamma)$, *and for every state* $s \in S$, *the average-price game* Γ *from* s *is determined and* $\mathsf{Val}(s) = G(s)$. *Both players have positional optimal strategies.*

Reachability-price games. A *reachability-price game* (Γ, F) consists of a priced game graph Γ and a set of *final* states $\mathsf{F} \subseteq S$. The goal of player Min is to reach a final state and the goal of player Max is to prevent it. Moreover, player Min wants to minimize the total price of reaching a final state, while player Max wants to maximize it. For a run $\rho = \langle s_0, s_1, s_2, \ldots \rangle$, we define $\mathsf{Stop}(\rho) = \inf_n \{ s_n : s_n \in \mathsf{F} \}$. The reachability-price payoff $\mathsf{P}(\rho)$ of the run $\rho = \langle s_0, s_1, s_2, \ldots \rangle$ is defined by $\mathsf{P}(\rho) = \sum_{i=0}^{\mathsf{Stop}(\rho)-1} \pi(s_i, s_{i+1})$ if $\mathsf{Stop}(\rho) < \infty$, and $\mathsf{P}(\rho) = \infty$ otherwise.

Optimality equations for reachability-price games. Let $P : S \rightarrow \mathbb{R}$ and $D : S \rightarrow \mathbb{N}$. We say that (P, D) is a solution of the *optimality equations* for the reachability-price game (Γ, F), denoted by $(P, D) \models Opt_{Reach}(\Gamma, \mathsf{F})$, if the following conditions hold for all states $s \in S$. If $s \in \mathsf{F}$ then $P(v) = D(v) = 0$; if $s \in S^{Min} \setminus \mathsf{F}$ then

$$P(s) = \min_{(s,s') \in E} \{ \pi(s, s') + P(s') \},$$

$$D(s) = \min_{(s,s') \in E} \{ 1 + D(s') : P(s) = \pi(s, s') + P(s') \},$$

and the analogous two equations hold, with max instead of min, for all $s \in S^{Max} \setminus \mathsf{F}$. Intuitively, in the equations above, $P(s)$ and $D(s)$ capture "optimal price to reach a final state" and "optimal number of steps to reach a final state with optimal price" from state $s \in S$, respectively.

Let $W^{Max} \subseteq S$ be the set of non-final states from which player Max can prevent ever reaching a final state. This set can be easily computed in time $O(|S| + |E|)$ for a finite game graph Γ. Moreover, let $W^{Min} \subseteq S \setminus W^{Max}$ be the set of states which have a negative value in the average-price game obtained from Γ by removing all states from the set W^{Max}. It is easy to argue that for all $s \in W^{Max}$, we have $\mathsf{Val}(s) = +\infty$, and for all $s \in W^{Min}$, we have $\mathsf{Val}(s) = -\infty$. Let $S^{fin} = S \setminus (W^{Max} \cup W^{Min})$ and let Γ^{fin} be the priced game graph obtained from Γ by restricting to the set of states S^{fin}.

Theorem 4. *For every* finite *priced game graph* Γ, *there is a pair of functions* $P :$ $S^{fin} \rightarrow \mathbb{R}$ *and* $D : S^{fin} \rightarrow \mathbb{N}$, *such that* $(P, D) \models Opt_{Reach}(\Gamma^{fin}, \mathsf{F})$, *and for every state* $s \in S^{fin}$, *the reachability-price game* Γ *from* s *is determined and* $\mathsf{Val}(s) = P(s)$.

Strategy improvement algorithms [17,13,21] can be used to prove Thms 3 and 4, and to compute solutions of optimality equations $Opt_{Avg}(\Gamma)$ and $Opt_{Reach}(\Gamma^{fin}, \mathsf{F})$.

Corollary 5. *Average-price and reachability-price games on finite priced game graphs are decidable and have computable optimal strategies.*

3   Games on Hybrid Automata with Strong Resets

We introduce hybrid automata with strong resets and define zero-sum hybrid games on these automata, which fit in the general framework presented in Sec. 2.2. The key result is that optimality equations characterize the game values of average-price and reachability-price hybrid games (Thms 7 and 11). This allows us to later prove the main result of this paper, i.e., that these games are positionally determined and decidable.

Our definition of a hybrid automaton varies from that used in [12,10], as we hide the dynamics of the system into guard functions. This approach allows for cleaner and more succinct notation and exposition, without loss of generality.

Priced hybrid automata with strong resets. Let L be a finite set of *locations*. Fix $n \in \mathbb{N}$ and define the set of *states* $S = L \times \mathbb{R}^n$. Let A be a finite set of *actions* and define the set of *times* $T = \mathbb{R}_{\oplus}$ We refer to action-time pairs $(a, t) \in A \times T$ as *timed actions*. A *priced hybrid automaton with strong resets (PHASR)* $\mathcal{H} = \langle L, A, G, R, \pi \rangle$ consists of finite sets L of *locations* and A of *actions*, a *guard* function $G : A \to 2^{S \times T}$, a *reset* function $R : A \to 2^S$, and a continuous *price* function $\pi : S \times (A \times T) \to \mathbb{R}$. We say that $\mathcal{H}$ is a *definable PHASR* if the sets G, R, and the function π are definable.

For states $s, s' \in S$ and a timed action $(a, t) \in A \times T$, we write $s \xrightarrow{a}_t s'$ iff $(s, t) \in G(a)$ and $s' \in R(a)$. If $s, s' \in S$, $\tau = (a, t) \in A \times T$, and $s \xrightarrow{a}_t s'$ then we write $s \xrightarrow{\tau} s'$. We define the *move* function $M : S \to 2^{A \times T}$ by $M(s) = \{(a, t) : (s, t) \in G(a)\}$. Note that M is definable if G is definable. A *run* from state $s \in S$ is a sequence $\langle s_0, \tau_1, s_1, \tau_2, s_2, \ldots \rangle \in S \times ((A \times T) \times S)^\omega$, such that $s_0 = s$, and for all $i \geq 0$, we have $s_i \xrightarrow{\tau_{i+1}} s_{i+1}$.

We say that the hybrid automaton is *price-bounded* if there exists a constant $B \geq 0$, such that for all $s \in S$ and $\tau \in M(s)$, we have $|\pi(s, \tau)| \leq B$. For technical convenience, we only consider price-bounded hybrid automata in this paper. Without it, it would be necessary to account for non-determinacy. This would have a negative effect on clarity of the paper.

Hybrid games with strong resets. A *hybrid game with strong resets (HGSR)* $\Gamma = \langle \mathcal{H}, M^{\mathrm{Min}}, M^{\mathrm{Max}} \rangle$ consists of a PHASR $\mathcal{H} = \langle L, A, G, R, \pi \rangle$, a *Min-move* function $M^{\mathrm{Min}} : S \to 2^{A \times T}$ and a *Max-move* function $M^{\mathrm{Max}} : S \times (A \times T) \to 2^{A \times T}$. We require that for all $s \in S$, we have $M^{\mathrm{Min}}(s) \subseteq M(s)$, and that for all $\tau \in M^{\mathrm{Min}}(s)$, we have $M^{\mathrm{Max}}(s, \tau) \subseteq M(s)$. W.l.o.g., we assume that for all $s \in S$, we have $M^{\mathrm{Min}}(s) \neq \emptyset$, and that for all $\tau \in M^{\mathrm{Min}}(s)$, we have $M^{\mathrm{Max}}(s, \tau) \neq \emptyset$. If $\mathcal{H}$ and the move functions are definable then, we say that Γ is *definable*.

A hybrid game with strong resets is played in rounds. In every round, the following three steps are performed by the two players Min and Max from the current state $s \in S$.

1. Player Min proposes a timed action $\tau \in M^{\mathrm{Min}}(s)$.
2. Player Max responds by choosing a timed action $\tau' = (a', t') \in M^{\mathrm{Max}}(s, \tau)$.
3. Player Max chooses a state $s' \in R(a')$, i.e., such that $s \xrightarrow{\tau'} s'$. The state s' becomes the current state for the next round.

A *play* of the game Γ from state $s \in S$ is a sequence $\langle s_0, \tau_1, \tau_1', s_1, \tau_2, \tau_2', s_2, \ldots \rangle \in S \times ((A \times T) \times (A \times T) \times S)^\omega$, such that $s_0 = s$, and for all $i \geq 0$, we have $\tau_{i+1} \in$

$\mathsf{M}^{\mathrm{Min}}(s_i)$ and $\tau'_{i+1} \in \mathsf{M}^{\mathrm{Max}}(s_i, \tau_{i+1})$. Note that if $\langle s_0, \tau_1, \tau'_1, s_1, \tau_2, \tau'_2, s_2, \ldots \rangle$ is a play then the sequence $\langle s_0, \tau'_1, s_1, \tau'_2, s_2, \ldots \rangle$ is a run of the hybrid automaton $\mathcal{H}$.

A hybrid game with strong resets can be viewed as a game on a priced game graph. The set of states S' is a subset of: $\mathsf{S} \cup (\mathsf{S} \times (\mathsf{A} \times \mathsf{T})) \cup ((\mathsf{A} \times \mathsf{T}))$. The E' relation is defined as follows: $(s, (s, \tau)) \in \mathsf{E}'$ iff $\tau \in \mathsf{M}^{\mathrm{Min}}(s)$, and $((s, \tau), \tau') \in \mathsf{E}$ iff $\tau' \in \mathsf{M}^{\mathrm{Max}}(s, \tau)$, and $((a', t'), s') \in \mathsf{E}'$ iff $s' \in \mathsf{R}(a')$. We define $\Gamma' = ((\mathsf{S}', \mathsf{E}'), \mathsf{S}, \mathsf{S}' \setminus \mathsf{S}, \pi')$, where $\pi'((s, \tau), (a', t')) = \pi(s, t')$, and 0 for all other edges. Additionally we require that $\mathsf{S}' \setminus \mathsf{S}$ contains all states reachable from S and does not contain those that are not. For all $(a, t), (a', t') \in \mathsf{S}'$, if $a = a'$ then $(a, t)\mathsf{E}' = (a', t')\mathsf{E}'$.

It is clear that plays of Γ directly correspond to runs on Γ'. Moreover, any run of Γ' uniquely determines a run of $\mathcal{H}$. To recall the definitions of strategies, payoff functions and game values, see Sec. 2.2. We define payoffs of Γ' runs as functions of the uniquely determined $\mathcal{H}$ runs.

In the following, we lift the concept of reachability-price and average-price games, as defined in Sec. 2.3, to hybrid games with strong resets. We show that values of these games are characterizable by optimality equations and we argue that if the game is determined, ε-optimal positional strategies are definable.

Average-price hybrid games. The goals of players Min and Max in an average-price game are to minimize and maximize, respectively, the average price per round of a play. This corresponds to defining the lower and upper payoffs as follows. For a run $\rho = \langle s_0, s_1, \ldots \rangle$ of $\mathcal{H}$, we define the lower payoff P_* and the upper payoff P^* by

$$\mathsf{P}_*(\rho) = \liminf_{n \to \infty} \frac{1}{n} \sum_{i=0}^{n-1} \pi(s_i, \tau_{i+1}), \qquad \mathsf{P}^*(\rho) = \limsup_{n \to \infty} \frac{1}{n} \sum_{i=0}^{n-1} \pi(s_i, \tau_{i+1}).$$

As we did in the case of finite game graphs (Thm 3), we prove determinacy and characterize the values of average-price games on hybrid automata with strong resets by optimality equations involving gain and bias. Let $G, B : \mathsf{S} \cup (\mathsf{S} \times (\mathsf{A} \times \mathsf{T})) \cup \mathsf{A} \to \mathbb{R}$. We say that (G, B) is a solution to *average-price optimality equations*, denoted by $(G, B) \models \mathrm{Opt}_{\mathrm{Avg}}(\Gamma)$, if the following equations hold for all $s \in \mathsf{S}$. If $s \in \mathsf{S}$, then

$$G(s) = \min_{\tau \in \mathsf{M}^{\mathrm{Min}}(s)} \{G(s, \tau)\}, \tag{1}$$

$$B(s) = \inf_{\tau \in \mathsf{M}^{\mathrm{Min}}(s)} \{-G(s) + B(s, \tau) : G(s, \tau) = G(s)\}; \tag{2}$$

if $s \in \mathsf{S}$ and $\tau \in \mathsf{M}^{\mathrm{Min}}(s)$, then

$$G(s, \tau) = \max_{(a', t') \in \mathsf{M}^{\mathrm{Max}}(s, \tau)} \{G(a')\}, \tag{3}$$

$$B(s, \tau) = \sup_{(a', t') \in \mathsf{M}^{\mathrm{Max}}(s, \tau)} \{\pi(s, a', t') - G(s, \tau) + B(a') : G(a') = G(s, \tau)\}; \tag{4}$$

and if $a \in \mathsf{A}$

$$G(a) = \max_{s \in \mathsf{R}(a)} \{G(s)\}, \qquad B(a) = \sup_{s \in \mathsf{R}(a)} \{-G(a) + B(s) : G(s) = G(a)\}.$$

Note that the above optimality equations refer to Γ', which allows us to model optimal choices that both players make in all steps of the hybrid game. Also note that in the definition of gain we use min and max rather than inf and sup. This is valid because gain has a finite range, namely $G(A)$, and A is finite.

Remark 6. Observe that if Γ is definable then the left hand sides of the optimality equations are definable functions of the right hand side arguments.

Theorem 7. *If* $(G, B) \models Opt_{Avg}(\Gamma)$ *then for every state* $s \in S$, *the average-price hybrid game* Γ *from* s *is determined and we have* $\mathsf{Val}(s) = 3 \cdot G(s)$. *Moreover, for every* $\varepsilon > 0$, *positional* ε-*optimal strategies exist for both players.*

The factor of 3 in the statement of Thm 7 is due to the fact that the value of gain is subtracted in each of the three bias equations. This is necessary because a round of a hybrid game Γ is encoded by a sequence of three edges in the finite graph $\widehat{\Gamma}$ (introduced in Sec. 4). This is a technical detail needed in the proof of Thm 17.

Corollary 8. *If there exists* (G, B) *such that* $(G, B) \models Opt_{Avg}(\Gamma)$ *and* Γ *definable then positional* ε-*optimal strategies are definable.*

The theorem and corollary follow from the following two lemmas and their proofs, which imply that for all states $s \in S$, we have that $\mathsf{Val}^*(s) \leq 3 \cdot G(s)$ and $\mathsf{Val}_*(s) \geq 3 \cdot G(s)$, respectively.

Lemma 9. *Let* $(G, B) \models Opt_{Avg}(\Gamma)$. *Then for all* $\varepsilon > 0$, *there is* $\mu_\varepsilon \in \Pi_{Min}$, *such that for all* $\chi \in \Sigma_{Max}$ *and for all* $s \in S$, *we have* $\mathsf{P}^*(\mathsf{Play}(s, \mu_\varepsilon, \chi)) \leq 3 \cdot G(s) + \varepsilon$.

Lemma 10. *Let* $(G, B) \models Opt_{Avg}(\Gamma)$. *Then for all* $\varepsilon > 0$, *there is* $\chi_\varepsilon \in \Pi_{Max}$, *such that for all* $\mu \in \Sigma_{Min}$ *and for all* $s \in S$, *we have* $\mathsf{P}_*(\mathsf{Play}(s, \mu, \chi_\varepsilon)) \geq 3 \cdot G(s) - \varepsilon$.

We prove Lem. 9 by observing that for every $\varepsilon' > 0$, player Min can choose $\tau \in \mathsf{M}^{Min}(s)$ in such away that: $G(s) = G(s, \tau)$ and $B(s) \geqslant B(s, \tau) - \varepsilon'$, We call this choice ε'-optimal. To complete the proof, we prove that if $\mu_\varepsilon \in \Pi^{Min}$ is such that for every, $s \in S$ $\mu_\varepsilon(s)$ is ε-optimal, then μ_ε is ε-optimal. The proof of Lem. 10 is similar.

Reachability-price hybrid games. A *hybrid reachability-price game with strong resets* (Γ, F) consists of a hybrid game with strong resets Γ and of a (definable) set $\mathsf{F} \subseteq S$ of *final* states.

For a run $\rho = \langle s_0, s_1, s_2, \ldots \rangle$ of $\mathcal{H}$, we define $\mathsf{Stop}(\rho) = \inf_n \{s_n : s_n \in \mathsf{F}\}$. The reachability-price payoff $\mathsf{P}(\rho)$ is defined by $\mathsf{P}(\rho) = \sum_{i=0}^{\mathsf{Stop}(\rho)-1} \pi(s_i, \tau_{i+1})$ if $\mathsf{Stop}(\rho) < \infty$, and $\mathsf{P}(\rho) = \infty$ otherwise.

As in the case of finite reachability-price games, we prove determinacy and characterize game values using optimality equations (Thm 4). We adapt the optimality equations in the same way as for average-price hybrid games. We write $(P, D) \models Opt_{Reach}(\Gamma, \mathsf{F})$ to denote a solution of the *reachability-price optimality equations*.

Theorem 11. *If* $(P, D) \models Opt_{Reach}(\Gamma, \mathsf{F})$ *then for every state* $s \in S$, *the reachability-price hybrid game* (Γ, F) *from state* s *is determined and we have* $\mathsf{Val}(s) = P(s)$. *Moreover, for every* $\varepsilon > 0$, *positional* ε-*optimal strategies exist for both players.*

Corollary 12. *If there exists* (P, D) *such that* $(P, D) \models Opt_{Reach}(\Gamma, \mathsf{F})$ *and* Γ *definable then positional* ε-*optimal strategies are definable.*

4   A Finite Abstraction

We introduce a finitary equivalence relation over the state space of the hybrid game Γ. It is used to construct a finite priced game graph $\widehat{\Gamma}$.

For $s \in S$ and $(a,t) \in M^{\text{Min}}(s)$, we define

$$A^{\text{Max}}(s, (a,t)) = \{a' \in A : (a', t') \in M^{\text{Max}}(s, (a,t)) \text{ for some } t' \in T\},$$

i.e., $A^{\text{Max}}(s, (a,t))$ is the set of actions $a' \in A$, such that there is a valid response $(a', t') \in A \times T$ of player Max to the proposal (a,t) of player Min. For $s \in S$ and $t \in T$, let

$$A^{\text{MinMax}}(s,t) = \{(a, A^{\text{Max}}(s, (a,t))) : (a,t) \in M^{\text{Min}}(s)\},$$

i.e., the set $A^{\text{MinMax}}(s,t)$ is the set of all pairs $(a, A') \in A \times 2^A$, such that player Min can propose the timed action (a,t) from state s, and the set of actions, appearing in valid responses of player Max to the proposal (a,t) of player Min, is exactly A'.

Let $\mathcal{R} = \{R_1, R_2, \ldots, R_n\}$ be such that $R_i \subseteq S$ for all i. For $s, s' \in S$, we define $s \sim_{\mathcal{R}} s'$ to hold iff the following conditions are satisfied: for all $i = 1, 2, \ldots, n$, we have that $s \in R_i$ iff $s' \in R_i$; $A^{\text{MinMax}}(s, T) = A^{\text{MinMax}}(s', T)$.

We will use $\mathcal{R} = \{R(a)\}_{a \in A}$ for average-price games and $\mathcal{R} = \{F\} \cup \{R(a)\}_{a \in A}$ for reachability-price games. If the set $\mathcal{R}$ is understood from the context, or if for the purpose of our discussion the exact identity of the set $\mathcal{R}$ is not important then, we often write simply $\sim$ instead of $\sim_{\mathcal{R}}$. Note that the second condition in the definition of $\sim$ states that the functions $A^{\text{MinMax}}(s, \cdot), A^{\text{MinMax}}(s', \cdot) : T \to A \times 2^A$ have the same ranges. Therefore, if $Q \in S/\sim$, then it makes sense to set $A^{\text{MinMax}}(Q, T)$ to be the range of the function $A^{\text{MinMax}}(s, \cdot)$ for any $s \in Q$.

Remark 13. Observe that $\sim$ is an equivalence relation on the set of states S, and that there are finitely many equivalence classes of $\sim$. Moreover, if Γ is definable then every equivalence class is also definable.

From Γ to the finite game. The main goal of this section is to define a finite game graph $\widehat{\Gamma}$ whose plays correspond to sequences of rounds, each of which consists of the following steps. Let $a'' \in A$ be the *current* action.

1. Max chooses $Q \in S/\sim$ such that $Q \subseteq R(a'')$.
2. Min chooses a pair $(a, A') \in A^{\text{MinMax}}(Q, T)$.
3. Max chooses an action $a' \in A'$, which becomes the current action.

Note that, unlike in the hybrid game Γ, here in every step players make choices out of finite sets of options. It is instructive to think of mapping choices made by the players in steps 3, 1, and 2 of the hybrid game Γ to steps 1, 2, and 3 of the finite game $\widehat{\Gamma}$ in the following way.

1. Max's choice of $s \in R(a'')$ is mapped to his choice of the equivalence class $[s]_\sim$.
2. Min's choice of $(a,t) \in M^{\text{Min}}(s)$ is mapped to his choice of $(a, A^{\text{Max}}(s, (a,t)))$.
3. Max's choice of $(a', t') \in M^{\text{Max}}(s, (a,t))$ is mapped to his choice of a'.

The above finitary abstraction of choices made by players in every round of the hybrid game $\Gamma = (\mathcal{H}, \mathsf{M}^{\mathrm{Min}}, \mathsf{M}^{\mathrm{Max}})$ is formalized by the following finite game graph $\widehat{\mathcal{H}} = (\widehat{\mathsf{S}}, \widehat{\mathsf{E}})$, where:

$$\widehat{\mathsf{S}} = \mathsf{A} \cup \mathsf{S}/\!\!\sim \cup \left\{ (Q, a, A') \, : \, Q \in \mathsf{S}/\!\!\sim \text{ and } (a, A') \in \mathsf{A}^{\mathrm{MinMax}}(Q, \mathsf{T}) \right\},$$

$$\widehat{\mathsf{E}} = \left\{ (a, Q) \, : \, Q \subseteq \mathsf{R}(a) \right\} \cup \left\{ \left(Q, (Q, a, A')\right) \, : \, (a, A') \in \mathsf{A}^{\mathrm{MinMax}}(Q, \mathsf{T}) \right\}$$
$$\cup \left\{ \left((Q, a, A'), a'\right) \, : \, a' \in A' \right\}.$$

We define the finite game graph $\widehat{\Gamma} = (\widehat{\mathcal{H}}, \widehat{\mathsf{S}}^{\mathrm{Min}}, \widehat{\mathsf{S}}^{\mathrm{Max}}, \widehat{\pi})$, where $(\widehat{\mathsf{S}}^{\mathrm{Min}}, \widehat{\mathsf{S}}^{\mathrm{Max}})$ is a partition of $\widehat{\mathsf{S}}$ and $\widehat{\pi} : \widehat{\mathsf{E}} \to \mathbb{R}$ is a price function. Let $\widehat{\mathsf{S}}^{\mathrm{Min}} = \mathsf{S}/\!\!\sim$ and let $\widehat{\mathsf{S}}^{\mathrm{Max}} = \widehat{\mathsf{S}} \setminus \widehat{\mathsf{S}}^{\mathrm{Min}}$. The price function $\widehat{\pi}$ is defined to be 0 for edges of the form (a, Q) or $\left(Q, (Q, a, A')\right)$, and for edges of the form $\left((Q, a, A'), a'\right)$ we define

$$\widehat{\pi}\left((Q, a, A'), a'\right) = \sup_{s \in Q} \; \inf_{t \in \mathsf{T}^{\mathrm{Min}}_{s,(a,A')}} \; \sup_{t' \in \mathsf{T}^{\mathrm{Max}}_{s,(a,t),a'}} \; \pi(s, (a', t')), \text{ where}$$

$$\mathsf{T}^{\mathrm{Min}}_{s,(a,A')} = \{ t \in \mathsf{T} \, : \, (a, t) \in \mathsf{M}^{\mathrm{Min}}(s) \text{ and } A' = \mathsf{A}^{\mathrm{Max}}(s, (a, t)) \},$$

$$\mathsf{T}^{\mathrm{Max}}_{s,(a,t),a'} = \{ t' \in \mathsf{T} \, : \, (a', t') \in \mathsf{M}^{\mathrm{Max}}(s, (a, t)) \}.$$

The set $\mathsf{T}^{\mathrm{Min}}_{s,(a,A')}$ is the set of times t, such that if Min proposes the timed action (a, t) from state s, then A' is the set of actions which occur in valid responses of Max. Similarly, the set $\mathsf{T}^{\mathrm{Max}}_{s,(a,t),a'}$ is the set of times $t' \in \mathsf{T}$, for which the timed action (a', t') is a valid response of Max to the proposal (a, t) of Min.

Note that the value of $\widehat{\pi}$ always exists. This follows from the assumption that hybrid automata with strong resets under consideration are price-bounded.

Theorem 14. *If Γ is definable then the finite priced game graph $\widehat{\Gamma}$ is also definable.*

Discussion. In the hybrid game Γ, each step of a round has a hybrid nature, i.e., consists of both a discrete and a continuous component. In the first two steps, players Min and Max make a discrete choice of an action followed by a continuous choice of time. In the last step, player Max makes a discrete choice of an equivalence class (recall the $\sim$ equivalence), followed by a continuous choice of a state in that class.

The construction of $\widehat{\Gamma}$ is built upon an idea to separate the discrete and continuous choices of both players. This separation is achieved by reconstructing the round of a game in such a way that first players make their discrete choices (in three steps) and then they make their continuous choices, which must be sound with respect to the discrete choices made earlier.

In $\widehat{\Gamma}$, the discrete steps of the reconstructed round are encoded in the choices of edges. The continuous choices are not present, however. Instead, we set the prices of edges as if, after making the discrete choices, the players were making optimal continuous choices (with respect to the discrete ones). This reduces the problem of solving a hybrid game Γ to a finite problem. The correctness of this approach will follow from Thms 17 and 20, which can be found in Sec. 5.

Example 15. To make the construction of $\widehat{\Gamma}$ clearer, we provide a simple example. Let $V_1 = \{(x, y) : x + y \geqslant 10\}, V_2 = \mathbb{R}^2 \setminus V_1, V_3 = \{(x, y) : y + x^2 \leqslant 0\}, I_1 = (1, 2),$ $I_2 = (3, 4)$ and $I_3 = (5, 6)$. We define the hybrid automaton $\mathcal{H} = \langle \mathsf{L}, \mathsf{A}, \mathsf{G}, \mathsf{R}, \pi \rangle$ as follows: $\mathsf{L} = \{\ell\}, \mathsf{A} = \{a, b\}, \mathsf{S} = \mathsf{L} \times \mathbb{R}^2, \mathsf{G} = \{a\} \times (\mathsf{S} \times I_3) \cup \{b\} \times (\mathsf{L} \times V_3) \times I_2,$ $\mathsf{R} = \mathsf{A} \times (\mathsf{L} \times V_1)$, and the price function is given by $\pi(x, y, \mathsf{A}, t) = -(t + x^2 + y^2)$. Fig 1(a-c) provides more insight into the definition of $\mathcal{H}$.

Recall that $\mathsf{M}(s) = \{(c, t) : (s, t) \in \mathsf{G}(c)\}$. We define Γ by setting $\mathsf{M}^{\mathrm{Min}}(s) = \mathsf{M}(s) \cap \{a\} \times \mathsf{T}$ and if $t \in I_1$ then $\mathsf{M}^{\mathrm{Max}}(s, a, t) = \{(a, t)\}$ otherwise, if $t \in I_3$ then $\mathsf{M}^{\mathrm{Max}}(s, a, t) = \{(a, t)\} \cup \{b\} \times I_2$.

Now we can construct the equivalence $\sim_{\mathcal{R}}$, where $\mathcal{R} = \{\mathsf{R}(a), \mathsf{R}(b)\}$. All elements of $\mathsf{L} \times V_1$ are contained in both $\mathsf{R}(a)$ and $\mathsf{R}(b)$. If we look at the set $\mathsf{A}^{\mathrm{MinMax}}(s, \mathsf{T})$ then it is easy to see that for all $s \in \mathsf{L} \times (V_1 \setminus V_3)$ it is equal to $\{(a, \{a\})\}$, and for all elements $s \in \mathsf{L} \times V_3$, to $\{(a, \{a\}), (a, \{a, b\})\}$. On the other hand, elements $s \in \mathsf{L} \times V_2$ are not contained in any set in $\mathcal{R}$, and the set $\mathsf{A}^{\mathrm{MinMax}}(s, \mathsf{T})$ is alway equal to $\{(a, \{a\})\}$. This gives us three equivalence classes of $\sim_{\mathcal{R}}$, namely $Q_1 = \mathsf{L} \times V_3, Q_2 = \mathsf{L} \times (V_1 \setminus V_3)$ and $Q_3 = \mathsf{L} \times V_2$. The finite priced game graph $\widehat{\Gamma}$ obtained from Γ using $\sim_{\mathcal{R}}$ is depicted on Fig 1(d).

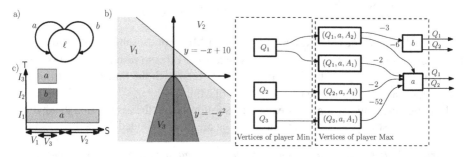

Fig. 1. a) Graph structure underlying $\mathcal{H}$. b) State space of $\mathcal{H}$. c) Guard function of $\mathcal{H}$. d) The priced game graph $\widehat{\Gamma}$ obtained from Γ through finite abstraction. A_1 stands for $\{(a, \{a\})\}$ and A_2 for $\{(a, \{a\}), (a, \{a, b\})\}$. Edge price is omitted when it is equal to zero.

5 Solving Average-Price and Reachability-Price Games

The key result of this section is that solutions of optimality equations for the average-price game $\widehat{\Gamma}$ and for the reachability-price game $(\widehat{\Gamma}, \widehat{\mathsf{F}})$ on the finite priced game graph $\widehat{\Gamma}$ coincide with the solutions of the optimality equations for the hybrid average-price game Γ and of the hybrid reachability-price game (Γ, F) respectively (Thms 17 and 20). In addition (by Thms 7 and 11) it follows that average-price and reachability-price hybrid games are positionally determined and decidable (Cor. 19 and 21).

Average-price games. The following are the optimality equations for the average-price game on the finite priced game graph $\widehat{\Gamma}$. For $Q \in S/\sim = \widehat{S}^{\mathrm{Min}}$, we have:

$$\widehat{G}(Q) = \min_{(Q, (Q, a, A')) \in \widehat{\mathsf{E}}} \{\widehat{G}(Q, a, A')\},$$

$$\widehat{B}(Q) = \min_{(Q,(Q,a,A'))\in\widehat{E}} \{-\widehat{G}(Q) + \widehat{B}(Q, a, A') \ : \ \widehat{G}(Q) = \widehat{G}(Q, a, A')\};$$

for $(Q, a, A') \in (S/\sim \times A \times 2^A) \subseteq \widehat{S}^{Max}$, we have:

$$\widehat{G}(Q, a, A') = \max_{((Q,a,A'),a')\in\widehat{E}} \{\widehat{G}(Q, a, A')\},$$

$$\widehat{B}(Q, a, A') = \max_{((Q,a,A'),a')\in\widehat{E}} \{\widehat{\pi}((Q, a, A'), a') - \widehat{G}(Q, a, A') + \widehat{B}(a') \ :$$

$$\widehat{G}(Q, a, A') = \widehat{G}(a')\};$$

and for $a \in A \subseteq \widehat{S}^{Max}$, we have:

$$\widehat{G}(a) = \max_{(a,Q)\in\widehat{E}} \{\widehat{G}(Q)\}, \qquad \widehat{B}(a) = \max_{(a,Q)\in\widehat{E}} \{-\widehat{G}(a) + \widehat{B}(Q) \ : \ \widehat{G}(a) = \widehat{G}(Q)\}.$$

Our goal is to show that a solution $(\widehat{G}, \widehat{B})$ of $\mathrm{Opt}_{Avg}(\widehat{\Gamma})$ can be used to obtain a solution (G, B) of $\mathrm{Opt}_{Avg}(\Gamma)$. Recall that a solution of optimality equations $\mathrm{Opt}_{Avg}(\Gamma)$ for a hybrid average-price game is a pair (G, B) of functions $G, B : S \cup (S \times (A \times T)) \cup A \to \mathbb{R}$.

Proposition 16. *If Γ is a hybrid average-price game, then for all states $s \in S$ and for all $\tau \in M^{Min}(s)$, the values $G(s), B(s), G(s, \tau)$, and $B(s, \tau)$ satisfying equations (1–4), respectively, are uniquely determined and first-order definable (provided that Γ is definable) from the (finitely many) values $\{G(a), B(a) \ : \ a \in A\}$.*

Theorem 17. *Let Γ be a hybrid average-price game and let $(\widehat{G}, \widehat{B}) \models \mathrm{Opt}_{Avg}(\widehat{\Gamma})$. If $G, B : S \cup (S \times (A \times T)) \cup A \to \mathbb{R}$ satisfy equations (1–4), and for all $a \in A$, it holds that $G(a) = \widehat{G}(a)$ and $B(a) = \widehat{B}(a)$, then $(G, B) \models \mathrm{Opt}_{Avg}(\Gamma)$.*

Example 18. Recall the game graph $\widehat{\Gamma}$ from Ex. 15. Fig 2 depicts the optimal choices of both players in the average-price game and the solution to the optimality equations for finite average-price games. The value of the game from every state is $-2/3$, because $(\widehat{G}, \widehat{B}) \models \mathrm{Opt}_{Avg}(\widehat{\Gamma})$.

We use the solutions to $\mathrm{Opt}_{Avg}(\widehat{\Gamma})$ to obtain solutions to $\mathrm{Opt}_{Avg}(\Gamma)$. We set $G \equiv -\frac{2}{3}$, $B(a) = \widehat{B}(a) = 0$ and $B(b) = \widehat{B}(b) = 0$. The remaining values are uniquely determined by these. One can see that the value of the average-price game on Γ is -2 and that the players have ε-optimal strategies as follows: from every state in Q_1 player Min should play $(a, 6-\varepsilon)$, and from every state in $Q_2 \cup Q_3$, Min should play $(a, 2-\varepsilon)$. Player Max on the other hand has always to play Min's choice unless he is in the state (s, a, t) and $t > 5$, when he should make the move $(b, 3 + \varepsilon)$. From every state in A, Max should choose choose to play $(0, 0) \in Q_2$.

Corollary 19. *Definable average-price hybrid games with strong resets are decidable.*

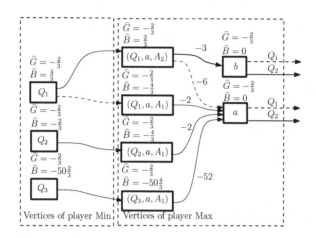

Fig. 2. Solid arrows denote the optimal strategies of both players. Above each vertex one can find its gain and bias.

Reachability-price games. As in the case of average-price hybrid games the solutions to the optimality equations for the finite game $(\widehat{\Gamma}, \widehat{F})$ coincide with the solutions to the optimality equations for the hybrid game (Γ, F). The main results are as follows, and is proved in a similar fashion as Thm 17.

Theorem 20. *Let* $(\widehat{P}, \widehat{D}) \models Opt_{Reach}(\widehat{\Gamma}, \widehat{F})$, *where* (Γ, F) *is a hybrid reachability-price game. If for all* $a \in A$, *we set* $P(a) = \widehat{P}(a)$ *and* $D(a) = \widehat{D}(a)$, *then there are unique extensions of* $P, D : A \to \mathbb{R}$ *to* $P, D : S \cup (S \times (A \times T)) \cup A \to \mathbb{R}$ *such that* $(P, D) \models Opt_{Reach}(\Gamma, F)$.

Corollary 21. *Definable reachability-price hybrid games with strong resets are decidable.*

Computability of ε-optimal strategies. Definable average-price and reachability-price admit ε-optimal strategies. We present the following computability result.

Theorem 22. *If Γ is a definable hybrid game with strong resets then, if in the average-price (reachability-price) game a player can always make a rational ε-optimal move, then ε-optimal strategies are computable.*

References

1. van der Schaft, A.J., Schumacher, H.: An introduction to hybrid dynamical systems. Lecture Notes in Control and Information Sciences, vol. 251. Springer, Heidelberg (1999)
2. Alur, R., Courcoubetis, C., Henzinger, T.A., Ho, P.H., Nicollin, X., Olivero, A., Sifakis, J., Yovine, S.: The algorithmic analysis of hybrid systems. Theoretical Computer Science 138, 3–34 (1995)
3. Alur, R., Dill, D.: A theory of timed automata. Theoretical Computer Science 126, 183–235 (1994)

4. Henzinger, T.A.: The theory of hybrid automata. In: Logic in Computer Science, LICS 1996, pp. 278–292. IEEE Computer Society Press, Los Alamitos (1996)
5. Lafferriere, G., Pappas, G.J., Sastry, S.: O-minimal hybrid systems. Mathematics of Control, Signals, and Systems 13, 1–21 (2000)
6. Brihaye, T., Michaux, C.: On the expressiveness and decidability of o-minimal hybrid systems. Journal of Complexity 21, 447–478 (2005)
7. Gentilini, R.: Reachability problems on extended o-minimal hybrid automata. In: Pettersson, P., Yi, W. (eds.) FORMATS 2005. LNCS, vol. 3829, pp. 162–176. Springer, Heidelberg (2005)
8. Alur, R., La Torre, S., Pappas, G.J.: Optimal paths in weighted timed automata. In: Di Benedetto, M.D., Sangiovanni-Vincentelli, A.L. (eds.) HSCC 2001. LNCS, vol. 2034, pp. 49–62. Springer, Heidelberg (2001)
9. Behrmann, G., Fehnker, A., Hune, T., Larsen, K.G., Pettersson, P., Romijn, J., Vaandrager, F.: Minimum-cost reachability for priced timed automata. In: Di Benedetto, M.D., Sangiovanni-Vincentelli, A.L. (eds.) HSCC 2001. LNCS, vol. 2034, pp. 147–161. Springer, Heidelberg (2001)
10. Bouyer, P., Brihaye, T., Chevalier, F.: Weighted o-minimal hybrid systems are more decidable than weighted timed automata! In: Artemov, S.N., Nerode, A. (eds.) LFCS 2007. LNCS, vol. 4514, pp. 69–83. Springer, Heidelberg (2007)
11. Church, A.: Logic, arithmetic and automata. In: Proceedings of the International Congress of Mathematicians, pp. 23–35 (1962)
12. Bouyer, P., Brihaye, T., Chevalier, F.: Control in o-minimal hybrid systems. In: Logic in Computer Science, LICS 2006, pp. 367–378. IEEE Computer Society Press, Los Alamitos (2006)
13. Jurdziński, M., Trivedi, A.: Reachability-time games on timed automata. In: Arge, L., Cachin, C., Jurdziński, T., Tarlecki, A. (eds.) ICALP 2007. LNCS, vol. 4596, pp. 838–849. Springer, Heidelberg (2007)
14. Brihaye, T., Michaux, C., Rivière, C., Troestler, C.: On o-minimal hybrid systems. In: Alur, R., Pappas, G.J. (eds.) HSCC 2004. LNCS, vol. 2993, pp. 219–233. Springer, Heidelberg (2004)
15. Brihaye, Th.: A note on the undecidability of the reachability problem for o-minimal dynamical systems. Mathematical Logic Quarterly 52, 165–170 (2006)
16. Adler, B.T., de Alfaro, L., Faella, M.: Average reward timed games. In: Pettersson, P., Yi, W. (eds.) FORMATS 2005. LNCS, vol. 3829, pp. 65–80. Springer, Heidelberg (2005)
17. Puterman, M.L.: Markov Decision Processes. Discrete Stochastic Dynamic Programming. Wiley, Chichester (1994)
18. Meer, K., Michaux, C.: A survey on real structural complexity theory. Bulletin of the Belgian Mathematical Society. Simon Stevin 4, 113–148 (1997)
19. Blum, L., Shub, M., Smale, S.: On a theory of computation and complexity over the real numbers: NP-completeness, recursive functions and universal machines. American Mathematical Society. Bulletin. New Series 21, 1–46 (1989)
20. Tarski, A.: A Decision Method for Elementary Algebra and Geometry. University of California Press (1951)
21. Filar, J., Vrieze, K.: Competitive Markov Decision Processes. Springer, Heidelberg (1997)

Timed Automata with Integer Resets: Language Inclusion and Expressiveness

P. Vijay Suman[1], Paritosh K. Pandya[1], Shankara Narayanan Krishna[2], and Lakshmi Manasa[2]

[1] Tata Institute of Fundamental Research, India
{vsuman,pandya}@tifr.res.in
[2] Indian Institute of Technology, Bombay, India
{krishnas,manasa}@cse.iitb.ac.in

Abstract. In this paper, we consider a syntactic subset of timed automata called integer reset timed automata (IRTA) where *resets* are restricted to occur at integral time points. We argue with examples that the notion of global sparse time base used in time triggered architecture and distributed web services can naturally be modelled/specified as IRTA. As our main result, we show that the language inclusion problem $L(\mathcal{A}) \subseteq L(\mathcal{B})$ for a timed automaton $\mathcal{A}$ and an IRTA $\mathcal{B}$ is decidable with EXPSPACE complexity. The expressive power and the closure properties of IRTA are also summarized. In particular, the IRTA are (highly succinct but) expressively equivalent to 1-clock deterministic IRTA and they are closed under boolean operations.

1 Introduction

Timed automata [AD94] are an extension of finite state automata with real-valued clocks. They have emerged as a standard theoretical model for real-time systems, and their formal properties have been well studied [AD94, AM04].

Unfortunately, many of the nice properties of finite state automata are lost when going to timed automata. Specifically, timed automata are not closed under complementation or determinization, and the crucial language inclusion question $L(\mathcal{A}) \subseteq L(\mathcal{B})$ is undecidable for timed automata. This prevents the effective use of timed automata themselves as property specification language in model checking.

Timed automata incorporate a global notion of time where the time is dense and all the clocks are perfectly synchronized. In distributed real-time systems this assumption is unrealistic and alternative models of timed computations such as time triggered architecture [KB01] are used in practice. The main features of this model are:

1. Time is dense and global. However, all nodes in a cluster work with global but *sparse time base* where dense time is broken into granular intervals of time of fixed precision.

F. Cassez and C. Jard (Eds.): FORMATS 2008, LNCS 5215, pp. 78–92, 2008.
© Springer-Verlag Berlin Heidelberg 2008

2. It is impossible to give ordering of time stamps of events at different nodes which occur within a single granule. Events occurring in different granules can be ordered based on the time stamps.

Inspired by this notion of sparse time base, in this paper we propose a subclass of timed automata called *Integer Reset Timed Automata* (IRTA) where clock resets are restricted to occur at integer valued time points. This is achieved by requiring that all reset transitions have a condition of the form $x = c$ as a conjunct in their guard where c is an integer. Note that in IRTA, the transitions which do not reset any clock can occur at any time point and IRTA are more general than integer timed automata.

IRTA incorporate the notion of sparse time base which is taken to be the set of natural numbers and time granules are unit time intervals. The only valid quantitative time constraints on events are with respect to the integral values of time where clock resets occur. Exploiting this, we show in the paper that IRTA cannot distinguish between the time stamps of events occurring within a unit open interval $(i, i+1)$. Example 2 presents a case study [MRD+08] of modelling end-to-end latency of a vehicle control system with multiple interacting ECUs working in a time triggered fashion. The resulting model is naturally an IRTA.

Sparse time bases are also used in the quantitative timing constraints which feature in the specification of distributed business processes and web services (e.g. see [KPP06]). Such constraints are typically given with respect to a sparse time base which provide globally available set of reference time points to all agents. Each such constraint can be naturally modelled as an IRTA. For example, consider the property: *Once check is deposited, the balance will be cleared by the end of the third day.* This can be modelled as the IRTA (with silent actions) shown in Figure 3. Here, clock x is reset every 24 hours. Once the check is deposited (at any arbitrary dense time point) a state change occurs and there are no more resets of clock x. The constraint on 'balance cleared' event is $x \leq 72$. Note that this constraint is with respect to the start of the day on which check was deposited and not the time of depositing the check. Similarly, in the specification of business processes (see [KPP06]), we have properties such as *Meeting must take place within 7 days of receiving the notification but not before 3 days.* In calendar automata [DS04] too the time constraints are with reference to calendar dates which can be considered as the sparse time base. Thus, we believe that IRTA constitute a useful and interesting sub-class of timed automata.

In this paper, we mainly focus on the decision problems and closure properties of IRTA. We show that the timed language of an IRTA over an alphabet Σ can be precisely represented symbolically by a regular language over an extended alphabet $\Sigma \cup \{\delta, \checkmark\}$. Such languages are called regular delta-tick languages. We also give a technique of conservatively overapproximating the timed language of a timed automaton by a regular delta-tick language. Utilizing this, we give a decision procedure with EXPSPACE complexity to check whether $L(\mathcal{A}) \subseteq L(\mathcal{B})$ for a timed automaton $\mathcal{A}$ and an IRTA $\mathcal{B}$. This is achieved by reducing the question to language containment of two regular delta-tick languages. We also remark that the method extends immediately to ϵ-IRTA which are IRTA with silent transitions [BPGD98], with the same complexity. The ϵ-IRTA are quite useful in modeling periodic clock constraints that occur in time triggered systems.

We also investigate the expressive power of IRTA. We can show that the IRTA are expressively equivalent to deterministic 1-clock IRTA. However, the known reduction from IRTA to 1-clock deterministic IRTA seems to result into a three exponent blowup in the automaton size [SPKM07]. We also show that IRTA are closed under boolean operations.

Related work. We propose a subclass IRTA of timed automata which are suitable for modelling distributed real-time systems working with global and sparse time base. Such a notion of time occurs in time-triggered architecture [KB01] and timing specification of business processes and web services [KPP06]. In a more comprehensive treatment of time triggered architecture, Krcál *et al* [KMTY04] have proposed a model of network of timed automata working in time triggered fashion which directly incorporates the buffering of signals between nodes. Moreover, they deal with the sparse time base using a notion of digitization. Our treatment of time is quite different where we give a weak subclass of timed automata and investigate its properties. Example 2 illustrates modelling of timed triggered systems using IRTA. A work closer to our approach uses the calendar automata to model and verify timed triggered protocol [DS04]. However, calendar automata are like discrete event simulation systems with event queues and infinite state verification techniques have to be used in their analysis. By comparison IRTA fit well within the theoretical framework for timed automata. It is also useful to have silent transitions in IRTA, giving ϵ-IRTA. Silent transitions in timed automata were investigated by [BPGD98]. Decision problems for timed automata with silent transitions have also been studied [BHR07].

We have shown that the language inclusion question $L(\mathcal{A}) \subseteq L(\mathcal{B})$ is decidable with EXPSPACE complexity for timed automaton $\mathcal{A}$ and ϵ-IRTA $\mathcal{B}$. This question is undecidable for timed automata in general and it has been shown to be decidable but with non-primitive-recursive complexity when $\mathcal{B}$ is a 1-clock timed automaton. [OW04, OW05].

For the class of deterministic timed automata [AD94] the language inclusion question is decidable and in PSPACE. However, the question whether a given timed automaton is determinizable is undecidable [Tri06, Fin06]. In general, finding determinizable sub-classes of timed automata is an interesting but difficult quest. In their pioneering work Alur *et al* [AFH99] have shown that a subclass of timed automata called Event Recording Automata (ERA) can indeed be determinized with one exponential blowup in the automaton size. This has been extended to the semantic model of input-determined automata [DT04]. We show with examples that in terms of expressive power ERA and IRTA are incomparable. While, IRTA can also be determinized to 1-clock deterministic IRTA, the available method [SPKM07] seems to result in a blowup of the automaton size by 3 exponents!

The rest of the paper is organized as follows. Section 2 introduces IRTA as a subclass of timed automata. The delta-tick word representation of timed words is given in Section 3. The construction of the delta-tick automaton $\mathcal{RMA}$ for a given timed automaton $\mathcal{A}$ is presented in Section 4. The decidability of language inclusion $L(\mathcal{A}) \subseteq L(\mathcal{B})$ for IRTA $\mathcal{B}$ is also shown in Section 4. The expressiveness and closure properties of IRTA are explored in Section 5. The paper ends with a discussion.

2   Integer Reset Timed Automata

Definition 1 (Timed Word). *A finite timed word over Σ is defined as $\rho = (\sigma, \tau)$, where $\sigma = \sigma_1 \ldots \sigma_n$ is a finite sequence of symbols in Σ and $\tau = \tau_1 \ldots \tau_n$ is a finite monotone sequence of real numbers. τ_i represents the time stamp of the occurrence of the event corresponding to the symbol σ_i. A timed language L is a set of timed words. Let $untime(L) = \{\sigma \mid (\sigma, \tau) \in L\}$. The set of all timed words over a set of symbols S is denoted by TW_S.*

For convenience of presentation we assume a default initial time stamp $\tau_0 = 0$, prefixed to any sequence of time stamps $\tau = \tau_1 \ldots \tau_n$.

Definition 2 (Timed Automata). *A timed automaton $\mathcal{A}$ is a tuple $(L, L_0, \Sigma, C, E, F)$ where (i) L is a finite set of locations, (ii) $L_0 \subseteq L$ is the set of initial locations, (iii) Σ is a finite set of symbols (called alphabet), (iv) C is a finite set of real valued clocks, (v) $E \subseteq L \times L \times \Sigma \times \Phi(C) \times 2^C$ is the set of transitions. An edge $e = (l, l', a, \varphi, \lambda)$ represents a transition from the source location l to the target location l' on input symbol a. The set $\lambda \subseteq C$ gives the set of clocks that are reset with the transition and, φ is a guard over C, and (vi)$F \subseteq L$ is the set of final locations.*

Let x represent a clock in C and c represent a natural number. $\Phi(C)$ is the set of constraints φ defined by

$$\varphi \quad := \quad x \leq c \mid x \geq c \mid x < c \mid x > c \mid \varphi \wedge \varphi$$

Note that the constraint $x = c$ is equivalent to $x \leq c \wedge x \geq c$.

Definition 3 (Clock Interpretation). *Let C be the set of clocks. A clock interpretation $\nu : C \rightarrow \mathbb{R}_{\geq 0}$ maps each clock $x \in C$ to a non-negative real number.*

A state of $\mathcal{A}$ is a pair (l, ν) such that $l \in L$ and ν is a clock interpretation over C. The state space of $\mathcal{A}$ is $L \times \mathbb{R}_{\geq 0}^{|C|}$. The state of a timed automaton can change in 2 ways:

1. *Due to elapse of time:* for a state (l, ν) and a real-number $t \geq 0$, $(l, \nu) \xrightarrow{t} (l, \nu + t)$. This kind of transition is called a *timed transition*.
2. *Due to a location-switch:* for a state (l, ν) and an edge $(l, l', a, \varphi, \lambda)$ such that $\nu \models \varphi$, $(l, \nu) \xrightarrow{a} (l', \nu[\lambda := 0])$. We call such a transition, a *Σ-transition*.

Here $(\nu + t)(x) = \nu(x) + t$ and, $\nu[\lambda := 0](x) = 0$, $\forall x \in \lambda$, and remains unchanged $\forall x \in (C \backslash \lambda)$.

Definition 4 (Run, Word, Language). *A run r of a timed automaton is a sequence of alternating timed and Σ transitions:* $(l_0, \nu_0) \xrightarrow{\tau_1} (l_0, \nu_1) \xrightarrow{e_1}$ $(l_1, \nu_1') \xrightarrow{\tau_2 - \tau_1} (l_1, \nu_2) \cdots (l_{n-1}, \nu_{n-1}') \xrightarrow{\tau_n - \tau_{n-1}} (l_{n-1}, \nu_n) \xrightarrow{e_n} (l_n, \nu_n')$ *with* $l_0 \in L_0$ *and* ν_0 *is such that* $\nu_0(x) = 0$, $\forall x \in C$. *The run r is accepting iff* $l_n \in F$. *Corresponding to each run, there is a timed word* $(\sigma_1, \tau_1), (\sigma_2, \tau_2), \cdots, (\sigma_n, \tau_n)$ *where σ_i is the event or symbol corresponding to e_i, and τ_i is the time stamp of σ_i. A finite timed word $\rho = (\sigma, \tau)$ is accepted by $\mathcal{A}$ iff there exists an accepting run over $\mathcal{A}$, the word corresponding to which is ρ. The timed language $L(\mathcal{A})$ accepted by $\mathcal{A}$ is defined as the set of all finite timed words accepted by $\mathcal{A}$.* □

Corresponding to a state (l, ν), we have the configuration $(l, \nu)^t$, where t is the time at which (l, ν) arises in the given run. We use the terms state and configuration interchangeably. The above run can be written as $(l_0, \nu_0)^0 \xrightarrow{\tau_1} (l_0, \nu_1)^{\tau_1} \xrightarrow{e_1}$ $(l_1, \nu_1')^{\tau_1} \xrightarrow{\tau_2 - \tau_1} (l_1, \nu_2)^{\tau_2} \cdots (l_{n-1}, \nu_{n-1}')^{\tau_{n-1}} \xrightarrow{\tau_n - \tau_{n-1}} (l_{n-1}, \nu_n)^{\tau_n} \xrightarrow{e_n} (l_n, \nu_n')^{\tau_n}$.

Theorem 1. *[AD94] Given a timed automaton $\mathcal{A}$ one can build a finite state automaton $\mathcal{RA}$, called the region automaton, such that $L(\mathcal{RA}) = untime(L(\mathcal{A}))$.*

Definition 5 (Integer Reset Timed Automata). *An integer reset timed automaton (IRTA) is a timed automaton in which every edge $e = (l, l', a, \varphi, \lambda)$ is such that λ is nonempty only if φ contains at least one atomic constraint of the form $x = c$, for some clock x.* □

Example 1. The automaton $\mathcal{A}$ in Figure 1 is an IRTA.

Example 2. Figure 2 shows timed automata based model (taken from [MRD$^+$08]) of a system which is a chain of n tasks working under the time triggered architecture. The model is an abstraction derived for the worst-case end-to-end latency estimation of a vehicle control system with multiple ECUs. Tasks cannot directly communicate control signals to each other and they only interact through buffered messages (temporal firewalling). Each task works according to predetermined time schedule based on the sparse time base. In our example, each task i executes periodically with an integer period T_i. On being triggered, it polls its input buffer and if input is available it carries out internal computation which can require upto E_i time. It then generates output signal for the following task $i + 1$

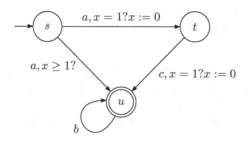

Fig. 1. An IRTA $\mathcal{A}$

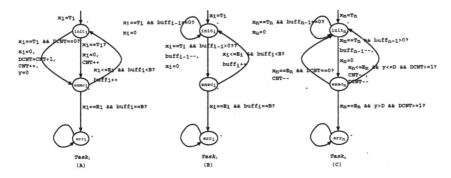

Fig. 2. Task Chain Model for End-to-end Latency Verification of a Multi-ECU Vehicular Control System in UPPAAL. Each task is an IRTA.

which is buffered. Note that the output signal can occur at any dense time point. The model reaches an error location if there is buffer overflow or, if the end-to-end latency exceeds the deadline D. The figure gives the UPPAAl [BLL+95] model of the system which was used to carry out experiments on model checking worst case end-to-end latency [MRD+08]. *It can be observed that the model naturally falls under the subclass IRTA of timed automata as the reset of clock x_i occurs with the constraint $x_i = T_i$. Thus, IRTA are useful in specifying and modelling time triggered systems.* □

Timed automata with silent transitions were studied by [BPGD98]. We adapt them to IRTA.

Definition 6 (ϵ-IRTA). *An ϵ-IRTA is an IRTA which can also have edges of the form $e = (l, l', \epsilon, \varphi, \lambda)$ such that $\epsilon \notin \Sigma$. Such an edge represents a silent or non-observable transition. We use ϵ-IRTA to represent the class of such automata.*

Example 3. Figure 3 shows an ϵ-IRTA which models the following property: *Once check is deposited, the balance will be cleared by the end of the third day.* Such properties arise in timing specification of business processes and distributed web services [KPP06].

Lemma 1. *ϵ-IRTA are strictly more expressive than IRTA.*

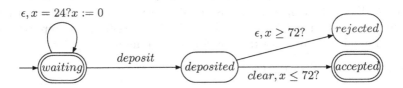

Fig. 3. The bank transaction property as IRTA

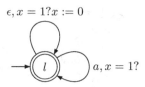

$$\epsilon, x = 1?x := 0$$

$$a, x = 1?$$

Fig. 4. ϵ-IRTA : $\mathcal{A}_1$

Proof. There exists no IRTA which accepts the timed language $L(\mathcal{A}_1)$, where $\mathcal{A}_1$ is the ϵ-IRTA in Figure 4. In fact, $\mathcal{A}_1$ is the classical example of an ϵ-Timed automaton whose language cannot be accepted by any timed automaton [BPGD98]. $\qquad\square$

Let t be a nonnegative real number. We use $int(t)$ and $fr(t)$ to denote respectively the integral part and the fractional part of t.

Proposition 1. *Let $\mathcal{A} = (L, L_0, \Sigma, C, E, F)$ be a timed automaton which restricts clock resets to integral time points, and let ν be an interpretation in a given run over $\mathcal{A}$. Then $\forall x, y \in C,\ fr(\nu(x)) = fr(\nu(y))$.*

Proof (Outline). By induction over the length of runs. Initial states satisfy this property and each transition preserves the property. Detailed proof can be found in the extended version of this paper [SPKM08].

The main result of the paper is stated below. The proof of this theorem as well as an analysis of the complexity will be developed over the next two sections.

Theorem 2. *If $\mathcal{A}$ is a timed automaton and $\mathcal{B}$ is an IRTA then, $L(\mathcal{A}) \subseteq L(\mathcal{B})$ is decidable using exponential space.* $\qquad\square$

3   Untiming Integer Reset Timed Automata

Our aim is to symbolically represent timed word where the time stamps of events which occur in any open interval $(i, i+1)$ need not be distinguished. With this aim we can represent the timed word ρ over Σ by an untimed word $f(\rho)$ over $\Sigma \cup \{\delta, \checkmark\}$. In $f(\rho)$ a $\checkmark$ occurs at every integral time point and all the Σ events of ρ which occur at this time point immediately follow the $\checkmark$. Moreover, before every $\checkmark$ denoting the integral point i, there is a δ denoting the open interval $(i-1, i)$ and all events of ρ which occur within this open interval follow the symbol δ. Example 4 illustrates this representation. The formal definition of representation function f is given below. Firstly we define a $\delta\checkmark$-representation for a real number τ, and its extension for two real numbers $\tau_1 \le \tau_2$.

Definition 7. *Let $int(\tau) = k$.*

$$dt(\tau) \triangleq \begin{cases} (\delta\checkmark)^k & \text{if } \tau \text{ is integral,} \\ (\delta\checkmark)^k \delta & \text{if } \tau \text{ is non-integral,} \end{cases}$$

Let $\tau_1 \leq \tau_2$ be two real numbers. Then $dte(\tau_1, \tau_2)$ is the $\delta\checkmark$-pattern that is to be right concatenated to $dt(\tau_1)$ to get $dt(\tau_2)$.   □

For example, if $\tau_1 = 1.6$ and $\tau_2 = 2.7$, then $dt(\tau_1) = \delta\checkmark\delta$ while $dt(2.7) = \delta\checkmark\delta\checkmark\delta$. Therefore, $dte(\tau_1, \tau_2) = \checkmark\delta$.

Definition 8. *Given a timed word $\rho = (\sigma, \tau)$, the map $f(\rho)$ is defined as the (untimed) word $w_1\sigma_1 w_2\sigma_2 \ldots w_n\sigma_n$, where each w_i is $dte(\tau_{i-1}, \tau_i)$.*   □

Example 4. For example, let $\rho_1 = (a, 1.2), (b, 3.5), (c, 4), (d, 4.5), (e, 4.5), (f, 5.6),$ $(g, 5.8))$ and $\rho_2 = (a, 0), (b, 0), (c, 0.5), (c, 0.6), (d, 2)$ be two timed words. Then, $f(\rho_1) = \delta\checkmark\delta a\checkmark\delta\checkmark\delta b\checkmark c\delta de\checkmark\delta fg$ and $f(\rho_2) = ab\delta cc\checkmark\delta\checkmark d$.

Definition 9. *Two timed words ρ and ρ' are said to be f-equivalent, denoted by $\rho \cong \rho'$, iff $f(\rho) = f(\rho')$.*   □

Proposition 2. *Let $\rho = (\sigma_1, \tau_1) \ldots (\sigma_n, \tau_n)$ and $\rho' = (\sigma'_1, \tau'_1) \ldots (\sigma'_n, \tau'_n)$ be two timed words. Then $\rho \cong \rho'$ iff $\forall 1 \leq i \leq n$, (i) $\sigma_i = \sigma'_i$, (ii) $int(\tau_i) = int(\tau'_i)$, and (iii) $fr(\tau_i) = 0$ iff $fr(\tau'_i) = 0$.*

Proof. See the extended version of this paper [SPKM08].   □

The following theorem states that IRTA are closed with respect to f-equivalence. Thus, the time stamps of events occurring within the same open interval $(i, i+1)$ cannot be distinguished by an IRTA.

Theorem 3. *If $\mathcal{A}$ is an IRTA and $\rho \cong \rho'$ then, $\rho \in L(\mathcal{A})$ iff $\rho' \in L(\mathcal{A})$.*

Proof. Let $\rho = (\sigma, \tau)$ and $\rho' = (\sigma', \tau')$ such that $\rho \cong \rho'$. Let r be a (accepting) run $(l_0, \nu_0) \xrightarrow{\tau_1} (l_0, \nu_1) \xrightarrow{e_1} (l_1, \nu'_1) \xrightarrow{\tau_2 - \tau_1} (l_1, \nu_2) \xrightarrow{e_2} \ldots \xrightarrow{\tau_n - \tau_{n-1}} (l_{n-1}, \nu_n) \xrightarrow{e_n} (l_n, \nu'_n)$ of $\mathcal{A}$ over ρ. We show by induction on the length of the run that there is a corresponding (accepting) run of $\mathcal{A}$ over ρ'. For a clock x, $\nu_n(x) = \tau_n - \tau_j$, where either j is the largest index less than n such that e_j resets x, or x was never reset, in which case τ_j is 0. In either case, since $\mathcal{A}$ is an IRTA, τ_j is integral. Hence $\nu_n(x) = int(\tau_n) + fr(\tau_n) - \tau_j$.

By induction hypothesis, we know that there is a partial run $(l_0, \mu_0) \xrightarrow{\tau'_1}$ $(l_0, \mu_1) \xrightarrow{e_1} (l_1, \mu'_1) \xrightarrow{\tau'_2 - \tau'_1} (l_1, \mu_2) \xrightarrow{e_2} \ldots \xrightarrow{\tau'_{n-1} - \tau'_{n-2}} (l_{n-2}, \mu_{n-1}) \xrightarrow{e_{n-1}} (l_{n-1}, \mu'_{n-1})$ $\xrightarrow{\tau'_n - \tau'_{n-1}} (l_{n-1}, \mu_n)$ over ρ' in $\mathcal{A}$ such that $\nu_i \models \varphi_i$ iff $\mu_i \models \varphi_i$, $i \leq n - 1$. As $int(\tau_i) = int(\tau'_i)$ and $fr(\tau_i), fr(\tau'_i)$ agree on zeroness for all $i \leq n$, it is clear that for a clock x, $\mu_n(x) = int(\tau'_n) + fr(\tau'_n) - \tau'_j = int(\tau_n) + fr(\tau'_n) - \tau_j$. Therefore, $int(\mu_n(x)) = int(\nu_n(x))$ and $fr(\mu_n(x))$ and $fr(\nu_n(x))$ agree on zeroness. Hence $\nu_n \models \varphi_n$ iff $\mu_n \models \varphi_n$. From this, as $(l_{n-1}, \nu_n) \xrightarrow{e_n} (l_n, \nu'_n)$ we have $(l_{n-1}, \mu_n) \xrightarrow{e_n} (l_n, \mu'_n)$ which can extend the partial run to full run over ρ'.   □

Proposition 3. *1. If $\mathcal{A}$ is a timed automaton $f^{-1}(f(L(\mathcal{A}))) \supseteq L(\mathcal{A})$.*
2. If $\mathcal{A}$ is an IRTA, $f^{-1}(f(L(\mathcal{A}))) = L(\mathcal{A})$.

Proof. 1 follows from the fact that f is a total function w.r.t. the domain of all timed words. 2 follows from the fact that if $\mathcal{A}$ is an IRTA then, $L(\mathcal{A})$ is closed w.r.t. f (i.e. If $f(\rho) = f(\rho')$ then $\rho \in L(\mathcal{A}) \Leftrightarrow \rho' \in L(\mathcal{A})$). ☐

Theorem 4. *If $\mathcal{A}$ is a timed automaton and $\mathcal{B}$ is an integer reset timed automaton then, $L(\mathcal{A}) \subseteq L(\mathcal{B})$ iff $f(L(\mathcal{A})) \subseteq f(L(\mathcal{B}))$.*

Proof. The forward direction follows from the fact that f is monotone increasing. For the reverse, assume that $f(L(\mathcal{A})) \subseteq f(L(\mathcal{B}))$. Since f^{-1} is monotone increasing, it follows that $f^{-1}(f(L(\mathcal{A}))) \subseteq f^{-1}(f(L(\mathcal{B})))$. From Proposition 3, we have $L(\mathcal{A}) \subseteq f^{-1}(f(L(\mathcal{A})))$, and also $f^{-1}(f(L(\mathcal{B}))) = L(\mathcal{B})$. Hence $L(\mathcal{A}) \subseteq L(\mathcal{B})$. ☐

4   Language Inclusion Problem for IRTA

Given a timed automaton $\mathcal{A}$ over alphabet Σ, we construct a marked timed automaton $\mathcal{MA}$ over the alphabet $\Sigma \cup \{\delta, \checkmark\}$. The automaton $\mathcal{MA}$ essentially mimics the runs of $\mathcal{A}$. But a time elapse move in $\mathcal{A}$ is mimicked by punctuating it by suitable occurrences of intermediate δ and $\checkmark$ events as prescribed in Section 3. Basically, a $\checkmark$ occurs at every integral time point i and there is a single δ in the interval $(i, i+1)$. A fresh clock n is used in $\mathcal{MA}$ to keep track of whether the current time is integral or non-integral. Each location l of $\mathcal{A}$ gives rise to two locations l^0, l^+ in $\mathcal{MA}$. The $\mathcal{MA}$ automaton enters the l_0 configuration exactly at integral time points by performing the $\checkmark$ event. All Σ transitions of $\mathcal{A}$ which can occur at integral points are enabled to occur from l^0 without elapse of time. Moreover, after a nondeterministic delay in open interval $(0, 1)$ the automaton moves to from l^0 to location l^+ on a δ event. All the Σ transitions of $\mathcal{A}$ which can occur at non-integral time point from l are enabled to occur in $\mathcal{MA}$ from the location l^+. The Figure 5 shows how a transition in $\mathcal{A}$ is transformed to transitions in $\mathcal{MA}$.

We formally define the construction of MA below.

Definition 10. *Given the timed automaton $\mathcal{A} = (L, L_0, \Sigma, C, E, F)$, we construct a marked timed automaton $\mathcal{MA}$ augmented with $\delta, \checkmark$, denoted as $\mathcal{MA} = (L', L_0', \Sigma \cup \{\delta, \checkmark\}, C \cup \{n\}, E', F')$ such that (i) $n \notin C$, (ii) $L' = L^0 \cup L^+$ where*

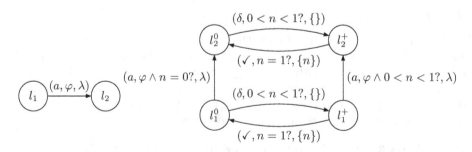

Fig. 5. Corresponding transitions in $\mathcal{A}$ and $\mathcal{MA}$

for $\alpha \in \{0, +\}$, $L^\alpha = \{l^\alpha | l \in L\}$, *(iii)* $L'_0 = \{l^0 | l \in L_0\}$, *(iv)* $F' = \{l^0, l^+ | l \in F\}$, *(v)* E' *is defined as follows:*

$$E' = \{(l^0, l'^0, a, \varphi \wedge n = 0?, \lambda) \mid (l, l', a, \varphi, \lambda) \in E\}$$
$$\cup \ \{(l^+, l'^+, a, \varphi \wedge 0 < n < 1?, \lambda) \mid (l, l', a, \varphi, \lambda) \in E\}$$
$$\cup \ \{(l^0, l^+, \delta, 0 < n < 1?, \emptyset)\} \cup \{(l^+, l^0, \checkmark, n = 1?, \{n\})\}.$$

Note that the language $L(\mathcal{MA})$ is a subset of $TW_{\Sigma \cup \{\delta, \checkmark\}}$. The following example illustrates a run of $\mathcal{A}$ and one of the corresponding runs of $\mathcal{MA}$.

Example 5. The Figure 6 shows a timed automaton $\mathcal{A}$ and its corresponding $\mathcal{MA}$. A run of $\mathcal{A}$ on timed word $\rho = (a, 0.3)(b, 2.4)(c, 2.6)$ is given by $r = (s, (0, 0)) \xrightarrow{0.3} (s, (0.3, 0.3)) \xrightarrow{a} (t, (0, 0.3)) \xrightarrow{2.1} (t, (2.1, 2.4)) \xrightarrow{b} (u, (2.1, 0)) \xrightarrow{0.2} (u, (2.3, 0.2)) \xrightarrow{c} (u, (2.3, 0.2))$ where $(\nu(x), \nu(y))$ represents the clock valuation.

A corresponding run of $\mathcal{MA}$ is given by $r' = (s^0, (0, 0, 0)) \xrightarrow{0.15} (s^0, (0.15, 0.15, 0.15)) \xrightarrow{\delta} (s^+, (0.15, 0.15, 0.15)) \xrightarrow{0.15} (s^+, (0.3, 0.3, 0.3)) \xrightarrow{a} (t^+, (0, 0.3, 0.3)) \xrightarrow{0.7} (t^+, (0.7, 1.0, 1.0)) \xrightarrow{\checkmark} (t^0, (0.7, 1.0, 0)) \xrightarrow{0.5} (t^0, (1.2, 1.5, 0.5)) \xrightarrow{\delta} (t^+, (1.2, 1.5, 0.5)) \xrightarrow{0.5} (t^+, (1.7, 2.0, 1.0)) \xrightarrow{\checkmark} (t^0, (1.7, 2.0, 0)) \xrightarrow{0.2} (t^0, (1.9, 2.2, 0.2)) \xrightarrow{\delta} (t^+, (1.9, 2.2, 0.2)) \xrightarrow{0.2} (t^+, (2.1, 2.4, 0.4)) \xrightarrow{b} (u^+, (2.1, 0, 0.4)) \xrightarrow{0.2} (u^+, (2.3, 0.2, 0.6)) \xrightarrow{c} (u^+, (2.3, 0.2, 0.6))$ with (x, y, n) denoting the clock valuation in r'. It corresponds to the timed word $\rho' = (\delta, 0.15), (a, 0.3), (\checkmark, 1), (\delta, 1.5), (\checkmark, 2), (\delta, 2.2), (b, 2.4), (c, 2.6)$. Another such run gives the timed word $\rho'' = (\delta, 0.25), (a, 0.3), (\checkmark, 1), (\delta, 1.75), (\checkmark, 2), (\delta, 2.1), (b, 2.4), (c, 2.6)$. Note that $f(\rho) = untime(\rho') = untime(\rho'')$. □

Now we formally relate the runs of $\mathcal{A}$ with the runs of $\mathcal{MA}$. Recall that $(m, \mu)^t$ denotes that configuration (m, μ) occurs at time t.

Definition 11. *A configuration $(m, \mu)^t$ of $\mathcal{MA}$ is called consistent iff (i) $fr(\mu(n)) = fr(t)$ and (ii) $l \in L^0 \Leftrightarrow \mu(n) = 0$ and $l \in L^+ \Leftrightarrow \mu(n) \in (0, 1)$.*

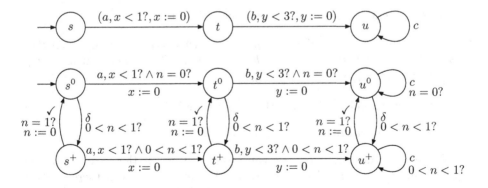

Fig. 6. $\mathcal{A}$ and corresponding $\mathcal{MA}$

Let $(l, \nu)^t$ be a configuration of $\mathcal{A}$. Then, the corresponding configuration of $\mathcal{MA}$, $h_1((l, \nu)^t)$ is given by the consistent configuration $(l^\alpha, \mu)^t$ where, μ agrees with ν for all $x \in C$. Let $(l^\alpha, \mu)^t$ be a configuration of $\mathcal{MA}$. Then, the corresponding configuration of $\mathcal{A}$ given by $h_2((l^\alpha, \mu)^t)$ is defined as $(l, \nu)^t$ where ν is the projection which restricts μ to clocks in C. □

Definition 12. A step in $\mathcal{A}$, $(l_1, \nu_1) \xrightarrow{\tau_2 - \tau_1} (l_2, \nu_2) \xrightarrow{e} (l_3, \nu_3)$ is a timed transition followed by a Σ-transition. Note that $l_1 = l_2$.

Let $(m_1, \mu_1)^{\tau_1}$ be consistent configuration of $\mathcal{MA}$. A superstep in $\mathcal{MA}$, $(m_1, \mu_1)^{\tau_1} \implies (m_2, \mu_2)^{\tau_2} \xrightarrow{e} (m_3, \mu_3)^{\tau_3}$ is obtained by making a sequence of time elapse and $\delta, \checkmark$ transitions (denoted by $(m_1, \mu_1)^{\tau_1} \implies (m_2, \mu_2)^{\tau_2}$) followed by a Σ-transition e. Note that $\tau_2 = \tau_3$.

Proposition 4. Let $(m_1, \mu_1)^{\tau_1} \implies (m_2, \mu_2)^{\tau_2} \xrightarrow{e} (m_3, \mu_3)^{\tau_3}$ be a superstep in $\mathcal{MA}$ where w is the timed $\delta, \checkmark$ word on which $(m_1, \mu_1)^{\tau_1}$ evolves into $(m_2, \mu_2)^{\tau_2}$. Let us denote this by $(m_1, \mu_1)^{\tau_1} \xRightarrow{w} (m_2, \mu_2)^{\tau_2} \xrightarrow{e} (m_3, \mu_3)^{\tau_3}$. Then,

- $(m_2, \mu_2)^{\tau_2}$ and $(m_3, \mu_3)^{\tau_3}$ are consistent, and
- For two timed $\delta, \checkmark$ words w, w', if we have $(m_1, \mu_1)^{\tau_1} \xRightarrow{w} (m_2, \mu_2)^{\tau_2}$ and $(m_1, \mu_1)^{\tau_1} \xRightarrow{w'} (m_2', \mu_2')^{\tau_2}$ then, $m_2 = m_2'$, $\mu_2 = \mu_2'$ and $untime(w) = untime(w') = dte(\tau_1, \tau_2)$. (see Definition 7)

Proof. See the extended version of this paper [SPKM08]. □

Remark 1. Given a configuration $(m_1, \mu_1)^{\tau_1}$ of $\mathcal{MA}$ and a time stamp τ_2, we obtain a unique configuration $(m_2, \mu_2)^{\tau_2}$ by a sequence of timed and $\delta, \checkmark$ transitions. It should be noted that the untimed $\delta, \checkmark$ word that takes the configuration $(m_1, \mu_1)^{\tau_1}$ to $(m_2, \mu_2)^{\tau_2}$ is unique. This is a form of determinacy of $\mathcal{MA}$ under time elapse.

Lemma 2. Let $(l_1, \nu_1)^{\tau_1} \xrightarrow{\tau_2 - \tau_1} (l_2, \nu_2)^{\tau_2} \xrightarrow{e} (l_3, \nu_3)^{\tau_3}$ be a step that occurs in $\mathcal{A}$ and let $(m_i, \mu_i)^{\tau_i} = h_1((l_i, \nu_i)^{\tau_i})$. Then, there exists a superstep $(m_1, \mu_1)^{\tau_1} \xRightarrow{w} (m_2, \mu_2)^{\tau_2} \xrightarrow{e} (m_3, \mu_3)^{\tau_3}$ in $\mathcal{MA}$.

Proof. See the extended version of this paper [SPKM08]. □

Lemma 3. Let $(m_1, \mu_1)^{\tau_1} \xRightarrow{\pi_1} (m_2, \mu_2)^{\tau_2} \xrightarrow{e} (m_3, \mu_3)^{\tau_3}$ be a superstep that occurs in $\mathcal{MA}$, and let $(l_i, \nu_i)^{\tau_i} = h_2((m_i, \mu_i)^{\tau_i})$. Then, there exists a step $(l_1, \nu_1)^{\tau_1} \xrightarrow{\tau_2 - \tau_1} (l_2, \nu_2)^{\tau_2} \xrightarrow{e} (l_3, \nu_3)^{\tau_3}$ over $\mathcal{A}$.

Proof. See the extended version of this paper [SPKM08]. □

Theorem 5. $untime(L(\mathcal{MA})) = f(L(\mathcal{A}))$

Proof. Using Lemmas 2 and 3, we can establish that (i) there exists an (accepting) run r over a timed word $\rho = (\sigma_1, \tau_1) \ldots (\sigma_n, \tau_n)$ in $\mathcal{A}$ iff there exists a corresponding (accepting) run r' over a timed word $\rho' = w_1(\sigma_1, \tau_1) \ldots w_n(\sigma_n, \tau_n)$ in $\mathcal{MA}$ such that (a) the configurations occurring after the supersteps in r' are the h_1 images of the configurations occurring after steps in r, (b) the configurations occurring after steps in r are the h_2 images of those occurring after supersteps in r', and (c)$untime(w_i) = dte(\tau_{i-1}, \tau_i)$. By definition of f, it is clear that $untime(\rho')$ is same as $f(\rho)$.   □

Recall that for a timed automaton $\mathcal{A}$, $\mathcal{R}\mathcal{A}$ represents its region automaton.

Corollary 1. $L(\mathcal{R}\mathcal{M}\mathcal{A}) = untime(L(\mathcal{M}\mathcal{A})) = f(L(\mathcal{A}))$.

Proof. Follows from Theorems 1 and 5.   □

Proof of Theorem 2. For a timed automaton $\mathcal{A}$ and IRTA $\mathcal{B}$, the language inclusion problem $L(\mathcal{A}) \subseteq L(\mathcal{B})$ reduces to $f(L(\mathcal{A})) \subseteq f(L(\mathcal{B}))$ by Theorem 4, and this further reduces to $L(\mathcal{R}\mathcal{M}\mathcal{A}) \subseteq L(\mathcal{R}\mathcal{M}\mathcal{B})$ by Corollary 1. Note that $\mathcal{R}\mathcal{M}\mathcal{A}$ and $\mathcal{R}\mathcal{M}\mathcal{B}$ are finite automata and their language inclusion is decidable using standard automata techniques.   □

Theorem 6. *If $\mathcal{A}$ is a timed automaton and $\mathcal{B}$ is an ϵ-IRTA then, $L(\mathcal{A}) \subseteq L(\mathcal{B})$ iff $f(L(\mathcal{A})) \subseteq f(L(\mathcal{B}))$.*

Proof (Outline). By treating ϵ as a visible special symbol and using Theorem 2 we get the result for timed words with ϵ and corresponding $\delta, \checkmark$ words with ϵ. Now ϵ can be erased from both.   □

Complexity. Let $\mathcal{A} = (L_1, L_{1_0}, \Sigma_1, C_1, E_1, F_1)$ be a timed automaton and let $\mathcal{B} = (L_2, L_{2_0}, \Sigma_2, C_2, E_2, F_2)$ be an IRTA or ϵ-IRTA. Let k_1, k_2 be the maximum constants appearing in constraints of $\mathcal{A}$ and $\mathcal{B}$. We construct the marked timed automaton $\mathcal{M}\mathcal{A} = (L_1', L_{1_0}', \Sigma_1', C_1', E_1', F_1')$ where $|L_1'| = 2 * |L_1|$, $|C_1'| = |C_1| + 1$. From [AD94], it follows that the number of locations in the region automaton $\mathcal{R}\mathcal{M}\mathcal{A}$ is $2.L_1.(2k_1 + 2)^{|C_1|+1}.(|C_1| + 1)!$. In case of $\mathcal{R}\mathcal{M}\mathcal{B}$, as the fractional parts of all the clocks are always equal and hence the number of clock regions reduces to $2.(k_2 + 1)^{|C_2|+1}$. Hence the number of locations in $\mathcal{R}\mathcal{M}\mathcal{B}$ is given by $4.L_2.(k_2 + 1)^{|C_2|+1}$. The problem $L(\mathcal{A}) \subseteq L(\mathcal{B})$ can be solved by checking $L(\mathcal{R}\mathcal{M}\mathcal{A}) \subseteq L(\mathcal{R}\mathcal{M}\mathcal{B})$. Thus the language inclusion problem of Theorem 2 can be solved in space $O(log_2(L_1.(2k_1 + 2)^{|C_1|+1}.(|C_1| + 1)! \times 2^{4.L_2.(k_2+1)^{|C_2|+1}}))$. Hence the problem is contained in nondeterministic EXPSPACE.

5   Expressiveness and Closure Properties

Lemma 4. *IRTA are closed under union and intersection.*

Proof. The construction techniques used for timed automata apply in the case of IRTA as well.   □

Lemma 5. *Given an IRTA $\mathcal{A}$, a deterministic one clock IRTA $Det(\mathcal{A})$ can be constructed such that $L(\mathcal{A}) = L(Det(\mathcal{A}))$.*

The detailed construction is involved and is given in [SPKM07]. However the size of the resultant automaton by this construction is triply exponential in the size of the original automaton. Using determinization we get the following result.

Corollary 2. *IRTA are closed under complementation.*

ERA represents Event Recording Automata which is a determinizable subclass of Timed Automata studied in [AFH99].

Lemma 6. *IRTA and ERA are incomparable. i.e. (1) ERA $\not\subseteq$ IRTA and (2) IRTA $\not\subseteq$ ERA.*

Proof. 1. The timed language accepted by the ERA in Figure 7 is given by $L_1 = \{(ab, \tau_1\tau_2) : \tau_2 - \tau_1 = 1\}$. Let $\rho = (ab, \tau)$ and $\rho' = (ab, \tau')$ be two timed words such that $\tau_1 = \tau_1' = 0.5$, $\tau_2 = 1.5$ and $\tau_2' = 1.6$. By Theorem 3, it follows that any integer reset timed automaton cannot distinguish between ρ and ρ'. But $\rho \in L_1$ and $\rho' \notin L_1$.

2. The timed language accepted by the integer reset timed automaton given in Figure 8 is given by $L_2 = \{(a^n, \tau\}$, where $n \geq 2$ and, $\tau_1 = 2$, $\tau_2 \in [2, 3]$ and for each $i \geq 3$, $\tau_i = i$. Let $\mathcal{A}$ be an ERA such that $L(\mathcal{A}) = L_2$. Since there is only one symbol $a \in \Sigma$, we can safely assume that $\mathcal{A}$ has only one clock x. By definition of ERA, $\mathcal{A}$ resets x at the occurrence of every a and hence at the second a too. And thus it cannot ensure that $\tau_3 - \tau_1 = 1$. So, $\rho = (a, 2)(a, 2.3)(a, 3.3) \in L(\mathcal{A})$ but $\rho \notin L_2$ and hence $L(\mathcal{A}) \neq L_2$.

Thus IRTA and ERA are incomparable. $\square$

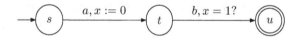

Fig. 7. Event Recording Automaton

Fig. 8. IRTA which is not an Event Recording Automaton

6   Discussion

We have identified a subclass of timed automata called IRTA as well as its extension with silent transitions called ϵ-IRTA. We have argued with examples that the notion of global but sparse time as used in time triggered architecture and distributed business processes can be naturally modeled in IRTA. Of course time triggered architecture contains several other orthogonal elements such as temporal firewalling, TDMA based message communication, and fault tolerance. Hence our paper is just a preliminary step in building formal models for reasoning about time triggered systems. We have focused mainly on formalizing the global, sparse time base.

We have shown that the language inclusion problem $L(\mathcal{A}) \subseteq L(\mathcal{B})$ is decidable with EXPSPACE complexity for timed automaton $\mathcal{A}$ and ϵ-IRTA $\mathcal{B}$. A lower bound for the problem remains to be given.

The class IRTA is expressively equivalent to 1-clock deterministic IRTA. However, the known reduction from IRTA to 1-clock deterministic IRTA results in blowup in the number of states by 3 exponents [SPKM07]. Thus, complementing IRTA may be expensive. This also shows that directly using deterministic IRTA for specification or verification may not be feasible due to large size of automata needed to express properties. No lower bound has been established for the determinization of IRTA and the issue remains open.

We have also shown that IRTA are closed under boolean operations. A similar proof shows that ϵ-IRTA are closed under union and intersection. However complementation of ϵ-IRTA remains open. Clearly, ϵ-IRTA are more expressive than IRTA and hence they cannot be determinized to 1-clock deterministic IRTA. We are investigating reduction from ϵ-IRTA to deterministic 1-clock IRTA extended with periodic constraints [CG00]. In this paper, we have worked with only the finite timed words and the theory of IRTA remains to be extended to infinite words. Also, a suitable logic for specifying properties of IRTA remains to be formulated.

We are currently working on an implementation of the decision procedure for language inclusion of IRTA proposed in this paper. Our aim is to tackle examples such as the end-to-end latency verification [MRD$^+$08] (originally verified using Uppaal) using the tool under construction. We also hope to verify timing properties of distributed web services and business processes modelled in BPEL4WS [KPP06].

Acknowledgements. This work was partially supported by General Motors India Science Lab sponsored project "Advanced Research on Formal Analysis of Hybrid Systems". The authors thank Kamal Lodaya for helpful comments.

References

[AD94]   Alur, R., Dill, D.L.: A theory of timed automata. Theoretical Computer Science 126(2), 183–235 (1994)

[AFH99]   Alur, R., Fix, L., Henzinger, T.A.: Event-clock automata: a determinizable class of timed automata. Theoretical Computer Science 211(1–2), 253–273 (1999)

[AM04]   Alur, R., Madhusudan, P.: Decision problems for timed automata: A survey. In: 4th Intl. School on Formal Mthods for Computer, Communication, and Software Systems: Real Time (2004)

[BHR07]   Bouyer, P., Haddad, S., Reynier, P.-A.: Undecidability results for timed automata with silent transitions. Research Report LSV-07-12, Laboratoire Spécification et Vérification, ENS Cachan, France, 22 pages (February 2007)

[BLL+95]   Bengtsson, J., Larsen, K., Larsson, F., Pettersson, P., Yi, W.: UPPAAL:
            A tool suite for automatic verification of real-time systems. In: Hybrid
            Systems, pp. 232–243 (1995)
[BPGD98]   Berard, B., Petit, A., Gastin, P., Diekert, V.: Characterization of the ex-
            pressive power of silent transitions in timed automata. Fundamenta Infor-
            maticae 36(2-3), 145–182 (1998)
[CG00]   Choffrut, C., Goldwurm, M.: Timed automata with periodic clock con-
            straints. Journal of Automata, Languages and Combinatorics 5(4), 371–
            404 (2000)
[DS04]   Dutertre, B., Sorea, M.: Modeling and verification of a fault-tolerant real-
            time startup protocol using calendar automata. In: FORMATS/FTRTFT,
            pp. 199–214 (2004)
[DT04]   D'Souza, D., Tabareau, N.: On timed automata with input-determined
            guards. In: FORMATS/FTRTFT, pp. 68–83 (2004)
[Fin06]   Finkel, O.: Undecidable problems about timed automata. In: Asarin,
            E., Bouyer, P. (eds.) FORMATS 2006. LNCS, vol. 4202, pp. 187–199.
            Springer, Heidelberg (2006)
[KB01]   Kopetz, H., Bauer, G.: The time-triggered architecture. In: Proceedings of
            the IEEE, Special Issue on Modeling and Design of Embedded Software
            (October 2001)
[KMTY04]   Krcál, P., Mokrushin, L., Thiagarajan, P.S., Yi, W.: Timed vs. time-
            triggered automata. In: Gardner, P., Yoshida, N. (eds.) CONCUR 2004.
            LNCS, vol. 3170, pp. 340–354. Springer, Heidelberg (2004)
[KPP06]   Kazhamiakin, R., Pandya, P., Pistore, M.: Representation, verification,
            and computation of timed properties in web. In: ICWS 2006: Proceedings
            of the IEEE International Conference on Web Services, Washington, DC,
            USA, pp. 497–504. IEEE Computer Society, Los Alamitos (2006)
[MRD+08]   Mohalik, S., Rajeev, A.C., Dixit, M.G., Ramesh, S., Suman, P.V., Pandya,
            P.K., Jiang, S.: Model checking based analysis of end-to-end latency in
            embedded, real-time systems with clock drifts. In: DAC 2008, Proceedings
            of Design Automaton Conference, Anaheim, California (2008)
[OW04]   Ouaknine, J., Worrell, J.: On the language inclusion problem for timed
            automata: Closing a decidability gap. In: LICS 2004: Proceedings of the
            19th Annual IEEE Symposium on Logic in Computer Science, Washing-
            ton, DC, USA, pp. 54–63. IEEE Computer Society, Los Alamitos (2004)
[OW05]   Ouaknine, J., Worrell, J.: On the decidability of metric temporal logic. In:
            LICS 2005: Proceedings of the 20th Annual IEEE Symposium on Logic in
            Computer Science, Washington, DC, USA, pp. 188–197. IEEE Computer
            Society, Los Alamitos (2005)
[SPKM07]   Suman, P.V., Pandya, P.K., Krishna, S.N., Manasa, L.: Determinization of
            timed automata with integral resets. Research Report TIFR-PPVS-GM-
            2007/4 (2007),
            http://www.tcs.tifr.res.in/~vsuman/TechReps/irtav4.pdf
[SPKM08]   Suman, P.V., Pandya, P.K., Krishna, S.N., Manasa, L.: Timed automata
            with integer resets: Langauge inclusion and expressiveness. Research Re-
            port TIFR-SPKG-GM-2008/1 (2008),
            http://www.tcs.tifr.res.in/ vsuman/
            TechReps/IrtaLangInclTechRep.pdf
[Tri06]   Tripakis, S.: Folk theorems on the determinization and minimization of
            timed automata. Inf. Process. Lett. 99(6), 222–226 (2006)

Complexity of Metric Temporal Logics with Counting and the Pnueli Modalities

Alexander Rabinovich

Sackler Faculty of Exact Sciences, Tel Aviv University, Israel 69978
rabinoa@post.tau.ac.il

Abstract. The common metric temporal logics for continuous time were shown to be insufficient, when it was proved in [7, 12] that they cannot express a modality suggested by Pnueli. Moreover no temporal logic with a finite set of modalities can express all the natural generalizations of this modality. The temporal logic with counting modalities (TLC) is the extension of until-since temporal logic $TL(\mathbf{U}, \mathbf{S})$ by "counting modalities" $C_n(X)$ and $\overleftarrow{C}_n$ ($n \in \mathbb{N}$); for each n the modality $C_n(X)$ says that X will be true at least at n points in the next unit of time, and its dual $\overleftarrow{C}_n(X)$ says that X has happened n times in the last unit of time. In [11] it was proved that this temporal logic is expressively complete for a natural decidable metric predicate logic. In particular the Pnueli modalities $Pn_k(X_1, \ldots, X_k)$, "there is an increasing sequence $t_1, \ldots, t_k$ of points in the unit interval ahead such that X_i holds at t_i", are definable in TLC.

In this paper we investigate the complexity of the satisfiability problem for TLC and show that the problem is PSPACE complete when the index of C_n is coded in unary, and EXPSPACE complete when the index is coded in binary. We also show that the satisfiability problem for the until-since temporal logic extended by Pnueli's modalities is PSPACE complete.

1 Introduction

The temporal logic that is based on the two modalities "Since" and "Until" is popular among computer scientists as a framework for reasoning about a system evolving in time. By Kamp's theorem [13] this logic has the same expressive power as the first order monadic logic of order, whether the system evolves in discrete steps or in continuous time. We will denote this logic by $TL(\mathbf{U}, \mathbf{S})$.

For systems evolving in discrete steps, this logic seem to supply all the expressive power needed. This is not the case for systems evolving in continuous time, as the logic cannot express metric properties like: "X will happen within one unit of time". The most straightforward extension which allows to express metric properties is to add modality which says that "X will happen exactly after one unit of time". Unfortunately, this logic is undecidable. Over the years different decidable extensions of $TL(\mathbf{U}, \mathbf{S})$ were suggested. Most extensively researched was $MITL$ [1, 2, 5]. Other logics are described in [3, 6, 14, 17]. We introduced the language QTL (quantitative temporal logic) [8, 9, 10], which extends the

F. Cassez and C. Jard (Eds.): FORMATS 2008, LNCS 5215, pp. 93–108, 2008.
© Springer-Verlag Berlin Heidelberg 2008

until-since temporal logic by two modalities: $\Diamond_1 X$ and $\overleftarrow{\Diamond}_1 X$. The formula $\Diamond_1 X$ (respectively $\overleftarrow{\Diamond}_1 X$) expresses that "$X$ will be true at some point during the next unit of time" (respectively, "X was true at some point during the previous unit of time"). These extensions of $TL(\mathbf{U}, \mathbf{S})$ have the same expressive power, which indicates that they capture a natural fragment of what can be said about the system which evolve in time. These "first generation" metric extensions of $TL(\mathbf{U}, \mathbf{S})$ can be called *simple metric temporal logics*.

A. Pnueli was probably the first person to question if these simple logics are expressive enough for our needs. The conjecture that they cannot express the property "X and then Y will both happen in the coming unit of time" is usually referred to as "Pnueli's conjecture" [2, 17].

In [7, 12] we proved Pnueli's conjecture, and we strengthened it significantly. To do this we defined for every natural k the "*Pnueli modality*" $Pn_k(X_1, \dots, X_k)$, which states that there is an increasing sequence $t_1, \dots, t_k$ of points in the unit interval ahead such that X_i holds at t_i. We also defined the weaker "*Counting modalities*" $C_k(X)$ which state that X is true at least at k points in the unit interval ahead (so that $C_k(X) = Pn_k(X, \dots, X)$). To deal with the past we define also the dual past modality, $\overleftarrow{Pn}_k(X_1, \dots, X_k)$: there is a decreasing sequence $t_1, \dots, t_k$ of points in the previous unit interval such that X_i holds at t_i, and $\overleftarrow{C}_k(X)$ which state that X was true at least at k points in the previous unit interval.

This yields a sequence of temporal logics TLP_n ($n \in \mathbb{N}$), where TLP_n is the standard temporal logic, with "Until" and "Since", and with the addition of the k-place modalities Pn_k and $\overleftarrow{Pn}_k$ for $k \leq n$. Similarly, TLC_n is the extension of $TL(\mathbf{U}, \mathbf{S})$ with the addition of modalities C_k and $\overleftarrow{C}_k$ for $k \leq n$. We note also that TLP_1 is just the logic QTL and it represents the simple metric logics.

Let TLP be the union of TLP_n and TLC be the union of TLC_n.

We proved in [7, 12] that:

1. The sequence of temporal logics TLP_n is strictly increasing in expressive power. In particular, $C_{n+1}(X)$ is not expressible in TLP_n
2. TLP and TLC are decidable and have the same expressive power. Moreover they are expressively equivalent to a natural decidable fragment of first-order logic.

In this paper we investigate the complexity of the satisfiability problem for TLP and TLC. In [16] it was shown that $TL(\mathbf{U}, \mathbf{S})$ is PSPACE complete. In [7, 10] we provided a polynomial satisfiability preserving translation from QTL to $TL(\mathbf{U}, \mathbf{S})$ and derived PSPACE completeness of QTL.

In this paper we first prove that the satisfiability problem for TLP is PSPACE complete.

When one write a TLC formula there are two natural possibility: to write index n of C_n in unary or in binary. We show that the satisfiability problem for TLC is PSPACE complete when the index of C_n is coded in unary, and EXPSPACE complete when the index is coded in binary.

Our results holds both when the interpretation of temporal variable is arbitrary and when we assume that they satisfy the finite variability assumption

(FVA) which states that no variable changes its truth-value infinitely many times in any bounded interval.

In [12] we proved that there is no temporal logic L with finitely many modalities definable in the monadic second-order logic expanded by $+1$ function such that over the reals L is at leats as expressive as TLC. Our conjecture was that this result can be extended to the non-negative reals. Our proofs refute this conjecture.

The paper is divided as follows: In Sect. 2, we recall definitions and previous results. In Sect. 3, we prove PSPACE completeness for TLP and as a consequence obtain PSPACE completeness for TLC under the unary coding of indexes. In Sect. 4, EXPSPACE completeness for TLC under the binary coding of indexes is proved. Section 5 contains additional complexity results and a discussion on the expressive power of TLC.

2 Preliminaries

First, we recall the syntax and semantics of temporal logics and how temporal modalities are defined using truth tables, with notations adopted from [4, 9].

Temporal logics use logical constructs called "modalities" to create a language that is free from quantifiers.

The syntax of a *Temporal Logic* has in its vocabulary a countably infinite set of *propositions* $\{X_1, X_2, \ldots\}$ and a possibly infinite set $B = \{O_1^{l_1}, O_2^{l_2}, \ldots\}$ of *modality names* (sometimes called "temporal connectives" or "temporal operators") with prescribed arity indicated as superscript (we usually omit the arity notation). $TL(B)$ denotes the *temporal logic based on modality-set B* (and B is called the *basis* of $TL(B)$). Temporal formulae are built by combining atoms (the propositions X_i) and other formulae using Boolean connectives and modalities (with prescribed arity). Formally, the syntax of $TL(B)$ is given by the following grammar:

$$\phi ::= X_i \mid \phi_1 \wedge \phi_2 \mid \phi_1 \vee \phi_2 \mid \phi_1 \leftrightarrow \phi_2 \mid \neg \phi_1 \mid O_i(\phi_1, \phi_2, \ldots, \phi_{l_i})$$

We will use (in our metalanguage) S, X, Y, Z to range over variables.

A *structure for Temporal Logic*, in this work, is the non negative real line with monadic predicates $\mathcal{M} = \langle \mathbb{R}^+, <, S_1, S_2, \ldots \rangle$, where the predicate S_i are the interpretation in $\mathcal{M}$ of the variable S_i. (All our complexity results can be easily adopted to the models over the whole real line $\mathbb{R}$.) Every modality $O^{(k)}$ is interpreted in the structure $\mathcal{M}$ as an operator $O_{\mathcal{M}}^{(k)} : [\mathbb{P}(\mathbb{R}^+)]^k \to \mathbb{P}(\mathbb{R}^+)$ which assigns "the set of points where $O^{(k)}[A_1, \ldots, A_k]$ holds" to the k-tuple $\langle A_1, \ldots, A_k \rangle \in \mathbb{P}(\mathbb{R}^+)^k$. ($\mathbb{P}(\mathbb{R}^+)$ denotes the set of all subsets of $\mathbb{R}^+$). Once every modality corresponds to an operator the semantics is defined by structural induction:

- for atomic formulas: $\mathcal{M}, t \models S$ iff $t \in S$.
- for Boolean combinations the definition is the usual one.
- for $O^{(k)}(\varphi_1, \cdots, \varphi_k)$

$$\mathcal{M}, t \models O^{(k)}(\varphi_1, \cdots, \varphi_k) \quad \text{iff} \quad t \in O_{\mathcal{M}}^{(k)}(A_{\varphi_1}, \cdots, A_{\varphi_k})$$

where $A_\varphi = \{\tau : \mathcal{M}, \tau \models \varphi\}$.

For the modality to be of interest the operator $O^{(k)}$ should reflect some intended connection between the sets A_{φ_i} of points satisfying φ_i and the set of points $O[A_{\varphi_1}, \ldots, A_{\varphi_k}]$. The intended meaning is usually given by a formula in an appropriate predicate logic:

Truth Tables: A formula $\overline{O}(t, X_1, \ldots X_k)$ in the predicate logic L is a *Truth Table* for the modality $O^{(k)}$ if for every structure $\mathcal{M}$

$$O_{\mathcal{M}}(A_1, \ldots, A_k) = \{\tau : \mathcal{M} \models \overline{O}[\tau, A_1, \ldots, A_k]\} .$$

2.1 Since-Until Temporal Logic

The modalities *until* and *since* are most commonly used in temporal logic for computer science. They are defined through the following truth tables:

- The modality $X\mathbf{U}\,Y$, "X *until* Y", is defined by

$$\psi(t_0, X, Y) \equiv \exists t_1 (t_0 < t_1 \wedge Y(t_1) \wedge \forall t(t_0 < t < t_1 \to X(t))).$$

- The modality $X\mathbf{S}\,Y$, "X *since* Y", is defined by

$$\psi(t_0, X, Y) \equiv \exists t_1 (t_0 > t_1 \wedge Y(t_1) \wedge \forall t(t_1 < t < t_0 \to X(t))).$$

Reynolds [16] proved.

Theorem 2.1. *The satisfiability problem for $TL(\mathbf{U}, \mathbf{S})$ over the reals is PSPACE complete.*

We will use standard abbreviations. E.g., $\Diamond X$ - sometimes in the future X holds - abbreviates $True\mathbf{U}X$; $\Box X$ - always in the future X holds - abbreviates $\neg(True\mathbf{U}\neg X)$; the past modalities $\overleftarrow{\Diamond} X$ -"X happened in the past", and $\overleftarrow{\Box} X$ - "X have been always true", are defined similarly. The modality *always* acts like the universal quantifier and is defined as

$$always(X): \quad \overleftarrow{\Box} X \wedge X \wedge \Box X.$$

$Llim(X)$ and $Rlim(X)$ abbreviate the formulas

$$Llim(X): \quad \neg(\neg X\mathbf{S}\,True)$$

$$Rlim(X): \quad \neg(\neg X\mathbf{U}\,True)$$

$Llim(X)$ holds at t if t is a left limit of X, i.e., for every $t_1 < t$ there is an X in the interval (t_1, t). $Rlim(X)$ holds at t if t is a right limit of X.

2.2   Three Metric Temporal Logics

We recall the definitions of three temporal logics: Quantitative Temporal Logic - QTL, Temporal Logic with Counting - TLC and Temporal Logic with Pnueli's modalities - TLP.

The logic QTL in addition to modalities $\mathbf{U}$ and $\mathbf{S}$ has two modalities $\Diamond_1 X$ and $\overleftarrow{\Diamond}_1 X$. These modalities are defined by the tables with free variable t_0:

$$\Diamond_1 X : \qquad \exists t((t_0 < t < t_0 + 1) \wedge X(t))$$

$$\overleftarrow{\Diamond}_1 X : \qquad \exists t((t - 1 < t < t_0) \wedge X(t)) \,)$$

In [7] it was proved.

Theorem 2.2. *The satisfiability problem for QTL is PSPACE complete.*

The logic TLP is the extension of $TL(\mathbf{U}, \mathbf{S})$ by an infinite set of modalities $Pn_k(X_1, \ldots, X_k)$ and $\overleftarrow{Pn}_k(X_1, \ldots, X_k)$. These modalities are defined by the tables with free variable t_0:

$$Pn_k(X_1, \ldots, X_k) : \qquad \exists t_1 \ldots \exists t_k (t_0 < t_1 < \cdots < t_k < t_0 + 1 \wedge \bigwedge_{i=1}^{k} X_i(t_i))$$

$$\overleftarrow{Pn}_k(X_1, \ldots, X_k) : \qquad \exists t_1 \ldots \exists t_k (t_0 - 1 < t_1 < \cdots < t_k < t_0 \wedge \bigwedge_{i=1}^{k} X_i(t_i))$$

Finally, the logic TLC - the temporal logic with counting modalities - is the extension of $TL(\mathbf{U}, \mathbf{S})$ by an infinite set of modalities $C_k(X)$ and $\overleftarrow{C}_k(X)$. These modalities are defined by the tables with free variable t_0:

$$C_k(X) : \qquad \exists t_1 \ldots \exists t_k (t_0 < t_1 < \cdots < t_k < t_0 + 1 \wedge \bigwedge_{i=1}^{k} X(t_i))$$

$$\overleftarrow{C}_k(X) : \qquad \exists t_1 \ldots \exists t_k (t_0 - 1 < t_1 < \cdots < t_k < t_0 \wedge \bigwedge_{i=1}^{k} X(t_i))$$

We recall the terminology that is used when comparing the expressive power of languages.

Let $\mathcal{C}$ be a class of structures and let L and L' be temporal logics.

1. L is *at least as expressive as* L' over a class $\mathcal{C}$ if for every formula φ of L' there is a formula ψ in L such that for every structure $\mathcal{M}$ in $\mathcal{C}$ and for every $\tau \in \mathcal{M}$: $\mathcal{M}, \tau \models \varphi$ iff $\mathcal{M}, \tau \models \psi$.
2. L and L' are *expressively equivalent* over $\mathcal{C}$ if L is at least as expressive as L' over $\mathcal{C}$ and L' is at least as expressive as L over $\mathcal{C}$.

We deal here with the temporal logics over the class of non-negative real numbers. We will say "L is *at least as expressive as* (respectively, is expressively equivalent to) L' if L is *at least as expressive as* (respectively, is expressively equivalent to) L' over this class.

The following theorem from [12] compares the expressive power of TLP, TLC and QTL.

Theorem 2.3 (Comparing the Expressive Power). TLP and TLC are *expressively equivalent*. TLP and TLC are *strictly more expressive than* QTL.

2.3   Size of Formulas

Usually the *size* of a formula is defined as its length (string representation) or the size of its directed acyclic graph representation (DAG). The logics TLC and TLP have infinite sets of modalities and therefore we have to agree how to code the names of modalities. There are two natural possibility: to write index k of C_k and Pn_k in unary or in binary. For TLP formulas this decision affects the size of the formulas up to a constant factor, and, therefore, it is not important, For TLC formulas the binary coding might be exponentially shorter than the unary coding. Our main results show that the satisfiability problem for TLC is PSPACE complete when the index of C_k is coded in unary, and EXPSPACE complete when the index is coded in binary.

Note that there might be an exponential gap in the size of a DAG representation of a formula and its length. Our proofs of upper bounds will be given for DAG representation (and hence the bounds are valid for string representations). Our proofs of lower bounds will be given for string representations (and hence the bounds are valid for DAG representation).

3   TLP Is PSPACE Complete

Theorem 3.1. *The satisfiability problem for TLP is PSPACE complete.*

The PSPACE hardness immediately follows from PSPACE hardness for the satisfiability problem for $TL(\mathbf{U}, \mathbf{S})$ which is a subset of TLP. Below we prove that the satisfiability problem is in PSPACE.

A structure $\mathcal{M}$ is called *proper* if it is an expansion of $\langle \mathbb{R}^+, <, \mathbb{N}, Even, Odd \rangle$ by unary predicates. Here $\mathbb{N}$, $Even$, and Odd are the sets of natural, even and odd numbers; these sets will be denoted by predicate names N, E, O.

In contrast to the fact that TLP is much more expressive than QTL over the class of all real structures and over the class of finite variability structures [7, 9], we are going to show that they are expressively equivalent over the class of proper structures. Moreover, there is a polynomial meaning preserving (over the proper structures) translation from TLP to QTL.

Lemma 3.2.   *1. For every k there is a QTL formula $\Psi_k(X_1, \ldots, X_k, N, E, O)$ which is equivalent over the proper structures to $Pn_k(X_1, \ldots, X_k)$. Furthermore, the size of Ψ_k is less than $100k^2$.*

2. *For every k there is a QTL formula $\overleftarrow{\Psi}_k(X_1, \ldots, X_k, N, E, O)$ which is equivalent over the proper structures to $\overleftarrow{Pn}_k(X_1, \ldots, X_k)$. Furthermore, the size of Ψ_k is less than $100k^2$.*

Proof. (1) For $i \leq j \leq k$ define formulas $\phi_{i,j}$ as follows:

$$\phi_{i,i} := (\neg N)\mathbf{U}X_i$$

$$\phi_{i,i+l+1} := (\neg N)\mathbf{U}\big(X_i \wedge \neg N \wedge \phi_{i+1,i+l+1}\big).$$

It is clear that the size of $\phi_{i,j}$ is less than $10(j - i + 1)$ and that $\phi_{i,j}$ holds at t iff there are $t < t_i < t_{i+1} < \cdots < t_j \leq n$, where n is the smallest integer greater than t, such that $\wedge_{l=i}^{j}X_l(t_l)$. Similarly, there are formulas $\overleftarrow{\phi}_{i,j}$ such that $\overleftarrow{\phi}_{i,j}$ holds at t iff there are $t > t_j > \cdots > t_i > n$, where n is the largest integer less than t, and $\wedge_{l=i}^{j}X_l(t_l)$ holds.

The formula Ψ_k which is equivalent to Pn_k over the proper structures can be defined as the disjunction of the following formulas:

1. $\phi_{1,k}$ - "$\phi_{1,k}$ holds at t if there are $t < t_1 < t_2 < \cdots < t_k \leq n$, where n is the smallest integer greater than t, such that $\wedge_{l=1}^{k}X_l(t_l)$".
2. $\bigvee_{n=1}^{k-1}(\neg N)\mathbf{U}E \wedge \phi_{1,n} \wedge \Diamond_1((\neg N)\mathbf{S}E \wedge \overleftarrow{\phi}_{n+1,k})$ - this covers the case when t is in an interval $[2m - 1, 2m]$ for some integer m. The n-th disjunct says that $\wedge_{l=1}^{n}X_l(t_l)$ holds for $t < t_1 < \cdots < t_n \leq 2m$ and in the interval $(2m, 2m+1)$ there are $t_{n+1} < \cdots < t_k < t + 1$ such that $\wedge_{l=n+1}^{k}X_l(t_l)$ holds.
3. $\bigvee_{n=1}^{k-1}(\neg N)\mathbf{U}O \wedge \phi_{1,n} \wedge \Diamond_1((\neg)NS O \wedge \overleftarrow{\phi}_{n+1,k})$ - this is similar to the previous disjunct, but deals with the intervals $[2m, 2m+1]$, where m is an integer.

This proves (1). The proof of (2) is similar.   □

Corollary 3.3. *TLP and QTL are expressively equivalent over the class of proper structures. Furthermore, for every TLP formula φ there is a QTL formula ψ which is equivalent to φ over the proper structures and $|\psi|$ is $O(|\varphi|^2)$.*

Proof. We define a meaning preserving translation Tr from *TLP* to *QTL*.

1. For variables $Tr(X) := X$.
2. If op is a Boolean connective $Tr(\varphi_1 op\varphi_2) := Tr(\varphi_1)op Tr(\varphi_2)$.
3. For until and since modalities $Tr(\varphi_1\mathbf{U}\varphi_2) := \big(Tr(\varphi_1)\big)\mathbf{U}\big(Tr(\varphi_2)\big)$, and $Tr(\varphi_1\mathbf{S}\varphi_2) := \big(Tr(\varphi_1)\big)\mathbf{S}\big(Tr(\varphi_2)\big)$.
4. $Tr(Pn_k(\varphi_1, \ldots, \varphi_k))$ is obtained by substitution of $Tr(\varphi_i)$ instead of X_i in Ψ_k; Similarly, $Tr(\overleftarrow{Pn}_k(\varphi_1, \ldots, \varphi_k))$ is obtained by substitution of $Tr(\varphi_i)$ instead of X_i in $\overleftarrow{\Psi}_k$.

It is clear that φ is equivalent to $Tr(\varphi)$ over the proper structures. In Ψ_k and in $\overleftarrow{\Psi}_k$ every variable appears at most k times, therefore the size (of the DAG representation) of $Tr(\varphi)$ is $O(|\varphi|^2)$.   □

The next lemma shows that the set of proper structures is definable by a *QTL* formula.

Lemma 3.4. *There is a QTL formula PROPER(Y, Z, U) such that* $\mathbb{R}^+, t \models$ *PROPER(N, E, O) iff N is the set of natural numbers, and E and O are the sets of even and odd numbers.*

Proof. (1) Let Nat(Y) be the conjunction of the following formulas:

1. $\overleftarrow{\Box}$ *False* $\rightarrow Y$ - "Y holds at zero".
2. $always(Y \rightarrow \Box_1 \neg Y)$ - "If Y holds at t then $\neg Y$ holds at all points in $(t, t+1)$".
3. $always(\neg Y \rightarrow \Diamond_1 Y)$ - "If Y does not hold at t then Y holds at some point in $(t, t+1)$".

It is clear that the set of naturals is unique set that satisfies Nat(Y).

(2) Let EVEN(Y, Z) be the conjunction of

1. Nat(Y) - "Y is the set of the natural numbers"
2. $always(Z \rightarrow Y)$ - "Z is a subset of the natural numbers".
3. $\overleftarrow{\Box}$ *False* $\rightarrow Z$ - "Z holds at zero".
4. $always(Z \rightarrow (\neg Y)U(Y \wedge \neg Z)$ - " if Z holds at a natural number n then it does not hold at the next natural number".
5. $always(\neg Z \wedge Y \rightarrow (\neg Y)U(Y \wedge Z)$ - " if Z does not hold at a natural number n then it holds at the next natural number".

It is clear that EVEN(N, E) holds iff N is the set of naturals and E is the set even numbers.

PROPER(Y, Z, U) can be defined as EVEN$(Y, Z) \wedge always(U \leftrightarrow (Y \wedge \neg Z))$. $\quad\Box$

Finally, to complete the proof of Theorem 3.1, observe that a *TLP* formula φ is satisfiable iff φ is satisfiable over a proper structure iff *PROPER(N, E, O)* $\wedge \varphi$ is satisfiable iff the *QTL* formula *PROPER(N, E, O)* $\wedge \psi$ is satisfiable, where ψ is constructed as in Corollary 3.3. Since, the satisfiability problem for *QTL* is in PSPACE we obtain that the satisfiability problem for *TLP* is in PSPACE and this completes the proof of Theorem 3.1.

As a consequence we obtain the following corollary.

Corollary 3.5. *The satisfiability problem for TLC is PSPACE complete under the unary coding.*

Proof. Note that $C_k(X)$ is equivalent to $Pn_k(X, X, \ldots, X)$. The translation from *TLC* to *TLP* based on this equivalence is linear in the size of DAG representation. Hence, by Theorem 3.1, *TLC* is in PSPACE.

The PSPACE hardness immediately follows from PSPACE hardness for the satisfiability problem for $TL(\mathbf{U}, \mathbf{S})$ which is a subset of *TLC*. $\quad\Box$

4   EXPSPACE Completeness for *TLC*

Theorem 4.1. *The satisfiability problem for TLC is EXPSPACE complete under the binary coding.*

The upper bound immediately follows from Corollary 3.5. Below we prove that the satisfiability problem is EXPSPACE hard. For every Turing Machine M which works in space 2^n and every input x of length n we construct a *TLC* formula $Acc_{M,x}$ which is satisfiable iff M accepts x. Moreover $Acc_{M,x}$ is computable from M and x in polynomial time. This proves EXPSPACE hardness with respect to the polynomial reductions.

A one-tape deterministic Turing machine M is $(Q, \; q_0, \; q_{acc}, \; q_{rej}, \; \Gamma, b, \; \nu)$, where Q is the set of states, $q_0, q_{acc}, q_{rej} \in Q$ are initial, accepting and rejecting states, Γ is the alphabet, $b \in \Gamma$ is the blank symbol and $\nu : ((Q \setminus \{q_{acc}, q_{rej}\}) \times \Gamma) \rightarrow (Q \times \Gamma \times \{-1, 0, 1\})$ is the transition function. If the head is over a symbol σ and M is in a state q and $\nu(q, \sigma) = \langle q'\sigma', d \rangle$, then M replace σ by σ' changes its state to q' and moves d cells to the right (if $d = -1$ then it moves one cell left). There is no transition from the accepting and rejecting states.

A configuration (or an instantaneous description) is a member of $\Gamma^* Q \Gamma^+$ and represents a complete state of the Turing machine.

Let $\alpha = xq\sigma y$ be a configuration, where $\sigma \in \Gamma$, $x, y \in \Gamma^*$ and $q \in Q$. We define $tape(\alpha) = x\sigma y$, and $state(\alpha) = q$. It describes that for $i \leq |tape(\alpha)|$, the i-th cell of the tape contains the i-th symbol of $tape(\alpha)$ and all other cells contain blank; the control state is q and the head is over the symbol σ at the position $|x| + 1$.

We deal with Turing machines which use at most 2^n tape cells on inputs of length n. A configuration α is an n-configuration if $tape(\alpha)$ has 2^n symbols. Hence, a computation of M on an input $x = x_1 \ldots x_n$ of length n can be described by a sequence $\alpha_1 \alpha_2 \ldots$ of n-configurations, where $\alpha_1 = q_0 x_1 x_2 \ldots x_n b^{2^n - n}$ is the initial n-configuration for the input x.

For n-configurations α and β we write $\alpha \rightarrow_M \beta$ if β is obtained from α according to the transition function of M. Whenever M is clear from the context we will write $\alpha \rightarrow \beta$. Note that if $\alpha \rightarrow \beta$ then $tape(\alpha)$ and $tape(\beta)$ have the same length.

A *computation sequence* is a sequence of configurations $\alpha_1 \ldots \alpha_k$ for which $\alpha_i \rightarrow \alpha_{i+1}$, $1 \leq i < k$. A configuration β is *reachable* from a configuration α if there exists a computation sequence $\alpha_1 \ldots \alpha_k$ with $\alpha = \alpha_1$ and $\beta = \alpha_n$.

Acceptance conditions. A configuration α is an accepting (respectively, rejecting) configuration if $state(\alpha)$ is accepting (respectively, rejecting) state. A computation sequence $\alpha_1 \ldots \alpha_m$ is accepting (respectively, rejecting) if α_m is accepting (respectively, rejecting).

We are going to encode computations of M over proper structures, i.e., over expansions of $\langle \mathbb{R}^+, <, \mathbb{N}, Even, Odd \rangle$ by monadic predicates. All these predicates will have finite variability and the EXPSPACE lower bound holds both under the finite variability and arbitrary interpretations. We will denote by $\mathcal{M}$ an expansion of $\langle \mathbb{R}^+, <, \mathbb{N} \rangle$ by unary predicates.

From now on we fix a Turing machine M with the alphabet $\{0, 1, b\}$ of space complexity $\leq 2^n$. W.l.o.g. we assume that M never moves to the left of the first input cell. All definitions and constructions below will be for this M.

Let $\alpha_1, \ldots, \alpha_k$ be a sequence of n-configurations (not necessary a computation sequence). The i-th configuration α_i will be encoded on the interval $(i-1, i)$ with integer end-points as follows: The interval will contain 2^n points $\tau_{i,j}$ such that $i - 1 < \tau_{i,1} < \tau_{i,2} < \cdots < \tau_{i,2^n} < i$ and the predicate T will hold exactly at these points in the interval. All other predicates described below will be subsets of T. A_0, A_1 and A_b will partition T; $\tau_{i,j}$ will be in A_0 (respectively, in A_1 or in A_b) if the j-th tape symbol of α_i is 0 (respectively 1, or blank). Predicates S_q for $q \in Q$ are interpreted in $(i - 1, i)$ as follows: $\tau_{i,j} \in S_q$ if q is the state of α_i and the head is over the j-th tape symbol.

Definition 4.2. *Let $\mathcal{M}$ be an expansion of $\langle \mathbb{R}^+, <, \mathbb{N} \rangle$ by predicates T, A_0, A_1, A_b, S_q for $q \in Q$. For $i \in \mathbb{N}$, we say that the interval $[i, i + 1]$ of $\mathcal{M}$ represents a legal n-configuration if*

1. *it contain 2^n points in T and all these points are inside $(i, i + 1)$.*
2. *A_0, A_1 and A_b partition T.*
3. *$\cup_{q \in Q} S_q \subseteq T$ and there is exactly one $q \in Q$ such that $S_q \cap [i, i + 1]$ is a singleton and for all $q' \neq q$, the set $S_{q'} \cap [i, i + 1]$ is empty.*

The following lemma is easy. We use there $\overrightarrow{S}$ for the tuple of predicate names $\langle S_q : q \in Q \rangle$.

Lemma 4.3. *1. There is a TLC formula $\varphi_0(N, T, A_0, A_1, A_b, \overrightarrow{S})$ which holds in a structure $\mathcal{M}$ iff there is $l \in \mathbb{N}$ such that for every $i < l$ the interval $[i, i + 1]$ represents a legal n-configuration, the configuration represented in the interval $[l - 1, l]$ is accepting or rejecting, and no $\tau \geq l$ is in $T \cup A_0 \cup A_1 \cup A_b \cup \cup_{q \in Q} S_q$. Furthermore, the size of φ_0 is $O(n)$.*
2. *For every $x = x_1 \ldots x_n \in \{0, 1\}^n$, there is a formula $INIT_x$ which holds in a structure $\mathcal{M}$ iff the interval $[0, 1]$ represents the initial n-configuration σ_0 with input x. Furthermore, the size of $INIT_x$ is $O(n)$.*

Our next task is to specify that the configuration represented in an interval $[i, i + 1]$ is obtained from the configuration represented in $[i - 1, i]$ according to the transition function of $\mathcal{M}$. We have to express (1) the head is moved properly and update the symbols under the head correctly and (2) all other symbols are unchanged.

The next lemma shows that the cells numbered from 1 to 2^n can be succinctly described by their binary representations.

Lemma 4.4. *There is a formula $\varphi_1(N, T, B_1, \ldots, B_n)$ such that if for every $i \in \mathbb{N}$ the interval $(i, i + 1)$ contains at most 2^n points from T then $\mathcal{M}, 0 \models \varphi_1$ iff for every $i \in \mathbb{N}$ and $\tau \in (i, i + 1)$: if τ is the j-th occurrence of T in this interval then $\tau \in B_l$ iff the l-th bit of the binary representation of $j - 1$ is one. Furthermore, the size of φ_1 is $O(n^2)$.*

Proof. φ_1 is $always(\psi_1)$, where ψ_1 is the conjunction of

1. $\vee B_l \rightarrow (T \wedge \neg N)$ - B_l are subsets of $T \setminus \mathbb{N}$.

2. $N \wedge (\neg N)\mathbf{U}(T \wedge \neg N) \rightarrow ((\neg N)\mathbf{U}(T \wedge \bigwedge_{l=1}^{n} \neg B_l))$ - the first occurrence of T in $(i, i+1)$ has binary representation $00\ldots 0$, i.e., is not in $\cup B_l$.

3. $T \wedge \neg N \wedge (\neg N)\mathbf{U}(T \wedge \neg N) \rightarrow \bigvee_k \gamma_k$, where γ_k is

$$(\neg B_k \wedge \bigwedge_{m=k+1}^{n} B_m) \rightarrow$$
$$((\neg T)\mathbf{U}(T \wedge (B_k \wedge \bigwedge_{m=k+1}^{n} \neg B_m) \wedge \bigwedge_{m=1}^{k-1}(B_m \rightarrow (\neg T)\mathbf{U}(T \wedge B_m))$$

The formula expresses that if τ is not the last occurrence of T in $(i, i+1)$ and its binary code has 0 at k-th place and 1 at places $k+1, \ldots n$ then the code of the next occurrence of T has 1 at k-th place and zero at places $k+1, \ldots, m$ and both occurrences have the same bit in the binary code at places $1, \ldots, k-1$.   □

Now we can express that the head moves properly, state is updated correctly and the type symbol under the head is updated correctly.

Lemma 4.5. *There is a formula φ_2 such that if $\mathcal{M}$ represents a terminating sequence of configurations $\alpha_1, \ldots, \alpha_l$ and $\mathcal{M}, 0 \models \varphi_1$, then[1] $\mathcal{M}, 0 \models \varphi_2$ iff*

for every $i < l$ if in α_i the head is over symbol σ at position j and the state is q and $\nu(q, \sigma) = \langle q'.\sigma', d \rangle$ then the state in the α_{i+1} is q' the head is at the position $j + d$, the symbol at position j is σ'.

Furthermore, the size of φ_2 is $O(n^2)$.

Proof. Let $\nu(q, \sigma) = \langle q'.\sigma', 1 \rangle$ and let $S := \vee_{q_1 \in Q} S_{q_1}$
    Let $\psi_{q,\sigma}$ be the conjunction of

1. the heads moved one position to the right: $S_q \wedge A_\sigma \rightarrow \bigvee_{k=1}^{n} \gamma'_k$ where γ'_k is obtained from γ_k after substitution of S instead T (see proof of Lemma 4.4).
2. The state and the symbols under the head were updated correctly: $S_q \wedge A_\sigma \rightarrow (\neg \vee_{q_1 \in Q} S_{q_1})\mathbf{U}(S_{q'} \wedge (\neg T)\mathbf{S}A_{\sigma'})$

When $\nu(q, \sigma) = \langle q'.\sigma', 0 \rangle$ and $\nu(q, \sigma) = \langle q'.\sigma', -1 \rangle$ the formula $\psi_{q,\sigma}$ is defined similarly.
    The desirable formula φ_2 can be defined as $always(\bigwedge_{q \notin \{q_a, q_r\}} \bigwedge_\sigma \psi_{q,\sigma})$.   □

The creative part of our proof is to show how to express succinctly that the symbols not under the head are unchanged. In order to do this we introduce the following notion.

Assume that $\mathcal{M}$ represent a terminating sequence of configuration $\alpha_1, \ldots, \alpha_l$. Recall that $\tau_{i,j} \in \mathbb{R}^+$ is the j-th occurrence of T in the interval $(i-1, i)$. We denote by $tape(\alpha_i)[j]$ the j-th symbol of $tape(\alpha_i)$. We say that $\mathcal{M}$ is *well-timed* if for all $i < l$ and $j \leq 2^n$ and some positive $\epsilon_{i,j}, \delta_{i,j}$:

$$\tau_{i+1,j} = \begin{cases} 1 + \tau_{i,j} + \epsilon_{i,j} & \text{if } tape(\alpha_i)[j] \text{ is } 0 \\ 1 + \tau_{i,j} - \delta_{i,j} & \text{if } tape(\alpha_i)[j] \text{ is } 1 \\ 1 + \tau_{i,j} & \text{if } tape(\alpha_i)[j] \text{ is blank} \end{cases} \qquad (Eq. \ WT)$$

First observe

---

[1] Until the end of this section φ_1 is the formula from Lemma 4.3. The scope of the definition of φ_2 from this lemma and formulas φ_3 and φ_4 from the following lemmas extends to the end of this section.

Lemma 4.6. *if* $\alpha_1 \ldots \alpha_l$, *is a terminating sequence of n-configuration, then there is a well-timed $\mathcal{M}$ which represents this sequence.*

Proof. Just choose $\tau_{1,j}$ as $\frac{j}{2^n+1}$ (for $j = 1, \ldots 2^n$) and choose $\epsilon_{i,j} = \delta_{i,j}$ as $\frac{1}{3l \times (2^n+1)}$. Define $\tau_{i+1,j}$ as in *Eq. WT*. Our choice of $\epsilon_{i,j}, \delta_{i,j}$ ensures that $i-1 < \tau_{i,1} < \tau_{i,2} < \cdots < \tau_{i,2^n} < i$ for all $i \leq l$.   □

Lemma 4.7. *There is a formula φ_3 such that $\mathcal{M} \models \varphi_3$ iff $\mathcal{M}$ is a well-timed sequence of n-configurations. Furthermore, the size of φ_3 is $O(n)$.*

Proof. Let ψ be the conjunction of the following formulas

1. $A_b \rightarrow (C_{2^n-1}(T) \wedge Llim(C_{2^n-1}(T)) \wedge Rlim(C_{2^n-1}(T)))$
2. $A_1 \rightarrow (C_{2^n}(T) \wedge Llim(C_{2^n+1}(T)) \wedge Rlim(C_{2^n}(T)))$
3. $A_0 \rightarrow (C_{2^n-1}(T) \wedge Llim(C_{2^n}(T)) \wedge Rlim(C_{2^n-1}(T)))$

(Recall that $Llim(X)$ (respectively, $Rlim(X)$) holds at t iff t is a left limit (respectively, a right limit of X), see Sect. 2.2)

Let $\mathcal{M}'$ represents an n-configuration α_i in $[i.i+1]$ and has 2^n occurrences of T in $[i+1, i+2]$ all the occurrences inside $(i+1, i+2)$. The crucial observation is that *Eq. WT* holds iff $\mathcal{M}', \tau \models \psi$ for every $\tau \in [i, i+1]$.

From ψ it is easy to construct φ_3. Just express that φ_0 holds, and ψ holds at all points except the points of the interval where the last configuration is represented.   □

We are now ready to specify that if a symbols is not under the head then in the next configuration it will be unchanged.

Lemma 4.8. *There is a formula φ_4 such that if $\mathcal{M}$ represents a well-timed terminating sequence of n-configurations $\alpha_1, \ldots, \alpha_l$ and $\mathcal{M}, 0 \models \varphi_1$, then $\mathcal{M}, 0 \models \varphi_4$ iff*

> *for every $i < l$ if in α_i the head is at position j, then $tape(\alpha_i)[m] = tape(\alpha_{i+1})[m]$ for every $m \neq j$.*

Furthermore, the size of φ_4 is $O(n)$.

Proof. Let ψ be the conjunction of the following formulas

1. $A_b \rightarrow (\overleftarrow{C}_{2^n-1}(T) \wedge Llim(\overleftarrow{C}_{2^n-1}(T)) \wedge Rlim(\overleftarrow{C}_{2^n-1}(T)))$
2. $A_1 \rightarrow (\overleftarrow{C}_{2^n}(T) \wedge Rlim(\overleftarrow{C}_{2^n+1}(T)) \wedge Llim(\overleftarrow{C}_{2^n}(T)))$
3. $A_0 \rightarrow (\overleftarrow{C}_{2^n-1}(T) \wedge Rlim(\overleftarrow{C}_{2^n}(T)) \wedge Llim(\overleftarrow{C}_{2^n-1}(T)))$

Assume that $\mathcal{M}$ is well-timed. Hence, *Eq. WT* holds. Then ψ holds at $\tau_{i+1,m}$ iff $tape(\alpha_i)[m] = tape(\alpha_{i+1})[m]$.

The head is at position m in σ_i iff at $\tau_{i+1,m}$ the following formula γ holds:

$$\gamma := \bigwedge_k (B_k \leftrightarrow ((\neg N)\mathbf{S}(N \wedge ((\neg N)\mathbf{S}(\vee_{q \in Q} S_q \wedge B_k)))))$$

Indeed, this formula says that B_k holds at τ iff in the previous interval B_k holds at the (unique) position where $\bigvee_{q \in Q} S_q$ holds (this is the position of the head in the configuration σ_i). Hence, $T \to ((\neg\gamma) \to \psi)$ holds in every point of the interval $[i+1, i+2]$ iff $tape(\alpha_i)[m] = tape(\alpha_{i+1})[m]$ for every m different from the head position in σ_i.

Finally, φ_4 should express that $T \to ((\neg\gamma) \to \psi)$ holds at all points except the points of the interval $[0,1]$. Note that $t \in [0,1]$ iff $\overleftarrow{\Diamond}(N \wedge \overleftarrow{\Diamond} N)$ holds at t. Hence, φ_4 can be defined as follows: $\varphi_4 := (\overleftarrow{\Diamond}(N \wedge \overleftarrow{\Diamond} N)) \to (T \to ((\neg\gamma) \to \psi))$ □

From Lemmas 4.3, 4.4, 4.5, 4.7, 4.8 we obtain:

Lemma 4.9. *For every $x \in \{0,1\}^n$ let $Acc_{M,x}$ be $INIT_x \wedge \varphi_0 \wedge \varphi_1 \wedge \varphi_2 \wedge \varphi_3 \wedge \varphi_4 \wedge \Diamond q_{acc}$. Then $\mathcal{M}, 0 \models Acc_{M,x}$ iff $\mathcal{M}$ represents a well-timed accepting computation sequence of M on x.*

The size $Acc_{M,x}$ is polynomial in the size of x, therefore this lemma together with Lemma 4.6 imply EXPSPACE hardness of the satisfiability problem for *TLC*.

5   Further Results

Often in the literature the temporal logics with modalities $\Diamond_{(m,n)}(X)$ for integers $m < n$ are considered. These modalities are defined by the truth tables:

$$\Diamond_{(m,n)}(X): \qquad \exists t((t_0 + m < t < t_0 + n) \wedge X(t))$$

The logic *QTLI* in addition to modalities **U** and **S** has infinity many modalities $\Diamond_{(m,n)}(X)$ for all integers $m < n$. The logic $QTLI_0$ is a fragment of *QTLI*; it has in addition to modalities **U** and **S** the modalities $\Diamond_{(0,n)}(X)$, $\Diamond_{(-n,0)}(X)$ for all natural n.

The logics *QTL*, $QTLI_0$ and *QTLI* have the same expressive power (under arbitrary interpretations) and are equivalent to the logic *MITL* introduced in [1]. However, there is an exponential succinctness gap (under the binary coding) between *QTL* and $QTLI_0$ and between $QTLI_0$ and *QTLI*. The next theorem characterize the complexity of these logics [1].

Theorem 5.1.   *1. The satisfiability problem for $QTLI_0$ is PSPACE complete under the binary coding.*
2. The satisfiability problem for QTLI is EXPSPACE complete under the binary coding.

The theorem was proved for the finite variability interpretation in [1] and for arbitrary interpretation in [8, 15].

In this section we consider temporal logics with the modalities $C_k^{(n,m)}(X)$ and $Pn_k^{(m,n)}(X_1, \ldots, X_k)$ for the integers $m < n$. These modalities are defined by the truth tables with free variable t_0:

$$Pn_k^{(m,n)}(X_1,\dots,X_k): \quad \exists t_1\dots\exists t_k(t_0+m \ll t_1 < \cdots < t_k < t_0+n \wedge \bigwedge_{i=1}^{k} X_i(t_i))$$

$$C_k^{(m,n)}(X): \qquad \exists t_1\dots\exists t_k(t_0+m < t_1 < \cdots < t_k < t_0+n \wedge \bigwedge_{i=1}^{k} X(t_i))$$

Note that Pn_k is equivalent to $Pn_k^{(0,1)}$ and C_k is equivalent to $C_k^{(0,1)}$

We consider the following temporal logics:

$$TLPI := TL(\mathbf{U}, \mathbf{S}, \{Pn_k^{(m,n)} : m < n\})$$

$$TLPI_0 := TL(\mathbf{U}, \mathbf{S}, \{Pn_k^{(0,n)}, Pn_k^{(-n,0)} : 0 < n\})$$

$$TLCI := TL(\mathbf{U}, \mathbf{S}, \{C_k^{(m,n)} : m < n\})$$

$$TLCI_0 := TL(\mathbf{U}, \mathbf{S}, \{C_k^{(0,n)}, C_k^{(-n,0)} : 0 < n\})$$

All these logics are expressively equivalent to TLC [11]. We investigate the complexity of the satisfiability problems for these logics under the unary and binary codings. Under the unary (respectively, binary) coding all the numbers which occur in the superscripts and subscripts of these modalities are coded in unary (respectively, in binary). The full version of this paper contains proofs of the results summarized in the following table:

Table 1. The complexity of the satisfiability problem

Logic	unary coding	binary coding
$TLPI_0$	PSPACE complete	PSPACE complete
$TLPI$	PSPACE complete	EXPSPACE complete
$TLCI_0$	PSPACE complete	EXPSPACE complete
$TLCI$	PSPACE complete	EXPSPACE complete

We conclude by a comparison of the expressive power of TLC and the expressive power of temporal logics with finitely many modalities.

Let $B = \{O_1^{l_1}, O_2^{l_2}, \dots\}$ be a finite set of modality names, and assume that every modality in B has a truth table definable in the monadic second-order logic of order with $\lambda x.x + 1$ function (we denote this logic by MLO^{+1}). MLO^{+1} is a very expressive (and undecidable) logic, and most of the modalities considered in the literature can be easily formalized in it. We proved in [12] that there is n (which depends on B) such that C_n is not expressible over the reals by a $TL(B)$ formulas. Hence, there is no temporal logic L which is at least as expressive as TLC over the reals, which has a finite set of modalities with truth tables in MLO^{+1}.

Our conjecture was that this result can be extended to the non-negative real line. However, the results of Sect. 3 refute this conjecture.

Indeed, let L be the temporal logic with the modalities $\mathbf{U}$, $\mathbf{S}$, $\Diamond_1 \overleftarrow{\Diamond}_1$, **nat** and **even**, where **nat** and **even** are zero-arity modalities interpreted as the sets of natural and even numbers respectively Corollary 3.3 shows that *TLP*, *TLC* and *QTL* are expressively equivalent over the class of proper structures, i.e., over the expansions of $\langle \mathbb{R}^+, <, \mathbb{N}, Even, Odd \rangle$ by unary predicates.

Hence, *L* is at least as expressive (over the class of non-negative real structures) as *TLC*. Over the non-negative reals, the modalities **nat** and **even** are easily definable by truth tables in MLO^{+1} (see Lemma 3.4). This refutes the conjecture.

Similarly to Corollary 3.3 one can show that *TLP*, *TLC* and *QTL* are expressively equivalent over the class of the expansions of $\langle \mathbb{R}, <, \mathbb{Z}, Even \rangle$ by unary predicates, where $\mathbb{Z}$ and *Even* are the sets of integers and even numbers. Hence, *QTL* with two additional zero-arity modalities for the set of integers and for the set of even numbers is at least as expressive as *TLC*. However, over the reals, these two modalities are not definable by truth tables in MLO^{+1}.

Acknowledgments

I am grateful to Yoram Hirshfeld for his insightful comments.

References

1. Alur, R., Feder, T., Henzinger, T.A.: The Benefits of Relaxing Punctuality. Journal of the ACM 43, 116–146 (1996)
2. Alur, R., Henzinger, T.A.: Logics and Models of Real Time: a survey. In: Huizing, C., de Bakker, J.W., Rozenberg, G., de Roever, W.-P. (eds.) REX 1991. LNCS, vol. 600, pp. 74–106. Springer, Heidelberg (1992)
3. Barringer, H., Barringer, R., Kuiper, R., Pnueli, A.: A really abstract concurrent model and its temporal logic. In: Proceedings of the 13th annual symposium on principles of programing languages, pp. 173–183 (1986)
4. Gabbay, D.M., Hodkinson, I., Reynolds, M.: Temporal Logics, vol. 1. Clarendon Press, Oxford (1994)
5. Henzinger, T.A.: It's about time: real-time logics reviewed. In: Sangiorgi, D., de Simone, R. (eds.) CONCUR 1998. LNCS, vol. 1466, pp. 439–454. Springer, Heidelberg (1998)
6. Henzinger, T.H., Raskin, J.F., Schobbens, P.Y.: The regular real time languages. In: Larsen, K.G., Skyum, S., Winskel, G. (eds.) ICALP 1998. LNCS, vol. 1443, pp. 580–591. Springer, Heidelberg (1998)
7. Hirshfeld, Y., Rabinovich, A.: A Framework for Decidable Metrical Logics. In: Wiedermann, J., Van Emde Boas, P., Nielsen, M. (eds.) ICALP 1999. LNCS, vol. 1644, pp. 422–432. Springer, Heidelberg (1999)
8. Hirshfeld, Y., Rabinovich, A.: Quantitative Temporal Logic. In: Flum, J., Rodríguez-Artalejo, M. (eds.) CSL 1999. LNCS, vol. 1683, pp. 172–187. Springer, Heidelberg (1999)
9. Hirshfeld, Y., Rabinovich, A.: Logics for Real Time: Decidability and Complexity. Fundam. Inform. 62(1), 1–28 (2004)
10. Hirshfeld, Y., Rabinovich, A.: Timer formulas and decidable metric temporal logic. Information and Computation 198(2), 148–178 (2005)

11. Hirshfeld, Y., Rabinovich, A.: An Expressive Temporal Logic for Real Time. In: Královič, R., Urzyczyn, P. (eds.) MFCS 2006. LNCS, vol. 4162, pp. 492–504. Springer, Heidelberg (2006)
12. Hirshfeld, Y., Rabinovich, A.: Expressiveness of Metric modalities for continuous time Logical methods in computer science 3(1) (2007)
13. Kamp, H.: Tense Logic and the Theory of Linear Order. Ph.D. thesis, University of California L.A (1968)
14. Manna, Z., Pnueli, A.: Models for reactivity. Acta informatica 30, 609–678 (1993)
15. Lutz, C., Walther, D., Wolter, F.: Quantitative temporal logics over the reals: PSPACE and below. Information and Computation 205(1), 99–123 (2007)
16. Reynolds, M.: The complexity of the temporal logic with until over general linear time (manuscript, 1999)
17. Wilke, T.: Specifying Time State Sequences in Powerful Decidable Logics and Time Automata. In: Langmaack, H., de Roever, W.-P., Vytopil, J. (eds.) FTRTFT 1994 and ProCoS 1994. LNCS, vol. 863, pp. 694–715. Springer, Heidelberg (1994)

MTL with Bounded Variability: Decidability and Complexity*

Carlo A. Furia and Matteo Rossi

Dipartimento di Elettronica e Informazione, Politecnico di Milano, Italy
{furia,rossi}@elet.polimi.it
http://home.dei.polimi.it/lastname/

Abstract. This paper investigates the properties of Metric Temporal Logic (MTL) over models in which time is dense but phenomena are constrained to have *bounded variability*. Contrary to the case of generic dense-time behaviors, MTL is proved to be fully decidable over models with bounded variability, if the variability bound is given. In these decidable cases, MTL complexity is shown to match that of simpler decidable logics such as MITL. On the contrary, MTL is undecidable if all behaviors with variability bounded by some generic constant are considered, but with an undecidability degree that is lower than in the case of generic behaviors.

1 Introduction

The designer of formal notations faces a perennial trade-off between expressiveness and complexity: on the one hand notations with high expressive power allow users to formalize complex behaviors with naturalness; on the other hand expressiveness usually comes with a significant price to pay in terms of complexity of the verification problem. This results in a continual search for the "best" compromise between these diverging features.

A paradigmatic instance of this general problem is the case of real-time temporal logics. Experience with real-time concurrent systems suggests that dense (or continuous) sets are a natural and effective modeling choice for the time domain. Also, Metric Temporal Logic (MTL) is often regarded as a suitable and natural extension of "classical" Temporal Logic to deal with real-time requirements. However, MTL is well-known to be undecidable over dense time domains [2].[1] In the literature, two main compromises have been adopted to overcome this impasse. One consists in the semantic accommodation of adopting the coarser discrete — rather than dense — time [2]. The other adopts the syntactic concession of restricting MTL formulas to a subset known as MITL [1]. More recently other syntactic adjustments have been studied [4].

In this paper we investigate other semantic compromises, in particular the use of models where time is dense but events are constrained to have only a *bounded variability*, i.e., their frequency of occurrence over time is bounded by some finite constant. We

---

* Work partially supported by the MIUR FIRB Projects: ArtDeco and "Applicazioni della Teoria degli Automi all'Analisi, Compilazione e Verifica di Software Critico e in Tempo Reale".
[1] With a few partial exceptions that will be discussed in the following.

F. Cassez and C. Jard (Eds.): FORMATS 2008, LNCS 5215, pp. 109–123, 2008.

show that MTL is fully decidable over such behaviors when the maximum variability rate is fixed *a priori*; in such cases we are also able to show that the complexity of decidability is the same as for the less expressive logic MITL, i.e., complete for **EXPSPACE**. On the contrary, if all behaviors with bounded variability are considered together, MTL becomes undecidable, but with a "lesser degree" of undecidability compared to the case of unconstrained behaviors. Our decidability results are based on the possibility of expressing of certain features of bounded variability in the expressive decidable temporal logics of [11]. Although the focus of this paper is on the more expressive *behavior* semantic model (also called signal, timed interval sequence, or trajectory) which is more expressive [5] but requires more sophisticated techniques, one can show that the same decidability and complexity results hold in the timed word case as well (where they were already partly implied by the results in [17]). For lack of space, several proofs and details are omitted from the paper but can be found in [9].

Related work. The complexity, decidability, and expressiveness of MTL over standard discrete and dense time models are well-known since the seminal work of Alur and Henzinger [2]. In [2] MTL is shown to be decidable over discrete time, with an **EXPSPACE**-complete decidability problem, and undecidable over dense time, with a Σ_1^1-complete decidability problem. These results hold regardless of whether a timed word or timed signal time model is assumed, with a peculiar, but significant exception: in a recent, unexpected, result, Ouaknine and Worrell showed that MTL is fully decidable over *finite* dense-timed words, if only future modalities are considered [14]. The practical usefulness of this result is unfortunately plagued by the prohibitively high nonprimitive-recursive complexity of the corresponding decidability problem.

In another very influential paper [1], Alur, Feder, and Henzinger showed that disallowing the expression of punctual (i.e., exact) time distances in MTL formulas renders the language fully decidable over dense time models. The corresponding MTL subset is called MITL and has an **EXPSPACE**-complete decidability problem. The decision procedure in [1] is based on a complex translation into timed automata; similar, but simpler, automata-based techniques have been studied by Maler et al. [13].

Hirshfeld and Rabinovich have reconsidered the work on MITL from a broader, more foundational, perspective built upon the standard timed behavior model [11]. Besides providing simpler decision procedures and proofs for a real-time temporal logic with the same expressive power as MITL, they have probed to what extent MITL can be made more expressive without giving up decidability. This lead to the introduction of the very expressive, yet decidable, monadic logic Q2MLO, and of the corresponding TLC temporal logic. In a nice analogy with classical results on linear temporal logic [10], TLC is expressively complete for all of Q2MLO (hence it subsumes MITL), and it has a **PSPACE**-complete decidability problem (or **EXPSPACE**-complete assuming a succinct encoding of constants used in formulas as it is customary in the majority of MITL literature) [16].

It is clear that TLC and MTL have incomparable expressive power; in particular the former disallows the expression of exact time distances. However, Bouyer et al. [4] have shown that it is possible to devise significantly expressive MTL fragments that are fully decidable (with **EXPSPACE** complexity) even if punctuality requirements are allowed to some extent. Also, for brevity we omit the summary of other, related complexity results for decidable real-time temporal logics over dense time domains recently developed by Lutz et al. [12].

Dense-timed words where the maximum number of events in a unit interval is fixed have been introduced by Wilke in [17]. More precisely, timed words over Σ where there are at most k positions over any unit interval are denoted by $\mathrm{TSS}_k(\Sigma)$ and called words of *bounded variability* k; in the following we introduce the class $T\Sigma T^\omega_{k,1}$ that can be seen to correspond to $\mathrm{TSS}_k(\Sigma)$. Wilke showed that, for every k, the monadic logic of distances $\mathcal{L}\mathrm{d}(\Sigma)$ is fully decidable over $\mathrm{TSS}_k(\Sigma)$. Wilke's results are based on translation into the monadic fragment $\overleftrightarrow{\mathcal{L}\mathrm{d}}(\Sigma)$, which ultimately corresponds to timed automata; also, they subsume the decidability of MTL over the same models. In this paper, we extend and generalize Wilke's result, and we discuss the complexity of the corresponding models.

The corresponding notion of dense-time *behaviors* with bounded variability has been introduced by Fränzle in [6] (where they are called *trajectories of n-bounded variability*). Fränzle shows that full Duration Calculus is undecidable even over such restricted behaviors, while some syntactic subsets of it become decidable; the decidability proofs exploit a characterization of certain behaviors with bounded variability by means of timed regular expressions.

In previous work [8,7], we introduced the notion of non-Berkeleyness:[2] a dense-time behavior is non-Berkeley for some $\delta > 0$ if δ time units elapse between any two consecutive state transitions. In this paper we show that this notion is similar, but different, than the notion of bounded variability; we also introduce a corresponding definition of non-Berkeleyness for timed words.

2 Words and Behaviors: A Semantic Zoo

The symbols $\mathbb{Z}$, $\mathbb{Q}$, and $\mathbb{R}$ denote the sets of integer, rational, and real numbers, respectively. For a set $\$$, $\$_{\sim c}$ with $\sim$ one of $<, \leq, >, \geq$ and $c \in \$$ denotes the subset $\{s \in \$ \mid s \sim c\} \subseteq \$$; for instance $\mathbb{Z}_{\geq 0} = \mathbb{N}$ denotes the set of nonnegative integers (i.e., naturals). An *interval* I of a set $\$$ is a convex subset $\langle l, u \rangle$ of $\$$ with $l, u \in \$$, $\langle$ one of $(, [, $ and $\rangle$ one of $),]$. An interval is *empty* iff it contains no points; an interval is *punctual* (or singular) iff $l = u$ and the interval is closed (i.e., it contains exactly one point). The *length* of an interval is given by $|I| = \max(u - l, 0)$. $-I$ denotes the interval $\langle -u, -l \rangle$, and $I \oplus t = t \oplus I$ denotes the interval $\langle t + l, t + u \rangle$, for any $t \in \$$. Correspondingly, we define the *length* $|\mathbf{x}|$ of $\mathbf{x}$ as $|\mathbf{x}| = n$.

2.1 Words and Behaviors

The two most popular models of real-time behavior [2,3] are the *timed word* (also called timed state sequence [17]) and the *timed behavior* (also called Boolean signal [13], timed interval sequence [1], or trajectory [6]). Let $\mathbb{T}$ be a time domain; in this paper we are interested in dense time domains, and in particular $\mathbb{R}$ and its mono-infinite subset $\mathbb{R}_{\geq 0}$. Also, let Σ be a set of atomic propositions.

---

[2] The name is an analogy with non-Zenoness [7].

Behaviors. A *(timed) behavior* over timed domain $\mathbb{T}$ and alphabet Σ is a function $b : \mathbb{T} \to 2^{\Sigma}$ which maps every time instant $t \in \mathbb{T}$ to the set of propositions $b(t) \in 2^{\Sigma}$ that hold at t. The set of all behaviors over time domain $\mathbb{T}$ and alphabet Σ is denoted by $\overline{\mathcal{B}\Sigma\mathbb{T}}$. For a behavior b let $\tau(b)$ denote the ordered (multi)set of its discontinuity points, i.e., $\tau(b) = \{x \in \mathbb{T} \mid b(x) \neq \lim_{t \to x^-} b(t) \vee b(x) \neq \lim_{t \to x^+} b(t)\}$, where each point that is both a right- and a left-discontinuity appears twice in $\tau(b)$. If $\tau(b)$ is discrete, we can represent it as an ordered sequence (possibly unbounded to $\pm\infty$); it will be clear from the context whether we are treating $\tau(b)$ as a sequence or as a set. Elements in $\tau(b)$ are called the *change* (or *transition*) instants of b. $\tau(b)$ can be unbounded to $\pm\infty$ only if $\mathbb{T}$ has the same property.

Words. An *infinite (timed) word* over time domain $\mathbb{T}$ and alphabet Σ is a sequence $(\Sigma \times \mathbb{T})^{\omega} \ni (\boldsymbol{\sigma}, \mathbf{t}) = (\sigma_0, t_0)(\sigma_1, t_1) \cdots$ such that: (1) for all $k \in \mathbb{N} : \sigma_k \in 2^{\Sigma}$, and (2) the sequence $\mathbf{t}$ of timestamps is strictly monotonically increasing. Every element (σ_n, t_n) in a word denotes that the propositions in the set σ_n hold at time t_n. The set of all infinite timed words over time domain $\mathbb{T}$ and alphabet Σ is denoted by $\overline{\mathcal{T}\Sigma\mathbb{T}^{\omega}}$. *Finite timed words* over time domain $\mathbb{T}$ and alphabet Σ are defined similarly as finite sequences in $(\Sigma \times \mathbb{T})^*$ and collectively denoted by $\mathcal{T}\Sigma\mathbb{T}^*$. Also, the set of all finite timed words of *length up to* n is denoted by $\mathcal{T}\Sigma\mathbb{T}^n = \{(\boldsymbol{\sigma}, \mathbf{t}) \in \mathcal{T}\Sigma\mathbb{T}^* \mid |\mathbf{t}| \leq n\}$.

2.2 Finite Variability and Non-zenoness

Since one is typically interested only in behaviors that represent physically meaningful behaviors, it is common to assume some regularity requirements on words and behaviors. In particular, it is customary to assume *non-Zenoness*, also called *finite variability* [11].

A behavior $b \in \overline{\mathcal{B}\Sigma\mathbb{T}}$ is non-Zeno iff $\tau(b)$ has no accumulation points; non-Zeno behaviors are denoted by $\mathcal{B}\Sigma\mathbb{T}$. It should be clear that every non-Zeno behavior can be represented through a canonical countable sequence of adjacent intervals of $\mathbb{T}$ such that b is constant on every such interval. Namely, for $b \in \mathcal{B}\Sigma\mathbb{T}$, $\iota(b)$ is an ordered sequence of intervals $\iota(b) = \{I_i = \langle^i l_i, u_i \rangle^i \mid i \in \mathbb{I}\}$ such that: (1) $\mathbb{I}$ is an interval of $\mathbb{Z}$ with cardinality $|\tau(b)| + 1$ (in particular, $\mathbb{I}$ is finite iff $\tau(b)$ is finite, otherwise $\mathbb{I}$ is denumerable); (2) the intervals in $\iota(b)$ form a partition of $\mathbb{T}$; (3) for all $i \in \mathbb{I}$ we have $\tau_i = u_i = l_{i+1}$; (4) for all $i \in \mathbb{I}$, for all $t_1, t_2 \in I_i$ we have $b(t_1) = b(t_2)$. Note that $\iota(b)$ is unique for any fixed $\tau(b)$ or, in other words, is unique up to translations of interval indices. Transitions at instants τ_i corresponding to singular intervals I_i are called *pointwise* (or *punctual*) transitions.

An *infinite* word $w \in \overline{\mathcal{T}\Sigma\mathbb{T}^{\omega}}$ is non-Zeno iff the sequence $\mathbf{t}$ of timestamps is diverging; non-Zeno infinite timed words are denoted by $\mathcal{T}\Sigma\mathbb{T}^{\omega}$. On the other hand, every *finite* timed word is non-Zeno.

2.3 Bounded Variability and Non-berkeleyness

In this paper we investigate behavior and words subject to regularity requirements that are stricter than non-Zenoness. In this section we introduce the two closely related — albeit different — notions of *bounded variability* and *non-Berkeleyness*.

Bounded variability. A *behavior* $b \in \mathcal{BST}$ has *variability bounded* by k, δ for $k \in \mathbb{N}_{>0}, \delta \in \mathbb{R}_{>0}$ iff it has at most k transition points over every open interval of size δ. The set of all behaviors in $\mathcal{BST}$ with variability bounded by k, δ is denoted by $\mathcal{BST}_{k,\delta}$. Formally, $\mathcal{BST}_{k,\delta} = \{b \in \mathcal{BST} \mid \forall t \in \mathbb{T} : |[t, t+\delta] \cap \tau(b)| \leq k\}$.

Similarly, a *word* $w \in \mathcal{TST}^\omega \cup \mathcal{TST}^*$ has *variability bounded* by k, δ iff for every closed interval of size δ there are at most k elements in w whose timestamps are within the interval. The set of all infinite (resp. finite) words with variability bounded by k, δ is denoted by $\mathcal{TST}^\omega_{k,\delta}$ (resp. $\mathcal{TST}^*_{k,\delta}$). With the notation introduced above, $\mathcal{TST}^\omega_{k,\delta} = \{w \in \mathcal{TST}^\omega \mid \forall i \in \mathbb{N} : t_{i+k} - t_i \geq \delta\}$ and $\mathcal{TST}^*_{k,\delta} = \{w \in \mathcal{TST}^\omega \mid \forall 0 \leq i \leq |w| - (k+1) : t_{i+k} - t_i \geq \delta\}$.

We also introduce the set of all behaviors (resp. infinite words, finite words) that are of *bounded variability for some k, δ* as $\mathcal{BST}_{\exists k \exists \delta} = \bigcup_{\substack{k \in \mathbb{N}_{>0} \\ \delta \in \mathbb{R}_{>0}}} \mathcal{BST}_{k,\delta}$ (resp. $\mathcal{TST}^\omega_{\exists k \exists \delta} = \bigcup_{\substack{k \in \mathbb{N}_{>0} \\ \delta \in \mathbb{R}_{>0}}} \mathcal{TST}^\omega_{k,\delta}, \mathcal{TST}^*_{\exists k \exists \delta} = \bigcup_{\substack{k \in \mathbb{N}_{>0} \\ \delta \in \mathbb{R}_{>0}}} \mathcal{TST}^*_{k,\delta})$.

Non-Berkeleyness. A *behavior* $b \in \mathcal{BST}$ is *non-Berkeley* for $\delta \in \mathbb{R}_{>0}$ iff every maximal constancy interval contains a closed interval of size δ. The set of all behaviors in $\mathcal{BST}$ that are non-Berkeley for δ is denoted by $\mathcal{BST}_\delta$; with the notation introduced above $\mathcal{BST}_\delta = \{b \in \mathcal{BST} \mid \forall I \in \iota(b) : \exists t \in I : [t, t+\delta] \subseteq I\}$.

Similarly, the set of infinite (resp. finite) *words* that are *non-Berkeley* for $\delta \in \mathbb{R}_{>0}$ is denoted by $\mathcal{TST}^\omega_\delta$ (resp. $\mathcal{TST}^*_\delta$) and is defined as $\mathcal{TST}^\omega_\delta = \{w \in \mathcal{TST}^\omega \mid \forall i \in \mathbb{N} : t_{i+1} - t_i \geq \delta\}$ (resp. $\mathcal{TST}^*_\delta = \{w \in \mathcal{TST}^* \mid \forall 0 \leq i \leq |w| - 2 : t_{i+1} - t_i \geq \delta\}$).

We also introduce the set of all behaviors (resp. infinite words, finite words) that are *non-Berkeley for some $\delta \in \mathbb{R}_{>0}$* as $\mathcal{BST}_{\exists \delta} = \bigcup_{\delta \in \mathbb{R}_{>0}} \mathcal{BST}_\delta$ (resp. $\mathcal{TST}^\omega_{\exists \delta} = \bigcup_{\delta \in \mathbb{R}_{>0}} \mathcal{TST}^\omega_\delta, \mathcal{TST}^*_{\exists \delta} = \bigcup_{\delta \in \mathbb{R}_{>0}} \mathcal{TST}^*_\delta)$.

Relations among classes. It is apparent that some of the various classes of behaviors that we introduced above are closely related. More precisely, the following inclusion relations hold.

Proposition 1. *For all $\delta' > \delta > 0$ and $k > k' \geq 2$:*

$$\mathcal{BST}_{1,\delta'} \subset \mathcal{BST}_{\delta'} \subset \mathcal{BST}_\delta \subset \mathcal{BST}_{k',\delta} \subset \mathcal{BST}_{k,\delta} \subset \mathcal{BST}_{\exists k \exists \delta} \subset \mathcal{BST} \quad (1)$$

$$\mathcal{BST}_\delta \subset \mathcal{BST}_{\exists \delta} \subset \mathcal{BST}_{\exists k \exists \delta} \subset \mathcal{BST} \quad (2)$$

$$\mathcal{BST}_{\exists \delta} \text{ and } \mathcal{BST}_{k',\delta} \text{ are incomparable} \quad (3)$$

$$\mathcal{TST}^\omega_{\delta'} \subset \mathcal{TST}^\omega_\delta = \mathcal{TST}^\omega_{1,\delta} \subset \mathcal{TST}^\omega_{k',\delta} \subset \mathcal{TST}^\omega_{k,\delta} \subset \mathcal{BST}_{\exists k \exists \delta} \subset \mathcal{TST}^\omega \quad (4)$$

$$\mathcal{TST}^\omega_\delta \subset \mathcal{TST}^\omega_{\exists \delta} \subset \mathcal{BST}_{\exists k \exists \delta} \subset \mathcal{TST}^\omega \quad (5)$$

$$\mathcal{TST}^\omega_{\exists \delta} \text{ and } \mathcal{TST}^\omega_{k',\delta} \text{ are incomparable} \quad (6)$$

$$\mathcal{TST}^*_{\delta'} \subset \mathcal{TST}^*_\delta = \mathcal{TST}^*_{1,\delta} \subset \mathcal{TST}^*_{k',\delta} \subset \mathcal{TST}^*_{k,\delta} \subset \mathcal{TST}^*_{\exists \delta} = \mathcal{TST}^*_{\exists k \exists \delta} = \mathcal{TST}^* \quad (7)$$

For lack of space, in the rest of the paper we will focus on behaviors, leaving the proofs of the corresponding results for words to [9]. Also, we will consider only behaviors (and words) that have bounded variability δ for some *rational* value of $\delta > 0$. This is due to the fact that even decidable logics such as MITL become undecidable if irrational constants are allowed [15]. It is also well-known that this is without loss of generality — as much as satisfiability is concerned — because formulas of common temporal logics are satisfiable iff they are satisfiable on behaviors (or words) with rational transition points [1].

3 MTL and Its Relatives

The main focus of this paper is the decidability of MTL over the classes of behaviors and words that we introduced in the previous section. Hence, this section introduces formally MTL and other closely related temporal logics that will be used to obtain the results of the following sections. For notational convenience, in this paper we usually denote MITL formulas as ψ and MTL formulas as ϕ.

3.1 MITL and MTL

Let us start with the Metric Interval Temporal Logic (MITL) [1], a decidable subset of MTL. MITL formulas are defined as follows, for $p \in \mathcal{P}$ an atomic proposition and I a non-singular interval of the nonnegative reals with rational (or unbounded) endpoints: $\psi := p \mid \neg\psi \mid \psi_1 \wedge \psi_2 \mid U_I(\psi_1, \psi_2) \mid S_I(\psi_1, \psi_2)$. Metric Temporal Logic (MTL) [2] is defined simply as an extension of MITL where singular intervals are allowed.

Abbreviations such as $\top, \bot, \vee, \Rightarrow, \Leftrightarrow$ are defined as usual. We drop the interval I in operators when it is $(0, \infty)$, and we represent intervals by pseudo-arithmetic expressions such as $> k, \geq k, < k, \leq k,$ and $= k$ for $(k, \infty), [k, \infty), (0, k), (0, k]$ and $[k, k]$, respectively. We also introduce a few derived temporal operators; in the following definitions I is an interval of the nonnegative reals with rational (or unbounded) endpoints. More precisely, the following definitions introduce MITL derived operators if I is taken to be non-singular and ϕ is an MITL formula; otherwise they introduce MTL derived operators. For both semantics we introduce the following derived operators: $\Diamond_I(\phi) = U_I(\top, \phi), \Box_I(\phi) = \neg\Diamond_I(\neg\phi), R_I(\phi_1, \phi_2) = \neg U_I(\neg\phi_1, \neg\phi_2), \bigcirc(\phi) = U(\phi, \top)$, as well as their past counterparts $\overleftarrow{\Diamond}_I(\phi) = S_I(\top, \phi), \overleftarrow{\Box}_I(\phi) = \neg\overleftarrow{\Diamond}_I(\neg\phi)$, $T_I(\phi_1, \phi_2) = \neg S_I(\neg\phi_1, \neg\phi_2), \overleftarrow{\bigcirc}(\phi) = S(\phi, \top)$, and $\text{Alw}(\phi) = \overleftarrow{\Box}(\phi) \wedge \phi \wedge \Box(\phi)$ and $\triangle(\phi) = \overleftarrow{\bigcirc}(\neg\phi) \wedge (\phi \vee \bigcirc(\phi))$.

Semantics. For $b \in \overline{\mathcal{B}\Sigma\mathbb{T}}$ (with $\Sigma = 2^{\mathcal{P}}$) and $t \in \mathbb{T}$ we define:[3]

$b(t) \models_{\mathbb{T}} p$ iff $p \in b(t)$

$b(t) \models_{\mathbb{T}} \neg\phi$ iff $b(t) \not\models_{\mathbb{T}} \phi$

$b(t) \models_{\mathbb{T}} \phi_1 \wedge \phi_2$ iff $b(t) \models_{\mathbb{T}} \phi_1$ and $b(t) \models_{\mathbb{T}} \phi_2$

$b(t) \models_{\mathbb{T}} U_I(\phi_1, \phi_2)$ iff there exists $d \in t \oplus I \cap \mathbb{T}$ such that $b(d) \models_{\mathbb{T}} \phi_2$
                                                                          and for all $u \in (t, d)$ it is $b(u) \models_{\mathbb{T}} \phi_1$

$b(t) \models_{\mathbb{T}} S_I(\phi_1, \phi_2)$ iff there exists $d \in -I \oplus t \cap \mathbb{T}$ such that $b(d) \models_{\mathbb{T}} \phi_2$
                                                                          and for all $u \in (d, t)$ it is $b(u) \models_{\mathbb{T}} \phi_1$

$b \models_{\mathbb{T}} \phi$ iff $b(0) \models_{\mathbb{T}} \phi$

Normal form over behaviors. In order to simplify the presentation of some of the following results, we present a normal form for MITL over behaviors, defined by the following grammar, where d is a positive rational number: $p \mid \neg\psi \mid \psi_1 \wedge \psi_2 \mid U(\psi_1, \psi_2) \mid$

---

[3] We assume that $0 \in \mathbb{T}$ without practical loss of generality.

$S(\psi_1, \psi_2) \mid \Diamond_{<d}(\psi) \mid \overleftarrow{\Diamond}_{<d}(\psi)$. The fact that every MITL formula can be expressed according to the syntax above follows from two results. [11, Th. 4.1, Prop. 4.2] showed that every generic MITL formula using intervals with integer endpoints can be translated into an equivalent one in the normal form above. Second, [1, Lm. 2.16] showed that every MITL using intervals with rational endpoints can be translated into an equi-satisfiable one with integer endpoints only; this is achieved by uniformly scaling the endpoints into integers. It is then clear that all our results for behaviors can assume formulas in this normal form. In addition, an analogous normal form for MTL can be defined by introducing the additional operators: $\Diamond_{=d}(\phi) \mid \overleftarrow{\Diamond}_{=d}(\phi)$.

For any MTL formula ϕ and behavior $b \in \mathcal{B\Sigma T}$, we define the derived behavior b_ϕ that represents the truth value of ϕ over b; namely:

$$b_\phi(t) = \begin{cases} b(t) \cup \{\phi\} & \text{if } b(t) \models_{\mathrm{T}} \phi \\ b(t) & \text{otherwise} \end{cases}$$

Also, the size $|\phi|$ of a formula ϕ is defined as the number of its atomic propositions, connectives, and temporal operators, multiplied by the size — assuming a binary encoding — of the largest finite constant appearing in intervals bounding temporal operators.

3.2   QITL: Decidable Extensions of MITL

Following [11,16], we introduce decidable extensions of MITL over behaviors. These extensions will be useful in the decidability proofs of Section 5.

We extend MITL by introducing modalities $\Diamond\!\!\!\!\!\Diamond^n_I(\psi_1, \ldots, \psi_n)$ for $n > 0$ and I a non-singular interval. We denote the corresponding temporal logics by $\text{QITL}(n)$, for $n > 0$. Also, we denote the temporal logic $\bigcup_{k>0} \text{QITL}(k)$ simply by QITL; note that QITL is essentially equivalent to the logic TLPI introduced in [16]. The semantics of the new operators is:

$b(t) \models_{\mathrm{T}} \Diamond\!\!\!\!\!\Diamond^n_I(\psi_1, \ldots, \psi_n)$ iff   there exist $t_1 < \cdots < t_n \in I \oplus t$
such that for all $1 \leq i \leq n$ it is $b(t_i) \models_{\mathrm{T}} \psi_i$

We also introduce the abbreviation $\Diamond\!\!\!\!\!\Diamond^n_I(\psi) = \Diamond\!\!\!\!\!\Diamond^n_I\left(\underbrace{\psi, \psi, \ldots, \psi}_{n \text{ times}}\right)$.

The small syntactic gap between QITL and TLPI can be easily bridged along the lines of [11] (see [9] for details). Hence, the following is a corollary of the complexity results for TLPI — with a succinct encoding of constants — presented in [16].

Proposition 2 (Decidability and Complexity of QITL**).** QITL *is decidable with an* **EXPSPACE**-*complete validity problem.*

4   Syntactic Definition of Regularity Constraints

In this section we show how to express the regularity constraints of bounded variability and non-Berkeleyness as MITL or QITL formulas. The following two sub-sections introduce two preliminary results.

4.1   From Non-berkeleyness to Bounded Variability

Let ϕ be any MTL formula and $b \in \mathcal{BET}_\delta$ a non-Berkeley behavior. While non-Berkeleyness is defined according to the behavior of atomic propositions in b, it is simple to realize that, in general, it cannot be lifted to the behavior of ϕ itself in b_ϕ. In other words, it may happen that b_ϕ is Berkeley (i.e., two adjacent transitions are less than δ time units apart) even if b is not.

However, b_ϕ is at least with variability bounded by $\theta(\phi), \delta$, where $\theta(\phi)$ can be computed from the structure of ϕ. More precisely, consider the following definition, where β is a Boolean combination of atomic propositions.

$$
\begin{aligned}
\theta(\beta) &= 2 \\
\theta(\neg\phi) &= \theta(\phi) \\
\theta(\phi_1 \wedge \phi_2) &= \theta(\phi_1) + \theta(\phi_2) \\
\theta(\mathsf{U}(\phi_1, \phi_2)) &= \theta(\phi_1) \\
\theta(\Diamond_{<\mathrm{d}}(\phi)) &= \theta(\phi) + 1 \\
\theta(\Diamond_{=\mathrm{d}}(\phi)) &= \theta(\phi)
\end{aligned}
$$

Note that $\theta(\phi) = O(|\phi|)$. Then, we can prove the following.

Lemma 1. *For any $b \in \mathcal{BET}_\delta$ and MTL formula ϕ, it is $b_\phi \in \mathcal{BET}_{\theta(\phi),\delta}$.*

Proof. Let b be a non-Berkeley behavior for $\delta > 0$, $J = [t, t+\delta]$ be any closed interval of size δ, and ϕ be a generic MTL formula. The proof goes by induction on the structure of ϕ; for brevity let us just consider the cases $\phi = \Diamond_{=\mathrm{d}}(\phi')$ and $\phi = \Diamond_{<\mathrm{d}}(\phi')$.

In the first case, clearly $\tau(\phi) = \ldots, x_{-1} - \mathrm{d}, x_0 - \mathrm{d}, x_1 - \mathrm{d}, \ldots, x_i - \mathrm{d}, \ldots$, where $\tau(\phi') = \ldots, x_{-1}, x_0, x_1, \ldots, x_i, \ldots$. Thus, $b_{\phi'} \in \mathcal{BET}_{\theta(\phi'),\delta}$ implies $b_\phi \in \mathcal{BET}_{\theta(\phi),\delta}$ as well, since $\theta(\phi) = \theta(\phi')$.

For the second case, let $x_1, \ldots, x_k = \tau(b_{\phi'}) \cap J$ be the transition points of $b_{\phi'}$ over J; by inductive hypothesis we know that $k \leq \theta' = \theta(\phi')$. Let us first consider the case: $x_i - x_{i-1} \geq \mathrm{d}$ for all $i = 2, \ldots, k + 1$. If also x_1 is a transition from false to true (see Figure 1 for an example with $k = 4$, where $x_i' = x_i - \mathrm{d}$), b_ϕ has the corresponding transition points $x_1 - \mathrm{d}, x_2, x_3 - \mathrm{d}, \ldots$; if instead x_1 is a transition from true to false, b_ϕ has the corresponding transition points $x_1, x_2 - \mathrm{d}, x_3, \ldots$. In particular, note that when $x_{i+1} - x_i = \mathrm{d}$ and ϕ' is false throughout (x_i, x_{i+1}), $x_i = x_{i+1} - \mathrm{d}$ is a punctual transition point for b_ϕ, and in fact it appears twice in $\tau(b_\phi)$. Overall, b_ϕ has at most all the transition points $b_{\phi'}$ has over J, plus one corresponding to $x_{k+1} - \mathrm{d}$. Since $\theta(\phi) = \theta(\phi') + 1$, we have that $b_\phi \in \mathcal{BET}_{\theta(\phi),\delta}$. Whenever $x_i - x_{i-1} < \mathrm{d}$ for some $i = 2, \ldots, k + 1$, the transition points of $b_{\phi'}$ may instead be fewer. In fact, if x_1 is a transition from false to true, for all odd $i = 3, \ldots, k+1$ such that $x_i - x_{i-1} < \mathrm{d}$, there are no transition points for b_ϕ between x_{i-1} and x_{i+1}. Similarly, if x_1 is a transition from true to false, for all even $i = 2, \ldots, k + 1$ such that $x_i - x_{i-1} < \mathrm{d}$, there are no transition points for b_ϕ between x_{i-1} and x_{i+1}. Overall, $\theta(\phi) = \theta(\phi') + 1$ is an upper bound on the number of transitions of b_ϕ over J in this case as well. $\square$

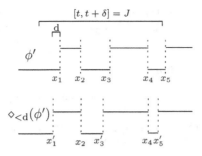

Fig. 1. $b_{\phi'}$ and $b_{\diamond_{<\mathrm{d}}(\phi')}$ over J

4.2 Describing Sequences of Transitions

Let us now introduce QITL formula $\mathsf{happ}(\phi, k, I)$ stating that formula ϕ takes exactly $k - 1$ consecutive transitions, eventually leading to true (i.e., it holds at the end of I). Formally, for every QITL formula ϕ, nonsingular interval I, and integer $k > 0$, we introduce the QITL formula:

$$\mathsf{happ}(\phi, k, I) = \diamondsuit_I^k \left(\underbrace{\phi', \neg\phi', \cdots, \phi, \neg\phi, \phi}_{k \text{ terms}} \right) \wedge \neg\diamondsuit_I^{k+1} \left(\underbrace{\phi', \neg\phi', \cdots, \phi, \neg\phi, \phi, \neg\phi}_{k+1 \text{ terms}} \right)$$

where $\phi' = \phi$ if k is odd and $\phi' = \neg\phi$ otherwise.

Next, we introduce a formula, built upon $\mathsf{happ}(\phi, k, I)$, to describe the case where we have *at most* n transitions over I. For every QITL formula ϕ, nonsingular interval I, and $n > 0$, we introduce the QITL formula:

$$\mathsf{yieldsT}(\phi, n, I) = \bigvee_{0 \le k \le n} \mathsf{happ}(\phi, k, I) \tag{8}$$

Lemma 2. *Let ϕ undergo at most n transitions over $t \oplus [\tau - \delta, \tau]$ for some $\tau > 0$, that is $\langle \tau(b_\phi) \cap t \oplus [\tau - \delta, \tau] \rangle \le n$; then $b(t + \tau) \models \phi$ iff $b(t) \models \mathsf{yieldsT}(\phi, n + 1, [\max(0, \tau - \delta), \tau])$.*

Proof. Let ϕ undergo exactly $k \le n$ transitions over $t \oplus [\tau - \delta, \tau]$, and let $I = [\max(0, \tau - \delta), \tau]$. Let us first consider the case $\tau - \delta > 0$, and thus $I = [\tau - \delta, \tau]$. If $b(t + \tau) \models \phi$ then one can check that $b(t) \models \mathsf{happ}(\phi, k + 1, [\tau - \delta, \tau])$, which implies $b(t) \models \mathsf{yieldsT}(\phi, n + 1, [\tau - \delta, \tau])$ according to (8). Conversely, if $b(t) \models \mathsf{yieldsT}(\phi, n + 1, [\tau - \delta, \tau])$ then $b(t) \models \mathsf{happ}(\phi, \tilde{k}, [\tau - \delta, \tau])$ for some $\tilde{k} \le n + 1$. In particular, it is $b(t) \models \mathsf{happ}(\phi, k + 1, I)$; hence $b(t + \tau) \models \phi$. Let us now assume $\tau - \delta \le 0$, and thus $I = [0, \tau] \subseteq [\tau - \delta, \tau]$. Then, ϕ undergoes exactly h transitions over $t \oplus I$, for some $h \le k \le n$. If $b(t + \tau) \models \phi$ then one can check that $b(t) \models \mathsf{happ}(\phi, h + 1, [0, \tau])$, which implies $b(t) \models \mathsf{yieldsT}(\phi, n + 1, [0, \tau])$ according to (8). Conversely, if $b(t) \models \mathsf{yieldsT}(\phi, n + 1, [0, \tau])$ then $b(t) \models \mathsf{happ}(\phi, \tilde{h}, [0, \tau])$ for some $\tilde{h} \le n + 1$. In particular, it is $b(t) \models \mathsf{happ}(\phi, h + 1, I)$; hence $b(t + \tau) \models \phi$. $\quad\square$

4.3 Syntactic Characterizations

This section defines non-Berkeleyness and bounded variability syntactically.

Non-Berkeleyness. The following formula χ_δ characterizes behaviors that are non-Berkeley for $\delta > 0$, that is $b \in \mathcal{BET}_\delta$ with $\Sigma = 2^{\mathcal{P}}$ iff $b \models \chi_\delta$.

$$
\chi_\delta \quad = \quad \mathsf{Alw}\left(\Diamond_{[0,\delta]}\left(\bigvee_{\beta \in 2^{\mathcal{P}}} \Box_{[0,\delta]}(\beta) \right) \wedge \left(\overleftarrow{\Box}(\bot) \Rightarrow \bigvee_{\beta \in 2^{\mathcal{P}}} \Box_{[0,\delta]}(\beta) \right) \right)
$$

Note that the second conjunct is needed only for time domains bounded to the left, where it holds precisely at the origin.

While χ_δ has size exponential in $|\mathcal{P}|$, it is possible to express non-Berkeleyness with a formula which is polynomial in $|\mathcal{P}|$. To this end, let us first define: $\mathsf{RT}(\beta) = \triangle(\beta) \wedge \beta \vee \triangle(\neg\beta) \wedge \neg\beta$, $\mathsf{LT}(\beta) = \triangle(\beta) \wedge \neg\beta \vee \triangle(\neg\beta) \wedge \beta$, $\mathsf{GT}(\beta) = \triangle(\beta) \vee \triangle(\neg\beta)$ that model a right-continuous, left-continuous, and generic transition of β, respectively. Then, we introduce:

$$
\chi_\delta^{\mathrm{R}} \quad = \quad \bigwedge_{\beta \in \Sigma}\left(\mathsf{RT}(\beta) \Rightarrow \bigwedge_{\gamma \in \Sigma}\left(\begin{array}{c} \Box_{(0,\delta)}(\neg\mathsf{GT}(\gamma)) \\ \wedge \\ \mathsf{GT}(\gamma) \Rightarrow \mathsf{RT}(\gamma) \\ \wedge \\ \Diamond_{(0,\delta]}(\mathsf{GT}(\gamma)) \Rightarrow \Diamond_{(0,\delta]}(\mathsf{LT}(\gamma)) \end{array} \right) \right)
$$

$$
\chi_\delta^{\mathrm{L}} \quad = \quad \bigwedge_{\beta \in \Sigma}\left(\mathsf{LT}(\beta) \Rightarrow \bigwedge_{\gamma \in \Sigma}\left(\begin{array}{c} \Box_{(0,\delta)}(\neg\mathsf{GT}(\gamma)) \\ \wedge \\ \mathsf{GT}(\gamma) \Rightarrow \mathsf{LT}(\gamma) \end{array} \right) \right)
$$

$$
\chi_\delta^{\mathrm{I}} = \overleftarrow{\Box}(\bot) \Rightarrow \bigwedge_{\beta \in \Sigma} \Box_{[0,\delta]}(\beta \vee \neg\beta)
$$

$$
\chi_\delta' \quad = \quad \mathsf{Alw}(\chi_\delta^{\mathrm{R}} \wedge \chi_\delta^{\mathrm{L}} \wedge \chi_\delta^{\mathrm{I}})
$$

χ_δ^{R} describes the non-Berkeley requirement about a right-continuous transition: no other transition can occur over $(0, \delta)$, if there is a transition at the current instant it must also be right-continuous, and if there is a transition at δ it must be left-continuous, so that a closed interval of size δ is fully contained between the two consecutive transitions. Similarly, χ_δ^{R} describes the non-Berkeley requirement about a left-continuous transition. Finally, χ_δ^{I} describes the non-Berkeley requirement at the origin of a time domain bounded to the left. It should be clear that $b \in \mathcal{BET}_\delta$ with $\Sigma = 2^{\mathcal{P}}$ iff $b \models \chi_\delta'$, and χ_δ' has size quadratic in $|\mathcal{P}|$.

Bounded variability. To describe bounded variability syntactically over behaviors, we first introduce QITL formula $\mathsf{pt}(k, I)$, for $k > 0$.

$$\mathsf{pt}(k, I) = \lozenge_I^k \left(\bigvee_{\beta \in \mathcal{P}} \left(\triangle(\beta) \wedge \bigcirc(\neg\beta) \vee \triangle(\neg\beta) \wedge \bigcirc(\beta) \right) \right)$$

$$\wedge \neg\lozenge_I^{k+1} \left(\bigvee_{\beta \in \mathcal{P}} \left(\triangle(\beta) \wedge \bigcirc(\neg\beta) \vee \triangle(\neg\beta) \wedge \bigcirc(\beta) \right) \right)$$

If we let $\mathsf{pt}(0, I) = \neg\lozenge_I^1 \left(\bigvee_{\beta \in \mathcal{P}} \left(\triangle(\beta) \wedge \bigcirc(\neg\beta) \vee \triangle(\neg\beta) \wedge \bigcirc(\beta) \right) \right)$, $\mathsf{pt}(k, I)$ states that there are exactly $k \geq 0$ *punctual* transitions of atomic propositions over interval I.

Second, we introduce QITL formula $\mathsf{gt}(k, I)$, for $k > 0$:

$$\mathsf{gt}(k, I) = \lozenge_I^k \left(\bigvee_{\beta \in \mathcal{P}} \left(\triangle(\beta) \vee \triangle(\neg\beta) \right) \right) \wedge \neg\lozenge_I^{k+1} \left(\bigvee_{\beta \in \mathcal{P}} \left(\triangle(\beta) \vee \triangle(\neg\beta) \right) \right)$$

If we let $\mathsf{gt}(0, I) = \neg\lozenge_I^1 \left(\bigvee_{\beta \in \mathcal{P}} \left(\triangle(\beta) \vee \triangle(\neg\beta) \right) \right)$, $\mathsf{gt}(k, I)$ states that there are exactly $k \geq 0$ (generic, i.e., punctual or not) transitions of atomic propositions over interval I.

Finally, the following formula $\chi_{k,\delta}$ characterizes behaviors with variability bounded by k, δ, that is $b \in \mathcal{BST}_{k,\delta}$ with $\Sigma = 2^{\mathcal{P}}$ iff $b \models \chi_{k,\delta}$.

$$\chi_{k,\delta}^{\mathsf{G}} = \bigvee_{\substack{0 \leq j \leq k \\ 0 \leq h \leq \lfloor j/2 \rfloor}} \mathsf{pt}(h, [0, \delta]) \wedge \mathsf{gt}(j - h, [0, \delta])$$

$$\chi_{k,\delta}^{\mathsf{I}} = \overleftarrow{\square}(\bot) \wedge \bigvee_{\beta \in \mathcal{P}} \begin{pmatrix} \beta \wedge \bigcirc(\neg\beta) \\ \vee \\ \neg\beta \wedge \bigcirc(\beta) \end{pmatrix} \Rightarrow \bigvee_{\substack{0 \leq j \leq k-2 \\ 0 \leq h \leq \lfloor j/2 \rfloor}} \begin{pmatrix} \mathsf{pt}(h, (0, \delta]) \\ \wedge \\ \mathsf{gt}(j - h, (0, \delta]) \end{pmatrix}$$

$$\chi_{k,\delta} = \mathrm{Alw}\left(\chi_{k,\delta}^{\mathsf{G}} \wedge \chi_{k,\delta}^{\mathsf{I}} \right)$$

More precisely, $\chi_{k,\delta}^{\mathsf{G}}$ applies to any time instant and requires that at most k transitions (weighted according to whether they are punctual or not) occur over any closed interval of size δ. On the other hand, $\chi_{k,\delta}^{\mathsf{I}}$ applies only at the origin of time domains that are bounded to the left: if there is a punctual transition at the origin, there must be at most $k - 2$ transitions over the residual interval $(0, \delta]$ (in fact, $\lim_{t \to 0^-} b(t)$ is undefined and hence different than $b(0)$); if not, it is clear that the general formula $\chi_{k,\delta}^{\mathsf{G}}$ is enough. Note that the size of $\chi_{k,\delta}$ is polynomial in $|\mathcal{P}|, k$.

5   Decidability Results

For simplicity, in this section we assume future-only MTL formulas. It is however clear that the results can be extended to MTL with past operators by providing a few additional details. We also assume formulas in normal form (introduced in Section 3.1).

5.1 MTL over Non-berkeley Behaviors

This section shows that MTL is decidable over non-Berkeley behaviors, by providing a translation from MTL formulas to QITL formulas.

Lemma 3. *For any MTL formula ϕ over any behavior $b \in \mathcal{B\Sigma T\delta}$, we have:*

$$\Diamond_{=d}(\phi) \quad \equiv \quad \text{yieldsT}(\phi, \theta(\phi) + 1, [\max(0, d - \delta), d])$$

Proof. Let $I = [\max(0, d-\delta), d]$. From Lemma 1, ϕ undergoes at most $\theta(\phi)$ transitions over $t \oplus I$. So, from Lemma 2, we have immediately that $b(t + d) \models \phi$ — i.e., $b(t) \models \Diamond_{=d}(\phi)$ — iff $b(t) \models \text{yieldsT}(\phi, \theta(\phi) + 1, I)$.   □

Decidability of MTL over non-Berkeley behaviors. It is now straightforward to prove the decidability of MTL over non-Berkeley behaviors. To this end, let us introduce the following translation function μ from MTL formulas to QITL formulas, where ψ is any MITL formula and ϕ is any MTL formula.

$$
\begin{aligned}
\mu(\psi) &\equiv & \psi \\
\mu(\neg\phi) &\equiv & \neg\mu(\phi) \\
\mu(\phi_1 \wedge \phi_2) &\equiv & \mu(\phi_1) \wedge \mu(\phi_2) \\
\mu(\mathsf{U}(\phi_1, \phi_2)) &\equiv & \mathsf{U}(\mu(\phi_1), \mu(\phi_2)) \\
\mu(\Diamond_{<d}(\phi)) &\equiv & \Diamond_{<d}(\mu(\phi)) \\
\mu(\Diamond_{=d}(\phi)) &\equiv & \text{yieldsT}(\mu(\phi), \theta(\phi) + 1, [\max(0, d - \delta), d])
\end{aligned}
$$

Theorem 1. *For any MTL formula ϕ, for any behavior $b \in \mathcal{B\Sigma T}_\delta$ for some $\delta > 0$, we have $b \models_T \phi$ iff $b \models_T \mu(\phi)$.*

Theorem 1, the decidability of MITL and QITL [1,11], and the syntactic characterization of non-Berkeleyness by means of the χ_δ formula, immediately imply the following.

Corollary 1. *For any $\delta > 0$, the satisfiability of MTL formulas is decidable over $\mathcal{B\Sigma T}_\delta$.*

Proof. Given a generic MTL formula ϕ, ϕ is satisfiable over $\mathcal{B\Sigma T}_\delta$ iff $\phi' = \phi \wedge \chi'_\delta$ is satisfiable over non-Zeno behaviors. In turn, by Theorem 1, ϕ' is satisfiable over non-Zeno behaviors iff $\phi'' = \mu(\phi) \wedge \chi'_\delta$ is. Since ϕ'' is a QITL formula, the theorem follows from Proposition 2.   □

5.2 MTL over Bounded Variably Behaviors

The results of the previous section can be extended to the case of behaviors with bounded variability along the following lines. First, consider the claim: for any $b \in \mathcal{B\Sigma T}_{k,\delta}$ and MTL formula ϕ, it is $b_\phi \in \mathcal{B\Sigma T}_{k+\theta(\phi),\delta}$. The claim can be proved similarly as for Lemma 1, where the base case for Boolean combinations β is changed into $2 + k$, whereas the inductive steps are essentially unaffected, provided the inductive hypothesis about the variability being bounded by θ is replaced by it being bounded by $\theta + k$. Correspondingly, we can introduce a translation μ' from MTL to QITL formulas which is obtained from μ by replacing $\theta(\phi)$ with $k + \theta(\phi)$. Finally, QITL formula $\mu'(\phi) \wedge \chi_{k,\delta}$ is satisfiable over $\mathcal{B\Sigma T}$ iff ϕ is satisfiable over $\mathcal{B\Sigma T}_{k,\delta}$. Hence, MTL is decidable over $\mathcal{B\Sigma T}_{k,\delta}$.

6   Related Results

This section discusses the expressiveness and complexity of MTL over non-Berkeley and bounded variably behaviors and words.

6.1   Expressiveness of MTL over Non-berkeley

The technique used in Section 5 to assess the decidability of MTL over non-Berkeley behaviors involved the translation of MTL formulas into QITL, a strict superset of MITL. This raises the obvious question of whether QITL is really needed in translating MTL to a decidable logic. A partial negative answer to this question can be provided by showing that MITL is strictly less expressive than MTL over non-Berkeley behaviors. This answer is only partial because we address expressiveness, not equi-satisfiability; that is, it might be possible to construct, for every MTL formula, a corresponding MITL formula which is equi-satisfiable over non-Berkeley behaviors but requires additional atomic propositions to be built. However, one can prove that for any $\delta > 0$, MTL is strictly more expressive than MITL over $\mathcal{BZT}_\delta$. We refer to [9] for some details of the (involved) proof.

6.2   Complexity of MTL over Non-berkeley

This section shows that the satisfiability problem for MTL formulas over non-Berkeley (and bounded variably) behaviors has the same complexity as the same problem for MITL over generic behaviors.

Theorem 2. *The satisfiability problem for MTL over $\mathcal{BZT}_\delta$ is **EXPSPACE**-complete.*

Proof. The fact that the problem is in **EXPSPACE** follows from the translation procedure of Section 3 from an MTL formula ϕ to an equi-satisfiable QITL formula of size polynomial in $|\phi|$, and from the complexity of QITL (Proposition 2).

The **EXPSPACE**-hardness of MTL satisfiability over non-Berkeley behaviors can be proved by reducing the corresponding problem over the integers, where integer-timed words are embedded into non-Berkeley behaviors. See [9] for details.   □

With a very similar justification we can prove the following.

Theorem 3. *The satisfiability problem for MTL over $\mathcal{BZT}_{k,\delta}$ is **EXPSPACE**-complete (assuming a unary encoding of k).*

7   Undecidability Results

MTL is decidable no more if we consider all non-Berkeley behaviors for any δ together. More precisely, the satisfiability problem for MTL over $\mathcal{BZT}_{\exists \delta}$ is Σ_1^0-complete; compare against the same problem over $\mathcal{BZT}$ where it is Σ_1^1-complete.

Theorem 4. *The satisfiability problem for MTL over $\mathcal{BZT}_{\exists \delta}$ is $\Sigma_1^0 = $ **RE**-complete.*

Proof. Let ϕ be a generic MTL formula. ϕ is satisfiable over $\mathcal{BST}_{\exists\delta}$ iff there exists a $\overline{\delta} > 0$ such that ϕ is satisfiable over $\mathcal{BST}_{\overline{\delta}}$. Given that $\mathcal{BST}_\gamma \supset \mathcal{BST}_{\overline{\delta}}$ for all $\gamma < \overline{\delta}$ (Proposition 1), and that the satisfiability of ϕ is decidable over $\mathcal{BST}_\gamma$ for any fixed $\gamma > 0$ (Corollary 1), the following procedure halts iff ϕ is satisfiable over $\mathcal{BST}_{\exists\delta}$: (1) let $d \leftarrow 1$; (2) decide if ϕ is satisfiable over $\mathcal{BST}_d$; (3) if not, let $d \leftarrow d/2$ and goto (2). This proves that the satisfiability problem for MTL over $\mathcal{BST}_{\exists\delta}$ is in **RE**.

To show **RE**-hardness, we reduce the halting problem for 2-counter machines to MTL satisfiability over $\mathcal{BST}_{\exists\delta}$. The key insight is that a halting computation is one where only a finite number of instructions is executed. Correspondingly it can be represented by a behavior where only a finite number of transitions occur within a finite amount of time; such behaviors are necessarily in $\mathcal{BST}_{\exists\delta}$ because the infimum over distances between transitions coincides with the minimum. See [9] for all details. $\square$

The above proof can be adapted with simple modifications to work for infinite timed words, as well as for the classes $\mathcal{BST}_{\exists k\exists\delta}$ and $\mathcal{TST}^\omega_{\exists k\exists\delta}$. On the contrary, undecidability does not carry over to finite words, where the problem is known to be decidable [14].

8 Summary

Table 1 summarizes the results on the expressiveness of MTL over various semantic classes. Cells without shade host previously known results; cells with a light shade are corollaries of known results; cells with a dark shade correspond to the main results discussed and proved in this paper.

As future work, it will be interesting to investigate the practical impact of the new decidability results of this paper. This will encompass, on the one hand, experimenting with implementations of decision algorithms to evaluate their performances on practical verification problems and, on the other hand, assessing which classes of systems can be naturally described with bounded variably models.

Table 1. Summary of the known results

	DECIDABILITY	COMPLEXITY
$\mathcal{BST}_\delta, \mathcal{BST}_{k,\delta}$	Yes	**EXPSPACE**-C
$\mathcal{BST}_{\exists\delta}, \mathcal{BST}_{\exists k\exists\delta}$	No	Σ^0_1-C
$\mathcal{BST}$	No	Σ^1_1-C
$\mathcal{TST}^\omega_\delta, \mathcal{TST}^\omega_{k,\delta}$	Yes	**EXPSPACE**-C
$\mathcal{TST}^\omega_{\exists\delta}, \mathcal{TST}^\omega_{\exists k\exists\delta}$	No	Σ^0_1-C
$\mathcal{TST}^\omega$	No	Σ^1_1-C
$\mathcal{TST}^*_\delta, \mathcal{TST}^*_{k,\delta}$	Yes	**EXPSPACE**-C
$\mathcal{TST}^*_{\exists\delta}, \mathcal{TST}^*_{\exists k\exists\delta}$	Yes	non-**PR**
$\mathcal{TST}^*$	Yes	non-**PR**

Acknowledgements. We thank Alexander Rabinovich for providing us with a draft of his recent work [16] and the anonymous reviewers of FORMATS for their detailed and insightful remarks.

References

1. Alur, R., Feder, T., Henzinger, T.A.: The benefits of relaxing punctuality. Journal of the ACM 43(1), 116–146 (1996)
2. Alur, R., Henzinger, T.A.: Real-time logics: Complexity and expressiveness. Information and Computation 104(1), 35–77 (1993)
3. Asarin, E., Caspi, P., Maler, O.: Timed regular expressions. Journal of the ACM 49(2), 172–206 (2002)
4. Bouyer, P., Markey, N., Ouaknine, J., Worrell, J.: The cost of punctuality. In: Proceedings of LICS 2007 (2007)
5. D'Souza, D., Prabhakar, P.: On the expressiveness of MTL in the pointwise and continuous semantics. Formal Methods Letters 9(1), 1–4 (2007)
6. M. Fränzle. Decidability of duration calculi on restricted model classes. Technical Report Kiel MF 21/1, Christian-Albrechts Universität Kiel (1996)
7. Furia, C.A., Pradella, M., Rossi, M.: Automated verification of dense-time MTL specifications via discrete-time approximation. In: Cuellar, J., Maibaum, T.S.E. (eds.) FM 2008. LNCS, vol. 5014, pp. 132–147. Springer, Heidelberg (2008)
8. Furia, C.A., Rossi, M.: Integrating discrete- and continuous-time metric temporal logics through sampling. In: Asarin, E., Bouyer, P. (eds.) FORMATS 2006. LNCS, vol. 4202, pp. 215–229. Springer, Heidelberg (2006)
9. Furia, C.A., Rossi, M.: MTL with bounded variability: Decidability and complexity. Technical report, DEI, Politecnico di Milano (May 2008)
10. Gabbay, D.M., Hodkinson, I., Reynolds, M.: Temporal Logic, vol. 1. Oxford University Press, Oxford (1994)
11. Hirshfeld, Y., Rabinovich, A.M.: Logics for real time: Decidability and complexity. Fundamenta Informaticae 62(1), 1–28 (2004)
12. Lutz, C., Walther, D., Wolter, F.: Quantitative temporal logics over the reals: PSPACE and below. Information and Computation 205(1), 99–123 (2007)
13. Maler, O., Nickovic, D., Pnueli, A.: From MITL to timed automata. In: Asarin, E., Bouyer, P. (eds.) FORMATS 2006. LNCS, vol. 4202, pp. 274–289. Springer, Heidelberg (2006)
14. Ouaknine, J., Worrell, J.: On the decidability and complexity of metric temporal logic over finite words. Logical Methods in Computer Science 3(1) (2007)
15. Rabinovich, A.: Temporal logics with incommensurable distances are undecidable. Information and Computation 205(5), 707–715 (2007)
16. Rabinovich, A.M.: Complexity of metric temporal logic with counting. In: Proceedings of FORMATS 2008. LNCS. Springer, Heidelberg (2008)
17. Wilke, T.: Specifying timed state sequences in powerful decidable logics and timed automata. In: Langmaack, H., de Roever, W.-P., Vytopil, J. (eds.) FTRTFT 1994. LNCS, vol. 863, pp. 694–715. Springer, Heidelberg (1994)

Timed Parity Games:
Complexity and Robustness*

Krishnendu Chatterjee[1], Thomas A. Henzinger[2,3], and Vinayak S. Prabhu[2]

[1] CCE, UC Santa Cruz
[2] EECS, UC Berkeley
[3] CCS, EPFL
{c_krish,vinayak}@eecs.berkeley.edu, tah@epfl.ch

Abstract. We consider two-player games played in real time on game structures with clocks and parity objectives. The games are *concurrent* in that at each turn, both players independently propose a time delay and an action, and the action with the shorter delay is chosen. To prevent a player from winning by blocking time, we restrict each player to strategies that ensure that the player cannot be responsible for causing a zeno run. First, we present an efficient reduction of these games to *turn-based* (i.e., nonconcurrent) *finite-state* (i.e., untimed) parity games. The states of the resulting game are pairs of clock regions of the original game. Our reduction improves the best known complexity for solving timed parity games. Moreover, the rich class of algorithms for classical parity games can now be applied to timed parity games.

Second, we consider two restricted classes of strategies for the player that represents the controller in a real-time synthesis problem, namely, *limit-robust* and *bounded-robust* strategies. Using a limit-robust strategy, the controller cannot choose an exact real-valued time delay but must allow for some nonzero jitter in each of its actions. If there is a given lower bound on the jitter, then the strategy is bounded-robust. We show that exact strategies are more powerful than limit-robust strategies, which are more powerful than bounded-robust strategies for any bound. For both kinds of robust strategies, we present efficient reductions to standard timed automaton games. These reductions provide algorithms for the synthesis of robust real-time controllers.

1 Introduction

Timed automata [2] are models of real-time systems in which states consist of discrete locations and values for real-time clocks. The transitions between locations are dependent on the clock values. *Timed automaton games* [9,6,12,11] are used to distinguish between the actions of several players (typically a "controller" and a "plant"). We consider two-player timed-automaton games with ω-regular objectives specified as *parity conditions*. The class of ω-regular objectives can

---

* This research was supported in part by the NSF grants CCR-0132780, CNS-0720884, and CCR-0225610, and by the European COMBEST project.

F. Cassez and C. Jard (Eds.): FORMATS 2008, LNCS 5215, pp. 124–140, 2008.

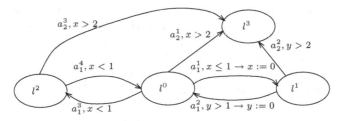

Fig. 1. A timed automaton game $\mathcal{T}$

express all safety and liveness specifications that arise in the synthesis and verification of reactive systems, and parity conditions are a canonical form to express ω-regular objectives [20]. The construction of a winning strategy for player 1 in such games corresponds to the *controller-synthesis problem for real-time systems* [10,17,22] with respect to achieving a desired ω-regular objective.

Timed-automaton games proceed in an infinite sequence of rounds. In each round, both players simultaneously propose moves, each move consisting of an action and a time delay after which the player wants the proposed action to take place. Of the two proposed moves, the move with the shorter time delay "wins" the round and determines the next state of the game. Let a set Φ of runs be the desired objective for player 1. Then player 1 has a winning strategy for Φ if she has a strategy to ensure that, no matter what player 2 does, one of the following two conditions holds: (1) time diverges and the resulting run belongs to Φ, or (2) time does not diverge but player-1's moves are chosen only finitely often (and thus she is not to be blamed for the convergence of time) [9,14]. This definition of winning is equivalent to restricting both players to play according to *receptive* strategies [3,19], which do not allow a player to block time.

In timed automaton games, there are cases where a player can win by proposing a certain strategy of moves, but where moves that deviate in the timing by an arbitrarily small amount from the winning strategy moves lead to her losing. If this is the case, then the synthesized controller needs to work with infinite precision in order to achieve the control objective. As this requirement is unrealistic, we propose two notions of *robust winning strategies*. In the first robust model, each move of player 1 (the "controller") must allow some jitter in when the action of the move is taken. The jitter may be arbitrarily small, but it must be greater than 0. We call such strategies *limit-robust*. In the second robust model, we give a lower bound on the jitter, i.e., every move of player 1 must allow for a fixed jitter, which is specified as a parameter for the game. We call these strategies *bounded-robust*. The strategies of player 2 (the "plant") are left unrestricted (apart from being receptive). We show that these types of strategies are in strict decreasing order in terms of power: general strategies are strictly more powerful than limit-robust strategies; and limit-robust strategies are strictly more powerful than bounded-robust strategies for *any* lower bound on the jitter, i.e., there are games in which player 1 can win with a limit-robust strategy, but there does not exist any nonzero bound on the jitter for which player 1 can win with a bounded-robust strategy. The following example illustrates this issue.

Example 1. Consider the timed automaton $\mathcal{J}$ in Fig. 1. The edges denoted a_1^k for $k \in \{1, 2, 3, 4\}$ are controlled by player 1 and edges denoted a_2^j for $j \in \{1, 2, 3\}$ are controlled by player 2. The objective of player 1 is $\square(\neg l^3)$, ie., to avoid l^3. The important part of the automaton is the cycle l^0, l^1. The only way to avoid l^3 in a time divergent run is to cycle in between l^0 and l^1 infinitely often. In addition player 1 may choose to also cycle in between l^0 and l^2, but that does not help (or harm) her. Due to strategies being receptive, player 1 cannot just cycle in between l^0 and l^2 forever, she must also cycle in between l^0 and l^1; that is, to satisfy $\square(\neg l^3)$ player 1 must ensure $(\square\diamond l^0) \wedge (\square\diamond l^1)$, where $\square\diamond$ denotes "infinitely often". But note that player 1 may cycle in between l^0 and l^2 as many (finite) number of times as she wants in between an l^0, l^1 cycle.

In our analysis below, we omit such l^0, l^2 cycles for simplicity. Let the game start from the location l^0 at time 0, and let l^1 be visited at time t^0 for the first time. Also, let t^j denote the difference between times when l^1 is visited for the $j+1$-th time, and when l^0 is visited for the j-th time. We can have at most 1 time unit between two successive visits to l^0, and we must have strictly more than 1 time unit elapse between two successive visits to l^1. Thus, t^j must be in a strictly decreasing sequence. Also, for player 1 to cycle around l^0 and l^1 infinitely often, we must have that all $t^j \geq 0$. Consider any bounded-robust strategy. Since the jitter is some fixed ε_j, for any strategy of player 1 which tries to cycle in between l^0 and l^1, there will be executions where the transition labeled a_1^1 will be taken when x is less than or equal to $1 - \varepsilon_j$, and the transition labeled a_1^2 will be taken when y is greater than $1 - \varepsilon_j$. This means that there are executions where t^j decreases by at least $2 \cdot \varepsilon_j$ in each cycle. But, this implies that we cannot having an infinite decreasing sequence of t^j's for any ε_j and for any starting value of t^0.

With a limit-robust strategy however, player 1 can cycle in between the two locations infinitely often, provided that the starting value of x is strictly less than 1. This is because at each step of the game, player 1 can pick moves that are such that the clocks x and y are closer and closer to 1 respectively. A general strategy allows player 1 to win even when the starting value of x is 1. The details can be found in [7].   □

Contributions. We first show that timed automaton parity games can be reduced to classical *turn-based* finite-state parity games. Since the timed games are *concurrent*, in that in each turn both players propose moves before one of the moves is chosen, our reduction to the untimed finite state game generates states that are pairs of clock regions. The reduction allows us to use the rich literature of algorithms for classical parity games to solve timed automaton parity games. While a solution for timed automaton games with parity objectives was already presented in [9], our reduction obtains a better computational complexity; we improve the complexity from roughly $O\left((M \cdot |C| \cdot |A_1| \cdot |A_2|)^2 \cdot (16 \cdot |S_{\mathsf{Reg}}|)^{d+2}\right)$ to roughly $O\left(M \cdot |C| \cdot |A_2| \cdot (32 \cdot |S_{\mathsf{Reg}}| \cdot M \cdot |C| \cdot |A_1|)^{\frac{d+2}{3}+\frac{3}{2}}\right)$, where M is the maximum constant in the timed automaton, $|C|$ is the number of clocks, $|A_i|$ is the number of player-i edges, $|A_i|^* = \min\{|A_i|, |L| \cdot 2^{|C|}\}$, $|L|$ is the number of of locations, $|S_{\mathsf{Reg}}|$ is the number of states in the region graph (bounded by

$|L| \cdot \prod_{x \in C}(c_x + 1) \cdot |C|! \cdot 2^{|C|})$, and d is the number of priorities in the parity index function. We note that the restriction to receptive strategies does not fundamentally change the complexity —it only increases the number of indices of the parity function by 2.

Second, we show that timed automaton games with limit-robust and bounded-robust strategies can be solved by reductions to general timed automaton games (with exact strategies). The reductions differentiate between whether the jitter is controlled by player 1 (in the limit-robust case), or by player 2 (in the bounded robust case). This is done by changing the winning condition in the limit-robust case, and by a syntactic transformation in the bounded-robust case. These reductions provide algorithms for synthesizing robust controllers for real-time systems, where the controller is guaranteed to achieve the control objective even if its time delays are subject to jitter. We also demonstrate that limit-robust strategies suffice for winning the special case of timed automaton games where all guards and invariants are strict (i.e., open). The question of the *existence* of a lower bound on the jitter for which a game can be won with a bounded-robust strategy remains open. The proofs of the results of the paper can be found in [7].

Related work. A solution for timed automaton games with receptive strategies and parity objectives was first presented in [9], where the solution is obtained by first demonstrating that the winning set can be characterized by a μ-calculus fixpoint expression, and then showing that only unions of clock regions arise in its fixpoint iteration. Our notion of bounded-robustness is closely related to the Almost-ASAP semantics of [24]. The work there is done in a one-player setting where the controller is already known, and one wants the know if the composition of the controller and the system satisfies a safety property in the presence of bounded jitter and observation delay. A similar model for hybrid automata is considered in [1]. The solution for the existence of bounded jitter and observation delay for which a timed system stays safe is presented in [23]. Various models of robust timed automata (the one-player case) are also considered in [4,5,13,15].

2   Timed Games

In this section we present the definitions of timed game structures, runs, objectives, and strategies in timed game structures.

Timed game structures. A *timed game structure* is a tuple $\mathcal{G} = \langle S, A_1, A_2, \Gamma_1, \Gamma_2, \delta \rangle$ with the following components.

- S is a set of states.
- A_1 and A_2 are two disjoint sets of actions for players 1 and 2, respectively. We assume that $\perp_i \notin A_i$, and write $A_i^\perp$ for $A_i \cup \{\perp_i\}$. The set of *moves* for player i is $M_i = \mathbb{R}_{\geq 0} \times A_i^{\perp_i}$. Intuitively, a move $\langle \Delta, a_i \rangle$ by player i indicates a waiting period of Δ time units followed by a discrete transition labeled with action a_i.
- $\Gamma_i : S \mapsto 2^{M_i} \setminus \emptyset$ are two move assignments. At every state s, the set $\Gamma_i(s)$ contains the moves that are available to player i. We require that $\langle 0, \perp_i \rangle \in$

$\Gamma_i(s)$ for all states $s \in S$ and $i \in \{1, 2\}$. Intuitively, $\langle 0, \perp_i \rangle$ is a time-blocking stutter move.

- $\delta : S \times (M_1 \cup M_2) \mapsto S$ is the transition function. We require that for all time delays $\Delta, \Delta' \in \mathbb{R}_{\geq 0}$ with $\Delta' \leq \Delta$, and all actions $a_i \in A_i^{\perp_i}$, we have (1) $\langle \Delta, a_i \rangle \in \Gamma_i(s)$ iff both $\langle \Delta', \perp_i \rangle \in \Gamma_i(s)$ and $\langle \Delta - \Delta', a_i \rangle \in \Gamma_i(\delta(s, \langle \Delta', \perp_i \rangle))$; and (2) if $\delta(s, \langle \Delta', \perp_i \rangle) = s'$ and $\delta(s', \langle \Delta - \Delta', a_i \rangle) = s''$, then $\delta(s, \langle \Delta, a_i \rangle) = s''$.

The game proceeds as follows. If the current state of the game is s, then both players simultaneously propose moves $\langle \Delta_1, a_1 \rangle \in \Gamma_1(s)$ and $\langle \Delta_2, a_2 \rangle \in \Gamma_2(s)$. If $a_1 \neq \perp_1$, the move with the shorter duration "wins" in determining the next state of the game. If both moves have the same duration, then the next state is chosen non-deterministically. If $a_1 = \perp_1$, then the move of player 2 determines the next state, regardless of Δ_i. We give this special power to player 1 as the controller always has the option of letting the state evolve in a controller-plant framework, without always having to provide inputs to the plant. Formally, we define the *joint destination function* $\delta_{\mathrm{jd}} : S \times M_1 \times M_2 \mapsto 2^S$ by

$$\delta_{\mathrm{jd}}(s, \langle \Delta_1, a_1 \rangle, \langle \Delta_2, a_2 \rangle) = \begin{cases} \{\delta(s, \langle \Delta_1, a_1 \rangle)\} & \text{if } \Delta_1 < \Delta_2 \text{ and } a_1 \neq \perp_1; \\ \{\delta(s, \langle \Delta_2, a_2 \rangle)\} & \text{if } \Delta_2 < \Delta_1 \text{ or } a_1 = \perp_1; \\ \{\delta(s, \langle \Delta_2, a_2 \rangle), \delta(s, \langle \Delta_1, a_1 \rangle)\} & \text{if } \Delta_2 = \Delta_1 \text{ and } a_1 \neq \perp_1. \end{cases}$$

The time elapsed when the moves $m_1 = \langle \Delta_1, a_1 \rangle$ and $m_2 = \langle \Delta_2, a_2 \rangle$ are proposed is given by $\mathsf{delay}(m_1, m_2) = \min(\Delta_1, \Delta_2)$. The boolean predicate $\mathsf{blame}_i(s, m_1, m_2, s')$ indicates whether player i is "responsible" for the state change from s to s' when the moves m_1 and m_2 are proposed. Denoting the opponent of player i by $\sim i = 3 - i$, for $i \in \{1, 2\}$, we define

$$\mathsf{blame}_i(s, \langle \Delta_1, a_1 \rangle, \langle \Delta_2, a_2 \rangle, s') = (\Delta_i \leq \Delta_{\sim i} \wedge \delta(s, \langle \Delta_i, a_i \rangle) = s') \wedge (i = 1 \rightarrow a_1 \neq \perp_1)$$

Runs. A *run* of the timed game structure $\mathcal{G}$ is an infinite sequence $r = s_0, \langle m_1^0, m_2^0 \rangle, s_1, \langle m_1^1, m_2^1 \rangle, \ldots$ such that $s_k \in S$ and $m_i^k \in \Gamma_i(s_k)$ and $s_{k+1} \in \delta_{\mathrm{jd}}(s_k, m_1^k, m_2^k)$ for all $k \geq 0$ and $i \in \{1, 2\}$. For $k \geq 0$, let $\mathsf{time}(r, k)$ denote the "time" at position k of the run, namely, $s_0, \langle m_1^0, m_2^0 \rangle, s_1, \langle m_1^1, m_2^1 \rangle, \ldots \mathsf{time}(r, k) = \sum_{j=0}^{k-1} \mathsf{delay}(m_1^j, m_2^j)$ (we let $\mathsf{time}(r, 0) = 0$). By $r[k]$ we denote the $(k+1)$-th state s_k of r. The run prefix $r[0..k]$ is the finite prefix of the run r that ends in the state s_k. Let Runs be the set of all runs of $\mathcal{G}$, and let $\mathsf{FinRuns}$ be the set of run prefixes.

Objectives. An *objective* for the timed game structure $\mathcal{G}$ is a set $\Phi \subseteq \mathsf{Runs}$ of runs. We will be interested in parity objectives. Parity objectives are canonical forms for ω-regular properties that can express all commonly used specifications that arise in verification.

Let $\Omega : S \mapsto \{0, \ldots, k-1\}$ be a parity index function. The parity objective for Ω requires that the maximal index visited infinitely often is even. Formally, let $\mathsf{InfOften}(\Omega(r))$ denote the set of indices visited infinitely often along a run r. Then the parity objective defines the following set of runs:

Parity$(\Omega) = \{r \mid \max(\mathsf{InfOften}(\Omega(r)))$ is even $\}$. A timed game structure $\mathcal{G}$ together with the index function Ω constitute a *parity timed game* (of *order* k) in which the objective of player 1 is Parity(Ω).

Strategies. A *strategy* for a player is a recipe that specifies how to extend a run. Formally, a *strategy* π_i for player $i \in \{1, 2\}$ is a function π_i that assigns to every run prefix $r[0..k]$ a move m_i in the set of moves available to player i at the state $r[k]$. For $i \in \{1, 2\}$, let Π_i be the set of strategies for player i. Given two strategies $\pi_1 \in \Pi_1$ and $\pi_2 \in \Pi_2$, the set of possible *outcomes* of the game starting from a state $s \in S$ is the set of possible runs denoted by Outcomes(s, π_1, π_2).

Receptive strategies. We will be interested in strategies that are meaningful (in the sense that they do not block time). To define them formally we first present the following two sets of runs.

- A run r is *time-divergent* if $\lim_{k \to \infty} \mathsf{time}(r, k) = \infty$. We denote by Timediv is the set of all time-divergent runs.
- The set Blameless$_i \subseteq$ Runs consists of the set of runs in which player i is responsible only for finitely many transitions. A run $s_0, \langle m_1^0, m_2^0 \rangle, s_1, \langle m_1^1, m_2^1 \rangle, \ldots$ belongs to the set Blameless$_i$, for $i = \{1, 2\}$, if there exists a $k \geq 0$ such that for all $j \geq k$, we have $\neg\, \mathsf{blame}_i(s_j, m_1^j, m_2^j, s_{j+1})$.

A strategy π_i is *receptive* if for all strategies $\pi_{\sim i}$, all states $s \in S$, and all runs $r \in$ Outcomes(s, π_1, π_2), either $r \in$ Timediv or $r \in$ Blameless$_i$. Thus, no what matter what the opponent does, a receptive strategy of player i cannot be responsible for blocking time. Strategies that are not receptive are not physically meaningful. A timed game structure $\mathcal{G}$ is *well-formed* if both players have receptive strategies. We restrict our attention to well-formed timed game structures. We denote Π_i^R to be the set of receptive strategies for player i. Note that for $\pi_1 \in \Pi_1^R, \pi_2 \in \Pi_2^R$, we have Outcomes$(s, \pi_1, \pi_2) \subseteq$ Timediv.

Winning sets. Given an objective Φ, let WinTimeDiv$_1^{\mathcal{G}}(\Phi)$ denote the set of states s in $\mathcal{G}$ such that player 1 has a receptive strategy $\pi_1 \in \Pi_1^R$ such that for all receptive strategies $\pi_2 \in \Pi_2^R$, we have Outcomes$(s, \pi_1, \pi_2) \subseteq \Phi$. The strategy π is said to be winning strategy. In computing the winning sets, we shall quantify over *all* strategies, but modify the objective to take care of time divergence. Given an objective Φ, let TimeDivBl$_1(\Phi) = ($Timediv $\cap\ \Phi) \cup ($Blameless$_1 \setminus$ Timediv$)$, i.e., TimeDivBl$_1(\Phi)$ denotes the set of runs such that either time diverges and Φ holds, or else time converges and player 1 is not responsible for time to converge. Let Win$_1^{\mathcal{G}}(\Phi)$ be the set of states in $\mathcal{G}$ such that for all $s \in$ Win$_1^{\mathcal{G}}(\Phi)$, player 1 has a (possibly non-receptive) strategy $\pi_1 \in \Pi_1$ such that for all (possibly non-receptive) strategies $\pi_2 \in \Pi_2$, we have Outcomes$(s, \pi_1, \pi_2) \subseteq \Phi$. The strategy π_1 is said to be winning for the non-receptive game. The following result establishes the connection between Win and WinTimeDiv sets.

Theorem 1 ([14]). *For all well-formed timed game structures $\mathcal{G}$, and for all ω-regular objectives Φ, we have* Win$_1^{\mathcal{G}}($TimeDivBl$_1(\Phi)) =$ WinTimeDiv$_1^{\mathcal{G}}(\Phi)$.

We now define a special class of timed game structures, namely, timed automaton games.

Timed automaton games. Timed automata [2] suggest a finite syntax for specifying infinite-state timed game structures. A *timed automaton game* is a tuple $\mathfrak{T} = \langle L, C, A_1, A_2, E, \gamma \rangle$ with the following components:

- L is a finite set of locations.
- C is a finite set of clocks.
- A_1 and A_2 are two disjoint sets of actions for players 1 and 2, respectively.
- $E \subseteq L \times (A_1 \cup A_2) \times \mathsf{Constr}(C) \times L \times 2^C$ is the edge relation, where the set $\mathsf{Constr}(C)$ of *clock constraints* is generated by the grammar: $\theta ::= x \leq d \mid d \leq x \mid \neg\theta \mid \theta_1 \wedge \theta_2$, for clock variables $x \in C$ and nonnegative integer constants d. For an edge $e = \langle l, a_i, \theta, l', \lambda \rangle$, the clock constraint θ acts as a guard on the clock values which specifies when the edge e can be taken, and by taking the edge e, the clocks in the set $\lambda \subseteq C$ are reset to 0. We require that for all edges $\langle l, a_i, \theta', l', \lambda' \rangle \neq \langle l, a_i', \theta'', l'', \lambda'' \rangle \in E$, we have $a_i \neq a_i'$. This requirement ensures that a state and a move together uniquely determine a successor state.
- $\gamma : L \mapsto \mathsf{Constr}(C)$ is a function that assigns to every location an invariant for both players. All clocks increase uniformly at the same rate. When at location l, each player i must propose a move out of l before the invariant $\gamma(l)$ expires. Thus, the game can stay at a location only as long as the invariant is satisfied by the clock values.

A *clock valuation* is a function $\kappa : C \mapsto \mathbb{R}_{\geq 0}$ that maps every clock to a nonnegative real. The set of all clock valuations for C is denoted by $K(C)$. Given a clock valuation $\kappa \in K(C)$ and a time delay $\Delta \in \mathbb{R}_{\geq 0}$, we write $\kappa + \Delta$ for the clock valuation in $K(C)$ defined by $(\kappa + \Delta)(x) = \kappa(x) + \Delta$ for all clocks $x \in C$. For a subset $\lambda \subseteq C$ of the clocks, we write $\kappa[\lambda := 0]$ for the clock valuation in $K(C)$ defined by $(\kappa[\lambda := 0])(x) = 0$ if $x \in \lambda$, and $(\kappa[\lambda := 0])(x) = \kappa(x)$ if $x \notin \lambda$. A clock valuation $\kappa \in K(C)$ *satisfies* the clock constraint $\theta \in \mathsf{Constr}(C)$, written $\kappa \models \theta$, if the condition θ holds when all clocks in C take on the values specified by κ. A *state* $s = \langle l, \kappa \rangle$ of the timed automaton game $\mathfrak{T}$ is a location $l \in L$ together with a clock valuation $\kappa \in K(C)$ such that the invariant at the location is satisfied, that is, $\kappa \models \gamma(l)$. We let S be the set of all states of $\mathfrak{T}$. Given a timed automaton game $\mathfrak{T}$, the definition of a associated timed game structure $[\![\mathfrak{T}]\!]$ is standard [9].

Clock regions. Timed automaton games can be solved using a region construction from the theory of timed automata [2]. For a real $t \geq 0$, let $\mathsf{frac}(t) = t - \lfloor t \rfloor$ denote the fractional part of t. Given a timed automaton game $\mathfrak{T}$, for each clock $x \in C$, let c_x denote the largest integer constant that appears in any clock constraint involving x in $\mathfrak{T}$ (let $c_x = 1$ if there is no clock constraint involving x). Two states $\langle l_1, \kappa_1 \rangle$ and $\langle l_1, \kappa_1 \rangle$ are said to be *region equivalent* if all the following conditions are satisfied: (a) $l_1 = l_2$, (b) for all clocks x, $\kappa_1(x) \leq c_x$ iff $\kappa_2(x) \leq c_x$, (c) for all clocks x with $\kappa_1(x) \leq c_x$, $\lfloor \kappa_1(x) \rfloor = \lfloor \kappa_2(x) \rfloor$, (d) for all clocks x, y with $\kappa_1(x) \leq c_x$ and $\kappa_1(y) \leq c_y$, $\mathsf{frac}(\kappa_1(x)) \leq \mathsf{frac}(\kappa_1(x))$ iff $\mathsf{frac}(\kappa_2(x)) \leq \mathsf{frac}(\kappa_2(x))$, and (e) for all clocks x with $\kappa_1(x) \leq c_x$, $\mathsf{frac}(\kappa_1(x)) = 0$ iff $\mathsf{frac}(\kappa_2(x)) = 0$. A *region* is an equivalence class of states with respect to the region equivalence relation. There are finitely many clock regions; more precisely, the number of clock regions is bounded by $|L| \cdot \prod_{x \in C}(c_x + 1) \cdot |C|! \cdot 2^{|C|}$.

Region strategies and objectives. For a state $s \in S$, we write $\mathsf{Reg}(s) \subseteq S$ for the clock region containing s. For a run r, we let the *region sequence* $\mathsf{Reg}(r) = \mathsf{Reg}(r[0]), \mathsf{Reg}(r[1]), \cdots$. Two runs r, r' are region equivalent if their region sequences are the same. An ω-regular objective Φ is a region objective if for all region-equivalent runs r, r', we have $r \in \Phi$ iff $r' \in \Phi$. A strategy π_1 is a *region strategy*, if for all runs r_1 and r_2 and all $k \geq 0$ such that $\mathsf{Reg}(r_1[0..k]) = \mathsf{Reg}(r_2[0..k])$, we have that if $\pi_1(r_1[0..k]) = \langle \Delta, a_1 \rangle$, then $\pi_1(r_2[0..k]) = \langle \Delta', a_1 \rangle$ with $\mathsf{Reg}(r_1[k] + \Delta) = \mathsf{Reg}(r_2[k] + \Delta')$. The definition for player 2 strategies is analogous. Two region strategies π_1 and π_1' are region-equivalent if for all runs r and all $k \geq 0$ we have that if $\pi_1(r[0..k]) = \langle \Delta, a_1 \rangle$, then $\pi_1'(r[0..k]) = \langle \Delta', a_1 \rangle$ with $\mathsf{Reg}(r[k] + \Delta) = \mathsf{Reg}(r[k] + \Delta')$. A parity index function Ω is a region (resp. location) parity index function if $\Omega(s_1) = \Omega(s_2)$ whenever $\mathsf{Reg}(s_1) = \mathsf{Reg}(s_2)$ (resp. s_1, s_2 have the same location). Henceforth, we shall restrict our attention to region and location objectives.

Encoding time-divergence by enlarging the game structure. Given a timed automaton game $\mathcal{T}$, consider the enlarged game structure $\widehat{\mathcal{T}}$ with the state space $\widehat{S} \subseteq S \times \mathbb{R}_{[0,1)} \times \{\text{TRUE}, \text{FALSE}\}^2$, and an augmented transition relation $\widehat{\delta} : \widehat{S} \times (M_1 \cup M_2) \mapsto \widehat{S}$. In an augmented state $\langle s, \mathfrak{z}, tick, bl_1 \rangle \in \widehat{S}$, the component $s \in S$ is a state of the original game structure $[\![\mathcal{T}]\!]$, $\mathfrak{z}$ is value of a fictitious clock z which gets reset to 0 every time it hits 1, $tick$ is true iff z hit 1 at last transition and bl_1 is true if player 1 is to blame for the last transition. Note that any strategy π_i in $[\![\mathcal{T}]\!]$, can be considered a strategy in $\widehat{\mathcal{T}}$. The values of the clock z, $tick$ and bl_1 correspond to the values each player keeps in memory in constructing his strategy. Any run r in $\mathcal{T}$ has a corresponding unique run $\widehat{r}$ in $\widehat{\mathcal{T}}$ with $\widehat{r}[0] = \langle r[0], 0, \text{FALSE}, \text{FALSE} \rangle$ such that r is a projection of $\widehat{r}$ onto $\mathcal{T}$. For an objective Φ, we can now encode time-divergence as: $\mathsf{TimeDivBl}_1(\Phi) = (\Box \Diamond \, tick \rightarrow \Phi) \wedge (\neg \Box \Diamond \, tick \rightarrow \Diamond \Box \neg \, bl_1)$. Let $\widehat{\kappa}$ be a valuation for the clocks in $\widehat{C} = C \cup \{z\}$. A state of $\widehat{\mathcal{T}}$ can then be considered as $\langle \langle l, \widehat{\kappa} \rangle, tick, bl_1 \rangle$. We extend the clock equivalence relation to these expanded states: $\langle \langle l, \widehat{\kappa} \rangle \, tick, bl_1 \rangle \cong \langle \langle l', \widehat{\kappa}' \rangle, tick', bl_1' \rangle$ iff $l = l'$, $tick = tick'$, $bl_1 = bl_1'$ and $\widehat{\kappa} \cong \widehat{\kappa}'$. Given a location l, and a set $\lambda \subseteq \widehat{C}$, we let $\widehat{R}[\mathrm{loc} := l, \lambda := 0]$ denote the region $\{\langle l, \widehat{\kappa} \rangle \in \widehat{S} \mid$ there exist l' and $\widehat{\kappa}'$ with $\langle l', \widehat{\kappa}' \rangle \in \widehat{R}$ and $\widehat{\kappa}(x) = 0$ if $x \in \lambda$, $\widehat{\kappa}(x) = \widehat{\kappa}'(x)$ if $x \notin \lambda \}$. For every ω-regular region objective Φ of $\mathcal{T}$, we have $\mathsf{TimeDivBl}_1(\Phi)$ to be an ω-regular region objective of $\widehat{\mathcal{T}}$.

We now present a lemma that states for region ω-regular objectives region winning strategies exist, and all strategies region-equivalent to a region winning strategy are also winning.

Lemma 1 ([8]). *Let $\mathcal{T}$ be a timed automaton game and $\widehat{\mathcal{T}}$ be the corresponding enlarged game structure. Let $\widehat{\Phi}$ be an ω-regular region objective of $\widehat{\mathcal{T}}$. Then,*

(1) there exists a region winning strategy for $\widehat{\Phi}$ from $\mathsf{Win}_1^{\widehat{\mathcal{J}}}(\widehat{\Phi})$, and (2) if π_1' is a strategy that is region-equivalent to a region winning strategy π_1, then π_1' is a winning strategy for $\widehat{\Phi}$ from $\mathsf{Win}_1^{\widehat{\mathcal{J}}}(\widehat{\Phi})$.

3   Exact Winning of Timed Parity Games

In this section we shall present a reduction of timed automaton games to turn-based finite game graphs. The reduction allows us to use the rich literature of algorithms for finite game graphs for solving timed automaton games. It also leads to algorithms with better complexity than the one presented in [9]. Let $\mathcal{J}$ be a timed automaton game, and let $\widehat{\mathcal{J}}$ be the corresponding enlarged timed game structure that encodes time divergence. We shall construct a finite state turn based game structure $\mathcal{J}^f$ based on regions of $\widehat{\mathcal{J}}$ which can be used to compute winning states for parity objectives for the timed automaton game $\mathcal{J}$. In this finite state game, first player 1 proposes a destination region $\widehat{R}_1$ together with a discrete action a_1. Intuitively, this can be taken to mean that in the game $\widehat{\mathcal{J}}$, player 1 wants to first let time elapse to get to the region $\widehat{R}_1$, and then take the discrete action a_1. Let us denote this intermediate state which specifies the desired region of player 1 in $\mathcal{J}^f$ by the tuple $\langle \widehat{R}, \widehat{R}_1, a_1 \rangle$. From this state in $\mathcal{J}^f$, player 2 similarly also proposes a move consisting of a region $\widehat{R}_2$ together with a discrete action a_2. These two moves signify that player i proposed a move $\langle \Delta_i, a_i \rangle$ in $\widehat{\mathcal{J}}$ from a state $\widehat{s} \in \widehat{R}$ such that $\widehat{s} + \Delta_i \in \widehat{R}_i$. The following lemma states that only the regions of $\widehat{s} + \Delta_i$ are important in determining the successor region in $\widehat{\mathcal{J}}$.

Lemma 2 ([8]). *Let $\mathcal{J}$ be a timed automaton game and let Y, Y_1', Y_2' be regions in the enlarged timed game structure $\widehat{[\mathcal{J}]}$. Suppose player-i has a move from $s_1 \in Y$ to $s_1' \in Y'$, for $i \in \{1, 2\}$. Then, one of the following cases must hold.*

1. *From all states $\widehat{s} \in Y$, there exists a player-1 move $m_1^{\widehat{s}}$ with $\widehat{\delta}(\widehat{s}, m_1^{\widehat{s}}) \in Y_1'$ such that for all moves $m_2^{\widehat{s}}$ of player-2 with $\widehat{\delta}(\widehat{s}, m_2^{\widehat{s}}) \in Y_2'$, we have $\mathsf{blame}_1(\widehat{s}, m_1^{\widehat{s}}, m_2^{\widehat{s}}, \widehat{\delta}(\widehat{s}, m_1^{\widehat{s}})) = \mathrm{TRUE}$ and $\mathsf{blame}_2(\widehat{s}, m_1^{\widehat{s}}, m_2^{\widehat{s}}, \widehat{\delta}(\widehat{s}, m_2^{\widehat{s}})) = \mathrm{FALSE}$.*
2. *From all states $\widehat{s} \in Y$, for all moves $m_1^{\widehat{s}}$ of player-1 with $\widehat{\delta}(\widehat{s}, m_1^{\widehat{s}}) \in Y_1'$, there exists a player-2 move $m_2^{\widehat{s}}$ with $\widehat{\delta}(\widehat{s}, m_2^{\widehat{s}}) \in Y_2'$ such that $\mathsf{blame}_2(\widehat{s}, m_1^{\widehat{s}}, m_2^{\widehat{s}}, \widehat{\delta}(\widehat{s}, m_2^{\widehat{s}})) = \mathrm{TRUE}$.*

By Lemma 2, given an initial state in $\widehat{R}$, for moves of both players to some fixed $\widehat{R}_1, \widehat{R}_2$, either the move of player 1 is always chosen, or player 2 can always pick a move such that player-1's move is foiled. Note that the lemma is asymmetric, the asymmetry arises in the case when time delays of the two moves result in the same region. In this case, not all moves of player 2 might work, but some will (e.g., a delay of player 2 that is the same as that for player 1).

Let $\widehat{S}_{\mathsf{Reg}} = \{x \mid X \text{ is a region of } \widehat{\mathcal{J}}\}$. Because of Lemma 2, we may construct a finite turn based game to capture the winning set.

A finite state turn based game G consists of the tuple $\langle (S, E), (S_1, S_2) \rangle$, where (S_1, S_2) forms a partition of the finite set S of states, E is the set of edges, S_1 is the set of states from which only player 1 can make a move to choose an outgoing edge, and S_2 is the set of states from which only player 2 can make a move. The game is bipartite if every outgoing edge from a player-1 state leads to a player-2 state and vice-versa. A bipartite turn based finite game $\mathcal{T}^f = \langle (S^f, E^f), (\widehat{S}_{\text{Reg}} \times \{1\}, \widehat{S}_{\text{Tup}} \times \{2\}) \rangle$ can be constructed to capture the timed game $\mathcal{T}$ (the full construction can be found in [7]). The state space S^f equals $\widehat{S}_{\text{Reg}} \times \{1\} \cup \widehat{S}_{\text{Tup}} \times \{2\}$. The set $\widehat{S}_{\text{Reg}}$ is the set of regions of $\widehat{\mathcal{T}}$. Each $\langle \widehat{R}, 1 \rangle \in \widehat{S}_{\text{Reg}} \times \{1\}$ is indicative of a state in the timed game $\widehat{\mathcal{T}}$ that belongs to the region $\widehat{R}$. Each $\langle Y, 2 \rangle \in \widehat{S}_{\text{Tup}} \times \{2\}$ encodes the following information: (a) the previous state of $\mathcal{T}^f$ (which corresponds to a region $\widehat{R}$ of $\widehat{\mathcal{T}}$), (b) a region $\widehat{R}'$ of $\widehat{\mathcal{T}}$ (representing an intermediate state which results from time passage in $\widehat{\mathcal{T}}$ from a state in the previous region $\widehat{R}$ to a state in $\widehat{R}'$), and (c) the desired discrete action of player 1 to be taken from the intermediate state in $\widehat{R}'$. An edge from $\langle \widehat{R}, 1 \rangle$ to $\langle Y, 2 \rangle$ represents the fact that in the timed game $\widehat{\mathcal{T}}$, from every state $\widehat{s} \in \widehat{R}$, player 1 has a move $\langle \Delta, a_1 \rangle$ such that $\widehat{s} + \Delta$ is in the intermediate region component $\widehat{R}'$ of $\langle Y, 2 \rangle$, with a_1 being the desired discrete action. From the state $\langle Y, 2 \rangle$, player 2 has moves to $\widehat{S}_{\text{Reg}} \times \{1\}$ depending on what moves of player 2 in the timed game $\widehat{\mathcal{T}}$ can beat the player-1 moves from $\widehat{R}$ to $\widehat{R}'$ according to Lemma 2.

Each $Z \in S^f$ is itself a tuple, with the first component being a location of $\mathcal{T}$. Given a location parity index function Ω on $\mathcal{T}$, we let Ω^f be the parity index function on $\mathcal{T}^f$ such that $\Omega^f(\langle l, \cdot \rangle) = \Omega(\langle l, \cdot \rangle)$. Another parity index function $\widehat{\Omega}^f$ with two more priorities can be derived from Ω^f to take care of time divergence issues, as described in [9]. Given a set $X = X_1 \times \{1\} \cup X_2 \times \{2\} \subseteq S^f$, we let $\mathsf{RegStates}(X) = \{\widehat{s} \in \widehat{S} \mid \mathsf{Reg}(\widehat{s}) \in X_1\}$. Theorem 2 shows that the turn based game $\mathcal{T}^f$ captures the timed automaton game $\mathcal{T}$.

Theorem 2. *Let $\widehat{\mathcal{T}}$ be an enlarged timed game structure, and let $\mathcal{T}^f$ be the corresponding finite game structure. Then, given an ω-regular region objective $\mathsf{Parity}(\Omega)$, we have $\mathsf{Win}_1^{\widehat{\mathcal{T}}}(\mathsf{TimeDivBl}_1(\mathsf{Parity}(\Omega))) = \mathsf{RegStates}(\mathsf{Win}_1^{\mathcal{T}^f}(\mathsf{Parity}(\widehat{\Omega}^f)))$.*

The state space of the finite turn based game can be seen to be at most $O(|\widehat{S}_{\text{Reg}}|^2 \cdot |L| \cdot 2^{|C|})$ (a discrete action may switch the location, and reset some clocks). We show that it is not required to keep all possible pairs of regions, leading to a reduction in the size of the state space. This is because from a state $\widehat{s} \in R$, it is not possible to get all regions by letting time elapse.

Lemma 3. *Let $\mathcal{T}$ be a timed automaton game, $\widehat{\mathcal{T}}$ the corresponding enlarged game structure, and $\widehat{R}$ a region in $\widehat{\mathcal{T}}$. The number of possible time successor regions of $\widehat{R}$ are at most $2 \cdot \sum_{x \in C} 2(c_x + 1) \leq 4 \cdot (M + 1) \cdot (|C| + 1)$, where c_x is the largest constant that clock x is compared to in $\widehat{\mathcal{T}}$, $M = \max\{c_x \mid x \in C\}$ and C is the set of clocks in $\mathcal{T}$.*

Complexity of reduction. Recall that for a timed automaton game $\mathcal{T}$, A_i is the set of actions for player i, C is the set of clocks and M is the largest constant in $\mathcal{T}$. Let $|A_i|^* = \min\{|A_i|, |L| \cdot 2^{|C|}\}$ and let $|\mathcal{T}_{\text{Constr}}|$ denote the length of the clock constraints in $\mathcal{T}$. The size of the state space of $\mathcal{T}^f$ is bounded by $|\widehat{S}_{\text{Reg}}| \cdot (1 + (M+1) \cdot (|C|+2) \cdot 2 \cdot (|A_1|^* + 1))$, where $|\widehat{S}_{\text{Reg}}| \leq 16 \cdot |L| \cdot \prod_{x \in C}(c_x + 1) \cdot |C+1|! \cdot 2^{|C|+1}$ is the number of regions of $\widehat{\mathcal{T}}$. The number of edges in $\mathcal{T}^f$ is bounded by $|\widehat{S}_{\text{Reg}}| \cdot ((M+1) \cdot (|C|+2) \cdot 2) \cdot (|A_1|^* + 1)[(1 + (|A_2|^* + 1) \cdot ((M+1) \cdot (|C|+2) \cdot 2)]$. The details can be found in [7].

Theorem 3. *Let $\mathcal{T}$ be a timed automaton game, and Ω be a region parity index function of order d. The set $\mathsf{WinTimeDiv}_1^{\mathcal{T}}(\mathsf{Parity}(\Omega))$ can be computed in time*

$$O\left((|\widehat{S}_{\text{Reg}}| \cdot |\mathcal{T}_{\text{Constr}}|) + [M \cdot |C| \cdot |A_2|^*] \cdot \left[2 \cdot |\widehat{S}_{\text{Reg}}| \cdot M \cdot |C| \cdot |A_1|^* \right]^{\frac{d+2}{3} + \frac{3}{2}} \right)$$

where $|\widehat{S}_{\text{Reg}}| \leq 16 \cdot |L| \cdot \prod_{x \in C}(c_x + 1) \cdot |C+1|! \cdot 2^{|C|+1}$, M is the largest constant in $\mathcal{T}$, $|\mathcal{T}_{\text{Constr}}|$ is the length of the clock constraints in $\mathcal{T}$, C is the set of clocks, $|A_i|^* = \min\{|A_i|, |L| \cdot 2^{|C|}\}$, and $|A_i|$ the number of discrete actions of player i for $i \in \{1,2\}$.

In Theorem 3, we have used the result from [18] which states that a turn based parity game with m edges, n states and d parity indices can be solved in $O(m \cdot n^{\frac{d}{3} + \frac{1}{2}})$ time. From Theorem 2, we can solve the finite state game $\mathcal{T}^f$ to compute winning sets for all ω-regular region parity objectives Φ for a timed automaton game $\mathcal{T}$, using *any* algorithm for finite state turn based games, e.g., strategy improvement, small-progress algorithms [21,16].

4   Robust Winning of Timed Parity Games

In this section we study restrictions on player-1 strategies to model robust winning, and show how the winning sets can be obtained by reductions to general timed automaton games. The results of Section 3 can then be used to obtain algorithms for computing the robust winning sets.

There is inherent uncertainty in real-time systems. In a physical system, an action may be prescribed by a controller, but the controller can never prescribe a single timepoint where that action will be taken with probability 1. There is usually some *jitter* when the specified action is taken, the jitter being non-deterministic. The model of general timed automaton games, where player 1 can specify exact moves of the form $\langle \Delta, a_1 \rangle$ consisting of an action together with a delay, assume that the jitter is 0. In subsection 4.1, we obtain robust winning sets for player 1 in the presence of non-zero jitter (which are assumed to be arbitrarily small) for each of her proposed moves. In subsection 4.2, we assume the jitter to be some fixed $\varepsilon_j \geq 0$ for every move that is known. The strategies of player 2 are left unrestricted. In the case of lower-bounded jitter, we also introduce a *response time* for player-1 strategies. The response time is the minimum delay between a discrete action, and a discrete action of the controller. We note that the set of player-1 strategies with a jitter of $\varepsilon_j > 0$ contains the set of player-1 strategies with a jitter of $\varepsilon_j/2$ and a response time of $\varepsilon_j/2$. Thus, the strategies of subsection 4.1 automatically have a response time greater than 0. The winning sets in both sections are hence robust towards the presence of jitter and response times.

4.1 Winning in the Presence of Jitter

In this subsection, we model games where the jitter is assumed to be greater than 0, but arbitrarily small in each round of the game.

Given a state s, a *limit-robust move* for player 1 is either the move $\langle \Delta, \perp_1 \rangle$ with $\langle \Delta, \perp_1 \rangle \in \Gamma_1(s)$; or it is a tuple $\langle [\alpha, \beta], a_1 \rangle$ for some $\alpha < \beta$ such that for every $\Delta \in [\alpha, \beta]$ we have $\langle \Delta, a_1 \rangle \in \Gamma_1(s)$. [1] Note that a time move $\langle \Delta, \perp_1 \rangle$ for player 1 implies that she is relinquishing the current round to player 2, as the move of player 2 will always be chosen, and hence we allow a singleton time move. Given a limit-robust move $mrob_1$ for player 1, and a move m_2 for player 2, the set of possible outcomes is the set $\{\delta_{jd}(s, m_1, m_2) \mid$ either (a) $mrob_1 = \langle \Delta, \perp_1 \rangle$ and $m_1 = mrob_1$; or (b) $mrob_1 = \langle [\alpha, \beta], a_1 \rangle$ and $m_1 = \langle \Delta, a_1 \rangle$ with $\Delta \in [\alpha, \beta]\}$. A *limit-robust strategy* π_1^{rob} for player 1 prescribes limit-robust moves to finite run prefixes. We let Π_1^{rob} denote the set of limit-robust strategies for player-1. Given an objective Φ, let $\mathsf{RobWinTimeDiv}_1^{\mathcal{T}}(\Phi)$ denote the set of states s in $\mathcal{T}$ such that player 1 has a limit-robust receptive strategy $\pi_1^{rob} \in \Pi_1^R$ such that for all receptive strategies $\pi_2 \in \Pi_2^R$, we have $\mathsf{Outcomes}(s, \pi_1^{rob}, \pi_2) \subseteq \Phi$. We say a limit-robust strategy π_1^{rob} is region equivalent to a strategy π_1 if for all runs r and for all $k \geq 0$, the following conditions hold: (a) if $\pi_1(r[0..k]) = \langle \Delta, \perp_1 \rangle$, then $\pi_1^{rob}(r[0..k]) = \langle \Delta', \perp_1 \rangle$ with $\mathsf{Reg}(r[k] + \Delta) = \mathsf{Reg}(r[k] + \Delta')$; and (b) if $\pi_1(r[0..k]) = \langle \Delta, a_1 \rangle$ with $a_1 \neq \perp_1$, then $\pi_1^{rob}(r[0..k]) = \langle [\alpha, \beta], a_1 \rangle$ with $\mathsf{Reg}(r[k]+\Delta) = \mathsf{Reg}(r[k]+\Delta')$ for all $\Delta' \in [\alpha, \beta]$. Note that for any limit-robust move $\langle [\alpha, \beta], a_1 \rangle$ with $a_1 \neq \perp_1$ from a state s, we must have that the set $\{s + \Delta \mid \Delta \in [\alpha, \beta]\}$ contains an open region of $\mathcal{T}$.

We now show how to compute the set $\mathsf{RobWinTimeDiv}_1^{\mathcal{T}}(\Phi)$. Given a timed automaton game $\mathcal{T}$, we have the corresponding enlarged game structure $\widehat{\mathcal{T}}$ which encodes time-divergence. We add another boolean variable to $\widehat{\mathcal{T}}$ to obtain another game structure $\widehat{\mathcal{T}}_{rob}$. The state space of $\widehat{\mathcal{T}}_{rob}$ is $\widehat{S} \times \{\text{TRUE}, \text{FALSE}\}$. The transition relation $\widehat{\delta}_{rob}$ is such that $\widehat{\delta}_{rob}(\langle \widehat{s}, rb_1 \rangle, \langle \Delta, a_i \rangle) = \langle \widehat{\delta}(\widehat{s}, \langle \Delta, a_i \rangle), rb_1' \rangle$, where $rb_1' = \text{TRUE}$ iff $rb_1 = \text{TRUE}$ and one of the following hold: (a) $a_i \in A_2^\perp$; or (b) $a_i = \perp_1$; or (c) $a_i \in A_1$ and $s + \Delta$ belongs to an open region of $\widehat{\mathcal{T}}$.

Theorem 4. *Given a state s in a timed automaton game $\mathcal{T}$ and an ω-regular region objective Φ, we have $s \in \mathsf{RobWinTimeDiv}_1^{\mathcal{T}}(\Phi)$ iff $\langle s, \cdot, \cdot, \cdot, \text{TRUE} \rangle \in \mathsf{Win}_1^{\widehat{\mathcal{T}}_{rob}}$ $(\Phi \wedge \Box(rb_1 = \text{TRUE}) \wedge (\Diamond\Box(tick = \text{FALSE}) \rightarrow (\Diamond\Box(bl_1 = \text{FALSE}))))$.*

We say a timed automaton $\mathcal{T}$ is *open* if all the guards and invariants in $\mathcal{T}$ are open. Note that even though all the guards and invariants are open, a player might still

---
[1] We can also have open or semi-open time intervals, the results do not change.

propose moves to closed regions, e.g., consider an edge between two locations l_1 and l_2 with the guard $0 < x < 2$; a player might propose a move from $\langle l_1, x = 0.2 \rangle$ to $\langle l_2, x = 1 \rangle$. The next theorem shows that this is not required of player 1 in general, that is, to win for an ω-regular location objective, player 1 only needs to propose moves to open regions of $\mathcal{T}$. Let $\mathsf{Constr}^*(C)$ be the set of clock constraints generated by the grammar: $\theta ::= x < d \mid x > d \mid x \geq 0 \mid x < y \mid \theta_1 \wedge \theta_2$, for clock variables $x, y \in C$ and nonnegative integer constants d. An *open polytope* of $\mathcal{T}$ is set of states X such that $X = \{\langle l, \kappa \rangle \in S \mid \kappa \models \theta\}$ for some $\theta \in \mathsf{Constr}^*(C)$. An open polytope X is hence a union of regions of $\mathcal{T}$. Note that it may contain open as well as closed regions. We say a parity objective $\mathsf{Parity}(\Omega)$ is an open polytope objective if $\Omega^{-1}(j)$ is an open polytope for every $j \geq 0$.

Theorem 5. *Let $\mathcal{T}$ be an open timed automaton game and let $\Phi = \mathsf{Parity}(\Omega)$ be an ω-regular location objective. Then,* $\mathsf{WinTimeDiv}_1^{\mathcal{T}}(\Phi) = \mathsf{RobWinTimeDiv}_1^{\mathcal{T}}(\Phi)$.

4.2   Winning with Bounded Jitter and Response Time

The limit-robust winning strategies described in subsection 4.1 did not have a lower bound on the jitter: player 1 could propose a move $\langle [\alpha, \alpha + \varepsilon], a_1 \rangle$ for arbitrarily small α and ε. In some cases, the controller may be required to work with a known jitter, and also a finite *response time*. Intuitively, the response time is the minimum delay between a discrete action and a discrete action of the controller. We model this scenario by allowing player 1 to propose moves with a single time point, but we make the jitter and the response time explicit and modify the semantics as follows. Player 1 can propose exact moves (with a delay greater than the response time), but the actual delay in the game will be controlled by player 2 and will be in a jitter interval around the proposed player-1 delay.

   Given a finite run $r[0..k] = s_0, \langle m_1^0, m_2^0 \rangle, s_1, \langle m_1^1, m_2^1 \rangle, \ldots, s_k$, let $\mathsf{TimeElapse}$ $(r[0..k]) = \sum_{j=p}^{k-1} \mathsf{delay}(m_1^j, m_2^j)$ where p is the least integer greater than or equal to 0 such that for all $k > j \geq p$ we have $m_2^j = \langle \Delta_2^j, \perp_2 \rangle$ and $\mathsf{blame}_2(s_j, m_1^j, m_2^j,$ $s_{j+1}) = \mathrm{TRUE}$ (we take $\mathsf{TimeElapse}(r[0..k]) = 0$ if $p = k$). Intuitively, $\mathsf{TimeElapse}$ $(r[0..k])$ denotes the time that has passed due to a sequence of contiguous pure time moves leading upto s_k in the run $r[0..k]$. Let $\varepsilon_j \geq 0$ and $\varepsilon_r \geq 0$ be given bounded jitter and response time (we assume both are rational). Since a pure time move of player 1 is a relinquishing move, we place no restriction on it. Player 2 can also propose moves such that only time advances, without any discrete action being taken. in this case, we need to adjust the remaining response time. Formally, an *ε_j-jitter ε_r-response bounded-robust strategy* π_1 of player 1 proposes a move $\pi_1(r[0..k]) = m_1^k$ such that either

- $m_1^k = \langle \Delta^k, \perp_1 \rangle$ with $\langle \Delta, \perp_1 \rangle \in \Gamma_1(S)$, or,
- $m_1^k = \langle \Delta^k, a_1 \rangle$ such that the following two conditions hold:
  - $\Delta^k \geq \max(0, \varepsilon_r - \mathsf{TimeElapse}(r[0..k]))$, and,
  - $\langle \Delta', a_1 \rangle \in \Gamma_1(s)$ for all $\Delta' \in [\Delta^k, \Delta^k + \varepsilon_j]$.

Given a move $m_1 = \langle \Delta, a_1 \rangle$ of player 1 and a move m_2 of player 2, the set of resulting states is given by $\delta_{jd}(s, m_1, m_2)$ if $a_1 = \bot_1$, and by $\{\delta_{jd}(s, m_1 + \epsilon, m_2) \mid \epsilon \in [0, \varepsilon_j]\}$ otherwise. Given an ε_j-jitter ε_r-response bounded-robust strategy π_1 of player 1, and a strategy π_2 of player 2, the set of possible outcomes in the present semantics is denoted by $\mathsf{Outcomes}_{jr}(s, \pi_1, \pi_2)$. We denote the winning set for player 1 for an objective Φ given finite ε_j and ε_r by $\mathsf{JRWinTimeDiv}_1^{\mathcal{T}, \varepsilon_j, \varepsilon_r}(\Phi)$. We now show that $\mathsf{JRWinTimeDiv}_1^{\mathcal{T}, \varepsilon_j, \varepsilon_r}(\Phi)$ can be computed by obtaining a timed automaton $\mathcal{T}^{\varepsilon_j, \varepsilon_r}$ from $\mathcal{T}$ such that $\mathsf{WinTimeDiv}_1^{\mathcal{T}^{\varepsilon_j, \varepsilon_r}}(\Phi) = \mathsf{JRWinTimeDiv}_1^{\mathcal{T}, \varepsilon_j, \varepsilon_r}(\Phi)$.

Given a clock constraint φ we make the clocks appearing in φ explicit by denoting the constraint as $\varphi(\overrightarrow{x})$ for $\overrightarrow{x} = [x_1, \ldots, x_n]$. Given a real number δ, we let $\varphi(\overrightarrow{x} + \delta)$ denote the clock constraint φ' where φ' is obtained from φ by syntactically substituting $x_j + \delta$ for every occurrence of x_j in φ. Let $f^{\varepsilon_j} : \mathsf{Constr}(C) \mapsto \mathsf{Constr}(C)$ be a function defined by $f^{\varepsilon_j}(\varphi(\overrightarrow{x})) = \mathsf{ElimQuant}\,(\forall \delta\,(0 \leq \delta \leq \varepsilon_j \to \varphi(\overrightarrow{x} + \delta)))$, where $\mathsf{ElimQuant}$ is a function that eliminates quantifiers (this function exists as we are working in the theory of reals with addition, which admits quantifier elimination). The formula $f^{\varepsilon_j}(\varphi)$ ensures that φ holds at all the points in $\{\overrightarrow{x} + \Delta \mid \Delta \leq \varepsilon_j\}$.

We now describe the timed automaton $\mathcal{T}^{\varepsilon_j, \varepsilon_r}$. The automaton has an extra clock z. The set of actions for player 1 is $\{\langle 1, e \rangle \mid e$ is a player-1 edge in $\mathcal{T}\}$ and for player 2 is $A_2 \cup \{\langle a_2, e \rangle \mid a_2 \in A_2$ and e is a player-1 edge in $\mathcal{T}\} \cup \{\langle 2, e \rangle \mid e$ is a player-1 edge in $\mathcal{T}\}$ (we assume the unions are disjoint). For each location l of $\mathcal{T}$ with the outgoing player-1 edges $e_1^1, \ldots, e_1^m$, the automaton $\mathcal{T}^{\varepsilon_j, \varepsilon_r}$ has $m+1$ locations: $l, l_{e_1^1}, \ldots, l_{e_1^m}$. Every edge of $\mathcal{T}^{\varepsilon_j, \varepsilon_r}$ includes z in its reset set. The invariant for l is the same as the invariant for l in $\mathcal{T}$. All player-2 edges of $\mathcal{T}$ are also player-2 edges in $\mathcal{T}^{\varepsilon_j, \varepsilon_r}$ (with the reset set being expanded to include z). The invariant for l_{e_j} is $z \leq \varepsilon_j$. If $\langle l, a_2, \varphi, l', \lambda \rangle$ is an edge of $\mathcal{T}$ with $a_2 \in A_2$, then then $\langle l_{e_j}, \langle a_2, e_j \rangle, \varphi, l', \lambda \cup \{z\} \rangle$ is a player-2 edge of $\mathcal{T}^{\varepsilon_j, \varepsilon_r}$ for every player-1 edge e_j of $\mathcal{T}$. For every player-1 edge $e_j = \langle l, a_1^j, \varphi, l', \lambda \rangle$ of $\mathcal{T}$, the location l of $\mathcal{T}^{\varepsilon_j, \varepsilon_r}$ has the outgoing player-1 edge $\langle l, \langle 1, e_j \rangle, f^{\varepsilon_j}(\gamma^{\mathcal{T}}(l)) \wedge (z \geq \varepsilon_r) \wedge f^{\varepsilon_j}(\varphi), l_{e_j}, \lambda \cup \{z\} \rangle$. The location l_{e_j} also has an additional outgoing *player-2* edge $\langle l_{e_j}, \langle 2, e_j \rangle, \varphi, l', \lambda \cup \{z\} \rangle$. The automaton $\mathcal{T}^{\varepsilon_j, \varepsilon_r}$ as described contains the rational constants ε_r and ε_j. We can change the timescale by multiplying every constant by the least common multiple of the denominators of ε_r and ε_j to get a timed automaton with only integer constants. Intuitively, in the game $\mathcal{T}^{\varepsilon_j, \varepsilon_r}$, player 1 moving from l to l_{e_j} with the edge $\langle 1, e_j \rangle$ indicates the desire of player 1 to pick the edge e_j from location l in the game $\mathcal{T}$. This is possible in $\mathcal{T}$ iff the (a) more that ε_r time has passed since the last discrete action, (b) the edge e_j is enabled for at least ε_j more time units, and (c) the invariant of l is satisfied for at least ε_j more time units. These three requirements are captured by the new guard in $\mathcal{T}^{\varepsilon_j, \varepsilon_r}$, namely $f^{\varepsilon_j}(\gamma^{\mathcal{T}}(l)) \wedge (z \geq \varepsilon_r) \wedge f^{\varepsilon_j}(\varphi)$. The presence of jitter in $\mathcal{T}$ causes uncertainty in when exactly the edge e_j is taken. This is modeled in $\mathcal{T}^{\varepsilon_j, \varepsilon_r}$ by having the location l_{e_j} be controlled entirely by player 2 for a duration of ε_j time units. Within ε_j time units, player 2 must either propose a move $\langle a_2, e_j \rangle$ (corresponding to one of its own moves a_2 in $\mathcal{T}$, or allow the action $\langle 2, e_j \rangle$ (corresponding to the original player-1 edge e_j) to be taken. Given a parity function $\Omega^{\mathcal{T}}$ on $\mathcal{T}$, the parity function $\Omega^{\mathcal{T}^{\varepsilon_j, \varepsilon_r}}$ is given by $\Omega^{\mathcal{T}^{\varepsilon_j, \varepsilon_r}}(l) = \Omega^{\mathcal{T}^{\varepsilon_j, \varepsilon_r}}(l_{e_j}) = \Omega^{\mathcal{T}}(l)$ for every player-1 edge e_j of $\mathcal{T}$. In computing the winning set for player 1, we need to modify blame_1 for technical reasons. Whenever an action of the form $\langle 1, e_j \rangle$ is taken, we blame player 2 (even though the action is controlled by player 1); and whenever an action of the form $\langle 2, e_j \rangle$ is taken, we blame player 1 (even though the action is controlled by player 2). Player 2 is blamed as usual for the actions $\langle a_2, e_j \rangle$. This modification is needed because player 1 taking the edge e_j in $\mathcal{T}$ is broken down into two stages in $\mathcal{T}^{\varepsilon_j, \varepsilon_r}$. If player 1 to be blamed for the edge $\langle 1, e_j \rangle$, then the following could happen: (a) player 1 takes the edge $\langle 1, e_j \rangle$ in $\mathcal{T}^{\varepsilon_j, \varepsilon_r}$ corresponding to her intention to take the edge e_j in $\mathcal{T}$ (b) player 2 then proposes her own move $\langle a_2, e_j \rangle$ from l_{e_j}, corresponding to her blocking the move e_j by a_2 in $\mathcal{T}$. If the preceeding scenario happens infinitely often, player 1 gets blamed infinitely often even though all she has done is signal her intentions infinitely often, but her actions have not been chosen. Hence player 2 is blamed for the edge $\langle 1, e_j \rangle$. If player 2 allows the intended player 1 edge by taking $\langle 2, e_j \rangle$, then we must blame player 1. We note that this modification is not required if $\varepsilon_r > 0$.

The construction of $\mathcal{T}^{\varepsilon_j, \varepsilon_r}$ can be simplified if $\varepsilon_j = 0$ (then we do not need locations of the form l_{e_j}). Given a set of states $\widetilde{S}$ of $\mathcal{T}^{\varepsilon_j, \varepsilon_r}$, let $\mathsf{JStates}(\widetilde{S})$ denote the projection of states to $\mathcal{T}$, defined formally by $\mathsf{JStates}(\widetilde{S}) = \{\langle l, \kappa \rangle \in S \mid \langle l, \widetilde{\kappa} \rangle \in \widetilde{S}$ such that $\kappa(x) = \widetilde{\kappa}(x)$ for all $x \in C\}$, where S is the state space and C the set of clocks of $\mathcal{T}$.

Theorem 6. *Let $\mathcal{T}$ be a timed automaton game, $\varepsilon_r \geq 0$ the response time of player 1, and $\varepsilon_j \geq 0$ the jitter of player 1 actions such that both ε_r and ε_j are rational constants. Then, for any ω-regular location objective $\mathsf{Parity}(\Omega^{\mathcal{T}})$ of $\mathcal{T}$, we have*

$$\mathsf{JStates}\left(\llbracket z = 0 \rrbracket \cap \mathsf{WinTimeDiv}_1^{\mathcal{T}^{\varepsilon_j, \varepsilon_r}}(\mathsf{Parity}(\Omega^{\mathcal{T}^{\varepsilon_j, \varepsilon_r}}))\right) = \mathsf{JRWinTimeDiv}_1^{\mathcal{T}, \varepsilon_j, \varepsilon_r}$$

$(\mathsf{Parity}(\Omega^{\mathcal{T}}))$, where $\mathsf{JRWinTimeDiv}_1^{\mathcal{T}, \varepsilon_j, \varepsilon_r}(\Phi)$ is the winning set in the jitter-response semantics, $\mathcal{T}^{\varepsilon_j, \varepsilon_r}$ is the timed automaton with the parity function $\Omega^{\mathcal{T}^{\varepsilon_j, \varepsilon_r}}$ described above, and $\llbracket z = 0 \rrbracket$ is the set of states of $\mathcal{T}^{\varepsilon_j, \varepsilon_r}$ with $\widetilde{\kappa}(z) = 0$.

An example which illustrates the differences between the various winning modes can be found in [7].

Theorem 7. *Let $\mathcal{T}$ be a timed automaton and Φ an objective. For all $\varepsilon_j > 0$ and $\varepsilon_r \geq 0$, we have $\mathsf{JRWinTimeDiv}_1^{\varepsilon_j, \varepsilon_r}(\Phi) \subseteq \mathsf{RobWinTimeDiv}_1(\Phi) \subseteq \mathsf{WinTimeDiv}_1(\Phi)$. All the subset inclusions are strict in general.*

Sampling semantics. Instead of having a response time for actions of player 1, we can have a model where player 1 is only able to take actions in an ε_j interval around sampling times, with a given time period $\varepsilon_{\mathsf{sample}}$. A timed automaton can be constructed along similar lines to that of $\mathcal{T}^{\varepsilon_j, \varepsilon_r}$ to obtain the winning set.

References

1. Agrawal, M., Thiagarajan, P.S.: Lazy rectangular hybrid automata. In: Alur, R., Pappas, G.J. (eds.) HSCC 2004. LNCS, vol. 2993, pp. 1–15. Springer, Heidelberg (2004)

2. Alur, R., Dill, D.L.: A theory of timed automata. Theor. Comput. Sci. 126(2), 183–235 (1994)

3. Alur, R., Henzinger, T.A.: Modularity for timed and hybrid systems. In: Mazurkiewicz, A., Winkowski, J. (eds.) CONCUR 1997. LNCS, vol. 1243, pp. 74–88. Springer, Heidelberg (1997)

4. Alur, R., Torre, S.L., Madhusudan, P.: Perturbed timed automata. In: Morari, M., Thiele, L. (eds.) HSCC 2005. LNCS, vol. 3414, pp. 70–85. Springer, Heidelberg (2005)

5. Bouyer, P., Markey, N., Reynier, P.A.: Robust analysis of timed automata via channel machines. In: Amadio, R. (ed.) FOSSACS 2008. LNCS, vol. 4962, pp. 157–171. Springer, Heidelberg (2008)

6. Cassez, F., David, A., Fleury, E., Larsen, K.G., Lime, D.: Efficient on-the-fly algorithms for the analysis of timed games. In: Abadi, M., de Alfaro, L. (eds.) CONCUR 2005. LNCS, vol. 3653, pp. 66–80. Springer, Heidelberg (2005)

7. Chatterjee, K., Henzinger, T.A., Prabhu, V.S.: Timed parity games: Complexity and robustness, CoRR abs/0805.4167 (2008)

8. Chatterjee, K., Henzinger, T.A., Prabhu, V.S.: Trading infinite memory for uniform randomness in timed games. In: HSCC 2008. LNCS. Springer, Heidelberg (2008)

9. de Alfaro, L., Faella, M., Henzinger, T.A., Majumdar, R., Stoelinga, M.: The element of surprise in timed games. In: Amadio, R., Lugiez, D. (eds.) CONCUR 2003. LNCS, vol. 2761, pp. 144–158. Springer, Heidelberg (2003)

10. D'Souza, D., Madhusudan, P.: Timed control synthesis for external specifications. In: Alt, H., Ferreira, A. (eds.) STACS 2002. LNCS, vol. 2285, pp. 571–582. Springer, Heidelberg (2002)

11. Faella, M., La Torre, S., Murano, A.: Automata-theoretic decision of timed games. In: Cortesi, A. (ed.) VMCAI 2002. LNCS, vol. 2294, pp. 94–108. Springer, Heidelberg (2002)

12. Faella, M., La Torre, S., Murano, A.: Dense real-time games. In: LICS 2002, pp. 167–176. IEEE Computer Society Press, Los Alamitos (2002)

13. Gupta, V., Henzinger, T.A., Jagadeesan, R.: Robust timed automata. In: Maler, O. (ed.) HART 1997. LNCS, vol. 1201, pp. 331–345. Springer, Heidelberg (1997)

14. Henzinger, T.A., Prabhu, V.S.: Timed alternating-time temporal logic. In: Asarin, E., Bouyer, P. (eds.) FORMATS 2006. LNCS, vol. 4202, pp. 1–17. Springer, Heidelberg (2006)

15. Henzinger, T.A., Raskin, J.-F.: Robust undecidability of timed and hybrid systems. In: Lynch, N.A., Krogh, B.H. (eds.) HSCC 2000. LNCS, vol. 1790, pp. 145–159. Springer, Heidelberg (2000)

16. Jurdzinski, M.: Small progress measures for solving parity games. In: Reichel, H., Tison, S. (eds.) STACS 2000. LNCS, vol. 1770, pp. 290–301. Springer, Heidelberg (2000)

17. Maler, O., Pnueli, A., Sifakis, J.: On the synthesis of discrete controllers for timed systems (an extended abstract). In: STACS 1995, pp. 229–242. Springer, Heidelberg (1995)

18. Schewe, S.: Solving parity games in big steps. In: Proc. FST TCS. Springer, Heidelberg (2007)

19. Segala, R., Gawlick, R., Søgaard-Andersen, J.F., Lynch, N.A.: Liveness in timed and untimed systems. Inf. Comput. 141(2), 119–171 (1998)

20. Thomas, W.: Languages, automata, and logic. In: Handbook of Formal Languages, ch. 7. Beyond Words, vol. 3, pp. 389–455. Springer, Heidelberg (1997)

21. Vöge, J., Jurdziński, M.: A discrete strategy improvement algorithm for solving parity games. In: Emerson, E.A., Sistla, A.P. (eds.) CAV 2000. LNCS, vol. 1855, pp. 202–215. Springer, Heidelberg (2000)
22. Wong-Toi, H., Hoffmann, G.: The control of dense real-time discrete event systems. In: Proc. of 30th Conf. Decision and Control, pp. 1527–1528 (1991)
23. Wulf, M.D., Doyen, L., Markey, N., Raskin, J.F.: Robustness and implementability of timed automata. In: Lakhnech, Y., Yovine, S. (eds.) FORMATS 2004 and FTRTFT 2004. LNCS, vol. 3253, pp. 118–133. Springer, Heidelberg (2004)
24. Wulf, M.D., Doyen, L., Raskin, J.F.: Almost asap semantics: from timed models to timed implementations. Formal Asp. Comput. 17(3), 319–341 (2005)

On Scheduling Policies for Streams of Structured Jobs*

Aldric Degorre and Oded Maler

VERIMAG-UJF-CNRS, 2 av. de Vignate, 38610 Gières, France
{Aldric.Degorre,Oded.Maler}@imag.fr

Abstract. We study a class of scheduling problems which combines the structural aspects associated with task dependencies, with the dynamic aspects associated with ongoing streams of requests that arrive during execution. For this class of problems we develop a scheduling policy which can guarantee bounded accumulation of backlog for all admissible request streams. We show, nevertheless, that no such policy can guarantee bounded latency for all admissible request patterns, unless they admit some laxity.

1 Introduction

The problem of efficient allocation of reusable resources over time, also known as *scheduling*, is a universal problem, appearing almost everywhere, ranging from the allocation of machines in a factory [6, 19, 22], allocation of processor time slots in a real-time system [9, 20], allocating communication channels in a network [16], or allocation of vehicles for transportation tasks [7]. Unfortunately, the study of scheduling problems is distributed among many academic communities and application domains, each focusing on certain aspects of the problem.

In the vast scheduling literature, one can, very roughly, identify two generic types of problems. In the first type, the work to be scheduled admits a *structure* which includes precedence constraints between tasks, but the problems are, more often than not, *static*: the work to be executed is known in advance and is typically finite. Examples of this type of problems are the job-shop problem motivated by manufacturing (linear precedence constraints, heterogeneous resources) [18, 19] or the task-graph scheduling problem, motivated parallel execution of programs (partially-ordered tasks, homogeneous resources) [14] (some recurrent aspects of scheduling are exhibited in program loop parallelization [13] but the nature of uncertainty there is different and rather limited).

On the other hand, in problems related to real-time systems [10] or in queuing theory [17], one is concerned with *infinite streams* of tasks which arrive either periodically or sporadically (or in a combination of both), satisfying some constraints on task arrival patterns. In many of these "dynamical" problems, the structural dimension of the problem is rather weak, and each request consists of

---

* This research was partially supported by the French MINLOGIC project ATHOLE.

F. Cassez and C. Jard (Eds.): FORMATS 2008, LNCS 5215, pp. 141–154, 2008.
© Springer-Verlag Berlin Heidelberg 2008

a monolithic amount of work. A notable exception is the domain of adversarial queuing theory [8] where some structure and uncertainty are combined.

In this paper we propose a model which combines the *dynamic* aspect associated with *request streams* whose exact content is not known in advance, with the *structural* aspects expressed by task dependencies. We define a scheduling problem where the demand for work is expressed as a stream of requests, each being a structured *job* taken from a finite set of types, hence such a stream can be viewed as a timed word over the the alphabet of job types. Each job type defines a finite partially-ordered set of tasks, each associated with a resource type and a duration. Such a stream is to be scheduled on an *execution platform* consisting of a finite number of resources (machines). A schedule is valid relative to a request stream if it satisfies *both* the precedence constraints imposed by the structure of the jobs and the resource constraints imposed by the number of resources available in the platform (and, of course, it does not execute jobs before they are requested).

The quality of a specific schedule is evaluated according to two types of measures, one associated with the evolution of the *backlog* over time, that is, the difference between the amount of work requested and the amount of work supplied, and the *latency*, the temporal distance between the arrival of a job instance and the termination of its execution. To model the uncertain external environment we use the concept of a *request generator*, a set of request streams satisfying some inter-arrival timing constraints. Such constraints can be expressed, for example, using timed automata [2], real-time logics [3] or timed regular expressions [4]. We restrict the discussion to *admissible* request streams that do not demand more work over time than the platform can offer. A *scheduling policy* (strategy) should produce a schedule for each admissible request stream, subject to *causality* constraints: the decision of the scheduler at a given moment can only be based on the *prefix* of the request stream it has seen so far.

After defining all these notions we prove two major fundamental results:

- Positive: we develop a scheduling policy which produces a bounded backlog schedule for any admissible request stream. Note that due to the precedence constraints between the tasks in the jobs, request stream admissibility does not, a priori, guarantee the existence of such a schedule. In fact, we show that a naive "oldest first" policy can accumulate an unbounded backlog for certain request streams. Our policy achieves this goal by making decisions that provide for pipelined execution whenever possible.
- Negative: there are admissible request streams for which no bounded-latency schedule (and hence no bounded-latency policy) exists.

The rest of the paper is organized as follows: in Sect. 2 we define our scheduling framework, in Sect. 3 we prove a negative result concerning the impossibility of bounded latency schedules. In Sect. 4 we extend the framework to include scheduling policies and in Sect. 5 we develop a scheduling strategy that guarantees bounded backlog. We conclude with a discussion of past and future work.

2   The Recurrent Scheduling Problem

2.1   General Definitions

We use timed words and timed languages to specify streams of requests for work. Intuitively, a timed word such as $\tilde{u} = 3 \cdot a_1 \cdot 2 \cdot a_2 \cdot a_3 \cdot 6$ consists of a passage of time of duration 3, followed by the event a_1, followed by a time duration 2, followed by the two events a_2 and a_3 and then a time duration of 6. We present some basic definitions and notations (see more formal details in [4]).

- A word over an event alphabet Σ is either ϵ, the empty word, or $u \cdot a$ where u is a word and $a \in \Sigma$. An ω-word is an infinite sequence $(a_i)_{i \in \mathbb{N}} \in \Sigma^\omega$.
- A timed word over Σ is a word over $\Sigma \cup \mathbb{R}_+$. The duration of a timed word u, denoted by $|u|$ is the sum of its elements that are taken from $\mathbb{R}_+$, for example $|\tilde{u}| = 11$. A timed ω-word is an infinite sequence $(a_i)_{i \in \mathbb{N}} \in (\Sigma \cup \mathbb{R}_+)^\omega$ such that its duration diverges.
- The concatenation of a word u and a word (or ω-word) v is denoted by $u \cdot v$.
- A word u is a prefix of v iff there exists w such that $v = u \cdot w$, which we denote $u \sqsubseteq v$. We say that u is a proper prefix of v, denoted by $u \sqsubset v$, if $u \neq v$.
- A word (or an ω-word) u is a suffix of v iff there exists w such that $v = w \cdot u$.

For a timed (ω-)word u over Σ

- By $u(a, i)$ we denote the time of the i-th occurrence of event $a \in \Sigma$ in the timed word u. Formally $u(a, i) = t$ if $u = v \cdot a \cdot w$ such that $|v| = t$ and v contains $i - 1$ occurrences of a. We let $u(a, i) = \infty$ when a occurs less than i times in u.
- The timed word $u_{[0,t]}$ is the longest prefix of u with duration t. Formally $u_{[0,t]} = t_0 \cdot a_0 \cdot t_1 \cdot a_1 \cdot \ldots \cdot t_i$ such that $\sum_{0 \le k \le i} t_k = t$ and there exists no discrete event a such that $t_0 \cdot a_0 \cdot t_1 \cdot a_1 \cdot \ldots \cdot t_i \cdot a$ is a prefix of w. For example, $\tilde{u}_{[0,4]} = 3 \cdot a_1 \cdot 1$ and $\tilde{u}_{[0,5]} = 3 \cdot a_1 \cdot 2 \cdot a_2 \cdot a_3 \cdot 0$.

Sets of timed (ω-)words over Σ are called timed (ω-)language. We denote the sets of such languages by $\mathcal{T}(\Sigma)$ and $\mathcal{T}_\omega(\Sigma)$, respectively.

2.2   Execution Platform, Jobs and Tasks

The execution platform determines our capacity to process work.

Definition 1 (Execution Platform). *An execution platform over a finite set* $M = \{m_1, \ldots, m_n\}$ *of resource (machine) types is a function* $R : M \to \mathbb{N}$.

Example: $\{m_1 \mapsto 2, m_2 \mapsto 4, m_3 \mapsto 1\}$ is an execution platform with three resource types m_1, m_2, m_3 having 2 instances of m_1, 4 instances of m_2, and 1 instance of m_3.[1]

---

[1] We will use the notation R_m for $R(m)$ and R when we want to treat the whole platform capacity as vector and make component-wise arithmetical operations. The same will hold for sets of functions indexed by the elements of M.

The *task* is the atomic unit of work, specified by the resource type it consumes and by its duration. The job is a unit of a larger granularity, consisting of tasks related by precedence constraints. Each job is an instantiation of a job type.

Definition 2 (Job Type). *A job type over a set M of resources is a tuple $J = \langle T, \prec, \mu, d \rangle$ such that $\prec \subseteq T \times T$ and $\langle T, \prec \rangle$ is a finite directed acyclic graph whose nodes are labelled by 2 functions: $\mu : T \to M$, which associates a task to the resource type it consumes, and $d : T \to \mathbb{R}_+ - \{0\}$ specifying task duration.*

As an example consider a job type where $T = \{a_1, a_2, a_3\}$, $\prec = \{(a_1 \prec a_3), (a_2 \prec a_3)\}$ $\mu = \{a_1 \mapsto m_1, a_2 \mapsto m_2, a_3 \mapsto m_3\}$, $d = \{a_1 \mapsto 3, a_2 \mapsto 2, a_3 \mapsto 1\}\rangle$, where a_1 needs resource m_1 for 3 time units, a_2 uses resource m_2 for 2 time units while a_3 consumes m_3 for 1 time unit. Task a_3 cannot start before both a_1 and a_2 terminate.

For a set $\mathcal{J} = \{\langle T_1, \prec_1, \mu_1, d_1 \rangle, ..., \langle T_n, \prec_n, \mu_n, d_n \rangle\}$ of job types, we let $T_{\mathcal{J}}, \prec_{\mathcal{J}}$,$\mu_{\mathcal{J}}$ and $d_{\mathcal{J}}$ denote, respectively, the (disjoint) union of T_i, $\prec_i$, μ_i and d_i, for $i = 1..n$. We call elements of $T_{\mathcal{J}}$ task types. When $\mathcal{J}$ is clear from the context we use notations T, $\prec$, μ and d.

Definition 3 (Initial Tasks, Rank). *An initial task a is an element of T such that there exists no $a' \in T$ with $a' \prec a$. The rank of task a is the number of edges of the longest path $a_0 \prec a_1 \prec ... \prec a$ such that a_0 is initial. Initial tasks have rank 0.*

2.3   The Demand

The sequence of jobs and tasks that should be executed on the platform is determined by a request stream.

Definition 4 (Request Streams and Generators). *A request stream over a set $\mathcal{J}$ of job types is a timed ω-word over $\mathcal{J}$. A request generator is a timed ω-language over $\mathcal{J}$.*

Each request stream presents a demand for work over time which should not exceed the platform capacity, otherwise the latter will be saturated.

Definition 5 (Work Requested by Jobs and Streams). *With each resource type m we define a function $W_m : \mathcal{J} \to \mathbb{R}_+$ so that $W_m(J)$ indicates the total amount of work on m demanded by job J, $W_m(J) = \sum_{\{a \in T_J : \mu(a) = m\}} d(a)$. We lift this function to request stream prefixes by letting $W(\epsilon) = 0$, $W(u \cdot t) = W(u)$ for $t \in \mathbb{R}_+$ and $W(u \cdot J) = W(u) + W(J)$ for $J \in \mathcal{J}$.*

We restrict our attention to request streams that do not ask for more work per time unit than the platform can provide, and, furthermore, do not present an unbounded number of requests in a bounded time interval.

Definition 6 (Admissible, Critical and Subcritical Request Streams) *A request stream σ is α-lax ($\alpha \in \mathbb{R}_+$) with respect to an execution platform R if* *for every* $t < t'$, $W(\sigma_{[0,t']}) - W(\sigma_{[0,t]}) \le \alpha(t'-t)R+b$ *for some constant* $b \in \mathbb{R}^n$. *A stream is admissible if it is α-lax for some $\alpha \le 1$, subcritical if it is α-lax for $\alpha < 1$ and critical if it is admissible but not subcritical. A request generator G is α-lax if every $\sigma \in G$ is α-lax.*

2.4 Schedules

Definition 7 (Schedule). *A schedule is a function* $s : T \times \mathbb{N} \to \mathbb{R}_+^\infty$ *(where* $\mathbb{R}_+^\infty = \mathbb{R}_+ \cup \{\infty\}$ *with the usual extension of the order and operations).*

The intended meaning of $s(a,i) = t$ is that the i-th instance of task a (which is part of the i-th instance of the job type to which it belongs) starts executing at time t. If we restrict ourselves to "non-overtaking" schedules[2] such that $s(a,i) \le s(a,i')$ whenever $i < i'$, we can view a schedule as a timed ω-word in $T_\omega(T)$. Likewise we can speak of finite prefixes $s_{[0,t]}$ which are timed words in $T(T)$.

Since tasks have fixed durations and cannot be preempted, a schedule determines uniquely which tasks are executed at any point in time and, hence, how many resources of each type are utilized, a notion formalized below.

Definition 8 (Utilization Function, Work Supplied). *The resource utilization function associated with every resource m is* $U_m : T_\omega(T) \times \mathbb{R}_+ \to \mathbb{N}$ *defined as* $U_m(s,t) = |\{(a,i) \in T \times \mathbb{N} : \mu(a) = m \wedge s(a,i) \le t < s(a,i)+d(a)\}|$. *The work supplied by a prefix of s is the accumulated utilization:* $W(s_{[0,t]}) = \int_0^t U(s,\tau)d\tau$.

Definition 9 (Valid Schedule). *A schedule s is valid for a request stream σ on an execution platform R if for any task instance (a,i)*

- *if J is the job type a belongs to, then $s(a,i) \ge \sigma(J,i)$ (no proactivity: jobs are executed after they are requested);*
- $\forall a', a' \prec a, s(a,i) \ge s(a',i) + d(a')$ *(job precedences are met);*
- $\forall t \in \mathbb{R}_+, U(s,t) \le R$ *(no overload: no more resource instances of a type are used than their total amount in the execution platform).*

The quality of a schedule can be evaluated in two principal and related (but not equivalent) ways, the first of which does not look at individual job instances but is based on the amount of work. During every prefix of the schedule there is a non-negative difference between the amount of work that has been requested and the amount of work that has been supplied. This difference can be defined in a "continuous" fashion like $\Delta_{\sigma,s}(t) = W(\sigma_{[0,t]}) - W(s_{[0,t]})$. An alternative that we will use, is based on the concept of *residue* or backlog, which is simply the set of requested tasks that have not yet started executing. It is not hard to see that a bounded residue is equivalent to a bounded difference between requested and supplied work.

Definition 10 (Residue, Bounded Residue Schedules). *The residue associated with a request stream σ and a valid schedule s at time t is* $\rho_{\sigma,s}(t) = \{(a,i) \in T \times \mathbb{N} : \sigma(a,i) \le t < s(a,i)\}$. *A valid schedule s is of bounded residue if there is a number c such that* $|\rho_{\sigma,s}(t)| \le c$ *for every t.*

---

[2] Note that non-overtaking applies only to tasks of the *same type*.

The second performance measure associated with a schedule is related to latency, the time an individual job has to wait between being requested and the completion time of its last task.

Definition 11 (Latency). *Given a request stream σ and a valid schedule s, the latency of a job instance (J, i) is $L_{J,i}(\sigma, s) = \max_{a \in T_J}\{(s(a, i) + d(a))\} - \sigma(J, i)$. The latency of s with respect to σ is $L(\sigma, s) = \sup_{J \in \mathcal{J}, i \in \mathbb{N}} L_{J,i}(\sigma, s)$.*

Note that it is possible that every job instance is served in finite time but the latency of the schedule is, however, infinite, that is, the sequence $\{L_{J,i}\}_{i \in \mathbb{N}}$ may diverge. Bounded residue does not imply bounded latency: we can keep one job waiting forever, while still serving all the others without accumulating backlog. But the implication holds in the other direction.

Lemma 1. *A valid schedule with bounded latency has a bounded residue.*

Proof. Let s be a valid schedule with latency $\lambda \in \mathbb{R}_+$. Let $V(t)$ be the total amount of work of the tasks that are in the residue at time t. Since all these tasks are supposed to be completed by $t + \lambda$ we have $V(t) \leq \lambda R$ which implies a bound on the residue. $\qquad\square$

2.5   The Running Example

We will use the following recurrent scheduling problem to construct the negative result and to illustrate our scheduling policy. Consider a platform over $M = \{m_1, m_2\}$ with $R(m_1) = R(m_2) = 1$. The set of job types is $\mathcal{J} = \{A, B\}$ whose respective sets of tasks $\{a_1 \prec a_2\}$ and $\{b_1 \prec b_2\}$ have all a unit duration. The difference between these job types is that A uses m_1 before m_2 while B uses m_2 before m_1 (see Fig. 1). As a request generator we consider $G = ((A \cdot 1) + (B \cdot 1))^\omega$, that is, every unit of time, an instance of either one of these jobs is requested (to simplify notations we will use henceforth A and B as a shorthand for $A \cdot 1$ and $B \cdot 1$, respectively). Since each job type requires exactly the amount of work offered by the platform, G is admissible and, in fact, critical. A bounded-residue schedule for such critical request streams should keep the machines busy *all the time* except for some intervals (that we call *utilization gaps*) whose sum of durations is bounded.

The reversed order of resource utilization in A and B renders these two job types *incompatible* in the sense that it is not easy to "pipeline" them on our platform. Intuitively at the moment a request stream switches from A to B, we

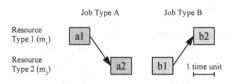

Fig. 1. The example

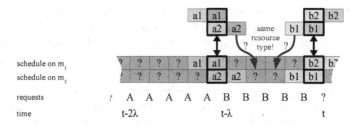

Fig. 2. An illustration of the fact that a request segment $A^\lambda \cdot B^\lambda$ implies a utilization gap in any schedule of latency λ or less. Before $t - \lambda$: job type A has been requested for a long time, so the residue contains only tasks from A. At $t - \lambda$: from now on, requests are of type B. After $t - 1$: if the latency is λ, there should be no more tasks from A in the residue. Now between $t - \lambda$ and $t - 1$, only suffixes of A and prefixes of B can be scheduled, and among those, at least one proper suffix.

may have tasks a_2 and b_1 ready for execution but only one instance of their common resource m_2 is free. Our scheduling policy will, nevertheless, manage to pipeline them but, as we show in the next section, bounded latency schedules are impossible.

3   Negative Result

Theorem 1. *Some admissible request streams admit no bounded-latency schedule.*

We prove the theorem using the following lemma, which shows that for any latency λ, the occurrence of a certain request pattern implies a unit increase in the residue and hence infinitely many consecutive repetitions of this pattern will imply an unbounded residue. The statement of the lemma and its proof are illustrated in Fig. 2.

Lemma 2. *Let σ be a request stream with a prefix of the form $\sigma_{[0,t]} = u \cdot A^\lambda \cdot B^\lambda$ and let s be a valid schedule for σ with latency λ. Then there is a utilization gap (an idle resource) of duration 1 or more in the interval $[t - \lambda - 1, t]$.*

Proof. Since the latency of s is λ, no task instance of B belongs to the residue $\rho_{\sigma,s}(t - \lambda - 1)$, so the only way to avoid a gap at time $t - \lambda - 1$ is to schedule an instance of a_1 and an instance of a_2. For the same reason, $\rho_{\sigma,s}(t - 1)$ contains no task instance of A, so that at time $t - 1$, s schedules b_1 and b_2. Moreover any task instance of B in the residue after $t - \lambda - 1$ is an instance that was requested since $t - \lambda$.

Now what happens in $[t - \lambda, t - 1]$? In that interval, the residue has task instances from requests for A made before $t - \lambda$ and from requests for B made since that time. Due to bounded latency all the instances from A are due for $t - 1$. We also know that, because $a_1 \prec a_2$, the residue has always more a_2 than a_1, and that their amount is the same only when all started job instances of A

are finished, which is not possible at $t-1$ because an a_1 is scheduled for $t-\lambda-1$ (and thus task a_2 of the same job instance cannot start before $t-\lambda$). In that interval we also schedule task instances from B the earliest of which can have started execution at $t-\lambda$. Thus, since $b_1 \prec b_2$, we cannot schedule more b_2 than b_1.

Summing up the quantity of work scheduled by s between $t-\lambda$ and t, we find that on m_1 we schedule n_{a_1} instances of a_1 and n_{b_2} instances of b_2 and on m_2 we schedule n_{a_2} instances of a_2 and n_{b_1} instances of b_1, satisfying $n_{a_2} > n_{a_1}$ and $n_{b_1} \geq n_{b_2}$. Thus m_2 performs at least one unit of work more than m_1 in the same interval, which is only possible if m_1 admits a utilization gap of duration 1.   □

Consider now a request stream that has infinitely many occurrences of the pattern $u \cdot A^\lambda \cdot B^\lambda$. A schedule with latency λ for this stream will have infinitely many gaps, and hence an unbounded residue, a fact which contradicts Lemma 1. Hence such a stream admits no schedule whose latency is λ or less.

Proof (of Theorem 1). Consider now any request stream σ in the language $L_\infty = \mathcal{J}^* \cdot A \cdot B \cdot B \cdot \mathcal{J}^* \cdot A \cdot A \cdot A \cdot B \cdot B \cdot B \cdot B \cdot \mathcal{J}^* \cdot A \cdot A \cdot A \cdot B \cdot B \cdot B \cdots$, where $\mathcal{J}$ stands for $(A+B)$. For every λ, σ has infinitely many prefixes of the form $u \cdot A^\lambda \cdot B^\lambda$ and cannot have a schedule of latency λ. Consequently it admits no bounded latency schedule.   □

Note that this impossibility result is not related to the dynamic aspect of the scheduling problem. Even a clairvoyant scheduler who knows the whole request stream in advance cannot find a bounded latency solution.

Note also that the language L_∞ is not pathological. If fact, in any reasonable way to induce probabilities on $(A+B)^\omega$, this language will have probability of 1. Hence we can say that critical systems having two incompatible jobs will almost surely admit only unbounded-latency schedules.

4   Scheduling Policies

Now we want to consider the act of scheduling as a dynamic process where a scheduler has to adapt its decisions to the evolution of the environment, here the incoming request stream. We want the scheduler to construct a schedule *incrementally* as requests arrive. The mathematical object that models the procedure of mapping request stream prefixes into scheduling decisions is called a scheduling *policy* or a *strategy*.

Formally speaking, a policy can be viewed as a timed transducer, a causal function $p : \mathcal{T}_\omega(\mathcal{J}) \to \mathcal{T}_\omega(T)$ which produces for each request stream σ a valid schedule $s = p(\sigma)$. Causality here means that the value of $s_{[0,t]}$ depends only on $\sigma_{[0,t]}$. We will represent the policy as a procedure p which, at each time instant t, looks at $\sigma_{[0,t]}$ and selects a (possibly empty) set of task instances to be scheduled for execution at time t, that is, $s(a,i) = t$ if $(a,i) \in p(\sigma_{[0,t]})$. We will use $s_{[0,t]} = p(\sigma_{[0,t]})$ to denote the schedule prefix constructed by successive applications of p during the interval $[0,t]$. We assume that each policy is designed to work with admissible request streams taken from a generator $G \subseteq \mathcal{T}_\omega(\mathcal{J})$.

Definition 12 (Scheduling policy). *A scheduling policy is a function* $p : \mathcal{T}(\mathcal{J}) \to 2^{T \times \mathbb{N}}$ *such that for every task instance* (a, i) *and a request stream prefix* σ, $(a, i) \in p(\sigma)$ *implies that* $(a, i) \notin p(\sigma')$ *for any* $\sigma' \sqsubset \sigma$. *A scheduling policy is valid for* σ *if for every* t, *the obtained schedule* $s_{[0,t]} = p(\sigma_{[0,t]})$ *satisfies the conditions of Definition 9, namely, no proactivity and adherence to precedence and resource constraints.*

We evaluate the overall performance of a policy based on the worst schedule it produces over the streams in the generator. Since we have just shown a negative result concerning latencies, we focus on the residue.

Definition 13 (Bounded Residue Policies). *A scheduling policy has a bounded residue relative to a generator* G *if it produces a bounded-residue schedule for every* $\sigma \in G$.

In the following, we use notation $\rho_{\sigma,p}$ instead of $\rho_{\sigma,p(\sigma)}$ to denote the residue resulting from the application of a policy p to a request stream (or prefix) σ.

5   Positive Result

In this section we show that any recurrent scheduling problem with an admissible request generator admits a policy in the sense of Sect. 4 which maintains the residue bounded. We emphasize again that the policy makes decisions at run time without knowing future requests.

5.1   Oldest-First Policy Does Not Work

To appreciate the difficulty, let us consider first a naive Oldest-First policy: whenever the number of tasks that are ready to use a resource is larger than the number of free instances of the resource, the available instances are granted to the older tasks among them. We show that this policy fails to guarantee bounded residues.

Theorem 2. *The Oldest-First policy cannot guarantee a bounded residue.*

In fact, this policy will lead to an unbounded residue schedule for request streams in the language L_∞ of the previous section as illustrated in Fig. 3 and proved below. The reason is, again, the incompatibility between the job types, which leads to infinitely many utilization gaps where a resource is free while none of the corresponding tasks in the residue is ready to utilize it. The result is a direct corollary of the following lemma:

Lemma 3. *A bounded residue schedule which conforms to the Oldest-First policy has a bounded latency.*

Note that we already proved the converse for arbitrary schedules and policies.

Proof. First we show that any task instance (a, i) that becomes eligible for execution at time t, is scheduled for execution within a bounded amount of time after t. This holds because, following the policy, the only tasks that can be executed between t and $s(a, i)$ are those that are already in the (bounded) residue at time t. Next we show, by induction on the rank of the tasks, that this fact implies that any task is executed within a bounded amount of time after its job is issued. This holds trivially for the initial tasks which become eligible for execution immediately when the job arrives and then holds for tasks of rank $n + 1$ by virtue of the bounded latency of tasks of rank n. Thus the latency of a bounded-residue schedule produced by the Oldest-First has to be bounded.   □

Since we have already shown that request streams in L_∞ do not admit bounded-latency schedules, a bounded residue strategy will lead to a contradiction and this proves Theorem 2. Like the case for Theorem 1, under reasonable probability assignments to jobs, one can show that the Oldest-First policy will almost surely lead to unbounded-residue schedules when applied to critical streams of incompatible jobs.

schedule on m_1	a1			b2	b2	a1	a1	a1			b2	b2	b2
schedule on m_2		a2	b1	b1			a2	a2	a2	b1	b1	b1	b1
residue on m_1	0	1	2	2	2	2	2	2	3	4	4	4	4
residue on m_2	1	1	1	1	2	3	3	3	3	3	3	3	3
requests	A	B	B	A	A	A	B	B	B	B	A	A	A

Fig. 3. Schedule generated by the "oldest first" policy on a stream in the language L_∞, described in 3. Here we see that a gap of length 2 is created on one of the resource types at every change of job type in the request stream, which makes the residue grow indefinitely.

5.2   A Bounded Residue Policy

Theorem 3. *Any admissible generator admits a bounded-residue scheduling policy.*

In order to circumvent the shortcomings of the "Oldest First" policy, we describe in the sequel a policy that eventually reaches the following situation: whenever a resource becomes free and the residue contains tasks that need it, at least one of those tasks will be ready for execution.

The policy is described in detail in Algorithm 1 and its proof is omitted due to space limitations. We explain the underlying intuition below. The policy separates the act of choosing which tasks to execute in the future from the act of actually starting them. The first decision is made upon job arrival while the second is made whenever a resource is free and a corresponding task has been selected. To this end we partition the residue into two parts. The first part P (the "pool") consists of requested task instances that have not yet been selected for execution. Among those, only task instances whose $\prec$-predecessors have already terminated are eligible for being selected and moved to the other part, which consists of n FIFO queues $\{Q_m\}_{m \in M}$, one for each resource type. The passage between the two is controlled by two types of events:

- Task termination: when a task (a, i) terminates, eligibility status of its successors in P is updated;
- Job arrival: when a job instance (J, i) arrives we pick the oldest[3] eligible instance $(a, j_a) \in P$ (if such exists) for every task type $a \in T_J$ such that $\mu(a) = m$, and move it to Q_m. Note that only initial tasks of (J, i) are eligible for being selected when (J, i) arrives, while for other task types only earlier instances can be chosen.

Whenever a resource of type m is free and Q_m is not empty, the first element is removed from Q_m and starts executing. This is sufficient to ensure a bounded residue. However, to improve the performance of the algorithm when the streams are subcritical, we also choose to start the oldest eligible task which requires m if an instance of m is released when Q_m is empty.

The intuition why this policy works is easier to understand when we look at critical request streams. For such streams, any job type which is requested often enough will eventually have instances of each of its tasks in Q and hence, whenever a resource is freed, there will always be some task ready to use it. This guarantees smooth pipelining and bounded residue for all admissible request streams. In Fig. 4 we can see how our policy schedules the request stream $\sigma_\infty = A \cdot B \cdot B \cdot A \cdot A \cdot A \cdots$.

Scheduling policies of the FIFO type have also been studied in the context of adversarial queuing and it has been shown under various hypothesis [12] that those were not stable, sometimes even for arbitrarily small loads. What makes our policy work is the fact that the act of queuing is triggered by a global event (arrival of a new job request) on which the actual choice of tasks to be queued depends. So the decision is somehow "conscious" of the global state of the system, as opposed to what happens in a classical FIFO network.

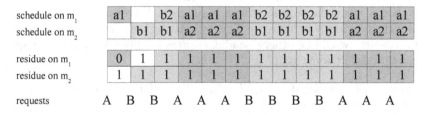

Fig. 4. The schedule generated by the bounded-residue policy for σ_∞. We can see that after the arrival of the second B, every resource is always occupied, and that the residue does not grow after that.

---

[3] Or one of the oldest if there are several of the same age.

Algorithm 1. The Bounded-Residue Policy

---

declarations
  req: jobType inputEvent   // events from σ
  free: resourceType inputEvent   // triggered when a resource is freed
  start: taskInstance outputEvent   // scheduling decisions
  P: taskInstance set   // pool, unselected tasks
  Q: resourceType $\rightarrow$ (taskInstance fifo)   // queues, selected tasks

procedure INIT
  $P = \emptyset$;
  for all $m \in M$ **do** $Q_m = \emptyset$

procedure STARTWORK(m: resourceType)
  if Q_m is not empty **then** $\alpha = \text{pop}(Q_m)$; **emit** $start(\alpha)$
  else   // for bounded latency against subcritical streams
    if P has eligible task instances requiring m **then**
      $\alpha = $ the oldest eligible task instance using m in P;
      $P = P - \{\alpha\}$; **emit** $start(\alpha)$

on $free(m)$ **do** startWork(m)

on $req(J)$ **do**
  for all $a \in T_J$ **do**
    $P = P \cup \{newInstance(a)\}$;
    if P has eligible task instances of type a **then**
      $\alpha = $ the oldest eligible task instance of a in P;
      $P = P - \{\alpha\}$; push(α, Q_m)   // select for execution
  for all $m \in M$ **do**
    for all free instances of m **do** startWork(m)

5.3   Bounded Latency for Subcritical Streams

We just showed that a policy could ensure bounded residues in the case of critical streams for which one needs full utilization. But criticality is just a limit case and for that reason it is interesting to know whether such a policy can adapt and behave better when the request stream is subcritical. Fortunately the answer is positive: the previously exhibited policy, by starting tasks which are not queued when a resource would be otherwise idle, ensures bounded latencies for request streams that admit some laxity.

Theorem 4. *The policy described by Algorithm 1 has a bounded latency when applied to any α-lax stream with $\alpha < 1$.*

Lemma 4. *There exists a time bound $T_{\alpha,m}$ such that any interval $[t, t + T_{\alpha,m}]$ admits a time instant where Q_m is empty, an instance of m is free and no new request arrives.*

Sketch of proof. Consider an interval of the form $[t, t + d]$ in which no machine of type m is idle. The quantity of work dequeued from Q_m is $R_m d$ and, due to laxity, the amount of work enqueued into Q_m is at most $(1 - \alpha)R_m d$. Hence the total contribution to the amount of work in Q_m is $(\alpha - 1)R_m d$ and for some sufficiently large d it will empty Q_m. □

Proof (of Theorem 4). We know that, when a task in the pool becomes the oldest task of the residue which is not queued, it becomes eligible in a bounded amount of time (all its predecessors must be in the queue). Thus we know that at most $T_{\alpha,m}$ units of time after that, this task is started (either queued or started to fill a gap). Since furthermore the residue (and hence the pool) is bounded (Thm. 3), there is a bound on the time it takes a task to become the oldest in the pool and hence to be executed. Thus we conclude that the latency of the policy is bounded. □

6 Discussion

We have proved some fundamental results on a model that captures, we believe, many real-world phenomena. Let us mention some related attempts to treat similar problems. The idea that verification-inspired techniques can be used to model and then solve scheduling problems that are not easy to express in traditional real-time scheduling models has been studied within the timed controller synthesis framework and applied to scheduling problems [1, 5, 21, 23]. What is common to all these approaches (including [15] which analyzes *given* policies that admit task preemption) is that the scheduler is computed using a verification/synthesis algorithm for timed automata, which despite several improvements [11] are intrinsically not scalable. The policy presented in this paper does not suffer from this problem, it only needs the request generator to be admissible. Explicit synthesis may still be needed in more complex settings.

In the future it would be interesting to investigate various extensions of the model and variations on the rules of the game, in particular, moving from worst-case reasoning to average case by using probabilistic request generators and evaluating policies according to expected backlog or latency. Finally, we intend to look closer at the question of "pipelinability", that is, the mutual compatibility of a set of job types. Results in this direction may lead to new design principles for request servers.

Acknowlegments. We thank anonymous referees for their comments. We are indebted to Viktor Schuppan for his great help in writing the paper.

References

1. Altisen, K., Gößler, G., Pnueli, A., Sifakis, J., Tripakis, S., Yovine, S.: A framework for scheduler synthesis. In: IEEE Real-Time Systems Symposium, pp. 154–163 (1999)
2. Alur, R., Dill, D.: A theory of timed automata. Theor. Comput. Sci. 126(2), 183–235 (1994)

3. Alur, R., Henzinger, T.: Logics and models of real time: A survey. In: REX Workshop, pp. 74–106 (1991)
4. Asarin, E., Caspi, P., Maler, O.: Timed regular expressions. J. ACM 49(2), 172–206 (2002)
5. Asarin, E., Maler, O., Pnueli, A.: Symbolic controller synthesis for discrete and timed systems. In: Hybrid Systems II, pp. 1–20 (1994)
6. Blazewicz, J., Ecker, K.H., Pesch, E., Schmidth, G., Weglarz, J.: Scheduling Computer and Manufacturing Processes, 2nd edn. Springer, Heidelberg (2001)
7. Bodin, L., Golden, B., Assad, A., Ball, M.: Routing and scheduling of vehicles and crews: The state of the art. Computers & OR 10(2), 63–211 (1983)
8. Borodin, A., Kleinberg, J., Raghavan, P., Sudan, M., Williamson, D.P.: Adversarial queuing theory. J. ACM 48(1), 13–38 (2001)
9. Bottazzo, G.: Hard Real-Time Computing Systems: Predictable Scheduling Algorithms and Applications, 2nd edn. Real-Time Systems Series. Springer, Heidelberg (2005)
10. Caccamo, M., Baker, T., Burns, A., Buttazzo, G., Sha, L.: Real-time scheduling for embedded systems. In: Hristu-Varsakelis, D., Levine, W. (eds.) Handbook of Networked and Embedded Control Systems, pp. 173–196. Birkhäuser, Basel (2005)
11. Cassez, F., David, A., Fleury, E., Larsen, K., Lime, D.: Efficient on-the-fly algorithms for the analysis of timed games. In: Abadi, M., de Alfaro, L. (eds.) CONCUR 2005. LNCS, vol. 3653, pp. 66–80. Springer, Heidelberg (2005)
12. Cholvi, V., Echagüe, J.: Stability of fifo networks under adversarial models: State of the art. Computer Networks 51(15), 4460–4474 (2007)
13. Darte, A., Robert, Y., Vivien, F.: Scheduling and Automatic Parallelization. Birkhauser, Boston (2000)
14. El-Rewini, H.: Partitioning and scheduling. In: Zomaya, A. (ed.) Parallel & Distributed Computed Handbook, ch. 9, pp. 239–273. McGraw-Hill, New York (1996)
15. Fersman, E., Mokrushin, L., Pettersson, P., Yi, W.: Schedulability analysis of fixed-priority systems using timed automata. Theor. Comput. Sci. 354(2), 301–317 (2006)
16. Gan, C.-H., Lin, P., Perng, N.-C., Kuo, T.-W., Hsu, C.-C.: Scheduling for time-division based shared channel allocation for UMTS. Wirel. Netw. 13(2), 189–202 (2007)
17. Hsu, G.-H.: A survey of queueing theory. Ann. Oper. Res. 24(1-4), 29–43 (1990)
18. Jain, A., Meeran, S.: A state-of-the-art review of job-shop scheduling techniques (1998)
19. Coffman Jr., E.G. (ed.): Computer and Job-Shop Scheduling Theory. J. Wiley, New York (1976)
20. Liu, C., Layland, J.: Scheduling algorithms for multiprogramming in a hard-real-time environment. J. ACM 20(1), 46–61 (1973)
21. Maler, O., Pnueli, A., Sifakis, J.: On the synthesis of discrete controllers for timed systems (an extended abstract). In: Mayr, E.W., Puech, C. (eds.) STACS 1995. LNCS, vol. 900, pp. 229–242. Springer, Heidelberg (1995)
22. Pinedo, M.: Planning and Scheduling in Manufacturing and Services. Springer Series in Operations Research and Financial Engineering. Springer, Heidelberg (2007)
23. Wong-Toi, H., Dill, D.: Synthesizing processes and schedulers from temporal specifications. In: Clarke, E., Kurshan, R.P. (eds.) CAV 1990. LNCS, vol. 531, pp. 272–281. Springer, Heidelberg (1991)

A Framework for Distributing Real-Time Functions

Frédéric Boniol[1], Pierre-Emmanuel Hladik[2], Claire Pagetti[1,3], Frédéric Aspro[4], and Victor Jégu[4]

[1] IRIT-ENSEEIHT, 2 rue C. Camichel, F31071 Toulouse - France
[2] LAAS, 135 av. de Rangueil, F31077 Toulouse - France
[3] ONERA-CERT, 2 av. E. Belin, F31055 Toulouse - France
[4] Airbus, Saint Martin du Touch, F31000 Toulouse - France
{frederic.boniol,claire.pagetti}@enseeiht.fr,
pehladik@laas.fr

Abstract. The design of critical embedded real-time systems requires high confidence in the architecture and the implemented functionalities. Classically, such functions are supported on a single monoprocessor, behavior of which is completely predictable, while the execution is totally deterministic. With the growing complexity of systems, it becomes quite unavoidable to implement these systems on distributed architectures. Scaling from mono to multiprocessor raises several issues which we address in this paper: we propose a simple executive model based on time triggered paradigm and an automated approach to allocate real-time tasks based on constraint resolution techniques. We illustrate the method on an industrial case study.

Keywords: Distributed systems, Constraint programming, Industrial case study.

1   Introduction

The use of digital embedded systems becomes natural for implementing highly critical systems. In the transport sector, numerous steps have been made, leading to the development of critical functions-by-wire and unmanned vehicles. Usually, this type of systems is based on a federated architecture of dedicated uniprocessor equipments: each one of these implements a critical function. With the increasing cost of energy, manufacturers generally try to optimize the power consumption, for instance by improving the aerodynamics and the weight of aircraft. This leads to flexible and unstable vehicles which need more accurate and complex control functions requiring more and more computing resources. Thus, in the next years, it will become unreasonable to expect to implement such control functions upon uniprocessor platforms. Additionally, next generation of embedded chips will evolve toward multicore architectures. Thus, efficient implementations on such multiprocessor or multicore platforms will require efficient tools and methods for carefully managing key resources, such as processor capacity, memory capacity, communication bandwidth, etc.

F. Cassez and C. Jard (Eds.): FORMATS 2008, LNCS 5215, pp. 155–169, 2008.
© Springer-Verlag Berlin Heidelberg 2008

Global Objective. Digital embedded systems are mainly composed of a *control software* (which implements the functions with a set of functional interacting tasks), a *hardware architecture* (which provides a set of processors, memories, buses, etc.), and an *executive model* (which schedules the execution of the tasks so that precedence, determinism and deadline constraints are satisfied). These different parts are often developed by several teams. Minimising modifications of the whole industrial process is thus a major purpose. Particularly, functional design has to be impacted as less as possible by hardware evolution. That purpose requires the definition of firstly an executive model that abstracts the hardware platform and that fits with the functional specifications assumptions, and secondly an automatic allocation method that maps the functional part onto the hardware architecture. Furthermore, the allocation method should be optimal in the sense that it should allocate as few resources as possible while guaranteeing the real-time requirements (deadlines and precedences). Obviously, in the case of realistic applications, this problem can note be treated manually. To overcome this difficulty, we show in this article that the allocation problem can be expressed (and solved) as a constraint satisfaction problem, even when considering very large applications.

Functional Hypotheses. We are interested in aeronautical functions which are mainly oriented control command and supervising. These functions are often specified by using synchronous block diagram languages such as Simulink (at the control design level) or SCADE[1] (at the software design level). From a semantic point of view, the notion of time used in these languages differs from that of non-synchronous languages in the following way: the notion of physical time is replaced by the notion of logical instant and with a partial order relation between blocks. Furthermore, the communication semantics often follows the global memory paradigm: blocks communicate through data flow; each data-flow has exactly one writer and several readers, and is supposed to be available immediately after produced. According to this functional model, we assume in this article that the functional specification to be allocated on the multiprocessor platform is modelled as a collection of simple multiperiodic real-time tasks, with precedence constraints, communicating through data flow; each task must be mapped on a single processor.

Scheduling Choices. Two main scheduling paradigms govern the implementation of real-time control systems: *on-line event-triggered* [Che02] and *off-line time-triggered* [GCG02]. On the one hand, event-triggered approaches, i.e., task executions are conducted by external or internal event, are efficient in terms of CPU usage, especially when release and execution times are not known precisely but are subject to variations. However, such an implementation generally requires the use of complex interfaces which are constrained by real-time operating systems and middleware; understanding its true behaviour becomes very complex. On the other hand, off-line time-triggered approaches, i.e., tasks are

---

[1] SCADE (Safety Critical Application Development Environment) is a tool-suite based on the data flow synchronous paradigm.

executed at time instants defined a priory, are efficient when dealing with ultra-dependable systems. Resulting implementation is very predictable (thus almost deterministic), easy to debug, and guarantees small bounded jitters. Its main drawback however lies in its lack of flexibility and in that it requires complex and non trivial pre-runtime schedule generation.

Aeronautical critical systems are subject to sound requirements that imply a particular care on the different components. The whole behaviour of the system should be predictable. This first requires strong *functional determinism*, which means that the program will always produce the same output sequence with respect to the same input sequence. The program must be *temporally determin-istic* as well, always having the same temporal behaviour and respecting hard real-time constraints. This is crucial to predict, prove and debug computed outputs for any given sequence of acquisitions, either by simulation or verification. Moreover, any designer of an aeronautical function has to ensure the quality of the development to the certification authorities.

For these reasons, static off-line non preemptive strategies are much more suited for such scheduling than others which generate non determinism. In this article, we assume a static time-triggered off-line scheduling approach, and we study the static allocation problem under such an assumption.

Mapping Problem. The *task mapping problem* consists in assigning (*allocat-ing*) each task to a processor and ordering (*scheduling*) the execution of these tasks such that all functional (precedence and deadline) and non functional (memory capacity, bandwidth network, processor capacity, etc.) constraints are met. Unfortunately, even in the simplified case when both the precedence constraints and the resource limitation constraints are ignored, the task mapping problem is essentially a bin-packing problem which is known to be NP-complete [GGJY76]. The global problem, when considering resource limitations is then, not surprisingly, intractable by exact methods. Consequently, much prior work on allocation and scheduling real-time tasks upon a multiprocessor platform have been made based upon specific heuristic approaches [PEP04]. If these methods are efficient for specif applications. However, they strogly suffer from a lack gnericity and adaptability. To cope with complexity, many non-guided search heuristics, like Simulated Annealing, can be used. These methods always maintain a current allocation by slight modifications in order to get a better one for the next iteration step. However, when considering very large applications (as presented section 4), these techniques often have difficulties in finding a first correct allocation (i.e., which satisfies the functional and non functional constraints). This is due to the size and the complex nature of the solution space.

Other recent approaches explore optimal techniques such as integer linear programming [Bar04] [FAB05] or constraint programming [SW00] [SK03] [Eke04] [HCDJ07]. Among these approaches, [CCM+03] and [SGR07] explore the allocation problem in the context of time triggered architectures. These methods provide an optimal allocation with respect to scheduling criteria (e.g., scheduling length). However, they often do not consider resource limitation constraints such as communication bandwidth or memory size.

Many other techniques are proposed based on constructive heuristics. However, most of these approaches focus on a particular aspect, such as the load balancing with the hope to keep the resources utilization low (e.g., network load). When dealing with a complete system, it is more suited to optimize multi criteria. We propose in this article to extend these constraint programming based methods by taking into account not only the temporal aspects (deadline and precedence) but also the resource limitation constraints (memory size, communication delay...). This extends the results obtained by [Eke04].

Contribution. In the context presented above, we have introduced an executive model that responds to the functional hypotheses: this model is built upon a temporal splitting into computation slices and communication slices. The allocation has then in charge to ensure that no two communicating tasks with precedence are placed on different processors at a same slice. This architectural solution is simple and deterministic, though flexible enough to provide the required services.

We also choose an exact solving approach based on constraint programming [RvBW06]. First, this technique has been widely used to solve a large range of combinatorial problems and it has proved quite effective in a variety of applications. Second, it provides a quite attractive framework for industrial use for many reasons:

declarativity: the variables, domains and constraints are simply described. Once the designer is usual with the programming, the coding of new constraints is quite friendly. When dealing with a complete system, there are several types of constraint. As an example, an aeronautical function can interact with other functions via the uni-sender multireceivers bus Arinc429: there is a bounded FIFO that stores messages to be sent and each message is sent in 0.5 ms. Thus, a constraint is that no message is lost because the FIFO is full. This type of constraint and more generally, many constraints to take into account can be encoded within the constraint programming framework. If we have chosen an ad hoc method, we would have to integrate any of these requirements. This is not suitable since during the design of a system, new requirements can emerge for many reasons, such as technological evolution, new implementation of a function or IMA integration;

genericity: it is not a problem-dependent technique, general rules are mechanically performed during the search. Once the problem is modelled, there are several tools and methods to find solutions. Moreover, it is also possible to express criteria of optimality such as smoothing;

adaptability: each constraint can be considered as independent and a model could be simply extended by merging these different constraints;

performance: in our context, we obtain the optimal theoretical performance that was computed by the incompressible path. However, optimisation is better handled with dedicated methods such as heuristics or branch-and-bound. It is then possible to combine the constraint programming declaration framework with optimised search techniques;

non-parametric ability: our approach is not sensitive to initial parameters that are huge difficulty for other search methods, i.e. temperature and cooling for simulated annealing, selection criteria and population size for genetic algorithm, enumeration order for branch-and-bound, etc.

In the paper, we detail how the problem of allocating a functional specification on a distributed architecture using the synchronous distributed executive model can be expressed as a constraint problem. We have applied our approach to different functions. We illustrate it in this paper on a particular case study composed of 762 tasks, subjected to 236 precedence constraints, and communicating by producing and consuming 3370 data. For solving the mapping problem of this case study on two multiprocessor platforms (composed respectively of 4 and 8 processors), we used the solver OPL [ILO] of ILOG Studio. OPL provides several searching strategies for integer domains with a large set of constraints, i.e. linear, global etc. A program is divided in two parts: a file .mod which contains the model and the constraints, a file .dat which contains exclusively the data. This separations allows to define a generic model for the material and executive architectures; and the user has just to change the .dat for each functional specification. We then show that OPL, with our formulation, finds quickly an allocation very close to the optimal one.

2   System Formal Description

To perform the tasks allocation, we first need to define formally the different components in the framework of the constraint programming. After a brief recall on the constraint programming, we model within this paradigm the system composed of a set of functions, an hardware architecture enriched with executive mechanisms that allow synchronisation between processors, a local sequencer on each processor, communication means between processors and with the environment.

2.1   Generalities on Constraint Programming

The constraint programming is a wide research area and several books, papers or courses can be found such as [RvBW06]. In a concise way, we can say that it manipulates *constraints* where a constraint is a logical relation between *variables*, values of which belong to a predefined *domain*. A *constraint satisfaction problem*, csp for short, is a problem modelled by a set of constraints laid on a set of variables. More formally, a csp is a tuple (X, D, C) where:

1. $X = \{x_1, \ldots, x_n\}$ is a set of variables;
2. D is a function that associates to each variable x_i its domain $D(x_i)$, i.e. the set of possible values of x_i;
3. $C = \{C_1, C_2, ..., C_k\}$ is the set of constraints. Each constraint C_j is a relation between some variables of X and reduces the values that can be taken simultaneously by the variables. The simplest constraints are comparisons defined over expressions of variables such as linear combinations, i.e. $x \leq y + z$.

More complex expressions such as min or max are also available. A global constraint is a dedicated constraint which allows to filter efficiently. In this paper we used only arithmetic and Boolean constraints.

Example 1. Here is a simple example of csp (X, D, C) describing the distribution of 4 tasks on 2 processors:

1. $X = \{x_1, x_2, x_3, x_4\}$ represents the set of the 4 tasks;
2. $D(x_1) = D(x_2) = D(x_3) = D(x_4) = \{0, 1\}$ corresponds to the variables domain. If x_i is equal to 0 it means that x_i is on the first processor, otherwise it is on the second one;
3. $C = \{x_1 = x_2, x_2 \neq x_4\}$ describes the constraints that x_1 and x_2 are on the same processor and that x_2 must not be on the same processor as x_4.

A solution to the problem is an assignment of a value in $D(x_i)$ to each variable x_i in X such that all constraints are satisfied. The solutions to a csp can be found by systematically searching through the possible assignments of values to variables. The variables are sequentially labeled and, as soon as all the variables relevant to a constraint are instantiated, the validity of the constraint is checked. If any of the constraints is violated, backtracking is performed to the most recently instantiated variable that still has available values. However, constraint programming offers more accurate methods to solve a csp. One of them is based on removing inconsistent values from domains of variables till a solution is found. This mechanism coupled with a backtracking scheme allows the search space to be explored in a *complete way*. For a more detailed explanation, we refer the reader to [RvBW06].

When there are several solutions, it is interesting to express some preferences among the solutions. For this, the idea is to define a numerical function from the set of solutions whose values depend on a quality criterion. The objective is then to maximise this function. In this case, we speak of a Constraint Satisfaction Optimisation Problem, csop for short.

Example 2. There are several solutions for the csp in example 1: $(x_1, x_2, x_3, x_4) \in \{(0, 0, 1, 1), (0, 0, 0, 1), (1, 1, 1, 0), (1, 1, 0, 0)\}$. When adding the criterion $f(A) = x_1 + x_3$, the csop has only one solution $\{(1, 1, 1, 0)\}$.

We now introduce the variables of the allocation problem with respect to the complete architecture.

2.2 Functional Architecture

The functional architecture is a set of communicating multiperiodic tasks partially constrained by a set of precedences.

Definition 1. *A functional architecture is a tuple* $\mathcal{F}onc = \langle\,\mathcal{N} \cup \{env_\Delta\},\ nb_pe\text{-}riods,\ periods,\ T_1,\ nb_tasks_T,\ vec_size,\ vec_wcet,\ nb_prec,\ prec,\ var_sent,\ nb_com,\ com,\ nb_input,\ nb_output,\ output\,\rangle\ where*

- $\mathcal{N}$ *is a set of atomic functional tasks, denoted by t^i_k where i refers to the period and k is an identifier. env_Δ is a functional abstraction of the environment and is assumed to produce periodically data to the system at period Δ;*
- nb_periods *is the number of periods, T_1 is the basic period of the specification and* periods *is a vector of size nb_periods elements of which are the relative periods of the tasks. Then, we have $periods[i] = T_i/T_1$. In the remainder of the paper, when we define an integer name, we assume that* Name *stands for the range 1..name. Thus, Nb_periods is used for the interval $[1..nb\_periods]$;*
- nb_tasks_T *is a vector such that for all $i \in Nb\_periods$, nb_tasks_T$[i]$ is the number of tasks of period T_i;*
- vec_size *(resp. vec_wcet) is matrix such that for all $(i,j) \in Nb\_periods \times Nb\_tasks[i]$, vec_size$[i][j]$ is the code size (resp. wcet (i.e., the worst case execution time)) of the j-th task of period T_i;*
- nb_prec *is a vector such that for all $i \in Nb\_periods$, nb_prec$[i]$ is the number of precedence between tasks of period T_i.* prec *is a matrix that depicts these precedences: for all $(i,j) \in Nb\_periods \times Nb\_prec[i]$, prec$[i][j] =< k,l >$ means that t^i_k has to be completed before t^i_l starts;*
- var_sent *is vector such that for all $i \in Nb\_periods$, var_sent$[i]$ is a list of pair $< k,l >$ that gives the number l of variables emitted by the task t^i_k.* nb_com *is a matrix such that for all $(i,j) \in Nb\_periods \times Nb\_periods$, nb_com$[i][j]$ is the number of exchanges from a task of period T_i to task of period T_j.* com *is a 3 dimensional matrix with for all $(i,j,k) \in Nb\_periods \times Nb\_periods \times Nb\_com[i][j]$, com$[i][j][k]$ is a pair of form (producer, consumer). Thus com$[i][j][k] =< p,l >$ means that t^j_l consumes at least one variable produced by t^i_p;*
- nb_input *(resp. nb_output$[i]$, for $i \in Nb\_periods$) is the number of inputs (resp. outputs) receives from (resp. emitted to) the environment. $\forall (i,j) \in Nb\_periods \times Nb\_output[i]$, output$[i][j] =< k,l >$ means that t^i_k emits l outputs.*

Let us denote by $HP = \mathrm{lcm}_i(periods[i])$ the hyper period of the functional architecture.

Note that the dependence relation *prec* is not necessarily related to the data-flow. Tasks are supposed to communicate asynchronously, following an "overwritting" communication mode: emitters write in a non blocking space (typically a buffer) (, and receivers always consume the last emitted value (or a default value if at the initial instant no value is receive).

Note also that we make an over approximation for the communications: we assume that if a variable produced by t_1 is consumed by a task t_2, then we send all the variables produced by t_1 to t_2. It is possible to encode the exact exchange but the complete problem was unsolved for our case study. If there is a solution for the over constrained problem, the solution handles for the real problem, which is fortunately the case for us.

Example 3. Let us consider the following functional architecture:

tasks (name,wcet,size)			data-flow		precedences		environment
10 ms	20 ms	40 ms					$\Delta = 2.5$ ms
t_1^1 1.2 10	t_1^2 1.5 5	t_1^3 1.4 15	var_0 12 t_1^1	t_1^3	t_1^1	t_2^1	i_1 $\quad t_1^1$
t_2^1 1.1 10	t_2^2 1.4 10	t_2^3 1 20		t_2^1	t_1^2	t_1^1	t_1^2
t_3^1 1.1 10	t_3^2 0.5 3			t_4^1			
t_4^1 0.5 3			var_1 15 t_1^2	t_1^3			o_1 $\quad t_2^3$
t_5^1 0.7 3				t_1^1			
			var_2 20 t_1^3	t_2^3			

The first macro column describes the set of tasks and each task is represented by a pair *(name, wcet, size)*. For instance, t_1^1 has period T_1, wcet 1.2 ms and size 10 bytes. This defines completely the set $\mathcal{N} = \{t_i^j | (i,j) \in [1,5] \times 1 \cup [1,3] \times 2 \cup [1,2] \times 3\}$. There are $nb\_periods = 3$ periods, $periods = [1,2,4]$, $nb\_tasks\_T[1] = 5$ of period 10 ms, $nb\_tasks\_T[2] = 3$ of period 20 ms and $nb\_tasks\_T[3] = 2$ of period 40 ms. We deduce that $HP = 40$ ms. The wcet of each function is stored in the vectors $vec\_wcet[1] = [12,11,11,5,7]$, $vec\_wcet[2] = [15,14,5]$, $vec\_wcet[3] = [15,14]$. The code sizes are given by $vec\_size[1] = [10,10,10,3,3]$, $vec\_size[2] = [5,10,3]$, $vec\_size[3] = [15,20]$.

The second macro column gives the data-flow which is represented by a tuple *(variable name, variable size, producer, list of consumers)*. For instance t_1^1 produces a variable var_0 which is consumed by t_1^3, t_2^1 and t_4^1. There is an emitter for each period that sends exactly one variable $var\_sent = [[<1,1>],[<1,1>],[<1,1>]]$. $com[1][1] = [<1,2>,<1,4>]$ and $com[1][3] = [<1,1>]$ for instance, other sub vectors can be deduced following the same way.

The third macro column depicts the precedence relation, for instance we have t_1^1 precedes t_2^1. The dependencies, with $nb\_prec = [1,1,0]$, are given by the vectors $prec[1] = [<1,2>]$, $prec[2] = [<1,2>]$.

The last macro column gives the exchange with the environment. The name i stands for input whereas o stands for output. There are one input used by t_1^1 and t_1^2; and an output produced by t_2^3. Thus, $nb\_input = [1,0,0]$, $nb\_output = [0,0,1]$ and $output[3] = [<2,1>]$.

Restrictions. In the following, we only consider causal functional architectures, i.e., such that the dependence relation defines an acyclic graph. This means that for all $n \in \mathcal{N}$, $(n,n) \notin prec^*$ where $prec^*$ is the transitive closure of $prec$.

We moreover assume that all considered functional architectures are well-formed. This means that the periods T_i are multiple of the the emission period Δ of the environment; each data is produced by one and only one task; each data is consumed by at least one task.

2.3   Hardware Architecture

Numerous architectures have been embedded, but in this article we consider a distributed architecture composed of computing resources communicating through

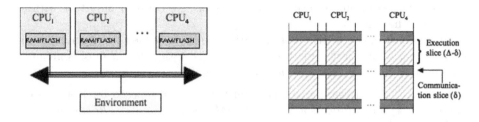

Fig. 1. Architecture and executive models

a commuted network as depicted in figure 1 on the left side. This network is constituted by a broadcast bus connecting all the resources.

We assume that each resource provides services to the functions that permit to sequence locally the tasks, to construct or receive exchange messages for the communication technology, to access the medium and so on. These services are abstracted for the modelling since their temporal costs are taken into account in the wcets and the communication rate.

Definition 2. *A hardware architecture is a tuple* $\mathcal{M}at = \langle$ *nb_proc, FlashMemory, SRamMemory, LinkRate* $\rangle$ *where*

– nb_proc *is the number of computing processors with a Flash and a SRam memories. The Flash contains the codes of nodes allocated on the resource whereas the SRam contains the data received and produced by these nodes;*
  • FlashMemory *is a vector such that for all* $i \in Nb\_proc$, *FlashMemory[i] gives the Flash memory size (in Bytes) of resource* i;
  • SRamMemory *is a vector such that for all* $i \in Nb\_proc$, *SRamMemory[i] gives the SRam memory size (in Bytes) of resource* i;
– LinkRate $\in \mathbb{N}$ *is the rate (in bits/s) of the broadcast bus.*

Distributed executive model. The global organisation of the distributed architecture defines the so-called *executive model*. For the critical and reactive context, this model should ensure determinism properties by construction. We propose an executive model almost synchronous based on time triggered principles.

The execution time on each resource is divided into sequential slices as depicted in figure 1 on the right side: processors execute alternatively and synchronously *execution* and *communication slices*. Tasks are executed during execution slices while data exchange between tasks located on different processors occurs during communication slices, i.e., between two execution slices. The slices begin and complete synchronously, i.e., at the same time, on all the processors.

The environment sends data with period Δ. Since Δ is the quickest rate, Δ is considered as the basic period of the system. Thus, the couples of execution and communication slices are repeated with period Δ. In this executive distributed model, we assume that all communication slices have the same size $\delta < \Delta$ and all execution slices have the same size $\Delta - \delta$. A task is non-preemtible and has to be completed during an execution slice. Thus, we consider only task with a wcet lower than $\Delta - \delta$.

To summarize, the distributed executive model is defined by the number of slices nb_slices, the basic period $huge\_delta$, the length $small\_delta$ of communication slices. Note that we have $nb\_slices * \Delta = T_1$.

Example 4. The hardware architecture of figure 1 is composed by 4 processors ($nb\_proc = 4$), each processor has a *FlashMemory* $= 40$ and *SRamMemory* $= 64$. The *LinkRate* is assumed to be at 100. The executive slicing gives by the conditions $nb\_slices = 4$, $huge\_delta = 25$ and $small\_delta = 2$.

3   Task Mapping Problem

The *task mapping problem* consists in allocating each task to a processor and in scheduling the execution of the tasks such that all functional and temporal constraints are respected. For the executive model defined below, each functional task in $\mathcal{N}$ has to be allocated not only on a resource but also on an execution slice. The aim of this section is to show that the mapping can be formalized as a constraint solving problem.

3.1   The Problem Variables

Fixed parameters. Some variables have constant values depending on the architecture and the function. The fixed parameters are given by the functional and hardware architectures. We introduce the data structure *Couple* for describing pairs, for the parameters *prec*, *var_sent*, *com[i][j]* and *output*. If x is of type *Couple*, we access to the fields *x.elt1* and *x.elt2*.

Variables. The variables describe the problem and the solver try to instantiate them while respecting the constraints and trying to optimize the criterion. The problem consists in allocating each task over one processor and one slice. There are two types of variables for the allocation:

1. $slice\_T[i][j]$ with $(i, j) \in Nb\_periods \times Nb\_tasks\_T[i]$ that allocates each task on the slice where it belongs. $slice\_T[i][j]$ is in the domain $1..(nb\_slices*periods[i])$;
2. $proc\_T[i][j]$ with $(i, j) \in Nb\_periods \times Nb\_tasks\_T[i]$ that allocates each task on the processor where it executes. $proc\_T[i][j]$ is in the domain Nb_proc.

We use intermediate variables to simplify the modelling and the computation:

1. the variable *var_proc* is a vector of Boolean such that $var\_proc[p][i][j]$, with $(p, i, j) \in Nb\_proc \times Nb\_periods \times Nb\_tasks\_T[i]$, is equal to 0 when the variables produced by t_j^i are not used by any task located on the processor p, meaning that the variables are not stored in the RAM of p;
2. *SizeRam* (resp. *SizeFlash*) is a vector of size Nb_proc determining the effective occupation of the RAM (resp. Flash) of each processor;
3. $com\_occupation[i][t]$ with $(i, t) \in Nb\_periods \times (Nb\_slices * periods[i])$, determines the number of emissions of the tasks of period T_i at slice t;
4. *com_occupation_max* and *cpu_occupation_max* are the variables to optimize.

3.2   The Constraints

The choice of the variables ensures that a task is allocated on a unique processor and a unique slice.

Precedence constraint. For all pair (t_1, t_2) in precedence, t_1 must execute and thus be allocated on a slice before the slice of t_2. This is given by the first condition. The second condition says that t_1 and t_2 can execute at the same slice if and only if they are on the same processor:

$$\forall k \in Nb\_periods, i \in Nb\_prec[k],$$
$$slice\_T[k][prec[k][i].elt1] \leq slice\_T[k][prec[k][i].elt2];$$
$$(slice\_T[k][prec[k][i].elt1] = slice\_T[k][prec[k][i].elt2]) \Rightarrow$$
$$(proc\_T[k][prec[k][i].elt1] = proc\_T[k][prec[k][i].elt2]$$

CPU occupation. For any slice in the hyper period and for any processor, the sum of the wcets of tasks executed on this slice and this processor is necessarily less than $\Delta - \delta$:

$$\forall t \in [1..(nb\_slices \times HP)], p \in Nb\_proc,$$
$$\sum_{i \in Nb\_periods, j \in Nb\_tasks\_T[i]} (proc\_T[i][j] = p) \times vec\_wcet[i][j]$$
$$\times (slice\_T[i][j] = t - ((t-1)/(nb\_slices \times HP/T_i) \times nb\_slices \times HP/T_i))$$
$$\leq huge\_delta - small\_delta$$

We mix Boolean expressions, such as $(proc\_T[i][j] = p)$ which is equal to 1 when the task t_j^i is on the processor p and 0 otherwise, and integer expressions. $(slice\_T[i][j] = t - ((t-1)/(nb\_slices \times HP/T_i) \times nb\_slices \times HP/T_i))$ is also a Boolean expression that tests if task t_j^i is on the slice t. Since $slice\_T[i]$ is defined for the slices $T_i \times nb\_slices$ and the computation is on the slices on the hyper period HP, we compute the translated slices where the task belonged.

No memory overflow. The allocation must respect the resource capacities in terms of storage. The sum of the tasks code size located on a resource should not exceed the Flash memory size.

$$\forall p \in Nb\_proc, \sum_{i \in Nb\_periods, j \in Nb\_tasks\_T[i]} (proc\_T[i][j] = p) \times vec\_size[i][j] \leq FlashMemory[p]$$

The sum of the tasks data size located on a resource should not exceed the SRam memory size. We need to be more careful when expressing this constraint since we should not count twice a same data which could be produced by a local task and consumed by an another local task. For this, we compute the intermediate predicates $var\_proc[p][i][j]$ which is equal to 1 when the variables produced by t_j^i are needed on processor p.

$$\forall p \in Nb\_proc, i \in Nb\_periods, j \in Nb\_tasks\_T[i],$$
$$var\_proc[p][i][j] = ((proc\_T[i][var\_sent[i][j].elt1] = p)$$
$$+ \sum_{l \in Nb\_com[i][j]} (com[i][j][l].elt1 = var\_sent[i][j].elt1) \times (proc\_T[i][com[i][j][l].elt2] = p)$$
$$\geq 1)$$

The variables produced by $var\_sent[i][j].elt1$ are on the processor p if the producer is itself on the processor, condition given by $(proc\_T[i][var\_sent[i][j].elt1] = p)$ or if one of the consumer is on the processor p. If the global sum is greater than one, it means that the producer or consumer is on processor p. Thus, for computing the occupation of the $SizeRam[k]$ we just have to add all the required variables on processor k. We also add the output allocated on the processor. The constraint is then to ensure that $SizeRam[k] \leq SRamMemory[k]$.

$$\forall k \in Nb\_proc,$$
$$SizeRam[k] = \sum_{i \in Nb\_periods, j \in Nb\_tasks\_T[i]} var\_proc[k][i][j] \times var\_sent[i][j].elt2$$
$$+ \sum_{i \in Nb\_periods, j \in Nb\_output[i]} (proc\_T[i][output[i,j].elt1]=k) \times output[i,j].elt2$$

Communication constraint. The last constraint concerns the communication slices duration. During a communication slice, time is spent emitting the variables.

$$\forall i \in Nb\_periods, \forall t \in [1..(nb\_slices \times periods[i])]$$
$$com\_occupation[i][t] = \sum_{j \in Nb\_tasks\_T[i]} (slice\_T[i][var\_sent[i][j].elt1] = t)$$
$$\times (\sum_{p \in Nb\_proc} var\_proc[p][i][j] >= 2) \times var\_sent[i][j].elt2$$
$$+ \sum_{j \in Nb\_output[i]} (slice\_T[i][output[i][j].elt1]=t) \times output[i][j].elt2$$

This computes for each slice t the number of variables emitted by tasks of period T_i. For any source of data allocated on the slice ($slice\_T[i][var\_sent[i][j].elt1] = t$), we test if the data is required on two different processors $var\_sent[i][j].elt2$ entailing that the data have to be sent. Moreover, we must take into account the outputs emitted at the slice t.

Globally, we obtain that for all slice, the number of variables emitted does not exceed the maximal number of variables, taking into account the inputs which are always emitted. This expressed by the constraint ($com\_occupation\_max + nb\_input) \times LinkRate \leq small\_delta$ where $com\_occupation\_max$ is the maximal number of internal variables exchanged during a slice:

$$\forall t \in [1..(nb\_slices \times HP)],$$
$$\sum_{i \in Nb\_periods} com\_occupationT[i][t-((t-1)/(nb\_slices \times HP/periods[i]) \times HP/periods[i])]$$
$$\leq com\_occupation\_max$$

Example 5. The example model is given in the page [Web]. The allocation is the following:

slice	1	2	3	4	5	6	7	8	9	10	11	12	13	14	15	16
P1	t_3^1				t_3^1	t_1^2		t_3^1					t_3^1	t_1^2		
P2	t_5^1				t_5^1		t_2^2	t_5^1					t_5^1,t_1^3			t_2^2
P3	t_4^1,t_3^2	t_1^1		t_4^1	t_1^1		t_4^1,t_3^2			t_1^1			t_4^1		t_1^1	
P4				t_2^1			t_2^1					t_2^1		t_2^3		t_2^1

The maximal CPU occupation is 18 and at most one variable is sent during a slice commmunication. The maximal Flash is 33 and RAMs contain at most 2 variables.

4   Case Study

We have applied the approach on a real avionics case study provided by Airbus and have obtained promising results for the distribution of the function.

Presentation. The function is composed of 762 tasks subjected to 236 precedences. The specification is given in a tabular, similar to the one of example 3, in the file `definition.csv` on the web page [Web]. The OPL code is also on the web page. In this example, we did not take into account the outputs. For the code size, we choose the same values as the wcet since we miss the information. The global uniprocessor occupation is of 8336.

Results. For solving the problem, we use a SUN station of 1600Mhz and with 1027Mo RAM. For finding optimal results, we first minimize *cpu_occupation_max* and then fix *cpu_occupation_max* to be this minimum and then minimize *com_occupation_max*. The results are summarized in the following tabular:

Number of processors	CPU occupation	number of data exchanged	RAM max size	Flash max size
4	2093	445	3028	14488
Optimisation	2093	339	2929	14470
Bounded Flash	2252	527	2980	9899
8	1047	787	2791	3398

For 4 processors, we obtain an optimal distribution in term of CPU, since 8336/4=2084. OPL does not converge and iterates indefinitely on the values. OPL has difficulties to distribute homogeneously on the slices and have the tendency to make packets. For improving the communication, we force, with additional constraints, to spread the tasks. The line *Optimisation* gives some improvements of the number of communications. The idea is to study the general solution founded and to impose the allocation of the non dependant nodes in different slices. The line *Bounded Flash* constrains the Flash to be bounded and to study the impact on the other resources occupation.

We then generate the code for 8 processors but in this case OPL was not able to solve the problem for insufficient RAM availability question. We then use a heuristic adapted to the context: we first allocate the tasks of period T_1, we then allocate the tasks of period T_2 while fixing tasks T_1 and so on. Again, we find a optimal repartition of the tasks.

It is hard to really measure the time spent by the solver since we interact with it. When fixing the bounds correctly, solving the problem takes a small amount of time. For instance, the computation needs 95s to find an optimal allocation for 4 processors.

5   Conclusion

This paper deals with the task mapping problem for aeronautical functions, i.e., it consists in assigning tasks to a set of processors and scheduling their execution such that all functional (precedence and deadline) and non functional (memory capacity, bandwidth network, processor capacity, etc.) constraints are met.

This problem is tackled by constraint programming to map automatically the functional architecture onto the hardware. We extended an existing method [Eke04] to assume a large diversity of functional specifications such as precedence constraints, communicating through data flow, memory (flash and ram) resource, etc. We illustrate it on a particular case study composed of 762 tasks, subjected to 236 precedence constraints, and communicating by producing and consuming 3370 data. Experimental results show that this method produces an efficient way to solve allocation problem.

The results produced by our experiments encourage us to go a step further. Future works concern the use of dedicated global constraint as cumulative one for memory constraints, i.e. a constraint which deals with bin packing problems. Another interesting work deals with the used of novel techniques to reduce the runtime of optimization algorithms, such as exclusion of symmetries in the solution space or local ad-hoc heuristics to reduce the amount of search in the last iteration of optimization.

References

[Bar04]   Baruah, S.K.: Partitioning real-time tasks among heterogeneous multiprocessors. In: ICPP 2004: Proceedings of the 2004 International Conference on Parallel Processing, pp. 467–474. IEEE Computer Society Press, Washington (2004)

[CCM+03]   Caspi, P., Curic, A., Maignan, A., Sofronis, C., Tripakis, S., Niebert, P.: From Simulink to SCADE/Lustre to TTA: a layered approach for distributed embedded applications. SIGPLAN Not. 38(7), 153–162 (2003)

[Che02]   Cheng, A.M.K.: Real-Time Systems: Scheduling, Analysis, and Verification. John Wiley & Sons, Inc., New York (2002)

[Eke04]   Ekelin, C.: An Optimization Framework for Scheduling of Embedded Real-Time Systems. PhD thesis, Chalmers University of Technology (2004)

[FAB05]   Fisher, N., Anderson, J.H., Baruah, S.: Task partitioning upon memory-constrained multiprocessors. In: RTCSA 2005: Proceedings of the 11th IEEE International Conference on Embedded and Real-Time Computing Systems and Applications, pp. 416–421. IEEE Computer Society Press, Washington (2005)

[GCG02]   Grolleau, E., Choquet-Geniet, A.: Off-line computation of real-time schedules using petri nets. Discrete Event Dynamic Systems 12(3), 311–333 (2002)

[GGJY76]   Garey, M.R., Graham, R.L., Johnson, D.S., Yao, A.C.: Resource constrained scheduling as generalized bin packing. Journal of Combinatorial Theory 21, 257–298 (1976)

[HCDJ07]   Hladik, P.-E., Cambazard, H., Déplanche, A.-M., Jussien, N.: Solving a real-time allocation problem with constraint programming. Journal of Systems and Software 5(4), 335–357 (2007)

[ILO]   ILOG. OPL Studio, http://www.ilog.com/products/oplstudio/

[PEP04]   Pop, P., Eles, P., Peng, Z.: Analysis and Synthesis of Distributed Real-Time Embedded Systems. Kluwer Academic Publishers, Dordrecht (2004)

[RvBW06]   Rossi, F., van Beek, P., Walsh, T. (eds.): Handbook of Constraint Pro-
           gramming. Elsevier, Amsterdam (2006)
[SGR07]   Sethu, R., Ganesan, P.V., Raravi, G.: A formal framework for the correct-
           by-construction and verification of distributed time triggered systems. In:
           IEEE Symposium on Industrial Embedded Systems (SIES 2007). IEEE
           Computer Society, Los Alamitos (2007)
[SK03]   Szymanek, R., Kuchcinski, K.: Partial task assignment of task graphs un-
           der heterogeneous resource constraints. In: Proceedings of the 40th con-
           ference on Design Automation (DAC 2003), pp. 244–249 (2003)
[SW00]   Schild, K., Würtz, J.: Scheduling of time-triggered real-time systems. Con-
           straints 5(4), 335–357 (2000)
[Web]   Web, http://www.cert.fr/anglais/deri/pagetti/FORMATS/

Formal Modeling and Scheduling of Datapaths of Digital Document Printers[*]

Georgeta Igna[2], Venkatesh Kannan[3], Yang Yang[1],
Twan Basten[1], Marc Geilen[1], Frits Vaandrager[2], Marc Voorhoeve[3],
Sebastian de Smet[4], and Lou Somers[4]

[1] Fac. of Electrical Engineering
Eindhoven University of Technology, the Netherlands
{Y.Yang,A.A.Basten,M.C.W.Geilen}@tue.nl
[2] Institute for Computing and Information Sciences
Radboud University Nijmegen, the Netherlands
{g.igna,f.vaandrager}@cs.ru.nl
[3] Fac. of Mathematics and Computer Science
Eindhoven University of Technology, the Netherlands
{V.Kannan,M.Voorhoeve}@tue.nl
[4] Océ Research & Development, the Netherlands
{sebastian.desmet,lou.somers}@oce.com

Abstract. We apply three different modeling frameworks — timed automata (UPPAAL), colored Petri nets and synchronous data flow — to model a challenging industrial case study that involves an existing state-of-the-art image processing pipeline. Each of the resulting models is used to derive schedules for multiple concurrent jobs in the presence of limited resources (processing units, memory, USB bandwidth,..). The three models and corresponding analysis results are compared.

1 Introduction

The Octopus project is a cooperation between Océ Technologies, the Embedded Systems Institute and several academic research groups in the Netherlands. The aim of Octopus is to define new techniques, tools and methods for the design of electromechanical systems like printers, which react in an adaptive way to changes during usage. One of the topics studied is the design of the datapath of printers/copiers. The datapath encompasses the complete trajectory of the image data from source (for example the network) to target (the imaging unit). Runtime changes in the environment (such as the observed image quality) may require the use of different algorithms in the datapath, deadlines for completion of computations may change, new jobs may suddenly arrive, and resource availability may change. To realize this type of behavior in a predictable way is a major challenge. In this paper, we report on the first phase of the project

[*] Research carried out in the context of the Octopus project, with partial support of the Netherlands Ministry of Economic Affairs under the Senter TS program.

F. Cassez and C. Jard (Eds.): FORMATS 2008, LNCS 5215, pp. 170–187, 2008.
© Springer-Verlag Berlin Heidelberg 2008

in which we studied a slightly simplified version of an existing state-of-the-art image processing pipeline that has been implemented in hardware, in particular the scheduling of multiple concurrent data flows.

1.1   The Case Study

Océ systems perform a variety of image processing functions on digital documents in addition to scanning, copying and printing. Apart from local use for scanning and copying, users can also remotely use the system for image processing and printing. A generic architecture of the system studied in this paper is shown in Fig. 1.

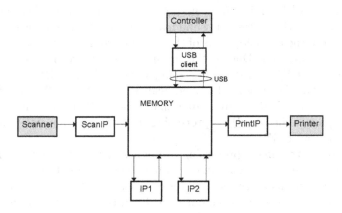

Fig. 1. Architecture of Océ system

The system has two ports for input: Scanner and Controller. Users locally come to the system to submit jobs at the Scanner and remote jobs enter the system via the Controller. These jobs use the image processing (IP) components (ScanIP, IP1, IP2, PrintIP), and system resources such as memory and a USB bus for executing the jobs. Finally, there are two places where the jobs leave the system: Printer and Controller.

The IP components can be used in different combinations depending on how a document is requested to be processed by the user. Hence this gives rise to different use cases of the system, that is, each job may use the system in a different way. The list of components used by a job defines the *datapath* for that job. Some examples of datapaths are:

- **DirectCopy:** Scanner $\rightsquigarrow$ ScanIP $\rightsquigarrow$ IP1 $\rightsquigarrow$ IP2 $\rightsquigarrow$ USBClient, PrintIP[1]
- **ScanToStore:** Scanner $\rightsquigarrow$ ScanIP $\rightsquigarrow$ IP1 $\rightsquigarrow$ USBClient
- **ScanToEmail:** Scanner $\rightsquigarrow$ ScanIP $\rightsquigarrow$ IP1 $\rightsquigarrow$ IP2 $\rightsquigarrow$ USBClient
- **ProcessFromStore:** USBClient $\rightsquigarrow$ IP1 $\rightsquigarrow$ IP2 $\rightsquigarrow$ USBClient

---

[1] If A $\rightsquigarrow$ B occurs in a datapath, then the start of the processing by A should precede the start of the processing by B.

- **SimplePrint:** USBClient $\rightsquigarrow$ PrintIP
- **PrintWithProcessing:** USBClient $\rightsquigarrow$ IP2 $\rightsquigarrow$ PrintIP

In the *DirectCopy* datapath, a job is processed in order by the components Scanner, ScanIP, IP1, and IP2, and then simultaneously sent to the Controller via the USBClient and to the printer through PrintIP. In the case of the *Process-FromStore* datapath, a remote job is sent by the Controller to the USBClient for processing by IP1 and IP2, after which the result is returned to the remote user via the USBClient and the Controller. The interpretation of the remaining datapaths is similar.

It is not mandatory that the components in the datapath process the job sequentially: the design of the system allows for a certain degree of parallelism. Scanner and ScanIP, for instance, may process a page in parallel. This is because ScanIP works fully streaming and has the same throughput as the Scanner. However, due to the characteristics of the different components, some additional constraints are imposed. Due to the nature of the image processing function that IP2 performs, IP2 can start processing a page only after IP1 has completed processing it. The dependency between ScanIP and IP1 is different. IP1 works streaming and has a higher throughput than ScanIP. Hence IP1 may start processing the page while ScanIP is processing it, with a certain delay due to the higher throughput of IP1.

In addition to the image processing components, two other system resources that may be scarce are memory and USB bandwidth. Execution of a job is only allowed if the entire memory required for completion of the job is available (and allocated) before its execution commences. Each component requires a certain amount of memory for its task and this can be released once computation has finished and no other component needs the information. Availability of memory is a critical factor in determining the throughput and efficiency of the system. Another critical resource is the USB. This bus has limited bandwidth and serves as a bridge between the USBClient and the memory. The bus may be used both for uploading and for downloading data. At most one job may upload data at any point in time, and similarly at most one job may download data. Uploading and downloading may take place concurrently. If only one job is using the bus, transmission takes place at a rate of *high* MByte/s. If two processes use the bus then transmission takes place at a slightly lower rate of *low* MByte/s[2]. This is referred to as the *dynamic* USB behavior. The *static* USB behaviour is the one in which the transmission rate is always *high* MByte/s.

The main challenge that we addressed in this case study was to compute efficient schedules that minimize the execution time for jobs and realize a good throughput. A related problem was to determine the amount of memory and USB bandwidth required, so that these resources would not become bottlenecks in the performance of the system.

---

[2] Approximately, *low* is 75% of *high*. The reason why it is not 50% is that the USB protocol also sends acknowledgment messages, and the acknowledgment for upward data can be combined with downward data, and vice versa.

1.2   Modelling and Analysis Approaches

We have applied and compared three different modeling methods: Timed Automata (TA), Colored Petri Nets (CPN), and Synchronous Data Flow (SDF). These methods are known to serve the purpose of investigating throughput and schedulability issues. The objective of our research was to see whether the three methods can handle this industrial case study, and to compare the quality, ease of construction, analysis efficiency, and predictive power of the models.

Timed Automata. A number of mature model checking tools, in particular UP-PAAL [4], are by now available and have been applied to the quantitative analysis of numerous industrial case studies [3]. In particular, timed automata technology has been applied successfully to optimal planning and scheduling problems [7,1], and performance analysis of distributed real-time systems [8,12]. A timed automaton is a finite automaton extended with clock variables, which are continuous variables with rate 1. A model consists of a network of timed automata. Each automaton has a set of nodes called *locations* connected by *edges*. A new location is reached after a condition, called *guard*, is satisfied or a synchronization with another automaton takes place via a *channel*. Another way to communicate in the network is by using shared variables.

Petri Nets. are used for modeling concurrent systems. They allow to both explore the state space and to simulate the behavior of the models created. We have used CPN Tools [11,10] as the sofware tool for the present case study and for performance analysis using simulation. Petri Nets are graphs with two types of nodes: *places* that are circular, and *transitions* that are rectangular. Directed arcs are used to connect places to transitions and vice versa. Objects or resources are modelled by *tokens*, which are distributed across the places representing a state of the system. The occurrence of events corresponds to firing a transition, consuming tokens from its *input* places and producing tokens at its *output* places. CPN (Colored Petri nets) is an extension where tokens have a value (color) and a time stamp. A third extension is hierarchy, with subnets depicted as transitions in nets higher in the hierarchy.

Synchronous Data Flow Graphs (SDFG). are widely used to model concurrent streaming applications on parallel hardware. An SDFG is a directed graph in which nodes are referred to as actors and edges are referred to as channels. Actors model individual tasks in an application and channels model communicated data or other dependencies between actors. When an actor fires, it consumes a fixed number of tokens (data samples) from all of its input channels (the consumption rates) and produces a fixed number of tokens on all of its output channels (the production rates). For the purpose of timing analysis, each actor in an SDFG is also annotated with a fixed (worst-case) execution time. A timed SDF specification of an application can be analyzed efficiently for many performance metrics, such as maximum throughput [6], latency or minimum buffer sizes. Analysis tools, like the freely available SDF3 [13], allow users to formally analyze the performance of those applications.

Outline of the Paper. In Sect. 2, the three models are explained. In Sect. 3, the analysis results are presented and compared. Sect. 4 gives conclusions and some directions for future research.

2   Modelling Approaches

2.1   Timed Automata

In the timed automata approach, each use case and each resource is described by an automaton, except for memory which is simply modelled as a shared variable.

All image processing components follow the same behavioral pattern, displayed in Fig. 2. Initially a component is in idle mode. As soon as the component is claimed by a job, it enters the running mode. A variable *execution_time* specifies how long the automaton stays in this mode. After this period has elapsed, the automaton jumps to the recovery mode, and stays there for *recover_time* time units. The template of Fig. 2 is parametrized by channel names *start_resource* and *end_resource*, which mark the start and termination of a component, and integer variables *execution_time* and *recover_time*, which describe the timing behavior.

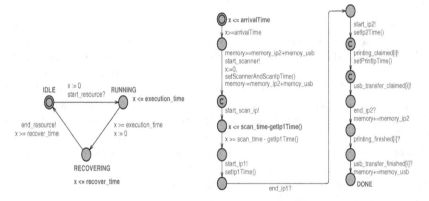

Fig. 2. Component template   **Fig. 3.** *DirectCopy* template

Each use case has been modeled using a separate automaton. As an example, the automaton for the *DirectCopy* use case is depicted in Fig. 3. A job may only claim the first component from its datapath after its arrival and when enough memory is available for all the processing in the datapath. This figure shows the way memory allocation and release is modelled. At the moment a component is claimed, the use case automaton specifies its execution time. The figure illustrates, also, the way we modelled the parallel activities done by IP2, USBClient and PrintIP.

USB. A challenging aspect in modelling the datapath was the USB because of its dynamic behaviour. Firstly we modelled this like a linear hybrid automaton

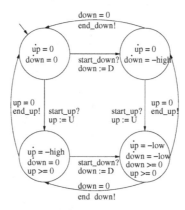

Fig. 4. Linear hybrid automaton model of USB bus

as can be seen in Fig. 4. Linear hybrid automata [2], are a slight extension of timed automata in which besides clocks, also other continuous variables are allowed with rates that may depend on the location. In the automaton of Fig. 4, there are two continuous variables: *up* and *down*, modeling the amount of data that needs to be uploaded and downloaded, respectively. In the initial state the bus is idle (derivatives $\dot{up}$ *and* $\dot{down}$ *are equal to* 0) and there are no data to be transmitted ($up = down = 0$). When uploading starts (event *start_up?*), variable *up* is set to U, the number of MBytes to be transmitted, and derivative $\dot{up}$ is set to $-high$. Uploading ends (*end_up!*) when there are no more data to be transmitted, that is, *up* has reached value 0. If during uploading via the USB, a download transfer is started, the automaton jumps to a new location in which *down* is set to D and both $\dot{up}$ and $\dot{down}$ are set to $-low$. The problem we face is that this type of hybrid behavior cannot be modeled directly in UPPAAL. There are dedicated model checkers for linear hybrid automata, such as HyTech [9], but the modeling languages supported by these tools are rather basic and the verification engine is not sufficiently powerful to synthesize schedules for our case study.

We experimented with several timed automaton models that approximate the hybrid model. In the simplest approximation, we postulate that the data rate is high, independently of the number of users. This behavior can simply be modelled using two instances of the resource template of Fig. 2. Our second "dynamic" model, displayed in Fig. 5, overapproximates the computation times of the hybrid automaton with arbitrary precision. Clock x records the time since the start of the last transmission. Integer variables *up* and *down* give the number of MBytes still to be transmitted. If an upward transmission starts in the initial state, *up* is set to U and x to 0. Without concurrent downward traffic, transmission will end at time $divide(up, high)$[3]. Now suppose that downward transmission starts somewhere in the middle of upward transmission, when clock

---

[3] Since in timed automata we may only impose integer bounds on clock variables, we use a function $divide(a, b)$, which gives the smallest integer greater or equal than $\frac{a}{b}$.

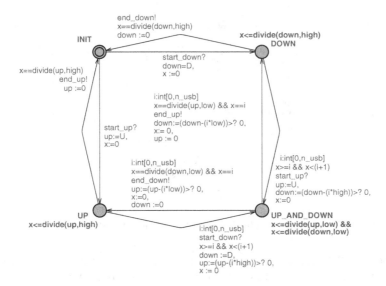

Fig. 5. Second timed automaton model of USB bus

x has value t. At this point still $up - high \cdot t$ MByte needs to be transmitted. In UPPAAL we cannot refer to the value of clocks in assignments to integer variables. However, and this is an interesting new trick, using the select statement[4] we may infer the largest integer i satisfying $i \leq t$. We update up to the maximum of $up - high \cdot i$ and 0, which is just a small overapproximation of the amount of data still to be transmitted, and reset x. The other transitions are specified in a similar style.

The UPPAAL verification engine is able to compute the fastest schedule for completing all jobs (without any a priori assumption about the scheduler such as first come first served). However, for more than 6 jobs, the computation times increase sharply due to state space explosion. The state explosion problem can be alleviated by declaring (some of) the *start_resource* channels to be urgent. In this way we impose a "non lazy" scheduling strategy in which a resource is claimed as soon as it has become available and some job needs it. This strategy reduces UPPAAL computation times from hours to minutes, with a risk of losing sometimes the optimal schedule.

2.2 CPN

In the Octopus project, the Petri Net approach takes an architecture oriented perspective to model the Océ system. The model, in addition to the system characteristics, includes the scheduling rules (First Come First Served is used when jobs enter the system) and is used to study the performance of the system through simulation. Each component in the system is modeled as a subnet. Since

---

[4] Adding a select statement $i : int[0, n\_usb]$ to a transition effectively amounts to having a different instance of the transition for each integer i in the interval $[0, n\_usb]$.

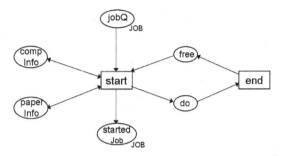

Fig. 6. Hierarchical subnet for components Scanner, ScanIP, IP1, IP2 and PrintIP

the processing time for all the components, except the USB, can be calculated before they start processing a job, the subnet for these components looks like the one shown in Fig. 6. The transitions *start* and *end* model the beginning and completion of processing a job, while the places *free* and *do* reflect the occupancy of the component. In addition, there are two places that characterise the subnet to each component: *compInfo* and *paperInfo*. The place *compInfo* contains a token with information about the component, namely the component ID, processing speed and the recovery time required by the component before starting the next job. The place *paperInfo* contains information on the number of bytes the particular component processes for a specific paper size. The values of the tokens at places *compInfo* and *paperInfo* remain constant after initialisation and govern the behaviour of the component. Since the behaviour of the USB is different from the other components, its model is different from the other components; it is discussed below.

In Fig. 6, the place *jobQ* contains tokens for the jobs that are available for the components to process at any instance of time. The color of a token of type *Job* contains information about the job ID, the use case and paper size of the job. Hence, the component can calculate the time required to process this job from the information available in the *Job* token, and the tokens at the places *compInfo* and *paperInfo*. Once the processing is completed, the transition *end* places a token at the place *free* after a certain delay, governed by the recovery time specific to each component, thus determining when the component can begin processing the next available job.

Fig. 7 shows an abstract view of the model. New jobs for the system can be created using the *Job Generator* subnet, which are placed as input to the *Scheduler* subnet at the place *newJob*. The *Scheduler* subnet models the scheduling rules, memory management rules and routes each job from one component to the next based on the datapath of the job. In this model, the scheduling rules are modeled as being global to system and not local to any of the components.

To start with, the *Scheduler* picks a new job that enters the system from the place *newJob* and estimates the amount of total memory required for executing this job. If enough memory is available, the memory is allocated (the memory resource is modelled as an integer token in the place *memory*) and the job is

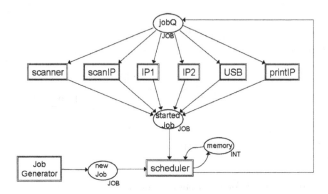

Fig. 7. Architectural view of the CPN model

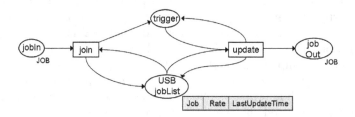

Fig. 8. CPN model for the USB

scheduled for the first component in the datapath of this job by placing a token of type *Job* in the place *jobQ*, which will be consumed by the corresponding component for processing. When a component starts processing a job, it immediately places a token in the *startedJob* place indicating this event. The *Scheduler* consumes this token to schedule the job to the next component in its datapath, adding a delay that depends on the component that just started, the next component in the datapath and the dependency explained in Sect. 1.1. Thus the logic in the *Scheduler* includes scheduling new jobs entering the system (from place *newJob*) and routing the existing jobs through the components according to the corresponding datapaths. As mentioned above, the *Scheduler* subnet also handles the memory management. This includes memory allocation and release for jobs that are executed.

USB. The USB model is different from that of the other components since the time required to transmit a job (upstream or downstream) is not constant and is influenced by other jobs that may be transmitted at the same time. The Petri Nets approach models the real-time behaviour of the USB explained in Sect. 1.1.

The CPN model of the USB works by monitoring two events observable in the USB: (1) a new job joining the transmission, and (2) completion of transmission of a job. Both events influence the transmission rates for any other jobs on the USB, and hence determine the transmission times for the jobs. In the model shown in Fig. 8, there are two transitions *join* and *update*, and two places *trigger* and *USBjobList*. The place *USBjobList* contains the list of jobs that are currently being transmitted over the USB. Apart from information about each job, it also contains the transmission rate currently assigned, the number of bytes remaining to be transmitted and the last time of update for each job. The transition *join* adds a new job waiting at the place *jobIn* that requests use of the USB (if it can be accommodated) to *USBjobList*, and places a token at the place *trigger*. This enables the transition *update* that checks the list of jobs at the place *USBjobList* and reassigns the transmission rates for all the jobs according to the number of jobs transmitted over the USB. The *update* transition also recalculates the number of bytes remaining to be transmitted for each job since the last update time, estimates the job that will finish next and places a timed token at *trigger*, so that the transition *update* can remove the jobs whose transmissions have completed. The jobs whose transmission over the USB is complete are placed in the place *jobOut*. Thus the transition *join* catches the event of new jobs joining the USB and the transition *update* catches the event of jobs leaving the USB, which are critical in determining the transmission time for a single job.

2.3   Synchronous Dataflow Graphs

In the SDF approach, we choose to model the Océ system from an application oriented perspective. In contrast to the two earlier approaches, we take a compositional approach that targets analysis efficiency for application at runtime. Since SDF is particularly well suited to optimize throughput for streaming applications, we focus on the scheduling problem for job sequences consisting of jobs with many iterations per use case (i.e., 100 pages of **DirectCopy**). The scheduling problem is tackled via a 2-phase methodology (see Fig. 9).

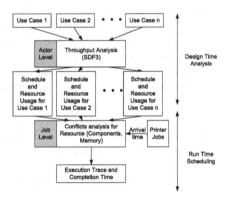

Fig. 9. Job scheduling using SDF models

Each use case is modeled as an SDF graph. Architecture information is included by annotating graph actors with resource usage information. In the **design time analysis** phase, we apply SDF3 [13] to generate a throughput-optimal schedule per use case. In the **runtime scheduling** phase, the schedule is computed based on arrival times of jobs. The schedule takes into account constraints (number of available components, memory amount) of the system. This 2-phase scheduling approach provides schedules and guaranteed job completion times for arbitrary job sequences. It avoids the complexity of analyzing all the details of a job sequence at runtime, which is infeasible in general, sacrificing some performance that might be obtainable via global optimization. The method can be seen as an instance of the Task Concurrency Management method of [14], providing predictability by the use of SDF as a modeling formalism.

Use Case Modeling. In the SDF approach, computations performed by the components of printer are modeled as actors. Actors are annotated with execution times and resource usage information. In order to model the appropriate delays between two concurrent computations running on different components of the printer, such delays are also explicitly modeled by means of actors. The USB communication is split into two actors: USB_Download and USB_Upload. The execution times of the USB actors are approximated conservatively by always assuming low bandwidth availability. Thus, use case analysis can be decoupled

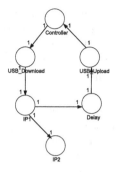

Fig. 10. ProcessFromStore

from job scheduling, sacrificing some accuracy in exchange for analysis efficiency. Fig. 10 shows the SDFG of **ProcessFromStore**, actor production and consumption rates are all 1 in this simple use case.

Job Scheduling and Completion Time Analysis. Using the SDF model to analyze the performance of a single job is straightforward. By ensuring composability through virtualization of the resources (every job gets its own, private share of the resources in system), multiple jobs can also be analyzed efficiently. However, as the components and memory can be shared between jobs, the existing techniques to analyze multiple jobs cannot be applied directly to the datapath analysis of a printer. How to model the behavior of concurrent jobs on the datapath of the printer in a non-virtualized way and how to calculate the completion time of those jobs is the challenge faced.

To analyze the datapath without virtualization, we make some assumptions. We conservatively assume that the resources needed by actors are claimed at the start of a firing and released at the end of firing, where the claim and release of a resource like the memory may happen in different actors. A waiting job can start if all the resources needed according to use case analysis can be reserved. The reservation of resources ensures that the execution time of all job tasks are fixed. As already mentioned, USB bandwidth is always assumed to be low. These assumptions make the system efficiently analyzable by limiting the dynamism in the datapath behavior, and allow the 2-phase scheduling approach explained above. The first phase is concerned with the actor level and uses throughput-optimal self-timed execution (data-driven, every actor fires as soon as it is enabled) as a scheduling strategy for a single SDF that represents a printer use case. Resource usage of each use case is calculated using this self-timed schedule. The second phase concerns job scheduling. Jobs are served in an FCFS (First Come First Served) way. If the resources required by a new job cannot be ensured at arrival time, the new job has to be postponed until the resources are available. Jobs can still be pipelined, overlapping in time, as illustrated below. Two types of resources, mutual exclusive and cumulative resources, are considered in a bit more detail. IP components are an example of mutual exclusive resources that can only be used by one job at a time, while

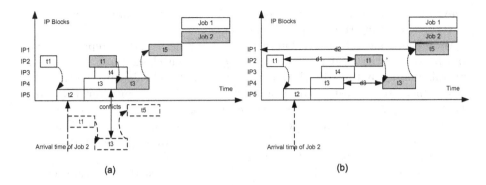

Fig. 11. Scheduling jobs with a conflict

shared memory is an example of a cumulative resource that can be used by many jobs as long as the total usage does not exceed the available amount.

Fig. 11 shows the scheduling of two jobs (J1 and J2) of different use cases with a component conflict (ignoring for now memory usage). The self-timed schedule and its resource usage are computed in phase one using the throughput analysis algorithm in SDF3. The work is done off-line, avoiding computation work at runtime. In phase two, the scheduler computes the earliest start time of the second job based on the phase one results and runtime information.

From Fig. 11(a), we see that J2 cannot start when it arrives at the printer due to a resource conflict on IP4. In order to maximize the resource usage, J2 has to start at a point that ensures that IP4 can be used by J2 as soon as it is released by J1. Fig.11(b) illustrates how to compute this specific point. As explained, when J1 starts its execution, all components and memory it needs are reserved. A system resource usage table is kept to store the release time of components. When J2 arrives, we initially assume it starts at the end of the last actor of J1 (t4 of J1 in Fig.11(b)). Then, we calculate the time distance between the current release time of components and the reservation of those components for J2. The start point then equals the end time of J1 minus the minimum of the computed distances (d3 in Fig.11(b)). In order to analyze memory conflicts, we store the memory usage of each use case as a list of time interval-memory quantity pairs. Fig.12 shows how to update system memory usage when a new job starts (q_i represents the amount of memory needed at time t_i). As a single job

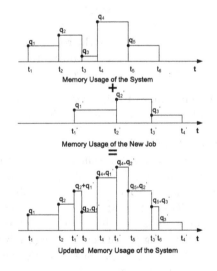

Fig. 12. Update memory usage

always fits in the memory, we only need to consider the overlap between a new job starting and any running jobs using memory.

We define a memory usage interval $MI_i = (q_i, [t_i, t_{i+1}))$ to represent that from t_i to t_{i+1} the used memory equals q_i. We can check those intersecting intervals iteratively to verify the memory constraint and calculate the time the job may need to be postponed. Assume that the memory constraint is q_c, and $MI_1 = (q_1, [t_1, t_3))$ belongs to the system and $MI_2 = (q_2, [t_2, t_4))$ to the new job. If $q_1 + q_2 < q_c$, we can check the next pair of overlapping intervals; else, we have to postpone the new job $t_3 - t_2$ and recheck all overlapping intervals. We can repeat these checks until the memory constraint is satisfied.

Observe that other exclusive or cumulative resources, like the USB connection, can be treated in the same way as outlined here.

3   Comparison

This section presents the results from comparing the analysis results for the three approaches. For this purpose, we have chosen a common arrival sequence of 7 one-page jobs shown below[5]:

JobID	Use case	Arrival time	Memory required
a6	PrintWithProcessing	0	12Y
a7	ProcessFromStore	0	24Y
a2	Scan2Email	1X	48Y
a3	Scan2Store	1X	36Y
a5	PrintWithProcessing	1X	12Y
a1	ProcessFromStore	2X	24Y
a4	ProcessFromStore	3X	24Y

The remainder of this section explains the results for both static and dynamic USB behaviour obtained via the three approaches.

Static USB behavior

CPN approach. Fig. 13 shows the execution of the jobs by the components with a total completion time of 24X. Even though jobs a6 and a7 arrive at the same time and request *USBdown* simultaneously, job a6 is chosen non-deterministically to use *USBdown* first at time 0. Such resource contentions can be observed for the IP components as well where job a5 waits for the *PrintIP* to become available as it is processing job a6, even though job a5 can be processed by *PrintIP* as soon as the *USBdown* is completed at 6X. The execution of the jobs is also influenced by the memory available in the system. Even though job a2 arrives before jobs a3, a5, a1 and a4, its execution commences only at time 15X, as shown in Fig. 13, because until 15X the memory available is less than that is required for job a2 of use case Scan2Email. This can be observed from Fig. 13 and Fig. 16, where

---

[5] Due to space limitations we only present one benchmark here. In fact, we studied several other benchmarks, for which we obtained similar results. The benchmark presented in this paper is the most challenging one that we studied thus far.

at time 15X execution of job a7 is completed, the memory required for job a2 is available and it is scheduled for processing by the scanner.

SDF approach. In the SDF approach, jobs are served in an FCFS way and are scheduled based on the strategy described before. The order of jobs is determined by the arrival time of each job. If jobs arrive at the same time, the order is determined non-deterministically. For the given arrival sequence, there are 12 possible orders for the 7 jobs ($2! \cdot 3! \cdot 1 \cdot 1 = 12$) and the best schedule has the shortest completion time, 27X, under 96Y of memory (see Fig. 14). From the figure, we can see that job a2 is postponed due to the memory limit. Since the static USB model optimistically assumes that USB bandwidth is high, in this experiment, we align with this assumption.

TA approach. UPPAAL computed an optimal schedule with completion time 22X, displayed in Fig. 15. The memory chart of Fig. 16 illustrates the use of the available memory in this schedule. At 10X memory is released when a2 is completed, and immediately afterwards, two jobs (a3 and a5) are started. The execution chart shows that IP2 is the critical resource, which is used optimally.

We conclude that UPPAAL managed to come up with the optimal schedule of 22X, CPN found a schedule of 24X, and SDF came up with a schedule of 27X. For the simulation based approach followed by the CPNTool, of course the result depends on the simulation time, and longer simulations lead to better schedules. The SDF approach follows a strict FIFO scheduling and hence the total completion time for the jobs is higher than for the optimal schedule. However, it is the only approach that is compositional, and hence it is expected to scale better to larger job sequences.

Dynamic USB behavior

CPN approach. As shown in Fig. 17, the total execution time is 25.5X as against 24X for the static USB behavior. Analysing the simulation results of the static and dynamic USB behavior, the difference in completion time is caused by the change in transmission rates of the USB.

TA approach. The result for the dynamic USB model is depicted in Fig. 18. The total completion time is 25X. It is easy to see that the only difference between this result and the one for the static model is caused by the changes in transmission rate when an upload and a download transmission occurs simultaneously. We claim that this is the optimal schedule for this dynamic behavior.

4   Conclusions and Future Work

We have applied three prominent state based modelling frameworks —UPPAAL, Colored Petri Nets, and Synchronous Data Flow— to a realistic industrial case study, and managed to compute schedules for a representative benchmark. Our preliminary conclusion is that Colored Petri Nets provide the most expressive modeling framework, whereas UPPAAL currently appears to be the most powerful tool for finding (optimal) schedules. However, this case study pushes UPPAAL to its limits and since the SDF approach, which is the only compositional one, is more scalable it is certainly possible that it will outperform UPPAAL on larger benchmarks. Such benchmarks can possibly also be tackled using UPPAAL Cora [5], a variant of UPPAAL that has been constructed to solve scheduling problems. We consider it too early for a definite comparison of modeling frameworks.

We have not embarked on the enterprise to formally relate the three different models. However, we can confirm the result of [8] that the construction of models of the same system using different tools helps to find bugs in the models, and thus contributes to improving the quality of the models.

From a modelling perspective, a very interesting feature in the Océ case study is definitely the USB bus. We consider it surprising that timed automata are able to deal so well with what at first sight appears to be a hybrid phenomenon. The select statement from UPPAAL is crucial in defining this model.

Future work includes the construction of more refined models of the same system. We want to develop better sense for what is the right level of modelling. Notable features that we want to model in more detail are the memory bus and memory fragmentation. We also want to study more realistic requirements on system performance such as larger number of use cases (involving for instance batches of several hundred pages), priorities between use cases, hard constraints on throughput, and runtime decision making whether new jobs can be accepted and how they should be scheduled.

References

1. Abdeddaïm, Y., Asarin, E., Maler, O.: Scheduling with timed automata. TCS 354(2), 272–300 (2006)
2. Alur, R., Courcoubetis, C., Halbwachs, N., Henzinger, T., Ho, P.-H., Nicollin, X., Olivero, A., Sifakis, J., Yovine, S.: The algorithmic analysis of hybrid systems. TCS 138, 3–34 (1995)
3. Behrmann, G., David, A., Larsen, K.: A tutorial on Uppaal. In: Bernardo, M., Corradini, F. (eds.) SFM-RT 2004. LNCS, vol. 3185, pp. 200–236. Springer, Heidelberg (2004)
4. Behrmann, G., David, A., Larsen, K.G., Håkansson, J., Pettersson, P., Yi, W., Hendriks, M.: Uppaal 4.0. In: QEST 2006, pp. 125–126. IEEE Computer Soceity Press, Los Alamitos (2006)
5. Behrmann, G., Larsen, K.G., Rasmussen, J.I.: Optimal scheduling using priced timed automata. SIGMETRICS Perform. Eval. Rev. 32(4), 34–40 (2005)
6. Ghamarian, A., Geilen, M., Stuijk, S., Basten, T., Moonen, A., Bekooij, M., Theelen, B., Mousavi, M.: Throughput analysis of synchronous data flow graphs. In: ACSD 2006, pp. 25–34. IEEE Computer Soceity Press, Los Alamitos (2006)
7. Hendriks, M., van den Nieuwelaar, N.J.M., Vaandrager, F.W.: Model checker aided design of a controller for a wafer scanner. STTT 8(6), 633–647 (2006)
8. Hendriks, M., Verhoef, M.: Timed automata based analysis of embedded system architectures. In: WPDRS 2006. IEEE, Los Alamitos (2006)
9. Henzinger, T.A., Ho, P.-H., Wong-Toi, H.: HyTech: A Model Checker for Hybrid Systems. STTT 1, 110–122 (1997)
10. Jensen, K.: Coloured Petri Nets. Basic Concepts, Analysis Methods and Practical Use. In: EATCS Monographs on Theoretical Computer Science. Springer, Heidelberg (1992)

11. Jensen, K., Kristensen, L.M., Wells, L.: Coloured Petri nets and CPN tools for modelling and validation of concurrent systems. In: STTT, vol. 9(3-4) (2007)
12. Perathoner, S., Wandeler, E., Thiele, L., Hamann, A., Schliecker, S., Henia, R., Racu, R., Ernst, R., Harbour, M.G.: Influence of different system abstractions on the performance analysis of distributed real-time systems. In: EMSOFT, New York, NY, USA, pp. 193–202 (2007)
13. Stuijk, S., Geilen, M., Basten, T.: SDF3: SDF For Free. In: ACSD 2006, pp. 276–278. IEEE CS Press, Los Alamitos (2006)
14. Wong, C., Marchal, P., Yang, P., Prayati, A., Catthoor, F., Lauwereins, R., Verkest, D., Man, H.D.: Task concurrency management methodology to schedule the mpeg4 1m1 player on a highly parallel processor platform. In: CODES, pp. 170–177. ACM, New York (2001)

A   Charts

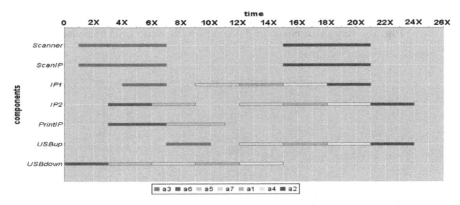

Fig. 13. Execution chart for CPN model with static USB behavior

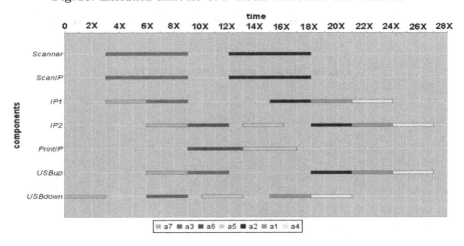

Fig. 14. Execution chart for SDF model with static USB behavior

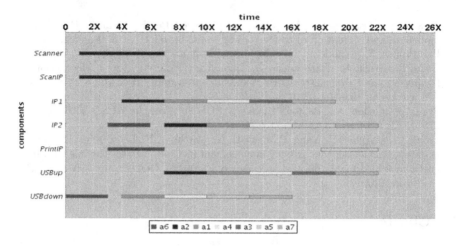

Fig. 15. Execution chart for TA model with static USB behavior

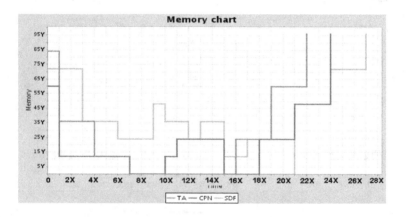

Fig. 16. Memory usage for static USB model

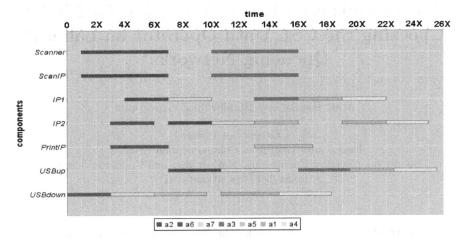

Fig. 17. Execution chart for CPN model with dynamic USB behavior

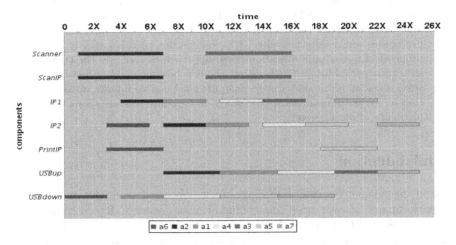

Fig. 18. Execution chart for TA model with dynamic USB behavior

A Uniformization-Based Algorithm for Model Checking the CSL Until Operator on Labeled Queueing Networks*

Anne Remke and Boudewijn R. Haverkort

University of Twente
Design and Analysis of Communication Systems
Faculty for Electrical Engineering, Mathematics and Computer Science
{anne,brh}@cs.utwente.nl

Abstract. We present a model checking procedure for the CSL until operator on the CTMCs that underly Jackson queueing networks. The key issue lies in the fact that the underlying CTMC is infinite in as many dimensions as there are queues in the JQN. We need to compute the transient state probabilities for all goal states and for all possible starting states. However, for these transient probabilities no computational procedures are readily available. The contribution of this paper is the proposal of a new uniformization-based approach to compute the transient state probabilities. Furthermore, we show how the highly structured state space of JQNs allows us to compute the possible infinite satisfaction set for until formulas. A case study on an e-business site shows the feasibility of our approach.

1 Introduction

Jackson queueing networks (JQNs) [9] are widely used to model and analyze the performance of computer and communication systems. Recently, we have presented detailed CSL model checking algorithms for QBDs [13] and in [12] (at Formats 2007) we presented a general approach to model check JQNs against continuous-stochastic logic (CSL)[1], [2]; note, however, that [12] only presented the principles of such an approach. This paper proposes an efficient iterative algorithm for the computation of the transient probabilities for any possible initial state on JQNs, which allows for model checking the CSL until operator on JQNs; the proposed algorithm generalizes our previous work for QBDs [13]. We elaborate on the form and the growth of the data structures, as needed for JQNs, that make our algorithm memory efficient. Furthermore, we explain that our algorithm is computationally efficient, as it uses just as many iterations as necessary to decide whether the transient probabilities meet a given probability bound.

* The work presented in this paper has been performed in the context of the MC=MC project (612.000.311), financed by the Netherlands Organization for Scientific Research (NWO). The authors thank Lucia Cloth for fruitful discussions on the topic.

F. Cassez and C. Jard (Eds.): FORMATS 2008, LNCS 5215, pp. 188–202, 2008.

Related work on transient analysis on queueing networks is mostly restricted to finite state spaces. For instance, Harrison [8] presents an iterative method to solve the time-dependent Kolmogorov equations of finite queueing networks. In [4] Buchholz applies uniformization to hierarchical queueing networks that have a finite structured state-space. We are not aware about any approach that tackles the problem we are solving with our new algorithm.

This paper is organized as follows: In Section 2 we introduce Jackson queueing networks and the partitioning of the underlying infinite state space. The general approach for model checking the time-bounded until operator on JQNs is discussed in Section 3, before we present the details of the uniformization-based algorithm on JQNs in Section 4. Section 5 shows how the presented algorithm can be used to facilitate model checking the CSL until operator. As a case study, we model an e-business site as JQN and analyze its scalability with the newly developed model checking techniques in Section 6 before we conclude in Section 7.

2   Jackson Queueing Networks

In the following we recapitulate some of the foundations needed for CSL model checking of Jackson queueing networks [9], as presented in [12]. A labeled JQN consists of a number of interconnected queues and is defined as follows:

Definition 1 (Labeled Jackson queueing network)
A labeled Jackson queueing network **JQN J** of order M (with $M \in \mathbb{N}^+$) is a tuple $(\lambda, \underline{\mu}, \mathbf{R}, L)$ with arrival rate λ, a vector of size M of service rates $\underline{\mu}$, a routing matrix $\mathbf{R} \in \mathbb{R}^{(M+1) \times (M+1)}$ and a labeling function L that assigns a set of valid atomic propositions from a fixed and finite set AP of atomic propositions to each state $\mathbf{s} = (s_1, s_2, \ldots, s_M)$.   □

The underlying state space of a JQN **J** of order M is a highly-structured *labeled infinite state continuous-time Markov chain*, $\mathcal{J}$, with state space $\mathsf{S} = \mathbb{N}^M$, that is infinite in M dimensions. Every state $\mathbf{s} \in \mathsf{S}$ is represented as an M-tuple $\mathbf{s} = (s_1, s_2, \cdots, s_M)$ and denoted the number of customers per queue. To deal with the underlying infinite state space we presented a partition into an infinite number of disjoint finite sets [12], such that with one step only the next higher or the next lower partition of the state space can be reached. A given corner point[1] $\overline{v}$ partitions the state space into rectangular shaped fronts, that are pairwise disjoint and situated like shells around each other. In an M dimensional JQN the front $F(\overline{v} + \overline{1})$ is a finite set of states defined by

$$F(\overline{v} + \overline{1}) = \{\mathbf{s} \in \mathsf{S} \mid \exists m (s_m = v_m + i) \land (\forall n \neq m (s_n \leq v_n + i))\}, \qquad (1)$$

with $m \in \{1, \ldots, M\}$. The number of states per front in a partitioning with corner point $\overline{v}$ equals:

$$|F(\overline{v})| = \prod_{m=1}^{M} (v_m + 1) - \prod_{m=1}^{M} v_m. \qquad (2)$$

---

[1] Denoted splitting vector in [12].

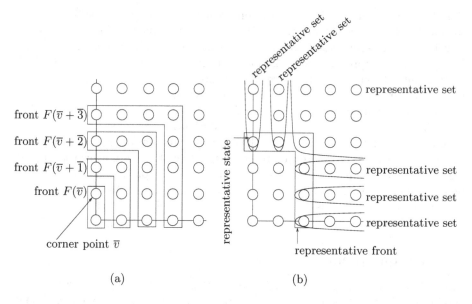

Fig. 1. (a) Partitioning of the underlying state space (b) Representative front, state and set according to Definition 2

In the following we introduce the concept of representative fronts, states and sets for JQNs, as visualized in Figure 1. A CSL state formula Φ is *independent* as of $\bar{g}$ if the validity of Φ remains the same in corresponding states in fronts $F(\bar{g}+\bar{\imath})$ for $i \geq 0$.

Definition 2 (Representative front, state and set)
For a JQN and a CSL formula that is independent as of $\bar{g}$ the notion of representatives is defined as follows: The front $F(\bar{g})$ is called *representative front* and denoted as $R(\bar{g})$. The states in the representative front are called *representative states* $r \in R(\bar{g})$. Each representative state r represents a distinct infinite set of states, denoted S_r, such that for all $r \in R(\bar{g})$ and for all $s \in S_r$ it holds that $r \models \Phi \Leftrightarrow s \models \Phi$. In general, in an M-dimensional JQN, there are M types of representative sets that account for 1 up to M infinite dimensions. A representative set S_r is called infinite in dimension m if and only if $r_m = g_m$, and restricted in dimension m otherwise. In case a representative state r equals $\bar{g}$ in k dimensions it represents a k-dimensional set S_r, such that

$$s \in S_r \Leftrightarrow \begin{cases} s_m \geq r_m, & \text{iff } r_m = g_m, \\ s_m = r_m, & \text{otherwise.} \end{cases} \qquad \square$$

Hence, a state s belongs to S_r when it takes the same value as r in the restricted dimensions and any value at least r_i in the infinite dimensions.

3 Time-Bounded Until Operator

Recall that the CSL path formula $\Phi\, \mathcal{U}^I \Psi$ is valid if a Ψ-state is reached on a path during the time interval I vial only Φ-states. As shown is [2], for model checking the time-bounded until operator with a time intervals of the form $I = [0, t]$, the future behavior of the JQN is irrelevant for the validity of φ, as soon as a Ψ-state is reached. Thus all Ψ-states can be made absorbing without affecting the satisfaction set of formula φ. On the other hand, as soon as a $(\neg\Phi \wedge \neg\Psi)$-state is reached, φ will be invalid, regardless of the future evolution. As a result of the above consideration, we may switch from checking the underlying CTMC $\mathcal{J}$ to checking a new, derived, Markov chain denoted as $\mathcal{J}[\Psi][\neg\Phi \wedge \neg\Psi] = \mathcal{J}[\neg\Phi \vee \Psi]$, where all states in the underlying Markov chain that satisfy the formula in square brackets are made absorbing. Model checking a formula involving the until operator then reduces to calculating the transient probabilities $\pi^{\mathcal{J}[\neg\Phi\vee\Psi]}(\mathsf{s}, \mathsf{s}', t)$ for all Ψ-states s'. Exploiting the partitioning of the underlying state space yields:

$$\mathsf{s} \models \mathcal{P}_{\bowtie p}(\Phi\, \mathcal{U}^{[0,t]}\Psi) \Leftrightarrow Prob^{\mathcal{J}}(\mathsf{s}, \Phi\, \mathcal{U}^{[0,t]}\Psi) \bowtie p$$

$$\Leftrightarrow \left(\sum_{i=0}^{\infty} \sum_{\mathsf{s}' \in Sat^{F(\mathbb{I})}(\Psi)} \pi^{\mathcal{J}[\neg\Phi\vee\Psi]}(\mathsf{s}, \mathsf{s}', t) \right) \bowtie p. \tag{3}$$

The transient probabilities are accumulated for the Ψ states in fronts $F(\bar{\imath})$ for $i \in \mathbb{N}$. The transient probability of being in each state of the infinite-state JQN for any possible initial state can be calculated with a new iterative uniformization-based method, which we present in the Section 4.

4 Uniformization with Representatives

We recapitulate the basic idea of uniformization with representatives as introduced in [13], before we present the details of applying uniformization with representatives to JQNs.

4.1 Uniformization

Uniformization is a well-known technique to compute the transient probabilities $\mathbf{V}(t)$ in a CTMC [7]. As standard property of uniformization, the finite time bound t is transformed to a finite number of steps n. The probability matrix $\mathbf{P}(\mathsf{s}, \mathsf{s}')$ for the uniformized DTMC is defined as

$$\mathbf{P}(\mathsf{s}, \mathsf{s}') = \frac{\mathbf{G}(\mathsf{s}, \mathsf{s}')}{\nu} \text{ for } \mathsf{s} \neq \mathsf{s}', \text{ and } \mathbf{P}(\mathsf{s}, \mathsf{s}) = \frac{\mathbf{G}(\mathsf{s}, \mathsf{s})}{\nu} + 1, \text{ for all } \mathsf{s}, \mathsf{s}'.$$

The uniformization constant ν must be at least equal to the maximum of absolute values of $\mathbf{G}(\mathsf{s}, \mathsf{s})$; for JQNs, the value $\nu = \lambda + \sum_{m=1}^{M} \mu_m$ suffices. Let $\mathbf{U}^{(k)}$ be the state probability distribution matrix after k epochs in the DTMC with transition matrix $\mathbf{P}$. That is, entry (i, j) of $\mathbf{U}^{(k)}$ is the probability that j is reached from i in k steps. $\mathbf{U}^{(k)}$ can be derived recursively as:

$$\mathbf{U}^{(0)} = \mathbf{I}, \quad \text{and} \quad \mathbf{U}^{(k)} = \mathbf{U}^{(k-1)}\mathbf{P}, \quad k \in \mathbb{N}^+. \tag{4}$$

Then, the matrix of transient state probabilities for the original CTMC at time t, can be calculated as:

$$\mathbf{V}(t) = \sum_{k=0}^{\infty} \psi(\nu t; k)\mathbf{P}^k = \sum_{k=0}^{\infty} \psi(\nu t; k)\mathbf{U}^{(k)}, \tag{5}$$

where $\psi(\nu t; k)$ is the probability of k events occurring in the interval $[0, t)$ in a Poisson process with rate ν. The probability distribution in the DTMC after k steps is described by $\mathbf{V}(0) \cdot \mathbf{P}^k$ (note that $\mathbf{V}(0) = \mathbf{I}$).

Note that matrices $\mathbf{V}(t)$ and $\mathbf{U}^{(k)}$, $k \in \mathbb{N}$, have infinite size. To avoid the infinite summation over the number of steps k, the sum (5) needs to be truncated. We denote the approximation of $\mathbf{V}(t)$ that has been calculated with up to $n+1$ terms of the summation with $\mathbf{V}^{(n+1)}(t)$:

$$\mathbf{V}^{(n+1)}(t) = \sum_{k=0}^{n+1} \psi(\nu t; k)\mathbf{U}^{(k)} = \mathbf{V}^{(n)}(t) + \psi(\nu t; n+1)\mathbf{U}^{(n+1)}. \tag{6}$$

Note that $\mathbf{V}^{(n)}(t)$ follows the structure of the previous $\mathbf{U}^{(m)}$ $(m \leq n)$ in terms of zeroes and non-zeroes because any non-zero entry in $\mathbf{V}^{(n)}$ corresponds to a non-zero in $\mathbf{U}^{(m)}(m \leq n)$. We denote a maximum bound on the error that possibly occurs in an entry of $\mathbf{V}(t)$ when the series is truncated after n steps as $\varepsilon_{t,\nu}^{(n)}$. For a given number of steps n, $\varepsilon_{t,\nu}^{(n)}$ increases linearly with $\nu \cdot t$ and decreases linearly with n:

$$\left\| \sum_{k=n+1}^{\infty} \psi(\nu t; k)\mathbf{U}^{(k)} \right\| \leq 1 - \sum_{k=0}^{n} e^{-\nu t}\frac{(\nu t)^k}{k!} = \varepsilon_{t,\nu}^{(n)}. \tag{7}$$

4.2 Finite Representation

In the following we will use uniformization to compute the transient probabilities to reach all possible goal states from all (starting) states in a JQN. The homogeneous probability matrix $\mathbf{P}$ contains the probability to reach a state s' from a state s within one step for all $s, s' \in S$. From every possible starting state, only n fronts can be reached with n steps. Hence, for a given number of steps n all states that are $n+1$ steps away from the origin $\hat{s}$ seem to be identical in the JQN. We only need to consider a finite part of the JQN, depending on the number of steps n. As we will see, the homogenous structure of the JQN and of the probability matrix implies that we obtain identical transient probabilities for states $s, s' \in S_r$ with $r \in R(\bar{l})$, within the error bounds of uniformization

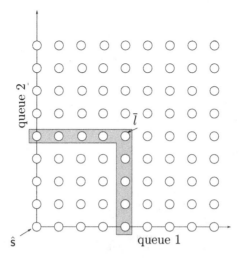

Fig. 2. Finite state space that needs to be considered for a given $\bar{l} = (4, 4)$

given n steps. In fact, we restrict the computation to a finite number of starting states and still perform a comprehensive transient analysis for every possible state as starting state. As shown in Figure 2, starting from every representative state $r \in R(\overline{n})$, still n steps can be undertaken in every direction without reaching beyond the origin $\hat{s}$. In a two-dimensional JQN the total amount of starting states we have to consider equals $(n + 1)^2$ and the total amount of goal states equals $(2n + 1)^2$. In an M dimensional setting $(l + 1)^M$ starting states and $(2l + 1)^M$ goal states have to be considered out of which $(l + 1)^M - l^M$ states are representative. The matrix $\mathbf{U}^{(n)}$ is the state probability matrix after n discrete epochs and $\mathbf{V}^{(n)}(t)$ holds the approximated transient probabilities after n steps. Note that these matrices remain two-dimensional for JQNs, as they represent all possible combinations of starting states and goal states. It is now sufficient to consider only starting states that belong to fronts $F(\bar{i})$ for $i \leq n$ for a finite representation of $\mathbf{U}^{(n)}$ and $\mathbf{V}^{(n)}(t)$. The size of the finite representation depends on the considered number of steps n, hence, on the time, the uniformization rate, and the required accuracy. We now address the growth of the matrices $\mathbf{U}^{(n)}$ in the course of the computation. Figure 3(a) shows that the dimension of the finite representation of $\mathbf{U}^{(0)}$ is: $\dim(\mathbf{U}^{(0)}) = (|F(\overline{0})|)^2 = (1^M - 0^M)^2 = 1$. Since $n = 0$, we cannot leave a state and the first front $R(\overline{0})$ is already a representative front. Figure 3(b) shows the dimension of the finite representation of $\mathbf{U}^{(1)}$. Since $n = 1$, we can reach the next higher or the next lower fronts. Thus, front $F(\overline{0})$ cannot be used as representative front, but we can use the next higher front $R(\overline{1})$ as representative front, as shown in Figure 3(b). Since $n = 1$, it is possible to reach the front $F(\overline{2})$ as well; thus we have to consider starting in one of the first two fronts $F(\bar{i})$ for $i = \{0, 1\}$ and ending up in one of the first three fronts $F(\bar{j})$ for $j = \{0, 1, 2\}$. The dimension of the finite representation of $\mathbf{U}^{(1)}$ depends on the fronts that contain the starting states and on the fronts containing the goal

(a)   0 steps

representative front $R(\overline{0})$

$F(\overline{0})$

$F(\overline{0})$ ▣ —— representative probabilities

(b)   1 steps

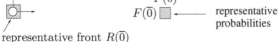

representative front $R(\overline{1})$

$F(\overline{0})\ R(\overline{1})\ F(\overline{2})$

$F(\overline{0})$

$R(\overline{1})$ representative probabilities

(c)   2 steps

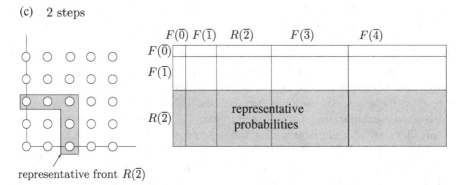

representative front $R(\overline{2})$

$F(\overline{0})\ F(\overline{1})\quad R(\overline{2})\qquad F(\overline{3})\qquad\quad F(\overline{4})$

$F(\overline{0})$

$F(\overline{1})$

$R(\overline{2})$ representative probabilities

Fig. 3. Considered part of the state space (left) and finite representation of $\mathbf{U}^{(n)}$ and $\mathbf{V}^{(n)}(t)$ (right), depending on the number of considered steps

states. The number of states of a given front can be calculated according to Equation (2). The dimension of $\mathbf{U}^{(1)}$ is given by:

$$\begin{aligned}
\dim(\mathbf{U}^{(1)}) &= \big(|F(\overline{0})| + |R(\overline{1})|\big) \times \big(|F(\overline{0})| + |R(\overline{1})| + |F(\overline{2})|\big) \\
&= \big(1^M - 0^M + 2^M - 1^M\big) \times \big(1^M - 0^M + 2^M - 1^M + 3^M - 2^M\big) \\
&= 2^M \times 3^M.
\end{aligned}$$

Figure 3(c) shows the finite representation of the matrix $\mathbf{U}^{(2)}$. From a given front, we can reach at most two more fronts in both directions. Picking the second front as new representative, ensures that we cannot reach beyond the origin $\hat{s}$. We have to attach another row of states to represent starting from the new representative front. Furthermore, we attach two more columns to account for the fronts $F(\overline{3})$ and $F(\overline{4})$ that can now be reached from the new representative front. In a general JQN, for a given number of steps n, the size of the matrix $\mathbf{U}^{(n)}$ is then

$$\dim(\mathbf{U}^{(n)}) = \left(\sum_{i=0}^{n} |F(\overline{i})| \right) \times \left(\sum_{j=0}^{2 \cdot n} |F(\overline{j})| \right) = (n+1)^M \times (2 \cdot n + 1)^M. \quad (8)$$

Note that, even though the left side of Figure 3 only shows the two dimensional case, ($M = 2$) the right side is also correctly depicted for an M dimensional setting. As before, the finite representation of the matrix $\mathbf{V}^{(n)}(t)$ has the same dimension as $\mathbf{U}^{(n)}$.

4.3   Uniformization with Representatives

We now proceed with the actual computation of the state probability matrix $\mathbf{U}^{(n)}$ and the approximated transient probability matrix $\mathbf{V}^{(n)}(t)$ according to (6). Starting with $n = 0$, and thus with the smallest finite portion of the JQN, cf. Figure 3(a), we increase n step by step, thus increasing accuracy and size of the considered finite representation of the JQN. However, in each iteration we always use the smallest possible representation. Considering n steps, the probability of starting in a state in the representative front $\mathbf{r} \in R(\overline{n})$ and ending in a state $\mathbf{s}'$ in one of the fronts $F(\overline{i})$, for $i \in \{0, \ldots, 2 \cdot n\}$, represents the probability of starting in a state $\mathbf{s} \in S_{\mathbf{r}}$ and ending in the corresponding state $\mathbf{s}''$. In order to increase the number of steps from $n - 1$ to n we first adapt the size of the data structure before computing the values for n steps. Moving from step $n - 1$ to n we have to add the front $F(\overline{n})$ that is going to be representative for n steps, to the set of starting states and the fronts $F(\overline{2n - 1})$ and $F(\overline{2n})$ to the set of goal states. First, the two new sets of columns of goal states are initialized with zero, as it is impossible to reach these states with $n - 1$ steps. Second, the new row of starting states $F(\overline{n})$ is initialized with the probabilities of the corresponding entries from front $R(\overline{n - 1})$ that is representative for $n - 1$ steps. Note that this holds for $\mathbf{U}^{(n)}$ and $\mathbf{V}^{(n)}(t)$. An entry $(\mathbf{s}, \mathbf{s}')$ in the new row of starting states $F(\overline{n})$ constitutes moving from a starting state $\mathbf{s}$ to a goal state $\mathbf{s}'$ with $\mathbf{s} \in F(\overline{n})$ and $\mathbf{s}' \in F(\overline{i})$ for $i = 0, \ldots 2n$. We first need to find the corresponding starting state $\mathbf{r} \in R(\overline{n - 1})$ such that $\mathbf{s} \in S_{\mathbf{r}}$. The corresponding goal state then is the state $\mathbf{s}''$ that is, in every dimension, exactly as far away from $\mathbf{r}$ than $\mathbf{s}'$ is from $\mathbf{s}$, $(\mathbf{r} - \mathbf{s}'' = \mathbf{s} - \mathbf{s}')$. Given a tuple of starting and goal state $(\mathbf{s}, \mathbf{s}')$ with $\mathbf{s} \in F(\overline{n})$, the corresponding tuple $(\mathbf{r}, \mathbf{s}'')$ with $\mathbf{r} \in R(\overline{n-1})$ is given by $\mathbf{r} = \mathbf{s} - \overline{h}(\mathbf{s})$ and $\mathbf{s}'' = \mathbf{s}' - \mathbf{s} + \mathbf{r}$, with

$$\overline{h}(\mathbf{s}) = \begin{cases} h_i = 1, & s_i = n, \\ h_i = 0, & s_i \neq n, \end{cases} \quad (9)$$

The matrices $\mathbf{U}^{(n)}$ and $\mathbf{V}^{(n)}(t)$ have a block structure, according to the fronts of a JQN; we denote the blocks that give the probabilities from states in front $F(\bar{\imath})$ to states in front $F(\bar{\jmath})$ as $\mathbf{U}_{\bar{\imath},\bar{\jmath}}^{(n)}$ and $\mathbf{V}_{\bar{\imath},\bar{\jmath}}(t)$. Note that $\mathbf{P}$ can also be organized according to this block structure. In iteration step n, we then need to multiply the enlarged representation of $\mathbf{U}^{(n-1)}$ with the square part of $\mathbf{P}$ that accounts for the one-step probabilities for all states in the first $2 \cdot n$ fronts. In general, for $n \geq 1, \mathbf{U}^{(n)}$ is computed as $\mathbf{U}^{(n-1)} \cdot \mathbf{P}$, cf. (4), as follows:

$$\mathbf{U}_{\bar{\imath},\bar{\jmath}}^{(n)} = \sum_{k=0}^{2n+1} \mathbf{U}_{\bar{\imath},\bar{k}}^{(n-1)} \cdot \mathbf{P}_{\bar{k},\bar{\jmath}}, \tag{10}$$

for $\bar{\imath} = \bar{0}, \ldots, \bar{n}$ and $\bar{\jmath} = \bar{0}, \ldots, 2 \cdot \bar{n}$. Due to the block structure of $\mathbf{V}^{(n)}(t)$, we can rewrite (6) as:

$$\mathbf{V}_{\bar{\imath},\bar{\jmath}}^{(n)}(t) = \mathbf{V}_{\bar{\imath},\bar{\jmath}}^{(n-1)}(t) + \psi(\nu t; n) \cdot \mathbf{U}_{\bar{\imath},\bar{\jmath}}^{(n)}, \tag{11}$$

again for $\bar{\imath} = \bar{0}, \ldots, \bar{n}$ and $\bar{\jmath} = \bar{0}, \ldots, 2 \cdot \bar{n} + \bar{1}$.

4.4 Complexity Issues

In the k-th iteration, we actually consider the states of the first k fronts as starting states and the states of the first $2 \cdot k$ fronts as goal states, resulting in matrices with $(k + 1)^M \times (2 \cdot k + 1)^M$ entries, as given by (8). If n is the maximum number of steps considered, the overall storage complexity for the three probability matrices $\mathbf{U}^{(n-1)}, \mathbf{U}^{(n)}, \mathbf{V}^{(n)}$ and the discrete transition matrix $\mathbf{P}$ is $\mathcal{O}(4n^{2 \cdot M})$. The k-th multiplication of matrix $\mathbf{U}^{(n-1)}$ with $\mathbf{P}$ is carried out in $\mathcal{O}(k^{6M})$. For n the maximum number of considered steps, the overall time complexity therefore equals $\mathcal{O}(n^{6 \cdot M+1})$. Note that the iteration costs per step increase. However, when full probability matrices of the size $\mathbf{U}^{(n)}$ and $\mathbf{V}^{(n)}$ are used throughout the complete computation, the iteration costs are much higher.

5 How to Stop?

For model checking an until-formula $\mathcal{P}_{\bowtie p}(\Phi \, \mathcal{U}^{[t_1,t_2]} \Psi)$ we have to compare for each starting state the probability to follow a $(\Phi \, \mathcal{U}^{[t_1,t_2]} \Psi)$-path with the probability bound p. In the transformed JQN $\mathcal{J}[\neg \Phi \vee \Psi]$ the set of goal states consists of all Ψ-states. We denote the probability to end up in a Ψ-state before time t, given starting state s, as $\gamma_s(t)$. For the time interval $I = [0, t]$, we have:

$$\gamma_s(t) = \sum_{i=0}^{\infty} \sum_{s' \in Sat^{F(\bar{\imath})}(\Psi)} \pi^{\mathcal{J}[\neg \Phi \vee \Psi]}(s, s', t).$$

Note that the vector $\gamma(t)$ consists of sub-vectors corresponding to the fronts of the JQN. The approximation of $\gamma_s(t)$ after n iterations is denoted $\gamma^{(n)}(t) = \mathbf{V}^{(n)}(t) \cdot \gamma(0)$, with

$$\gamma_s(0) = \begin{cases} 1, & s \models \Psi, \\ 0, & \text{otherwise.} \end{cases}$$

In principle, $\gamma^{(n)}(t)$ is of infinite size, but we can cut it to a finite representation, as from a representative front on, corresponding states have the same probability values. For all states $s \in S$, we add the computed transient probabilities to reach any Ψ-state and check whether the accumulated probability meets the bound p on a regular basis. The accumulated probability is always an underestimation of the actual probability. Recall that $\varepsilon_{t,\nu}^{(n)}$ is the maximum error of uniformization after n iteration steps (cf. (7)), such that $\gamma_s(t) \leq \gamma_s^{(n)}(t) + \varepsilon_{t,\nu}^{(n)}$ for time interval $I = [0,t]$. From (7) it follows that the value of $\varepsilon_{t,\nu}^{(n)}$ decreases as n increases. Exploiting the above inequality, we obtain the following stopping criteria:

$$
\begin{array}{ll}
\text{(a)} & \gamma_s^{(n)}(t) \geq p \Rightarrow \gamma_s(t) \geq p, \\
\text{(b)} & \gamma_s^{(n)}(t) < p - \varepsilon_{t,\nu}^{(n)} \Rightarrow \gamma_s(t) < p.
\end{array}
$$

These criteria can be exploited as follows. Starting with a small number of steps, we check whether for the current approximation one of the inequalities (a) or (b) holds for all starting states. If this is not the case we continue, check again, etc., until either of the stopping criteria holds. However, if for one of the starting states $s \in S$ we have $\gamma_s(t) = p$, the iteration never stops, as neither of the stopping criteria ever holds. However, this is highly unlikely to occur in practice. In case $(\neg \Phi \vee \Psi)$ is independent as of $\bar{g}$ and either (a) or (b) holds for all considered starting states with n steps, front $R(\bar{g} + \bar{n})$ is representative and the transient probabilities for all $s \in S_r$ computed with n steps will be the same. $\mathcal{P}_{\bowtie p}(\Phi \, \mathcal{U}^{[0,t]} \Psi)$ then is independent as of $\bar{g} + \bar{n}$. In that case, we check for all states $s \leq \bar{g} + \bar{n}$ whether the accumulated transient probability of reaching a Ψ-state meets the bound p. The representative states that satisfy $\mathcal{P}_{\bowtie p}(\Phi \, \mathcal{U}^{[0,t]} \Psi)$ form the representative satisfaction set $Sat^{R(\bar{g}+\bar{l})}(\mathcal{P}_{\bowtie p}(\Phi \, \mathcal{U}^{[0,t]} \Psi))$.

6   Case Study: An E-Business Site

Modeling an e-business site as Jackson queueing network facilitates analyzing its scalability. This is extremely important as customers become dissatisfied easily in case such a site is overloaded. We are able to model an e-business site in as much detail as shown in [10], however, we use a model with one queue per server instead of two, to keep the model concise. On the other hand, where [10] only analyzes average response times, we are able to analyze a wide range of more advanced measures, given by the logic CSL and the new analysis algorithm.

6.1   System Description and Model

Consider an online retail shop, where requests arrive from a potentially infinite customer base. The site itself consists of three servers: a web server, an application server and a database server. The requests are first dealt with by the web server that manages all the web pages and handles the direct interactions with the customer. The application server implements the core logic of the site and the database server stores persistent information about registered customers, prices and article descriptions. Arriving requests first visit the web server, after which they are either forwarded to the application server, routed back to the web server itself or leave the system, when they have been completed. Jobs that visit the application server are either forwarded to the database server or routed back to either the web server or the application server. From the database server, jobs are routed to either the application server or back to the database server itself. Note that requests can only leave the system via the web server. As illustrated in Figure 4, the associated JQN then consists of three unbounded queues modeling the buffer of the web server, the buffer of the application server and the buffer of the database server, respectively. Requests from the infinite population arrive according to a Poisson process with rate λ and are then routed as shown in Figure 4. The arrival rates per queue that follow from solving the traffic equation and the service rates per queue are given in Table 1.

To analyze the scalability of the e-business site, we define the CSL formula overflow to indicate that all queues are filled above a certain threshold as

$$\text{overflow} = (s_1 \geq \text{full}) \vee (s_2 \geq \text{full}) \vee (s_3 \geq \text{full}),$$

for different possible values of full. The atomic proposition

$$\text{no\_overflow} = \neg \text{overflow} = (s_1 < \text{full}) \wedge (s_2 < \text{full}) \wedge (s_3 < \text{full})$$

indicates that all queues contain less than full requests.

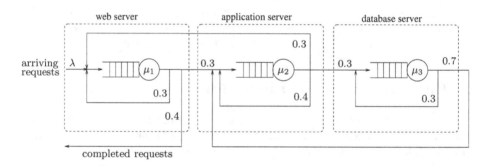

Fig. 4. Queueing network model for an online auction site

6.2   Model Checking Time-Bounded Until

Figure 5 shows the number of uniformization steps needed for model checking

$$Sat(\mathcal{P}_{\geq p}(\text{overflow } \mathcal{U}^{[0,t]} \text{ no\_overflow})) \text{ for } t = \{5; 10; 5\},$$

depending on the probability bound p. We show the number of iterations with the dynamic stopping criterion, as well as the a priori computed number of steps required for an error $\varepsilon_{t,\nu}^{(n)} = 10^{-7}$. Clearly, the a priori number of steps is independent of the probability bound p and increases with time bound t. After 0

Table 1. Numerical values for the parameters of the model

parameter	λ_1	λ_2	λ_3	μ_1	μ_2	μ_3
sec^{-1}	$\frac{5}{2}\cdot\lambda$	$\frac{5}{2}\cdot\lambda$	$\frac{15}{14}\cdot\lambda$	5	5	3

steps the comparison can be evaluated for $p = 0$ for all time bounds when using the dynamic stopping criterion. Then the number of iterations first increases steeply and the maximum number of iterations is reached for a probability bound at most 0.2 for all four time bounds. In general, the number of iteration steps using the dynamic stopping criterion decreases for larger p. Note that the step size of p, as shown in Figure 5 was taken to be 0.01. The number of iterations in Figure 5 clearly varies over time. A peak occurs whenever the computed probability for some state is really close to the probability bound p we have to compare with. The maximum number of iterations with the dynamic stopping criterion approximates the a priori computed number of steps for $\varepsilon_{t,\nu}^{(n)} = 1\cdot 10^{-7}$. For larger time bounds t, the difference between the number of iterations for the dynamic and the a priori stopping criterion increases, showing the efficiency gain using the dynamic stopping criterion.

In Table 2 the first group of rows show the minimum and maximum number of iterations, depending on the probability bound p, per time bound with the dynamic stopping criterion and the a priori computed number of iterations per time bound. The second group of rows then show the finite number of states

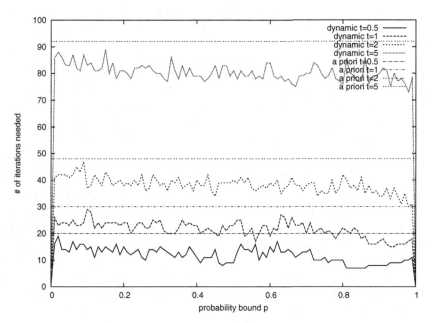

Fig. 5. Number of iterations needed for model checking $s \models \mathcal{P}_{\geq p}(\texttt{overflow}\ \mathcal{U}^{[0,t]}\ \texttt{no\_overflow})$ with the dynamic stopping criterion and with a priori error

Table 2. Numerical values for the parameters of the model

	t	dynamic		a priori
		min	max	$\varepsilon_{t,\nu}^{(n)} = 1 \cdot 10^{-6}$
	0.5	7	19	20
number of iterations	1	15	29	30
	2	30	47	48
	5	73	89	92
	0.5	7770	260130	273819
number of states in	1	23426	877975	1004731
$\mathcal{J}$	2	91881	2081156	2362041
	5	782246	1333300	1456935
	0.5	121768	252132	265821
number of states in	1	532276	869977	996733
$\mathcal{J}[\neg\Phi \vee \Psi]$	2	1406912	2073158	2354043
	5	782246	1325302	1448937
	0.5	$1.3 \cdot 10^{-1}$	$4.0 \cdot 10^{-7}$	$1 \cdot 10^{-7}$
uniformization error	1	$2.4 \cdot 10^{-2}$	$3.1 \cdot 10^{-7}$	$1 \cdot 10^{-7}$
$\varepsilon_{t,\nu}^{(n)}$	2	$1.5 \cdot 10^{-2}$	$1.0 \cdot 10^{-7}$	$1 \cdot 10^{-7}$
	5	$1.1 \cdot 10^{-3}$	$3.45 \cdot 10^{-7}$	$1 \cdot 10^{-7}$

that is considered of the underlying infinite Markov chain $\mathcal{J}$, depending on the number of iterations and again depending on the time bound t. The corresponding number of states in the absorbing Markov chain $\mathcal{J}[\neg\Phi \vee \Psi]$ is shown in third row. In the last group of rows, the numerical error $\varepsilon_{t,\nu}^{(n)}$ for the corresponding number of iterations is given.

Using the dynamic stopping criterion, the number of iterations that is necessary to decide whether $\mathsf{s} \models \mathcal{P}_{\geq p}(\texttt{overflow } \mathcal{U}^{[0,t]} \texttt{ no\_overflow})$ for all $s \in \mathsf{S}$ grows with increasing time bound t. This is due to the fact, that with a larger time bound more steps can be taken. With an increasing number of iterations also the considered finite part of the underlying infinite Markov chain grows. In contrast, with more iterations, the introduced numerical error $\varepsilon_{t,\nu}^{(n)}$ decreases. Therefore, the error bound in column *dynamic min* is larger than the error bound in column *dynamic max*. For time bound $t = 5$, $\varepsilon_{t,\nu}^{(n)} = 1.1 \cdot 10^{-7}$ is enough to decide that $\mathsf{s} \models \mathcal{P}_{\geq p}(\texttt{overflow } \mathcal{U}^{[0,t]} \texttt{ no\_overflow})$ for probability bound $p = 0.98$. Whereas $\varepsilon_{t,\nu}^{(n)} = 3.45 \cdot 10^{-7}$ is enough to decide this for all probability bounds $p \in \{0.0, 0.01, 0.02, \ldots, 0.99, 1.0\}$. However, this small error is only necessary to decide the validity of the CSL formula for probability bound $p = 0.15$. Note that the given number of iterations and the given error might not be enough to decide for every other probability bound. The last column of Table 2 shows the number of iterations that has to be undertaken to keep $\varepsilon_{t,\nu}^{(n)} \leq 1 \cdot 10^{-7}$. Figure 5 shows that an error of $1 \cdot 10^{-7}$ is always enough to decide whether $\mathsf{s} \models \mathcal{P}_{\geq p}(\texttt{overflow } \mathcal{U}^{[0,t]} \texttt{ no\_overflow})$ for all $s \in \mathsf{S}$. The number of states of the infinite Markov chain that has to be considered is always slightly larger than for the maximum in case the dynamic stopping criterion is used.

6.3 Tool Usage

To model check the time bounded until operator the JQN has been transformed manually into a stochastic Petri net [5]. To model the possible infinite population of the JQN, an additional place si added to the SPN from which all arrivals take place and to which all departures are routed. In case the inner formula $\neg\Phi \vee \Psi$ is independent of g and given the number of iterations is n, the place *finite* is initialized with $g + 2 \cdot n$ tokens. Then the CSPL implementation by Bell [3] is used to generate the underlying Markov chain and an implementation of the uniformization method for finite state Markov chains by Cloth [6] is used to compute the transient probabilities. A script then emulated the dynamic behavior of the algorithm. The time to compute the transient probabilities ranges from 0.4 seconds to 22 seconds for the different time bounds, when using the dynamic stopping criterion, and between 1.3 seconds and 26 seconds, when using the a priori stopping criterion.

7 Conclusion

In this paper we presented a model checking algorithm for efficiently checking the time-bounded until operator labeled Jackson queueing networks. Note that with this algorithm the until operator with time interval $[t_1, t_2]$ and with time interval $[t, t]$ can be model checked on JQNs along the same lines as presented for QBDs in [13]; even more details on this can be found in [11]. Hence, we have shown that it is possible to carry the idea of uniformization with representatives to other highly structured classes of infinite-state CTMCs as well.

Storage complexity and the computational complexity for doing uniformization with representatives on JQNs is much higher than for uniformization with representatives on QBDs. This is due to the fact that the state space of a QBD grows without bound in just one direction, whereas the state space of a JQNs grows without bound in as many directions as the JQN has queues.

Note that we used an approximate algorithm to construct a decision procedure for model checking the until operator. The approximate algorithm, uniformization, computes the transient probabilities for a given error bound. Comparing the computed probability with the given probability bound and the uniformization error allows us to decide for a given starting state whether or not a CSL formula that contains the until operator is valid.

References

1. Aziz, A., Sanwal, K., Brayton, R.: Model checking continuous-time Markov chains. ACM Transactions on Computational Logic 1(1), 162–170 (2000)
2. Baier, C., Haverkort, B.R., Hermanns, H., Katoen, J.-P.: Model-checking algorithms for continuous-time Markov chains. IEEE Transactions on Software Engineering 29(7), 524–541 (2003)
3. Bell, A.: Distributed evaluation of stochasic Petri nets. PhD thesis, Dept.of Computer Science, RWTH Aachen (2004)

4. Buchholz, P.: A class of hierarchical queueing systems and their analysis. Qeueing Systems 15, 59–80 (1994)
5. Ciardo, G.: Discrete-time Markovian stochastic Petri nets. In: Computations with Markov Chains, pp. 339–358. Raleigh (1995)
6. Cloth, L., Katoen, J.-P., Khattri, M., Pulungan, R.: Model checking Markov reward models with impulse rewards. In: Int. Conf. on Dependable Systems and Networks (DSN2005). IEEE Press, Los Alamitos (2005)
7. Gross, D., Miller, D.R.: The randomization technique as a modeling tool and solution procedure for transient Markov processes. Operations Research 32(2), 343–361 (1984)
8. Harrison, P.G.: Transient behaviour of queueing networks. Journal of Applied Probability 18(2), 482–490 (1981)
9. Jackson, J.R.: Networks of waiting lines. Operations Research 5(4), 518–521 (1957)
10. Menasce, D.A., Almeida, V.A.F., Dowdy, L.W.: Performance by Design. Prentice-Hall, Englewood Cliffs (2004)
11. Remke, A.: Model checking structured infinite Markov chains. PhD thesis, Dept.of Computer Science, University Twente (2008)
12. Remke, A., Haverkort, B.R.: CSL model checking algorithms for infinite-state structured Markov chains. In: Raskin, J.-F., Thiagarajan, P.S. (eds.) FORMATS 2007. LNCS, vol. 4763, pp. 336–351. Springer, Heidelberg (2007)
13. Remke, A., Haverkort, B.R., Cloth, L.: CSL model checking algorithms for QBDs. Theoretical Computer Science (2007)

Model Checking HML on Piecewise-Constant Inhomogeneous Markov Chains⋆

Joost-Pieter Katoen and Alexandru Mereacre

Software Modeling and Verification, RWTH Aachen University, Germany
{katoen,mereacre}@cs.rwth-aachen.de

Abstract. This paper presents a stochastic variant of Hennessy-Milner logic that is interpreted over (state-labeled) inhomogeneous continuous-time Markov chains (ICTMCs), i.e., Markov chains in which transition rates are functions over time t. For piecewise constant rate functions, the model-checking problem is shown to be reducible to finding the zeros of an exponential polynomial. Using Sturm sequences and Newton's method, we obtain an approximative model-checking algorithm which is linear in the size of the ICTMC, logarithmic in the number of bits precision, and exponential in the nesting depth of the formula.

1 Introduction

Continuous-time Markov chains (CTMCs) are applied in a large range of applications, ranging from transportation systems to systems biology, and are a popular model in performance and dependability analysis. These Markov chains are typically homogeneous, i.e., the rates that determine the speed of changing state as well as the probabilistic nature of mode transitions are constant. However, in some situations constant rates do not adequately model real behavior. This applies, e.g., to failure rates of hardware components (that usually depend on the component's age), battery depletion (where the power extraction rate non-linearly depends on the remaining amount of energy), and random phenomena that are subject to environmental influences such as temperature. In these circumstances, Markov models with *inhomogeneous* rates, i.e., rates that are time-varying functions, are more appropriate.

Whereas temporal logics and accompanying model-checking algorithms have been developed for CTMCs [5,4], and have resulted in a number of successful model checkers such as PRISM [16] and MRMC [15], the verification of time-inhomogeneous CTMCs (ICTMCs) has – to the best of our knowledge – not yet been investigated. This paper presents an initial step in that direction by presenting a stochastic variant of the well-known Hennessy-Milner Logic [11] (HML) for ICTMCs. The main ingredient is a simple probabilistic real-time extension of the modal operator $\langle \Phi \rangle$ in (state-based) HML: the formula $\langle \Phi \rangle^I_{\geq p}$ asserts that a Φ-state is reachable in the time interval I with likelihood at least p. The main

---

⋆ This research has taken place as part of the Research Training Group 1298 ALGO-SYN funded by the German Research Council.

F. Cassez and C. Jard (Eds.): FORMATS 2008, LNCS 5215, pp. 203–217, 2008.
ⓒ Springer-Verlag Berlin Heidelberg 2008

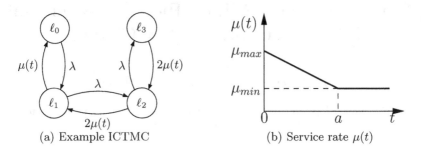

(a) Example ICTMC   (b) Service rate $\mu(t)$

Fig. 1. Queue with three capacities and two servers

technical difficulty is that the semantics of the stochastic variant of HML has to be defined on the underlying continuous state space of an ICTMC. This is similar to the semantics of timed CTL [2] over timed automata [3] which is typically interpreted over infinite-state timed transition systems. The adequacy of this extension is justified by the fact that, as for the discrete probabilistic variant of HML [18], logical equivalence corresponds to strong bisimulation. Opposed to CTMC model checking (where all rate functions are constant), restrictions have to be imposed on the rate functions in order to enable (approximate) model-checking algorithms for ICTMCs. It is shown that verifying our variant of HML for rate functions that are piecewise constant boils down to determining the zeros of an exponential polynomial. Using Laguerre's theorem [17] it can be established that this polynomial has at most five such zeros. By transforming the exponential polynomial into an equivalent (square-free) ordinary polynomial, Sturm sequences, as well as the well-known Newton's method are applied to obtain these zeros. This results in an approximative verification algorithm for stochastic HML which is exponential in the nesting depth of the formula (i.e., the number of $\langle \Phi \rangle^I_{\geq p}$ formulas in sequence), linear in the size of the ICTMC, linear in the number of pieces of a rate function, and logarithmic in the number of bits precision of Newton's method.

2   Preliminaries

Definition 1 (ICTMC). *An inhomogeneous continuous-time Markov chain (ICTMC) is a structure $\mathcal{C} = (\mathbb{L}, \ell_0, \mathbf{R}(t), AP, L)$ such that: $\mathbb{L}$ is a finite set of n locations, $\ell_0 \in \mathbb{L}$ is the initial location, $\mathbf{R}(t) = [R_{\ell,\ell'}(t)] \in \mathbb{R}^{n \times n}_{\geq 0}$ is a time-dependent rate matrix, where $R_{\ell,\ell'}(t)$ is the rate between locations $\ell, \ell' \in \mathbb{L}$ at time $t \in \mathbb{R}_{\geq 0}$, AP is a finite set of atomic propositions and L is the labeling function defined as $L : \mathbb{L} \to 2^{AP}$.*

Let diagonal matrix $\mathbf{E}(t) = \text{diag}\,[E_\ell(t)] \in \mathbb{R}^{n \times n}_{\geq 0}$, where $E_\ell(t) = \sum_{\ell' \in \mathbb{L}} R_{\ell,\ell'}(t)$ for all $\ell, \ell' \in \mathbb{L}$ i.e., $E_\ell(t)$ is the total exit rate of location ℓ at time t. We sometimes write $\ell \xrightarrow{\lambda(t)} \ell'$ as shorthand for $R_{\ell,\ell'}(t) = \lambda(t)$. Note that the only requirement for rates and exit rates is that they are integrable. If all rates (and thus exit rates) are constant, we obtain a CTMC.

The state of an ICTMC is determined by the current state of control (i.e., location), and the current instant of time. A state ξ of ICTMC C is a tuple (ℓ, x) where $\ell \in \mathbb{L}$ indicates the current location and $x \in \mathbb{R}_{\geqslant 0}$ the current time instant.

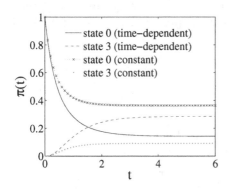

The state space $\mathbb{E}$ of an ICTMC is given by a disjoint union of subsets $\mathbb{E}_\ell$ of $\mathbb{R}_{\geqslant 0}$ for each location ℓ such that:

$$\mathbb{E} = \coprod_{\ell \in \mathbb{L}} \mathbb{E}_\ell = \bigcup_{\ell \in \mathbb{L}} \{(\ell, x) \mid x \in \mathbb{R}_{\geqslant 0}\}.$$

Let $\mathcal{E}$ denote the σ-field of subsets A of $\mathbb{E}$ which take the form $A = \coprod_{\ell \in \mathbb{L}} A_\ell$, where A_ℓ is a Borel set of $\mathbb{E}_\ell$ (defined as above). As the set $\mathbb{R}_{\geqslant 0}$ denotes the set of possible time points, the initial state $\xi_0 \in \mathbb{E}$ of C becomes $\xi_0 = (\ell_0, 0)$. For any state $\xi = (\ell, x)$ the projection $\xi_{\mathbb{L}}$ yields $\ell \in \mathbb{L}$, and projection $\xi_{\mathbb{R}}$ yields $x \in \mathbb{R}_{\geqslant 0}$. These projection functions are lifted to sets of states in a pointwise manner. For a set of states $A \subseteq \mathbb{E}$ and location $\ell \in \mathbb{L}$, let $A_\ell^{\mathbb{R}}$ denote the set $\{x \in \mathbb{R}_{\geqslant 0} \mid \xi \in A, \xi_{\mathbb{L}} = \ell, \xi_{\mathbb{R}} = x\}$.

Fig. 2. Transient distribution for ℓ_0 and ℓ_3

Example 1. Fig. 1(a) shows a queue with three capacities and two servers modeled by an ICTMC. The customers arrive as a Poisson process with rate λ and the service rate is a function $\mu(t)$ (see Fig. 1(b)). Initially the service rate starts at μ_{max} and decreases linearly until μ_{min} at time $t = a$. From that moment on, all customers are served with constant rate μ_{min}.

The transition probability (kernel) $\text{Pr} : \mathbb{E} \times \mathcal{E} \to [0, 1]$ of an ICTMC is a probability measure $\text{Pr}(\xi, \cdot)$ on $(\mathbb{E}, \mathcal{E})$ for each fixed $\xi \in \mathbb{E}$, and $\text{Pr}(\cdot, A)$ is a measurable function for each fixed $A \in \mathcal{E}$. In order to derive the transition probability function we note that the probability to take some transition $\ell \to \ell'$ ($\ell, \ell' \in \mathbb{L}$) with rate $R_{\ell,\ell'}(t)$ within Δt units of time at time t is given by:

$$\text{Prob}\{\ell \to \ell', t, \Delta t\} = \int_0^{\Delta t} R_{\ell,\ell'}(t + \tau) e^{-\int_0^\tau E_\ell(t+v)dv} d\tau. \tag{1}$$

As a next step, we rewrite Eq. (1) into:

$$\text{Prob}\{\ell \to \ell', t, \Delta t\} = \int_t^{t+\Delta t} R_{\ell,\ell'}(\tau) e^{-\int_t^\tau E_\ell(v)dv} d\tau. \tag{2}$$

It is not difficult to see that $\text{Prob}\{\ell \to \ell', t, \Delta t\}$ measures the probability to move from state $\xi = (\ell, t)$ to the set of states $A = \{(\ell', x) \mid x \in [t, t + \Delta t]\}$. For an arbitrary set of states A, Eq. (2) results in transition kernel:

$$\Pr(\xi, A) = \sum_{\ell' \in A_L} \int_{A_{\ell'}^{\mathbb{R}} \cap [0, \infty[\oplus \xi_{\mathbb{R}}} R_{\xi_L, \ell'}(\tau) e^{-\int_{\xi_{\mathbb{R}}}^{\tau} E_{\xi_L}(v) dv} d\tau, \tag{3}$$

where for any interval I (in our case $I = [0, \infty[)$, $I \oplus \xi_{\mathbb{R}} = \{x + \xi_{\mathbb{R}} \mid x \in I\}$. Note that the domain of the integral in Eq. (3) is composed of the sets $A_{\ell'}^{\mathbb{R}}$ and $[0, \infty[\oplus \xi_{\mathbb{R}}$. The latter set ensures that the probability to jump back in time is zero. From Eq. (3) we directly obtain that the probability to move from state ξ to the set A of states in the interval I is given by:

$$\Pr(\xi, A, I) = \sum_{\ell' \in A_L} \int_{A_{\ell'}^{\mathbb{R}} \cap I \oplus \xi_{\mathbb{R}}} R_{\xi_L, \ell'}(\tau) e^{-\int_{\xi_{\mathbb{R}}}^{\tau} E_{\xi_L}(v) dv} d\tau. \tag{4}$$

Proposition 1. *The transition kernel is a probability measure provided:*

$$\lim_{\tau \to \infty} \int_{\xi_{\mathbb{R}}}^{\tau} E_{\xi_L}(v) dv = \infty, \quad \text{for } \xi \in \mathbb{E}.$$

For every location $\ell \in \mathbb{L}$ the divergence of the integral from Proposition 1 or $\int_0^\infty E_\ell(v) dv$ can be tested by searching for a simpler function $h_\ell(v)$ such that $h_\ell(v) \leq E_\ell(v)$ for every $v \in [0, \infty[$ and for which we can easily show that $\int_0^\infty h_\ell(v) dv = \infty$.

Besides the transition kernel, for any ICTMC we can define the *transient probability distribution* which indicates the probability $\pi_j(t + \Delta t)$ to be in state j at time $t + \Delta t$:

$$\pi_j(t + \Delta t) = \sum_{i \in \mathbb{L}} \text{Prob}\{X(t) = i\} \cdot \text{Prob}\{X(t + \Delta t) = j \mid X(t) = i\}, \tag{5}$$

where $X(t)$ is a random variable indicating the location of the ICTMC at time t. Notice that $\text{Prob}\{X(t + \Delta t) = j \mid X(t) = i\}$ is a multi-step version of the transition kernel Pr as the number of transitions between states i and j can be arbitrary. For ICTMCs the transient behavior can also be described by a homogeneous system of ODEs (Chapman-Kolmogorov equations):

$$\frac{d\pi(t)}{dt} = \pi(t) \mathbf{Q}(t), \quad \sum_{i=1}^n \pi_i(t_0) = 1, \tag{6}$$

where $\mathbf{Q}(t) = \mathbf{R}(t) - \mathbf{E}(t)$ is the *infinitesimal generator* and the vector $\pi(t_0) = [\pi_1(t_0), \ldots, \pi_n(t_0)]$ is the initial condition.

Example 2. Fig. 2 depicts the transient probability distribution (see Eq. (5)) of states ℓ_0 and ℓ_3 from Fig. 1 for two cases: (1) a time-dependent rate function $\mu(t)$ with $\mu_{min} = 1$, $\mu_{max} = 2$ and $a = 3$, (2) a constant rate function $\mu(t) = 2$. For both cases $\lambda = 2$. Note the significant difference between the transient probabilities for these time-dependent and constant cases.

3   Continuous Hennessy-Milner Logic

Background. Hennessy-Milner Logic (HML) [11] is an action-based logic aimed at specifying properties of labeled transition systems. Its syntax is given by:

$$\Phi ::= \top \mid \Phi \wedge \Phi \mid \neg \Phi \mid \langle a \rangle \Phi,$$

where a is an action. The semantics is defined over process P. $P \models \langle a \rangle \Phi$ whenever for some process P', $P' \models \Phi$ and $P \xrightarrow{a} P'$.

Several probabilistic variants of HML exist. Larsen and Skou [18] have extended HML for discrete probabilistic systems by adding two new operators: Δ_a and $\langle a \rangle_p \Phi$ with $p \in [0,1] \cap \mathbb{Q}$. $P \models \Delta_a$ holds when $P \xrightarrow{a}$ and $P \models \langle a \rangle_p \Phi$ holds when $P \xrightarrow{a}_\nu S$ (ν is the probability to move from P to the set of processes S) such that $\nu \geq p$ and $\forall s \in S. s \models \Phi$. Recently, Parma & Segala [19] defined HML for probabilistic automata [21]. Clark *et al.* [7] defined a similar variant as Larsen and Skou for action-labeled CTMCs [14] where the probability p in $\langle a \rangle_p \Phi$ is replaced by a rate.

Syntax and semantics. Our logic for ICTMCs is inspired by Larsen and Skou's variant of HML. We consider a state-based variant of HML and include a notion of time. The Continuous Hennessy-Milner Logic (CHML) for ICTMCs is defined by the following grammar:

Definition 2 (Syntax). *For ICTMC $\mathcal{C}$ with state space $\mathbb{E}$, atomic proposition $a \in AP$, $p \in [0,1] \cap \mathbb{Q}$, interval $I \subseteq \mathbb{R}_{\geq 0}$ with rational bounds and $\trianglelefteq \in \{<, \leq, \geq, >\}$, the grammar of* **CHML** *is:*

$$\Phi ::= \top \mid a \mid \Phi \wedge \Phi \mid \neg \Phi \mid \langle \Phi \rangle^I_{\trianglelefteq p}.$$

Here, the formula $\langle \Phi \rangle^I_{\trianglelefteq p}$ asserts that a state satisfying Φ can be reached within the interval I with probability within the threshold of p.

Example 3. Consider the ICTMC from Fig. 1 with the labels $L(\ell_0) = empty$, $L(\ell_1) = \#1, L(\ell_2) = \#2$ and $L(\ell_3) = full$. The formula $\langle \#2 \rangle^{[1,4]}_{\geq 0.3} \wedge \neg \#1$ holds in any state ξ with $L(\xi_{\mathbb{L}}) = \{\neg \#1\}$, which may jump in a single transition to the state ξ' such that $L(\xi'_{\mathbb{L}}) = \{\#2\}$ in the interval $[1,4]$ with probability at least 0.3.

Applying the negation operator $\neg$ to the operator $\langle \cdot \rangle$ yields:

$$\neg \left(\langle \Phi \rangle^I_{\leq p} \right) = \langle \neg \Phi \rangle^I_{\geq 1-p} \quad \text{and} \quad \neg \left(\langle \Phi \rangle^I_{> p} \right) = \langle \neg \Phi \rangle^I_{< 1-p}.$$

It is important to note that CHML can be viewed as a sub-logic of Continuous Stochastic Logic (CSL)[5] with $\langle \Phi \rangle^I_{\trianglelefteq p}$ being equivalent to the next operator $\mathcal{P}_{\trianglelefteq p} (X^I \Phi)$ of CSL. The substantial difference between CHML and CSL is that the satisfaction relation for any CHML-formula is defined over the set of states of an ICTMC which is *uncountable*. This difference is due to the fact that the evolution of the ICTMC depends on (a global notion of) time, whereas in CTMCs this is not the case. The global time in ICTMCs implies a continuous state-space rather than a finite one as in CTMCs. Finally, the definition of CHML is more similar to the approach of Desharnais [8] where CSL is defined for continuous-time Markov processes. As opposed to the approach of Desharnais, in this paper we are more interested in model checking. Let $[\![\Phi]\!] = \{\xi \in \mathbb{E} \mid \xi \models \Phi\}$ denote the set of states satisfying Φ, where $\models$ is defined as follows:

Definition 3 (Semantics). *The relation $\models \subseteq \mathbb{E} \times \mathbf{CHML}$ is defined by:*

$$\begin{aligned}
\xi &\models \top &&\text{for all } \xi \in \mathbb{E}, &\qquad \xi &\models \neg\Phi &&\text{iff not } \xi \models \Phi,\\
\xi &\models a &&\text{iff } a \in L(\xi_{\mathrm{L}}), &\qquad & &&\\
\xi &\models \Phi \wedge \Psi &&\text{iff } \xi \models \Phi \text{ and } \xi \models \Psi, &\qquad \xi &\models \langle \Phi \rangle^{I}_{\trianglelefteq p} &&\text{iff } \mathrm{Pr}(\xi, [\![\Phi]\!], I) \trianglelefteq p.
\end{aligned}$$

In order for $\models$ to be well-defined, we need to address measurability.

Lemma 1. *For any formula $\Phi \in \mathbf{CHML}$ the set $[\![\Phi]\!]$ is measurable.*

The ICTMC $\mathcal{C}$ satisfies formula Φ, denoted $\mathcal{C} \models \Phi$, iff $\xi_0 \in [\![\Phi]\!]$.

Bisimulation. It is well-known that strong bisimulation coincides with HML equivalence. In a similar vein, Larsen and Skou [18] showed that their logic characterizes probabilistic bisimulation. Recently, we have defined a notion of bisimulation for ICTMCs [10] which has the same coinductive flavor as in the case of CTMCs [6] and IMCs [13]. Our bisimulation is a structural notion and is defined on the level of the syntax of ICTMCs rather than their underlying infinite state space. Let $R(\ell, C, t)$ be the sum of all outgoing rates from location ℓ to the set C of locations at time t given by $\sum_i \{| \lambda(t) \mid \ell \xrightarrow{\lambda(t)}_i \ell'', \ell'' \in C |\}$, where $\ell \xrightarrow{\lambda(t)}_i \ell''$ denotes the i'th transition from location ℓ to location ℓ'' labeled with $\lambda(t)$ and $\{| \cdots |\}$ denotes a multi-set.

Definition 4 (Bisimulation). *An equivalence $\mathcal{R} \subseteq \mathbb{L} \times \mathbb{L}$ is a bisimulation whenever for all $(\ell, \ell') \in \mathcal{R}$ it holds that $L(\ell) = L(\ell')$ and $R(\ell, C, t) = R(\ell', C, t)$ for all $t \in \mathbb{R}_{\geqslant 0}$ and $C \in \mathbb{L}/\mathcal{R}$. ℓ and ℓ' are bisimilar, denoted $\ell \sim \ell'$, if (ℓ, ℓ') is contained in some bisimulation $\mathcal{R}$.*

In [5] there is a well-known result which states that bisimulation (for CTMCs) preserves the validity of CSL formulas. A similar result can be obtained also for HML first, by lifting the notion of bisimulation to the set of states $\mathbb{E}$ as follows:

Definition 5. *An equivalence $\mathcal{R} \subseteq \mathbb{E} \times \mathbb{E}$ is an $\mathbb{E}$-bisimulation whenever for all $(\xi, \xi') \in \mathcal{R}$ holds $\xi_{\mathrm{L}} \sim \xi'_{\mathrm{L}}$ and $\xi_{\mathbb{R}} = \xi'_{\mathbb{R}}$. ξ and ξ' are $\mathbb{E}$-bisimilar, denoted $\xi \sim_{\mathbb{E}} \xi'$, if (ξ, ξ') is contained in some $\mathbb{E}$-bisimulation $\mathcal{R}$.*

Note that the $\mathbb{E}$-bisimulation is not the coarsest one. As for a constant rate matrix one can define a bisimulation such that any two states ξ and ξ' with $\xi_{\mathrm{L}} = \xi'_{\mathrm{L}}$ and $\xi_{\mathbb{R}} \neq \xi'_{\mathbb{R}}$ will be bisimilar while $\xi \nsim_{\mathbb{E}} \xi'$. On the other hand it is not difficult to see that the conditions for $\mathbb{E}$-bisimilarity in Definition 5 are sufficient to ensure $(\mathbb{E}/\sim_{\mathbb{E}})_{\mathrm{L}} = \mathbb{L}/\sim$.

Theorem 1. *For any formula* $\Phi \in \mathbf{CHML}$, *($\xi \models \Phi$ iff $\xi' \models \Phi$) iff $\xi \sim_E \xi'$.*

Due to this theorem, any verification results on $\mathcal{C}/\sim$, the quotient of $\mathcal{C}$ under $\sim$, carries over to $\mathcal{C}$ since $\mathcal{C}/\sim$ is bisimilar to $\mathcal{C}$. A bisimulation minimization algorithm for ICTMCs with piecewise constant rate functions has recently been proposed [10] and requires $\mathcal{O}\left(Nm \log n\right)$ time, where N is the number of constant pieces of the rate matrix $\mathbf{R}(t)$, and m, n are the number of transitions and locations of $\mathcal{C}$, respectively.

4 Model Checking Continuous Hennessy-Milner Logic

Continuous Hennessy-Milner Logic describes properties which can be verified for every state of $\mathbb{E}$. When one attempts to develop model-checking algorithms for CHML one has to consider that the state space $\mathbb{E}$ is in fact continuous (i.e., consists of uncountably many states). This is a main difference with logics for CTMCs, such as CSL, where the state space is denumerable since the behavior of a CTMC only depends on the current location and not on the amount of time spent there. Therefore, our aim is to group all states $\xi \in \mathbb{E}$, where $\xi \models \Phi$ into tuples $(\ell, \mathcal{I})$ with $\ell \in \mathbb{L}$ and $\mathcal{I} \subseteq \mathbb{R}_{\geqslant 0}$ - formed of a finite union of intervals:

$$\llbracket \Phi \rrbracket := \{(\ell, \mathcal{I}) \mid \ell \in \mathbb{L}, \mathcal{I} = \{\xi_{\mathbb{R}} \mid \xi \in \mathbb{E}, \xi \models \Phi, \xi_{\mathbb{L}} = \ell\}\} \setminus \{(\ell, \emptyset) \mid \ell \in \mathbb{L}\}.$$

Using the tuple (location-interval) representation we can form the satisfaction set of any propositional formula $\Phi \in \mathbf{CHML}$ as:

$$\llbracket \top \rrbracket = \{(\ell, \mathbb{R}_{\geqslant 0}) \mid \ell \in \mathbb{L}\} \quad \llbracket a \rrbracket = \{(\ell, \mathbb{R}_{\geqslant 0}) \mid \ell \in \mathbb{L}, a \in L(\ell)\}$$

$$\llbracket \Phi \wedge \Psi \rrbracket = \left\{\left(\ell, \llbracket \Phi \rrbracket_\ell^{\mathbb{R}} \cap \llbracket \Psi \rrbracket_\ell^{\mathbb{R}}\right) \mid \ell \in \mathbb{L}, \ell \in \llbracket \Phi \rrbracket_{\mathbb{L}} \cap \llbracket \Psi \rrbracket_{\mathbb{L}}\right\}$$

$$\llbracket \neg \Phi \rrbracket = \{(\ell, \mathbb{R}_{\geqslant 0}) \mid \ell \in \mathbb{L}\setminus\llbracket \Phi \rrbracket_{\mathbb{L}}\} \cup \{(\ell, \mathbb{R}_{\geqslant 0}\setminus\llbracket \Phi \rrbracket_\ell^{\mathbb{R}}) \mid \ell \in \llbracket \Phi \rrbracket_{\mathbb{L}}\}$$

As every element of the set $\llbracket \Phi \rrbracket$ is a tuple $(\ell, \mathcal{I})$ the intersection is done componentwise, i.e., per location ℓ and component $\mathcal{I}$.

Example 4. Consider the ICTMC from Fig. 1(a) and the sets $\llbracket \Phi \rrbracket = \{(\ell_0, [1, 2])\}$, $\llbracket \Psi \rrbracket = \{(\ell_3, [0, 5] \cup [8, \infty[)\}$. We have the following satisfaction sets:

$$\llbracket \neg \Phi \rrbracket = \{(\ell_0, [0, 1[\cup]2, \infty[), (\ell_1, \mathbb{R}_{\geqslant 0}), (\ell_2, \mathbb{R}_{\geqslant 0}), (\ell_3, \mathbb{R}_{\geqslant 0})\}$$

$$\llbracket \neg \Psi \rrbracket = \{(\ell_0, \mathbb{R}_{\geqslant 0}), (\ell_1, \mathbb{R}_{\geqslant 0}), (\ell_2, \mathbb{R}_{\geqslant 0}), (\ell_3,]5, 8[)\}$$

$$\llbracket \neg \Phi \wedge \neg \Psi \rrbracket = \{(\ell_0, [0, 1[\cup]2, \infty[), (\ell_1, \mathbb{R}_{\geqslant 0}), (\ell_2, \mathbb{R}_{\geqslant 0}), (\ell_3,]5, 8[)\}.$$

By using only the above four cases (initially we don't consider the formula $\langle \Phi \rangle_{\trianglelefteq p}^I$) it is not difficult to see that every set $\llbracket \Phi \rrbracket$ will be formed of finitely many tuples $(\ell, \mathcal{I})$ where $\mathcal{I} \subseteq \mathbb{R}_{\geqslant 0}$. The most challenging part is to find all tuples (elements) $(\ell, \mathcal{I})$ of the set $\llbracket \langle \Phi \rangle_{\trianglelefteq p}^I \rrbracket$.

Verifying $\langle \Phi \rangle^I_{\trianglelefteq p}$*-formulas.* Using Eq. (4), the set $[\![\langle \Phi \rangle^I_{\trianglelefteq p}]\!]$ for any $\Phi \in$ **CHML** is given by:

$$[\![\langle \Phi \rangle^I_{\trianglelefteq p}]\!] = \{\xi \in \mathbb{E} \mid \Pr(\xi, [\![\Phi]\!], I) \trianglelefteq p\} \quad \text{where} \tag{7}$$

$$\Pr(\xi, [\![\Phi]\!], I) = \sum_{\ell' \in [\![\Phi]\!]_{\mathbb{L}}} \int_{[\![\Phi]\!]^{\mathbb{R}}_{\ell'} \cap I \oplus \xi_{\mathbb{R}}} R_{\xi_{\mathbb{L}}, \ell'}(\tau) e^{-\int_{\xi_{\mathbb{R}}}^{\tau} E_{\xi_{\mathbb{L}}}(v)dv} d\tau. \tag{8}$$

Here our task is to group all $\xi \in [\![\langle \Phi \rangle^I_{\trianglelefteq p}]\!]$ into tuples $(\ell, \mathcal{I})$ such that $\ell \in [\![\langle \Phi \rangle^I_{\trianglelefteq p}]\!]_{\mathbb{L}}$ and $\mathcal{I} = [\![\langle \Phi \rangle^I_{\trianglelefteq p}]\!]^{\mathbb{R}}_{\ell}$. For every $\ell \in \mathbb{L}$, a two-step procedure corresponding to equations (7) and (8) follows:

1. Find the set $\mathcal{X}$ of solutions by solving the equation (recall that $\xi = (\ell, x)$)

$$\Pr((\ell, x), [\![\Phi]\!], I) = p, \tag{9}$$

   where $x \in \mathbb{R}_{\geq 0}$ is the unknown variable and
2. Find $\mathcal{I}$ by using $\mathcal{X}$ such that $\Pr((\ell, x^*), [\![\Phi]\!], I) \trianglelefteq p$ and $x^* \in \mathcal{I}$.

The second step is straightforward i.e., after computing the set $\mathcal{X}$ the interval $\mathcal{I}$ is computed by checking the condition $\Pr((\ell, x^*), [\![\Phi]\!], I) \trianglelefteq p$ for every sequential pair of solutions $x_i, x_{i+1} \in \mathcal{X}$ such that $x_i < x_{i+1}$ and $x^* = \frac{x_i + x_{i+1}}{2}$. The first step is a bit more problematic. The difficulty lies in computing the integral from Eq. (8) over a time-variant domain $[\![\Phi]\!]^{\mathbb{R}}_{\ell'} \cap I \oplus \xi_{\mathbb{R}}$ of a time-variant rate $R_{\xi_{\mathbb{L}}, \ell'}(\tau)$ and exit rate $E_{\xi_{\mathbb{L}}}(v)$. Moreover, we aim to obtain a finite set of solutions $\mathcal{X}$. In order to meet this challenge, we impose some conditions on the rate functions of ICTMCs.

We assume that the rates $R_{\ell, \ell'}(\tau)$ for any two locations ℓ and ℓ' are piecewise constant functions which are *right-continuous with left limits*. Formally, this means that $R_{\ell, \ell'}(\tau) = R^{(k)}_{\ell, \ell'}$ for every $\tau \in [t_k, t_{k+1}[$, where $t_{k+1} = t_k + \Delta t$ (here Δt is the time discretization parameter), $t_{N+1} = \infty$, $k \in \{1, \cdots, N\}$ and N is the total number of constant pieces. We thus obtain $E_{\ell}(\tau) = E^{(k)}_{\ell}$ for every $\tau \in [t_k, t_{k+1}[$. Notice that the restriction of rates to be right-continuous with left limits is not crucial as the values of the rates at discrete points are not relevant. This partition of the time-axis $\mathbb{R}_{\geq 0}$ will ensure that for every tuple $(\ell, \mathcal{I})$ in $[\![\langle \Phi \rangle^I_{\trianglelefteq p}]\!]$ the component $\mathcal{I}$ will consist of a finite union of disjoint intervals. In fact, later on it will be shown that for piecewise constant rate functions the set $\mathcal{X}$ is finite. Now consider the CHML-formula Φ from $[\![\langle \Phi \rangle^I_{\trianglelefteq p}]\!]$. Assume that in every tuple $(\ell', \mathcal{I})$ from $[\![\Phi]\!]$, $\mathcal{I} = [\![\Phi]\!]^{\mathbb{R}}_{\ell'}$ is a finite union of disjoint intervals i.e., $[\![\Phi]\!]^{\mathbb{R}}_{\ell'} = \biguplus_{i=1}^{\theta} \mathcal{I}^{(i)}_{\ell'}$, where θ is the total number of such intervals. Eq. (8) becomes:

$$\Pr((\ell, x), [\![\Phi]\!], I) = \sum_{\ell' \in [\![\Phi]\!]_{\mathbb{L}}} \sum_{i=1}^{\theta} \int_{\mathcal{I}^{(i)}_{\ell'} \cap I \oplus x} R_{\ell, \ell'}(\tau) e^{-\int_{x}^{\tau} E_{\ell}(v)dv} d\tau. \tag{10}$$

It is important to note that the intervals $\mathcal{I}^{(i)}_{\ell'}$ can be open, closed, or half-closed. Therefore, for the integral in Eq. (10) one has to consider the limit from the

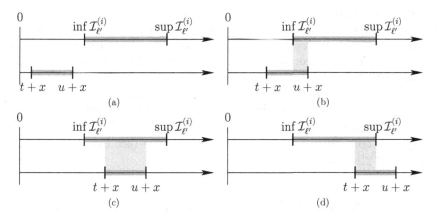

Fig. 3. The position of $\mathcal{I}_{\ell'}^{(i)}$ and $[t,u] \oplus x$ together with their intersection in (gray) for the case $\sup \mathcal{I}_{\ell'}^{(i)} - \inf \mathcal{I}_{\ell'}^{(i)} > u - t$

right, as well as from the left. In our case this is not necessary as all rates are right-continuous with left limits.

Until now we set the basis for solving Eq. (9) by considering a finite partition of the time-axis. The final step is to compute the integral from Eq. (10) over the time-variant domain $\mathcal{I}_{\ell'}^{(i)} \cap I \oplus x$ (by varying x the size of the integration domain changes). For this we take $I = [t,u]$ and as a result the integration domain $\mathcal{I}_{\ell'}^{(i)} \cap [t,u] \oplus x$ takes the form:

$$\mathcal{I}_{\ell'}^{(i)} \cap [t,u] \oplus x = \left[\max \left\{ \inf \mathcal{I}_{\ell'}^{(i)}, t+x \right\}, \min \left\{ \sup \mathcal{I}_{\ell'}^{(i)}, u+x \right\} \right]. \qquad (11)$$

Notice the interval in Eq. (11) is not necessary closed as its bounds depend on the interval $\mathcal{I}_{\ell'}^{(i)}$. For instance, if $\inf \mathcal{I}_{\ell'}^{(i)} > t + x$ and $\mathcal{I}_{\ell'}^{(i)}$ is left-open, then the integration domain will be also left-open.

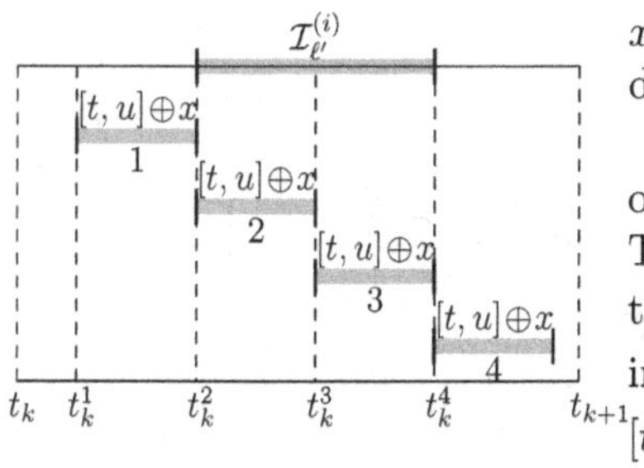

The interval in Eq. (11) strongly depends on the position of $\mathcal{I}_{\ell'}^{(i)}$ relative to $[t,u] \oplus x$. This means that there are several configurations given by $\sup \mathcal{I}_{\ell'}^{(i)}$, $\inf \mathcal{I}_{\ell'}^{(i)}$, t, and u. For instance, Fig. 3 depicts the position of $\mathcal{I}_{\ell'}^{(i)}$ and $[t,u] \oplus x$ when $\sup \mathcal{I}_{\ell'}^{(i)} - \inf \mathcal{I}_{\ell'}^{(i)} > u - t$. As you can see, the relative placement of both intervals in Fig. 3 is crucial for the computation of the integral from Eq. (10).

Fig. 4. Time point events

At the beginning of the section we have assumed that the rates are piecewise constant or more intuitively we have discretized the time-axis into intervals $[t_k, t_{k+1}[$ during which the rates are constant. This discretization gives us the possibility to find a closed-form expression for Eq. (10) that enables us to solve

Eq. (9). The derived expression will not contain the integral, but instead will be a linear combination of exponential functions as we will show below. Now by considering each interval $[t_k, t_{k+1}[$ separately we can derive an expression for $\Pr((\ell, x), \llbracket \Phi \rrbracket, I)$ by computing the integral from Eq. (10) with the condition that $x \in [t_k, t_{k+1}[$. As was shown before, the computation of the integral strongly depends on the integration domain. By varying x from t_k up to t_{k+1}, the interval $[t, u] \oplus x$ shifts as shown in Fig. 3. Note that different values of x mark the beginning of time when the intersection between $\mathcal{I}_{\ell'}^{(i)}$ and $[t, u] \oplus x$ will be empty or not. There are four of such time points (see Fig. 4) for the case $\sup \mathcal{I}_{\ell'}^{(i)} - \inf \mathcal{I}_{\ell'}^{(i)} > u - t$:

1. $t_k^1 = x$ - is the moment of time when $u + x \geq \inf \mathcal{I}_{\ell'}^{(i)}$,
2. $t_k^2 = x$ - is the moment of time when $t + x \geq \inf \mathcal{I}_{\ell'}^{(i)}$ and $[t, u] \oplus x \subseteq \mathcal{I}_{\ell'}^{(i)}$,
3. $t_k^3 = x$ - is the moment of time when $u + x \geq \sup \mathcal{I}_{\ell'}^{(i)}$,
4. $t_k^4 = x$ - is the moment of time when $t + x \geq \sup \mathcal{I}_{\ell'}^{(i)}$ and $\mathcal{I}_{\ell'}^{(i)} \cap [t, u] \oplus x = \emptyset$ when $t + x > \sup \mathcal{I}_{\ell'}^{(i)}$.

Note that in order to simplify the notations we do not indicate the indices ℓ' and i to t_k^j as it is clear that every t_k^j, $j \in \{1, \ldots, 4\}$ is computed respective to the interval $\mathcal{I}_{\ell'}^{(i)}$ i.e., for every ℓ' and i, the time point t_k^j will be different. Also if some time point t_k^j is not defined then $t_k^j = t_k$.

Using t_k^j we divide the interval $[t_k, t_{k+1}[$ into five sub-intervals $[t_k, t_k^1[$, $[t_k^1, t_k^2[$, $[t_k^2, t_k^3[$, $[t_k^3, t_k^4[$ and $[t_k^4, t_{k+1}[$. For each of the mentioned sub-intervals we can compute the integral from Eq. (10). Here we only consider the case when $k = N$ and $\sup \mathcal{I}_{\ell'}^{(i)} - \inf \mathcal{I}_{\ell'}^{(i)} > u - t$. For the remaining cases, the procedure is straightforward. Distinguish (as indicated above), the following five cases:

- $x \in [t_N, t_N^1[\Rightarrow \mathcal{I}_{\ell'}^{(i)} \cap [t, u] \oplus x = \emptyset$.
- $x \in [t_N^1, t_N^2[\Rightarrow \max\left\{\inf \mathcal{I}_{\ell'}^{(i)}, t + x\right\} = \inf \mathcal{I}_{\ell'}^{(i)}, \min\left\{\sup \mathcal{I}_{\ell'}^{(i)}, u + x\right\} = u + x,$

$$\int_{\inf \mathcal{I}_{\ell'}^{(i)}}^{u+x} R_{\ell,\ell'}(\tau) e^{-\int_x^\tau E_\ell(v) dv} d\tau = \frac{R_{\ell,\ell'}^{(N)}}{E_\ell^{(N)}} \left(e^{-\left(\inf \mathcal{I}_{\ell'}^{(i)} - x\right) E_\ell^{(N)}} - e^{-u E_\ell^{(N)}}\right).$$

- $x \in [t_N^2, t_N^3[\Rightarrow \max\left\{\inf \mathcal{I}_{\ell'}^{(i)}, t + x\right\} = t + x, \min\left\{\sup \mathcal{I}_{\ell'}^{(i)}, u + x\right\} = u + x,$

$$\int_{t+x}^{u+x} R_{\ell,\ell'}(\tau) e^{-\int_x^\tau E_\ell(v) dv} d\tau = \frac{R_{\ell,\ell'}^{(N)}}{E_\ell^{(N)}} \left(e^{-t E_\ell^{(N)}} - e^{-u E_\ell^{(N)}}\right).$$

- $x \in [t_N^3, t_N^4[\Rightarrow \max\left\{\inf \mathcal{I}_{\ell'}^{(i)}, t + x\right\} = t + x, \min\left\{\sup \mathcal{I}_{\ell'}^{(i)}, u + x\right\} = \sup \mathcal{I}_{\ell'}^{(i)},$

$$\int_{t+x}^{\sup \mathcal{I}_{\ell'}^{(i)}} R_{\ell,\ell'}(\tau) e^{-\int_x^\tau E_\ell(v) dv} d\tau = \frac{R_{\ell,\ell'}^{(N)}}{E_\ell^{(N)}} \left(e^{-t E_\ell^{(N)}} - e^{-\left(\sup \mathcal{I}_{\ell'}^{(i)} - x\right) E_\ell^{(N)}}\right).$$

- $x \in [t_N^4, \infty[\Rightarrow \mathcal{I}_{\ell'}^{(i)} \cap [t, u] \oplus x = \emptyset$.

For all five intervals the integral in Eq. (10) has the same form given by the expression $a_{N,\ell'}^{i,j} + b_{N,\ell'}^{i,j} e^{x E_\ell^{(N)}}$ (it is in fact a linear combination of exponential functions). The constants $a_{N,\ell'}^{i,j}$ and $b_{N,\ell'}^{i,j}$ corresponding to the interval $[t_N^j, t_N^{j+1}[$, $j \in \{1, 2, 3\}$ are formed by the expressions containing $R_{\ell,\ell'}^{(N)}$ and $E_\ell^{(N)}$. Given $a_{N,\ell'}^{i,j} + b_{N,\ell'}^{i,j} e^{x E_\ell^{(N)}}$ for each interval $[t_N^j, t_N^{j+1}[$, Eq. (10) can be simplified to:

$$\Pr((\ell, x), [\![\Phi]\!], I) = \sum_{\ell' \in [\![\Phi]\!]_\mathbb{L}} \sum_{i=1}^{\theta} \left(a_{N,\ell'}^{i,j} + b_{N,\ell'}^{i,j} e^{x E_\ell^{(N)}} \right) \chi_{\ell'}^{i,j}(x), \qquad (12)$$

where $\chi_{\ell'}^{i,j}(x) = 1$ for every $x \in [t_N^j, t_N^{j+1}[$ and 0 otherwise. Note that there is at most one solution (i.e., $|\mathcal{X}| \leq 1$) when solving Eq. (9) using Eq. (12) (i.e., the case when $k = N$).

Now we proceed with the interval $[t_k, t_{k+1}[$ for $k < N$. Here the general form of Eq. (10) becomes more complex as transition rates are not constant on the interval of time $[0, t_N[$. We obtain the following result, which is a major stepping-stone towards a model-checking algorithm for piecewise constant ICTMCs.

Theorem 2. *For any $x \in [t_k, t_{k+1}[$ and $k < N$, Eq. (10) takes the general form:*

$$\Pr((\ell, x), [\![\Phi]\!], I) = a_k^{(1)} e^{x b_1} + a_k^{(2)} e^{x b_2} + a_k^{(3)} e^{x b_3} + a_k^{(4)} e^{x b_4} + a_k^{(5)} e^{x b_5} + a_k^{(6)}, \quad (13)$$

where $a_k^{(i)}$ for $i = 1, \cdots, 6$ is constant and $b_1 = E_\ell^{(k)}$, $b_j = \left(b_1 - E_\ell^{(k_{j-1})} \right)$, for $j > 1$ with $k_1 = \lfloor \frac{t + t_k}{\Delta t} \rfloor + 1$, $k_2 = k_1 + 1$, $k_3 = \lfloor \frac{u + t_k}{\Delta t} \rfloor + 1$, $k_4 = k_3 + 1$.

Eq. (13) will be derived for every sub-interval $[t_k^j, t_k^{j+1}[$, $[t_k, t_k^1[$, and $[t_k^4, t_{k+1}[$, $j \in \{1, 2, 3\}$ also for the special case of the *two* intervals obtained from each $[t_k^1, t_k^2[$, $[t_k^2, t_k^3[$, and $[t_k^3, t_k^4[$. Actually for every $\mathcal{I}_{\ell'}^{(i)}$ the interval $[t_k, t_{k+1}[$ will be partitioned into at most eight sub-intervals on which different derivations of Eq. (13) will be obtained.

Example 5. Let us consider an ICTMC $\mathcal{C}$ with the set of locations $\mathbb{L} = \{\ell, \ell'\}$, where ℓ is the initial location of $\mathcal{C}$. There is a transition $\ell \to \ell'$ with rate $R_{\ell,\ell'}(\tau)$ and an exit rate $E_\ell(\tau)$ for location ℓ defined as:

1. $R_{\ell,\ell'}(\tau) = R_{\ell,\ell'}^{(1)}$, $E_\ell(\tau) = E_\ell^{(1)}$ when $\tau \in [0, 3[$ and
2. $R_{\ell,\ell'}(\tau) = R_{\ell,\ell'}^{(2)}$, $E_\ell(\tau) = E_\ell^{(2)}$ when $\tau \in [3, \infty[$,

$R_{\ell,\ell'}^{(1)}$, $R_{\ell,\ell'}^{(2)}$, $E_\ell^{(1)}$ and $E_\ell^{(2)}$ are constant. Here notice that $\Delta t = 3$ and $N = 2$. Assume we have the formula $\langle a \rangle_{\leq p}^{[0, \infty[}$, where $I = [0, \infty[$, $L(\ell') = a$, $a \in AP$ and $p \in [0, 1]$. We want to find an expression for $\Pr((\ell, x), [\![a]\!], [0, \infty[)$. Notice that in Eq. (10) $[\![a]\!] = \{(\ell', [0, \infty[)\}$, $[\![a]\!]_\mathbb{L} = \ell'$, $\theta_{\ell'} = 1$ and $\mathcal{I}_{\ell'}^{(1)} = [0, \infty[$. We consider two intervals $[t_1, t_2[= [0, 3[$ and $[t_2, \infty[= [3, \infty[$. First we take $x \in [0, 3[$ with $t_1^2 = t_1^3 = 0$, $\max \left\{ \inf \mathcal{I}_{\ell'}^{(i)}, t + x \right\} = t + x = x$, $\min \left\{ \sup \mathcal{I}_{\ell'}^{(i)}, u + x \right\} = \infty$. We get that $\Pr((\ell, x), [\![a]\!], [0, \infty[) =$

$$\int_x^\infty R_{\ell,\ell'}(\tau)e^{-\int_x^\tau E_\ell(v)dv}d\tau = \int_x^3 R_{\ell,\ell'}^{(1)}e^{-\int_x^\tau E_\ell^{(1)}dv}d\tau + \int_3^\infty R_{\ell,\ell'}^{(2)}e^{-\int_x^\tau E_\ell^{(2)}dv}d\tau =$$

$$\frac{R_{\ell,\ell'}^{(1)}}{E_\ell^{(1)}}\left(1 - e^{(x-3)E_\ell^{(1)}}\right) + \frac{R_{\ell,\ell'}^{(2)}}{E_\ell^{(2)}}e^{(x-3)E_\ell^{(2)}}.$$

Now we take $x \in [3,\infty[$ with $\max\left\{\inf \mathcal{I}_{\ell'}^{(i)}, t+x\right\} = x$, $\min\left\{\sup \mathcal{I}_{\ell'}^{(i)}, u+x\right\} = \infty$, $t_1^2 = t_1^3 = 3$ and we obtain

$$\Pr((\ell,x),[\![a]\!],[0,\infty[) = \int_x^\infty R_{\ell,\ell'}(\tau)e^{-\int_x^\tau E_\ell(v)dv}d\tau = \int_x^\infty R_{\ell,\ell'}^{(2)}e^{-\int_x^\tau E_\ell^{(2)}dv}d\tau = \frac{R_{\ell,\ell'}^{(2)}}{E_\ell^{(2)}}.$$

Using Theorem 2, we can solve Eq. (9) for every interval $[t_k, t_{k+1}[$ and $x \in [t_k, t_{k+1}[$ by means of:

$$a_k^{(1)}e^{xb_1} + a_k^{(2)}e^{xb_2} + a_k^{(3)}e^{xb_3} + a_k^{(4)}e^{xb_4} + a_k^{(5)}e^{xb_5} + a_k^{(6)} - p = 0. \qquad (14)$$

Like in Eq. (12) the values of $a_k^{(j)}$, $j \in \{1,\dots,6\}$ are formed by the expressions containing $R_{\ell,\ell'}^{(k)}$ and $E_\ell^{(k)}$. The following theorem of Laguerre [17] provides an interesting property about the number of real solutions (zeros) of Eq. (14). For any sequence $a_1, \cdots, a_V$ let $W(a_1, \cdots, a_V)$ denote the number of sign changes in $a_1, \cdots, a_V$ defined by the number of pairs a_{m-i}, a_m $(m \geq 1)$ such that $a_{m-v}a_m < 0$ and $a_{m-v} = 0$ for $v = 1, \cdots, i-1$

Theorem 3 (Laguerre [17]). *Let $f(x) = \sum_{i=1}^V a_i e^{xb_i}$ be an exponential polynomial, where $a_i, b_i \in \mathbb{R}$ and $b_1 < \cdots < b_V$. The number $Z(f)$ of real zeros of f is bounded by $Z(f) \leq W(a_1, \cdots, a_V)$, and $Z(f)$ is of the same parity as $W(a_1, \cdots, a_V)$.*

From Laguerre's theorem it follows that the number of zeros of Eq. (14) is bounded by *five*. Laguerre's theorem does however neither provide a recipe for obtaining the solutions nor the intervals containing the solution. To obtain an algorithmic way to compute the zeros, we transform the exponential polynomial in Eq. (14) to the equivalent polynomial representation $P(z) = \sum_{i=1}^6 c_i z^{n_i}$, where $n_1 > n_2 > n_3 > n_4 > n_5 > n_6$, n_1 - degree of P. Notice that the polynomial $P(z)$ can always be obtained because $b_i \in \mathbb{Q}_{\geqslant 0}$ in Eq. (14) can be represented as $b_i = m_i 10^{d_i}$ where $m_i, d_i \in \mathbb{Z}$. Therefore, transforming all $e^{xm_i 10^{d_i}}$'s to a common d_i and changing e^x to z yields $P(z)$.

Definition 6 (Sturm sequence). *Let $P(z)$ be a square-free (every root has multiplicity one) polynomial and $P'(z)$ denote its derivative. The Sturm sequence of $P(z)$ is the sequence $\{F_i(z)\}$ of polynomials defined by $F_0(z) = P(z)$, $F_1(z) = P'(z)$ and $F_i(z) = -\text{rem}(F_{i-2}(z), F_{i-1}(z))$ for $i > 1$, where $\text{rem}(F_{i-1}(z), F_{i-2}(z))$ is the remainder obtained by dividing $F_{i-2}(z)$ by $F_{i-1}(z)$.*

Notice if $P(z)$ is not square-free one can easily transform it to a square-free polynomial by computing the greatest common divisor of $P(z)$ and $P'(z)$.

Theorem 4 ([12]). *The number of real zeros of $P(z)$ in any interval $]a, b[$ is given by $W(F_0(a), F_1(a), \cdots, F_k(a)) - W(F_0(b), F_1(b), \cdots, F_k(b))$.*

Using the Sturm sequence we get the following algorithm which finds all real zeros $z_1, \cdots, z_m$ $(m \leq 5)$ of $P(z)$ in the interval $]a, b[$ with precision $\epsilon = 2^{-\mu}$.

Algorithm 1. Polynomial solver

Require: polynomial $P(z)$, interval $]a, b[$ and precision $\epsilon = 2^{-\mu}$
Ensure: $z_1, \cdots, z_m$
1: $P'(z) := \mathbf{derivative}(P(z))$
2: $\hat{P}(z) := \mathbf{gcd}(P(z), P'(z))$
3: $\hat{P}'(z) := \mathbf{derivative}\left(\hat{P}(z)\right)$
4: $\{F_0(z), F_1(z), \cdots, F_k(z)\} := \mathbf{Sturm}\left(\hat{P}(z), \hat{P}'(z)\right)$
5: $\{]a_1, b_1[, \cdots,]a_m, b_m[\} := \mathbf{Binarysearch}(\{F_0(z), F_1(z), \cdots, F_k(z)\},]a, b[)$
6: $\{z_1, \cdots, z_m\} := \mathbf{Newton}(\{]a_1, b_1[, \cdots,]a_m, b_m[\}, \epsilon)$
7: **return** $\{z_1, \cdots, z_m\}$

The above algorithm uses several functions. The *gcd* function computes the greatest common divisor of the polynomials $P(z)$ and $P'(z)$. The function *Binarysearch* divides the interval $]a, b[$ into subintervals $]a_i, b_i[$ using the bisection method [9] such that $z_i \in]a_i, b_i[$. Finally, the function *Newton* finds the approximate root z_i of $P(z)$ from $]a_i, b_i[$ with precision $\epsilon = 2^{-\mu}$, $\mu \in \mathbb{N}$ using the Newton method [9]. The first two lines in Alg. 1 are used to obtain a square free polynomial $\hat{P}(z)$.

Lemma 2. *The time complexity of Algorithm 1 is:*

$$\mathcal{O}\left(n_1^2 \log^2 n_1 (\log n_1 + s) + n_1 \log^2 n_1 \left|\log(\Delta t)\right| + n_1 \log \mu\right),$$

where n_1 is the degree of $P(z)$, s is the size in bits of the coefficients of $P(z)$ in the ring of integers, Δt is the time discretization parameter and μ is the number of bits-precision for the Newton method.

Proof. The running time of line 1 and 3 is $\mathcal{O}(n_1)$. The *gcd* (line 2) and the Sturm sequence (line 4) can be computed in $\mathcal{O}(n_1 \log^2 n_1)$ time [1]. Note that the minimal distance between any two zeros [20] of $P(z)$ is bounded from below by $2^{-\frac{n_1+2}{2}\log n_1 - sn_1 + s}$. Therefore, we get that the search-depth of *Binarysearch* is of order $\mathcal{O}(\left|\log(b-a)\right| + n_1 \log n_1 + sn_1)$. As every iteration of *Binarysearch* requires $\mathcal{O}(n_1 \log^2 n_1)$ time and by taking $b - a \leq \Delta t$, we get the running time of line 5 is $\mathcal{O}(n_1^2 \log^2 n_1(\log n_1 + s) + n_1 \log^2 n_1 \left|\log(\Delta t)\right|)$. The Newton method takes $\mathcal{O}(n_1 \log \mu)$ time as there are in total $\mathcal{O}(\log \mu)$ iterations and each iteration requires $\mathcal{O}(n_1)$ time. The final time-complexity is obtained by combining the running-times of all functions in Algorithm 1 and the fact that $m \leq 5$.

Assume that θ (number of intervals of $[\![\Phi]\!]_{\ell'}^{\mathbb{R}}$) in Eq. (10) is bounded by M.

Lemma 3. *For every tuple $(\ell, \mathcal{I})$ of $[\![\, \langle \Phi \rangle^I_{\leq p} \,]\!]$ and interval $[t_k, t_{k+1}[$ such that $\mathcal{I} \subseteq [t_k, t_{k+1}[$, $\mathcal{I}$ is given by a union of at most $21nM + 3$ disjoint intervals where n is the number of locations.*

Proof. We already know that for every $\mathcal{I}_{\ell'}^{(i)}$ the interval $[t_k, t_{k+1}[$ will partitioned into a maximum of eight sub-intervals. From Eq. (10) we get that the total number of sub-intervals is $8nM$. Taking the intersection (due to the double summation in Eq. (10)) of all $8nM$ sub-intervals we obtain a smaller set of $8 + \sum_{j=1}^{nM-1}(8-1) = 7nM + 1$ sub-intervals on which we have to solve Eq. (14). By solving Eq. (14) or its equivalent Eq. (9) we get that for every $\mathcal{I}$, such that $\Pr((\ell, x), [\![\Phi]\!], I) \leq p$ and $x \in \mathcal{I}$, will be formed of maximum three intervals (due to a bound of five for the number of zeros in Eq. (14)). Therefore, for every tuple $(\ell, \mathcal{I})$ of $[\![\, \langle \Phi \rangle^I_{\leq p} \,]\!]$, $\mathcal{I}$ will be a disjoint union of at most $21nM + 3$ intervals.

We complete this section by addressing the time-complexity of the CHML model checking of ICTMCs. Now we take the formula $\Phi = \langle \ldots \langle a \rangle^{I_1}_{\leq p_1} \ldots \rangle^{I_h}_{\leq p_h}$ (without conjuction operator), where h is the nesting level of Φ and $a \in AP$. It is clear that every component $\mathcal{I}$ such that the tuple $(\ell, \mathcal{I})$ is in the set $[\![\Phi]\!]$, will be a disjoint union of $\mathcal{O}\left(21^h n^h\right)$ intervals.

Theorem 5. *The time complexity of model-checking CHML-formula Φ with nesting level h on an ICTMC with a piecewise constant rate matrix (N pieces):*

$$\mathcal{O}\left(21^h n^h N \cdot \left(n_1^2 \log^2 n_1 (\log n_1 + s) + n_1 \log^2 n_1 |\log(\Delta t)| + n_1 \log \mu + h \log n\right)\right),$$

where n is the total number of locations, n_1 is the bound for the polynomial degree, s is the size in bits of the coefficients of polynomials in the ring of integers, Δt is the time discretization parameter and μ is the number of bits-precision for the Newton method.

Proof. The theorem follows from Lemma 2 and 3. Also, we include the time complexity $\mathcal{O}\left(21^h n^h h \log n\right)$ of sorting the bounds of all $\mathcal{O}\left(21^h n^h\right)$ intervals.

5 Concluding Remarks

This paper presented a stochastic variant of Hennessy-Milner logic for inhomogeneous continuous-time Markov chains, and introduced an approximative verification algorithm for the setting in which rates are piecewise constant functions. Moreover, we have shown that the complexity of the model checking algorithm is exponential in the nesting depth of the formula and linear in the size of the ICTMC. Currently CHML is limited to the $\langle \cdot \rangle^I_{\leq p}$ operator. It is possible to add the time-bounded reachability as in CSL by means of transient probability distribution Eq. (6), but without any nesting. Therefore, future work will consist of investigating time-bounded reachability as well as long-run operators for ICTMCs.

References

1. Aho, A.V., Hopcroft, J.E., Ullman, J.D.: Design and Analysis of Computer Algorithms. Addison-Wesley, Reading (1974)
2. Alur, R., Courcoubetis, C., Dill, D.L.: Model-checking for real-time systems. In: Proceedings of the Fifth Annual IEEE Symposium on Logic in Computer Science, pp. 414–425 (1990)
3. Alur, R., Dill, D.L.: A theory of timed automata. Theoretical Computer Science 126(2), 183–235 (1994)
4. Aziz, A., Sanwal, K., Singhal, V., Brayton, R.: Model checking continuous time Markov chains. ACM Trans. on Comp. Logic 1(1), 162–170 (2000)
5. Baier, C., Haverkort, B.R., Hermanns, H., Katoen, J.-P.: Model-checking algorithms for continuous-time Markov chains. IEEE Trans. on Softw. Eng. 29(6), 524–541 (2003)
6. Buchholz, P.: Exact and ordinary lumpability in finite Markov chains. J. of Applied Probability 31, 59–75 (1994)
7. Clark, G., Gilmore, S., Hillston, J., Ribaudo, M.: Exploiting modal logic to express performance measures. In: Haverkort, B.R., Bohnenkamp, H.C., Smith, C.U. (eds.) TOOLS 2000. LNCS, vol. 1786, pp. 247–261. Springer, Heidelberg (2000)
8. Desharnais, J., Panangaden, P.: Continuous stochastic logic characterizes bisimulation of continuous-time Markov processes. J. Log. Algebr. Program 56(1-2), 99–115 (2003)
9. Hamming, R.W.: Numerical Methods for Scientists and Engineers. McGraw-Hill, New York (1973)
10. Han, T., Katoen, J.-P., Mereacre, A.: Compositional modeling and minimization of time-inhomogeneous Markov chains. In: Hybrid Systems: Computation and Control. LNCS, vol. 4981, pp. 244–258. Springer, Heidelberg (2008)
11. Hennessy, M., Milner, R.: Algebraic laws for nondeterminism and concurrency. J. ACM 32(1), 137–161 (1985)
12. Henrici, P., Kenan, W.R.: Applied & *Computational Complex Analysis: Power Series Integration Conformal Mapping Location of Zero.* John Wiley & Sons, Chichester (1988)
13. Hermanns, H.: Interactive Markov Chains: The Quest for Quantified Quality. LNCS, vol. 2428. Springer, Heidelberg (2002)
14. Hillston, J.: A Compositional Approach to Performance Modeling. Cambridge University Press, Cambridge (1996)
15. Katoen, J.-P., Khattri, M., Zapreev, I.S.: A Markov reward model checker. In: Quantitative Evaluation of Systems (QEST), pp. 243–245. IEEE CS Press, Los Alamitos (2005)
16. Kwiatkowska, M.Z., Norman, G., Parker, D.A.: Probabilistic symbolic model checking using PRISM: a hybrid approach. J. on Software Tools for Technology Transfer 6(2), 128–142 (2004)
17. Laguerre, E.: Sur la théorie des équations numériques. J. Math. Pures Appl. 9, 99–146 (1883); (3e série)
18. Larsen, K.G., Skou, A.: Bisimulation through probabilistic testing. Inf. Comput. 94(1), 1–28 (1991)
19. Parma, A., Segala, R.: Logical characterizations of bisimulations for discrete probabilistic systems. In: Seidl, H. (ed.) FOSSACS 2007. LNCS, vol. 4423, pp. 287–301. Springer, Heidelberg (2007)
20. Reif, J.H.: An $\mathcal{O}\left(n\log^3 n\right)$ algorithm for the real root and symmetric tridiagonal eigenvalue problems. In: 34th Annual IEEE Conference on Foundations of Computer Science (FOCS 1993), pp. 626-635 (1993)
21. Segala, R.: Modeling and Verification of Randomized Distributed Real-Time Systems. PhD thesis, MIT, Dept. of Electrical Eng. and Computer Sci. (1995)

Convergence Verification: From Shared Memory to Partially Synchronous Systems⋆

K. Mani Chandy, Sayan Mitra, and Concetta Pilotto

California Institute of Technology
Pasadena, CA 91125
{mani,mitras,cetta}@caltech.edu

Abstract. Verification of partially synchronous distributed systems is difficult because of inherent concurrency and the potentially large state space of the channels. This paper identifies a subclass of such systems for which convergence properties can be verified based on the proof of convergence for the corresponding discrete-time shared state system. The proof technique extends to the class of systems in which an agent's state evolves continuously over time. The proof technique has been formalized in the PVS interface for timed I/O automata and applied to verify convergence of a mobile agent pattern formation algorithm.

1 Introduction

In a partially synchronous distributed system a collection of processes interact by exchanging messages. Sent messages are either lost or delivered within a constant but unknown time bound. This model of communication presents an interesting and realistic middle-ground between the two extremes of completely synchronous (lock-step execution) and asynchronous (unbounded message delay) models. The model is particularly appropriate for a wide class of systems including those employing wireless communication and mobile agents. Algorithms and impossibility results for problems such as mutual exclusion and consensus [10] in this model have been studied extensively (see, for example, Chapters 24-25 of [16] and the bibliographic notes).

Partially synchronous systems are difficult to understand and reason about because of their inherent concurrency and message delays. Formal models, in particular variants of Timed Automata [2,13], have been used to model and analyze such systems, however, there have been few applications of formal verification techniques in checking correctness. Typically these systems present difficulty for model checking because of the huge state space which includes the (potentially large number of) messages in transit. Nevertheless, in a recent paper [11] the time to reach agreement of a consensus protocol has been model checked with UP-PAAL [5] by exploiting a key compositional property of the protocol. Two other partially synchronous distributed algorithms have been model checked in [14].

⋆ The work is funded in part by the Caltech Information Science and Technology Center and AFOSR MURI FA9550-06-1-0303.

F. Cassez and C. Jard (Eds.): FORMATS 2008, LNCS 5215, pp. 218–232, 2008.

In this paper, we study partially synchronous distributed systems (with possibly continuous state spaces), with the aim of verifying *convergence*. Such systems arise in sensor networks, mobile robotics, and unmanned vehicle coordination applications, and convergence properties capture the requirement that the distributed system iteratively computes a certain function. For example, the requirement that a set of mobile robots get arbitrarily close to a particular spatial pattern through communication is a convergence property.

Techniques based on analyzing the Eigen values of state-transition matrices [18,6] that have been used for verifying convergence of completely synchronous systems, cannot be applied in a straightforward way to highly nondeterministic partially synchronous systems. The main contributions of this paper are: (i) a methodology for transforming a shared state distributed system—in which processes can read each other's state instantaneously—to a corresponding partially synchronous system, such that the convergence properties of the original system are preserved in the latter, (ii) a substantial verification case study carried out within the Tempo/PVS framework [4,1] based on the above theory.

We begin in Section 2 by describing *Shared State (SS)* systems—a general discrete-time model for distributed systems in which each process can change its state by reading the states of some subset of other processes. A change of state can be nondeterministic and each process is free to change its state at any point in time, independent of the others. We adapt a theorem from Tsitsiklis [20], to obtain a sufficient condition for proving convergence of such shared state systems. Given a shared state system $\mathcal{A}$, this sufficient condition requires us to find a collection of shrinking invariant sets for $\mathcal{A}$. Next, in Section 3, we present a natural transformation of the given shared state system $\mathcal{A}$ to a partially synchronous system $\mathcal{B}$. The partially synchronous system is modeled as a Timed Input/Output Automaton [13]. In Section 4, we show that if $\mathcal{A}$ converges, then under some assumptions about the structure of the invariant sets of $\mathcal{A}$ and message losses in $\mathcal{B}$, $\mathcal{B}$ also converges. Our proof relies critically on properties of the collection of shrinking invariants that are used in the theorem of [20].

In Section 5, we apply the above theory to verify convergence of a partially synchronous pattern formation protocol for mobile agents. First, we specify the shared state version of the protocol in PVS and verify its convergence using the pre-existing PVS metatheory [17] . We obtain the partially synchronous version of the pattern formation system; this is specified in PVS using the PVS/-TIOA toolset [15] and we show that it satisfies the assumptions required for convergence.

2   Preliminaries

In this section we present a standard discrete-time model for shared state distributed systems and state a well-known theorem for proving convergence.

Standard notations are used for natural numbers $\mathbb{N} = \{0, 1, \ldots, \}$ and the set of reals $\mathbb{R}$. For $N \in \mathbb{N}$, the set $\{0, 1, 2, \ldots, N\}$ is denoted by $[N]$. For a set A,

$A_\perp \triangleq A \cup \{\perp\}$. The set of finite sequences of length N (and infinite sequences) of elements in A is denoted by A^N (and resp., A^ω). For $a \in A^N, i \in [N-1]$, the ith element of a is denoted by a_i. The same notation is used for infinite sequences. For any $x \in A, i \in [N], a \in A^{N+1}$, $[a|a_i := x]$ denotes the (unique) element $a' \in A^{N+1}$ satisfying: for all $j \in [N]$, if $j = i$ then $a'_j = x$ else $a'_j = a_j$.

A *Labeled Transition System* $\mathcal{A}$ is a quadruple $(S, S_0, A, \rightarrow)$ where (a) S is a set of *states*, (b) $S_0 \subseteq S$ is a set of *start states*, (c) A is a set of *actions*, and (d) $\rightarrow \subseteq S \times A \times S$ is a set of *transitions*. For $(s, a, s') \in \rightarrow$ we write $s \xrightarrow{a} s'$. An *execution* α of $\mathcal{A}$ is an (finite or infinite) alternating sequence of states and actions $s_0 a_1 s_1 a_2 \ldots$, such that $s_0 \in S_0$ and for all i, $s_i \xrightarrow{a_{i+1}} s_{i+1}$. An LTS is said to be *action deterministic* if for any $s, s', s'' \in S, a \in A$, if $s \xrightarrow{a} s'$ and $s \xrightarrow{a} s''$ then $s' = s''$. Thus, each action $a \in A$ is associated with a unique *state transition function* $f_a : S \rightarrow S$, such that if $s \xrightarrow{a} s'$ then $s' = f_a(s)$.

Convergence. In order to define convergence of an execution to a state $s^* \in S$ we have to introduce some notion of "closeness" of states to s^*. One straightforward way to do this, and the approach we take in presenting this paper, is to assume that S is equipped with a metric d. An infinite execution α *converges* to s^* with respect to d, if for every $\epsilon > 0$, there is a suffix of α such that for every state s in this suffix $d(s, s^*) \leq \epsilon$. Convergence to a subset $S^* \subseteq S$ is defined by extending the definition of d in the obvious way. We remark that for defining convergence to s^* or to a subset S^* of S, it is not necessary for S to be a metric space, and it suffices to have a topological structure around s^* (or S^*). The results presented in this paper carry over to this more general setting.

For verifying convergence, we restrict our attention to executions in which certain classes of actions occur infinitely often. This motivates the notion of fair executions. For a set of actions A, a *fairness condition* $\mathcal{F}$ is a finite collection $\{F_i\}_{i=1}^n$, $n \in \mathbb{N}$, where each F_i is a nonempty subset of A. An infinite sequence of actions $a \in A^\omega$ to be $\mathcal{F}$-*fair* iff $\forall F \in \mathcal{F}, n \in \mathbb{N}, \exists m \in \mathbb{N}, m > n$, such that $a_m \in F$. An infinite execution $\alpha = s_0, a_0, s_1, a_1, \ldots$ is $\mathcal{F}$-*fair* exactly when the corresponding sequence of actions $a_0, a_1, \ldots$ is $\mathcal{F}$-fair. Under a given fairness condition $\mathcal{F}$, an LTS $\mathcal{A}$ is said to *converge* to s^* if every $\mathcal{F}$-fair execution converges to s^*.

Usually a convergence proof is carried out by showing the existence of a Lyapunov-like function that is nonnegative and decreases along all executions of the system. The following theorem from [20], translated to our setting, provides a general sufficient condition for proving convergence in terms of a collection of invariant sets (sublevel sets of a Lyapunov function).

Theorem 1. *Consider an LTS $\mathcal{A}$ and a fairness condition $\mathcal{F}$ for $\mathcal{A}$. Suppose there exists a well ordered set $(T, <)$ with smallest element 0 and a collection of sets $\{P_k \subseteq S | k \in T\}$ satisfying:*

C1. (Monotonicity) $\forall\ k, l \in T, k > l \Rightarrow P_k \subsetneq P_l$.
C2. (Granularity) $\forall\ \epsilon > 0, \exists\ k \in T$, such that $\forall s \in P_k, d(s, s^*) \leq \epsilon$.
C3. (Initial) $S_0 \subseteq P_0$.
C4. (Invariance) $\forall\ s, s' \in S, a \in A, k \in T$ if $s \xrightarrow{a} s'$ and $s \in P_k$ then $s' \in P_k$.

C5. (Progress) $\forall \, k \in T$, *if* $P_k \neq \{s^*\}$ *then* $\exists \, F \in \mathcal{F}$, *such that* $\forall \, a \in F$, $\forall \, s \in P_k, s' \in$
S, $s \xrightarrow{a} s' \Rightarrow s' \in P_l$, *for some* $l > k$.

Then all $\mathcal{F}$-fair executions of $\mathcal{A}$ converge to s^* with respect to d.

It turns out that under some weak assumptions about the stability of $\mathcal{A}$, these conditions are also necessary for convergence of $\mathcal{A}$. C1 requires that the sequence of predicates is monotonically stronger. C2 states that for every $\epsilon > 0$ there exists a a set P_k that is contained in the ϵ-ball around s^*. C4 requires that the P_k's are invariant under the transitions of $\mathcal{A}$. Finally, C5 requires that for any state s in P_k (other than s^*) there exists a fair set F in $\mathcal{F}$, such that any action in F takes the system to a state P_l, where $l > k$.

Shared State Systems. A distributed system consists of a finite collection of LTSs executing and communicating in parallel. In a shared state (distributed) system a process can read but not modify the states of other asynchronous processes. Formally, a *shared state distributed system* with $N + 1$ processes is an action deterministic LTS $(S, S_0, A, \rightarrow)$ with the following additional structure:

(a) $S \triangleq X^{N+1}$, where X is a set of *process states*. For each $s \in S, i \in [N]$, s_i is called the state of the ith process.
(b) $S_0 = \{x_0\}$, where $x_0 \in X^{N+1}$ is the vector of initial SS process states,
(c) The set of actions A is partitioned into disjoint sets $\{A_i\}_{i \in [N]}$ such that for all $s, s' \in S, a \in A_i$, if $s \xrightarrow{a} s'$ then $\forall \, j \in [N] \setminus \{i\}$, $s_j = s'_j$.

An action $a \in A_i$ corresponds to process i reading the current states of a subset of other agents and updating its own state. For each action $a \in A_i$ we denote the state transition function f_a restricted to the ith component (mapping X^{N+1} to X) by f_{ia}. That is, if $s \xrightarrow{a} s'$ then $s' = [s|s_i = f_{ia}(s)]$. Function f_{ia} is a function of the states of some subset of processes and is independent of the states of other processes; this is captured by the *dependency function* $D : A \rightarrow 2^{[N]}$ as follows: for any pair of states $s, u \in S$, $i \in [N]$, and any action $a \in A$, if for all $j \in D(a)$, $s_j = u_j$ then the $f_{ia}(s) = f_{ia}(u)$. That is, the post-state of action a depends on the jth state component of the pre-state only if $j \in D(a)$. We say that j is a *neighbor* of i exactly when there exists $a \in A_i$ such that j is in $D(a)$.

3   Partially Synchronous Systems

In this section, we present the model for partially synchronous distributed systems and describe a natural translation of shared state systems to this model. In a partially synchronous distributed system a fixed set of processes communicate by sending messages over a broadcast channel. A message broadcast by process i at some time t is delivered to some (possibly empty) subset of processes; all (if any) deliveries are within $t + b$, where b is a parameter of the broadcast channel.

Timed I/O Automata. We formally model partially synchronous distributed systems as Timed Input/Output Automata (TIOA) [13]. A Timed I/O Automaton is a non-deterministic state transition system in which the states may change either (a) instantaneously through a transition, or (b) continuously over an interval of time following a *trajectory*. We give the essential definitions for the TIOA framework and refer the reader to [13] for the details. A variable structure is used to specify the states of a TIOA. Let V be a set of variables. Each variable $v \in V$ is associated with a type which defines the set of values v can take. The set of valuations of V is denoted by $val(V)$. A *trajectory* for a set of variables V models continuous evolution of values of the variables. Formally, a trajectory τ maps a left-closed interval of $\mathbb{R}_{\geq 0}$ with left endpoint 0 to $val(V)$. The domain τ is denoted by $\tau.dom$. A trajectory is *closed* if $\tau.dom = [0,t]$ for some $t \in \mathbb{R}_{\geq 0}$, in which case we define $\tau.\mathsf{ltime} \triangleq t$ and $\tau.\mathsf{lstate} \triangleq \tau(t)$.

A TIOA $\mathcal{B} = (V, S, S_0, A, \mathcal{D}, \mathcal{T})$ consists of (a) A set V of *variables*. (b) A set $S \subseteq val(V)$ of *states*. (c) A set $S_0 \subseteq S$ of *start states*. (d) A set A of *actions* partitioned into *input, output* and *internal* actions I, O, and H, (e) A set $\mathcal{D} \subseteq S \times A \times S$ of *discrete transitions*. An action $a \in A$ is said to be *enabled* at s iff $(s, a, s') \in \mathcal{D}$. (f) A set $\mathcal{T}$ of trajectories for V that is closed[1] under prefix, suffix and concatenation. In addition, for every $\mathbf{s} \in S$, $\mathcal{A}$ must satisfy the following two nonblocking conditions: (i) $\forall a \in I$, a is enabled at $\mathbf{s}$, and (ii) $\exists \tau \in \mathcal{T}$, such that $\tau(0) = \mathbf{s}$ and either $\tau.dom = [0, \infty)$ or τ is closed and $\exists a \in O \cup H$ enabled at $\tau.\mathsf{ltime}$.

An *execution fragment* of $\mathcal{B}$ is a finite or infinite alternating sequence of trajectories and actions $\tau_0 a_1 \tau_1 a_2 \ldots$, such that for all i in the sequence, $\tau_i.\mathsf{lstate} \overset{a_{i+1}}{\to} \tau_{i+1}(0)$. We define the first state of α, to be $\alpha.\mathsf{fstate} \triangleq \tau_0(0)$, and for a closed α, its last state to be $\alpha.\mathsf{lstate} \triangleq \tau_n.\mathsf{lstate}$, where τ_n is the last trajectory in α, and $\alpha.\mathsf{ltime} \triangleq \sum_i \tau_i.\mathsf{ltime}$. An execution fragment α is *admissible* if $\alpha.\mathsf{ltime} = \infty$. An execution fragment is an *execution* if $\tau_0(0) \in S_0$.

Given a shared state system $\mathcal{A} = (S, x_0, A, \to)$ for processes indexed by $[N]$ we define a natural translation of $\mathcal{A}$ to the partially synchronous setting. The partially synchronous system corresponding to a given shared state system $\mathcal{A}$ is a TIOA $\mathcal{B}$ obtained by composing a set of Process$_i$ TIOAs—one for each $i \in [N]$—and an TIOA LBCast which models the communication channels.

Generic process. First, we specify a TIOA Process$_i$ for each participating process $i \in [N]$. The code in Figure 1 specifies this automaton using the TIOA Language [12]. The specification is parameterized by (a) an uninterpreted type X, (b) a element x_{0i} of X representing the initial state of process i, (c) a collection of functions $g_{ia} : X_\perp^{N+1} \to X$, for $i \in [N], a \in A_i$ representing the actions of i, and (d) nonnegative real-valued parameters l and w dealing with timing. In order to obtain the process corresponding to $\mathcal{A}$, these parameters are instantiated as follows: (i) the type X equals the process state set of $\mathcal{A}$, (ii) x_{0i} is set

---

[1] See Sections 3-4 of [13] for formal definitions of the trajectory closure properties and the statements of the enabling conditions.

to the ith component of the start state of $\mathcal{A}$, (iii) for each $a \in A_i$, and for any $x : X, y : \mathtt{Array}[[N] \to X_\perp]$

$$g_{ia}(x, y) \triangleq \begin{cases} f_{ia}([y|y_i := x]) & \text{if } \forall j \in D(f_{ia}), y[j] \neq \perp \\ x & \text{otherwise.} \end{cases}$$

Process$_i$ has the following state **variables**: (a) x_i is a discrete variable of type X and is initialized to x_{0i} (b) y_i records state information about other processes received through messages. It is an array of type $X_\perp$ indexed by $[N]$ and initialized to $\perp$; $y_i[j]$ is the last message (if any) that i received from j (c) now_i, a continuous variable of type $\mathbb{R}_{\geq 0}$ and initialized to 0, models real time, and (d) $earliest_i$, a discrete variable of type $\mathbb{R}_{\geq 0}$ and initialized to l, is the earliest time for the next broadcast by process i. The initial state is defined by the initial valuations of the variables.

The **transitions** for send$_i$ and receive$_{ij}$ actions are specified in **precondition-effect** style in lines 15–23. (a) receive$_{ij}(m)$ models the delivery of message m to Process$_i$ from Process$_j$ over the broadcast channel. When this action occurs, the jth component of the history variable y_i is updated to m, and the state variable x_i is updated according to a nondeterministically chosen function g_{ia}. (b) A send$_i(m)$ action models the broadcasting of message m. This action *can* occur whenever $x_i = m$ and now exceeds $earliest_i$. When this action does occur, $earliest_i$ is advanced to $now_i + l$.

Finally, the state of Process$_i$ changes over an interval of time according to the **trajectories** specified in lines 11–13. Along any trajectory, x_i and $earliest_i$ remain constant and now_i increases monotonically at the same rate as real-time. The **stop when** condition states that no trajectory continues beyond the time point at which now_i equals $earliest + w$. This forces the trajectory to stop, which along with condition (ii) in the definition of TIOA forces a send to occur.

signature		1			14
output send$_i(m : X)$			**transitions**		
input receive$_{ij}(m : X)$, **where** $j \in [N]$		3	**input** receive$_{ij}(m)$		16
			eff $y_i[j] := m$;		
variables		5	**let** $a :=$ **choose** A_i		18
$x_i : X := x_{0i}$;			$x_i := g_{ia}(x, y)$		
$y_i : \mathtt{Array}[[N] \to X_\perp]$		7			20
initially $\forall j \in [N], y[j] := \perp$			**output** send$_i(m)$		
$earliest_i : \mathbb{R}_{\geq 0} := l; now_i : \mathbb{R}_{\geq 0} := 0$		9	**pre** $m = x_i \wedge now_i \geq earliest_i$		22
			eff $earliest_i := now_i + l$		
trajectories		11			
evolve $d(now_i) = 1$					
stop when $now_i \geq earliest_i + w$		13			

Fig. 1. Process$_i$ TIOA with parameters $X, x_0, A_i, \{g_{ia}\}_{a \in A_i}, l, w : \mathbb{R}_{\geq 0}$

Channel. The LBCast automaton of Figure 2 specifies the local broadcast-based communication layer of the system. For any $b \in \mathbb{R}_{\geq 0}$, LBCast($b$) ensures that any message sent by $\mathsf{Process}_i$ at time t is received by some subset of other processes within $[t, t+b]$.

A *timed message* is a pair consisting of a message of type X and a deadline of type $\mathbb{R}_{\geq 0}$. For a timed message p, the message and the deadline are denoted by $p.msg$ and $p.dl$. LBCast has two state variables: (a) *buffer* is a two dimensional array of sets of timed messages; it is initialized to be empty. $buffer[i, j]$ is the set of messages (time stamped with a deadline) sent by i to j, that are in transit. (b) *now* is a continuous variable of type $\mathbb{R}_{\geq 0}$ and it models real time.

The state of LBCast changes through the occurrence of send, receive, and drop actions as follows: (a) $\mathsf{receive}_{ij}(m)$ models the delivery of message m sent by $\mathsf{Process}_j$ to $\mathsf{Process}_i$. This action can occur when there exists $dl \in \mathbb{R}_{\geq 0}$ (actually $\geq now$) such that the timed message $\langle m, dl \rangle$ is in $buffer[j, i]$. As a result of this action *some* message m (with deadline $dl' \geq now$) is removed from $buffer[j, i]$. (b) $\mathsf{send}_i(m)$ models the broadcasting of message m by $\mathsf{Process}_i$. The effect of this action is that the timed message $\langle m, now + b \rangle$ is added to $buffer[i, j]$ for every $j \in \mathcal{I}$. (c) $\mathsf{drop}_{ij}(m)$ models the loss of message m in transit from i to j. This action is enabled as long as the message m is in transit, and the effect is that the message is removed from $buffer[i, j]$.

Along any trajectory of LBCast (see lines 26–29), *buffer* remains constant and *now* increases monotonically at the same rate as real-time. The **stop when** condition enforces the delivery deadline of non-dropped messages by forcing the receive actions to occur.

```
signature                                    1       buffer[j, i] := buffer[j, i] \ ⟨m, dl'⟩;
  input send_i(m : X), where i ∈ [N]                                                                16
  output receive_ij(m : X), where i, j ∈ [N]  3       input send_i(m)
  internal drop_ij(m : X, dl : ℝ≥0)                   eff for j ∈ [N]  do                           18
                                              5         buffer[i, j] := buffer[i, j] ∪ ⟨m, now + b⟩
variables                                             od                                            20
  buffer : Array[i, j : [N], Set[X × ℝ≥0]] := {}  7
  now : ℝ≥0 := 0                                      internal drop_ij(m, dl)                        22
                                              9         pre ⟨m, dl⟩ ∈ buffer[i, j] ∧ dl ≥ now
transitions                                           eff buffer[i, j] := buffer[i, j] \ ⟨m, dl⟩    24
  output receive_ij(m)                       11
    pre ∃ dl : ℝ≥0, ⟨m, dl⟩ ∈ buffer[j, i]          trajectories                                    26
    eff dl' := choose                         13       evolve d(now) = 1
      {dl ∈ ℝ≥0 | ⟨m, dl⟩ ∈ buffer[j, i]}            stop when ∃ m : X, dl ∈ ℝ≥0, i, j : I,         28
                                                        ⟨m, dl⟩ ∈ buffer[i, j] ∧  dl = now
```

Fig. 2. $\mathsf{LBCast}_{i,j}$ TIOA with parameter $X, b : \mathbb{R}_{\geq 0}$

Complete system. The partially synchronous system corresponding to $\mathcal{A}$ is the composed TIOA $\mathcal{B} = \|_{i \in [N]} \mathsf{Process}_i \| \mathsf{LBCast}$. Let the set of states of $\mathcal{B}$ be $\mathcal{S}$. The values of the real-time related variables such as now_i's *earliest*$_i$, diverge along the admissible executions of $\mathcal{B}$. In studying convergence of $\mathcal{B}$ we are really interested in the behavior of the x_i and the y_i variables and the messages in *buffer* without their time stamps. Hence, we define a projection function *untime*: for any state $s \in \mathcal{S}$, *untime*(s) is an object that is identical to s except that the components corresponding to $now, now_i, earliest_i$ are removed, every timed message p is replaced by $p.msg$, and all $\perp$ values are removed from the history variables y_i's. We denote this projected state space of B by S_B and its elements by $\mathbf{s}, \mathbf{u}$. Each $\mathbf{s} \in S_B$ corresponds to a particular valuation for each non-time-related state variable of B. These variable valuations are denoted by the usual $(.)$ notation. For example, the valuations of the variables x_i and $buffer$ at a state $\mathbf{s}$ are denoted by $\mathbf{s}.x_i$ and $\mathbf{s}.buffer$. We define a metric on S_B based on the metric d on S_A as follows:

$$U(\mathbf{s}) \triangleq \Pi_{i=0}^{N} \left\{ \{\mathbf{s}.x_i\} \cup_{j \in [N]} \{\mathbf{s}.y_j[i] \mid \mathbf{s}.y_j[i] \neq \perp\} \cup_{j \in [N]} \mathbf{s}.buffer[i,j] \right\}$$

$$d_B(\mathbf{s}_1, \mathbf{s}_2) \triangleq \max_{r_1 \in U(\mathbf{s}_1), r_2 \in U(\mathbf{s}_2)} d(r_1, r_2)$$

An admissible execution α is said to converge to a untimed state $\mathbf{s}^* \in S_B$ if $untime(\alpha(t)) \rightarrow \mathbf{s}^*$ with respect to the metric d_B, as $t \rightarrow \infty$[2]. Automaton B converges to $\mathbf{s}^*$ if all its admissible executions converge.

4   Verification of the Partially Synchronous Systems

Throughout this section we assume that A is a shared state system and B is the corresponding partially synchronous system obtained using the translation scheme of the previous section. We denote the set of states of A by S_A and the individual states by s, u, etc. We assume that A converges to a state $s^* \in S_A$ with respect to the metric d and a fairness condition $\mathcal{F}$. We assume that convergence of A is proved using Theorem 1. Therefore, we know that there exists a well ordered set $(T, <)$ with a smallest element 0 and a collection of sets $\{P_k \subseteq S \mid k \in T\}$ satisfying the conditions C1-5.

We define the following relation $\mathcal{R} \subseteq S_B \times S_A$:

$$\mathcal{R}(\mathbf{s}, s) \triangleq (\forall i \in [N], s_i = \mathbf{s}.x_i \vee \exists j \in [N], s_i \in \mathbf{s}.buffer[i,j] \cup \mathbf{s}.y_j[i])$$

For each i, the i-th component of s can be one of the following: (i) the state of the i-th process in $\mathbf{s}$, (ii) a message in transit from i to some j in $\mathbf{s}.buffer$, (iii) the state of the history variable $\mathbf{s}.y_j[i]$ for some other process j. If $\mathcal{R}(\mathbf{s}, s)$ then we say that s is an *asynchronous view* of $\mathbf{s}$. Given $\mathbf{s} \in S_B$, we define $\mathcal{R}(\mathbf{s}) \triangleq \{s \in S_A \mid \mathcal{R}(\mathbf{s}, s)\}$. We define $\mathbf{s}^* \triangleq \{\mathbf{s} \in S_B \mid \forall s \in \mathcal{R}(\mathbf{s}) \;\; s = s^*\}$.

In the remainder of this section we shall prove that B converges to $\mathbf{s}^*$ with respect to the metric d_B. We make the following two assumptions about the structure of the P_k's and message losses. For any specific problem these assumptions become proof obligations which must be discharged.

Assumption 1. *Consider any two states $s, u \in S$, a process index $i \in [N]$, and an action $a \in A_i$. For any $k, l \in T$, $l > k$, if $P_k(s)$ and $P_k(u)$ hold, then:*

B1. $P_k([s|s_i := f_{ia}(s)]) \Rightarrow P_k([u|u_i := f_{ia}(s)])$, *and*
B2. $P_l([s|s_i := f_{ia}(s)]) \Rightarrow P_l([u|u_i := f_{ia}(s)])$.

---

[2] $\alpha(t) \triangleq \alpha'.\mathsf{lstate}$, where α' is the longest prefix of α with $\alpha'.\mathsf{ltime} = t$.

Assumption 2. *For any $i, j \in [N]$ with i a neighbor of j, along any admissible execution α of $\mathcal{B}$, for any time t, there exists $\zeta > l + w + b$ such that j receives at least one message sent after time t from i within time $t + \zeta$.*

All processes execute send messages within w time. Hence, every every agent i receives at least one message from every neighbor in the interval $[t, t + \zeta]$. Next, we define a sequence $Q_k, k = 0, 1, 2, \ldots$ of predicates on states of $S_{\mathcal{B}}$ based on the predicates P_k on $S_{\mathcal{A}}$. Informally, Q_k holds for a state $\mathbf{s}$ exactly when all asynchronous view of $\mathbf{s}$ satisfy P_k.

$$Q_k(\mathbf{s}) \stackrel{\Delta}{=} (\forall s \in S_{\mathcal{A}}, \mathcal{R}(\mathbf{s}, s) \Rightarrow P_k(s)).$$

We now show that the conditions C1-5 are satisfied by the collection of sets Q_k. The proof for the next lemma uses C1-3 property of $\{P_k\}$ and appears in the full version of the paper which is available online.

Lemma 1. *The collection $\{Q_k\}$ satisfies C1-3.*

Lemma 2. $\forall k \in T, \mathbf{s}, \mathbf{s}' \in S_{\mathcal{B}}, a \in A_{\mathcal{B}}$, *if* $\mathbf{s} \stackrel{a}{\to} \mathbf{s}'$ *and* $Q_k(\mathbf{s})$ *then* $Q_k(\mathbf{s}')$.

Proof. Assuming $Q_k(\mathbf{s})$ holds for some $k \in T$, we show that $Q_k(\mathbf{s}')$ also holds. The proof is straightforward for $a = \mathsf{drop}$, $a = \mathsf{send}$, and for a closed trajectory of $\mathcal{B}$. Consider the case where $a = \mathsf{receive}_{ij}(m)$, $i, j \in [N]$ and $m \in X$. In order to show that $Q_k(\mathbf{s}')$, we consider any $u \in S_{\mathcal{A}}$ and assume that $\mathcal{R}(\mathbf{s}', u)$ holds. Then, it suffices to deduce $P_k(u)$.

Let the state of process i in the pre-state $\mathbf{s} \in S_{\mathcal{B}}$ be (x, y). Then its post-state is (x', y), where $x' = f_{ia}([y|y_i := x])$. We define the corresponding pre-state $s \in S_{\mathcal{A}}$ as $[y|y_i := x]$. From the definition of $\mathcal{R}$, it is follows that $\mathcal{R}(\mathbf{s}, s)$ holds. From the definition of Q and C4 we have these two implications:

$$Q_k(\mathbf{s}) \wedge \mathcal{R}(\mathbf{s}, s) \Rightarrow P_k(s) \qquad P_k(s) \Rightarrow P_k([s|s_i := f_{ia}(s)])$$

Assume that u is an asynchronous view of $\mathbf{s}'$. Then u is an asynchronous view of $\mathbf{s}$ with u_i either unchanged, or replaced by $f_{ia}(s)$. Hence:

$$\mathcal{R}(\mathbf{s}', u) \Rightarrow \mathcal{R}(\mathbf{s}, u) \vee (\exists v : \mathcal{R}(\mathbf{s}, v) \wedge (u = [v|v_i := f_{ia}(s)]))$$
$$Q_k(\mathbf{s}) \wedge \mathcal{R}(\mathbf{s}', u) \Rightarrow (Q_k(\mathbf{s}) \wedge \mathcal{R}(\mathbf{s}, u)) \vee (\exists v : Q_k(\mathbf{s}) \wedge \mathcal{R}(\mathbf{s}, v) \wedge (u = [v|v_i := f_{ia}(s)]))$$
$$\Rightarrow P_k(u) \vee (\exists v : P_k(v) \wedge (u = [v|v_i := f_{ia}(s)])) \quad \text{[From Q definition]}$$
$$\Rightarrow P_k(u) \quad \text{[from $B1$, and $P_k(s)$]}.$$

Lemma 3. *For all $k \in T$, if $P_k \neq \{s^*\}$ and $\mathbf{s} \in Q_k$ then there exists $l > k$ and a closed execution fragment α of $\mathcal{B}$ such that*

$$(untime(\alpha.\mathsf{fstate}) = \mathbf{s}) \wedge (untime(\alpha.\mathsf{lstate}) \in Q_l) \wedge (\alpha.\mathsf{ltime} \leq 2 \cdot \zeta)$$

Proof. Let us fix $k \in T$. By C5, there exists $l \in T, l > k$ and a transition function f_{ia} of $\mathcal{A}$ such that for all $s \in S_{\mathcal{A}}$ $P_k(s) \Rightarrow s' = [s \mid s_i := f_{ia}(s)] \in P_l$. We define a new relation $R' \subseteq S_{\mathcal{B}} \times S_{\mathcal{A}}$ as follows:

$$\mathcal{R}'(\mathbf{s}, s) \stackrel{\Delta}{=} \exists u, v \in S_{\mathcal{A}} : \mathcal{R}(\mathbf{s}, u) \wedge \mathcal{R}(\mathbf{s}, v) \wedge s = [v|v_i := f_{ia}(u)]$$

Thus $\mathcal{R}'(\mathbf{s}, s)$ holds exactly when s is an asynchronous view v of $\mathbf{s}$ except that the i-th agent's state is $f_{ia}(u)$ where u is itself an asynchronous view of $\mathbf{s}$. We define $Q'_k(\mathbf{s}) \triangleq (\forall u \in S_{\mathcal{A}} : \mathcal{R}'(\mathbf{s}, u) \Rightarrow P_l(u))$. If $\mathbf{s} \in Q_k \cap Q'_k$, then for all i, $\mathbf{s}.x_i$ satisfies P_l and any asynchronous view of $\mathbf{s}$ satisfies P_k.

Claim. $Q_k \cap Q'_k$ is invariant under the transitions and trajectories of $\mathcal{B}$.
Proof of Claim. The proof is straightforward for an actions drop, send and trajectories of $\mathcal{B}$. Consider an action $a = \text{receive}_{j,k}(m)$. We consider two cases $i = j$ and $i \neq j$. Consider the case when $i = j$. All $\mathbf{s}.x$ satisfies P_l. From C4, P_l is invariant under transitions of $\mathcal{A}$. Hence all $\mathbf{s}'.x$ satisfy P_{k+1}. Therefore $\mathbf{s}' \in Q'_k$. Consider the case $j \neq i$. Applying Lemma 2, $\mathbf{s}' \in Q_k$ holds. Hence, for all $s' \in \mathcal{R}(s')$ we have that $s' \in P_k(s')$ and by B2, $\mathbf{s}' \in Q'_k$.

We define α as the concatenation of two fragments α_1 and α_2. We show that

1. $\exists$ a closed execution fragment α_1 with $untime(\alpha_1.\text{fstate}) \in Q_k$ and $\alpha_1.\text{ltime} \geq \zeta$ such that $untime(\alpha_1.\text{lstate}) \in Q_k \cap Q'_k$.
2. $\forall$ closed execution fragments α_2 with $untime(\alpha_2.\text{fstate}) \in Q'_k \cap Q_k$ and $\alpha_2.\text{ltime} \geq \zeta$, $untime(\alpha_2.\text{lstate}) \in Q_l$.

Part 1. By Assumption 2, i receives at least one message from all its neighbors by time $t + \zeta$. Denote by $\mathbf{s}' = untime(\alpha_1.lstate)$ and assume that $\mathbf{s}'$ is obtained by executing g_{ia}. By Lemma 2, $\mathbf{s}' \in Q_k$. Denote by $s' \in S_{\mathcal{A}}$ any state of $\mathcal{A}$ such that $\mathcal{R}'(\mathbf{s}', s')$. It suffices to show that $s' \in P_l$. By definition of $\mathcal{R}'$, there exists u, v such that $\mathcal{R}(\mathbf{s}', u) \wedge \mathcal{R}(\mathbf{s}', v) \wedge s' = [v \mid v_i := f_{ia}(u)]$. Since $Q_k(\mathbf{s}')$ holds, it follows that $u \in P_k$ and $v \in P_k$. By C5, $P_k(u) \Rightarrow P_l([u \mid u_i := f_{ia}(u)])$. Hence, by B2, $s' \in P_l$ with $s' = [v \mid v_i := f_{ia}(u)])$.

Part 2. Fix a closed execution fragment α_2 with start state $untime(\alpha_2.\text{fstate}) \in Q'_k \cap Q_k$. Assume that α_2 ends at time $\alpha_2.\text{ltime} \geq \zeta$. We denote $untime(\alpha_2.\text{lstate})$ by $\mathbf{s}'$. We will show that $\mathbf{s}' \in Q_{k+1}$ holds. By Claim 1, $\mathbf{s}' \in Q'_k$. Let s' be any state in $\mathcal{R}(\mathbf{s}')$. It suffices to show that $s' \in P_l$ holds. By Assumption 2 (noting that $\zeta \geq b$), for all j, k $\mathbf{s}'.x$, $\mathbf{s}'.y_j[k]$, and $\mathbf{s}'.buffer[j, k]$ contain information sent at or after time 0 and this information satisfies P_l. This is because starting from time 0 the x variables satisfy P_l and by time ζ the old messages and local copies are updated with values that satisfy P_l. Hence, any asynchronous view of $\mathbf{s}'$ satisfies P_l. Hence, $P_l(s')$ holds.

Theorem 2. *If $\mathcal{A}$ converges to s^* with respect to d, then under Assumptions B1-2 and 2, $\mathcal{B}$ converges to $\mathbf{s}^*$.*

Proof. It is straightforward to see that $\mathcal{B}$ is indeed a labeled transition system with set of states $\mathcal{S}$, start states defined by the start states of $\mathcal{A}$, set of actions $A_{\mathcal{B}} \cup T_{\mathcal{B}}$, and transitions $(s, a, s') \in \to$ if and only if (i) $(s, a, s') \in \mathcal{D}_{\mathcal{B}}$ or (ii) $\exists \tau \in T_{\mathcal{B}}$, with $\tau(0) = s$ and $\tau.\text{lstate} = s'$. Therefore, Theorem 1's sufficient conditions for convergence are applicable to $\mathcal{B}$ with fairness conditions replaced by time bounded progress guarantees. From Assumptions B1-2 and convergence of $\mathcal{A}$ we obtain a collection $\{Q_k\}$ of invariant sets of $\mathcal{B}$ which satisfy conditions 1-4. Assumption 2 and Lemma 3 imply that $\mathcal{B}$ makes progress.

5   Verifying Convergence of a Pattern Formation Protocol

We verify a class of pattern formation protocols for mobile agents. Starting from arbitrary locations in a space, the goal of such a protocol is to make the agents converge to some predefined spatial pattern. Distributed pattern formation protocols have been studied extensively, but typically under the assumption that the agents can communicate synchronously (see, for example [9,6,8,18]). In this paper, we present the verification of a simple one-dimensional algorithm. Several generalizations of this protocol have been presented in [7].

The shared state protocol is modeled as a LTS $\mathcal{A} = (S, S_0, A, \rightarrow)$, where (a) $S = \mathbb{R}^{N+1}$, (b) $S_0 \in \mathbb{R}^{N+1}$ (c) $A = \cup_{i \in [N]} A_i$, where $A_i \subseteq \{(i, \mathsf{avg}_{l,r}) \mid l < i < r\}$. (d) $f_{i\ \mathsf{avg}_{l,r}} : \mathbb{R}^{N+1} \rightarrow \mathbb{R}$ such that for $s \in S$, $f_{i\ \mathsf{avg}_{l,r}}(s) = \frac{r-i}{r-l}s_l + \frac{i-l}{r-l}s_r$. Note that for every $l < i$ and $r > i$, the object $(i, \mathsf{avg}_{l,r})$ may not be an action for agent i; A_i is some subset of such actions. Action $(i, \mathsf{avg}_{l,r}) \in A_i$ changes the state of the ith agent according to the function $f_{i,\mathsf{avg}_{l,r}}$. This function depends on the states of agents l and r, that is $D((i, \mathsf{avg}_{l,r})) = \{l, r\}$. We adopt the notations from Section 2 to $\mathcal{A}$. For instance, for a state $s \in S$, we denote the ith component as s_i. It is easy to check that $\mathcal{A}$ is a shared state system. At a particular state s of $\mathcal{A}$, we say that agent i is *located* at s_i. Throughout this section, mid denotes the value $\frac{N}{2}$.

We define a state $s^* \in S$ as follows: $\forall i \in [N]$, $s_i^* \triangleq s_{00}\frac{N-i}{N} + s_{0N}\frac{i}{N}$. This specifies a particular pattern where agents are located, in order, at equidistant points on a straight with extremes s_{00} and s_{0N}. We set $\mathcal{F} = \{A_i\}_{i \in [N]}$. It turns out that $\mathcal{F}$-fair executions of $\mathcal{A}$ converges to the state s^* with respect to the Euclidean metric on S. In the remainder of this section, we shall first verify this property and show how this result carries over to the convergence of the partially synchronous version of $\mathcal{A}$.

5.1   Convergence of Shared State Protocol

First, we introduce the deviation profile of a state of $\mathcal{A}$ which in turn will be used to define a sequence of predicates which satisfy C1-5. For any $x \in \mathbb{R}$ and $i \in [N]$, we define $e_i(x) \triangleq |x - s_i^*|$. Given $s \in S_{\mathcal{A}}$, $i \in [N]$, $m \in \mathbb{N}$, we define the following two symmetric predicates:

$$L_{m,j}(s) \triangleq \forall l \leq j \quad e_l(s_l) \leq C \cdot \beta^m \left(1 - \frac{1}{2^l}\right)$$

$$R_{m,j}(s) \triangleq \forall r \geq N - j \quad e_r(s_r) \leq C \cdot \beta^m \left(1 - \frac{1}{2^{N-r}}\right)$$

where $\beta \triangleq \left(1 - \frac{1}{2^N}\right)$, and C is chosen such that the $L_{0,\frac{N}{2}}$ and $R_{0,\frac{N}{2}}$ predicates are satisfied at the start state s_0. For any state s, if $L_{m,j}(s)$ holds then the deviations of the agent locations at s from those at s^* is upper-bounded by the deviation

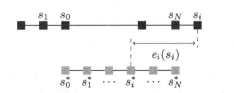

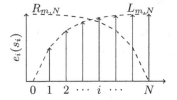

Fig. 3. Deviation from s^*. Left and Right deviation profiles.

profile function (shown in Figure 3) increasing from 0 to j. Symmetrically, the predicate $R_{m,j}(s)$ holds if the deviations are decreasing from $N - j$ to N.

For a state $s \in S_\mathcal{A}$, we define $max(s) \triangleq \max_{i \in [N]} e_i(s_i)$ and $M_m(s) \triangleq \langle max(s) \leq C \cdot \beta^m \rangle$. We define $d(s, s^*) \triangleq max(s)$. For any $j \in [mid]$, we define the following symmetric predicates: $\mathcal{L}_{m,j}(s) \triangleq M_m(s) \wedge L_{m,j}(s) \wedge L_{m-1,mid}(s)$ and $\mathcal{R}_{m,j}(s) \triangleq M_m(s) \wedge R_{m,j}(s) \wedge R_{m-1,mid}(s)$.

These predicates partition $[N]$ into three groups as: for all $i \in [j]$, the deviation for agent i is upper bounded by the profile function defined by $C \cdot \beta^m$; for $i \in \{j + 1 \ldots mid\}$ the upper bound is $C \cdot \beta^{m-1}$; and for the remaining, the deviations do not have any upper bound other than one given by the first part of the predicate ($\leq C \cdot \beta^m$). For $i \in [N]$, we define the left profile function $lp_{m,j}(i)$ as $C \cdot \beta^m \left(1 - \frac{1}{2^i}\right)$ if $i \leq j$, equals to $C \cdot \beta^{m-1} \left(1 - \frac{1}{2^i}\right)$ if $j < i \leq mid$ and $C \cdot \beta^m$ otherwise. This function is concave.

Lemma 4. *Let T be the set $\mathbb{N} \times [mid]$ equipped with lexicographic ordering ($\leq_{lex}$). The collections $\{\mathcal{L}_{m,j}\}$ and $\{\mathcal{R}_{m,j}\}$ indexed by T satisfy C1-4.*

Proof. C1. Consider any state $s \in \mathcal{L}_{m_2,j_2}$ and any pair $[m_1, j_1] \leq_{lex} [m_2, j_2]$. If $m = m_1 = m_2$, $s \in \mathcal{L}_{m,j_2} \Rightarrow s \in \mathcal{L}_{m,j_1}$ since the profile holds up to j_2, it is valid up to j_1 (for all $j_1 \leq j_2$). When $m_1 < m_2$, $s \in \mathcal{L}_{m_2,j_2} \Rightarrow s \in \mathcal{L}_{m_1,j_1}$ for all $j_1, j_2 \leq mid$; this is because for all i $lp_{m_2,j_2}(i) \leq lp_{m_1,j_1}(i)$ since $\beta^{m_2} < \beta^{m_2 - 1} \leq \beta^{m_1}$. For C2, for all ϵ we set k to be any value satisfying $C \cdot \beta^k \leq \epsilon$. Hence, $\forall s$ satisfying $\mathcal{L}_{k,0}$ we have that $max(s) \leq C \cdot \beta^k < \epsilon$. C3 follows from the definition of C. C4. Assume without loss of generality $s \in \mathcal{L}_{m,j}$ and $a = (i, \text{avg}_{l,r})$. For all $j \neq i$, s'_j satisfies $\mathcal{L}_{m,j}$, since $s'_j = s_j$. Assume $i \leq j$. The value s'_i satisfies $\mathcal{L}_{m,j}$ as well, and $e_i(s'_i)$ is upper bounded by

$$\frac{r - i}{r - l} e_l(s_l) + \frac{i - l}{r - l} e_r(s_r) \leq \frac{r - i}{r - l} \left(1 - \frac{1}{2^l}\right) C \cdot \beta^m + \frac{i - l}{r - l} C \cdot \beta^m \leq C \cdot \beta^m \left(1 - \frac{1}{2^i}\right)$$

An analogous argument is used to prove the case when $i > j$.

Condition C5 is only partially satisfied by these predicates; for any m and $j < mid$, for all $\mathcal{L}_{m,j}$ (resp. $\mathcal{R}_{m,j}$) there exists an action such that the execution of this action take the system to $\mathcal{L}_{m,j+1}$ (resp. $\mathcal{R}_{m,j+1}$). The following relationships among $\mathcal{L}$ and $\mathcal{R}$ are used for showing C5. The proofs appears in the full version.

Lemma 5. $\forall m \in \mathbb{N}, \quad \mathcal{L}_{m,mid} \cap \mathcal{R}_{m,mid} = \mathcal{L}_{m+1,0} \cap \mathcal{R}_{m+1,0}$

Lemma 6. $\forall j < mid$ (a) $\exists a_1$ such that $\forall s \overset{a_1}{\rightarrow} s'$ and $\forall m \in \mathbb{N}, s \in \mathcal{L}_{m,j} \Rightarrow s' \in \mathcal{L}_{m,j+1}$. (b) $\exists a_2$ such that $\forall s \overset{a_2}{\rightarrow} s'$ and $\forall m \in \mathbb{N}, s \in \mathcal{R}_{m,j} \Rightarrow s' \in \mathcal{R}_{m,j+1}$.

Lemma 5 implies that the left and right profile predicates satisfy C1-4, but in order to prove C5 we require both these predicates hold simultaneously. This motivates our next definition. For state $s \in S_{\mathcal{A}}, m \in \mathbb{N}, j \in [mid-1], b \in \{0,1\}$, we define: $\mathcal{P}_{m,j,b}(s) \overset{\Delta}{=} \mathcal{L}_{m,j+b}(s) \wedge \mathcal{R}_{m,j}(s)$. All indices from 0 to $j+b$ and from $N-j$ to N belong to the profile defined by $C \cdot \beta^m$, while the indices between $(j+b)+1$ and $(N-j)-1$ belong to profile defined by $C \cdot \beta^{m-1}$.

Lemma 7. Let T be the set $\mathbb{N} \times [mid-1] \times \{0,1\}$ equipped with lexicographic ordering ($\leq_{lex}$). The collection $\{\mathcal{P}_{m,j,b}\}$ indexed by T satisfies C1-5.

Proof. It is straightforward to check using Lemma 4 that the sequence of predicates satisfy C1-4. C5. Applying Part (a) of Lemma 6,

$$s \in \mathcal{P}_{m,j,0} \Rightarrow s \in \mathcal{L}_{m,j} \wedge s \in \mathcal{R}_{m,j} \Rightarrow s' \in \mathcal{L}_{m,j+1} \wedge s' \in \mathcal{R}_{m,j} \Leftrightarrow s' \in \mathcal{P}_{m,j,1}.$$

for any m, j with $j \leq mid - 1$, let a_1 be any action in A_{j+1}. Without loss of generality, we assume $a_1 = (j+1, \mathsf{avg}_{l,r})$. Using part (b) of Lemma 6, we obtain

$$s \in \mathcal{P}_{m,j,1} \Rightarrow s \in \mathcal{L}_{m,j+1} \wedge s \in \mathcal{R}_{m,j} \Rightarrow s' \in \mathcal{L}_{m,j+1} \wedge s' \in \mathcal{R}_{m,j+1} \Leftrightarrow s' \in \mathcal{P}_{m,j+1,0}.$$

Next, for any m, j with $j < mid - 1$, let a_2 be any action in $A_{N-(j+1)}$. Again, without loss of generality, let $a_2 = (N-(j+1), \mathsf{avg}_{l,r})$. Finally from Lemma 5, $s \in \mathcal{P}_{m,mid-1,1} \Rightarrow s \in \mathcal{P}_{m+1,0,0}$. Since both A_{j+1} and $A_{N-(j+1)}$ are in the fairness condition $\mathcal{F}$, we obtain the required result.

Lemma 7 and Theorem 1 imply that all $\mathcal{F}$-fair executions of $\mathcal{A}$ converge to s^*.

5.2 Convergence of the Partially Synchronous Protocol

From the shared state protocol for patten formation described in Section 5.1, we first obtain the corresponding $\mathsf{Process}_i$ automaton based on the translation scheme of Section 3. In particular, $\mathsf{Process}_i$ is a TIOA specified by the code in Figure 1 with $X = \mathbb{R}, x_0 = s_{0i}$ and $g_{i\ avg_{l,r}} : \mathbb{R}^3 \to \mathbb{R}$. The $g_{i\ avg_{l,r}}$ functions are obtained from the $f_{i\ avg_{l,r}}$ functions using the transformation of Equation 1. The communication channel for the system is modeled by LBCast of Figure 2 with $X = \mathbb{R}$ and some value for b. The complete partially synchronous system specification is the TIOA obtained by composing $\mathsf{Process}_i$'s with LBCast. Finally, the convergence state $\mathbf{s}^*$ and $d_{\mathcal{B}}$ for $\mathcal{B}$ are obtained from s^*, d of $\mathcal{A}$ using the definitions in 3. It is easily checked that the collection of predicates $\{\mathcal{P}_{m,j,b}\}$ satisfy Assumptions 1 and 2. Therefore, from Theorem 2, we conclude that $\mathcal{B}$ converges to $\mathbf{s}^*$. In fact, we observe that the system $\mathcal{B}$ converges under the following weaker assumption about message losses:

Assumption 3. *For any agent i, for any time t there exists $\zeta > 0$, such that i receives at least one message sent after time t from some agent $l < i$ ($r > i$, respectively) within time $t + u$ with $(i, \mathsf{avg}_{l,r}) \in A_i$.*

This is weaker than Assumption 2 since each process i receives at least one message from some pair (neighbor) and not necessarily all pairs in A_i. The progress property is still guaranteed because by the system makes progress executing any action of A_i.

5.3   Verification in PVS Theorem Prover

We have developed a PVS [19] theory for verifying partially synchronous pattern formation protocols within the exiting Timed I/O Automata/PVS framework [3,15]. The theory formalizes partially synchronous systems as described in this paper, and we have verified the convergence of the example presented here. The PVS theory files and the related documentation are available from http://www.infospheres.caltech.edu/papers. The the proofs presented in this section have been mechanically checked using the PVS theorem prover. The invariance of the $\mathcal{P}$ predicates are proved using the standard inductive proof technique followed by a case analysis on the actions (and trajectories) of the automaton in question. We also prove the convergence of the partially synchronous system directly under Assumption 3. An appropriately changed version of Lemma 5 holds in the partially synchronous settings as well. In order to do so, we prove a set of basic lemmas about LBCast that are used repeatedly. One example, of such a basic lemma is that if all the input messages satisfy a certain predicate, then within bounded time the values stored in the *buffer* satisfy the same predicate

6   Discussion

Designing and verifying partially synchronous distributed algorithms is complicated because of their inherent concurrency and message delays. We have presented a methodology for transforming a shared state distributed system— in which processes can read each other's state without delay—to a partially synchronous system, such that the convergence of the former carry over to the latter, under certain assumptions. Checking Assumption 1 is easy when it can be expressed as a conjunction of predicates on individual process states. It would be interesting to explore relaxations of this assumption. Assumption 2 is fairly weak, however, it is possible to weaken it further for specific protocols—as it is observed in the presented case study. We implemented the theory in PVS and have applied this methodology to verify the convergence of a mobile-agent pattern pattern formation protocol operating on partially synchronous communication. Several generalizations of the translation scheme and the convergence theorem are possible; some more immediate than others. The processes participating in the partially synchronous system could have clocks with bounded drift. We could also define arbitrary continuous trajectories for the main state variables x_i as long as Assumption 1 is satisfied.

References

1. Tempo toolset, version 0.2.2 beta (January 2008), http://www.veromodo.com/
2. Alur, R., Dill, D.L.: A theory of timed automata. Theoretical Computer Science 126, 183–235 (1994)
3. Archer, M., Heitmeyer, C., Sims, S.: TAME: A PVS interface to simplify proofs for automata models. In: Proceedings of UITP 1998 (July 1998)
4. Archer, M., Lim, H., Lynch, N., Mitra, S., Umeno, S.: Specifying and proving properties of timed I/O automata using Tempo. Design Aut. for Emb. Sys (to appear, 2008)
5. Bengtsson, J., Larsen, K.G., Larsson, F., Pettersson, P., Yi, W.: UPPAAL in 1995. In: Margaria, T., Steffen, B. (eds.) TACAS 1996. LNCS, vol. 1055, pp. 431–434. Springer, Heidelberg (1996)
6. Blondel, V., Hendrickx, J., Olshevsky, A., Tsitsiklis, J.: Convergence in multiagent coordination consensus and flocking. In: CDC-ECC, pp. 2996–3000 (2005)
7. Blondel, V., Hendrickx, J., Olshevsky, A., Tsitsiklis, J.: Formations of mobile agents with message loss and delay (preprint, 2007),
   http://www.ist.caltech.edu/~mitras/research/2008/asynchcoord.pdf
8. Chatterjee, S., Seneta, E.: Towards consensus: some convergence theorems on repeated averaging. J. Applied Probability 14(1), 89–97 (1977)
9. Clavaski, S., Chaves, M., Day, R., Nag, P., Williams, A., Zhang, W.: Vehicle networks: achieving regular formation. In: ACC (2003)
10. Dwork, C., Lynch, N., Stockmeyer, L.: Consensus in the presence of partial synchrony. J. ACM 35(2), 288–323 (1988)
11. Hendriks, M.: Model checking the time to reach agreement. In: Pettersson, P., Yi, W. (eds.) FORMATS 2005. LNCS, vol. 3829, pp. 98–111. Springer, Heidelberg (2005)
12. Kaynar, D., Lynch, N., Mitra, S., Garland, S.: TIOA Language. MIT Computer Science and Artificial Intelligence Laboratory, Cambridge (2005)
13. Kaynar, D.K., Lynch, N., Segala, R., Vaandrager, F.: The Theory of Timed I/O Automata. Synthesis Lectures on CS. Morgan Claypool (November 2005)
14. Lamport, L.: Real-time model checking is really simple. In: Borrione, D., Paul, W. (eds.) CHARME 2005. LNCS, vol. 3725, pp. 162–175. Springer, Heidelberg (2005)
15. Lim, H., Kaynar, D., Lynch, N., Mitra, S.: Translating timed I/O automata specifications for theorem proving in PVS. In: Pettersson, P., Yi, W. (eds.) FORMATS 2005. LNCS, vol. 3829, pp. 17–31. Springer, Heidelberg (2005)
16. Lynch, N.A.: Distributed Algorithms. Morgan Kaufmann Publishers Inc., San Francisco (1996)
17. Mitra, S., Chandy, K.M.: A formalized theory for verifying stability and convergence of automata in pvs. In: TPHOLs 2008 (to appear, 2008)
18. Olfati-Saber, R., Fax, J., Murray, R.: Consensus and cooperation in networked multi-agent systems. Proc. of the IEEE 95(1), 215–233 (2007)
19. Owre, S., Rajan, S., Rushby, J., Shankar, N., Srivas, M.: PVS: Combining specification, proof checking, and model checking. In: Alur, R., Henzinger, T.A. (eds.) CAV 1996. LNCS, vol. 1102, pp. 411–414. Springer, Heidelberg (1996)
20. Tsitsiklis, J.N.: On the stability of asynchronous iterative processes. Theory of Computing Systems 20(1), 137–153 (1987)

Compositional Abstraction in Real-Time Model Checking*

Jasper Berendsen and Frits Vaandrager

ICIS, Radboud University Nijmegen
P.O. Box 9010, 6500 GL Nijmegen, the Netherlands
J.Berendsen@cs.ru.nl, F.Vaandrager@cs.ru.nl

Abstract. The idea to use simulations (or refinements) as a compositional abstraction device is well-known, both in untimed and timed settings, and has already been studied theoretically and practically in many papers during the last three decades. Nevertheless, existing approaches do not handle two fundamental modeling concepts which, for instance, are frequently used in the popular UPPAAL model checker: (1) a parallel composition operator that supports communication via shared variables as well as synchronization of actions, and (2) committed locations. We describe a framework for compositional abstraction based on simulation relations that does support both concepts, and that is suitable for UPPAAL. Our approach is very general and the only essential restriction is that the guards of input transitions do not depend on external variables. We have applied our compositional framework to verify the Zeroconf protocol for an arbitrary number of hosts.

1   Introduction

In this article, we describe a framework for compositional abstraction based on simulation relations that is suitable for the popular model checker UPPAAL [1]. The idea to use simulations (or refinements) as a compositional abstraction device is well-known, both in untimed and timed settings, and has already been studied theoretically and practically in many articles during the last three decades, see for instance [2, 3, 4, 5, 6, 7, 8, 9, 10, 11]. Nevertheless, when we attempted to apply these existing approaches to fight state space explosions in a model of an industrial protocol [12], we ran into the problem that they do not handle two fundamental modeling concepts that are frequently used in UPPAAL.

The first concept is an (asynchronous) parallel composition operator that supports communication via both shared variables and synchronization of actions. Models for reactive systems typically either support communication via shared variables (TLA [13], Reactive Modules [14], etc), or communication via synchronization of actions (CCS [15], I/O automata [3], etc). We are only aware of five studies of compositionality in which the two types of communication are

---

* Research supported by NWO/EW project 612.000.103 Fault-tolerant Real-time Algorithms Analyzed Incrementally (FRAAI) and DFG/NWO bilateral cooperation project Validation of Stochastic Systems (VOSS2).

F. Cassez and C. Jard (Eds.): FORMATS 2008, LNCS 5215, pp. 233–249, 2008.

combined [8, 16, 17, 18, 19]. It is well known that both types of communication can be defined in terms of each other. A shared variable can be modeled
as a separate process/automaton that communicates with its environment via
read/write synchronization actions. However, in this approach the evaluation of,
for instance, an integer expression may involve a sequence of interactions with
shared variable automata. This blows up the state space and makes it more
difficult to understand the model. Conversely, synchronization of actions can
be modeled in a shared variable setting using some auxiliary flag variables and
handshake transitions of the synchronizing automata. But again this blows up
the state space and makes it harder to understand the model. The UPPAAL
model checker supports both shared variables and synchronization of actions,
and this feature is extremely helpful for building tractable models of complex
systems.

When combining shared variables and synchronization of actions, one has to
deal with the scenario, illustrated in Fig. 1, in which the transitions involved in
a synchronization assign different values to a shared variable.

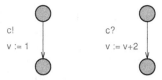

Fig. 1. Combining shared variables and synchronization of actions

One simple (but restrictive) approach, pursued by Lynch et al [16], is to
impose syntactic conditions which ensure that the scenario does not occur: for
each shared variable only one automaton gets write permission, and the other
automata may read the variable but not assign a new value to it. A slightly
more general approach is taken by Jensen et al [8], where the variables of each
automaton are classified as *readable* and/or *writable*. Two automata may share
writable variables, but in this case a synchronizing transition may only occur if
both automata assign the same values to these variables. In practice, this means
that multi-writer variables can only be updated via internal (non-synchronizing)
transitions. As we describe in [20], the approach of [8] is flawed since parallel
composition is not associative; as a result a connection with the standard UP-
PAAL semantics cannot be established. In the framework of Sociable Interfaces
of De Alfaro et al [18], the output transition selects the next value of the global
variables, and the input transition is used only to determine the next value of the
local variables. The transition relation associated with the output action must
respect the constraints specified by the transition relation associated with the input action. In the example of Fig. 1 this is only the case when $v = -1$ before the
synchronization. As we point out in [21], also the parallel composition of [18] is
not associative (disproving Theorem 4) in the sense that there exist modules M_1,
M_2 and M_3 such that $M_1 \otimes (M_2 \otimes M_3)$ is defined but $(M_1 \otimes M_2) \otimes M_3$ is not. A
general, process algebraic approach is presented by Groote & Ponse [17]. In this
elegant approach one can basically define the desired effect of a synchronization

for any pair of actions $c!$ and $c?$. However, due to the linking of action names to effects on the global state space, the behavioral equivalence proposed in [17] is extremely fine and not suited as a compositional abstraction device: two configurations can only be related if they assign identical values to all variables. An approach suitable for hybrid systems is presented in [19]. Here synchronization can take place between multiple automata. Automata that synchronize need to agree on their shared external variables both before and after the transitions. Therefore passing information during synchronization is not possible in the same way as in our setting.

In this article, we present a very general approach that is consistent with the actual treatment of synchronization in UPPAAL, and that supports compositional abstraction. Unlike [8, 16, 17, 18, 19], UPPAAL deals with the situation of Fig. 1 by first performing the assignment on the output transition $c!$, followed by the assignment on the input transition $c?$. This means that after occurrence of the synchronization transition v will have the value 3. Following UPPAAL, we describe synchronization of automata by a rule of the form

$$\frac{r \xrightarrow{c!} r' \qquad s[r'] \xrightarrow{c?} s'}{r \| s \xrightarrow{\tau} r'[s'] \| s'} \tag{1}$$

Here $s[r']$ denotes state s but with the shared variables updated according to r'. In UPPAAL, a synchronization may only occur if the guards of both transitions hold, and only if this is the case the assignments are carried out. This means that if we add a guard $v \neq 1$ to the rightmost transition in Fig. 1, synchronization will be possible starting from any state satisfying this predicate. In a semantics with rule (1), however, synchronization will no longer be possible since after the assignment on the output transitions has been performed, the guard of the input transition no longer holds. In order to rule out this scenario (which we have never observed in practical applications), our approach imposes the restriction that guards of input transitions do not refer to external (shared) variables. Guards of input transitions may depend on the internal variables, so in general our automata are certainly not input enabled.

The second modeling concept, which is not handled by any existing framework but needed for industrial applications, is the notion of a *committed location*. In UPPAAL, locations of a timed automaton can be designated as *committed*. If one automaton in a network of automata is in a committed location, time may not progress and the next transition (if any) has to start from a committed location. Committedness is useful to specify that certain transitions need to be executed *atomically* without intervening transitions from other components. Also, excluding certain behavior with committed locations may lead to serious reductions in the state space of a model [22]. In this article, we present a compositional semantics for committedness. This is achieved by distinguishing, at the semantic level, between committed and uncommitted transitions. Our rules for describing committed locations involve negative antecedents and are similar to the rules that have been proposed in the process algebra literature to describe priorities [23, 24, 25]: a component may only perform an internal transition, denoted by a τ, if other components may *not* perform a committed transition. Although there are some subtle differences at the technical level, basically our results show that one may view committedness as a form of priority.

We define the semantics of timed automata in terms of *timed transition systems (TTSs)*. These are labeled transition systems (LTSs) equipped with a bit of additional structure to capture relevant information about state variables, committedness of transitions, and real-time behavior. On TTSs we define the operations of parallel composition and a CCS style restriction operator. An important sanity check for our definitions is that, for any network of timed automata, the (noncompositional) UPPAAL semantics (as defined in the UPPAAL 4.0 help menu) is isomorphic to the (compositional) semantics obtained by associating TTSs to the timed automata in the network, composing these TTSs in parallel, applying a restriction operator, and then considering the underlying LTS. That is, if $\mathcal{N} = \langle \mathcal{A}_1, \ldots, \mathcal{A}_n \rangle$ is a network of timed automata then

$$\mathsf{LTS}(\mathcal{N}) \ \cong \ \mathsf{LTS}((\mathsf{TTS}(\mathcal{A}_1)\| \cdots \|\mathsf{TTS}(\mathcal{A}_n))\backslash\mathcal{C}),$$

where $\backslash\mathcal{C}$ facilitates hiding of internal synchronization. A key lemma needed to prove this result is associativity of parallel composition.

We define an abstraction relation on TTSs in terms of *timed step simulations*. These induce a behavioral preorder $\preceq$ that is somewhere in between strong and weak simulation. If $\mathcal{T}_1 \preceq \mathcal{T}_2$, then $\mathcal{T}_2$ can either mimic the transitions of $\mathcal{T}_1$ or (in case of an internal transition) do nothing, but it may not add internal transitions that are not present in $\mathcal{T}_1$. We establish that $\mathcal{T}_1 \preceq \mathcal{T}_2$ implies $\mathcal{T}_1\|\mathcal{T}_3 \preceq \mathcal{T}_2\|\mathcal{T}_3$. We briefly summarize the use of our compositional framework in the verification of the Zeroconf protocol for an arbitrary number of hosts [26]. Without our techniques, UPPAAL can only verify instances with three hosts.

Section 2 introduces timed transition systems. In Sect. 3, we define timed step simulations and establish that the induced preorder is compositional. Section 4 presents networks of timed automata and defines their semantics both noncompositionally (as in UPPAAL) and compositionally in terms of TTSs. Also, the consistency of the two semantics is established and we briefly discuss the application of our framework. Finally, Sect. 5 discusses some extensions and future research. For lack of space, some technical details and all proofs can be found in [27].

2   Timed Transition Systems

In this section, we introduce the semantic model of timed transitions systems (TTSs). Basically, a TTS is a labeled transition system equipped with a bit of additional structure to support shared variables and committed transitions: states are defined as valuations of variables, and transitions may be committed, which gives them priority in a parallel composition. TTSs can be placed in parallel and may communicate by means of shared variables and synchronization of actions. Like in CCS [15], two transitions may synchronize when their actions are complementary, leading to an internal transition in the composition.

Just to fix notation, we first recall the definition of a labeled transition system. Since we consider systems that communicate via shared variables, we find it convenient to model states as functions that map state variables to values in their domain. We also introduce a basic vocabulary for overriding and updating of functions that we need to describe shared variable communication. After these preliminaries, we present the definition of a timed transition system, the operations of parallel composition and restriction, and establish some key properties of these operations, in particular associativity of parallel composition. All the proofs of this section have been deferred to [27] Throughout this article, we write $\mathbb{R}_{\geq 0}$ for the set of nonnegative real numbers, $\mathbb{N}$ for the set of natural numbers, and $\mathbb{B} = \{1, 0\}$ for the set of Booleans. We let d range over $\mathbb{R}_{\geq 0}$, i, j, k, n over $\mathbb{N}$, and $b, b', \ldots$ over $\mathbb{B}$.

We consider labeled transition systems with several types of state transitions, corresponding to different sets of actions. We assume a set $\mathcal{C}$ of *channels* and let c range over $\mathcal{C}$. The set of *external actions* is defined as $\mathcal{E} \triangleq \{c!, c? \mid c \in \mathcal{C}\}$. Actions of the form $c!$ are called *output actions* and actions of the form $c?$ are called *input actions*. We let e range over $\mathcal{E}$. We assume the existence of a special *internal action* τ, and write $\mathcal{E}_\tau$ for $\mathcal{E} \cup \{\tau\}$, the set of *discrete actions*. We let α range over $\mathcal{E}_\tau$. Finally, we assume a set of *durations* or *time-passage actions*, which in this article are just the nonnegative real numbers in $\mathbb{R}_{\geq 0}$. We write *Act* for $\mathcal{E}_\tau \cup \mathbb{R}_{\geq 0}$, the set of *actions*, and let $a, a', \ldots$ range over *Act*.

The following definition is standard, except maybe for our specific choice of a universe of transition labels.

Definition 1 (LTS). *A labeled transition system (LTS) is a tuple* $\mathcal{L} = \langle S, s^0, \longrightarrow \rangle$, *where* S *is a set of states,* $s^0 \in S$ *is the initial state, and* $\longrightarrow \subseteq S \times Act \times S$ *is the transition relation. We let* $q, r, s, t \ldots$ *range over states, and write* $s \xrightarrow{a} t$ *if* $(s, a, t) \in \longrightarrow$. *We refer to* s *as the source of the transition, and to* t *as the target. We say that an a-transition is enabled in* s, *notation* $s \xrightarrow{a}$, *whenever* $s \xrightarrow{a} t$, *for some* t. *A state* s *is reachable iff there exist states* $s_1, \ldots s_n$ *such that* $s_1 = s^0$, $s_n = s$ *and, for all* $i < n$ *there exists an a s.t.* $s_i \xrightarrow{a} s_{i+1}$.

We write $dom(f)$ to denote the domain of a function f. If also X is a set, then we write $f \lceil X$ for the restriction of f to X, that is, the function g with $dom(g) = dom(f) \cap X$ such that $g(z) = f(z)$ for each $z \in dom(g)$. For functions f and g, we let $f \rhd g$ denote the *left-merge*, the combined function where f overrides g for all elements in the intersection of their domains.[1] Formally, we define $f \rhd g$ to be the function with $dom(f \rhd g) = dom(f) \cup dom(g)$ satisfying, for all $z \in dom(f \rhd g)$, $(f \rhd g)(z) \triangleq$ if $z \in dom(f)$ then $f(z)$ else $g(z)$. We define the dual *right-merge* operator by $f \lhd g \triangleq g \rhd f$. Two functions f and g are *compatible*, notation $f \heartsuit g$, if they agree on the intersection of their domains, that is, $f(z) = g(z)$ for all $z \in dom(f) \cap dom(g)$. For compatible functions f and

---

[1] Essentially, this is the overriding operator "$\oplus$" from Z. On finite domains, the operator is also defined in VDM, where it is written †. We prefer not to use a symmetric symbol for an asymmetric (non commutative) operator.

g, we define their *merge* by $f\|g \triangleq f \rhd g$. Whenever we write $f\|g$, we implicitly assume $f \heartsuit g$. We write $f[g]$ for the *update* of function f according to g, that is, $f[g] \triangleq (f \lhd g) \lceil dom(f)$.

We assume a universal set $\mathcal{V}$ of typed *variables*, with a subset $\mathcal{X} \subseteq \mathcal{V}$ of *clock variables* or *clocks*. Clocks have domain $\mathbb{R}_{\geq 0}$. We let y range over $\mathcal{V}$ and x over $\mathcal{X}$. A *valuation* for a set $V \subseteq \mathcal{V}$ is a function that maps each variable in V to an element in its domain. We let $u, v, w, \ldots$ range over valuations, and write $Val(V)$ for the set of valuations for V. For valuation $v \in Val(V)$ and duration $d \in \mathbb{R}_{\geq 0}$, we define $v \oplus d$ to be the valuation for V that increments clocks by d, and leaves the other variables untouched, that is, for all $y \in V$,

$$(v \oplus d)(y) \triangleq \text{if } y \in \mathcal{X} \text{ then } v(y) + d \text{ else } v(y) \text{ fi}$$

A subset $P \subseteq Val(V)$ of valuations is called a *property over* V. Let $W \supseteq V$ and $v \in Val(W)$. We say that P *holds in* v, notation $v \models P$, if $v\lceil V \in P$. A property P over V is *left-closed* w.r.t. time-passage if, for all $v \in Val(V)$ and $d \in \mathbb{R}_{\geq 0}$, $v \oplus d \models P \Rightarrow v \models P$. We say that property P over V *does not depend on* a set of variables $W \subseteq V$ if, for all $v \in Val(V)$ and $u \in Val(W)$, $v \models P \Leftrightarrow v[u] \models P$. We write $\{y_1 \mapsto z_1, \ldots, y_n \mapsto z_n\}$ for the valuation that assigns value z_i to variable y_i, for $i = 1, \ldots, n$.

The state variables of a TTS are partitioned into external and internal variables. Internal variables may only be updated by the TTS itself and not by its environment. This in contrast to external variables, which may be updated by both the TTS and its environment. A new element in our definition of a TTS is that transitions are classified as either *committed* or *uncommitted*. Committed transitions have priority over time-passage transitions and over internal transitions that are not committed. Interestingly, whereas in UPPAAL committedness is an attribute of locations, it must be treated as an attribute of transitions in order to obtain a compositional semantics. This issue is further discussed in [27].

We are now ready to formally define our notion of a timed transition system.

Definition 2 (TTS). *A* timed transition system (TTS) *is a tuple*

$$\mathcal{T} = \langle E, H, S, s^0, \longrightarrow^1, \longrightarrow^0 \rangle,$$

where $E, H \subseteq \mathcal{V}$ *are disjoint sets of external and internal variables, respectively,* $V = E \cup H$, $S \subseteq Val(V)$, *and* $\langle S, s^0, \longrightarrow^1 \cup \longrightarrow^0 \rangle$ *is an LTS.*

We write $r \xrightarrow{a,b} s$ *if* $(r, a, s) \in \longrightarrow^b$. *The boolean value* b *determines whether or not a transition is committed. We often omit* b *when it equals 0. A state* s *of a TTS is called committed, notation* $Comm(s)$, *iff it has an enabled outgoing committed transition, that is,* $s \xrightarrow{a,1}$ *for some* a. *We write* LTS$(\mathcal{T})$ *to denote the underlying LTS of* $\mathcal{T}$. *We require the following axioms to hold, for all* $s, t \in S$, $a, a' \in Act$, $b \in \mathbb{B}$, $d \in \mathbb{R}_{\geq 0}$ *and* $u \in Val(E)$,

$$s \xrightarrow{a,1} \wedge s \xrightarrow{a',b} \Rightarrow a' \in \mathcal{E} \vee (a' = \tau \wedge b) \qquad \text{(Axiom I)}$$

$$s[u] \in S \qquad\qquad\qquad\qquad \text{(Axiom II)}$$

$$s \xrightarrow{c?,b} \;\Rightarrow\; s[u] \xrightarrow{c?,b} \qquad\qquad \text{(Axiom III)}$$

$$s \xrightarrow{d} t \;\Rightarrow\; t = s \oplus d \qquad\qquad \text{(Axiom IV)}$$

Axiom I states that in a committed state neither time-passage steps nor un-committed τ's may occur. The axiom implies that committed transitions always have a label in $\mathcal{E}_\tau$. Note that a committed state may have outgoing uncommitted transitions with a label in $\mathcal{E}$. The reason is that, for instance, an uncommitted $c!$-transition may synchronize with a committed $c?$-transition from some other component, and thereby turn into a committed τ-transition.

In general, the states of a TTS constitute a proper subset of the set of all valuations of the state variables. This feature is used to model the concept of location invariants in timed automata: if a timed automaton has, for instance, a location invariant $x \leq 1$ then this automaton may never reach a state in which $x > 1$; semantically speaking states in which $x \leq 1$ does not hold simply do not exist. In a setting with shared variable communication, complications may arise if one component wants to update a shared variable in a way that violates the location invariant of another component. In UPPAAL, a state transition is only possible if the location invariant holds in the target state. Our position is that models in which state transitions may violate location invariants are bad models. Therefore, and also because it simplifies the technicalities, we postulate in Axiom II that if the external variables of a state are changed, the result is again a state.

Axiom III states that enabledness of input transitions is not affected by changing the external variables. This is a key property that we need in order to obtain compositionality, we will discuss this axiom in more detail below. Axiom IV, finally, asserts that if time advances with an amount d, all clocks also advance with an amount d, and the other variables remain unchanged.

We now introduce the operations of parallel composition and restriction on TTSs. In our setting parallel composition is a partial operation that is only defined when TTSs are *compatible*: the initial states must be compatible functions and the internal variables of one TTS may not intersect with the variables of the other. We can avoid the restriction on the internal variables via a straightforward renaming procedure, but this would complicate the definitions.

From now on, if we have multiple indexed systems (TTSs, or later timed automata), then we use the indices also to denote the components of individual systems. For example, we let E_i denote the set of external variables of T_i.

Definition 3 (Parallel composition). *Two TTSs T_1 and T_2 are compatible if $H_1 \cap V_2 = H_2 \cap V_1 = \emptyset$ and $s_1^0 \heartsuit s_2^0$. In this case, their parallel composition $T_1 \| T_2$ is the tuple $T = \langle E, H, S, s^0, \longrightarrow^1, \longrightarrow^0 \rangle$, where $E = E_1 \cup E_2$, $H = H_1 \cup H_2$, $S = \{r \| s \mid r \in S_1 \wedge s \in S_2 \wedge r \heartsuit s\}$, $s^0 = s_1^0 \| s_2^0$, and $\longrightarrow^1$ and $\longrightarrow^0$ are the least relations that satisfy the rules in Fig. 2. Here i, j range over $\{1, 2\}$, r, r' range over S_i, s, s' range over S_j, b, b' range over $\mathbb{B}$, e ranges over $\mathcal{E}$ and c over $\mathcal{C}$.*

$$\frac{r \xrightarrow{e,b}_i r'}{r\|s \xrightarrow{e,b} r' \rhd s} \; \textbf{EXT}$$

$$\frac{r \xrightarrow{c!,b}_i r' \quad s[r'] \xrightarrow{c?,b'}_j s' \quad i \neq j}{\Large Comm(r) \vee Comm(s) \Rightarrow b \vee b'} \; \textbf{SYNC}$$
$$r\|s \xrightarrow{\tau,b\vee b'} r' \lhd s'$$

$$\frac{r \xrightarrow{\tau,b}_i r' \quad Comm(s) \Rightarrow b}{r\|s \xrightarrow{\tau,b} r' \rhd s} \; \textbf{TAU}$$

$$\frac{r \xrightarrow{d}_i r' \quad s \xrightarrow{d}_j s' \quad i \neq j}{r\|s \xrightarrow{d} r'\|s'} \; \textbf{TIME}$$

Fig. 2. Rules for parallel composition of TTSs

The external and internal variables of the composition are simply obtained by taking the union of the external and internal variables of the components, respectively. The states (and start state) of a composed TTS are obtained by merging the states (resp. start state) of the components (viewed as functions). The interesting part of the definition consists of the transition rules. Rule **EXT** states that an external transition of a component induces a corresponding transition of the composition. The component that takes the transition may override some of the shared variables. Observe that, since $r' \rhd s = r'\|s[r']$, and since $s[r']$ is a state of $\mathcal{T}_{3-i}$ by Axiom II, it follows that $r' \rhd s$ is a state of $\mathcal{T}$. Similarly, rule **TAU** states that an internal transition of a component induces a corresponding transition of the composition, except that an uncommitted transition may only occur if the other component is in an uncommitted state. Rule **SYNC** describes the synchronization of components. If $\mathcal{T}_i$ has an output transition from r to r', and if $\mathcal{T}_j$ has a corresponding input transition from s, updated by r', to s', the composition has a τ transition to $r' \lhd s'$. The synchronization is committed iff one of the participating transitions is committed. However, an uncommitted synchronization may only occur if both components are in an uncommitted state. By Axiom II for $\mathcal{T}_j$ it follows that in rule **SYNC** $s[r']$ is a state of $\mathcal{T}_j$, and by $r' \lhd s' = r'[s']\|s'$ and Axiom II for $\mathcal{T}_i$ it follows that in rule **SYNC** $r' \lhd s'$ is a state of $\mathcal{T}$. Rule **TIME**, finally, states that a time step d of the composition may occur when both components perform a time step d. Observe that $r\heartsuit s$ and Axiom IV for both $\mathcal{T}_1$ and $\mathcal{T}_2$ imply $r'\heartsuit s'$. One may check that composition is a well-defined operation on TTSs.

Commutativity and associativity are highly desirable properties for parallel composition operators. However, associativity becomes very tricky in a setting with both shared variables and synchronization of actions. In [20, 21], we have shown that the composition operators defined in two published papers [8, 18] is not associative. We claim that the parallel composition operator defined in this article is both commutative and associative. Commutativity is immediate from the symmetry in the definitions. The proof of associativity is more involved and presented in [27]. A key step needed in order to make this proof tractable is to first derive a series of basic laws for $\rhd$, $\|$, $.[.]$ and $\heartsuit$.

Theorem 1. *Composition of compatible TTSs is commutative and associative.*

The next definition introduces a standard restriction operator, very similar to the one in CCS [15]. The restriction operator *internalizes* a set of channels so that no further TTSs may synchronize on it.

Definition 4 (Restriction). *Given a TTS $\mathcal{T}$ and a set $C \subseteq \mathcal{C}$ of channels, we define $\mathcal{T} \backslash C$ to be the TTS that is identical to $\mathcal{T}$, except that all transitions with a label in $\{c!, c? \mid c \in C\}$ have been removed from the transition relations.*

We write $\Sigma(\mathcal{T})$ for the set of channels that occur in transitions of $\mathcal{T}$. Using this notation, we can formulate restriction laws, as in CCS [15][p80], such as $(\mathcal{T} \| \mathcal{T}') \backslash C = \mathcal{T} \| (\mathcal{T}' \backslash C)$ if $\Sigma(\mathcal{T}) \cap C = \emptyset$

3   Compositional Abstraction

In our approach, timed step simulations capture what it means that one TTS is an abstraction of another. In this section, we formally define timed step simulations and establish compositionality of the induced preorder.

A timed step simulation relates the states of two TTSs that have the same external interface, that is, the same sets of external variables. Initial states must always be related. Also, related states must agree on their external variables, and the relation must be preserved by consistently changing the external variables. If the detailled system does a step, then either this can be simulated by an identical step in the abstract system that preserves the relation, or the detailled step is an internal computation step that preserves the simulation relation. Finally, abstract level committed states may only be related to detailled level committed states.

Definition 5 (Timed step simulation). *Two TTSs $\mathcal{T}_1$ and $\mathcal{T}_2$ are comparable if they have the same external variables, that is $E_1 = E_2$. Given comparable TTSs $\mathcal{T}_1$ and $\mathcal{T}_2$, we say that a relation $R \subseteq S_1 \times S_2$ is a timed step simulation from $\mathcal{T}_1$ to $\mathcal{T}_2$, provided that $s_1^0 R s_2^0$ and if $s R r$ then*

1. *$s \lceil E_1 = r \lceil E_2$,*
2. *$\forall u \in Val(E_1) : s[u] \; R \; r[u]$,*
3. *if $Comm(r)$ then $Comm(s)$,*
4. *if $s \xrightarrow{a,b} s'$ then either there exists an r' such that $r \xrightarrow{a,b} r'$ and $s' R r'$, or $a = \tau$ and $s' R r$.*

We write $\mathcal{T}_1 \preceq \mathcal{T}_2$ when there exists a timed step simulation from $\mathcal{T}_1$ to $\mathcal{T}_2$.

It is straightforward to prove that $\preceq$ is a preorder on the class of TTS, that is, $\preceq$ is reflexive and transitive. Our first main theorem states that $\preceq$ is a precongruence for parallel composition. This means that timed step simulations can be used as a compositional abstraction device.

Theorem 2. *Let $\mathcal{T}_1, \mathcal{T}_2, \mathcal{T}_3$ be TTSs with $\mathcal{T}_1$ and $\mathcal{T}_2$ comparable, $\mathcal{T}_1 \preceq \mathcal{T}_2$, and both $\mathcal{T}_1$ and $\mathcal{T}_2$ compatible with $\mathcal{T}_3$. Then $\mathcal{T}_1 \| \mathcal{T}_3 \preceq \mathcal{T}_2 \| \mathcal{T}_3$.*

The timed step simulation preorder $\preceq$ is in general not a precongruence for restriction. The problem is that the restriction operator removes transitions: this may affect enabledness of committed transitions and invalidate the property that high-level committed states may only be related to low-level committed states. In the theorem below, we explicitly add the condition needed for compositionality: if a state is committed in T_1 it should still be committed in $T_1 \backslash C$.

Theorem 3. *Let T_1 and T_2 be comparable TTSs such that $T_1 \preceq T_2$. Let $C \subseteq \mathcal{C}$. If, for all states s of T_1, $Comm(s) \Rightarrow \exists a \in \mathcal{E}_\tau - \{c!, c? \mid c \in C\} : s \xrightarrow{a,1}_1$ then $T_1 \backslash C \preceq T_2 \backslash C$.*

In practice, the side condition of Theorem 3 is unproblematic, for instance because in committed locations of components in a network only output transitions are enabled, and the corresponding input transitions are always enabled in other components. In such a network, a committed state always enables a committed τ-transition, which implies the side condition.

4   Networks of Timed Automata

In this section, we introduce networks of timed automata (NTA), a mathematical model for describing real-time systems inspired by the UPPAAL modeling language. We present two different definitions of the semantics of NTAs and establish their equivalence. The first definition is not compositional and closely follows the UPPAAL semantics (as defined in the UPPAAL 4.0 help menu). The second definition constructs an LTS compositionally by first associating a TTS to each TA in the network, composing these, applying a restriction operator, and then considering the underlying LTS.

An NTA consists of a number of timed automata that may communicate via synchronization of transition labels and via a global set of multi-reader/multi-writer variables. Our model supports committed locations and a restricted form of urgency by allowing internal transitions to be urgent.[2] Our definition of timed automata abstracts from syntactic details and the various restrictions from UPPAAL that are needed to make model checking decidable. These aspects that are not relevant for our compositionality result. However, in order to obtain compositionality, we need to impose some axioms on timed automata that are not required by UPPAAL. Also, several UPPAAL features have not been incorporated within our NTA model, in particular broadcast channels, urgent synchronization channels, and priorities. We expect that these features can be incorporated in our approach (at the price of complicating the definitions) but it remains future work to work out the details.

Definition 6 (TA). *A timed automaton (TA) is defined to be a tuple $\mathcal{A} = \langle L, K, l^0, E, H, v^0, I, \longrightarrow, \longrightarrow^u \rangle$, where L is a set of locations, $K \subseteq L$ is a set of*

---

[2] Urgent internal transitions can be encoded in UPPAAL by declaring a special urgent broadcast channel **urg**, labeling urgent internal transitions by **urg!**, and ensuring that no transitions carry the label **urg?**. Urgent internal transitions are very convenient for modeling systems since they allow one to specify that a component reacts instantaneously to some change of the external variables.

committed locations, $l^0 \in L$ is the initial location, $E, H \subseteq \mathcal{V}$ are disjoint sets of external and hidden variables, respectively, $V = E \cup H$, $v^0 \in Val(V)$ is the initial valuation, $I : L \rightarrow 2^{Val(V)}$ assigns a left-closed invariant property to each location such that $v^0 \models I(l^0)$,

$$\longrightarrow \subseteq L \times 2^{Val(V)} \times \mathcal{E}_\tau \times (Val(V) \rightarrow Val(V)) \times L$$

is the transition relation, and $\longrightarrow^u \subseteq \longrightarrow$ is the urgent transition relation. We let $l, \ldots$ range over locations, write $l \xrightarrow{g,\alpha,\rho} l'$ if $(l, g, \alpha, \rho, l') \in \longrightarrow$, refer to l as the source of the transition, to l' as the target, to g as the guard, and to ρ as the update (or reset) function. We require:

$$I(l) \text{ does not depend on } E \qquad\qquad (\text{Axiom V})$$

$$l \xrightarrow{g,c?,\rho} l' \quad \Rightarrow \quad g \text{ does not depend on } E \qquad\qquad (\text{Axiom VI})$$

$$\forall l \in K \; \forall v \in I(l) \; \exists (l \xrightarrow{g,\alpha,\rho} l') : v \models g \wedge \rho(v) \models I(l') \qquad (\text{Axiom VII})$$

$$l \xrightarrow{g,\alpha,\rho}{}^u l' \quad \Rightarrow \quad \alpha = \tau \wedge g \text{ does not depend on } \mathcal{X} \qquad (\text{Axiom VIII})$$

Recall that a property P is left-closed if, for all $v \in Val(V)$ and $d \in \mathbb{R}_{\geq 0}$, $v \oplus d \models P \Rightarrow v \models P$. In UPPAAL, left-closedness of location invariants is ensured syntactically by disallowing lower bounds on clocks in invariants. Axiom V asserts that location invariants do not depend on external variables. This restriction is not imposed by UPPAAL, but run-time errors may occur in UPPAAL when one automaton modifies external variables in a way that violates the location invariant of another automaton. Although it may be possible to come up with a compositional semantics for a setting without Axiom V, it is clear that the axiom eliminates a number of technical complications. We are not aware of UPPAAL applications in which the axiom is violated. Axiom VI asserts that the guards of input transitions do not depend on external variables. This is a key axiom that we need for our approach to work: it ensures that the update function of an output transition does not affect the enablesness of matching input transitions. Axiom VII states that in a committed location always at least one transition is possible. We need this axiom to ensure that a state in the TTS semantics of a timed automaton is committed iff the corresponding location is committed. The axiom is a prerequisite for what is called time reactivity in [28] and timelock freedom in [29], that is, whenever time progress stops there exists at least one enabled transition. UPPAAL does not impose this axiom, but we would like to argue that any model that does not satisfy it is a bad model. Axiom VIII, finally, states that only internal transitions can be urgent and that the guards of urgent transitions may not depend on clocks. The constraint that urgent transitions may not depend on clocks is syntactically enforced in UPPAAL by requiring that clock variables may not occur in the guards of urgent transitions.

A network of timed automata can now be defined as a finite collection of compatible timed automata:

Definition 7 (NTA). *Two timed automata A_1 and A_2 are compatible if $H_1 \cap V_2 = H_2 \cap V_1 = \emptyset$ and $v_1^0 \heartsuit v_2^0$. A network of timed automata (NTA) consists of a finite collection $\mathcal{N} = \langle A_1, \ldots, A_n \rangle$ of pairwise compatible timed automata.*

The operational semantics of NTAs can be defined in terms of labeled transition systems.

Definition 8 (LTS semantics of NTA). *Let* $\mathcal{N} = \langle \mathcal{A}_1, \ldots, \mathcal{A}_n \rangle$ *be an NTA. Let* $V = \bigcup_i (V_i \cup \{\mathsf{loc}_i\})$, *with for each* i, loc_i *a fresh variable with type* L_i. *The semantics of* $\mathcal{N}$, *notation* $\mathsf{LTS}(\mathcal{N})$, *is the LTS* $\langle S, s^0, \longrightarrow \rangle$, *where*

$$S = \{v \in Val(V) \mid \forall i : v \models I_i(v(\mathsf{loc}_i))\},$$
$$s^0 = v_1^0 \| \cdots \| v_n^0 \| \{\mathsf{loc}_1 \mapsto l_1^0, \ldots, \mathsf{loc}_n \mapsto l_n^0\},$$

and $\longrightarrow$ *is defined by the rules in Fig. 3. We use the convention that if an update function* $\rho : Val(W) \to Val(W)$ *is applied to a valuation* $v \in Val(W')$ *with* $W \subset W'$, *it only affects the variables in* W, *that is* $\rho(v) \triangleq v[\rho(v \lceil W)]$.

Definition 8 describes the semantics of an NTA in terms of an LTS. The states of this LTS are valuations of a set V of variables. This set V contains the variables of all TAs and also, for each TA $\mathcal{A}_i$, a special variable loc_i to store the current location of $\mathcal{A}_i$. The set of states S only contains valuations in which the location invariants for all TAs hold. The initial state s^0 is the state where all automata are in their initial location and all variables have their initial value.

The transition relation $\longrightarrow$ contains two kinds of transitions: delay transitions and action transitions. We have a delay transition $s \xrightarrow{d} s'$ iff s contains no committed locations, no urgent transition is enabled in s, and s' is obtained from s by incrementing all clocks with d and leaving the other variables unchanged, that is $s' = s \oplus d$. Note that, since s' is a state, s' satisfies the location invariants. In fact, since we require that location invariants are left-closed, we have that,

$$\frac{\begin{array}{c} l \xrightarrow{g,\tau,\rho}_i l' \\ s(\mathsf{loc}_i) = l \\ s \models g \end{array} \quad \begin{array}{c} s' = \rho(s)[\{\mathsf{loc}_i \mapsto l'\}] \\ (\forall k : s(\mathsf{loc}_k) \notin K_k) \vee l \in K_i \end{array}}{s \xrightarrow{\tau} s'} \quad \mathbf{TAU}$$

$$\frac{\begin{array}{cc} l_i \xrightarrow{g_i,c!,\rho_i} l_i' & l_j \xrightarrow{g_j,c?,\rho_j} l_j' \\ s(\mathsf{loc}_i) = l_i & s(\mathsf{loc}_j) = l_j \\ s \models g_i & s \models g_j \end{array} \quad \begin{array}{c} s' = \rho_j(\rho_i(s))[\{\mathsf{loc}_i \mapsto l_i', \mathsf{loc}_j \mapsto l_j'\}] \\ (\forall k : s(\mathsf{loc}_k) \notin K_k) \vee l_i \in K_i \vee l_j \in K_j \\ i \neq j \end{array}}{s \xrightarrow{\tau} s'} \quad \mathbf{SYNC}$$

$$\frac{s' = s \oplus d \quad \forall k : s(\mathsf{loc}_k) \notin K_k \quad \nexists(l \xrightarrow{g,\tau,\rho}_i^u l') : s(\mathsf{loc}_i) = l \wedge s \models g}{s \xrightarrow{d} s'} \quad \mathbf{TIME}$$

Fig. 3. UPPAAL style LTS semantics of an NTA

for all $d' \in [0, d]$, $s \oplus d'$ satisfies the location invariants. Also, since the guards of urgent transitions may not depend on clocks, we have that, for all $d' \in [0, d]$, $s \oplus d'$ does not enable any urgent transition.

For action transitions there are two cases: internal transitions and binary synchronizations. We have an internal transition $s \xrightarrow{\tau} s'$ if there is an automaton $\mathcal{A}_i$ that enables an internal transition $l \xrightarrow{g, \tau, \rho} l'$: $s(\mathsf{loc}_i) = l$ and $s \models g$. We require that either l is committed or no location in s is committed. Furthermore, s' is obtained from s by assigning to loc_i the value l', and applying the update function ρ. We have a synchronization transition $s \xrightarrow{\tau} s'$ if there are distinct components $\mathcal{A}_i$ and $\mathcal{A}_j$ that enable an output transition $l_i \xrightarrow{g_i, c!, \rho_i} l'_i$ and input transition $l_j \xrightarrow{g_j, c?, \rho_j} l'_j$, respectively. We require that either l_i or l_j is committed, or no location in s is committed. State s' is obtained from s by first applying update ρ_i and then update ρ_j. In addition the location variables are updated.

The key step towards a *compositional* semantics of NTAs is the definition below, which associates a TTS to an individual TA. Essentially this is a simplified version of Definition 8 in which a transition is made committed iff it originates from a committed location.

Definition 9 (TTS semantics of TA). *Let $\mathcal{A} = \langle L, K, l^0, E, H, v^0, I, \longrightarrow \rangle$ be a TA. The TTS associated to $\mathcal{A}$, notation $\mathsf{TTS}(\mathcal{A})$, is the tuple*

$$\langle E, H \cup \{\mathsf{loc}\}, S, s^0, \longrightarrow^1, \longrightarrow^0 \rangle,$$

where loc is a fresh variable with type L, $W = E \cup H \cup \{\mathsf{loc}\}$, $S = \{v \in \mathit{Val}(W) \mid v \models I(v(\mathsf{loc}))\}$, $s^0 = v^0 \| \{\mathsf{loc} \mapsto l^0\}$, and the transitions are defined by the rules in Fig. 4.

We can check that the structure that we have just defined is indeed a TTS. We now come to our second main theorem, which states that a compositional semantics of NTAs defined in terms of TTSs coincides (modulo isomorphism) with the noncompositional UPPAAL style semantics of Definition 8.

Theorem 4. *Let $\mathcal{N} = \langle \mathcal{A}_1, \ldots, \mathcal{A}_n \rangle$ be an NTA. Then*

$$\mathsf{LTS}(\mathcal{N}) \cong \mathsf{LTS}((\mathsf{TTS}(\mathcal{A}_1) \| \cdots \| \mathsf{TTS}(\mathcal{A}_n)) \backslash \mathcal{C}).$$

$$\frac{l \xrightarrow{g, \alpha, \rho} l' \quad s(\mathsf{loc}) = l \quad s \models g \quad s' = \rho(s)[\{\mathsf{loc} \mapsto l'\}] \quad b \Leftrightarrow (l \in K)}{s \xrightarrow{\alpha, b} s'} \quad \textbf{ACT}$$

$$\frac{s' = s \oplus d \quad s(\mathsf{loc}) \notin K \quad \nexists(l \xrightarrow{g, \tau, \rho}{}^u l') : s(\mathsf{loc}) = l \wedge s \models g}{s \xrightarrow{d, 0} s'} \quad \textbf{TIME}$$

Fig. 4. TTS semantics of a TA

In the remainder of this section, we briefly discuss how the previous results may help to alleviate the state space explosion problem. Simulation preorders preserve a rich class of properties (for instance, for Kripke structures all $\forall$CTL* properties, see [30]), but for simplicity we limit ourselves here to verification of invariants.

Definition 10 (Invariants). *Let $\mathcal{L} = \langle S, s^0, \longrightarrow \rangle$ be an LTS with $S \subseteq Val(V)$, for some set of variables V. Let P be a property over a subset of the variables of V. We say that P is an* invariant *of $\mathcal{L}$, notation $\mathcal{L} \models \forall \square P$, iff, for all reachable states s of $\mathcal{L}$, $s \models P$.*

By extension, we say that P is an invariant *of an NTA $\mathcal{N}$, notation $\mathcal{N} \models \forall \square P$, iff it is an invariant of $\mathsf{LTS}(\mathcal{N})$, and that P is an* invariant *of a TTS $\mathcal{T}$, notation $\mathcal{T} \models \forall \square P$, iff it is an invariant of $\mathsf{LTS}(\mathcal{T})$.*

Timed step simulations preserve invariant properties in one direction: if an invariant property holds for the abstract system, we may conclude it also holds for the concrete system.

Theorem 5. *Let $\mathcal{T}_1$ and $\mathcal{T}_2$ be comparable TTSs such that $\mathcal{T}_1 \preceq \mathcal{T}_2$. Let P be a property over the external variables of $\mathcal{T}_1$ and $\mathcal{T}_2$. If $\mathcal{T}_2 \models \forall \square P$, then $\mathcal{T}_1 \models \forall \square P$.*

Since our compositional semantics is consistent with the UPPAAL semantics, we can apply our abstraction results to networks of UPPAAL automata as follows. With abuse of notation write $\mathcal{A}_1 \| \cdots \| \mathcal{A}_i \preceq \mathcal{B}_1 \| \cdots \| \mathcal{B}_j$ if $\mathsf{LTS}(\mathcal{A}_1) \| \cdots \| \mathsf{LTS}(\mathcal{A}_i) \preceq \mathsf{LTS}(\mathcal{B}_1) \| \cdots \| \mathsf{LTS}(\mathcal{B}_j)$. Assume that $\mathcal{A}_1 \| \cdots \| \mathcal{A}_i \preceq \mathcal{B}_1 \| \cdots \| \mathcal{B}_j$, and the timed automata on the right-hand-side are simpler than those on the left-hand-side. Then, by the definitions and straightforward application of Theorems 2, 3 (assuming the side condition holds), 4 and 5,

$$\langle \mathcal{B}_1, \ldots, \mathcal{B}_j, \mathcal{A}_{i+1}, \ldots, \mathcal{A}_n \rangle \models \forall \square P \quad \Rightarrow \quad \langle \mathcal{A}_1, \ldots, \mathcal{A}_n \rangle \models \forall \square P$$

Thus, instead of model checking $\langle \mathcal{A}_1, \ldots, \mathcal{A}_n \rangle$ it suffices to model check the simpler system obtained by substituting $\mathcal{B}_1, \ldots, \mathcal{B}_j$ for $\mathcal{A}_1, \ldots, \mathcal{A}_i$. Variations of this result can be obtained by using the restriction laws of CCS.

We have successfully used this approach in order to analyze Zeroconf, a protocol for dynamic configuration of IPv4 link-local addresses defined by the IETF [12, 26]. Below we briefly summarize the different types of abstractions that we applied, and which all can be formally justified using timed step simulations: (1) Weakening guards and location invariants of component timed automata. Use of this type of "overapproximations" can be automatically checked using a general purpose theorem prover. (2) After weakening guards and location invariants, state variables that are not mentioned in the global invariant and that are no longer tested in guards, can be omitted. Again such transformations can be automatically checked using a general purpose theorem prover. (3) In order to verify instances of the protocol with an arbitrary number of hosts, we applied the "Spotlight" principle of [31] and abstracted all hosts except two into a "chaos" automaton, a very coarse abstraction with a single state that enables every action at any time. It should be routine to check this transformation formally using a proof assistant. (4) At some point, we abstracted one automaton by a composition of two automata. Unlike the other abstractions, proving correctness of this abstraction by hand turned out to be nontrivial. With help of Thomas Chatain, we succeeded to prove existence of a timed step simulation fully automatically using UPPAAL-TIGA [32], a branch of UPPAAL that is able to solve timed games on NTAs. It turns out that a timed step simulation corresponds to a winning strategy for a certain timed game. By using the abstractions, UPPAAL was able to verify the Zeroconf for an arbitrary number of hosts. Without our techniques, UPPAAL can only handle instances with three hosts.

5   Future Work

Our framework deals with an important part of the UPPAAL modeling language, and is for instance suitable for dealing with the Zeroconf protocol. Nevertheless, several features have not been dealt with, notably:

- *Urgent channels.* Our approach supports urgent internal transitions but not general urgent channels as in UPPAAL. Shared variables in combination with urgent internal transitions are very expressive, though, and we have never felt the need to use urgent synchronization channels in any of the numerous UPPAAL applications that we have been involved in. We expect that urgent channels can be easily incorporated using the concept of timed ready simulations from [7].

- *Broadcast communication.* General broadcast communication, as supported by UPPAAL, does not have a neat semantics: the order in which automata are declared influences the semantics of a network. It should be possible though to identify a well-behaved subset (for instance, by requiring that the variables modified by different input actions be disjoint). Once this has been done, we expect that the results of this paper can easily be generalized.

- *Priorities.* UPPAAL supports channel priorities. As we have shown, committed locations induce a priority mechanism, and we expect that channel priorities can be described in an analogous manner.

Conceptually there are no major difficulties involved in generalizing our results to a setting which includes these features, but the proofs will become tedious and long. Since UPPAAL is extended all the time, we envisage that proof assistants such as Isabelle and PVS will become indispensable for establishing correctness of verification methods.

Although from a theoretical viewpoint implementing our framework may be less interesting, from a practical viewpoint it is all the more. We envisage a version of UPPAAL that maintains networks of timed automata at different levels of abstraction, and which can automatically prove correctness of abstractions using UPPAAL-TIGA and theorem proving technology.

Since we phrased our compositionality results very abstractly in terms of timed transition systems, which may (or may not) have time-passage transitions and may (or may not) have committed transitions, our results can be reused directly in the design of other practical modeling languages with both shared variables and synchronization of actions.

References

1. Behrmann, G., David, A., Larsen, K.: A tutorial on Uppaal. In: Bernardo, M., Corradini, F. (eds.) SFM-RT 2004. LNCS, vol. 3185, pp. 200–236. Springer, Heidelberg (2004)
2. Milner, R.: An algebraic definition of simulation between programs. In: Proceedings 2nd Joint Conference on Artificial Intelligence, pp. 481–489. British Computer Society Press, London (1971)
3. Lynch, N., Tuttle, M.: Hierarchical correctness proofs for distributed algorithms. In: Proceedings of the 6th Annual ACM Symposium on Principles of Distributed Computing, August 1987, pp. 137–151 (1987); A full version is available as MIT Technical Report MIT/LCS/TR-387
4. Jonsson, B.: Simulations between specifications of distributed systems. In: Baeten, J., Groote, J. (eds.) CONCUR 1991. LNCS, vol. 527, pp. 346–360. Springer, Heidelberg (1991)
5. Abadi, M., Lamport, L.: The existence of refinement mappings. Theoretical Computer Science 82(2), 253–284 (1991)
6. Lynch, N., Vaandrager, F.: Forward and backward simulations, I: Untimed systems. Information and Computation 121(2), 214–233 (1995)
7. Jensen, H.: Abstraction-Based Verification of Distributed Systems. PhD thesis, Department of Computer Science, Aalborg University, Denmark (June 1999)
8. Jensen, H., Larsen, K., Skou, A.: Scaling up Uppaal: Automatic verification of real-time systems using compositionality and abstraction. In: Joseph, M. (ed.) FTRTFT 2000. LNCS, vol. 1926, Springer, Heidelberg (2000)
9. Griffioen, W., Vaandrager, F.: A theory of normed simulations. ACM Transactions on Computational Logic 5(4), 577–610 (2004)
10. Frehse, G.: Compositional Verification of Hybrid Systems using Simulation Relations. PhD thesis, Radboud University Nijmegen (October 2005)
11. Kaynar, D., Lynch, N., Segala, R., Vaandrager, F.: The Theory of Timed I/O Automata. Synthesis Lecture on Computer Science, p. 101. Morgan & Claypool Publishers (2006) ISBN 159829010X
12. Gebremichael, B., Vaandrager, F., Zhang, M.: Analysis of the Zeroconf protocol using Uppaal. In: Proceedings 6th Annual ACM & IEEE Conference on Embedded Software (EMSOFT 2006), Seoul, South Korea, October 22-25, 2006, pp. 242–251. ACM Press, New York (2006)
13. Lamport, L.: The temporal logic of actions. ACM Transactions on Programming Languages and Systems 16(3), 872–923 (1994)
14. Alur, R., Henzinger, T.: Reactive Modules. Formal Methods in System Design 15(1), 7–48 (1999)
15. Milner, R.: Communication and Concurrency. Prentice-Hall International, Englewood Cliffs (1989)
16. Lynch, N., Segala, R., Vaandrager, F., Weinberg, H.: Hybrid I/O automata. In: Alur, R., Henzinger, T., Sontag, E. (eds.) Hybrid Systems III. LNCS, vol. 1066, pp. 496–510. Springer, Heidelberg (1996)
17. Groote, J., Ponse, A.: Process algebra with guards. Combining Hoare logic with process algebra. Formal Aspects of Computing 6, 115–164 (1994)
18. de Alfaro, L., da Silva, L.D., Faella, M., Legay, A., Roy, P., Sorea, M.: Sociable interfaces. In: Gramlich, B. (ed.) FroCos 2005. LNCS (LNAI), vol. 3717, pp. 81–105. Springer, Heidelberg (2005)

19. van Beek, D.A., Reniers, M.A., Schiffelers, R.R.H., Rooda, J.E.: Foundations of a compositional interchange format for hybrid systems. In: Bemporad, A., Bicchi, A., Buttazzo, G. (eds.) HSCC 2007. LNCS, vol. 4416, pp. 587–600. Springer, Heidelberg (2007)
20. Berendsen, J., Vaandrager, F.: Parallel composition in a paper of Jensen, Larsen and Skou is not associative. Technical note (September 2007), http://www.ita.cs.ru.nl/publications/papers/fvaan/BV07.html
21. Berendsen, J., Vaandrager, F.: Parallel composition in a paper by De Alfaro e.a. is not associative. Technical note available electronically (May 2008), http://www.ita.cs.ru.nl/publications/papers/fvaan/BV07.html
22. Bhat, G., Cleaveland, R., Lüttgen, G.: Dynamic priorities for modeling real-time. In: Togashi, A., Mizuno, T., Shiratori, N., Higashino, T. (eds.) FORTE. IFIP Conference Proceedings, vol. 107, pp. 321–336. Chapman & Hall, Boca Raton (1997)
23. Cleaveland, R., Lüttgen, G., Natarajan, V.: A process algebra with distributed priorities. Theor. Comput. Sci. 195(2), 227–258 (1998)
24. Phillips, I.: CCS with priority guards. In: Larsen, K.G., Nielsen, M. (eds.) CONCUR 2001. LNCS, vol. 2154, pp. 305–320. Springer, Heidelberg (2001)
25. Aceto, L., Bloom, B., Vaandrager, F.: Turning SOS rules into equations. LICS 1992 Special Issue of Information and Computation 111(1), 1–52 (1994)
26. Berendsen, J., Gebremichael, B., Vaandrager, F., Zhang, M.: Formal specification and analysis of zeroconf using Uppaal. Report ICIS-R07032, Institute for Computing and Information Sciences, Radboud University Nijmegen (December 2007)
27. Berendsen, J., Vaandrager, F.: Compositional abstraction in real-time model checking. Technical Report ICIS-R07027, Institute for Computing and Information Sciences, Radboud University Nijmegen (2007), http://www.ita.cs.ru.nl/publications/papers/fvaan/BV07.html
28. Sifakis, J.: The compositional specification of timed systems - a tutorial. In: Halbwachs, N., Peled, D.A. (eds.) CAV 1999. LNCS, vol. 1633, pp. 2–7. Springer, Heidelberg (1999)
29. Bowman, H.: Modelling timeouts without timelocks. In: Katoen, J.-P. (ed.) AMAST-ARTS 1999, ARTS 1999, and AMAST-WS 1999. LNCS, vol. 1601, p. 20. Springer, Heidelberg (1999)
30. Grumberg, O., Long, D.: Model checking and modular verification. ACM Trans. Program. Lang. Syst. 16(3), 843–871 (1994)
31. Wachter, B., Westphal, B.: The Spotlight Principle: On Process-Summarizing State Abstractions. In: Podelski, A., Cook, B. (eds.) VMCAI 2007. LNCS, vol. 4349. Springer, Heidelberg (2007)
32. Cassez, F., David, A., Fleury, E., Larsen, K., Lime, D.: Efficient on-the-fly algorithms for the analysis of timed games. In: Abadi, M., de Alfaro, L. (eds.) CONCUR 2005. LNCS, vol. 3653, pp. 66–80. Springer, Heidelberg (2005)

On Conformance Testing for Timed Systems

Julien Schmaltz[1,2,*] and Jan Tretmans[1,2]

[1] Radboud University Nijmegen
Institute for Computing and Information Sciences
PO Box 9010 6500GL Nijmegen, The Netherlands
[2] Embedded System Institute
PO Box 513 5600 MB Eindhoven, The Netherlands
{julien,tretmans}@cs.ru.nl

Abstract. Conformance testing for labeled transition systems starts with defining when an implementation conforms to its specification. One of the formal theories for model-based testing uses the implementation relation **ioco** for this purpose. A peculiar aspect of **ioco** is to consider the absence of outputs as an observable action, named *quiescence*. Recently a number of real-time extensions of **ioco** have been proposed in the literature. Quiescence and the observation of arbitrary delays are issues when defining such extensions. We present two new timed implementation relations and show their relation with existing ones. Based on these new definitions and using several examples, we show the subtle differences, and the consequences that small modifications in the definitions can have on the resulting relations. Moreover, we present conditions under which some of these implementation relations coincide. The notion of *M-quiescence*, i.e., if outputs occur in a system they occur before a delay M, turns out to be important in these conditions.

1 Introduction

One of the emerging and promising techniques for automating the testing process is *model-based testing*. A *model* specifying the desired behavior of the *implementation under test* (IUT) is used for test generation and test result analysis. One theory for model-based testing uses labeled transition systems as models, and an *implementation relation* called **ioco** which formally defines when an IUT is correct with respect to its specification model [12, 13]. The implementation relation **ioco** expresses that an IUT conforms to its specification if the IUT never produces an output that cannot be produced by the specification. In addition, the notion of *quiescence* is used to express silence, i.e., the absence of outputs. An IUT may only be quiescent if the specification can be quiescent. Testing according to **ioco** involves testing the ordering of events and timing properties are not considered. The correct behavior of many systems – *e.g.* embedded systems and communication protocols – depends on real-time properties, for which a real-time implementation relation is required.

* Funded by EU projects FP6 MCRTN TAROT and FP7 STREP QUASIMODO.

F. Cassez and C. Jard (Eds.): FORMATS 2008, LNCS 5215, pp. 250–264, 2008.

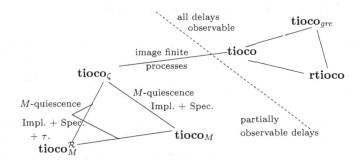

Fig. 1. Global Overview

Real-time extensions of **ioco** have already been defined [2, 3, 4, 6, 7, 11]. These extensions differ in particular in their treatment of quiescence and their assumptions regarding the observation of arbitrary delays. In this paper, we study various timed **ioco** relations and relate them to each other. These relations subtly differ in their definitions and we show under which conditions they are equivalent. In the comparison, we introduce two new relations. The relation **tioco** considers that all delays are observable. The relation **tioco**$_\zeta$ considers that only delays up to some bound are observable.

The relations considered in this paper are shown in Fig. 1. Two equivalent relations are connected by a line. Annotations on this line are conditions under which the equivalence holds. On the right hand side of the picture, we find the relations where any delay is an observable action. We define **tioco** in Section 3. Section 4 shows that *relativized conformance* **rtioco** defined by Larsen, Mikucionis, Nielsen, and Skou [11] is equivalent to **tioco**. This also holds for the relation defined by Krichen and Tripakis [7] which we refer to as **tioco**$_{gre}$.

On the other side of the dotted line, relations assume that delays are only observable to some bound M. Then, the notion of *M-quiescence* introduced by Brandán-Briones and Brinksma [3, 4] is important. A system is M-quiescent if outputs occur within a maximum delay M after the previous action. Section 5 introduces *quiescence, M-quiescence, unbounded delays*, and their relations. Those concepts serve as a basis when considering partially observable delays. Section 6 defines **tioco**$_\zeta$ which restricts to unbounded delays instead of arbitrary delays. It is shown that this is sufficient if implementations are image finite. Section 7 shows that **tioco**$_\zeta$, and thus **tioco**, coincide with **tioco**$_M$ defined by Brandán-Briones and Brinksma [3, 4] if implementations and specifications are assumed to be M-quiescent. An alternative definition of quiescence, which is closer to the untimed definition of quiescence, leads to the relation **tioco**$_M^{\mathcal{R}}$. If in addition to M-quiescence of outputs for implementations and specifications, internal τ-steps are assumed to be M-quiescent, i.e., τ-steps always occur within delay M, then this relation coincides with the other ones.

The last section, Section 8, presents our conclusions and some further work. Section 2 recapitulates the model of Timed Input/Output Transition Systems, on which our work, analogous to the other above mentioned papers, is based.

2   Timed Input/Output Transition Systems

Timed Input Output Transition Systems (TIOTS) are labeled transition systems extended with time. Labels are either an observable action (input or output), a time passage action, or the internal (unobservable) action τ. Time passage actions range over time domain $\mathcal{D}$ (here the nonnegative reals $\mathbb{R}_{\geq 0}$ [1]).

Definition 1. *A TIOTS $\mathcal{A}$ is a 6-tuple $\langle \mathcal{Q}, q_0, \mathcal{L}_I, \mathcal{L}_U, \mathcal{D}, \mathcal{T} \rangle$ where $\mathcal{Q}$ is a non-empty set of states, q_0 is the initial state, $\mathcal{L}_I$ is the set of input actions (noted $?a$), $\mathcal{L}_U$ is the set of output actions (noted $!x$), we have $\mathcal{L}_I \cap \mathcal{L}_U = \emptyset$, $\mathcal{D}$ is the set of time passage actions, and $\mathcal{T} \subseteq \mathcal{Q} \times (\mathcal{L}_\tau \cup \mathcal{D}) \times \mathcal{Q}$ is the transition relation (where $\mathcal{L} = \mathcal{L}_I \cup \mathcal{L}_U$ and $\mathcal{L}_\tau = \mathcal{L} \cup \{\tau\}$) constrained by the following properties:*

Time Additivity (TiAdd):

$\forall q_1, q_3 \in \mathcal{Q}, \forall d_1, d_2 \in \mathcal{D} : \exists q_2 : q_1 \xrightarrow{d_1} q_2 \xrightarrow{d_2} q_3 \ \equiv q_1 \xrightarrow{d_1+d_2} q_3$

Null Delay (NuDe): $\forall q_1, q_2 \in \mathcal{Q} : q_1 \xrightarrow{0} q_2 \equiv q_1 = q_2$

Time Determinism (TiDet)

$\forall q_1, q_2, q_3 \in \mathcal{Q} : q_1 \xrightarrow{d} q_2$ **and** $q_1 \xrightarrow{d} q_3$ **then** $q_2 = q_3$

Letting time pass moves a TIOTS to a new state. State $q(d)$ denotes the state reached from q after d time units. Sometimes, state q is written as $q(0)$. The set of all finite (resp. infinite) sequences over $\mathcal{L}_\tau \cup \mathbb{R}_{\geq 0}$ is noted $(\mathcal{L}_\tau \cup \mathbb{R}_{\geq 0})^*$ (resp. $(\mathcal{L}_\tau \cup \mathbb{R}_{\geq 0})^\omega$). The empty sequence is noted ϵ. The sequence $d \cdot \mu$ is often written (d, μ). If there exists at least one reachable state from state q by performing a sequence l, we write $q \xrightarrow{l}$. Otherwise, we write $q \xrightarrow{l} \!\!\!\!/\;$. A path π is a finite or infinite sequence of transitions. The set of all finite (resp. infinite) paths of a TIOTS $\mathcal{A}$ is noted $\mathbf{paths}(\mathcal{A})$ (resp. $\mathbf{paths}^\omega(\mathcal{A})$). Let $\sigma \in (\mathcal{L} \cup \mathbb{R}_{\geq 0})^*$, $\mu \in \mathcal{L}_U$, and $d_1, d_2 \in \mathbb{R}_{\geq 0}$. We define the generalized transition relation as the minimal relation satisfying the following rules:

$$(\mathbf{T}\epsilon) \ q \xRightarrow{\epsilon} q \qquad\qquad (\mathbf{T}\tau) \ q \xRightarrow{\sigma} q' \text{ if } q \xRightarrow{\sigma} q_1 \xrightarrow{\tau} q'$$

$$(\mathbf{T}\mu) \ q \xRightarrow{\sigma \cdot \mu} q' \text{ if } q \xRightarrow{\sigma} q_1 \xrightarrow{\mu} q' \ (\mathbf{T}d) \ q \xRightarrow{d_1+d_2} q' \text{ if } q \xRightarrow{d_1} q_1 \xRightarrow{d_2} q'$$

A timed trace σ is a sequence of actions and delays. There can be two successive delays, e.g., $\sigma = ?a \cdot d_1 \cdot d_2 \cdot !x$. It would be more natural to normalize to timed traces with no consecutive delays, for instance $\sigma = ?a \cdot (d_1 + d_2) \cdot !x$.

Definition 2. Normalized Timed Traces. *Let $A = \langle \mathcal{Q}, q_0, \mathcal{L}_I, \mathcal{L}_U, \mathbb{R}_{\geq 0}, \mathcal{T} \rangle$ be a TIOTS. We have* $\mathbf{nttraces}(\mathcal{A}) \triangleq \{\sigma \in (\mathbb{R}_{\geq 0} \cdot \mathcal{L})^* \cdot (\epsilon + \mathbb{R}_{\geq 0}) | q_0 \xRightarrow{\sigma} \}$.

It is possible to associate to each timed trace a normalized one. As shown in [3], the set of normalized timed traces characterizes the set of all timed traces.

---

[1] In general, the time domain could be different than the non-negative reals. Formally, a time domain is "a totally ordered, well-founded additive monoid with neutral element 0 that is also the minimum of the ordering, and with $d + d' \leq d$ iff $d' = 0$"[2].

We define the operator **after**$_t$ to compute the set of states reachable after performing a timed trace $\sigma \subset (\mathcal{L} \cup \mathbb{R}_{\geq 0})^*$.

$$q \textbf{ after}_t \sigma \triangleq \{q' \mid q \overset{\sigma}{\Longrightarrow} q'\}; \quad \mathcal{Q} \textbf{ after}_t \sigma \triangleq \bigcup_{q \in \mathcal{Q}} (q \textbf{ after}_t \sigma)$$

To represent realistic systems and to reason in a precise manner, the following restrictions on the TIOTS are made.

A TIOTS is *strongly convergent* if and only if there is no infinite τ-paths.

$$\textbf{(StroConv)} \qquad \forall \pi \in \textbf{paths}^\omega(\mathcal{A}) : \exists q_i, \mu \in \pi : q_i \overset{\mu}{\to} \wedge \mu \neq \tau \qquad (1)$$

A TIOTS has no forced input, if, when waiting for inputs to make progress, it has always the possibility to let time pass. Formally, a system has no forced input if from every state and for any possible delay D there exists a trace with no input and the sum of the delays equals D.

$$\textbf{(noFI)} \forall q \in \mathcal{Q}, \forall D \in \mathbb{R}_{\geq 0}, \exists \sigma \in (\mathcal{L}_U \cup \{\tau\} \cup \mathbb{R}_{\geq 0})^* : q \overset{\sigma}{\to} \wedge \sum_{\mu \in \sigma, \mu \in \mathbb{R}_{\geq 0}} \mu = D \quad (2)$$

Any TIOTS is assumed to be strongly convergent and to have no forced input. Note that the "no forced input" implies "time divergence". The definition of the latter generalizes Equation 2 by removing the restriction to traces with output and internal states. It considers traces with inputs as well.

3   The tioco Relation

Any implementation is assumed to be an *input enabled* TIOTS, i.e., to accept all inputs at all times.

Definition 3. Input Enabled TIOTS. *A TIOTS $\mathcal{A} = \langle \mathcal{Q}, q_0, \mathcal{L}_I, \mathcal{L}_U, \mathbb{R}_{\geq 0}, \mathcal{T} \rangle$ is input enabled if and only if $\forall q \in \mathcal{Q}, \forall a \in \mathcal{L}_I : q \overset{a}{\Longrightarrow} .$*

The set **out**$_t$ of a state q is a set of traces of length two: an output action μ and the delay d that is possible before this output action, or a delay d together with '$-$' to denote a delay that is not followed by an output action. Here, we consider any delay to be an observable action. If there can be more than one delay before an action, the set **out**$_t$ contains all the possibilities.

$$\textbf{out}_t(q) \triangleq \{(d, \mu) \mid \mu \in \mathcal{L}_U \wedge d \in \mathbb{R}_{\geq 0} \wedge q \overset{(d,\mu)}{\Longrightarrow} \} \cup \{(d, -) \mid d \in \mathbb{R}_{\geq 0} \wedge q \overset{d}{\Longrightarrow} \}$$
$$(3)$$

This notation is overloaded to apply to a set of states.

$$\textbf{out}_t(\mathcal{Q}) \triangleq \bigcup_{q \in \mathcal{Q}} \textbf{out}_t(q) \qquad (4)$$

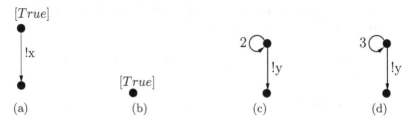

Fig. 2. Implementation examples

Example 1. Consider the examples[2] in Fig. 2. For example (a), $\mathbf{out}_t(q_0) = \{(d, !x) \mid d \in \mathbb{R}_{\geq 0}\} \cup \{(d, -) \mid d \in \mathbb{R}_{\geq 0}\}$. For example (b), $\mathbf{out}_t(q_0) = \{(d, -) \mid d \in \mathbb{R}_{\geq 0}\}$. For example (c), $\mathbf{out}_t(q_0) = \{(d, !y) \mid d \bmod 2 = 0\} \cup \{(d, -) \mid d \in \mathbb{R}_{\geq 0}\}$. Note that $\{(d, -) \mid d \in \mathbb{R}_{\geq 0}\}$ is a consequence of time additivity. Similarly, for example (d), $\mathbf{out}_t(q_0) = \{(d, !y) \mid d \bmod 3 = 0\} \cup \{(d, -) \mid d \in \mathbb{R}_{\geq 0}\}$.

For an implementation i satisfying the test hypothesis and a specification s, i is **tioco** correct w.r.t. s, if the output set of i after every normalized timed trace of s is a subset of the output set of s after the same normalized timed trace.

$$i \text{ tioco } s \equiv \forall \sigma \in \mathbf{nttraces}(s), \mathbf{out}_t(i \text{ after}_t \sigma) \subseteq \mathbf{out}_t(s \text{ after}_t \sigma) \qquad (5)$$

Example 2. Let consider example (a) in Fig. 2 a specification and example (b) in the same figure an implementation. As they both accept all possible delays in their initial state, they are conforming according to our implementation relation.

Consider example (c) in Fig. 2 a specification and example (d) in Fig. 2 an implementation. Implementation (d) is not a valid implementation of specification (c), because it can output !y after 3 time units, and the specification only allows outputs after even numbers.

4   Relating tioco with Similar Relations

The conformance relation **rtioco** has been developed by Larsen Mikucionis, Nielsen, and Skou [5, 11] at the University of Aalborg, Denmark. The main feature of this relation is to consider the environment of the IUT explicitly. The conformance is then shown under such an environment. Test generation for the relation **rtioco** is implemented in the tool UPPAAL-TRON [10] which uses Timed Automata in UPPAAL's syntax.

Definition 4. *Given e, i, and t be input-enabled TIOTS, the **rtioco** relation is:*

$$i \text{ rtioco}_e s \triangleq \forall \sigma \in \mathbf{nttraces}(e) : \mathbf{out}_{aa}((i, e) \text{ after}_t \sigma) \subseteq \mathbf{out}_{aa}((s, e) \text{ after}_t \sigma)$$

where $\mathbf{out}_{aa}(q) \triangleq \{\mu \in \mathcal{L}_U \cup \mathbb{R}_{\geq 0} \mid q \xrightarrow{\mu} \}$

---

[2] Examples are sometimes drawn using the Timed Automata [1] notation. Invariants and guards – noted $[\varphi]$ – restrict the amount of time that can be spent in a state or that a transition is available. The clock is reset on all transitions.

To compare our approach with **rtioco** we assume the most general environment. In contrast to the **rtioco** relation, we do not assume input-enabled specifications. Thus, we have to reduce the traces of the least restrictive environment – i.e., all traces over the input and output actions – to traces that are accepted by the specification. We compare our relation to the following:

$$i \ \textbf{rtioco} \ s \triangleq \forall \sigma \in \textbf{nttraces}(s) : \textbf{out}_{aa}(i \ \textbf{after}_t \ \sigma) \subseteq \textbf{out}_{aa}(s \ \textbf{after}_t \ \sigma) \quad (6)$$

The next proposition proves that **tioco** and **rtioco** are equivalent.

Proposition 1. $i \ \textbf{tioco} \ s \equiv i \ \textbf{rtioco} \ s$

Proof. Both relations consider the same set of timed traces (specification). Thus, we only need to prove the mutual inclusion of the sets of outputs.

1. $(d, -) \in \textbf{out}_t(q) \equiv d \in \textbf{out}_{aa}(q)$ by definitions of $\textbf{out}_t$ and $\textbf{out}_{aa}$.
2. $(d, l) \in \textbf{out}_t(q) \equiv d \in \textbf{out}_{aa}(q) \wedge l \in \textbf{out}_{aa}(q \ \textbf{after}_t \ d)$. From the left hand side we obtain that $q \xrightarrow{d} \bullet \xrightarrow{l} \bullet$. It equivalently follows that $d \in \textbf{out}_{aa}(q)$ and $l \in \textbf{out}_{aa}(q \ \textbf{after}_t \ d)$.

Our **tioco** relation is similar to the relation – named **tioco**$_{gre}$ in this paper – developed by Krichen and Tripakis [7]. The **tioco**$_{gre}$ relation does not consider the environment explicitly. The models considered in **tioco**$_{gre}$ are less restrictive than for **rtioco**. Krichen and Tripakis' relation includes non-deterministic and partially-observable timed automata. Their definition of the set of outputs is slightly different. They define the set of all delays which can elapse in state q as the set of all the possible sums over traces without input or output action:

$$elapse(q) \triangleq \{t > 0 \mid \exists \sigma \in \{\tau\}^* : \sum_{\mu \in \sigma, \mu \in \mathbb{R}_{\geq 0}} \mu = t \wedge q \xrightarrow{t} \} \quad (7)$$

Then, they define the set of outputs of state q as the union of $elapse(q)$ with the output actions outgoing from q without internal steps.

$$\textbf{out}_{gre}(q) = \{\mu \in \mathcal{L}_U \mid q \xrightarrow{\mu} \} \cup elapse(q) \quad (8)$$

The **tioco**$_{gre}$ relation is then defined over the timed traces of the specification:

$$i \ \textbf{tioco}_{gre} \ s \triangleq \forall \sigma \in \textbf{ttraces}(s) : \textbf{out}_{gre}(i \ \textbf{after}_t \ \sigma) \subseteq \textbf{out}_{gre}(s \ \textbf{after}_t \ \sigma) \quad (9)$$

Recently, Krichen and Tripakis proved [9] that the **tioco**$_{gre}$ can capture **rtioco** by modeling the assumption on the environment separately and taking the composition with the specification [9]. They prove the following proposition:

Proposition 2. *Let s,i and e be three input-enabled TIOTS. We have*

$$i \ \textbf{rtioco}_e \ s \equiv (i \| e) \ \textbf{tioco}_{gre} \ (s \| e)$$

where $\|$ denotes a parallel composition (see [9] for more details).

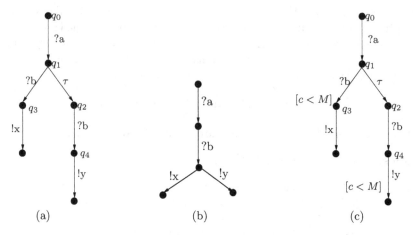

Fig. 3. Quiescence: examples

From this proposition and Proposition 6, it easily follows that under the least restrictive environment **tioco**$_{gre}$ and **tioco** are equivalent.

Brandán Briones and Brinksma proposed the **tioco**$_M$ relation as an extension of the **ioco** relation [3, 4]. This relation includes the notion of quiescence and assumes that delays are only observable up to some limit. Before going further in the comparisons, we introduce this notion and related concepts. In Section 7, we discuss the relation between partially and fully observable delays.

5   M-Quiescence, Quiescence and Unbounded Delays

Quiescence. We introduce quiescence as defined in the **tioco**$_M$ relation [2, 3, 4] (presented in Section 7). A quiescent state is a state where the system is unable to produce an output now or in the future, without receiving an input first.

Definition 5. Quiescence. $\delta(q) \triangleq \forall \mu \in \mathcal{L}_U, \forall d \in \mathbb{R}_{\geq 0} : q \overset{(d,\mu)}{=\!\!\!=\!\!\!\not\Rightarrow}$

Example 3. The initial state of example (b) in Fig 2 is quiescent, as no output is ever produced. All initial states of the remaining examples of the same figure are not quiescent, as an output can be produced at (almost) any time.

As pointed out by Bohnenkamp and Belinfante [2] this definition of quiescence differs from the original notion introduced in the **ioco** theory [12]. We recall the original definition of quiescence, noted δ_0.

Definition 6. Untimed Quiescence $\delta_0(q) \triangleq \forall \mu \in \mathcal{L}_U \cup \{\tau\} : q \overset{\mu}{\longrightarrow}\!\!\!\not$

The difference is that in the original definition, states with an outgoing internal transition are not quiescent, whereas in the above timed definition, such states are quiescent. Before illustrating these differences on examples, we introduce a "repaired" definition – noted $\delta_\mathcal{R}$ – closer to the original one.

Definition 7. Quiescence "repaired".

$$\delta_{\mathcal{R}}(q) \triangleq \forall \mu \in \mathcal{L}_U \cup \{\tau\}, \forall d \in \mathbb{R}_{\geq 0} : q \xrightarrow{(d,\mu)} \not\rightarrow$$

Example 4. Consider the examples in Fig. 3 as untimed transition systems. Let consider example (a). According to the original untimed definition of quiescence (δ_0), we have $\delta_0(q_0)$ and $\neg\delta_0(q_1)$. Regarding example (b), we have $\delta_0(q_0)$ and $\delta_0(q_1)$. Let us now consider that an arbitrary amount of time can be spent in every state. In example (a), state q_1 is now quiescent according to Def. 5. We have $\delta(q_1)$, as well as $\delta(q_0)$ and $\delta(q_2)$. In example (b), no new quiescent state is introduced. According to the "repaired" timed definition (Def. 7), quiescent states correspond to those of the untimed case, i.e., we have $\neg\delta_{\mathcal{R}}(q_1)$ in example (a).

This detail in the definition of quiescence has an important impact. We discuss this in more details in Section 7.

M-quiescence. The idea behind M-quiescence is to consider that delays up to M are observable and that no output is ever produced after M [4]. Formally, a system is M-quiescent if and only if once M time units have passed without observable action, then no output will *ever* be produced.

Definition 8. M-quiescence. *Let* $\mathcal{I} = \langle \mathcal{Q}, q_0, \mathcal{L}_I, \mathcal{L}_U, \mathbb{R}_{\geq 0}, \mathcal{T} \rangle$ *be a TIOTS.* $\mathcal{I}$ *is M-quiescent if and only if:* $\forall q \in \mathcal{Q}, \forall \mu \in \mathcal{L}_U, \forall d \geq M : q \overset{(d,\mu)}{\Longrightarrow} \not\rightarrow$

Example 5. Examples (a), (c), and (d) in Fig. 2 can produce an output at any time, and are therefore not M-quiescent for any $M \in \mathbb{R}_{\geq 0}$. Example (b) is M-quiescent for any $M \in \mathbb{R}_{\geq 0}$, as no output is ever produced.

Unbounded Delays. Let us consider example (a) in Fig. 2 to be a specification. This system specifies that an output may be produced at *any time*. Intuitively, a valid implementation could choose between producing the output or never producing any output (example (b) in Fig. 2). A conformance relation based on any of the aforementioned definition of quiescence would not consider example (b) as a valid implementation of example (a). We introduce the notion of "unbounded delays" as a new action, which is given a new symbol: ζ. Formally, a state accepts any finite delay, if it accepts all possible delays:

Definition 9. Unbounded Delay (UD). $\zeta(q) \triangleq \forall d \in \mathbb{R}_{\geq 0} : q \overset{d}{\Longrightarrow}$

Example 6. For all examples in Fig 2, initial states satisfy the above definition. If we assume that an arbitrary time can be spent in any state of the examples in Fig. 3, all these states also satisfy the above definition.

Quiescence and Unbounded Delays. If a state is quiescent, then it can accept any finite unbounded delay. We prove this proposition using Def. 5 for quiescence. The proposition also holds for Def. 7 and the proof is very similar.

Proposition 3. $\delta(q) \Rightarrow \zeta(q)$

Proof. Assume $\delta(q)$. From property **noFI** (Equation 2), we can find from $q -$ and for any possible time $D-$ a trace without an input action such that the sum of its delay equals D. Because state q is quiescent, this trace has also no output action. So, traces in Equation 2 have no output action, and we have:

$$\forall D \in \mathbb{R}_{\geq 0}, \exists \sigma \in (\mathbb{R}_{\geq 0} \cup \{\tau\})^* : q \xrightarrow{\sigma} \wedge \sum_{\mu \in \sigma, \mu \in \mathbb{R}_{\geq 0}} \mu = D \qquad (10)$$

We choose an arbitrary delay d and eliminate the universal quantifier in the definition of ζ. Then, we conclude by instantiating the universal quantifier of our hypothesis (Equation 10) with this arbitrary d.

Example (a) in Fig. 2 shows that "unbounded delay" does not imply quiescence. Its initial state is ζ because it accepts all possible delays. It is not δ, because $!x$ can be output at any time.

Quiescence and M-quiescence. In the context of M-quiescent systems, quiescence is equivalent to accept M time units, i.e., considering timed traces with occurrences of quiescence is equivalent to consider normal traces (without δ's).

To be more precise, we need to consider traces where quiescence (δ) appears exactly after M time units. We denote by $\Delta(\mathcal{A})$, the δ-closure of TIOTS $\mathcal{A}$ where a self-loop transition is added to every state satisfying Def. 5.

$$\mathbf{nttraces}_M^\Delta(\mathcal{A}) \triangleq \mathbf{nttraces}(\Delta(\mathcal{A})) \cap (\mathbb{R}_{\geq 0} \cdot \mathcal{L} + M \cdot \delta)^* \cdot (\epsilon + \mathbb{R}_{\geq 0}) \qquad (11)$$

The next proposition shows that for any normalized timed suspension trace σ, one can build a trace $\hat{\sigma}$ equivalent to σ but where every occurrence of δ has been removed. Every occurrence of (M, δ) in σ is replaced by $(M, -)$ in $\hat{\sigma}$.

Definition 10. $\forall \sigma \in \mathbf{nttraces}_M^\Delta(\mathcal{A})$ *such that* $\sigma = \sigma_1 \cdot (M, \delta) \cdot (d, \mu) \cdot \sigma_2$, *where* σ_1 *does not contain any occurrence of* δ *and* $\mu \in \mathcal{L}_I$, $\hat{\sigma} = \sigma_1 \cdot (M + d, \mu) \cdot \hat{\sigma_2}$. *And for all other* $\sigma \in \mathbf{nttraces}_M^\Delta(\mathcal{A})$, $\hat{\sigma} = \sigma$.

Proposition 4. $\forall \sigma \in \mathbf{nttraces}_M^\Delta(\mathcal{A}) : q \xRightarrow{\sigma} q'$ *iff* $q \xRightarrow{\hat{\sigma}} q'$.

Proof. By induction over $\hat{\sigma}$.

$\Rightarrow$ We consider all q_1' and q_2' such that $q \xRightarrow{\sigma_1 \cdot (M, \delta)} q_1' \xRightarrow{(d, \mu)} q_2'$, which can be further expanded to $q \xRightarrow{\sigma_1 \cdot M} q_1' \xrightarrow{\delta} q_1'$. Thus, we have $q \xRightarrow{\sigma_1 \cdot M} q_1' \xRightarrow{(d, \mu)} q_2'$. Finally, we get $q \xRightarrow{\sigma_1 \cdot (M+d, \mu)} q_2'$ and the induction hypothesis concludes.

$\Leftarrow$ We consider all q_1' and q_2' such that $q \xRightarrow{\sigma_1 \cdot M} q_1' \xRightarrow{(d, \mu)} q_2'$. From M-quiescence (Def. 8), it follows that $\delta(q_1')$. One can add a self-loop transition to every q_1' and $q \xRightarrow{\sigma_1 \cdot (M, \delta)} q_1'$. The induction hypothesis concludes the case.

Example (a) in Fig. 4 shows an non M-quiescent system where Proposition 4 does not hold. State q_3 is quiescent but state q_1 is not. Therefore, after execution the trace $(0, ?a) \cdot (M, \delta)$ only state q_3 is reached. After execution trace $(0, ?a) \cdot M$, states q_3 and q_1 are reached.

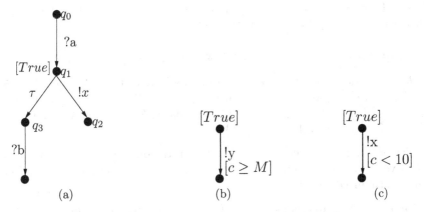

Fig. 4. Quiescence and M-quiescence: examples

Quiescence, M-quiescence and Unbounded delays. For M-quiescent systems, unbounded delay is equivalent to quiescence after M. Adding the guard $[c < M]$ to the output transition of Example (a) in Fig. 2 turns this system into an M-quiescent system. In the initial state, ζ is a possible output for **tioco**$_\zeta$ and (M, δ) is also present in the output set of **tioco**$_M$ (noted **out**$_M$ and defined by Equation 13 in Section 7).

Proposition 5. *Let q be M-quiescent. We have $\zeta(q) \equiv (M, \delta) \in$ **out**$_M(q)$*

Proof. We proceed in two steps:

$\Rightarrow$ $\zeta(q)$ implies that q accepts any delay, in particular it accepts M time units: $q \xrightarrow{M}$. Because of M-quiescence (Def. 8), we have $\forall d \geq M : q \overset{(d,\mu)}{=\!=\!\not\Rightarrow}$ and according to Def. 5, $\delta(q(M))$. Consequently, $\delta \in$ **out**$_M(q)$.

$\Leftarrow$ We consider the contrapositive. From $\neg\zeta(q)$ we obtain $\exists d : q \xrightarrow{d} \not\!\!\rightarrow$. By time additivity, we have $\forall d' \geq d : q \overset{d'}{=\!\!\not\Rightarrow}$. From "no forced input" (Equation 2), there is an output before d, i.e., $\exists \mu \in \mathcal{L}_U, d'' \leq d : q \overset{(d'',\mu)}{=\!=\!=\!\Rightarrow}$. Because of M-quiescence, $d'' \leq M$ and $\delta \notin$ **out**$_M(q)$.

6 The tioco$_\zeta$ Relation and Its Relation to tioco

The implementation relations introduced so far consider that all delays are observable. In practice, one would like to bound this set by some maximum observable delay. This is achieved by relation **tioco**$_\zeta$ where only delays up to a bound M are observable. The bound M is not an explicit parameter of the **tioco**$_\zeta$ relation. Its result does not depend on M, which is – as discussed in Section 7 – the main difference with the **tioco**$_M$ relation.

The set of outputs is composed of outputs associated with their possible delay, together with symbol ζ if all delays are accepted.

$$\mathbf{out}_\zeta(q) \triangleq \{(d, \mu) \mid \mu \in \mathcal{L}_U \wedge d \in \mathbb{R}_{\geq 0} \wedge q \xrightarrow{(d,\mu)} \} \cup \{\zeta \mid \zeta(q)\}$$

Example 7. Consider Fig. 2. For example (a), we have $\mathbf{out}_\zeta(q_0) = \{(d, !x) \mid d \in \mathbb{R}_{\geq 0}\} \cup \{\zeta\}$. For example (b), we have $\mathbf{out}_\zeta(q_0) = \{\zeta\}$. For example (c), we have $\mathbf{out}_\zeta(q_0) = \{(d, !y) \mid d \bmod 2 = 0\} \cup \{\zeta\}$. Similarly, for example (d), we have $\mathbf{out}_\zeta(q_0) = \{(d, !y) \mid d \bmod 3 = 0\} \cup \{\zeta\}$.

An implementation i is $\mathbf{tioco}_\zeta$ correct w.r.t. s, if the output set of i – including ζ – after every normalized timed trace of s is a subset of the output set of s after the same normalized timed trace.

$$i \; \mathbf{tioco}_\zeta \; s \equiv \forall \sigma \in \mathbf{nttraces}(s), \mathbf{out}_\zeta(i \; \mathbf{after}_t \; \sigma) \subseteq \mathbf{out}_\zeta(s \; \mathbf{after}_t \; \sigma) \quad (12)$$

Example 8. If we consider the examples in Fig. 2 and Example 2. The $\mathbf{tioco}_\zeta$ produces the same results. Indeed, if we compare the different sets of outputs (see Example 1 and 7), we observe that the only difference is that $\{(d, -) \mid d \in \mathbb{R}_{\geq 0}\}$ is replaced by ζ. This reduction of the output set is exactly the purpose of $\mathbf{tioco}_\zeta$.

As suggested by the previous example, the next proposition shows that our reduction to partially observable delays is sound w.r.t. the $\mathbf{tioco}$ relation.

Fig. 5. Image Finiteness and $\mathbf{tioco}_\zeta$

This is not generally true. Let us consider specification (s) and implementation (i) in Fig. 5. After $?a$ the specification may produce $!x$ at any integer time. Note that the specification *always* produces $!x$. Consequently, there is no state q after $?a$ such that $\zeta(q)$ holds. Nevertheless, any delay (*i.e.*, $(d, -)$) is contained in the output set. After $?a$, the implementation can choose between producing $!x$ at any integer time, or to never produce $!x$. Therefore, the state reached after $?a$ satisfies $\zeta(q)$. According to $\mathbf{tioco}$, i is conforming to s, as delays and actions are included in the output set of both systems. Because ζ is in the output set of the implementation after $?a$ and not in the output set of the specification, i is not conforming to s according to $\mathbf{tioco}_\zeta$.

To relate $\mathbf{tioco}$ and $\mathbf{tioco}_\zeta$, we assume TIOTS to be *image finite*.

Definition 11. *A TIOTS $\mathcal{A}$ is* image finite *iff* $\forall \mathcal{Q} \subseteq \mathcal{Q}_{\mathcal{A}}, \forall \sigma \in \mathbf{nttraces}(\mathcal{A})$, $\exists N \in \mathbb{N} : |\mathcal{Q} \, \mathbf{after}_t \, \sigma| < N$.

Proposition 6. *Let i be input-enabled. Assume i and s are image finite.*
$i \, \mathbf{tioco} \, s \equiv i \, \mathbf{tioco}_\zeta \, s$

Proof. We prove each part separately and consider their contrapositive form. Because both relations consider the same set of traces, we only need to reason about the respective output sets. The interesting case is when the output sets of i and s always contain the same output actions. They differ in the presence of ζ or delays, which are not followed by an output action.

1. $\neg(i \, \mathbf{tioco} \, s) \Rightarrow \neg(i \, \mathbf{tioco}_\zeta \, s)$. Let us assume σ such that $\mathbf{out}_t(i \, \mathbf{after}_t \, \sigma) \not\subseteq \mathbf{out}_t(s \, \mathbf{after}_t \, \sigma)$. So, there is a delay in the output set of i that is not in the output set of s. This delay is either followed by an input action or followed by no action. Because of "no forced input" and image finiteness, there must exist a state that accepts all delays. So, $\zeta \in \mathbf{out}_\zeta(i \, \mathbf{after}_t \, \sigma)$. Regarding the specification, because of time additivity and image finiteness, there exists no state that accepts all delays. So, $\zeta \notin \mathbf{out}_\zeta(s \, \mathbf{after}_t \, \sigma)$.
2. $\neg(i \, \mathbf{tioco}_\zeta \, s) \Rightarrow \neg(i \, \mathbf{tioco} \, s)$. Let us assume σ such that $\mathbf{out}_\zeta(i \, \mathbf{after}_t \, \sigma) \not\subseteq \mathbf{out}_\zeta(s \, \mathbf{after}_t \, \sigma)$. Assume ζ is in the set of outputs of the implementation. This implies that all possible delays are in $\mathbf{out}_t(i \, \mathbf{after}_t \, \sigma)$. Because ζ is not in the outputs of the specification, it follows by definition of ζ and image finiteness that there exists a delay d such that all delays greater than d are not accepted by the specification. This delay is then a reason for $\neg(i \, \mathbf{tioco} \, s)$.

7 Relation between $\mathbf{tioco}_\zeta$, $\mathbf{tioco}_M$, and $\mathbf{tioco}_M^{\mathcal{R}}$

The main characteristics of the $\mathbf{tioco}_M$ relation [3, 4] are the notions of M-quiescence, quiescence and the fact that it is parameterized by duration M. This relation applies to the specifications models defined in Section 2 and relies on the same $\mathbf{after}_t$ operator and the test hypothesis of the $\mathbf{tioco}_\zeta$ relation.

The set of outputs is parameterized by M. It collects all possible output actions, but only quiescence (Def. 5) that appears exactly after M time units.

$$\mathbf{out}_M(q) \triangleq \{(d,l) \mid l \in \mathcal{L}_U \wedge d \in \mathbb{R}_{\geq 0} \wedge q \xrightarrow{(d,l)} \} \cup \{(M,\delta) \mid q \xrightarrow{(M,\delta)} \} \quad (13)$$

Example 9. Consider the examples in Fig 2. For example (a), $\mathbf{out}_M(q_0) = \{(d,!x) \mid d \in \mathbb{R}_{\geq 0}\}$. Similarly, for examples (c) and (d), we obtain $\mathbf{out}_t$ without the time domain $\mathbb{R}_{\geq 0}$. For example (b), $\mathbf{out}_M(q_0) = \{(M,\delta)\}$. Consider example (b) in Fig. 4. We have $\mathbf{out}_M(q_0) = \{(d,!y) \mid d \geq M$, for any value of M. Consider example (c) in Fig. 4. Let us assume $M = 10$. Then, we have $\mathbf{out}_M(q_0) = \{(d,!x) \mid d \leq 10\} \cup \{(10,\delta)\}$. Now, if we assume $M = 5$, the occurrence of $(10,\delta)$ is removed from the output set. We have $\mathbf{out}_M(q_0) = \{(d,!x) \mid d \leq 10\}$.

An implementation i is **tioco**$_M$ correct w.r.t. s, if the output set of i after every normalized timed suspension trace of s (i.e., including quiescence) is a subset of the output set of s after the same normalized timed suspension trace.

$$i \ \mathbf{tioco}_M \ s \equiv$$
$$\forall \sigma \in \mathbf{nttraces}_M^{\Delta}(s), \mathbf{out}_M(\Delta(i) \ \mathbf{after}_t \ \sigma) \subseteq \mathbf{out}_M(\Delta(s) \ \mathbf{after}_t \ \sigma)$$

Example 10. Examples (a), (c) and (d) in Fig. 2 are not M-quiescent as outputs $!x$ or $!y$ can be produced after (almost) any time units. Therefore, they do not belong to the set of valid implementations – but are valid specifications – considered by **tioco**$_M$, for any value of M. In contrast, example (b) is M-quiescent, for any value of M. Because example (b) is quiescent and not example (a), the former is not a valid implementation of the later.

We now assume that specifications *and* implementations are M-quiescent. Under this assumption, we prove that **tioco**$_\zeta$ and **tioco**$_M$ are equivalent. This shows that under the assumption of M-quiescence, the introduction of quiescence is superfluous. It also justifies the fact that there is no need to introduce ζ's in the traces used in the definition of **tioco**$_\zeta$.

Theorem 1. *Let i be input-enabled, and let i and s be M-quiescent. Then, i tioco$_\zeta$ s $\equiv$ i tioco$_M$ s.*

Proof. We prove the contrapositive. From Proposition 4, we can construct $\hat{\sigma}$ for any $\sigma \in \mathbf{nttraces}_M^{\Delta}(s)$ such that $q_0 \overset{\sigma}{\Longrightarrow} q'$ iff $q_0 \overset{\hat{\sigma}}{\Longrightarrow} q'$. Then, the proof reduces to the equivalence of output set membership. The interesting case is when the reason for non-conformance is the presence of (M, δ) or ζ. This equivalence follows directly from Proposition 5.

The relation **tioco**$_M^{\mathcal{R}}$ corresponds to the **tioco**$_M$ relation but considers the "repaired" definition of quiescence, see Definition 7. This slight modification in the set of outputs modifies the result of the relation (see Example 11 below).

$$\mathbf{out}_M^{\mathcal{R}}(q) \triangleq \{(d, l) \mid l \in \mathcal{L}_U \wedge d \in \mathbb{R}_{\geq 0} \wedge q \overset{(d,l)}{\Longrightarrow} \} \cup \{(M, \delta_{\mathcal{R}}) \mid q \overset{(M, \delta_{\mathcal{R}})}{\Longrightarrow} \}$$

Example 11. Consider examples (b) and (c) in Fig. 3 and assume that the outputs of example (b) are M-quiescent. After the trace $(0, ?a) \cdot (M, \delta_{\mathcal{R}}) \cdot (2, ?b)$, specification (c) is in state q_4 (we have $\neg\delta_{\mathcal{R}}(q_1)$ and $\delta_{\mathcal{R}}(q_2)$) and $!y$ is the only possible output. After the same trace, implementation (b) is in state q_2 and can produce $!x$ which is not allowed. Hence, $\neg(b \ \mathbf{tioco}_M^{\mathcal{R}} \ c)$. In contrast, we have $\delta(q_1)$, and after the trace $(0, ?a) \cdot (M, \delta) \cdot (2, ?b)$, specification (c) is in states q_3 and q_4. We have $b \ \mathbf{tioco}_M \ c$, and $b \ \mathbf{tioco}_\zeta \ c$ as well.

Example 11 shows that if two systems are **tioco**$_\zeta$-conforming (equivalently, conforming according to all previous relations introduced in this paper) then they are not necessary **tioco**$_M^{\mathcal{R}}$-conforming, even if the specification *and* the implementation are M-quiescent. Proposition 7 below shows the other direction. Any two systems that are **tioco**$_M^{\mathcal{R}}$-conforming are also **tioco**$_\zeta$-conforming.

Proposition 7. *Let i be input-enabled, and let i and s be M-quiescent. Then,* i **tioco**$_M^{\mathcal{R}}$ $s \Rightarrow i$ **tioco**$_\zeta$ s.

Proof. We prove the contrapositive and considers the **tioco**$_M$ relation because it considers the same set of traces: $\neg(i$ **tioco**$_M$ $s) \Rightarrow \neg(i$ **tioco**$_M^{\mathcal{R}}$ $s)$. We assume σ such that **out**$_M(i$ **after**$_t$ $\sigma) \not\subseteq$ **out**$_M(s$ **after**$_t$ $\sigma)$. The only difference between **out**$_M$ and **out**$_M^{\mathcal{R}}$ is quiescence. So, we assume that δ is in the **out**$_M$ of the implementation and not in the **out**$_M$ of the specification. The only difference between δ and $\delta_{\mathcal{R}}$ is the internal step. Let consider $\sigma \cdot \epsilon$. Then, we have $\delta_{\mathcal{R}} \in$ **out**$_M^{\mathcal{R}}(i$ **after**$_t$ $\sigma \cdot \epsilon)$. Because δ is not in the **out**$_M$ of the specification, there must be (d, μ), with $\mu \in \mathcal{L}_U$, such that $(d, \mu) \in$ **out**$_M(s$ **after**$_t$ $\sigma)$. Obviously, we also have $(d, \mu) \in$ **out**$_M^{\mathcal{R}}(s$ **after**$_t$ $\sigma \cdot \epsilon)$.

The other direction is generally not true, as there may be internal steps after M time units. If we assume that internal steps are M-quiescent too, and occur always before delay M – we can prove the other direction.

Proposition 8. *Assume s, i to be M-quiescent TIOTS where internal steps never occur after M time units. We have i* **tioco**$_\zeta$ $s \Rightarrow i$ **tioco**$_M^{\mathcal{R}}$ s.

Proof. We consider the equivalent **tioco**$_M$ relation and the contrapositive. As τ-steps (assumption) and outputs (M-quiescence, Def. 8) never occur after M time units, we have $\forall q, (M, \delta_{\mathcal{R}}) \in$ **out**$_M^{\mathcal{R}}(q)$. By definition, $\delta_{\mathcal{R}}$ (Def. 7) implies δ (Def. 5). Hence, $\forall q, (M, \delta) \in$ **out**$_M(q)$.

8   Conclusion and Future Work

We discussed several implementation relations for timed input/output transition systems occurring in the literature. We added our own timed implementation relations, and we showed under which conditions these relations coincide. The summary of these relationships between relations is given in Figure 1. The discussion of these relationships turned to concentrate around the subtle differences between observations of delays, unbounded delays, quiescence in different variants, and M-quiescence. The presented implementation relations and their relationships can form the basis for a theory of timed model-based testing. They may serve to compare the corresponding test generation algorithms and tools.

This paper only discussed and compared implementation relations. The next step is the design of test generation algorithms which are sound and exhaustive with respect to these implementation relations, and the development of tools implementing these algorithms. A couple of such tools already exist: UPPAAL-TRON [10], Timed-TorX [2], and TTG [8].

Other interesting issues which have not been answered in this paper, are to what extent the conditions and assumptions posed on implementations and specifications (input-enabledness, M-quiescence on implementations and/or specifications, τ-M-quiescence) are realistic and feasible. Also the compatibility with untimed **ioco**, which is an important issue in [3, 4], needs further elaboration.

References

1. Alur, R., Dill, D.L.: A theory of timed automata. Theoretical Computer Science 126(2), 183–235 (1994)
2. Bohnenkamp, H., Belinfante, A.: Timed Testing with TorX. In: Fitzgerald, J.S., Hayes, I.J., Tarlecki, A. (eds.) FM 2005. LNCS, vol. 3582, pp. 173–188. Springer, Heidelberg (2005)
3. Brandan-Briones, L.: Theories for Model-based Testing: Real-time and Coverage. PhD thesis, University of Twente, Enschede, The Netherlands (2007)
4. Brandán Briones, L., Brinksma, E.: A Test Generation Framework for quiescent Real-Time Systems. In: Grabowski, J., Nielsen, B. (eds.) FATES 2004. LNCS, vol. 3395, pp. 64–78. Springer, Heidelberg (2005)
5. Hessel, A., Larsen, K.G., Mikucionis, M., Nielsen, B., Pettersson, P., Skou, A.: Testing Real-Time Systems Using UPPAAL. In: Hierons, R.M., Bowen, J.P., Harman, M. (eds.) FORTEST. LNCS, vol. 4949, pp. 77–117. Springer, Heidelberg (2008)
6. Khoumsi, A., Jéron, T., Marchand, H.: Test cases generation for nondeterministic real-time systems. In: Petrenko, A., Ulrich, A. (eds.) FATES 2003. LNCS, vol. 2931, pp. 131–146. Springer, Heidelberg (2004)
7. Krichen, M., Tripakis, S.: Black-box conformance testing for real-time systems. In: Graf, S., Mounier, L. (eds.) SPIN 2004. LNCS, vol. 2989, pp. 109–126. Springer, Heidelberg (2004)
8. Krichen, M., Tripakis, S.: An expressive and implementable formal framework for testing real-time systems. In: Khendek, F., Dssouli, R. (eds.) TestCom 2005. LNCS, vol. 3502, pp. 209–225. Springer, Heidelberg (2005)
9. Krichen, M., Tripakis, S.: Interesting properties of the real-time conformance relation tioco. In: Barkaoui, K., Cavalcanti, A., Cerone, A. (eds.) ICTAC 2006. LNCS, vol. 4281, pp. 317–331. Springer, Heidelberg (2006)
10. Larsen, K.G., Mikucionis, M., Nielsen, B., Skou, A.: Testing real-time embedded software using uppaal-tron: an industrial case study. In: EMSOFT 2005: Proceedings of the 5th ACM international conference on Embedded software, pp. 299–306. ACM, New York (2005)
11. Larsen, K.G., Mikucionis, M., Nielsen, B.: Online Testing of Real-Time Systems using Uppaal. In: Grabowski, J., Nielsen, B. (eds.) FATES 2004. LNCS, vol. 3395, pp. 79–94. Springer, Heidelberg (2005)
12. Tretmans, J.: Test Generation with Inputs, Outputs and Repetitive Quiescence. Software - Concepts and Tools 17(3), 103–120 (1996)
13. Tretmans, J.: Model Based Testing with Labelled Transition Systems. In: Hierons, R.M., Bowen, J.P., Harman, M. (eds.) FORTEST. LNCS, vol. 4949, pp. 1–38. Springer, Heidelberg (2008)

Relevant Timed Schedules / Clock Valuations for Constructing Time Petri Net Reachability Graphs

Hanifa Boucheneb[1] and Kamel Barkaoui[2]

[1] Laboratoire VeriForm, Department of Computer Engineering,
École Polytechnique de Montréal, P.O. Box 6079, Station Centre-ville, Montréal,
Québec,Canada, H3C 3A7
hanifa.boucheneb@polymtl.ca
[2] Laboratoire CEDRIC, Conservatoire National des Arts et Métiers,
192 rue Saint Martin, Paris Cedex 03, France
kamel.barkaoui@cnam.fr

Abstract. We consider here time Petri nets (the TPN model) and two of its state space abstractions: the state class graph (SCG) and the zone based graph (ZBG). We show that only some time points of the clock/firing domains of abstract states are relevant to construct a TPN reachability graph. Moreover, for the state class graph method, the graph computed using relevant time points is smaller than the SCG.

1 Introduction

Time Petri nets are a simple yet powerful formalism useful to model and verify concurrent systems with time constraints (real time systems). In time Petri nets, a firing interval is associated with each transition specifying the minimum and maximum times it must be maintained enabled, before its firing. Its firing takes no time but may lead to another marking.

To use enumerative analysis techniques with time Petri nets, an extra effort is required to abstract their generally infinite state spaces. Abstraction techniques aim to construct by removing some irrelevant details, a finite contraction of the state space of the model, which preserves properties of interest. For best performances, the contraction should also be the smallest possible and computed with minor resources too (time and space). The preserved properties are usually verified using standard analysis techniques on the abstractions [8].

Several state space abstraction methods have been proposed, in the literature, for time Petri nets. The well known are: the *state class graph (SCG)* [3], the *geometric region graph (GRG)* [8,10], the *strong state class graph (SSCG)* [3], the *zone based graph (ZBG)* [6], the *Integer state class graph* [9], and the *atomic state class graphs (ASCGs)* [3,5]. These abstractions may differ mainly in the characterization of states (interval states in the SCG, clock states in all others), the agglomeration criteria of states, the representation of the agglomerated states (abstract states), the kind of properties they preserve and their size.

F. Cassez and C. Jard (Eds.): FORMATS 2008, LNCS 5215, pp. 265–279, 2008.

These abstractions are finite for all bounded time Petri nets. However, abstractions based on clocks are less interesting than the interval based abstractions when only linear properties are of interest. They are, in general, larger and their computation takes more time. Indeed, abstractions based on clocks do not enjoy naturally the finiteness property for bounded TPNs with unbounded intervals as it is the case for abstractions based on intervals. The finiteness is enforced using an approximation operation, which may involve some overhead computation.Interval based abstractions are however not appropriate for constructing abstractions preserving branching properties (ASCGs) [3]. Indeed, this construction, based on splitting abstract states, is not possible on interval abstract states (the union of intervals is irreversible) whereas it is possible on clock abstract states. Together, the mentioned remarks suggest that the interval characterization of states is more appropriate to construct abstractions preserving linear properties but is not appropriate to construct abstractions preserving branching properties.

We consider here the SCG and the ZBG methods and show that only some time points of the clock/firing domains are relevant to construct a reachability graph for TPNs. We also show that, for the state class method, the graph computed, using these relevant time points, is in general smaller than the SCG.

The rest of the paper is organized as follows. In section 3, we present the TPN model and its semantics. In section 4, we first present the state class graph method and show that only some time points (timed schedules) of each state class firing domain are essential to compute a TPN reachability graph. Afterwards, we establish a useful firing rule which computes, using essential timed schedules of a state class, those of its successors. In addition, we show, by means of an example, that two different state classes may have identical essential timed schedules. The timed schedule based graphs (TSBG) can be seen as a contraction the SCG where state classes sharing the same essential timed schedules are grouped in the same node. In section 5, we show how to extend our approach to the zone based graph method. In addition, we show here how to group, in one step, two distinct operations used to compute the ZBG state zones (discrete successor and relaxation). The relaxation of an abstract state consists in extending it with all states reachable from its states by time progression.

2   Time Petri Nets

A time Petri net is a Petri net augmented with time intervals associated with transitions. Formally, a *TPN* is a tuple $(P, T, Pre, Post, M_0, Is)$ where P and T are finite sets of places and transitions such that $(P \cap T = \emptyset)$, Pre and $Post$ are the backward and the forward incidence functions $(Pre, Post : P \times T \longrightarrow \mathbb{N}, \mathbb{N}$ is the set of nonnegative integers), M_0 is the initial marking $(M_0 : P \longrightarrow \mathbb{N})$, and Is is the static firing bound function $(Is : T \rightarrow Q^+ \times (Q^+ \cup \{\infty\}))$, Q^+ is the set of nonnegative rational numbers. $Is(t_i)$ specifies the lower $\downarrow Is(t_i)$ and the upper $\uparrow Is(t_i)$ bounds of the static firing interval of transition t_i.

Let M be a marking and t_i a transition. Transition t_i is enabled for M iff all required tokens for firing t_i are present in M, i.e.: $\forall p \in P, M(p) \geq Pre(p, t_i)$.

Transition t_i can be multi-enabled in M (i.e., $\forall p \in P, M(p) \geq 2 \times Pre(p, t_i)$). The multi-enabledness of t_i can be considered as different enabled transitions which are either totaly independent or managed so as to fire the oldest one first and disable (in case of conflict) the most recent one first. Without loss of generality, for reasons of clarity in this paper, if a transition remains enabled after its firing, it is considered newly enabled. We denote by $En(M)$ the set of all transitions enabled for M, i.e.: $En(M) = \{t_i \in T \mid \forall p \in P, Pre(p, t_i) \leq M(p)\}$.

If M results from firing some transition t_f from some marking, $New(M, t_f)$ denotes the set of all transitions newly enabled in M, i.e.:
$New(M, t_f) = \{t_i \in En(M) \mid t_i = t_f \vee \exists p \in P, M(p) - Post(p, t_f) < Pre(p, t_i)\}$.

Let $t_i, t_j \in En(M)$. t_i and t_j are in conflict in M iff $\exists p \in P, M(p) < Pre(p, t_i) + Pre(p, t_j)$. The firing of one of them will disable the other. We denote $conf(t_i, M)$ the set of transitions in conflict with t_i in M (with $t_i \in conf(t_i, M)$).

There are two known characterizations for the TPN state. The first one, based on clocks, associates with each transition t_i of the model a *clock* to measure the time elapsed since t_i became enabled most recently. The TPN *clock state* is a couple (M, ν), where M is a marking and ν is a clock valuation function, $\nu : En(M) \rightarrow \mathbb{R}^+$. For a clock state (M, ν) and $t_i \in En(M)$, $\nu(t_i)$ is the value of the clock associated with transition t_i. The initial clock state is $s_0 = (M_0, \nu_0)$ where $\nu_0(t_i) = 0$, for all $t_i \in En(M_0)$. The TPN clock state evolves either by time progression or by firing transitions. When a transition t_i becomes enabled, its clock is initialized to zero. The value of this clock increases synchronously with time until t_i is fired or disabled by the firing of another transition. t_i can fire, if the value of its clock is inside its static firing interval $Is(t_i)$. It must be fired immediately, without any additional delay, when the clock reaches $\uparrow Is(t_i)$. The firing of a transition takes no time, but may lead to another marking (required tokens disappear while produced ones appear).

Let $s = (M, \nu)$ and $s' = (M', \nu')$ be two clock states of a TPN, $\theta \in \mathbb{R}^+$ and $t_f \in T$. We write $s \xrightarrow{\theta} s'$, also denoted $s + \theta$, iff state s' is reachable from state s after a time progression of θ time units, i.e.:
$$\bigwedge_{t_i \in En(M)} \nu(t_i) + \theta \leq \uparrow Is(t_i), \quad M' = M, \quad \text{and} \quad \forall t_j \in En(M'), \nu'(t_j) = \nu(t_j) + \theta.$$

We write $s \xrightarrow{t_f} s'$ iff state s' is immediately reachable from state s by firing transition t_f, i.e.: $t_f \in En(M)$, $\nu(t_f) \geq \downarrow Is(t_f)$,
$\forall p \in P, M'(p) = M(p) - Pre(p, t_f) + Post(p, t_f)$, and $\forall t_i \in En(M'), \nu'(t_i) = 0$, if $t_i \in New(M', t_f)$, $\nu'(t_i) = \nu(t_i)$, otherwise

The second characterization, based on intervals, defines the TPN state as a marking and a function which associates with each enabled transition the time interval in which the transition can fire [3]. The TPN state is defined as a pair $s = (M, I)$, where M is a marking and I is a firing interval function $(I : En(M) \rightarrow Q^+ \times (Q^+ \cup \{\infty\}))$. The lower and upper bounds of the interval $I(t_i)$ are denoted $\downarrow I(t_i)$ and $\uparrow I(t_i)$. The initial state of the TPN model is $s_0 = (M_0, I_0)$ where $I_0(t_i) = Is(t_i)$, for all $t_i \in En(M_0)$. The TPN state evolves either by time progressions or by firing transitions. When a transition t_i becomes enabled, its firing interval is set to its static firing interval $Is(t_i)$. The bounds of this interval decrease synchronously with time, until t_i is fired or disabled by another firing. t_i can fire if the lower bound of its firing interval reaches 0 but must fire, without any additional delay, if the upper bound of its firing interval reaches 0. The firing of a transition takes no time but may lead to another marking.

Let $s = (M, I)$ and $s' = (M', I')$ be two interval states of the TPN model, $\theta \in \mathbb{R}^+$ and $t_f \in T$. We write $s \xrightarrow{\theta} s'$, also denoted $s + \theta$, iff state s' is reachable from state s after a time progression of θ time units, i.e.: $\bigwedge_{t_i \in En(M)} \theta \leq \uparrow I(t_i)$, $M' = M$, and $\forall t_j \in En(M'), I'(t_j) = [Max(\downarrow I(t_j) - \theta, 0), \uparrow I(t_j) - \theta]$.

We write $s \xrightarrow{t_f} s'$ iff state s' is immediately reachable from state s by firing transition t_f, i.e.: $t_f \in En(M)$, $\downarrow I(t_f) = 0$, $\forall p \in P, M'(p) = M(p) - Pre(p, t_f) + Post(p, t_f)$, and $\forall t_i \in En(M'), I'(t_i) = Is(t_i)$, if $t_i \in New(M', t_f)$, $I'(t_i) = I(t_i)$, otherwise.

The TPN state space is the structure $(S, \rightarrow, s_0)$, where: s_0 is the initial clock/interval state of the TPN and $S = \{s | s_0 \xrightarrow{*} s\}$ ($\xrightarrow{*}$ being the reflexive and transitive closure of the relation $\rightarrow$ defined above) is the set of reachable states of the model. A *run* in the TPN state space $(\mathcal{S}, \rightarrow, s_0)$, starting from a state s, is a maximal sequence $s_1 \xrightarrow{\theta_1 \ t_1} s_2 \rightarrow \ldots$, such that $s_1 = s$. A marking M is reachable iff $\exists s \in \mathcal{S}$ s.t. its marking is M. Runs of the TPN are all runs starting from the initial state s_0.

Enumerative analysis methods of the TPN model are based on abstractions preserving properties of interest (reachability, linear or branching properties). We interest here to abstractions which preserving linear properties of the TPN. In such abstractions, we distinguish three levels of abstraction. In the first level, states reachable by time progression may be either represented (ZBG) or abstracted (SCG, GRG, SSCG). In the second level, states reachable by the same firing sequence independently of their firing times are agglomerated in the same node. In the third level, the agglomerated states are then considered modulo some relation of equivalence (firing domain of the SCG [3], approximations of the ZBG [6] and the SSCG [3].

In general, an abstract state consists of some finite or infinite set of states sharing the same marking. It is defined by a marking and a conjunction of constraints characterizing either a dense firing/clock domain [3,6,10] or a discrete clock domain [9]. Dense domains are convex and usually represented by means of *difference bound matrices* DBMs, by giving for each pair of variables (clocks or delays) the upper bound of their difference. Though the same domain may be expressed by different conjunctions of constraints, equivalent formulae have a unique form, called canonical form[1]. Canonical forms make operations needed to compute and compare abstract states much more simple. In [9], authors have

---

[1] A canonical form of a DBM is the representation with tightest bounds on all differences between time variables (clocks or delays).

shown that integer clock states[2] of each abstract state are sufficient to compute a TPN reachability graph. An abstract state is represented by its integer states. The number of integer states of an abstract state is finite but depends on bounds of clocks which, in turn, depends on the finite bounds of the TPN intervals. The main advantage of this discrete approach is the possibility to extend this approach to non-convex domains (DBMs are known to be not closed under union). Its drawback is that the number of integer states is very sensitive to the length of firing intervals. Such a situation may have a bad impact on the computation time of successor abstract states. We focus, in the following, on the SCG and the ZBG and show that only some time points of clock/firing domains are essential to compute reachability graphs for the TPN.

3   Essential Time Points of Firing Domains

3.1   The State Class Method

In the state class method, the abstract state, called state class, is defined as a pair $\alpha = (M, FD)$, where M is the common marking of states agglomerated in the state class and FD is a formula which characterizes the union of all firing domains of these states. Each transition which is enabled in M is a variable with the same name in FD representing its firing delay. The initial state class is $\alpha_0 = (M_0, FD_0)$ where $FD_0 = \bigwedge_{t_i \in En(M_0)} \downarrow Is(t_i) \leq t_i \leq \uparrow Is(t_i))$.

The domain of FD is convex and has a unique canonical form represented by the pair (M, D), where D is a DBM of order $|En(M) \cup \{o\}|$ defined by: $\forall (x, y) \in (En(M) \cup \{o\})^2$, $d_{xy} = Sup_{FD}(x - y)$, where o represents the value 0.

Two state classes are said to be equal iff they share the same marking and their firing domains are equal (i.e.: their formulae are equivalent). Proposition 1 below shows how to compute directly the canonical form of each reachable state class in $O(n^2)$, n being the number of transitions enabled in the state class (see [4] for the proof).

Proposition 1. Let $\alpha = (M, D)$ be a state class in canonical form and $t_f \in T$.
1) t_f is firable from α (i.e.: $succ(\alpha, t_f) \neq \emptyset$) iff $t_f \in En(M) \wedge \underset{t_i \in En(M)}{Min} d_{t_i t_f} = 0$.

2) If $succ(\alpha, t_f) \neq \emptyset$ then its firing leads to the state class $succ(\alpha, t_f) = (M', D')$ computed as follows:
2.1) $\forall p \in P, M'(p) = M(p) - Pre(p, t_f) + Post(p, t_f)$;
2.2) $\forall t_i, t_j \in En(M')$,

$$d'_{t_i o} = \begin{cases} \uparrow Is(t_i) & \text{if } t_i \in New(M', t_f) \\ d_{t_i t_f} & \text{otherwise} \end{cases} \quad d'_{o t_i} = \begin{cases} - \downarrow Is(t_i) & \text{if } t_i \in New(M', t_f) \\ \underset{t_u \in En(M)}{Min} d_{t_u t_i} & \text{otherwise} \end{cases}$$

$$d'_{t_i t_j} = \begin{cases} 0 & \text{if } t_i \text{ is } t_j \\ d'_{t_i o} + d'_{o t_j} & \text{if } t_i, t_j \in New(M', t_f) \wedge t_i \text{ is not } t_j \\ Min(d_{t_i t_j}, d'_{t_i o} + d'_{o t_j}) & \text{otherwise} \end{cases}$$

---

[2] An integer clock state is a state whose clock values are integer numbers.

Formally, the SCG of a TPN is a structure $(\mathcal{C}, \twoheadrightarrow, \alpha_0)$, where $\alpha_0 = (M_0, FD_0)$ is the initial state class, $\forall t_i \in T, \alpha \xrightarrow{t_i} \alpha'$ iff $\alpha' = succ(\alpha, t_i) \neq \emptyset$ and $\mathcal{C} = \{\alpha \mid \alpha_0 \xrightarrow{*} \alpha\}$. The SCG is finite for all bounded TPNs and preserves linear properties [3].

For example, Fig. 1 shows a TPN and its SCG. This SCG consists of 17 classes, given in Table 1, and 21 edges.

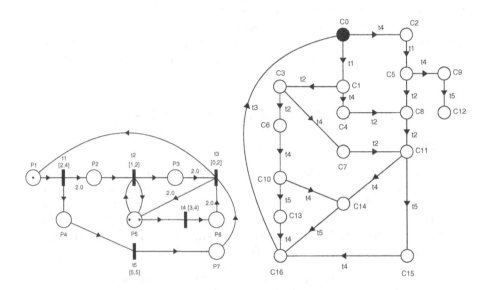

Fig. 1. A TPN and its state class graph

Table 1. State classes of the SCG in Fig. 1

C0: $P1 + 2P5$	$2 \le t1 \le 4$	$3 \le t4 \le 4$	$-2 \le t1 - t4 \le 1$
C1: $2P2 + P4 + 2P5$	$1 \le t2 \le 2$	$5 \le t5 \le 5$	$0 \le t4 \le 2$
	$-4 \le t2 - t5 \le -3$	$-1 \le t2 - t4 \le 2$	$3 \le t5 - t4 \le 5$
C2: $P1 + P5 + P6$	$0 \le t1 \le 1$	$3 \le t4 \le 4$	$-4 \le t1 - t4 \le -2$
C3: $P2 + P3 + P4 + 2P5$	$1 \le t2 \le 2$	$0 \le t4 \le 1$	$3 \le t5 \le 4$
	$-3 \le t2 - t5 \le -1$	$0 \le t2 - t4 \le 2$	$3 \le t5 - t4 \le 4$
C4: $2P2 + P4 + P5 + P6$	$0 \le t2 \le 2$	$3 \le t4 \le 4$	$3 \le t5 \le 5$
	$-4 \le t2 - t4 \le -1$	$-4 \le t2 - t5 \le -3$	$-1 \le t5 - t4 \le 2$
C5: $2P2 + P4 + P5 + P6$	$1 \le t2 \le 2$	$2 \le t4 \le 4$	$5 \le t5 \le 5$
	$-3 \le t2 - t4 \le 0$	$-4 \le t2 - t5 \le -3$	$1 \le t5 - t4 \le 3$
C6: $2P3 + P4 + 2P5$	$0 \le t4 \le 0$	$3 \le t5 \le 3$	
C7: $P2 + P3 + P4 + P5 + P6$	$0 \le t2 \le 2$	$3 \le t4 \le 4$	$3 \le t5 \le 4$
	$-4 \le t2 - t4 \le -1$	$-3 \le t2 - t5 \le -1$	$-1 \le t5 - t4 \le 1$
C8: $P2 + P3 + P4 + P5 + P6$	$1 \le t2 \le 2$	$3 \le t4 \le 4$	$3 \le t5 \le 4$
	$-3 \le t2 - t4 \le -1$	$-3 \le t2 - t5 \le -1$	$-1 \le t5 - t4 \le 1$
C9: $2P2 + P4 + 2P6$	$3 \le t5 \le 3$		
C10: $2P3 + P4 + P5 + P6$	$3 \le t4 \le 4$	$3 \le t5 \le 3$	$-1 \le t5 - t4 \le 0$
C11: $2P3 + P4 + P5 + P6$	$3 \le t4 \le 4$	$1 \le t5 \le 3$	$-3 \le t5 - t4 \le 0$
C12: $2P2 + 2P6 + P7$	$true$		
C13: $2P3 + P5 + P6 + P7$	$0 \le t4 \le 1$		
C14: $2P3 + P4 + 2P6$	$0 \le t5 \le 0$		
C15: $2P3 + P5 + P6 + P7$	$0 \le t4 \le 3$		
C16: $2P3 + 2P6 + P7$	$0 \le t3 \le 2$		

3.2   Timed Schedules of Firing Domains

Let $\alpha = (M, D)$ be a state class. We define, in the following, the notion of timed schedule of D (i.e. α) and some operations on timed schedules.

Definition 1. *Let A and B be two vectors of $(Q^+ \cup \{\infty\})^{|T|}$.*

- *$Min(A, B)$ (resp. $Max(A, B)$) is the vector X (resp. Y) of $(Q^+ \cup \{\infty\})^{|T|}$ defined by: $\forall t_i \in T, x_{t_i} = Min(a_{t_i}, b_{t_i})$ (resp. $y_{t_i} = Max(a_{t_i}, b_{t_i})$).*
- *Let $E_1, E_2 \subseteq T$ be two disjoint sets of transitions ($E_1 \cap E_2 = \emptyset$). $A_{[E_1:=\downarrow Is, E_2:=\uparrow Is]}$ is the vector B of $(Q^+ \cup \{\infty\})^{|T|}$ defined by:*

$$\forall t_i \in T, b_{t_i} = \begin{cases} a_{t_i} & \text{if } t_i \in T - (E_1 \cup E_2) \\ \downarrow Is(t_i) & \text{if } t_i \in E_1 \\ \uparrow Is(t_i) & \text{otherwise} \end{cases}$$

- *A is a timed schedule of D (of α) iff $\forall t_i \in En(M), -d_{ot_i} \leq a_{t_i} \leq d_{t_i o}$ and $\forall t_i, t_j \in En(M), a_{t_i} - a_{t_j} \leq d_{t_i t_j}$.*
- *If A is a timed schedule of D, its relaxed form, denoted $\overrightarrow{A}$, is the vector defined by: $\forall t_i \in T, \overrightarrow{a}_{t_i} = \begin{cases} a_{t_i} - \underset{t_k \in En(M)}{Min} a_{t_k} & \text{if } t_i \in En(M) \\ a_{t_i} & \text{otherwise} \end{cases}$*

Lemma 1. *Let α be a state class, A and B two timed schedules of α[3]. Then: $Min(A, B)$ and $Max(A, B)$ are timed schedules of α.*

Proof. We give the proof for $Min(A, B)$. The proof for $Max(A, B)$ is similar. By assumption, A and B are timed schedules of α, i.e., $\forall t_i \in En(M)$, (1) $-d_{ot_i} \leq a_{t_i} \leq d_{t_i o}$, and (2) $-d_{ot_i} \leq b_{t_i} \leq d_{t_i o}$, $\forall t_i, t_j \in En(M)$, (3) $a_{t_i} - a_{t_j} \leq d_{t_i t_j}$, and (4) $b_{t_i} - b_{t_j} \leq d_{t_i t_j}$. Relations (1) and (2) implies that: $\forall t_i \in En(M), -d_{ot_i} \leq Min(a_{t_i}, b_{t_i}) \leq d_{t_i o}$ Let us show that: $\forall t_i, t_j \in En(M), Min(a_{t_i}, b_{t_i}) - Min(a_{t_j}, b_{t_j}) \leq d_{t_i t_j}$ Case $a_{t_i} \leq b_{t_i}$ and $a_{t_j} \leq b_{t_j}$: $Min(a_{t_i}, b_{t_i}) - Min(a_{t_j}, b_{t_j}) = a_{t_i} - a_{t_j} \leq d_{t_i t_j}$ Case $b_{t_i} \leq a_{t_i}$ and $b_{t_j} \leq a_{t_j}$: $Min(a_{t_i}, b_{t_i}) - Min(a_{t_j}, b_{t_j}) = b_{t_i} - b_{t_j} \leq d_{t_i t_j}$ Case $b_{t_i} \leq a_{t_i}$ and $a_{t_j} \leq b_{t_j}$: $Min(a_{t_i}, b_{t_i}) - Min(a_{t_j}, b_{t_j}) = b_{t_i} - a_{t_j} \leq a_{t_i} - a_{t_j} \leq d_{t_i t_j}$ Case $a_{t_i} \leq b_{t_i}$ and $b_{t_j} \leq a_{t_j}$: $Min(a_{t_i}, b_{t_i}) - Min(a_{t_j}, b_{t_j}) = a_{t_i} - b_{t_j} \leq b_{t_i} - b_{t_j} \leq d_{t_i t_j}$. □

Lemma 2. *Let $\alpha = (M, D)$ be a state class, $t_j \in En(M)$ and $\rho(t_j)$ a vector of $(Q^+ \cup \{\infty\})^{|T|}$ defined by: $\forall t_i \in T, \rho(t_j)_{t_i} = \begin{cases} d_{t_i t_j} - d_{ot_j} & \text{if } t_i \in En(M) \\ \uparrow Is(t_i) & \text{otherwise} \end{cases}$*

Then $\rho(t_j)$ is a timed schedule of α.

Proof. Note first that the following relation holds for any state class $\alpha = (M, D)$ in canonical form: $\forall x, y, z \in En(M) \cup \{o\}, d_{xz} \leq d_{xy} + d_{yz}$.

We have to show that: $\forall t_i \in En(M)$, 1) $-\rho(t_j)_{t_i} \leq d_{ot_i}$, 2) $\rho(t_j)_{t_i} \leq d_{t_i o}$ and 3) $\forall t_i, t_k \in En(M), \rho(t_j)_{t_i} - \rho(t_j)_{t_k} \leq d_{t_i t_k}$.

Relations 1) and 2) are respectively derived from relations $\rho(t_j)_{t_i} = d_{t_i t_j} - d_{ot_j}$, $d_{t_i t_j} \leq d_{t_i o} + d_{ot_j}$ and $d_{ot_j} \leq d_{ot_i} + d_{t_i t_j}$. Relation 3) is derived from relations $\rho(t_j)_{t_i} - \rho(t_j)_{t_k} = d_{t_i t_j} - d_{t_k t_j}$ and $d_{t_i t_j} \leq d_{t_i t_k} + d_{t_k t_j}$. □

---

[3] Note that transitions not enabled are represented in time vectors but not considered.

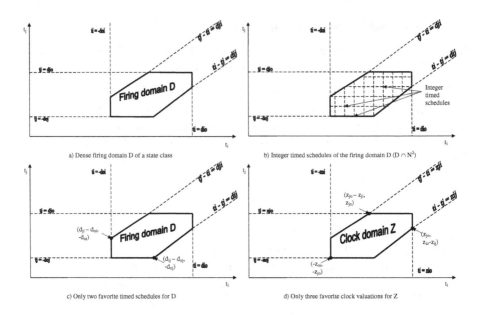

a) Dense firing domain D of a state class

b) Integer timed schedules of the firing domain D (D ∩ N²)

c) Only two favorite timed schedules for D

d) Only three favorite clock valuations for Z

Fig. 2. Dense, discrete clock/firing domains and their favorite time points

Intuitively, $\rho(t_j)$ is the timed schedule of α with the smallest firing delay for t_j (i.e. $-d_{ot_j}$) and the biggest firing delays for other enabled transitions (i.e. $d_{t_it_j} - d_{ot_j}$). $\rho(t_j)$ is called the favorite timed schedule of t_j in α. The favorite timed schedules of α are those of its enabled transitions (i.e. $\{\rho(t_j), t_j \in En(M)\}$). Fig. 2 shows respectively the firing domain (Fig. 2.a) of a state class, its integer states (Fig. 2.b) and its favorite timed schedules (Fig. 2.c).

3.3 Favorite Schedule Based Graphs

In this section, we show that favorite timed schedules of a state class are sufficient to compute its firing sequences. Moreover, these favorite timed schedules are also sufficient to compute those of all successor state classes. The following proposition establishes a firing rule based on the favorite timed schedules.

Proposition 2. *Let $\alpha = (M, D)$ be a state class, ρ its favorite timed schedule function and t_f a transition of T.*

1) $succ(\alpha, t_f) \neq \emptyset$ iff $t_f \in En(M)$ and $\overrightarrow{\rho(t_f)}_{t_f} = 0$.

2) If $succ(\alpha, t_f) \neq \emptyset$ then the favorite timed schedule function ρ' of $succ(\alpha, t_f) = (M', D')$ is computed as follows: Let $E = New(M', t_f) \cup conf(t_f, M)$.

$$\forall t_j \in En(M'), \rho'(t_j) = \begin{cases} (Min(\overrightarrow{\rho(t_j)}, \overrightarrow{\rho(t_f)}))_{[\emptyset, E:=\uparrow Is]} & \text{if } t_j \notin New(M', t_f) \\ \overrightarrow{\rho(t_f)}_{[\{t_j\}:=\downarrow Is, (E-\{t_j\}):=\uparrow Is]} & \text{otherwise} \end{cases}$$

Proof. The proof is based on Proposition 1.

1) By definition, $\forall t_f \in En(M), \overrightarrow{\rho(t_f)}_{t_f} = \rho(t_f)_{t_f} - \underset{t_i \in En(M)}{Min} \rho(t_f)_{t_i} = - \underset{t_i \in En(M)}{Min} d_{t_it_f}$.

It follows that relation $\overrightarrow{\rho(t_f)}_{t_f} = 0$ is equivalent to: $\underset{t_i \in En(M)}{Min} d_{t_i t_f} = 0$.

2) Let $\alpha' = (M', D') = succ(\alpha, t_f)$. By definition: (i) $\forall t_i, t_j \in En(M'), \rho'(t_j)_{t_i} = d'_{t_i t_j} - d'_{ot_j}$. Proposition 1 states that: $\forall t_i, t_j \in En(M')$,

$$d'_{t_i t_j} = \begin{cases} 0 & \text{if } t_i \text{ is } t_j \\ Min(d_{t_i t_j}, d_{t_i t_f} + \underset{t_u \in En(M)}{Min} d_{t_u t_j}) & \text{if } t_i, t_j \notin New(M', t_f) \wedge \ t_i \text{ is not } t_j \\ \uparrow Is(t_i) - \downarrow Is(t_j) & \text{if } t_i, t_j \in New(M', t_f) \wedge \ t_i \text{ is not } t_j \\ d_{t_i t_f} - \downarrow Is(t_j) & \text{if } t_i \notin New(M', t_f) \wedge \ t_j \in New(M', t_f) \\ \uparrow Is(t_i) + \underset{t_u \in En(M)}{Min} d_{t_u t_j} & \text{otherwise} \end{cases}$$

and $\forall t_j \in En(M'), d'_{ot_j} = \begin{cases} \underset{t_u \in En(M)}{Min} d_{t_u t_j} & \text{if } t_j \notin New(M', t_f) \\ - \downarrow Is(t_j) & \text{otherwise} \end{cases}$.

It follows that: $d'_{t_i t_j} - d'_{ot_j} =$

$$\begin{cases} - \underset{t_u \in En(M)}{Min} d_{t_u t_j} & \text{if } t_j \notin New(M', t_f) \wedge \quad t_i \text{ is } t_j \\ \downarrow Is(t_i) & \text{if } t_j \in New(M', t_f) \wedge \quad t_i \text{ is } t_j \\ Min(d_{t_i t_j} - \underset{t_u \in En(M)}{Min} d_{t_u t_j}, d_{t_i t_f}) & \text{if } t_i, t_j \notin New(M', t_f) \wedge \quad t_i \text{ is not } t_j \\ \uparrow Is(t_i) & \text{if } t_i \in New(M', t_f) \wedge \quad t_i \text{ is not } t_j \\ d_{t_i t_f} & \text{otherwise} \end{cases}$$

Since, $\forall t_j, t_i \in En(M), \overrightarrow{\rho(t_j)}_{t_i} = d_{t_i t_j} - \underset{t_u \in En(M)}{Min} d_{t_u t_j}, \overrightarrow{\rho(t_j)}_{t_j} = - \underset{t_u \in En(M)}{Min} d_{t_u t_j}$

and $\underset{t_u \in En(M)}{Min} d_{t_u t_f} = 0$, it follows that $\overrightarrow{\rho(t_f)}_{t_i} = d_{t_i t_f}$. Then: $\forall t_i, t_j \in En(M')$,

$$\rho'(t_j)_{t_i} = \begin{cases} Min(\overrightarrow{\rho(t_j)}_{t_i}, \overrightarrow{\rho(t_f)}_{t_i}) & \text{if } t_i, t_j \notin New(M', t_f) \\ \uparrow Is(t_i) & \text{if } t_i \in New(M', t_f) \wedge \ t_i \text{ is not } t_j \\ \downarrow Is(t_i) & \text{if } t_i \in New(M', t_f) \wedge \ t_i \text{ is } t_j \\ \overrightarrow{\rho(t_f)}_{t_i} & \text{otherwise} \end{cases}$$

and $\forall t_i \in T - En(M'), \rho'(t_j)_{t_i} = \uparrow Is(t_i)$ $\square$

The above proposition states that the firability test of some transition t_f, from a state class α, consists in testing whether the delay of t_f in its favorite timed schedule (i.e. $\rho(t_f)$) is smaller than delays of other enabled transitions. Note that, there is no need to test other favorite timed schedules. In case t_f is firable, the favorite timed schedules of the successor state class can be computed using those of α. The favorite timed schedule of each enabled transition has to be updated so as to take into account the fact that t_f is fired before others. The favorite timed schedule of a not newly enabled transition t_j is derived from the minimum of the relaxed favorite timed schedules of t_f and t_j in α. Note that according with Lemma 1, these relaxed favorite timed schedules and their minimum belong to the relaxed form of α. The favorite timed schedule of each newly enabled transition t_j is derived from the relaxed form of the favorite timed schedule of t_f in α.

Let $\simeq_1$ and $\simeq_2$ be two relations over the SCG defined by:
$\forall \alpha_1 = (M_1, D_1), \alpha_2 = (M_2, D_2) \in \mathcal{C}$,
$\alpha_1 \simeq_1 \alpha_2$ iff $M_1 = M_2 \wedge \rho_1 = \rho_2$ and $\alpha_1 \simeq_2 \alpha_2$ iff $M_1 = M_2 \wedge \overrightarrow{\rho_1} = \overrightarrow{\rho_2}$.

Lemma 3. $\simeq_1$ and $\simeq_2$ are bisimulation relations over the SCG.

Proof. (sketch of proof) Using Proposition 2, we show that $\forall \alpha_1, \alpha_2 \in \mathcal{C}, t_f \in T$, if $((\alpha_1 \simeq_1 \alpha_2 \vee \alpha_1 \simeq_2 \alpha_2) \wedge succ(\alpha_1, t_f) \neq \emptyset)$ then $succ(\alpha_2, t_f) \neq \emptyset$ and their successors by t_f have the same favorite timed schedules.   □

Formally, the timed schedule based graph (TSBG) (resp. the relaxed timed schedule based graph (RTSBG)) is the quotient graph of the SCG w.r.t. $\simeq_1$ (resp. $\simeq_2$), defined above.

As an example, we report, in Table 2, the favorite timed schedules, in relaxed form, of state classes of the SCG shown in Fig. 1. Let us explain how to compute the favorite timed schedules of the successor of C_0 by t_4. Firing t_4 from C_0 leads to class C_2 where transitions t_1 and t_4 are enabled (t_4 is newly enabled but t_1 is not). Favorite timed schedules of C_2 are computed as follows:

$\rho_2(t_1)_{t_1} = Min(\overrightarrow{\rho_0(t_1)}_{t_1}, \overrightarrow{\rho_0(t_4)}_{t_1}) = 0$ and $\rho_2(t_1)_{t_4} = \uparrow Is(t_4) = 4$.
$\rho_2(t_4)_{t_1} = \overrightarrow{\rho_0(t_4)}_{t_1} = 1$ and $\rho_2(t_4)_{t_4} = \overrightarrow{\rho_0(t_4)}_{t_4} = 3$.

Notice that classes C_{13} and C_{15} have the same favorite timed schedules. The gain in both size and time may be much more significant. As an example, for one of the producer-consumer models given in [4], sizes (nodes /edges/times) of the SCG, TSBG and RTSBG are respectively 14086/83375/1.38, 13841/82288/1.15 and 9267/54977/0.76. For this model, there are at least 4 enabled transitions in each marking. Note also that timed schedule graphs allow a gain in space needed to represent each state class.

Lemma 4. *(i) TSBG is smaller than SCG; (ii) RTSBG is smaller than TSBG.*

Proof. (i): The proof is immediate as the TSBG is the quotient graph of the SCG w.r.t. $\simeq_1$ and two different SCG state classes may have the same favorite timed schedules (see the previous example). (ii): The RTSBG can also be seen as the quotient graph of the TSBG w.r.t. some relation of equivalence over the TSBG. Moreover, for the TPN shown in Fig. 1, both the TSBG and RTSBG are smaller than the SCG.   □

Table 2. Relaxed favorite timed schedules of state classes of the SCG in Fig. 1

C0:	$\overrightarrow{\rho_0}\ t_1\ t_4$ t_1 0 1 t_4 2 0	C1:	$\overrightarrow{\rho_1}\ t_2\ t_4\ t_5$ t_2 0 2 0 t_4 1 0 0 t_5 4 5 3	C2:	$\overrightarrow{\rho_2}\ t_1\ t_4$ t_1 0 0 t_4 4 2	C3:	$\overrightarrow{\rho_3}\ t_2\ t_4\ t_5$ t_2 0 2 2 t_4 0 0 0 t_5 3 4 3
C4:	$\overrightarrow{\rho_4}\ t_2\ t_4\ t_5$ t_2 0 0 0 t_4 4 1 4 t_5 4 3 3	C5:	$\overrightarrow{\rho_5}\ t_2\ t_4\ t_5$ t_2 0 0 0 t_4 3 0 2 t_5 4 3 1	C6:	$\overrightarrow{\rho_6}\ t_4\ t_5$ t_4 0 0 t_5 3 3	C7:	$\overrightarrow{\rho_7}\ t_2\ t_4\ t_5$ t_2 0 0 0 t_4 4 1 2 t_5 3 2 1
C8:	$\overrightarrow{\rho_8}\ t_2\ t_4\ t_5$ t_2 0 0 0 t_4 3 1 2 t_5 3 2 1	C9:	$\overrightarrow{\rho_9}\ t_5$ t_5 0	C10:	$\overrightarrow{\rho_{10}}\ t_4\ t_5$ t_4 0 1 t_5 0 0	C11:	$\overrightarrow{\rho_{11}}\ t_4\ t_5$ t_4 0 3 t_5 0 0
C12:	*true*	$C13, C15$:	$\overrightarrow{\rho_{13}}\ t_4$ t_4 0	C14:	$\overrightarrow{\rho_{14}}\ t_5$ t_5 0	C16:	$\overrightarrow{\rho_{16}}\ t_3$ t_3 0

4   Essential Time Points of Clock Domains

4.1   The State Zone Method

In the *Zone Based Graph (ZBG)*[6], all clock states reachable by runs supporting the same firing sequence are agglomerated in the same node and considered modulo some over-approximation operation [1,6]. This operation is used to ensure the finiteness of the ZBG for Bounded TPNs with unbounded firing intervals. An abstract state, called state zone, is defined as a pair $\beta = (M, FZ)$ combining a marking M and a formula FZ which characterizes the clock domains of all states agglomerated in the state zone. In FZ, the clock of each enabled transition for M is represented by a variable with the same name. The domain of FZ is convex and has a unique canonical form represented by the pair (M, Z), where Z is a DBM of order $|En(M) \cup \{o\}|$ defined by: $\forall (x, y) \in (En(M) \cup \{o\})^2$, $z_{xy} = Sup_{FZ}(x - y)$, where o represents the value 0. State zones of the ZBG are in relaxed form.

We first focus on the construction of the ZBG without considering the over-approximation operation. Afterwards, we show how to handle the case of TPNs with unbounded firing intervals.

The initial state zone is the pair $\beta_0 = (M_0, FZ_0)$, where M_0 is the initial marking and $FZ_0 = \bigwedge\limits_{t_i, t_j \in En(M_0)} 0 \le t_i = t_j \le \underset{t_u \in En(M_0)}{Min} \uparrow Is(t_u)$.

Proposition 3 below establishes a firing rule which computes directly, in canonical and relaxed form, a successor of a state zone in $O(n^2)$, n being the number of its enabled transitions. Note that this firing rule is somewhat the adaptation to the case of relaxed clock abstract states, of the one given in [5] for the SSCG. Indeed, unlike the SSCG, in the ZBG, state zones are in relaxed form. Our contribution here consists in combining, in one step, two operations: the discrete successor of a state zone and its relaxation.

Proposition 3. *Let $\beta = (M, \overrightarrow{FZ})$ be a relaxed state zone in canonical form, $\overrightarrow{Z}$ its DBM and t_f a transition.*

1) t_f is firable from β (i.e. $sucz(\beta, t_f) \neq \emptyset$) iff: $t_f \in En(M)$ and $\downarrow Is(t_f) \le \overrightarrow{Z}_{t_f o}$

2) If $sucz(\beta, t_f) \neq \emptyset$, its firing leads to $\beta' = (M', \overrightarrow{Z'})$ computed as follows:

2.1) $\forall p \in P, M'(p) = M(p) - Pre(p, t_f) + Post(p, t_f)$

2.2) $\forall t_i, t_j \in En(M')$,

$$z'_{o t_i} = \begin{cases} 0 & \text{if } t_i \in New(M', t_f) \\ Min(\overrightarrow{z}_{o t_i}, \overrightarrow{z}_{t_f t_i} - \downarrow Is(t_f)) & \text{otherwise} \end{cases}$$

$$z'_{t_j o} = \begin{cases} 0 & \text{if } t_i \in New(M', t_f) \\ \overrightarrow{z}_{t_j o} & \text{otherwise} \end{cases}$$

$$z'_{t_j t_i} = \begin{cases} 0 & \text{if } t_i \text{ is } t_j \vee t_i, t_j \in New(M', t_f) \\ \overrightarrow{z}_{t_j o} & \text{if } \{t_i, t_j\} \cap New(M', t_f) = \{t_i\} \\ \overrightarrow{z}_{o t_i} & \text{if } \{t_i, t_j\} \cap New(M', t_f) = \{t_j\} \\ Min(\overrightarrow{z}_{t_j t_i}, \overrightarrow{z}_{t_j o} + \overrightarrow{z}_{t_f t_i} - \downarrow Is(t_f)) & \text{otherwise} \end{cases}$$

$$\overrightarrow{z'}_{o t_i} = z'_{o t_i}, \; \overrightarrow{z'}_{t_j t_i} = z'_{t_j t_i} \text{ and } \overrightarrow{z'}_{t_j o} = \underset{t_u \in En(M')}{Min}(\uparrow Is(t_u) + \overrightarrow{z'}_{t_j t_u})$$

Proof. (sketch of proof) The proof is based on constraint graphs [5]. $\overrightarrow{FZ}$ is consistent and can be represented by a constraint graph G. G has no negative cycle and the weight of the shortest path, in G, from a node x to a node y is equal to $\overrightarrow{z}_{xy}$.

1) Transition t_f is firable from β iff t_f is enabled in M and the following formula is consistent: $\overrightarrow{FZ} \wedge (t_f \geq\downarrow Is(t_f))$. In other words, the constraint graph of $\overrightarrow{FZ}$ completed with edge $(o, t_f, -\downarrow Is(t_f))$ has no negative cycle. Since before adding this edge, the graph did not contain any negative cycle, the completed graph will have no negative cycle iff, the shortest cycle going through the added edge is not negative: $-\downarrow Is(t_f) + \overrightarrow{z}_{t_f,o} \geq 0$.

2) State zone $(M, \overrightarrow{Z'}) = sucz(\beta, t_f)$ can be computed from the constraint graph of $\overrightarrow{Z}$ as follows: a) Add edge $(o, t_f, -\downarrow Is(t_f))$; b) Rename node t_f and all nodes associated with transitions conflicting with t_f for M (to avoid having different nodes with the same name); c) For each transition t_n newly enabled in M', add a new node t_n and both arcs $(t_n, o, 0)$ and $(o, t_n, 0)$. This corresponds to the constraint: $t_n = 0$.

For each couple (x, y) of $(En(M') \cup \{o\})^2$, z'_{xy} is the weight of the shortest path from node x to node y, in the completed constraint graph:

- If t_i is not newly enabled, the shortest path from node o to node t_i is the shortest path among those going through the added edge $(o, t_f, -\uparrow Is(t_f))$ and those going through old edges (i.e.: $z'_{ot_i} = Min(z_{ot_i}, z_{t_f t_i} - \downarrow Is(t_f)))$. Otherwise, its value is 0.
- If t_j is not newly enabled, the shortest path from node t_j to node o is the shortest path among those going through old edges (i.e.: $z'_{t_j o} = z_{t_j o}.$). Otherwise, its value is 0.
- If t_i and t_j are not newly enabled, the shortest path from node t_j to node t_i is the shortest path among those going through the added edge and those which do not pass through this edge, i.e., $z'_{t_j t_i} = Min(z_{t_j t_i}, z_{t_j o} + z_{t_f t_i} - \downarrow Is(t_f))$.
- If t_i is t_j or t_i and t_j are newly enabled, $z'_{t_i t_j} = 0$.
- If t_i is newly enabled and t_j is not, i.e., $z'_{t_i t_j} = z'_{ot_j}$ and $z'_{t_j t_i} = z'_{t_j o}$.

Finally, to obtain $\overrightarrow{Z'}$, it suffices to consider the constraint graph of Z' and to replace edges $(t_j, o, z'_{t_j o}), t_j \in En(M')$ with $(t_j, o, \uparrow Is(t_j)), t_j \in En(M')$. Then:

$$\forall t_i, t_j \in En(M'), \overrightarrow{z'}_{t_j t_i} = z'_{t_j t_i}, \overrightarrow{z'}_{ot_i} = z'_{ot_i} \text{ and } \overrightarrow{z'}_{t_j o} = \underset{t_u \in En(M')}{Min} \uparrow Is(t_u) + z'_{t_j t_u}.$$
□

4.2 Essential States of Zones

Let $\beta = (M, Z)$ be a state zone and $t_j \in En(M)$. Similarly to the SCG, for the ZBG, the clock valuation in β [4], which favors t_j is the one with the highest clock value for t_j ($z_{t_j o}$) and the lowest clock values for other enabled transitions. The

---

[4] $A \in (Q^+ \cup \{\infty\})^{|T|}$ is a clock valuation of $\beta = (M, Z)$ iff $\forall t_i \in En(M)$, $-a_{t_i} \leq z_{ot_i}$, $a_{t_i} \leq z_{t_i o}$ and $\forall t_i, t_k \in En(M)$, $a_{t_i} - a_{t_k} \leq z_{t_i t_k}$.

favorite clock valuation of t_j denoted $\eta(t_j)$ is defined by:

$$\forall t_i \in T, \ \eta(t_j)_{t_i} = \begin{cases} z_{t_j o} - z_{t_j t_i} & \text{if } t_1 \in En(M) \\ 0 & \text{otherwise} \end{cases}$$

We also define the minimal clock valuation $\eta(o)$ by:

$$\forall t_i \in En(M), \eta(o)_{t_i} = \begin{cases} -z_{ot_i} & \text{if } t_1 \in En(M) \\ 0 & \text{otherwise} \end{cases}$$

Let $\eta(t_j)$ be a clock valuation of a state zone $\beta = (M, Z)$. The relaxed form of $\eta(t_j)$ is the clock valuation denoted $\overrightarrow{\eta(t_j)}$ defined by: $\forall t_i \in En(M)$,

$$\overrightarrow{\eta(t_j)}_{t_i} = \eta(t_j)_{t_i} + (\underset{t_u \in En(M)}{Min} \uparrow Is(t_u) - \eta(t_j)_{t_u}).$$

Lemma 5. $\eta(t_j)$ and $\eta(o)$ are clock valuations of β.

Proof. $\eta(t_j)$: We have to show that $\forall t_i \in En(M)$,
1) $-\eta(t_j)_{t_i} \le z_{ot_i}$, 2) $\eta(t_j)_{t_i} \le z_{t_i o}$ and 3) $\forall t_i, t_k \in En(M), \eta(t_j)_{t_i} - \eta(t_j)_{t_k} \le z_{t_i t_k}$.
Relations 1), 2) and 3) are derived from relations: $\eta(t_j)_{t_i} = z_{t_j o} - z_{t_j t_i}, z_{t_j o} \le z_{t_i o} + z_{t_j t_i}$,
$z_{t_j t_i} \le z_{t_j o} + z_{ot_i}, \eta(t_j)_{t_i} - \eta(t_j)_{t_k} = -z_{t_j t_i} + z_{t_j t_k}$ and $z_{t_j t_k} \le z_{t_j t_i} + z_{t_i t_k}$.
$\eta(o)$: $\forall t_i, t_k \in En(M), \eta(o)_{t_i} = -z_{ot_i} \le z_{t_i o}$ and $\eta(o)_{t_i} - \eta(o)_{t_k} \le -z_{ot_i} + z_{ot_k} \le z_{t_i t_k}$. □

The favorite clock valuations of β are those of its enabled transitions and the one of o (i.e., $\{\eta(o)\} \cup \{\eta(t_j), t_j \in En(M)\}$) (see Fig 2.d). As an example, the favorite clock valuation η_0 of the ZBG initial state zone is:
$\forall t_i, t_j \in En(M_0), \eta_0(t_j)_{t_i} = \underset{t_k \in En(M_0)}{Min} \uparrow Is(t_k)$ and $\forall t_i \in En(M_0), \eta_0(o)_{t_i} = 0$.

4.3   Essential Clock Valuation Based Graphs

The following proposition establishes a firing rule based on the favorite clock valuations of a state zone.

Proposition 4. Let $\beta = (M, \overrightarrow{Z})$ be a state zone, η its favorite clock valuation function and t_f a transition of T.
1) $sucz(\beta, t_f) \ne \emptyset$ iff $t_f \in En(M) \ \wedge \ \eta(t_f)_{t_f} \ge \downarrow Is(t_f)$.
2) If $sucz(\beta, t_f) \ne \emptyset$ then the favorite clock valuation function η' of $\beta' = sucz(\beta, t_f) = (M', \overrightarrow{Z'})$ is computed as follows: Let $\triangle_f = \eta(t_f)_{t_f} - \downarrow Is(t_f)$ and $E = New(M', t_f) \cup conf(t_f, M)$.
2.1) $\eta'(o) = Max(\eta(o), \eta(t_f) - \triangle_f)_{[E:=0]}$.

2.2) $\forall t_j \in En(M'), \eta'(t_j) = \begin{cases} \overrightarrow{\eta'(o)} & \text{if } t_j \in New(M', t_f) \\ \overrightarrow{Max(\eta(t_j), \eta(t_f) - \triangle_f)_{[E:=0]}} & \text{otherwise} \end{cases}$

Proof. (sketch of proof) The proof is based on rewriting Proposition 3 by means of η using the following relations: $\overrightarrow{z}_{t_f o} = \eta(t_f)_{t_f}, \forall t_j, t_i \in En(M), \overrightarrow{z}_{t_j o} = \eta(t_j)_{t_j}, \overrightarrow{z}_{ot_i} = -\eta(o)_{t_i}$ and $\overrightarrow{z}_{t_j t_i} = \eta(t_j)_{t_j} - \eta(t_j)_{t_i}$. Let $\triangle_f = \eta(t_f)_{t_f} - \downarrow Is(t_f)$. Note that before relaxing a zone, clocks of newly enabled transitions are all set to zero[5].

---

[5] The relaxation does not affect lower bounds of clocks and bounds of clock differences but it however may affect the upper bounds of clocks of enabled transitions.

$\forall t_i, t_j \in En(M')$,

1) $\overrightarrow{z}'_{ot_i} = z'_{ot_i} = \begin{cases} 0 & \text{if } t_i \in New(M', t_f) \\ Min(-\eta(o)_{t_i}, \triangle_f - \eta(t_f)_{t_i}) & \text{otherwise} \end{cases}$

$\forall t_i \notin En(M'), \eta'(o)_{t_i} = 0$. Then: $\eta'(o) = (Max(\eta(o), \eta(t_f) - \triangle_f))_{[E:=0]}$.

2) $z'_{t_j o} = \begin{cases} 0 & \text{if } t_j \in New(M', t_f) \\ \eta(t_j)_{t_j} & \text{otherwise} \end{cases}$

3) $\overrightarrow{z}'_{t_j t_i} = \begin{cases} 0 & \text{if } t_i \text{ is } t_j \ \vee \ t_i, t_j \in New(M', t_f) \\ Min(-\eta(o)_{t_i}, \triangle_f - \eta(t_f)_{t_i}) & \text{if } \{t_i, t_j\} \cap New(M', t_f) = \{t_j\} \\ \eta(t_j)_{t_j} & \text{if if } \{t_i, t_j\} \cap New(M', t_f) = \{t_i\} \\ \eta(t_j)_{t_j} + Min(-\eta(t_j)_{t_i}, \triangle_f - \eta(t_f)_{t_i}) & \text{otherwise} \end{cases}$

Let $A(t_j) = (Max(\eta(t_j), \eta(t_f) - \triangle_f))_{[New(M', t_f):=0]}$. Using $A(t_j)$, we obtain[6]:

$\overrightarrow{z}'_{t_j t_i} = \begin{cases} -\eta'(o)_{t_i} & \text{if } t_i \text{ is } t_j \ \vee \ t_j \in New(M', t_f) \\ \eta(t_j)_{t_j} - A(t_j)_{t_i} & \text{otherwise} \end{cases}$

Proposition 3 states that: $\overrightarrow{z}'_{t_j o} = \underset{t_u \in En(M')}{Min} (\uparrow Is(t_u) + \overrightarrow{z}'_{t_j t_u})$

It follows that: $\eta'(t_j)_{t_i} = \overrightarrow{z}'_{t_j o} - \overrightarrow{z}'_{t_j t_i} =$

$\begin{cases} \underset{t_u \in En(M')}{Min} (\uparrow Is(t_u) - \eta'(o)_{t_u}) + \eta'(o)_{t_i} & \text{if } t_j \in New(M', t_f) \\ \underset{t_u \in En(M')}{Min} (\uparrow Is(t_u) - A(t_j)_{t_u}) + A(t_j)_{t_i} & \text{otherwise} \end{cases}$

Then: $\eta'(t_j)_{t_i} = \overrightarrow{z}'_{t_j o} - \overrightarrow{z}'_{t_j t_i} = \begin{cases} \overrightarrow{\eta'(o)}_{t_i} & \text{if } t_j \in New(M', t_f) \\ \overrightarrow{A(t_j)}_{t_i} & \text{otherwise} \end{cases}$ $\square$

To ensure the convergence of the ZBG, one can use any approximation operation [1,7], which preserves markings and timed traces, since the DBM of every state zone can be retrieved from its favorite clock valuations (see the proof of Proposition 4). We can also consider state zones modulo the following relation of equivalence denoted $\simeq_3$ defined on the favorite clock valuation functions: Let $\beta_1 = (M_1, Z_1), \beta_2 = (M_2, Z_2)$ be two state zones and η_1, η_2 their respective favorite clock valuation functions.
$\beta_1 \simeq_3 \beta_2$ iff $M_1 = M_2 \ \wedge \ \forall t_i \in En(M_1), \forall x \in En(M_1) \cup \{o\}$,

$$\begin{cases} Min(\eta_1(x)_{t_i}, \downarrow Is(t_i)) = Min(\eta_2(x)_{t_i}, \downarrow Is(t_i)) & \text{if } \uparrow Is(t_i) = \infty \\ \eta_1(x)_{t_i} = \eta_2(x)_{t_i} & \text{otherwise} \end{cases}$$

Lemma 6. $\simeq_3$ *preserves markings and timed traces of the TPN.*

Proof. It suffices to show that $\forall x \in En(M_1) \cup \{o\}, \eta_1(x)$ and $\eta_2(x)$ have the same interval state. The firing interval I_1^x of $\eta_1(x)$ is defined by:$\forall t_i \in En(M_1), I_1^x(t_i) = [Max(0, \downarrow Is(t_i) - \eta_1(x)_{t_i}), \uparrow Is(t_i) - \eta_1(x)_{t_i}]$. It follows that $\beta_1 \simeq_3 \beta_2$ implies that $\forall x \in En(M_1) \cup \{o\}, I_1^x = I_2^x$. $\square$

Formally, the clock valuation based graph (CVBG) is the quotient graph of the ZBG w.r.t. the relation of equivalence $\simeq_3$ above. The resulting graph is finite since

---

[6] Note that $\forall t_j \in En(M'), \forall t_i \in New(M', t_f), A(t_j)_{t_i} = 0$.

with $\simeq_3$, clock values beyond some bounded limits are ignored when state zones are compared. For lack of space, we let as a future work the comparison and investigation of combination of $\simeq_3$ with state zone approximations [1,7].

5 Conclusion

In this paper, we considered two state space abstractions of the TPN: the SCG and the ZBG. For the SCG, we showed that only some timed schedules of each state class (one timed schedule per transition) are relevant to compute a TPN reachability graph (TSBG). In addition, the resulting graph is smaller than the SCG. For the ZBG, we first proposed a firing rule that computes, in one step, state zones in canonical and relaxed form. Afterwards, we showed that only some clock valuations of each state zone (one clock valuation per transition plus the minimal clock valuation) are relevant to compute a TPN reachability graph (CVBG). To ensure the finiteness of the CVBG, we proposed a relation of equivalence over it which preserves markings and timed traces of the TPN.

In the near future, we will investigate the implementation of the TSBG and CVBG using binary decision diagrams or other appropriate data structures. We will also investigate the contraction of the CVBG.

References

1. Behrmann, G., Bouyer, P., Larsen, K.G., Pelànek, R.: Lower and upper bounds in zone-based abstractions of timed automata. International Journal on Software Tools for Technology Transfer 8(3), 204–215 (2006)
2. Bengtsson, J.: Clocks, DBMs and States in Timed Systems, PhD thesis, Dept. of Information Technology, Uppsala University (2002)
3. Berthomieu, B., Vernadat, F.: State class constructions for branching analysis of time Petri nets. In: Garavel, H., Hatcliff, J. (eds.) TACAS 2003. LNCS, vol. 2619, pp. 442–457. Springer, Heidelberg (2003)
4. Boucheneb, H., Rakkay, H.: A more efficient time Petri net state space abstraction preserving linear properties. In: Proc. of the seventh International Conference on Application of Concurrency to System Design (ASCD 2007), pp. 61–70. IEEE Computer Society, Los Alamitos (2007)
5. Boucheneb, H., Hadjidj, R.: CTL* model checking for time Petri nets. Journal of Theoretical Computer Science TCS 353(1-3), 208–227 (2006)
6. Gardey, G., Roux, O.H., Roux, O.F.: State space computation and analysis of time Petri nets. Theory and Practice of Logic Programming (TPLP), Special Issue on Specification Analysis and Verification of Reactive Systems 6(3), 301–320 (2006)
7. Boucheneb, H., Gardey, G., Roux, O.H.: TCTL model checking of time Petri nets, Technical Report IRCCyN number RI 2006-14 (2006)
8. Penczek, W., Pólrola, A.: Specification and Model Checking of Temporal Properties in Time Petri Nets and Timed Automata. In: Cortadella, J., Reisig, W. (eds.) ICATPN 2004. LNCS, vol. 3099, pp. 37–76. Springer, Heidelberg (2004)
9. Popova-Zeugmann, L., Schlatter, D.: Analyzing paths in time Petri nets. Fundamenta Innformaticae 37, 311–327 (1999)
10. Yoneda, T., Schlingloff, B.H.: Efficient Verification of Parallel Real-Time Systems. Formal Methods in System Design 11(2), 187–215 (1997)

Parametric Model-Checking of Time Petri Nets with Stopwatches Using the State-Class Graph*

Louis-Marie Traonouez, Didier Lime, and Olivier H. Roux

Institute of Research in Communications and Cybernetics of Nantes,
1 rue de la Noë, BP 92101, 44321 Nantes Cedex 03, France
{Louis-Marie.Traonouez,Didier.Lime,Olivier-h.Roux}@irccyn.ec-nantes.fr

Abstract. In this paper, we propose a new framework for the parametric verification of time Petri nets with stopwatches controlled by inhibitor arcs. We first introduce an extension of time Petri nets with inhibitor arcs (ITPNs) with temporal parameters. Then, we define a symbolic representation of the parametric state space based on the classical state class graph method. The parameters of the model are embedded into the firing domains of the classes, that are represented by convex polyhedra. Finally, we propose semi-algorithms for the parametric model-checking of a subset of parametric TCTL formulae on ITPNs. We can thus generate the set of the parameter valuations that satisfy the formulae.

Keywords: Time Petri nets, stopwatches, model-checking, parameters, state-class graph.

Introduction

Formal methods are widely used in the conception of real-time systems. Methods such as model-checking allow the verification of a system by exploring the state-space of a model. A popular class of models is Petri nets and their extensions among which Time Petri nets (TPNs) [1] are a widely used time extension in which transitions can be fired within a time interval.

In order to take into account the global complexity of systems, we can use models that encompass the notion of actions that can be suspended and resumed. This implies extending traditional clock variables by "stopwatches". Several extensions of TPNs address this issue, such as Preemptive-TPNs [2] or Inhibitor Hyperarc TPNs (ITPNs) [3]. ITPNs introduce special inhibitor arcs that control the progress of transitions. These models all belong to the class of TPNs extended with stopwatches (SwPNs)[4].

The model-checking of these models has become more and more efficient. It nevertheless requires a complete knowledge of the system. Consequently, the verification of the behavior must be done after the conception when the global system and its environment are known. On the one hand, it increases the complexity of the conception and the verification of systems. For too complex systems this can lead to a combinatory explosion. Besides, if the system is proven wrong

---

* Work supported by the French Government under grant ANR-SETI-06-003.

F. Cassez and C. Jard (Eds.): FORMATS 2008, LNCS 5215, pp. 280–294, 2008.

or if the environment changes, this complex verification process must be carried out again. On the other hand, getting a complete knowledge of a system can be impossible. In many important applications, a system is defined by parameters that are in relation with several other systems. In the existing tools for modelling and verification, parameters are often used, however they must be instantiated to perform analyses. The next development step of the technology is to be able to directly analyze a parametric model.

Related Works. Parametric analysis of real-time systems has been studied in [5]. They introduce Parametric Timed Automata (PTA) and prove that, in the general case, the emptiness problem is undecidable. On this subject, in [6] the authors prove that for a particular class of PTA called L/U automata this emptiness problem is decidable. They also give a model-checking algorithm that use parametric Difference Bound Matrices. Parametric model-checking can be used to generate a set of constraints on the parameters such that the property is verified. In discrete time, parametric model-checking of PTA has been studied in [7], and some decidability results have been found. On hybrid automata, state-space exploration algorithms have been extended to allow a parametric analysis and implemented in the tool HYTECH [8].

Another approach developed in [9] focuses on the verification of parametric TCTL formulae on clock automata. They consider unbounded parameters that take their value among integers and the problem is proved decidable. In [10], this approach is used in parametric TPNs, but with bounded parameters. However, they consider and analyze a region graph for each parameter valuation.

Our Contribution. In this context, we propose to study the parametric model-checking problem on time Petri nets and more generally on ITPNs. We consider unbounded parameters and thus, we need a proper abstraction of the state-space of the parametric model. In TPNs, considering that the time is dense, the state-space of the model is infinite, but it can be represented by a finite partition as in the state-class graph [11]. We therefore extend the state-class graph construction with parameters and define parametric state-classes that represent at the same time the temporal domain and the parameter domain. Although the state-class graph does not preserve timed properties, there exists methods [12] to verify a subset of TCTL with this abstraction. We consider this subset of formulae and extend it with parameters. Then, we propose and prove semi-algorithms for parametric model-checking.

Outline of the Paper. In section 1, we present our parametric extension of ITPNs (PITPNs). Then, in section 2, we introduce some decidability and undecidability results. Section 3 defines the parametric state-class graph of PITPNs. In section 4, we study the parametric model-checking of a subset of TCTL with parameters. Finally, in 5 we discuss our solution to the parametric model-checking problem.

Due to the lack of place proofs of theorems and algorithms are not included in this paper but can be found in the internal report based on this article [13].

1   Parametric Time Petri Nets with Inhibitor Arcs

1.1   Notations

The sets $\mathbb{N}$, $\mathbb{Q}^+$ and $\mathbb{R}^+$ are respectively the sets of natural, non-negative rational and non-negative real numbers. An interval I of $\mathbb{R}^+$ is a $\mathbb{Q}$-interval iff its left endpoint $I^\uparrow$ belongs to $\mathbb{Q}^+$ and its right endpoint $I^\downarrow$ belongs to $\mathbb{Q}^+ \cup \{\infty\}$. We denote by $\mathcal{I}(\mathbb{Q})$ the set of $\mathbb{Q}$-intervals of $\mathbb{R}^+$.

1.2   Formal Definitions of PITPNs

We parameterize the ITPN model with a set of temporal parameters $Par = \{\lambda_1, \lambda_2, \ldots, \lambda_l\}$ by replacing some of the temporal bounds of the transitions by parameters. These parameters are considered as constant variables in the semantics, and take their values among rationals.

Some initial constraints are given on the parameters. These constraints define the domain $D_p \subseteq \mathbb{Q}^{+Par}$ of the parameters which is a convex polyhedron. These constraints must at least specify that for all parameters valuations in D_p, the minimum bounds of the firing intervals of the transitions are inferior to the maximum bounds. Additional linear constraints may of course be given.

A *valuation* of the parameters is a function $\nu : Par \rightarrow \mathbb{Q}^+$, such that $[\nu(\lambda_1)\ \nu(\lambda_2) \ldots \nu(\lambda_l)]^\top \in D_p$, which is equivalent to say that ν is a point of D_p. We will also write that $\nu = [\lambda_1\ \lambda_2 \ldots \lambda_l]^\top$.

A *linear constraint* over the parameters is an expression $\gamma = \sum_{i=0}^l a_i * \lambda_i \sim b$, where $\forall 0 \leq i \leq l$, $a_i, b \in \mathbb{R}$ and $\sim \in \{=, <, >, \leq, \geq\}$. A convex polyhedron is a conjunction of linear constraints.

A *parametric time interval* is a function $J : D_p \rightarrow \mathcal{I}(\mathbb{Q}^+)$ that associates to each parameter valuation a $\mathbb{Q}$-interval. The set of parametric time intervals over Par is denoted by $\mathcal{J}(Par)$.

Definition 1. *A parametric time Petri net with inhibitor arcs (PITPN) is a tuple* $\mathcal{N} = \langle P, T, Par, {}^\bullet(.), (.)^\bullet, {}^\circ(.), M_0, J_s, D_p \rangle$, *where:*

 - $P = \{p_1, p_2, \ldots, p_m\}$ *is a non-empty finite set of* places,
 - $T = \{t_1, t_2, \ldots, t_n\}$ *is a non-empty finite set of transitions,*
 - $Par = \{\lambda_1, \lambda_2, \ldots, \lambda_l\}$ *is a finite set of parameters,*
 - ${}^\bullet(.) \in (\mathbb{N}^P)^T$ *is the backward incidence function,*
 - $(.)^\bullet \in (\mathbb{N}^P)^T$ *is the forward incidence function,*
 - ${}^\circ(.) \in (\mathbb{N}^P)^T$ *is the inhibition function,*
 - $M_0 \in \mathbb{N}^P$ *is the initial marking of the net,*
 - $J_s \in (\mathcal{J}(Par))^T$ *is the function that associates a parametric firing interval to each transition,*
 - $D_p \subseteq \mathbb{Q}^{+Par}$ *is a convex polyhedron that is the domain of the parameters.*

A *marking* M of the net is an element of $\mathbb{N}^P$ such that $\forall p \in P, M(p)$ is the number of tokens in the place p.

A transition t is said to be *enabled* by the marking M if $M \geq^\bullet t$, (*i.e.* if the number of tokens in M in each input place of t is greater or equal to the value on the arc between this place and the transition). We denote it by $t \in$ enabled (M).

A transition t is said to be *inhibited* by the marking M if the place connected to one of its inhibitor arc is marked with at least as many tokens than the weight of the considered inhibitor arc between this place and t: $0 < {}^\circ t \leq M$. We denote it by $t \in$ inhibited (M). Practically, inhibitor arcs are used to stop the elapsing of time for some transitions: an inhibitor arc between a place p and a transition t means that the stopwatch associated to t is stopped as long as place p is marked with enough tokens.

A transition t is said to be *active* in the marking M if it is enabled and not inhibited by M.

Example 1. In the figure 1 an example of PTPN is given that includes three parameters a, b and c.

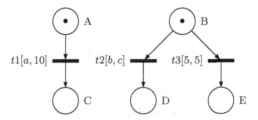

Fig. 1. A parametric time Petri net

1.3   Semantics of Parametric Time Petri Nets with Inhibitor Arcs

The semantics of a Parametric Time Petri net with Inhibitor Arcs $\mathcal{N}$ is defined for a parameter valuation $\nu \in D_p$, as the non-parametric ITPN obtained when replacing in $\mathcal{N}$ all the parameters by their valuation.

Definition 2 (Semantics of a PITPN). *Given a PITPN $\mathcal{N} = \langle P, T, Par,$ $^\bullet(.), (.)^\bullet, {}^\circ(.), M_0, J_s, D_p \rangle$, and a valuation $\nu \in D_p$, the semantics $[\![\mathcal{N}]\!]_\nu = \langle P, T,$ $^\bullet(.), (.)^\bullet, {}^\circ(.), M_0, I_s \rangle$ of $\mathcal{N}$ is a ITPN such that $\forall t \in T$, $I_s(t) = J_s(t)(\nu)$.*

We now recall the semantics of an ITPN.

A transition t is said to be *firable* when it has been enabled and not inhibited for at least $I_s(t)^\uparrow$ time units.

A transition t_k is said to be *newly* enabled by the firing of the transition t_i from the marking M, and we denote it by $\uparrow$ enabled (t_k, M, t_i), if the transition is enabled by the new marking $M - {}^\bullet t_i + t_i^\bullet$ but was not by $M - {}^\bullet t_i$, where M is the marking of the net before the firing of t_i. Formally:

$$\uparrow \text{enabled}\,(t_k, M, t_i) = ({}^\bullet t_k \leq M - {}^\bullet t_i + t_i^\bullet)$$
$$\wedge ((t_k = t_i) \vee ({}^\bullet t_k > M - {}^\bullet t_i))$$

By extension, we will denote by $\uparrow$ enabled (M, t_i) the set of transitions newly enabled by firing the transition t_i from the marking M.

Definition 3. *A state of a ITPN is a pair $q = (M, I)$ in which M is a marking and I is a function called the* interval *function. Function $I \in (\mathcal{I}(\mathbb{Q}))^T$ associates a temporal interval with every transition enabled at M.*

The semantics of an ITPN is defined as a timed transition system (TTS) [14], in which two kinds of transitions may occur: *time* transitions when time passes and *discrete* transitions when a transition of the net is fired.

Definition 4 (Semantics of an ITPN). *The semantics of a time Petri net with inhibitor arcs $\mathcal{N} = \langle P, T, {}^\bullet(.), (.)^\bullet, {}^\circ(.), M_0, I_s \rangle$ is defined as the TTS $\mathcal{S}_{\mathcal{N}} = \langle Q, q_0, \rightarrow \rangle$ such that:*

- $Q = \mathbb{N}^P \times (\mathcal{I}(\mathbb{Q}))^T$,
- $q_0 = (M_0, I_s)$,
- $\rightarrow \in Q \times (T \cup \mathbb{R}^+) \times Q$ *is the transition relation including a time transition relation and a discrete transition relation.*
  The time transition relation is defined $\forall d \in \mathbb{R}^+$ by:

$(M, I) \xrightarrow{d} (M, I')$ *iff* $\forall t_i \in T$,
$$\begin{cases} I'(t_i) = \begin{cases} I(t_i) & \text{if } t_i \in \text{enabled}\,(M) \text{ and } t_i \in \text{inhibited}\,(M) \\ I'(t_i)^\uparrow = \max(0, I(t_i)^\uparrow - d), \text{ and } I'(t_i)^\downarrow = I(t_i)^\downarrow - d \text{ otherwise,} \end{cases} \\ M \geq^\bullet t_i \Rightarrow I'(t_i)^\downarrow \geq 0 \end{cases}$$

The discrete transition relation is defined $\forall t_i \in T$ by:

$(M, I) \xrightarrow{t_i} (M', I')$ *iff* $\begin{cases} t_i \in \text{enabled}\,(M) \text{ and } t_i \notin \text{inhibited}\,(M), \\ M' = M - {}^\bullet t_i + t_i^\bullet, \\ I(t_i)^\uparrow = 0, \\ \forall t_k \in T, I'(t_k) = \begin{cases} I_s(t_k) & \text{if } \uparrow\text{enabled}\,(t_k, M, t_i) \\ I(t_k) & \text{otherwise} \end{cases} \end{cases}$

A *run* ρ of length $n \geq 0$ in $\mathcal{S}_{\mathcal{N}}$ is a finite or infinite sequence of alternating time and discrete transitions of the form

$$\rho = q^0 \xrightarrow{d_0} q^0 + d_0 \xrightarrow{t_0} q^1 \xrightarrow{d_1} q^1 + d_1 \xrightarrow{t_1} \cdots q^n \xrightarrow{d_n} \cdots$$

We write *first*(ρ) the first state of a run ρ. A run is *initial* if *first*$(\rho) = q_0$. A run ρ of $\mathcal{N}$ is an initial run of $\mathcal{S}_{\mathcal{N}}$. For a state q, the set of all the infinite runs starting from q is denoted by $\pi(q)$. The set of all the runs of $\mathcal{N}$ is $\pi(q_0)$.

For a state q^i in ρ the absolute time elapsed (relative to the initial state) is time$(q) = d_0 + d_1 + \cdots + d_{i-1}$. For a run ρ the total elapsed time in ρ is time$(\rho) = \sum_{i=0}^n d_i$. In this paper we restrict ourselves to non-zeno ITPN, which means that the elapsed time is diverging (i.e. $\forall \rho \in \pi(q_0), \text{time}(\rho) = \infty$), and by extension to non-zeno PITPN (i.e. such that $\forall \nu \in D_p, [\![\mathcal{N}]\!]_\nu$ is non zeno).

2   Decidability of Parametric TPNs

In this section, we give some results concerning the decidability of the emptiness and reachability problems for bounded parametric time Petri nets (without inhibitor arcs). The case of PITPNs is of little interest since these problems are already known undecidable for bounded ITPNs [4].

Let us consider lower/upper bound (L/U) bounded parametric TPNs i.e. every parameter occurring in the PTPN is either the lower bound of some of the time intervals or their upper bound, but there exists no pair of intervals I_1, I_2 and no parameter λ such that $\lambda = I_1^\uparrow$ and $\lambda = I_2^\downarrow$.

Theorem 1. *The emptiness and reachability problems for bounded L/U parametric TPNs are decidable.*

Proof (Theorem 1). The structural and syntactical translation proposed in [15] from a TPN into a bisimilar timed automaton (TA) can straightforwardly be extended from L/U PTPNs to L/U parametric TA [6]. Therefore, since the emptiness and reachability problems are decidable for L/U parametric TA [6], they also are decidable for L/U PTPNs.

Theorem 2. *The emptiness and reachability problems for bounded parametric TPNs are undecidable.*

Proof (Theorem 2). The structural and syntactical translation preserving timed language acceptance proposed in [16] from a TA into a bounded TPN can straightforwardly be extended to parametric TA. Thus, for every parametric TA, we can compute a parametric TPN that accepts the same timed language. Since the emptiness problem (and then, the reachability problem) is undecidable for parametric TA [5], it is also undecidable for parametric TPNs.

3   The Parametric State-Class Graph of a PITPN

Since the state-space of a non-parametric TPN is generally infinite in dense-time, it is required to abstract the time by merging some states into some equivalence classes. Consequently, symbolic representations of the state-space are used. One of the approaches to partition the state-space in a finite set of infinite state classes is the state-class graph [11]. This approach has been extended for ITPNs in [3].

However, there also exists an infinite number of parameter valuations. Thus, in the same way, we need to use symbolic representations of the parameter domains. In time Petri nets or timed automata, the time domain of an abstract state can be efficiently encoded by a difference bound matrix (DBM). This is why, in the parametric timed automata proposed in [6], the authors define parametric DBMs in which they encode both the time domain and the parameter domain. When considering stopwatch time Petri nets, the firing domain of a class is a general polyhedron and cannot necessarily be represented by a DBM. Consequently, in the parametric state-classes of PITPNs we will use polyhedra, which describe both the transition variable domains and the parameter domains.

3.1   Parametric State-Classes

Definition 5. *A parametric state-class C of a PITPN is a pair (M, D) where M is a marking of the net and D is a firing domain represented by a (convex) polyhedron involving $l + n$ variables, with n being the number of transitions enabled by the marking of the class and l the number of parameters in the net.*

A point (ν, ν') of the firing domain is constituted by a valuation ν of the parameters in Par and a valuation ν' of the firing times θ of enabled transitions. The set of those variables θ of D will be noted Θ.

We denote by $D_{|Par}$ the projection of a firing domain D on the set of parameters:

$$D_{|Par} = \{\nu \in \mathbb{Q}^{+l} \mid \exists \nu' \in \mathbb{R}^n \text{ s.t. } (\nu, \nu') \in D\}$$

This definition can be extended to any arbitrary subset of variables of D.

3.2   Computation of the Parametric State-Class Graph

The parametric state-class graph is computed similarly to the non-parametric case. Parameters are embedded into the firing domain of the initial class, and the operations that compute the successor classes do not concern the parameters. However, throughout the computation of the graph, the domain of the parameters in a class will be automatically reduced to consider only the valuations that make this class reachable.

Definition 6 (Firability). *Let $C = (M, D)$ be a parametric state-class of a PITPN. A transition t_i is said to be firable from C iff there exists a solution (ν, ν') of D, such that $\forall j \in \{1, \ldots, n\} - \{i\}$, s.t. $t_j \in$ enabled (M) and $t_j \notin$ inhibited (M), $\nu'(\theta_i) \leq \nu'(\theta_j)$. We will write this: $t_i \in$ firable (C).*

Now, given a parametric class $C = (M, D)$ and a firable transition t_f, the parametric class $C' = (M', D')$ obtained from C by the firing of t_f, which we write $C' = succ(C, t_f)$, is given by

  - $M' = M - {}^\bullet t_f + t_f^\bullet$
  - D' is computed along the following steps, and noted $\text{next}(D, t_f)$
    1. intersection with the firability constraints : $\forall j$ s.t. t_j is active, $\theta_f \leq \theta_j$
    2. variable substitutions for all enabled transitions that are *active* t_j: $\theta_j = \theta_f + \theta'_j$,
    3. elimination (using for instance the Fourier-Motzkin method) of all variables relative to transitions disabled by the firing of t_f,
    4. addition of inequations relative to newly enabled transitions

$$\forall t_k \in \uparrow \text{enabled}\,(M, t_f), \ J_s(t_k)^\uparrow \leq \theta'_k \leq J_s(t_k)^\downarrow$$

Case of a point : Let $C = (M, D)$ be a parametric state-class of a PITPN, $x = [\lambda_1 \ldots \lambda_l \ \theta_1 \ldots \theta_n]^\top$ be a point of D and t_f be a transition firable from $(M, \{x\})$. The successor of $\{x\}$ by the firing t_f from marking M is given by

$$\text{next}(\{x\}, t_f) = \left\{ \forall i \in [1..n] \ \begin{bmatrix} \lambda_1 \\ \vdots \\ \lambda_l \\ \theta'_1 \\ \vdots \\ \theta'_n \end{bmatrix} \ \middle| \ \begin{array}{l} \theta'_i \in I_s(t_i) \text{ if } \uparrow \text{enabled}\,(t_i, M, t_f) \\ \theta'_i = \theta_i \text{ if } t_i \in \text{enabled}\,(M) \\ \quad \text{and } t_i \in \text{inhibited}\,(M) \\ \quad \text{and not } \uparrow \text{enabled}\,(t_i, M, t_f) \\ \theta'_i = \theta_i - \theta_f \text{ otherwise} \end{array} \right\}$$

The next operator straightforwardly extends to finite or infinite unions of points.

The parametric state-class graph is generated by iteratively applying the function that computes the successors of a state-class:

Definition 7. *Given a PITPN $\mathcal{N}$, the parametric state-class graph of $\mathcal{N}$ is the transition system $\mathcal{G}(\mathcal{N}) = \langle \mathcal{C}, \rightarrow\!\!\!\rightarrow, C_0 \rangle$ such that:*

- *$C_0 = (M_0, D_0)$ is the initial class such that $D_0 = D_p \wedge \{\theta_k \in J_s(t_k) \mid t_k \in$ enabled $(M_0)\}$*
- *$C \xrightarrow{t} C'$ iff $t \in$ firable (C) and $C' = succ(C, t)$,*
- *$\mathcal{C} = \{C | C_0 \rightarrow\!\!\!\rightarrow^* C\}$, where $\rightarrow\!\!\!\rightarrow^*$ is the reflexive and transitive closure of $\rightarrow\!\!\!\rightarrow$.*

3.3   Valuation of the Parametric State-Class Graph

From the parametric state-class graph of a PITPN it is possible to choose a valuation of the parameters and to replace in the graph all the parameters by their value. Then, we obtain a non-parametric graph. However, some firing domains of the classes may become empty, which means that the class is not reachable for this valuation. Those classes must be removed from the non-parametric graph. The graph finally obtained corresponds to the state-class graph of the ITPN obtained for this valuation.

Definition 8 (Valuation of a Parametric State-Class). *Let $C = (M, D)$ be a parametric state-class of a PITPN $\mathcal{N}$ and let $\nu \in D_p$ be a valuation of the parameters of $\mathcal{N}$. The valuation of C by ν is a non-parametric class $[\![C]\!]_\nu = (M, [\![D]\!]_\nu)$ where*

$$[\![D]\!]_\nu = \{\nu' \in \mathbb{R}^n \mid (\nu, \nu') \in D\}$$

The valuation of the parametric state-class graph is obtained by valuating the classes of the graph, starting from the initial class and stopping if the firing domains become empty.

Definition 9 (Valuation of the Parametric State-Class Graph). *Given a PITPN $\mathcal{N}$ and a valuation $\nu \in D_p$, $[\![\mathcal{G}(\mathcal{N})]\!]_\nu = (\mathcal{C}_\nu, \rightarrow\!\!\!\rightarrow, [\![C_0]\!]_\nu)$ where:*

- *$[\![C_0]\!]_\nu$ is the valuation of the initial class C_0 of $\mathcal{G}(\mathcal{N})$,*
- *$[\![C]\!]_\nu \xrightarrow{t} [\![C']\!]_\nu$ iff $C = (M, D), C' = (M', D') \in \mathcal{G}(\mathcal{N}) C \xrightarrow{t} C'$ and $[\![D']\!]_\nu \neq \emptyset$*
- *$\mathcal{C}_\nu = \{[\![C]\!]_\nu \mid [\![C_0]\!]_\nu \rightarrow\!\!\!\rightarrow^* [\![C]\!]_\nu\}$, where $\rightarrow\!\!\!\rightarrow^*$ is the reflexive and transitive closure of $\rightarrow\!\!\!\rightarrow$.*

The theorem 3 establishes that the valuation of the parametric state-class graph of a PITPN matches the non-parametric state-class graph of the ITPN obtained for the same parameter valuation. Theorem 4 allows to directly determine the accessibility condition of a parametric state-class.

Theorem 3. *Given a PITPN $\mathcal{N}$ and a valuation $\nu \in D_p$, then*

$$[\![\mathcal{G}(\mathcal{N})]\!]_\nu = \mathcal{G}([\![\mathcal{N}]\!]_\nu).$$

Theorem 4. *Given a PITPN $\mathcal{N}$ and a valuation $\nu \in D_p$, let $C = (M, D)$ be a parametric state-class in $\mathcal{G}(\mathcal{N})$. Then*

$$[\![C]\!]_\nu \in [\![\mathcal{G}(\mathcal{N})]\!]_\nu \ \text{ iff } \ \nu \in D_{|Par}.$$

4   Parametric Model-Checking

The model-checking problem consists in checking that a model $\mathcal{N}$ satisfies a property ϕ expressed in a given logic, which is more formally written $\mathcal{N} \models \phi$. The answer to this problem is either *true* or *false*. Concerning the parametric model-checking problem, given a parametric model $\mathcal{N}$ and a property ϕ, which may also be parameterized, we want to determine the set of parameter valuations $F(\mathcal{N}, \phi)$ such that $\forall \nu \in F(\mathcal{N}, \phi)$ the non-parametric model $[\![\mathcal{N}]\!]_\nu$ obtained for the valuation ν satisfies the non-parametric property $[\![\phi]\!]_\nu$ obtained for the same valuation. This set will be represented by a set of constraints on the parameters of the problem.

4.1   Parametric TCTL Formulae

Like ITPN, we parameterize TCTL formulae by allowing that the bounds of the temporal intervals of the formulae are parameters. The parameters used in the formulae are added to the set of parameters of the PITPN in study. Besides, we consider only a subset of TCTL formulae for which "on-the-fly" model-checking algorithms have already been proposed for TPNs [12]. This subset is sufficient to verify many interesting problems (reachability, safety, bounded liveness...).

First, we recall the syntax and semantics of TCTL formulae in the context of TPNs (or ITPNs).

Definition 10 (TCTL for TPN). *The grammar of TCTL formulae is:*

$$TCTL ::= \mathcal{P} \mid \neg\varphi \mid \varphi \Rightarrow \psi \mid \exists\varphi\mathcal{U}_I\psi \mid \forall\varphi\mathcal{U}_I\psi$$

where $\varphi, \psi \in TCTL$, $I \in \mathcal{I}(\mathbb{Q}^+)$, $\mathcal{P} \in PR$, and $PR = \{\mathcal{P} \mid \mathcal{P} : M \to \{true, false\}\}$ is the set of propositions on the marking on the net.

We use the following abbreviations $\exists\Diamond_I\varphi = \exists\mathbf{true}\mathcal{U}_I\varphi$, $\forall\Diamond_I\varphi = \forall\mathbf{true}\mathcal{U}_I\varphi$, $\exists\Box_I\varphi = \neg\forall\Diamond_I\neg\varphi$ and $\forall\Box_I\varphi = \neg\exists\Diamond_I\neg\varphi$.

We define the bounded time response by $\varphi \leadsto_I \psi = \forall\Box(\varphi \Rightarrow \forall\Diamond_I\psi)$.

TCTL formulae are interpreted on the states of a model $\mathcal{M} = (\mathcal{S}_\mathcal{N}, \mathcal{V})$, where $\mathcal{S}_\mathcal{N}$ is the state space of the TPN and $\mathcal{V} : \mathcal{S}_\mathcal{N} \to 2^{PR}$ is a function that evaluates the marking of a state, such that $\mathcal{V}(q) = \{\mathcal{P} \in PR \mid \mathcal{P}(M) = true\}$. Now, let $q \in \mathcal{S}_\mathcal{N}$ be a state and $\rho \in \pi(q)$ a run starting from q, such that $\rho = q^0 \xrightarrow{d_0} q^0 + d_0 \xrightarrow{t_0} q^1 \xrightarrow{d_1} q^1 + d_1 \xrightarrow{t_1} \cdots$. We define $\rho^* : \mathbb{R}^+ \to \mathcal{S}_\mathcal{N}$ by $\rho^*(r) = q^i + \delta$ if $r = \sum_{j=0}^{i-1} d_j + \delta$, with $i \geq 0$ and $0 \leq \delta < d_i$.

Definition 11 (Semantics of TCTL). *Given a TPN $\mathcal{N}$ and its model $\mathcal{M} = (\mathcal{S}_\mathcal{N}, \mathcal{V})$, the truth value of a TCTL formula for a state $q \in \mathcal{S}_\mathcal{N}$ is*

- $q \models \mathcal{P}$ iff $\mathcal{P} \in \mathcal{V}(q)$,
- $q \models \neg\varphi$ iff $q \not\models \varphi$,
- $q \models \varphi \Rightarrow \psi$ iff $q \not\models \varphi \vee q \models \psi$,
- $q \models \exists\varphi\mathcal{U}_I\psi$ iff $\exists\rho \in \pi(q)$, $\exists r \in I$ s.t. $\rho^*(r) \models \psi$ and $\forall r' < r$, $\rho^*(r') \models \varphi$
- $q \models \forall\varphi\mathcal{U}_I\psi$ iff $\forall\rho \in \pi(q)$, $\exists r \in I$, s.t. $\rho^*(r) \models \psi$ and $\forall r' < r$, $\rho^*(r') \models \varphi$

Given a model $\mathcal{M} = (\mathcal{S}_\mathcal{N}, \mathcal{V})$, for a marking proposition $\mathcal{P} \in PR$ and a state $q = (M, I) \in \mathcal{S}_\mathcal{N}$, we use the notation $M \models \mathcal{P}$ if $\mathcal{P} \in \mathcal{V}(q)$ and $M \not\models \mathcal{P}$ if $\mathcal{P} \notin \mathcal{V}(q)$.

Finally, a TPN $\mathcal{N}$ satisfies a TCTL formula ϕ if and only if $q_0 \models \phi$.

We present now the syntax and semantics of Parametric TCTL (PTCTL) formulae for PITPN.

Definition 12 (PTCTL for PITPN). *The grammar of PTCTL formulae is:*

$$PTCTL ::= \exists\varphi\mathcal{U}_J\psi \mid \forall\varphi\mathcal{U}_J\psi \mid \exists\Diamond_J\varphi \mid \forall\Diamond_J\varphi \mid \exists\Box_J\varphi \mid \forall\Box_J\varphi \mid \varphi \leadsto_{J_r} \psi$$

where $\varphi, \psi \in PR$, $J, J_r \in \mathcal{J}(Par)$ are parametric time intervals, with the restriction that $J_r = [0, b]$ with $b \in \mathbb{Q}^+ \cup Par$, or $J_r = [0, \infty[$.

The semantics of PTCTL formulae are defined similarly to the semantics of PITPNs. Given a valuation, the parameters in the formulae are replaced by their value to obtain a TCTL formula, which is interpreted on the ITPN obtained for this valuation.

Definition 13 (Semantics of PTCTL). *Let $\mathcal{N}$ be a PITPN and ϕ be a PTCTL formulae and $\nu \in D_p$ be a valuation of the parameters of $\mathcal{N}$ (which are shared with ϕ). $[\![\phi]\!]_\nu$ is the TCTL formula obtained when replacing in ϕ the parametric time interval J (or J_r) by the $\mathbb{Q}$-interval $J(\nu)$ (or $J_r(\nu)$).*
Then $\mathcal{N}$ satisfy ϕ for the valuation ν if and only if $[\![\mathcal{N}]\!]_\nu \models [\![\phi]\!]_\nu$.

4.2   Extending the Parametric State-Class Graph with a Global Clock

In the state-class graph, the firing domain of a class gives the firing dates of the transitions with the entrance in the class as a time origin. Timed properties are difficult to verify in this context. In order to easily check timed properties with the state class graph abstraction, it is necessary to be able to evaluate the time that has elapsed between classes. For this purpose, we propose to extend the parametric state-classes with an additional variable noted θ_c. This variable is initialized to zero in the initial class, and then decreases when time flows, like a transition variable [1] . However, the variable will not constrain the transitions variables when determining the firability constraints. Then, for all classes, the time elapsed from the initialization of θ_c to the entrance in the class is: $\tau_c = -\theta_c$.

---

[1] The value of this variable will always be non-positive. But this is not a problem in the computation of the state-classes. The alternative would be to initialize it, not to zero, but to a sufficiently large value, but this value is hard to determine.

Definition 14. *An extended parametric state-class C of a PITPN is a class whose firing domain D is extended with an additional variable $\theta_c \in \Theta$.*

The definition of the firability of an extended class is not modified. The firability constraints indeed only involve the variables θ_i where $\forall i \in \{1, \ldots, n\}$, $t_i \in T$. The next operator is redefined for an extended class such that for a point $x = [\lambda_1 \ldots \lambda_l \ \theta_1 \ldots \theta_n \ \theta_c]^\top$ of D, in $\mathsf{next}((\{x\}, t_f))$ we have $\theta'_c = \theta_c - \theta_f$.

The extended parametric state-class graph $\mathcal{G}_c(\mathcal{N})$ is then computed iteratively in a similar way, starting from the initial class $C_0 = (M_0, D_0)$ where

$$D_0 = D_p \wedge \{\theta_k \in J(t_k) \mid t_k \in \mathsf{enabled}\,(M_0)\} \wedge \{\theta_c = 0\}$$

Finally, given an extended parametric state-class $C = (M, D)$, we are able to determine:

- $\tau_{min}(C)$, the absolute minimum time elapsed when entering the class. This a function of the parameters Par of the net $\tau_{min}(C) : D_p \to \mathbb{Q}^+$, such that $\tau_{min}(C)(\nu) = \min_{x=(\nu,\nu') \in D}(\tau_c)$. It can be expressed as the maximum between the minimum values of τ_c and it is necessarily positive and finite.
- $\tau_{max}(C)$, the absolute maximum time elapsed when entering the class. This a function on the parameters Par of the net $\tau_{max}(C) : D_p \to \mathbb{Q}^+ \cup \{\infty\}$, such that $\tau_{max}(C)(\nu) = \max_{x=(\nu,\nu') \in D}(\tau_c)$. It can be expressed as the minimum between the maximum values of τ_c and it is necessarily positive but may be infinite if there is no maximum time.

If $[\![C]\!]_\nu \in [\![\mathcal{G}_c(\mathcal{N})]\!]_\nu$, let $q \in [\![C]\!]_\nu$ be a state. Then the elapsed time of the state is such that $\tau_{min}(C)(\nu) \leq \mathsf{time}(q) \leq \tau_{max}(C)(\nu)$.

Example 2. In the PTPN of the figure 1, we can exhibit the two following extended classes:

$$\mathbf{C_0} = (\mathbf{M_0}, \mathbf{D_0}) :$$
$$M_0 = (A, B)$$
$$D_0 = \begin{cases} 0 \leq a \leq \theta_1 \leq 10, \\ 0 \leq b \leq \theta_2 \leq c, \\ \theta_3 = 5, \theta_c = 0. \end{cases} \xrightarrow{t_1}$$

$$\mathbf{C_1} = (\mathbf{M_1}, \mathbf{D_1}) :$$
$$M_1 = (B, C)$$
$$D_1 = \begin{cases} \theta_3 - \theta_c = 5, \\ b \leq \theta_2 - \theta_c \leq c, \\ -5 \leq \theta_c \leq -a, \\ 0 \leq \theta_2, 0 \leq a, 0 \leq b. \end{cases}$$

Thus, the elapsed time after the firing of t_1 is such that $\tau_{min}(C_1) = a$ and $\tau_{max}(C_1) = \min(5, c)$.

4.3   Principles of Parametric Model-Checking with the State-Class Graph

Given a PITPN $\mathcal{N}$ and a PTCTL property ϕ, in the parametric model-checking problem we want to characterize the set $F(\mathcal{N}, \phi)$ of all the parameters valuations that resolve the problem, which is defined by:

$$F(\mathcal{N}, \phi) = \{\nu \in D_p \mid [\![\mathcal{N}]\!]_\nu \models [\![\phi]\!]_\nu\}$$

To achieve this we are going to recursively compute, on each extended class $C = (M, D)$, a logical predicate on the parameters that corresponds to the verification of the property on the current class and its successors. This predicate represents the set: $F^\phi(C) = \{\nu \in D_{|Par} \mid [\![C]\!]_\nu \models [\![\phi]\!]_\nu\}$

We begin by giving an interpretation of the verification of a PTCTL formula ϕ on an extended parametric state class C, which we write $[\![C]\!]_\nu \models [\![\phi]\!]_\nu$.

Formulae $\phi = \exists\varphi\mathcal{U}_J\psi$ or $\phi = \forall\varphi\mathcal{U}_J\psi$: For a valuation $\nu \in D_{|Par}$ and a state $q \in [\![C]\!]_\nu$, we define $[\![\phi[J - time(q)]]\!]_\nu$ as the TCTL formula obtained after replacing in ϕ, the parametric time interval J by $J(\nu) - time(q)$. Then, according to the form of the PTCTL formula ϕ we define:

- if $\phi = \exists\varphi\mathcal{U}_J\psi$, then $[\![C]\!]_\nu \models [\![\phi]\!]_\nu$ iff $\exists q \in [\![C]\!]_\nu$, $q \models [\![\phi[J - time(q)]]\!]_\nu$
- if $\phi = \forall\varphi\mathcal{U}_J\psi$, then $[\![C]\!]_\nu \models [\![\phi]\!]_\nu$ iff $\forall q \in [\![C]\!]_\nu$, $q \models [\![\phi[J - time(q)]]\!]_\nu$

Formulae $\phi = \varphi \leadsto_{J_r} \psi$: We extend the PITPN $\mathcal{N}$ with an additional place named P_{LT} that will be marked if and only if we are looking for ψ. We denote by $\mathcal{N}_{LT}$ the resulting PITPN. In this model, the successor $C' = (M', D') = succ_{LT}(C, t)$ of an extended parametric state-class $C = (M, D) \in \mathcal{G}_c(\mathcal{N}_{LT})$ by a transition $t_f \in firable\,(C)$, is given by:

- $M' = M - {}^\bullet t_f + t_f^\bullet$ and $\begin{cases} \text{if } (M' \models \varphi \text{ and } M' \not\models \psi) \text{ then } M'(P_{LT}) = 1, \\ \text{else if } (M \models \psi) \text{ then } M'(P_{LT}) = 0, \\ \text{else } M'(P_{LT}) = M(P_{LT}) \end{cases}$
- $D' = next(D, t_f)$ and
  if $(M(P_{LT}) = 0$ or $M \models \psi)$ then the clock variable θ_c is reset to zero.

On this model we define that $[\![C]\!]_\nu \models [\![\phi]\!]_\nu$ if and only if $\forall q \in [\![C]\!]_\nu$, $\forall \rho \in \pi(q)$,

$$M(P_{LT}) = 1 \Rightarrow \begin{cases} \exists 0 \leq r_1 \leq J_r(\nu)^\downarrow - time(q) \text{ s.t. } \rho^*(r_1) \models \psi \text{ and} \\ \forall r_2 \geq r_1\ \rho^*(r_2) \models M(P_{LT}) = 1 \Rightarrow \exists r_3 \geq r_2 \\ \qquad \text{s.t. } r_3 - r_2 \leq J_r(\nu)^\downarrow \text{ and } \rho^*(r_3) \models \psi \end{cases}$$

$$M(P_{LT}) = 0 \Rightarrow \begin{cases} \forall r_2 \geq 0\ \rho^*(r_2) \models M(P_{LT}) = 1 \Rightarrow \exists r_3 \geq r_2 \\ \qquad \text{s.t. } r_3 - r_2 \leq J_r(\nu)^\downarrow \text{ and } \rho^*(r_3) \models \psi \end{cases}$$

In this model, $time(q)$ refers to the time elapsed since the last reinitialization of θ_c. We notice that when the time has been reset (then $time(q) = 0$) the two definitions above are equivalent and correspond to $q \models [\![\phi]\!]_\nu$.

Finally, the theorem 5 states that we are able to resolve the parametric model-checking problem if we compute the set of solutions on the initial class.

Theorem 5. *Given a PITPN $\mathcal{N}$ and a PTCTL formula ϕ, $F(\mathcal{N}, \phi) = F^\phi(C_0)$, where C_0 is the initial class of the extended parametric state class graph of $\mathcal{N}$.*

4.4   Parametric Model-Checking Semi-algorithms

To verify PTCTL formulae we propose three semi-algorithms according to the form of the formulae. These algorithms recursively characterize, for each class C, the set $F^\phi(C)$. This set is represented by conjunctions or disjunctions of linear constraints on the parameters. We use a disjunctive normal form (i.e. a disjunction of convex polyhedra).

Algorithm EU: This semi-algorithm is designed for formulae whose form is $\phi = \exists \varphi \mathcal{U}_J \psi$, where $J \in \mathcal{J}(Par)$. Let be $C = (M, D) \in \mathcal{G}_c(\mathcal{N})$, we compute:

$$F_{EU}^{\phi}(C) = D_{|Par} \wedge \{\tau_{min}(C) \le J^{\downarrow}\} \wedge \left(\left(M \models \psi \wedge \{\tau_{max}(C) \ge J^{\uparrow}\} \right) \right.$$

$$\vee \left(M \models \varphi \wedge M \models \psi \wedge \left(\text{firable}(C) = \emptyset \vee \right. \right.$$

$$\left(\bigvee_{\substack{t \in \text{firable}(C) \\ C' = (M', D') = succ(C,t)}} (\{\tau_{max}(C') \ge J^{\uparrow}\} \wedge D'_{|Par})) \right) \right)$$

$$\left. \vee \left(M \models \varphi \wedge \text{firable}(C) \ne \emptyset \wedge \left(\bigvee_{\substack{t \in \text{firable}(C) \\ C' = succ(C,t)}} F_{EU}^{\phi}(C') \right) \right) \right)$$

This formula establishes three conditions in disjunction to prove the formula ϕ:

– The first disjunction is used when C verifies ψ but not ϕ. Thus, the elapsed time must be entailed in the interval J as soon as we get into the class.
– The second case is when both ϕ and ψ are verified. Comparing to the first one it allows to wait in the class.
– The third disjunction is used when only ϕ is verified. In this case we have to compute the successors of C.

Example 3. In the net of the figure 1 we check the formula:
$\phi_1 = \exists \Diamond_{[0,inf[}(M(D) = 1)$. The result is $F_{EU}^{\phi_1}(C_0) = \{b <= 5\}$.

Algorithm AU: This semi-algorithm is designed for formulae whose form is $\phi = \forall \varphi \mathcal{U}_J \psi$, where $J \in \mathcal{J}(Par)$. Let be $C = (M, D) \in \mathcal{G}_c(\mathcal{N})$, we compute:

$$F_{AU}^{\phi}(C) = D_{|Par} \wedge \begin{Bmatrix} \tau_{max}(C) \le J^{\downarrow} \\ \tau_{max}(C) \ne \infty \end{Bmatrix} \wedge \left(\left(M \models \psi \wedge \{\tau_{min}(C) \ge J^{\uparrow}\} \right) \right.$$

$$\vee \left(M \models \varphi \wedge M \models \psi \wedge \left(\text{firable}(C) = \emptyset \vee \right. \right.$$

$$\left(\bigwedge_{\substack{t \in \text{firable}(C) \\ C' = (M', D') = succ(C,t) \\ D'' = D' \wedge \{\theta_c > -J^{\uparrow}\}}} (F_{AU}^{\phi}(M', D'') \vee \neg D''_{|Par})) \right) \right)$$

$$\left. \vee \left(M \models \varphi \wedge \text{firable}(C) \ne \emptyset \wedge \left(\bigwedge_{\substack{t \in \text{firable}(C) \\ C' = (M', D') = succ(C,t)}} (F_{AU}^{\phi}(C') \vee \neg D'_{|Par})) \right) \right) \right)$$

Similarly, there are three conditions in disjunction. Unlike previously,. in the second one successors are computed, but only on the points of the class for which the property has not been verified yet. The conditions $\neg D'_{|Par}$ or $\neg D''_{|Par}$ forbid the accessibility of the class if it does not verify the property.

Example 4. In the net of the figure 1 we check the formula:
$\phi_2 = \forall \Diamond_{[0,inf[}(M(D) = 1)$. The result is $F_{AU}^{\phi_2}(C_0) = \{c < 5\}$.

Algorithm LT: This semi-algorithm is designed for formulae whose form is $\phi = \varphi \rightsquigarrow_{J_r} \psi$, where $J_r \in \mathcal{J}(Par)$ such that $J_r = [0, b]$ with $b \in \mathbb{Q}^+ \cup Par$, or $J_r = [0, \infty[$. Let be $C = (M, D) \in \mathcal{G}_c(\mathcal{N}_{LT})$, we compute:

$$F_{LT}^\phi(C) = D_{|Par} \wedge \left(M(P_{LT}) = 0 \vee \left\{ \begin{matrix} \tau_{max}(C) \leq J_r^\downarrow \\ \tau_{max}(C) \neq \infty \end{matrix} \right\} \right)$$

$$\wedge \left(\left(\mathsf{firable}\,(C) = \emptyset \wedge \left(M(P_{LT}) = 0 \vee M \models \psi \right) \right) \vee \right.$$

$$\left. \left(\mathsf{firable}\,(C) \neq \emptyset \wedge \left(\bigwedge_{\substack{t \in \mathsf{firable}(C) \\ C' = (M', D') = succ_{LT}(C, t)}} (F_{LT}^\phi(C') \vee \neg D'_{|Par}) \right) \right) \right)$$

This algorithm is similar to F_{AU} when $J^\uparrow = 0$. However analysis only stops if no successor is found.

5 Discussion

The semi-algorithms presented in this paper have been implemented in the tool ROMEO [17], a software for time Petri nets analysis. For polyhedra manipulation, the Parma Polyhedra Library [18] is used to represent the firing domains of the parametric state-classes and the logical formulae computed by the model-checking algorithms. These formulae are represented as powersets of convex polyhedra, that is to say a finite disjunction of polyhedra.

As mentioned before, the parametric model-checking problem is undecidable. Indeed the parametric state-class graph of a PITPN may be infinite. Additionally, to determine the whole set of parameters valuations that satisfy a formula, it would be in general necessary to analyze every parametric state-class. Nevertheless, some methods can help with the termination. In this way, if a parametric state-class $C = (M, D)$ is included in another class $C' = (M', D')$ (i.e. $M = M'$ and $D \subseteq D'$), it can be shown that $F_{EU}^\phi(C) \subseteq F_{EU}^\phi(C')$, and on the contrary that $F_{AU}^\phi(C') \subseteq F_{AU}^\phi(C) \vee \neg D_{|Par}$ and $F_{LT}^\phi(C') \subseteq F_{LT}^\phi(C) \vee \neg D_{|Par}$. As a result, in our "on-the-fly" model-checking approach it will not be necessary to analyze the whole state-class graph, but we will be able to stop the analysis of successors when finding included parametric state-classes.

Conclusion

In this paper, we have introduced a parametric extension of time Petri nets with stopwatches where the temporal bounds of the firing intervals are replaced by temporal parameters. We have proposed a symbolic representation of the state-space of these parametric models which is based on a parametric extension of the state-class graph. Upon this abstraction we have developed semi-algorithms for the parametric model-checking of parametric TCTL formulae.

In our future works we want to integrate this parametric approach in the development cycle of real-time systems through the functional decomposition of the systems. On concrete examples, a parametric decomposition combined with a projection of the formulae to verify can be useful in the development process. We hope to succeed in the elaboration of a formal framework for this method so that the process could be automated.

References

1. Merlin, P.: A study of the recoverability of computing systems. PhD thesis, Department of Information and Computer Science, Univ. of California, Irvine (1974)
2. Bucci, G., Fedeli, A., Sassoli, L., Vicario, E.: Time state space analysis of real-time preemptive systems. IEEE trans. on Soft. Eng. 30(2), 97–111 (2004)
3. Roux, O.H., Lime, D.: Time Petri nets with inhibitor hyperarcs. Formal semantics and state space computation. In: Cortadella, J., Reisig, W. (eds.) ICATPN 2004. LNCS, vol. 3099, pp. 371–390. Springer, Heidelberg (2004)
4. Berthomieu, B., Lime, D., Roux, O.H., Vernadat, F.: Reachability problems and abstract state spaces for time petri nets with stopwatches. Discrete Event Dynamic Systems 17(2), 133–158 (2007)
5. Alur, R., Henzinger, T.A., Vardi, M.Y.: Parametric real-time reasoning. In: ACM Symposium on Theory of Computing, pp. 592–601 (1993)
6. Hune, T., Romijn, J., Stoelinga, M., Vaandrager, F.W.: Linear parametric model checking of timed automata. In: Margaria, T., Yi, W. (eds.) TACAS 2001. LNCS, vol. 2031. Springer, Heidelberg (2001)
7. Bruyère, V., Raskin, J.F.: Real-time model-checking: Parameters everywhere. CoRR abs/cs/0701138 (2007)
8. Henzinger, T.A., Ho, P.H., Wong-Toi, H.: HYTECH: A model checker for hybrid systems. Int. Journal on Soft. Tools for Technology Transfer 1(1–2), 110–122 (1997)
9. Wang, F.: Parametric timing analysis for real-time systems. Inf. Comput. 130(2), 131–150 (1996)
10. Virbitskaite, I., Pokozy, E.: Parametric behaviour analysis for time petri nets. In: Malyshkin, V.E. (ed.) PaCT 1999. LNCS, vol. 1662, pp. 134–140. Springer, Heidelberg (1999)
11. Berthomieu, B., Diaz, M.: Modeling and verification of time dependent systems using time Petri nets. IEEE trans. on Soft. Eng. 17(3), 259–273 (1991)
12. Hadjidj,R.,Boucheneb,H.:On-the-fly tctl model checking for time petri nets using state class graphs. In: ACSD, pp. 111–122. IEEE Computer Society, Los Alamitos (2006)
13. Traonouez, L.M., Lime, D., Roux, O.H.: Parametric model-checking of time petri nets with stopwatches using the state-class graph. Technical Report RI2008-3, IR-CCyN, Nantes, France (2008)
14. Larsen, K.G., Pettersson, P., Yi, W.: Model-checking for real-time systems. In: Fundamentals of Computation Theory, pp. 62–88 (1995)
15. Cassez, F., Roux, O.H.: Structural translation from Time Petri Nets to Timed Automata – Model-Checking Time Petri Nets via Timed Automata. The journal of Systems and Software 79(10), 1456–1468 (2006)
16. Bérard, B., Cassez, F., Haddad, S., Lime, D., Roux, O.H.: Comparison of the expressiveness of timed automata and time Petri nets. In: Pettersson, P., Yi, W. (eds.) FORMATS 2005. LNCS, vol. 3829. Springer, Heidelberg (2005)
17. Roux, O.H., Didier Lime, G.G., Magnin, M.: Roméo (2006),
    http://romeo.rts-software.org
18. Bagnara, R., Hill, P.M., Zaffanella, E.: The Parma Polyhedra Library. Quaderno 457, Dipartimento di Matematica, Università di Parma, Italy (2006)

Author Index

Lecture Notes in Computer Science

Sublibrary 1: Theoretical Computer Science and General Issues

For information about Vols. 1– 4942
please contact your bookseller or Springer

Vol. 5073: O. Gervasi, B. Murgante, A. Laganà, D. Taniar, Y. Mun, M.L. Gavrilova (Eds.), Computational Science and Its Applications – ICCSA 2008, Part II. XXIX, 1280 pages. 2008.

Vol. 5072: O. Gervasi, B. Murgante, A. Laganà, D. Taniar, Y. Mun, M.L. Gavrilova (Eds.), Computational Science and Its Applications – ICCSA 2008, Part I. XXIX, 1266 pages. 2008.

Vol. 5065: P. Degano, R. De Nicola, J. Meseguer (Eds.), Concurrency, Graphs and Models. XV, 810 pages. 2008.

Vol. 5062: K.M. van Hee, R. Valk (Eds.), Applications and Theory of Petri Nets. XIII, 429 pages. 2008.

Vol. 5059: F.P. Preparata, X. Wu, J. Yin (Eds.), Frontiers in Algorithmics. XI, 350 pages. 2008.

Vol. 5058: A.A. Shvartsman, P. Felber (Eds.), Structural Information and Communication Complexity. X, 307 pages. 2008.

Vol. 5050: J.M. Zurada, G.G. Yen, J. Wang (Eds.), Computational Intelligence: Research Frontiers. XVI, 389 pages. 2008.

Vol. 5045: P. Hertling, C.M. Hoffmann, W. Luther, N. Revol (Eds.), Reliable Implementation of Real Number Algorithms: Theory and Practice. XI, 239 pages. 2008.

Vol. 5038: C.C. McGeoch (Ed.), Experimental Algorithms. X, 363 pages. 2008.

Vol. 5036: S. Wu, L.T. Yang, T.L. Xu (Eds.), Advances in Grid and Pervasive Computing. XV, 518 pages. 2008.

Vol. 5035: A. Lodi, A. Panconesi, G. Rinaldi (Eds.), Integer Programming and Combinatorial Optimization. XI, 477 pages. 2008.

Vol. 5029: P. Ferragina, G.M. Landau (Eds.), Combinatorial Pattern Matching. XIII, 317 pages. 2008.

Vol. 5028: A. Beckmann, C. Dimitracopoulos, B. Löwe (Eds.), Logic and Theory of Algorithms. XIX, 596 pages. 2008.

Vol. 5022: A.G. Bourgeois, S.Q. Zheng (Eds.), Algorithms and Architectures for Parallel Processing. XIII, 336 pages. 2008.

Vol. 5018: M. Grohe, R. Niedermeier (Eds.), Parameterized and Exact Computation. X, 227 pages. 2008.

Vol. 5015: L. Perron, M.A. Trick (Eds.), Integration of AI and OR Techniques in Constraint Programming for Combinatorial Optimization Problems. XII, 394 pages. 2008.

Vol. 5011: A.J. van der Poorten, A. Stein (Eds.), Algorithmic Number Theory. IX, 455 pages. 2008.

Vol. 5010: E.A. Hirsch, A.A. Razborov, A. Semenov, A. Slissenko (Eds.), Computer Science – Theory and Applications. XIII, 411 pages. 2008.

Vol. 5008: A. Gasteratos, M. Vincze, J.K. Tsotsos (Eds.), Computer Vision Systems. XV, 560 pages. 2008.

Vol. 5004: R. Eigenmann, B.R. de Supinski (Eds.), OpenMP in a New Era of Parallelism. X, 191 pages. 2008.

Vol. 5000: O. Grumberg, H. Veith (Eds.), 25 Years of Model Checking. VII, 231 pages. 2008.

Vol. 4996: H. Kleine Büning, X. Zhao (Eds.), Theory and Applications of Satisfiability Testing – SAT 2008. X, 305 pages. 2008.

Vol. 4988: R. Berghammer, B. Möller, G. Struth (Eds.), Relations and Kleene Algebra in Computer Science. X, 397 pages. 2008.

Vol. 4985: M. Ishikawa, K. Doya, H. Miyamoto, T. Yamakawa (Eds.), Neural Information Processing, Part II. XXX, 1091 pages. 2008.

Vol. 4984: M. Ishikawa, K. Doya, H. Miyamoto, T. Yamakawa (Eds.), Neural Information Processing, Part I. XXX, 1147 pages. 2008.

Vol. 4981: M. Egerstedt, B. Mishra (Eds.), Hybrid Systems: Computation and Control. XV, 680 pages. 2008.

Vol. 4978: M. Agrawal, D.-Z. Du, Z. Duan, A. Li (Eds.), Theory and Applications of Models of Computation. XII, 598 pages. 2008.

Vol. 4975: F. Chen, B. Jüttler (Eds.), Advances in Geometric Modeling and Processing. XV, 606 pages. 2008.

Vol. 4974: M. Giacobini, A. Brabazon, S. Cagnoni, G.A. Di Caro, R. Drechsler, A. Ekárt, A.I. Esparcia-Alcázar, M. Farooq, A. Fink, J. McCormack, M. O'Neill, J. Romero, F. Rothlauf, G. Squillero, A.Ş. Uyar, S. Yang (Eds.), Applications of Evolutionary Computing. XXV, 701 pages. 2008.

Vol. 4973: E. Marchiori, J.H. Moore (Eds.), Evolutionary Computation, Machine Learning and Data Mining in Bioinformatics. X, 213 pages. 2008.

Vol. 4972: J. van Hemert, C. Cotta (Eds.), Evolutionary Computation in Combinatorial Optimization. XII, 289 pages. 2008.

Vol. 4971: M. O'Neill, L. Vanneschi, S. Gustafson, A.I. Esparcia Alcázar, I. De Falco, A. Della Cioppa, E. Tarantino (Eds.), Genetic Programming. XI, 375 pages. 2008.

Vol. 4967: R. Wyrzykowski, J. Dongarra, K. Karczewski, J. Wasniewski (Eds.), Parallel Processing and Applied Mathematics. XXIII, 1414 pages. 2008.

Vol. 4963: C.R. Ramakrishnan, J. Rehof (Eds.), Tools and Algorithms for the Construction and Analysis of Systems. XVI, 518 pages. 2008.

Vol. 4962: R. Amadio (Ed.), Foundations of Software Science and Computational Structures. XV, 505 pages. 2008.

Vol. 4961: J.L. Fiadeiro, P. Inverardi (Eds.), Fundamental Approaches to Software Engineering. XIII, 430 pages. 2008.

Vol. 4960: S. Drossopoulou (Ed.), Programming Languages and Systems. XIII, 399 pages. 2008.

Vol. 4959: L. Hendren (Ed.), Compiler Construction. XII, 307 pages. 2008.

Vol. 4957: E.S. Laber, C. Bornstein, L.T. Nogueira, L. Faria (Eds.), LATIN 2008: Theoretical Informatics. XVII, 794 pages. 2008.

Vol. 4943: R. Woods, K. Compton, C. Bouganis, P.C. Diniz (Eds.), Reconfigurable Computing: Architectures, Tools and Applications. XIV, 344 pages. 2008.